Advanced SQL:1999

Understanding Object-Relational and Other Advanced Features

The Morgan Kaufmann Series in Data Management Systems

Series Editor: Jim Gray, Microsoft Research

Advanced SQL:1999—Understanding Object-Relational and Other Advanced Features
Jim Melton

Database Tuning: Principles, Experiments, and Troubleshooting Techniques
Dennis Shasha and Philippe Bonnet

SQL:1999—Understanding Relational Language Components
Jim Melton and Alan R. Simon

Information Visualization in Data Mining and Knowledge Discovery
Edited by Usama Fayyad, Georges G. Grinstein, and Andreas Wierse

Transactional Information Systems: Theory, Algorithms, and the Practice of Concurrency Control and Recovery
Gerhard Weikum and Gottfried Vossen

Spatial Databases: With Application to GIS
Philippe Rigaux, Michel Scholl, and Agnès Voisard

Information Modeling and Relational Databases: From Conceptual Analysis to Logical Design
Terry Halpin

Component Database Systems
Edited by Klaus R. Dittrich and Andreas Geppert

Managing Reference Data in Enterprise Databases: Binding Corporate Data to the Wider World
Malcolm Chisholm

Data Mining: Concepts and Techniques
Jiawei Han and Micheline Kamber

Understanding SQL and Java Together: A Guide to SQLJ, JDBC, and Related Technologies
Jim Melton and Andrew Eisenberg

Database: Principles, Programming, and Performance, Second Edition
Patrick O'Neil and Elizabeth O'Neil

The Object Data Standard: ODMG 3.0
Edited by R. G. G. Cattell and Douglas K. Barry

Data on the Web: From Relations to Semistructured Data and XML
Serge Abiteboul, Peter Buneman, and Dan Suciu

Data Mining: Practical Machine Learning Tools and Techniques with Java Implementations
Ian H. Witten and Eibe Frank

Joe Celko's SQL for Smarties: Advanced SQL Programming, Second Edition
Joe Celko

Joe Celko's Data and Databases: Concepts in Practice
Joe Celko

Developing Time-Oriented Database Applications in SQL
Richard T. Snodgrass

Web Farming for the Data Warehouse: Exploiting Business Intelligence and Knowledge Management
Richard D. Hackathorn

Database Modeling and Design, Third Edition
Toby J. Teorey

Management of Heterogeneous and Autonomous Database Systems
Edited by Ahmed Elmagarmid, Marek Rusinkiewicz, and Amit Sheth

Object-Relational DBMSs: Tracking the Next Great Wave, Second Edition
Michael Stonebraker and Paul Brown, with Dorothy Moore

A Complete Guide to DB2 Universal Database
Don Chamberlin

Universal Database Management: A Guide to Object/Relational Technology
Cynthia Maro Saracco

Readings in Database Systems, Third Edition
Edited by Michael Stonebraker and Joseph M. Hellerstein

Understanding SQL's Stored Procedures: A Complete Guide to SQL/PSM
Jim Melton

Principles of Multimedia Database Systems
V. S. Subrahmanian

Principles of Database Query Processing for Advanced Applications
Clement T. Yu and Weiyi Meng

Advanced Database Systems
Carlo Zaniolo, Stefano Ceri, Christos Faloutsos, Richard T. Snodgrass, V. S. Subrahmanian, and Roberto Zicari

Principles of Transaction Processing for the Systems Professional
Philip A. Bernstein and Eric Newcomer

Using the New DB2: IBM's Object-Relational Database System
Don Chamberlin

Distributed Algorithms
Nancy A. Lynch

Active Database Systems: Triggers and Rules For Advanced Database Processing
Edited by Jennifer Widom and Stefano Ceri

Migrating Legacy Systems: Gateways, Interfaces, and the Incremental Approach
Michael L. Brodie and Michael Stonebraker

Atomic Transactions
Nancy Lynch, Michael Merritt, William Weihl, and Alan Fekete

Query Processing for Advanced Database Systems
Edited by Johann Christoph Freytag, David Maier, and Gottfried Vossen

Transaction Processing: Concepts and Techniques
Jim Gray and Andreas Reuter

Building an Object-Oriented Database System: The Story of O_2
Edited by François Bancilhon, Claude Delobel, and Paris Kanellakis

Database Transaction Models for Advanced Applications
Edited by Ahmed K. Elmagarmid

A Guide to Developing Client/Server SQL Applications
Setrag Khoshafian, Arvola Chan, Anna Wong, and Harry K. T. Wong

The Benchmark Handbook for Database and Transaction Processing Systems, Second Edition
Edited by Jim Gray

Camelot and Avalon: A Distributed Transaction Facility
Edited by Jeffrey L. Eppinger, Lily B. Mummert, and Alfred Z. Spector

Readings in Object-Oriented Database Systems
Edited by Stanley B. Zdonik and David Maier

Advanced SQL:1999

Understanding Object-Relational and Other Advanced Features

Jim Melton
Oracle Corporation

MORGAN KAUFMANN PUBLISHERS

AN IMPRINT OF ELSEVIER SCIENCE

AMSTERDAM BOSTON LONDON NEW YORK
OXFORD PARIS SAN DIEGO SAN FRANCISCO
SINGAPORE SYDNEY TOKYO

Senior Acquisitions Editor	Lothlórien Homet
Publishing Services Manager	Edward Wade
Project Management	Yonie Overton
Editorial Assistants	Mona Buehler and Corina Derman
Cover Design	Ross Carron Design
Front Cover Image	NASA/JPL/University of Arizona
Text Design, Composition, and Illustration	Rebecca Evans, Evans & Associates
Copyeditor	Beth Berkelhammer
Proofreader	Sharilyn Hovind
Indexer	Richard Evans, Infodex Indexing Services, Inc.
Printer	The Maple-Vail Book Manufacturing Group

QA 76.73 .S67 M422 2003

Designations used by companies to distinguish their products are often claimed as trademarks or registered trademarks. In all instances in which Morgan Kaufmann Publishers is aware of a claim, the product names appear in initial capital or all capital letters. Readers, however, should contact the appropriate companies for more complete information regarding trademarks and registration.

Morgan Kaufmann Publishers
An imprint of Elsevier Science
340 Pine Street, Sixth Floor
San Francisco, CA 94104-3205
www.mkp.com

© 2003 by Elsevier Science (USA)
All rights reserved.
Printed in the United States of America

07 06 05 04 03 5 4 3 2 1

No part of this publication may be reproduced, stored in a retrieval system, or transmitted in any form or by any means—electronic, mechanical, photocopying, or otherwise—without the prior written permission of the publisher.

Library of Congress Control Number: 2002107329
ISBN: 1-55860-677-7

This book is printed on acid-free paper.

AUG 1 2 2003

To my friends and colleagues:

Len Gallagher, the longtime (and long-suffering) Rapporteur who led the Database Languages Rapporteur Group through the publications of SQL-86/SQL-87, SQL-89, and SQL-92.

Stephen Cannan, the Convenor of WG3 who shepherded a recalcitrant bunch of technologists through difficult periods to achieve the publication of SQL:1999 and the coming publication of the next generation of the standard.

Phil Shaw, the first editor of the SQL standard who, through his technical excellence and sheer perseverance, is properly known as the "father of the SQL standard."

I am proud and enriched to have worked with each and all of them.

Jim

Foreword

Jim Gray
Microsoft Research

In the last decade, SQL has evolved from the pure-relational model to a post-relational model. This book is a lucid explanation of that evolution. At its core, the old SQL is tables-of-rows-and-columns. The new SQL adds typed-tables, each containing a set of objects accessed via methods. This is an enormous advance in the utility and applicability of the SQL language—and it goes a long way toward reducing the impedance mismatch between databases and programming languages.

SQL's new object model is the basis of the extensions to text, spatial, image and data mining data types and methods. SQL has also grown to support OLAP (on-line analytic processing) operations and functions, as well as better integration with Java, and to have cleaner support for data links (external files as values) and data wrappers (foreign data sources).

All these changes are documented in the SQL standards. Unfortunately, those standards are written by language lawyers and are very difficult to read. Fortunately, Jim Melton, who is the editor of the SQL:1999 standard (and the SQL-92 standard), is also able to write lucid descriptions that most of us can read. Jim wrote a previous volume that explained the "classical" aspects of SQL:1999: the table-row-column stuff.[1] This book explains the post-relational SQL:1999 aspects: objects, links, wrappers, and OLAP. It also hints at the progress in the emerging topics of XML, text, spatial, image, and data mining.

SQL must interoperate with almost all languages, it must be persistent, and it has to worry about security and schema evolution. These are not issues that most

1 Jim Melton and Alan Simon, *SQL:1999—Understanding Relational Language Components* (San Francisco: Morgan Kaufmann Publishers, 2002).

object-oriented systems need to address, but they are central to SQL. Consequently, designing the SQL object model was a pioneering and extremely delicate task. Melton does a wonderful job describing the issues the designers faced and explaining why they chose the path they did. He gives one of the more insightful discussions of the concepts and issues that underlie object models. In the end, you come away understanding the tradeoffs the designers made and have a clear understanding of the final design. The result is quite elegant.

The SQL:1999 standard will influence commercial products for years to come. This book is an excellent guidepost for features that products will likely add in the future. It also gives a vendor-neutral and very readable view of the SQL language. Hence, the book will be an indispensable reference both for expert SQL users and for SQL implementers.

Contents

Preface

A Word about SQL, Databases, and Programmers

SQL is undoubtedly the most widely accepted and implemented interface language for relational database systems. Some years ago, Michael Stonebraker (responsible for relational and object-relational implementations such as Ingres, Postgres, and Illustra) referred to SQL as "intergalactic dataspeak" (a fact that serves as the inspiration for the covers of all of my SQL-related books). Indeed, like Fortran, C, COBOL, and Java, SQL may be among the most widely used and understood computer languages around.

The fourth version of the ANSI and ISO standard for SQL has now been published, and all programmers concerned with relational database applications will be affected by it. Because of the influence of the relational model of data, few programmers are unaware of relational database systems and many use them daily. Programmers using almost any modern enterprise- or workgroup-class system will be affected by SQL:1999, whether their applications use Oracle 9i, IBM's DB2, Microsoft's SQL Server, Sybase's Adaptive Server, or any of several other popular database systems.

Why I Wrote This Book

Most of the books on SQL with which I am familiar are oriented toward end users who might type queries into an interactive terminal, or they are critiques of the language. Neither approach is really adequate for the broad variety of use that typically characterizes SQL programming. Moreover, with the increasing use of SQL, many people are learning the language without the benefit (or disadvantage) of knowing the earlier SQL-86, SQL-89, or SQL-92. I believe that there is a need for a book that presents the entire SQL language from the novice level through the expert level. In taking such an approach, I wanted to focus not on interactive SQL use, but primarily on the ways in which real applications will use the language.

SQL:1999, however, has many different aspects—deriving from the many uses to which SQL is put in business and industry today. As a result, a single volume covering the entire SQL:1999 language would be unreasonably intimidating and not a little expensive. I have thus chosen to partition the subject into two volumes. The first volume, *Basic SQL:1999: Understanding Relational Language Components*, was jointly authored by me and my longtime friend and colleague, Alan Simon; it was released in May 2001 and covers (as the title implies) the essential relational components of SQL:1999. This volume builds on that basic material to address the object facilities of the language, along with several of the other new aspects of SQL that are included in the 1999 edition of the standard.

Who Should Read It

Because of the orientation and style chosen for the book, I believe that it will be useful to a broad range of readers. Application programmers are my primary audience, but I also kept in mind the needs of database administrators and designers as well as system analysts.

I hope that the book will be a helpful resource to programmers at every level. In addition, system designers and implementers can benefit from knowing the design rationale and choices represented in the standard. I have included some fairly esoteric material from the SQL:1999 standard with the intent to present it more clearly than the standard does. This may be of help to engineers building the SQL DBMS systems that implement SQL:1999.

How This Book Is Organized

Conformance to the SQL-92 standard was based on three "levels" of the language, ranging from features broadly used in older systems to those that have not been and may never be widely implemented. SQL:1999, by contrast, requires implementation of a single set of features—called *Core SQL*—in order for conformance to be claimed. The majority of SQL:1999's features are not included in Core SQL; however, a number of them are grouped into *packages* to which conformance may be claimed once Core SQL:1999 has been implemented. While

SQL-92 was published in a single (admittedly large) document, SQL:1999 was partitioned into several different documents with dependencies among them.

The combination of having been broken into packages and multiple documents, along with SQL's large size and complexity, means that no linear treatment of it can ever succeed completely. Printed books, unfortunately, are inherently linear. I have attempted to organize the book so that you can read it cover to cover if you are so inclined. However, I realize that most readers don't approach technical books like this. Instead, you might prefer to skip around and first read certain chapters or sections that are of particular interest to you, or that contain information required for your current projects. Both the amount of material in each chapter and the structure of the discussions are intended to facilitate this kind of "real-world" use.

This volume starts off with a brief review of SQL:1999 and the scope of the standard, followed immediately by an in-depth discussion of SQL's object facilities, including structured user-defined types, typed tables, and user-defined routines and routine invocation. These chapters are intended primarily to cover the use of SQL:1999's object capabilities in environments other than those using the Java programming language (but see three paragraphs hence). Some of the SQL syntax presented in these chapters contains Java-specific clauses, which are shown in the BNF, but there is little discussion of how the features are used in a Java environment (although a few footnotes highlight especially important differences).

This is followed by material contained in a new part of SQL that deals with management of external data (and, not coincidentally, known as SQL/MED), which is covered in some detail. While the specifications of SQL/MED are only partly relevant to applications programmers and database administrators, I believe that a good understanding of the design of this aspect of SQL will aid those readers.

I then move into a detailed discussion of SQL's new OLAP (on-line analytical processing) features, recently processed as an *amendment* to the original SQL:1999 publication. This volume continues with a high-level discussion of a second multipart standard—SQL/MM, or SQL Multimedia and Application Packages—that is specified as layers built atop SQL:1999.

This volume then includes a relatively brief review of two additional new parts of the SQL standard that bring the database world together with the Java language. (This material is covered in depth by *Understanding SQL and Java Together: A Guide to SQLJ, JDBC, and Related Technologies*, written by me and another longtime friend and colleague, Andrew Eisenberg.)

The final substantive chapter introduces a part of the SQL standard that is still under initial development and that is not part of SQL:1999 (it is anticipated to be published as part of the next generation of the SQL standard). This material addresses the ways in which SQL and XML can be used together and is included because of the great promise that XML shows for use in data management environments.

The book concludes with a short chapter suggesting future directions in which the SQL standard might go, followed by several appendices containing supplementary information about the SQL standard that will be of interest to many readers.

This book, along with its companion first volume, *SQL:1999: Understanding Relational Language Components*, is meant to be used in place of the SQL:1999 standard and is not merely a rehash of that standard. While the standard is designed to tell vendors how to write an SQL DBMS, this book is intended to tell application writers how to *use* such a DBMS. If you are interested in the details of the language specification, Appendix C, "Relevant Standards Bodies," tells you how to buy a copy of the standard for your own use.

However, this book is not a substitute for product documentation. It discusses the entire SQL:1999 language, not just those parts implemented by a specific vendor or at any specific point in time. You will frequently need documentation for your specific products to write your applications. On the other hand, it may also give you some idea of what your system may be capable of in future incarnations.

Examples

One thing that distinguishes this book from most others is the nature of the example application. The great majority of database books seem to choose one of two example applications that are used to illustrate language features—a payroll application or a parts database. I have long since tired of these applications and tried to find something that would be a bit more fun. I am a great fan of music and of the cinema, so I decided to design a database based on a hypothetical movie and music store and write example code to extract information from and manipulate data in that database. Appendix A, "An SQL:1999 Example Using UDTs," presents the database definition (schema) and the queries that are used for this application.

Not every concept that requires illustration lends itself to the music and video application, so some of the examples use a variety of different concepts, ranging from coordinate systems to airplane construction.

Syntax Notation

Anybody who has ever read a programming language manual or a textbook about a language knows that the authors always need to present the syntax of the language elements (the statements, for example) in *some* form. One of the most common techniques for this is the use of some variation of Backus-Naur Form (BNF), which is used extensively in this book.

I use two different styles when I give you the syntax of various parts of the SQL language. One form is the more formal BNF that is actually used in the SQL standard itself. It is distinguished from the other forms in its use of angle brackets (< and >) to identify nonterminal symbols of the grammar. (A nonterminal symbol is one that is further resolved in the grammar; a terminal symbol is one that has no further breakdown.) This more formal notation is usually quite complete, specifying every detail of the syntax. For example, let's consider here a short, hypothetical example of the more formal notation (for a USA-style mailing address):

```
<mailing address> ::=
    <street number> <space> <street name> [ <space> <street type> ]
    <city name> <space> <state code> <space> <zip code>

<street number> ::= <digit>... [ <letter> ]

<street name> ::= <character string>

<street type> ::=
    Street
  | Avenue
  | Lane

<city name> ::= <character string>

<state code> ::=
    'AK'
  | !! 49 codes omitted here (including DC, for the District of Columbia)
  | 'WY'

<zip code> ::=
    <digit> <digit> <digit> <digit> <digit>
    [ <hyphen> <digit> <digit> <digit> <digit> ]
```

That preceding bit of syntax provides several pieces of information. First, it says that a `<mailing address>` (a BNF nonterminal symbol) is made up of two mandatory pieces of syntax followed by an optional one, which is followed in turn by three more mandatory ones. It allows the (mandatory) `<street number>` to be an arbitrary number of digits, optionally followed by a single letter. A `<street type>` is allowed to be one of exactly three alternatives. The BNF in this volume takes advantage of notation used by the SQL standard for a BNF comment—the two consecutive exclamation points (`!!`). Note also that I did *not* tell you (in this BNF excerpt) what a `<space>`, a `<digit>`, or a `<hyphen>` is or what a `<character string>` is, even though a complete language syntax specification would have to do so.

The other, more casual, form doesn't use the angle brackets, but depends on a (natural language) interpretation of the various terms used in the syntax being described. The same (USA-style mailing address) example expressed using the more casual style would look like this:

```
mailing-address ::=
    street-number street-name [ street-type ]
    city-name state-code zip-code

street number ::= digit... [ letter ]

street-name> ::= character string

street-type ::=
    Street
  | Avenue
  | Lane

city-name ::= character string

state-code ::= one of the 51 codes approved by the postal service

zip-code ::=
    5-digit-code [ - 4-digit-extension ]
```

This casual style includes almost the same information as the formal style, but I take for granted more ability on your part to intuitively understand my meaning, including leaving out BNF productions for spaces and using actual punctuation marks instead of BNF nonterminal symbols that represent such marks (e.g., "`-`" instead of "`<hyphen>`").

In a few cases, where it seems appropriate that different alternatives for one piece of syntax deserve to be considered almost as though they were complete separate entities, I use bullets to break up the syntax, like this:

```
<mailing address> ::=
    <USA mailing address>
  | <Canada mailing address>
  | <Japan mailing address>
```

- `<USA mailing address> ::= ...`
- `<Canada mailing address> ::= ...`
- `<Japan mailing address> ::= ...`

The bullets have no intrinsic meaning for BNF purposes—they are used strictly to help you visually distinguish between several alternatives easily.

I should clarify the use of ellipses (`...`) in the syntax examples. In formal BNF, an ellipsis is used specifically to indicate that the preceding token (or, when the ellipsis follows a right curly brace, }, or a right square bracket,], the preceding group of tokens) is repeated an arbitrary number of times. In the three bullets just preceding, the ellipses are used for a different purpose: to avoid having to define just what each of those three sorts of mailing addresses are!

Additional Information Resources

Many vendors of SQL database management systems allow their products to be downloaded from their Web sites, usually allowing use in a limited situation, often for a limited time period. The documentation for such products is almost always available on the companies' Web sites as well, often without even having to download and install the products themselves. Even though no vendor has made a formal claim (at the time I write these words) of Core SQL:1999 conformance, it may be very helpful to use those products while you learn SQL:1999.

As you will see in Appendix C, "Relevant Standards Bodies," it is possible to purchase copies of the various documents that make up SQL:1999 by visiting certain Web sites. It may also be possible (but will certainly be more expensive if so) to purchase copies of the SQL:1999 standard documents in hardcopy form.

Relevant Products

No known SQL DBMS conforms to Core SQL:1999 at the time this book goes to press, but a number of vendors are known to be pursuing conformance. The vendors that I believe are actively pursuing conformance, or are likely to be doing so even though I may not have concrete knowledge of it, include

- Hitachi
- IBM
- Microsoft
- Mimer
- Oracle
- Sybase

There may be others—in fact, there almost certainly are—but I have little or no awareness of them.

Typographical Conventions

A quick note on the typographical conventions used in the book:

- Type in this font (Stone Serif) is used for all ordinary text, as well as for SQL identifiers appearing in that text.
- *Type in this font (Stone Serif Italic) is used for terms that I define or for emphasis.*
- `Type in this font (Letter Gothic) is used for all examples, syntax presentation, SQL identifiers, and Java identifiers that appear in ordinary text.`
- **`Type in this font (Letter Gothic Bold) is used to highlight especially interesting parts of some examples.`**

Acknowledgments

Writing this book, like writing any book, was a labor of love—with the emphasis all too often on "labor." It's difficult and time-consuming, even though the end result is usually rather rewarding (not financially, in most cases!). It's exceedingly rare to do it alone—the assistance of others is necessary and certainly invaluable: for reviews, for trying out ideas and phraseology, and just for offering encouragement. I cannot fail to acknowledge and express my gratitude to the wonderful and talented people who reviewed this book and offered help throughout the process. I especially want to thank the following people (alphabetized by last name) for their extensive reviews, which heavily influenced the content and accuracy of this book:

- Mark Ashworth, now working for IBM, who is the original and current editor of SQL/MM Spatial and is now editor of Full-Text and Still Image as well. Mark's understanding of spatial systems and of the Spatial standard is unsurpassed and his help is greatly appreciated.
- M. Faisal, my Oracle colleague who specializes in full-text systems and frequently represents the USA in SQL/MM Full-Text meetings. His knowledge of that standard resulted in a far better description of its capabilities.
- Christopher Farrar of IBM is a former longtime participant in the United States committee responsible for SQL (NCITS H2) and an acknowledged expert in many aspects of the standard. Chris's knowledge of Java and its interaction with the SQL standard was invaluable.
- Art Kaufmann is another NCITS H2 participant, as well as an implementer of SQL products. Art's thorough review, especially of the chapters related to SQL/MED, were invaluable. Several other chapters also benefited from his attention.
- IBM's Jan-Eike Michels also participates in NCITS H2, giving special attention to the SQL/MED specifications. Jan-Eike's reviews of the SQL/MED chapters were especially important in finding and resolving subtle errors and unclear text.
- Peter Pistor long represented Germany to the international group responsible for SQL (ISO/IEC JTC1/SC32/WG3) and for SQL/MM (WG4). His keen eye for detail and his sensitivity to how English language is understood by native speakers of other languages contributed greatly to improvements in accuracy and clarity.
- Paul Scarponcini participates in NCITS H2, largely in support of the SQL/MM standard, for which he also represents the USA in WG4. Paul is among the world's experts in the use of SQL's object facilities because of his participation in the SQL/MM work, supported by Bentley Systems, Inc. His review of every chapter of this volume resulted in many improvements, particularly in the user-defined type and SQL/MM chapters.
- Frank Symonds of Informix (now part of IBM) offered me his insights based on concurrent implementation of SQL:1999's structured user-defined types

and other aspects of the language. His reviews improved the accuracy and clarity of several chapters.

- Fred Zemke, Oracle's primary member of H2 and a regular USA delegate to JTC1/SC32/WG3, is an expert on more aspects of the SQL standard than most people ever read, and one of the most focused people I know. Fred was a principle author of the SQL/OLAP specifications, and his review of that material in this book was thorough and irreplaceable.

Of course, all errors that remain in the book (and I have no illusions that I found and eliminated all errors in a topic this complex) are solely my responsibility.

Last, but not least, I offer my gratitude to Åke Persson, one of the best SQL parsing experts whom I have ever known. His SQL:1999 parser (available at *http://www.mimer.com*) helped me find and correct a number of errors in the examples used in this book.

I also wish to thank Diane Cerra, Belinda Breyer, Mona Buehler, and others at Morgan Kaufmann Publishers for their outstanding support during the conception, writing, and production of this book. Whenever asked, Diane provided feedback and suggestions about the content and style of the book (and was amazingly tolerant—but encouraging—when I all too often missed deadlines). Belinda was ever present to answer questions, always found time to track down information that I'd misplaced, and ensured that the chapters were quickly reviewed. Mona kept information flowing between Morgan Kaufmann and me and ensured that I received every review that was submitted. Yonie Overton worked substantial production miracles during the production process for this book, and she was always there to answer my questions, calm my nerves, and generally keep production on schedule. My thanks also go to Rebecca Evans, who has promptly and accurately typeset all of my books for Morgan Kaufmann. To these and others, I am most grateful.

As with any large project—of which writing a book is among the larger—other aspects of life are sorely neglected. I cannot overstate my gratitude and appreciation to my Significant Other, Barbara Edelberg, for being so incredibly tolerant of the absurd workload that a book adds to an already busy schedule and for being so supportive, picking up the slack in keeping a household full of Shelties and Corgis running smoothly without my full participation. It might not be true that I couldn't have done it without her help, but I would really rather not have to find out! And the companionship, love, and attention from our Shelties, our Corgi, and our sole remaining cat helped me remember that we're supposed to work in order to live and not the other way around. Thanks!

Chapter 1

Introduction to SQL:1999

1.1 Introduction

The decade of the 1990s was notable for many significant events in multiple areas of information technology: client/server computing; the evolution of the Internet from an academic and research network into the foundation of e-commerce and e-business; the growth of business intelligence and data warehousing; the emergence of the World Wide Web as a medium for commerce; widespread adoption of packaged software for enterprise applications, call center management, sales force automation, and customer relationship management (CRM); and many other advances that have made information technology, circa the turn of the century, exponentially more pervasive in business and society than a mere decade earlier.

One common component of all of the above occurrences is relational database technology with database management system (DBMS) products based on SQL. Today it seems a foregone conclusion that nearly every new data-intensive application will be built on top of a relational database and that access to that database's contents will be through a dialect of SQL. Barely a decade ago, though, relational database technology was just beginning to be mature enough that production-quality, high-data-volume applications could be built and deployed by IT organizations. Those organizations needed confidence that their applications wouldn't crumble under the demands of industrial-strength information systems. Even though SQL had already established its dominance in the relational database world by the early 1990s, there were still plenty of doubters among data center managers, information systems strategists, and "old world" application developers who questioned whether relational DBMSs—and, by extension, SQL—would ever extend beyond departmental computing that was then dominated by minicomputers and early client/server systems.

What a difference a decade makes. Today, existing applications that are built on earlier, non–relational database technology or on file systems are dismissively called *legacy applications,* the inference being that they not only feature older, antiquated technologies and capabilities, but that they are significantly less valuable to an organization than their more modern counterparts. And it is difficult to imagine any new application, on any size platform, that wouldn't be built using SQL and a relational DBMS.

In 1999, work was completed on the latest version of the SQL standard, known as SQL:1999. This book—along with its preceding companion volume[1]—will teach you what you need and want to know about the SQL language and the 1999 standard. First, however, the subject of database management systems and associated concepts warrants introduction. Readers who have experience working with relational technology may wish to briefly skim this chapter and skip ahead to Chapter 2, "User-Defined Types," where SQL:1999's structured user-defined data types are introduced.

1.2 What Is SQL?

SQL (correctly pronounced "ess cue ell," instead of the somewhat common "sequel") is a *data sublanguage* for access to relational databases that are managed by relational database management systems (RDBMSs). Many books and articles "define" SQL by parenthetically claiming that the letters stand for *Structured Query Language.* While this was true for the original prototypes, it is not true of the standard. When the letters appear in product names, they have often been assigned this meaning by the product vendors, but we believe that users are ill-served by claims that the word *structured* accurately describes the language overall. I've heard recent claims that the letters stand for *Standard Query Language,* but that's at best a myth. The letters are not an abbreviation or an acronym, merely the result of the evolution from the name used in early research projects. If you *really* need the name to be an acronym, I suggest that it could simply stand for

1 Jim Melton and Alan R. Simon, *SQL:1999: Understanding Relational Language Components* (San Francisco: Morgan Kaufmann Publishers, 2001).

SQL Query Language, one of those recursive acronyms (another is GNU, which I'm told is an acronym for *GNU's Not Unix*).

The 1999 edition of the SQL standard introduces many significant new features into the language, but the most eagerly awaited enhancement is the addition of user-defined type support, often considered to provide "object-oriented SQL" capabilities. The largest fraction of this volume addresses those new features.

1.2.1 SQL Versus Object-Oriented Database Systems

The rigidity of the relational model with its mathematical underpinnings (discussed in Volume 1) made it impossible to include complex user-defined data types, methods, encapsulation, and all the other aspects of object orientation[2] . . . right?

Not exactly, as it turned out. As time slipped away from the 1970 publication of Dr. Codd's paper describing the relational model, many database product strategists and technologists increasingly questioned the merits of trying to adhere strictly to the core relational model in the face of increasingly complex applications, dramatic advances in hardware and software technology, and an ever more competitive product landscape.

The result has been commercial products that are primarily relational in their respective foundations—that is, they are built around the familiar table-and-column structure—but, at the same time, those products are augmented with the capabilities and structures (user-defined data types, encapsulation, etc.) that have been found in commercial object-oriented database management systems (OODBMSs) since the late 1980s. The best of both worlds, many agree, has been the outcome of producing products that are commonly referred to as *extended relational,* or *object-relational,* database management systems (that is, their core capabilities are extended with those from the object-oriented world).

Of course, not everyone agrees with this trend and the results. Many relational "purists" decry the ever continuing move away from the rigid foundations of the relational model and implementation of an architecture that they claim is (with more than a little justification) not soundly based on mathematical foundations. It may be worth observing that SQL has always gone beyond the relational model. Its support for duplicate rows and null values is frequently criticized by relational purists, so it's inevitable that some observers will not approve of adding object-oriented facilities to SQL. Regardless, the world of extended relational DBMS products is here to stay, and the publication of the SQL:1999 standard with its object-oriented extensions has codified and formalized this technology direction.

2 These and other related terms are defined in section 1.4 and in Chapter 2, "User-Defined Types."

You probably won't be surprised to learn that SQL's inclusion of object capabilities doesn't precisely match the object facilities in any other language or system. (You might be disappointed if, for example, you are intimately familiar with some particular language like C++ or OQL, but that's a different issue.) I discuss SQL's object model in section 1.4.

1.2.2 ODMG and OQL

During the mid- and late 1980s, even as the relational model was taking hold and commercial RDBMS products were beginning to be commonly used, many technology planners and implementers were quick to point out the deficiencies of the relational model in the context of "real world" applications. Specifically, it was noted that neither complex nor user-defined data types could be easily supported using the available numeric, character string, and date-oriented data types available within SQL. Nor did the rigid mathematical foundations of the relational model support the extensibility needed for applications such as computer-aided design (CAD), computer-aided manufacturing (CAM), or spatial and geographic systems, for example. Such applications utilize data that is difficult to force into SQL's tabular structures.

A divide emerged between two competing "camps"—those who insisted that the relational model was *the* future of database technology, no questions asked, versus others who insisted that the relational model was proving to be increasingly unsuitable for "modern" applications. At that time, object-oriented languages were coming into vogue, and the principles of object orientation were quickly carried over into the world of databases.

While work on SQL began to address these requirements in the very early 1990s, the object-oriented database adherents formed a consortium called the Object Database Management Group (ODMG) with the purpose of defining an object-oriented database model and language (the language is known as OQL, which most people correlate with *Object Query Language*). While the specification work was generally considered a significant accomplishment (the most recent version is version 3.0[3]) and was very successful in its technological goals, the language was not a significant commercial success. OQL was implemented in several OODBMS products, but rarely in a complete form. One of the most important characteristics of OQL and of the ODMG model is that retrieval of information from the underlying OODBMS is expressed in OQL, but creation, modification, and deletion of that data is done directly through the host programming language, which is always an object-oriented programming language.

3 R. G. G. Cattell et al., *The Object Database Standard: ODMG 3.0* (San Francisco: Morgan Kaufmann Publishers, 2000).

It's very important to note that unlike the relational model, with its rigid mathematical precision and formal definition (though, as we noted, RDBMS products have always "taken liberties" with the underlying foundations), there is no standard definition for what object orientation is—or isn't. This volume discusses the principles of object orientation in some detail, particularly as they apply to SQL:1999; it also describes the SQL object model (but does not explicitly compare and contrast it to other object models, although the relationship with the Java object model is discussed).

It is also important to note, though, that before this convergence of the relational and object-oriented worlds, the prevailing sentiment within the database world was relational versus object-oriented, with proponents of each model claiming the superiority of their preferred approach as well as the shortcomings of the alternative model. SQL:1999, along with the products that implement it, demonstrate conclusively that an object-relational approach to data management fulfils a great many of the requirements of "modern" applications.

1.3 The Structure and Goals of This Book

Unlike most books that address the SQL language, this book takes the long view. Time is required for standard language features to be introduced into commercial products, and rather than concentrate on the features that products *X* and *Y* might include in their current versions, I have chosen to focus on a *standards orientation* toward SQL.

Because of the large size of SQL:1999, it is quite unlikely that any single product will ever implement the entire language. The standard itself acknowledges this reality by specifying only one required conformance capability for SQL:1999, called *Core SQL*. All features of the language that are not in Core SQL are optional; conformance to some of them may be claimed in packages of features, while conformance to others may be claimed individually.

I have chosen to document the entire SQL:1999 standard, not just the new features that did not appear in SQL-92. I believe that it's unfair to ask someone new to relational technology to use one book (and one style) to get started and then another to pursue more advanced topics. (And, of course, the very size of the language makes such an approach unrealistic.) Instead, I believe that such readers are better served by having all of the material available in one volume, in one style, fully integrated.

How might this comprehensive presentation affect the reader who is already intimately familiar with SQL-92? I have tried to ensure that the material in this book distinguishes those components of SQL:1999 that were "inherited" from

SQL-92 from those that are new to SQL:1999. Accordingly, experienced SQL programmers can easily skip over the material with which they are familiar and concentrate only on truly new information. Part of the organizational structure involves a division of the content into two volumes, the first of which covers SQL's more traditional features, while this volume addresses a number of facilities that are arguably "nonrelational" in nature. The language features described in this volume, in particular, have very little overlap with SQL-92.

Now that I've introduced SQL, let's turn our focus to the purpose of this book.

1.3.1 Volume 1: Relational Language Components

Before summarizing the purpose and content of this book, I'd like to give you a brief overview of the preceding volume, *SQL:1999: Understanding Relational Language Components*. Naturally, I think it would be worth your while to acquire a copy of Volume 1, as its material is genuinely a prerequisite for the material in this volume. However, if you are thoroughly familiar with the relational aspects of SQL:1999 from some other source, then you have the necessary information to successfully use this volume.

Volume 1 offers readers the relational model in some detail and provides an introduction to SQL and its variations from that model. The introductory material is followed by an explanation of SQL:1999's built-in data types and its *distinct* user-defined types (in this volume, I cover the other alternative: structured user-defined types), its expressions and operators (including, for example, the *constructed* types ROW and ARRAY, regular expression support in a new predicate, and recursive queries), language embedding, dynamic execution and call-level interface, and most other "traditional" aspects of the SQL language.

1.3.2 Volume 2: Object-Relational and Other Advanced Features

The contents of this volume are based on the presumption that you are familiar with the material in Volume 1, or that you are willing to refer to that volume (or an equivalent resource) if you encounter material herein with which you are not reasonably comfortable.

The bulk of this volume covers SQL:1999's *structured* user-defined types, focusing on their object capabilities—including their definition, their uses, the ways in which their methods are specified and invoked, the privileges required to successfully utilize them, and what implementations must do in order to claim conformance to these facilities.

While on the subject of object orientation, I briefly review aspects of the SQL standard in its relationship with the Java programming language. This material is covered in depth in a different book,[4] so the treatment in this volume is strictly minimal.

I then move on to the subject of using SQL to access non-SQL data sources, which is addressed by a new part of the SQL standard known as SQL/MED (Management of External Data). Because the very intent of SQL/MED is to allow applications to use SQL to access non-SQL data, only part of the material in the SQL/MED chapters of this volume is directly relevant to application programmers; the remainder of these chapters will probably be of more interest to engineers who build SQL DBMS products.

In subsequent chapters, you'll learn about SQL's new OLAP (On-Line Analytical Processing) capabilities, published in 2000 as an amendment to SQL:1999, as well as about other new parts of SQL that have been very recently published (and, in some cases, not yet published—meaning that it is not yet appropriate to refer to such material as a *standard*—such as SQL/XML, in which facilities for supporting the use of SQL and XML together are specified).

This volume also reviews a separate standard, SQL Multimedia and Application Packages (SQL/MM), that is specified as *applications* of SQL:1999 and its structured user-defined types. SQL/MM is, like SQL, a multipart standard. In SQL/MM's case, however, the various parts have little or no dependencies on one another. Instead, each part specifies a "type library" for a specific type of nontraditional data. Parts of SQL/MM currently available or nearing publication include Full-Text, Spatial, Still Image, and Data Mining.

Finally, I end with a brief look at the future of SQL (and SQL/MM), trying to interpret the mist, chips, and cracks in my old crystal ball to give you something to which you can look forward!

1.4 The SQL Object Model

As you read in section 1.2.1, SQL's object model is not identical to the object model of any other object-oriented programming language or any other object-oriented database management system. However, while defining the SQL:1999 object model, the standards participants carefully examined a number of other languages and systems, trying to learn from the successes and failures of those other efforts. In the end, I believe that SQL's object model bears a modest resemblance to that of the Java programming language, but with adaptations required by SQL's nature as a database management system language, the existence of persistent metadata, and its inherent persistence of data.

4 Jim Melton and Andrew Eisenberg, *Understanding SQL and Java Together: A Guide to SQLJ, JDBC, and Related Technologies* (San Francisco: Morgan Kaufmann Publishers, 2000).

SQL's object model includes two distinguishable components. The first is *structured user-defined types,* which give you a way to define a new data type that can be more complex than SQL's built-in types such as INTEGER, DECIMAL, CHARACTER, DATE, or BLOB. When you define a structured UDT (an abbreviation for *user-defined type* that I'll use frequently), you must define not only the data elements that it contains, but also its semantics—behaviors that are evoked using a method invocation interface.

The second major component is *typed tables*. SQL has always had tables, of course, but tables prior to SQL:1999 were always multisets (or sets) of rows, each of which was defined to have multiple columns. Naturally, those "ordinary" tables remain in SQL:1999, but a new type of table has been added. A typed table is one whose rows *are* instances (or, if you prefer, values) of a particular structured user-defined type with which the table has been explicitly associated. It is by combining structured user-defined types and typed tables that a true object model is manifested in SQL.

1.4.1 An Overview of Object Orientation

The relational model of data[5] is a widely accepted, formal data model with a sound mathematical foundation. While there are countless enhancements and improvements that have been proposed (and, in many cases, adopted) for the relational model, it is prudent to say that there is only one *data model* for relational data. It is also correct to say that SQL's data model, although not strictly identical to the relational model, is certainly founded on the relational model. (SQL permits duplicate rows, which the relational model prohibits; SQL also endorses null values and three-valued logic, which do not appear in the formal relational model.)

By contrast, there is no one universally accepted *object model* or *object data model.* Instead, there are a number of characteristics of object orientation that are generally (but not always universally) accepted as part of *a given* object model, while specific object models frequently add additional characteristics. Regrettably, it often seems that specific object models are defined more by example than by rigor. Nonetheless, there are certainly characteristics that appear in so many object models that I will dare to say that they are central to the definition of object orientation.

---

5 Dr. E. F. Codd, "A Relational Model of Data for Large Shared Data Banks," *Communications of the ACM,* Vol. 13, No. 6, June 1970, pp. 377–387.

In 1989, several papers were produced in an effort to lay the groundwork for inserting object technology into the database world. One of these[6] proposed that true object-oriented programming language capabilities should form the foundation for creation of object-oriented database systems. Another[7] proposed the addition of extension to relational systems that provided better support for user-defined types and complex data structures. A third[8] argued for retaining the relational aspects of SQL, but extending its type system to include complex types. SQL's relational model includes many of the ideas taken from all of those papers.

The Computer Science and Engineering Handbook[9] says, "The [object] model is based on the concept of encapsulating data, and code that operates on those data, in an object."

In 1990, Khoshafian and Abnous[10] asserted that the three most fundamental characteristics of object orientation are

1. Abstract data types (the ability to define classes of data comprising data structures and operations on them whose details are hidden from the users of the types),
2. Inheritance (the ability to share structure and behavior among related types), and
3. Object identity (the real-world characteristic that every entity is uniquely identifiable).

The purposes of object orientation, they tell us, include improved modeling of the application's worldview and increased ability to reuse application code in other applications. Program modularity is also an important benefit of object orientation.

I like to clarify the first of those three fundamental characteristics by emphasizing the notion of *encapsulation,* the mechanism that hides the details of those data structures and operations.

---

6 Malcolm Atkinson et al., "The Object-Oriented Database System Manifesto," *Proceedings of the First International Conference on Deductive and Object-Oriented Databases,* 1989.

7 Michael Stonebraker et al., "Third-Generation Database System Manifesto," *SIGMOD Record,* Vol. 19, No. 3, Sept. 1990, pp. 31–44.

8 Chris Date and Hugh Darwen, "The Third Manifesto," *SIGMOD Record,* Vol. 24, No. 1, March 1995, pp. 39–49.

9 Avi Silbershatz et al., "Data Models," in *The Computer Science and Engineering Handbook,* ed. Allen B. Tucker, Jr. (Boca Raton, Fla. CRC Press, 1996), p. 985.

10 Setrag Khoshafian and Razmik Abnous, *Object Orientation: Concepts, Languages, Databases, User Interfaces* (New York: John Wiley & Sons, 1990).

Oscar Nierstrasz further enhances[11] those fundamental characteristics by the addition of

4. Polymorphism and overloading (the ability to distinguish between two or more operations having the same name that have different semantics or that operate on values of different types).

Finally, in an excellent introduction to Java programming,[12] we learn that Alan Kay gives five basic characteristics of Smalltalk (the first successful object-oriented language):

1. Everything is an object.
2. A program is a bunch of objects telling each other what to do by sending messages.
3. Each object has its own memory made up of other objects.
4. Every object has a type.
5. All objects of a particular type can receive the same messages.

Looking at all of these statements about object models and languages, it's easy to see a theme. As we'll see, SQL's object model honors that theme, while adding its own spin where needed. (I observe that SQL's approach to "sending messages" involves explicit routine invocation, which most observers seem to feel is a satisfactory way to provide that facility.) I mentioned earlier that SQL's object model has a close resemblance to Java's in several ways; the relationship of the object models is covered in Chapter 2, "User-Defined Types."

1.4.2 Structured User-Defined Types

SQL's term for the concept that Khoshafian and Abnous called "abstract data type" is "structured user-defined type." The use of the different terminology is historical and isn't significant to the definition of SQL's object model (although I note in passing that the name "abstract data type" was used for several years during the development of SQL:1999). In Volume 1 (Chapter 4, "Basic Data Definition Language (DDL)"), SQL's user-defined types were introduced, drawing a

11 Oscar Nierstrasz, "A Survey of Object-Oriented Concepts," in *Object-Oriented Concepts, Databases, and Applications,* eds. Won Kim and Frederick H. Lochovsky (New York: ACM Press, 1989), pp. 3–11.

12 Bruce Eckel, *Thinking in Java,* second edition (Upper Saddle River, N.J.: Prentice-Hall, 2000).

distinction between *distinct* types and *structured* types. Volume 1 addressed distinct types in detail, while the discussion of structured types was deferred to this volume.

I'll cover UDTs in detail in Chapter 2, "User-Defined Types," so this section serves as an introduction to and a survey of that facility in SQL:1999.

SQL:1999's Framework[13] (the part of the SQL standard that defines common terms and concepts) introduces structured user-defined types thus: "A *structured type* is a named, user-defined data type. A value of a structured type comprises a number of *attribute values*." It goes on, of course, to add a more comprehensive definition and description of structured types, including the fact that attributes have data types of their own. As you will see in the next subsection, structured user-defined types are accessed through SQL-invoked routines, but this section focuses on the way their content is represented.

From that definition, we see that structured user-defined types contain attributes that have values—in other words, data associated with a structured user-defined type is stored in attributes of the type. (I'm getting tired of writing the complete phrase "structured user-defined type" so frequently, and you're probably tired of reading it again and again; henceforth, I'll default to the shorthand UDT unless I have some particular reason to distinguish structured types from distinct types.) If you're a C programmer, then you'll be comfortable with a comparison between a C `struct` and the attributes of an SQL UDT. In many ways, though, SQL's UDTs have more in common with Java's classes.

Of course, each attribute of a UDT has a specific data type. One attribute can have data type INTEGER, another can be CHARACTER(50), and another can be ARRAY[100] (with an array element type specified, of course). To further increase the flexibility and power of UDTs, an attribute of one UDT can have as its data type another UDT. For example, you might define a structured user-defined type called, say, `ADDRESS` to represent postal addresses for your customers. You might then define a second structured user-defined type named `CUSTOMER` to represent the customers themselves. A natural attribute of a customer is his or her address; thus, part of the definition of `CUSTOMER` would be an attribute whose data type is `ADDRESS`.

SQL:1999 permits you to nest such UDT usages as deeply as you desire (although specific implementations of the language will undoubtedly have limits on such nesting). In the United States, one attribute of an address is the ZIP code, which is typically made up of two fields separated by a hyphen, so it would be reasonable to define another UDT named `ZIP_CODE` and give that as the data type of the `ZIP` attribute of the `ADDRESS` type.

---

13 ISO/IEC 9075-1:1999, *Information technology—Database languages—SQL—Part 1: Framework (SQL/Framework)* (Geneva: International Organization for Standardization, 1999).

1.4.3 Attributes and Methods

In section 1.4.2, I suggested that there is an analogy between an SQL UDT and a C `struct`. However, a C `struct` has only data associated with it; there are no semantics associated with that data other than those associated with the data itself and those given it by the application that uses it.

By contrast, an SQL UDT comprises not only data but behaviors defined in the form of SQL-invoked routines. Java programmers will immediately recognize the analogy, but SQL goes a bit further than Java—the semantics of SQL UDTs (as well as of SQL's distinct types) can be provided through routines written entirely in SQL (using SQL/PSM's procedural statements),[14] or through routines written in any of the several programming languages that are supported by the SQL standard (and any others supported by specific products). By contrast, Java requires that its methods all be written in a single programming language: Java.

SQL provides several sorts of SQL-invoked routines: procedures, (ordinary) functions, and—most important for UDTs—methods. In Chapter 4, "Routines and Routine Invocation," I'll cover the similarities and the differences in considerable detail. For now, the relevant observation is that a method is an SQL-invoked routine that is very closely associated with a specific UDT and that is intended to provide behaviors of that UDT.

Instances of SQL's UDTs (that is, values whose data types are some UDT) thus contain *state* in the form of data stored in attributes and *behaviors* in the form of SQL-invoked routines that are associated with the UDT. UDTs, however, are *encapsulated* in SQL:1999—meaning that their internal details are obscured from the view of applications—by automatic provision of routines used to access and modify the values of attributes. In other words, applications do not directly retrieve the value of an attribute of a UDT, but code that specifies such a retrieval is implicitly converted to invocation of an *observer* method that returns the attribute's value to the application; modification of an attribute is similarly handled by a *mutator* method. This mechanism allows UDT authors to redefine the details of their UDTs by providing explicit methods that simulate the actions of the automatically generated observers and mutators.

1.4.4 Inheritance

In section 1.4.1, we saw that Khoshafian and Abnous included in their definition of object orientation a characteristic called *inheritance,* which they defined as the

14 ISO/IEC 9075-4:1999, *Information technology—Database languages—SQL—Part 4: Persistent Stored Modules (SQL/PSM)* (Geneva: International Organization for Standardization, 1999).

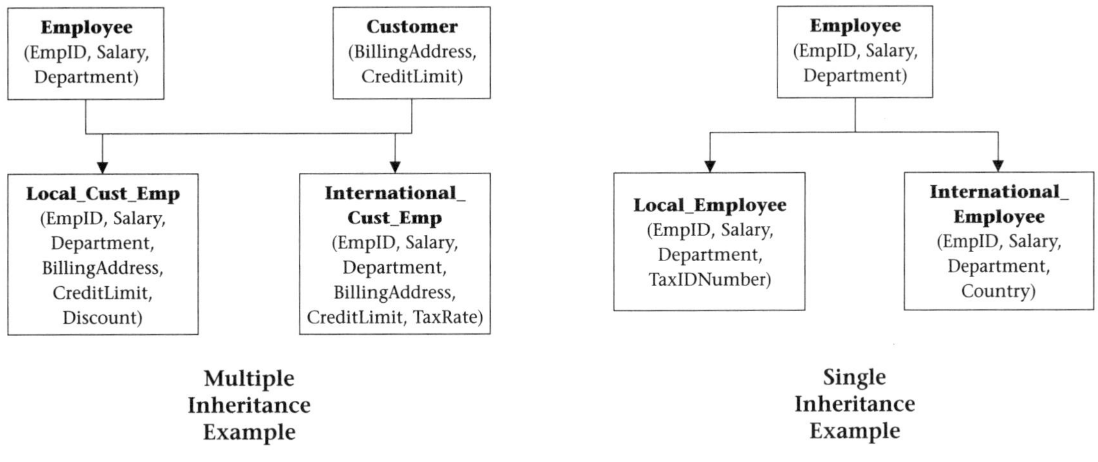

Figure 1.1 Multiple and Single Inheritance

ability to share structure and behavior among related types. In fact, inheritance is perhaps the most common characteristic among object models. In general, the word means that one type can be defined in terms of another type, inheriting all of the characteristics of that other type, as well as potentially adding new characteristics particular to the new type.

SQL/Framework defines inheritance in the following manner: "A structured type may be defined to be a *subtype* of another structured type, known as its *direct supertype*. A subtype *inherits* every attribute of its direct supertype and may have additional attributes of its own." Although that definition doesn't cite behaviors explicitly, SQL:1999's inheritance includes more than attributes—methods of supertypes are also inherited by subtypes.

Many object-oriented systems permit attributes and methods to be inherited from multiple supertypes; systems with this capability are said to support *multiple inheritance*. For example, the movie and video store that forms the basis of my sample application has several employees; naturally (if I am to remain in business), it also has customers. The database through which I manage the store includes UDTs for both employees and customers. However, some of my employees are also customers, so the question naturally arises: How do I represent a single entity that is both a customer and an employee? Systems that support multiple inheritance would allow creation of a new UDT, say `CUST_EMP`, that inherits all attributes and methods of my `CUSTOMER` type and all attributes and methods of my `EMPLOYEE` type. Figure 1.1 illustrates the relationships of types in a type hierarchy when multiple inheritance is supported and when single inheritance is supported.

Unfortunately, multiple inheritance works best in the environment of a single computer system, that is, in the absence of distribution over a communications network. Limited multiple inheritance capabilities can be provided in a distributed environment, but such environments generally impose serious performance problems on multiple-inheritance systems (the performance issues are related to the difficulties in dispatching a specific method to operate on an object whose most specific subtype is unknown until runtime). As a consequence, the specifications for several recent object-oriented systems, notably Java and SQL, have eschewed multiple inheritance in favor of a *single inheritance* facility. (Java provides a limited form of multiple inheritance through its distinction between *interface* and *implementation*; SQL:1999 does not provide that distinction, although it is being discussed for inclusion in some future version of the standard.)

1.4.5 Polymorphism

As you read in section 1.4.1, another attribute of object-oriented systems lies in polymorphism and overloading, which provide the ability to distinguish between two or more operations having the same name that have different semantics or that operate on values of different types. Most programmers are intimately familiar with polymorphism, even if they don't apply that word to describe the concept: If you've ever programmed in a language that allows you to add two integers using the familiar + operator *and* allows you to add two floating point numbers using that same operator, then you've already experienced the benefits of polymorphism. In this case, the + operator provides different (although conceptually similar) functions based on the data types of its arguments; for example, an integer addition usually makes use of different hardware circuitry than a floating point addition. SQL provides polymorphism of several operators across its built-in types (but not for user-defined types, even for familiar operators such as +).

The word derives from the Greek πολιμορφοσ (in Latin characters, that's *polimorphos*), meaning "many forms." You saw in Volume 1 of this book that Webster's Third New International Dictionary defines the related word *polymorphic* to mean "having or assuming various forms, characters, styles, or functions." In that definition, the use of *functions* is especially appropriate for our purposes, since SQL uses the word *polymorphism* to describe a characteristic of SQL-invoked functions and methods. SQL permits you to define more than one routine with a given routine name, as long as each such routine has either a different number of parameters or parameters with different data types. Whenever you execute a routine invocation that specifies the name of such a routine, SQL's routine resolution algorithm (covered in Chapter 4, "Routines and Routine Invocation") selects one particular routine, among the routines with the specified name, based on the number of arguments provided in the routine invocation and the data types of those arguments.

The most powerful use of polymorphism in SQL occurs along with the use of inheritance: a `PlayClip` method designed to play a clip from a music source whose identity is passed as an argument might effectively play clips from a subtype of "music source," such as CD or MusicDVD. On the other hand, you might choose to write a *different* version of `PlayClip` that handles DTD DVDs differently, but you can continue to use the name `PlayClip` regardless of the kind of music source you identify when you call the routine. The underlying routine invocation algorithm chooses the particular version of `PlayClip` that gets invoked based on the particular data passed into the routine invocation.

1.4.6 Typed Tables

To this point, my description of SQL's structured user-defined types has concentrated on the use of UDTs as values of a particular type. SQL permits the definition of a column in a table to have some UDT, say `ADDRESS`, as the type of that column in the same manner that it permits that column to have the data type INTEGER. The value stored in that column in each row of the table is an `ADDRESS` value or an INTEGER value, depending on the data type specified for the column. Similarly, you can define parameters of SQL-invoked routines, SQL variables, and attributes of other UDTs to have data types that are user-defined types.

But all of those uses of UDTs are as *values* and not as *objects*.

The final piece of the object-orientation puzzle, as you saw in section 1.4.1, is object identity, the real-world characteristic that every entity is uniquely identifiable. In the context of an object-oriented programming or database environment, that means that instances of abstract data types must have a unique identifier by which they can be referenced. SQL:1999 allows you to define and use UDTs whose instances do not have unique identities, and those instances are treated purely as values, not much different from instances of SQL's INTEGER, CHARACTER, or TIMESTAMP data types. But SQL also allows you to create instances of UDTs that have unique identity.

You may not be surprised to learn that in SQL:1999, UDT instances gain a unique identity only by placing them into a table. After all, the table is SQL's most fundamental data structure. In SQL:1999, a new kind of table has been introduced.

The definition of structured user-defined types includes this statement: "One or more base tables can be created based on a structured type." When a base table is created "based on a structured type," that table is called a *typed table* (it is sometimes called a *table of type*). Every row of a typed table *is* an instance (or a value, if you wish) of the UDT of which the table is a type. The table has one column derived from each attribute of the UDT (that is, the data type of the column is the data type of the associated attribute, the name of the column is the name of the attribute, and the values stored in the rows of the column are the values of the instances of the attribute in the instances of the type); it also has one additional column, called a *self-referencing column*. (As you'll see in Chapter 3, "Typed Tables," the term *self-referencing* was chosen to highlight the fact that each value stored in that column is a unique reference to the row in which it is stored—it is effectively an object identifier that uniquely identifies the UDT instance stored in the row of the table!)

As discussed in Chapter 3, "Typed Tables," SQL:1999 provides inheritance in the form of typed tables that corresponds closely with inheritance among the UDTs that are associated with those typed tables.

1.5 Conforming to SQL:1999 Object Facilities

As you would expect, the addition of object capabilities to SQL involved a bit of complexity. In order to make sense of the many different aspects involved, the SQL standardization groups identified and labeled a number of features associated with object orientation. Several of those features have been collected into two packages of features specifically associated with object facilities. (You can read more about SQL's features and packages in Volume 1 of this book, in Appendix C, "The SQL:1999 Annexes.")

One package, known as PKG006, "Basic object support," provides enough features for a minimal sort of "object-oriented SQL" implementation. The other, PKG007, "Enhanced object support," naturally requires PKG006 as a prerequisite and adds several significant features to the object support offered by an SQL implementation. In this section, I'm going to summarize the packages and each of their features. (While it's impossible to know just what those features provide without understanding what requirements they place on an implementation, the names and brief descriptions provided here should give you an idea of what the packages imply for an implementation.) You'll learn in Chapter 2, "User-Defined Types," and Chapter 3, "Typed Tables," about the actual language features that underlie these packages.

PKG006 contains a mere five features:

- Feature S023, "Basic structured types," supplies the ability to define UDTs and their methods without a number of advanced features.
- Feature S041, "Basic reference types," gives applications the ability to define and use references to instances of UDTs that appear in typed tables.
- Feature S051, "Create table of type," provides the ability to create typed tables.
- Feature S151, "Type predicate," allows an application to determine the precise type (in a type hierarchy) of an instance of some UDT.
- Feature T041, "Basic LOB data type support," supports the definition of SQL's LARGE OBJECT types (but not operations on them other than storage and retrieval).

PKG007 adds nine additional features:

- Feature S024, "Enhanced structured types," adds to Feature S023 a number of advanced UDT capabilities, including the ability to write methods in languages other than SQL, to compare two instances of a UDT, and to pass UDT instances to and from various routines.
- Feature S043, "Enhanced reference types," extends Feature S041 by permitting scoped references and automatic checking of reference validity, as well as other enhanced features.
- Feature S071, "SQL-paths in function and type name resolution," allows the use of SQL-paths to influence SQL's routine resolution algorithm.
- Feature S081, "Subtables," increases the power of Feature S051 by allowing typed tables to be arranged into a table hierarchy analogous to the type hierarchy of the associated UDTs.
- Feature S111, "ONLY in query expressions," gives applications the ability to retrieve *only* instances of a specific type and not instances of any of its subtypes.
- Feature S161, "Subtype treatment," provides the capability to instruct the SQL environment to assume that the value of some UDT instance is actually an instance of a specific subtype.
- Feature S211, "User-defined cast functions," supports syntax allowing type definers to define routines that cast UDT instances to and from other types.

- Feature S231, "Structured type locators," assists in accessing UDT instances from host programs.
- Feature S241, "Transform functions," supports syntax allowing type definers to define routines that transform values between UDTs and SQL's predefined data types.

1.6 Relationship to Products

The menagerie of SQL products on the marketplace has shrunk in recent years, as the relational database industry consolidates. At the time that this volume was written, Informix Software had recently been purchased by IBM, further reducing the number of independent players. (IBM announced that the Informix database products that it acquired in that purchase would continue to be supported for some period, but it seems doubtful that the products will be the subject of extensive new development.)

Of the remaining commercial SQL products, both Oracle and IBM have delivered implementations of various portions of SQL:1999's object capabilities. Neither has, to my knowledge, formally announced conformance to Core SQL:1999; without that conformance claim, they cannot *formally* claim conformance to PKG006, "Basic object support," much less PKG007, "Enhanced object support." In spite of that detail, both companies' products do support significant, although somewhat different, subsets of the features in those packages. It appears to me that Oracle's support has emphasized the use of structured user-defined types as rows of typed tables, while IBM's tends more toward the use of those UDTs as the types of columns in ordinary tables. Both directions are obviously useful and I would not be at all surprised to see both vendors enhancing their products by including the missing features.

Other major relational vendors (for example, Microsoft) have either not made clear their intentions regarding support for SQL:1999's structured user-defined types, or they have indicated only limited support for them. Sybase, for example, focuses on using Java as the underpinnings of its object-relational strategy and depends heavily on SQL-Java-related capabilities that are discussed in Chapter 8, "SQL/OLB and SQL/JRT."

While today (as I write this volume), IBM and Oracle (and, with a different orientation, Sybase) are the primary choices for acquiring an object-relational SQL system, there are other vendors from whom we have not yet heard, and the possibility always exists that one or more additional products will show up on the market.

1.7 Chapter Summary

This chapter included

- A brief introduction to object orientation and SQL's interpretation of the object model.
- An introduction to SQL:1999's structured user-defined types at a very high level, giving a preview of the material that will be covered in significantly more detail in other chapters.
- A review of the features that an SQL implementation must provide in order to claim conformance to object-oriented SQL.
- A survey of the support that you will find in SQL products that are actually on the market.

Chapter 2

User-Defined Types

2.1 Introduction

In this chapter, I'll tell you about user-defined types in general and about SQL's approach to them. First, I'll give you a solid overview of the facility and the supporting technology in SQL, after which I'll cover the subject in substantial detail.

In particular, in this chapter, I'll tell you what user-defined types are and why you might want to use them in your applications. Then I'll get more specific and show you SQL's UDT facilities, with examples of creating UDTs and manipulating instances of those UDTs. This discussion includes the creation and use of user-defined functions and methods that applications can use to invoke appropriate behaviors of those UDT instances. (However, details of SQL's routine definition and invocation are found in Chapter 4, "Routines and Routine Invocation.")

I'll also let you see how SQL's UDTs can be used as the data types of columns in tables and even the types of SQL variables. In addition, you'll see how a UDT can be declared to be the "data type" of an entire table—such that the table's columns are intimately related to the UDT's attributes. In Chapter 3, "Typed Tables," I'll cover the subject in greater detail.

Before finishing up, I'll give you an overview of the SQL object model, comparing and contrasting it (to some degree, at least) with Java's object model.

Finally, I'll discuss the implementation issues and some limitations on SQL's user-defined type facilities—both the technical limitations and the economic ones. The discussion of the technical limitations may be the most interesting to programmers, but the economic limitations are equally important and actually may have more influence on what products support. Don't neglect this section, since it has the potential to affect your organization's use of the technology.

2.2 What Are UDTs?

The term *user-defined type* may seem to be pretty much self-explanatory, but I'll expand on it anyway. The use of *type* is, of course, meant to imply "data type," that is, a data type that can be the type of some piece of data in the environment under discussion. In an SQL environment, this would normally be the data type of a column in a table, of an SQL variable in an SQL-invoked routine written in SQL, or of a parameter to an externally invoked SQL routine (which, as discussed in Volume 1 of this book, is little more than a fancy name for the implicit procedures generated for embedded SQL statements).

The inclusion of the phrase *user-defined* implies—obviously, I suppose, to most people—that the type isn't *built in* to the database system, but is defined in some other manner. Before examining user-defined types specifically, let's take a brief look at the history that brought us to this discussion.

2.2.1 Evolution of Type Systems

SQL database systems have always had a selection of built-in data types that are available for use in applications. They range from types specified in the SQL standard (like INTEGER and SMALLINT, CHARACTER and CHARACTER VARYING, and DATE, TIME, and TIMESTAMP) to proprietary types defined by individual database system products (such as Sybase's SMALLMONEY and IMAGE types or Oracle's NUMBER and RAW types). These built-in types served applications well for quite a few years, since SQL database systems were used principally to manage "traditional" data: data that is naturally represented using numbers, character strings, and datetime values.

However, as time passed, users of SQL database systems began to encounter the need to represent and manage more complex data—such as very large text documents on which search operations more complex than equality (and similar comparisons) could be performed, graphics and other image data, spatial and geographic information, and so forth. At first, the vendors of SQL systems responded by supporting "large object" types (LOBs, usually BLOBs for binary data and CLOBs for character data, although the names given to these types often varied from vendor to vendor). While these types made it possible to store large data items in a single cell (a name I use to describe the intersection of a column and a row, even though the SQL standard has no word for that concept) of a table, the database systems rarely supported any operations, including comparisons, on such data. If any operations were supported, they tended to be simple ones such as substring, concatenation, and basic comparisons (often limited to equality and inequality). In other words, the semantics of the data stored in such cells were not handled by the database system; they were left to the applications to tackle.

As a result of customer dissatisfaction with this state of affairs, SQL database system vendors began to explore other approaches to handling the requirements being expressed by their users. Some vendors responded fairly quickly by providing support for certain specific types of data—text, geospatial data, images, and time series data were among the most common—and often did so by tightly coupling their products with special-purpose modules that dealt specifically with those selected data types. This approach proved very successful because it focused on the most popular complex data types for which support was being demanded by large customers.

But customers and vendors alike recognized that this approach would satisfy requirements only for so long. For one thing, it was unlikely that this technique would continue to be successful if it were applied to dozens of specialized types. Instead, a more generalized approach was required. The answer (obvious to some, but not all, observers) was deceptively simple: build into SQL engines the capability to allow application builders to define their own specialized data types, especially including code to provide the semantics of those types. Some vendors used a pure SQL approach to providing this capability, while others used a hybrid approach that allowed SQL to invoke code written in another programming language, sometimes even supporting data types of that other language directly in the SQL engine.

Which brings me to user-defined types!

Even though they were not defined by users per se, one could argue that the few specialized types some vendors supported (in those special-purpose modules that I mentioned a couple of paragraphs ago) were user-defined types since they weren't exactly built-in from the database engine's point of view. However, I would dispute this definition, since I believe that the term should be reserved for types that can be defined flexibly enough to allow the creation of new behaviors not envisioned by the original authors of those special-purpose modules. Note, if you will, that I do *not* insist that *end users* be allowed to define either types or behaviors on them! The term *user-defined* does not have to imply end users; I am quite happy with the term applying to types defined by (or whose behaviors are defined by) system administrators, builders of commercial application packages, or authors other than end users.

In fact, I would argue that very few end users would even *want* to define their own types or behaviors! Most end users—by whom I mean the armies of application developers who are responsible for the majority of corporations' data processing and information systems—are far too busy trying to respond to business requirements thrown at them daily to want to spend time inventing new data types. Instead, I anticipate that information systems groups are likely to assign responsibilities for inventing these new data types to a small number of system programmers or database administrators, who will design the types and their behaviors to make available to the application programmers, who, in turn, will use them to build the bread-and-butter applications needed by their organizations. The SQL/MM standard discussed in Chapter 10, "SQL Multimedia and Application Packages," is an example of a standard defined using SQL's structured types. In defining SQL/MM, experts in the specific data domain participated to specify the necessary behaviors and algorithms for a particular application domain.

2.2.2 Introducing User-Defined Types

"Well," I can hear some of you asking, "exactly *what* is a user-defined type?"—not an unexpected question . . . especially since I just said that it doesn't have to be a type defined by a user at all!

Here's a working definition: A user-defined type is a type that is not built into a database system or programming language, but that can be defined as part of an application development effort, often (but not always) with behaviors provided by its definition.

Hmmm . . . "Do you really mean that user-defined types aren't required to have user-defined behaviors?" Right! As will be seen later in this chapter, SQL's user-defined type capabilities allow an application (or a database) to define a new type that is identical in most respects to some existing, built-in type. That's a pretty limited definition of user-defined type, I admit, but it does have its uses, as we'll see in section 2.4.1. As you'll see, these types—called *distinct* types—are permitted, but not required, to have user-defined behaviors, which distinguishes them from the other category of user-defined types—*structured types*—that have only user-defined behaviors.

Aside from such restricted types, most of what you'll see called *user-defined types* (or *abstract data types,* a phrase once employed in SQL:1999 during its development period) are likely to have some structure associated with them (comparable to the C programming language's `struct`) and also to have several user-defined functions to provide behaviors of the types. This could be as simple as a type for "temperature" that stores a single value, possibly an integer, and allows its users to store and retrieve the value in their choice of degrees Fahrenheit, degrees Celsius, or Kelvins. Or, it could be as complex as a type associated with "spatial data" having dozens or hundreds of data components and hundreds of functions to manipulate those components in various ways. It might even be a representation of a business entity, such as an employee, a department, an invoice, or a movie. (You *had* to see that coming!)

2.3 Using Objects: GUIs, Languages, and Major Applications

Before I launch into the technical details of SQL:1999's structured user-defined types, it may be interesting to look at a few areas of technology where object-oriented facilities are frequently used and consider the applicability of SQL's UDTs to those uses.

One of the first ways in which many people encounter object technology is in the graphical user interface (GUI) of the Windows operating system or of the Apple operating system, or X Windows on Unix and other operating systems. The event-driven nature of object-oriented systems fits very naturally with the requirements of GUIs, and the developers of those systems and of the applications that interface with them were quick to adopt the technology.

When object-oriented features were first being used in GUIs, the selection of programming languages supporting such features was rather limited. The fact that C has long been a popular language for implementing operating system–level programs such as GUIs may have contributed to the development of a major C extension, C++, as an object-oriented programming language (OOPL). While there are many critics of C++ as a language, it nonetheless has many adherents and is arguably one of the most popular OOPLs in use today.

However, some critics of C++ have been extremely successful in the creation of another language that shares many characteristics of C: Java. Java's designers believe that the language avoids many of the problems they perceive in C++ and that it addresses a number of important security issues associated with use of the Internet and the World Wide Web. In a very short period of time (even by information technology standards), Java has become extremely popular; it is difficult today to find serious Web application programmers who are not familiar with the language—which, as we shall see later in this chapter, strongly influenced the design of SQL:1999's object-related features. As a result of this popularity, both C++ and Java are being widely deployed for building system applications and for developing end-user applications.

Packaged applications, such as those provided by Oracle, PeopleSoft, SAP, and others, are not widely recognized as being based on object technology. Indeed, many such applications are not presently built using object-oriented capabilities (although some are). While I don't claim to have any inside information about the plans of companies building this sort of application system, I feel confident that most or all of them are actively moving toward the use of objects in their products. Why? For the simple reason that this class of application depends very heavily on being able to reuse design and code, sharing data among hundreds or thousands of application modules, and providing extreme customizability and maintainability. Object technology is widely agreed to be one of the most important ways of achieving those goals.

2.4 Three Kinds of UDTs

As I said in section 2.2.2, SQL:1999 provides more than one sort of user-defined type. While SQL provides a very powerful variation called *structured types* (which I'll introduce more thoroughly in section 2.4.2 and spend the bulk of the chapter discussing in detail), it also provides a more limited variant called *distinct types*. The discussion of distinct types is relatively short, since the subject was covered in detail in Volume 1 of this book; in fact, I'm including it only for the sake of completeness. Most of this chapter's space, and energy, is spent on structured types.

2.4.1 Distinct Types

A *distinct type* is a data type that is based on a single built-in data type, such as INTEGER, but whose values cannot be directly mixed in operations with that built-in type or with other distinct types based on that built-in type. (I say that they cannot be *directly* mixed because it is possible to cast a value of a distinct type to its underlying built-in type, after which it can be combined in operations with values of that built-in type.) Distinct types are first-class types, meaning that they can be used to define columns, variables, and so on, just like any SQL built-in type. They provide *strong typing* in the SQL language (in which typing is traditionally viewed as moderately strong at best, since you are allowed to mix data types in expressions within fairly generous bounds).

The best way to explain SQL's distinct types is by example. Consider an application that gathers information about people who buy music CDs and videotapes in an effort to learn how to predict, based on their demographics, what products people will be interested in hearing more about. This application—let's call it DEMOGRAPH—might gather quite a variety of data in hope that a data mining product could use it to uncover unexpected relationships.

DEMOGRAPH might choose to collect both a person's shoe size rounded to the nearest integer size *and* the person's IQ. (Okay, shoe size is unlikely to have much correlation with taste in music, but who knows!) It seems unlikely that DEMOGRAPH would ever want to compare anybody's shoe size with their IQ (now, now . . . no jokes about which one is larger for your buddy down the hall!), nor is it likely that we'd want to add them together, multiply them, or otherwise mix them in any sort of expression. If both values were collected into columns whose data types were declared to be INTEGER, however, there would be no protection against a programmer making an error and mixing those values in a single expression.

On the other hand, in SQL:1999, if a database designer declares two distinct types as shown in Example 2.1, then appropriate column definitions could be created as shown in Example 2.2.

Example 2.1 *Distinct Types*

```
CREATE TYPE shoe_size AS INTEGER FINAL;
CREATE TYPE iq AS INTEGER FINAL;
```

Example 2.2 *Table Definition Using Distinct Types*

```
CREATE TABLE demograph_people (
  name            CHARACTER VARYING(50),
  footsies        shoe_size,
  smarts          iq,
  last_purchase   DECIMAL(5,2) )
```

(Don't worry about the keyword FINAL; it's required in distinct type definitions by SQL:1999 for arcane reasons not relevant to this discussion.) The *source type* of the two distinct types defined above is INTEGER, but we can't blissfully use instances of the two types as though they were ordinary integer values. In fact, that table definition makes it impossible to *accidentally* write something like Example 2.3.

Example 2.3 *Incorrect Use of Distinct Types*

```
SELECT   name
FROM     demograph_people
WHERE    footsies > smarts
```

Any such mixing of the columns `footsies` and `smarts` in an expression (including a predicate like the one in the WHERE clause) will cause a syntax error. On the other hand, if your application really, *really* wants to do something like this, SQL:1999 provides a way to do so deliberately, as seen in Example 2.4.

Example 2.4 *Syntactically Correct (but Perhaps Nonsensical) Use of Distinct Types*

```
SELECT   name
FROM     demograph_people
WHERE    CAST(footsies TO INTEGER) > CAST(smarts TO INTEGER)
```

By coding the explicit CAST expressions, you've told SQL that you know what you're doing and it's not an accident for which a syntax error should be raised. In fact, SQL goes a bit further than the examples so far illustrate. It's similarly forbidden to raise your IQ or even compare your IQ as indicated in Example 2.5, because the + operator does not support adding integer values to IQ values or comparing IQ values with integer values.

Example 2.5 *Invalid Attempt to Raise an IQ and to Compare a Shoe Size*

```
SELECT   name, iq + 20
FROM     demograph_people
WHERE    footsies > 7
```

Again, casting the IQ value to an INTEGER before performing the operation—and, where the result is required to be an IQ value, casting the resulting INTEGER value back to an IQ value—is the right way to go, as illustrated in Example 2.6.

Example 2.6 *Valid Attempt to Raise an IQ and to Compare a Shoe Size*

```
SELECT   name, CAST ( iq AS INTEGER ) + 20
FROM     demograph_people
WHERE    CAST ( footsies AS INTEGER ) > 7
```

In SQL:1999, distinct types are made more powerful by allowing database designers to create user-defined comparisons, user-defined casts, and other sorts of user-defined functions based on the distinct types in the database. Such functions, if defined, provide at least part of the distinct type's semantics. It's beyond the scope of this book to go into that level of detail about distinct types, though; if you're interested in it, I urge you to acquire one of the SQL:1999 books that are (or soon will be) available.

By the way, if you are familiar with SQL-92, you've probably learned something about its *domain* capabilities. While SQL:1999 retains that facility (and makes no statement about its relationship to distinct types), I believe that distinct types provide a much better solution to the problems that domains attempted to solve. Based on this belief, it is possible that future generations of the SQL standard may first deprecate and then delete domains entirely, in spite of the existence of users who take advantage of domains' macro-like behaviors.

2.4.2 Structured UDTs as Values

As indicated earlier, the other sort of user-defined type supported in SQL:1999 is the structured type; you should infer from its name that values of such types are permitted to have—and usually do have—internal structure to them. For example, a structured type named `address` might contain several components: `number`, `street_name`, `apartment_number`, `city`, `state_or_region`, `country`, and `postal_code`. Similarly, a type named `movie` might contain components such as `title`, `length`, and `description`. Instances of SQL's structured types are values, no less than instances of SQL's INTEGER type are values. As you'll see in section 2.4.3, values of a structured type may, under certain circumstances, take on some characteristics of objects, but they are first and foremost values of their user-defined type.

In SQL:1999, users may create any number of structured types and use them as first-class types in their databases and applications. (Reminder: I use the phrase *first-class type* to indicate a data type that can be used as the data type of database columns, SQL variables, and so forth.) In addition to an internal structure, SQL's structured types can be associated with specific user-defined functions that are used for all comparisons of instances of the type, for casting values of the type to and from other types, and for implementing all sorts of behaviors (that is, semantics) of the type.

Syntax 2.1 contains the syntax of the CREATE TYPE statement. Please don't be too intimidated by the many different parts of this statement. I'll get to them all in due time. My purpose in giving you the entire syntax now is so that I can refer back to it as I get to each component in the discussion of structured types throughout the rest of this chapter.

Syntax 2.1 *CREATE TYPE Syntax*

```
CREATE TYPE type-name [ UNDER supertype-name ]
    [ <external Java type clause> ]
    [ AS representation ]
    [ [ NOT ] INSTANTIABLE ]
    [ NOT ] FINAL
    [ reference-type-specification ]
    [ <ref cast option> ]
    [ cast-option ]
    [ method-specification-list ]
```

The `<external Java type clause>` is, as its name suggests, relevant only for types defined using Java, which is addressed in detail in another book[1] and is thus discussed only sparingly here.

1 Jim Melton and Andrew Eisenberg, *Understanding SQL and Java Together: A Guide to SQLJ, JDBC, and Related Technologies* (San Francisco: Morgan Kaufmann Publishers, 2000).

2.4.3 Structured UDTs as Objects

As stated in section 2.4.2, instances of SQL:1999's structured user-defined types are essentially *values*. Sure, they have many of the characteristics that many object-oriented systems give to their objects (instances of their classes), such as type hierarchies, user-provided behaviors, and so forth. But they're missing an important characteristic of true objects: a unique identity.

The essential purpose of an object in an object-oriented programming language or other system is to represent some real-world entity, and all real-world entities are unique "things" with their own unique "self." (Of course, we all recognize that some "things" in the real world are incredibly anonymous, such as the ants in our backyards or the cornflakes in the boxes we purchase at the market. Such entities are rarely given names or handles with which they can be identified from a distance, but merely holding two of them in your hands should persuade you that they are different "things" and not merely two "pointers" to the same individual entity.)

The way that instances of SQL:1999 structured types become part of an "object" environment is through their insertion into a special sort of SQL table, called a *typed table,* which is covered in detail in Chapter 3, "Typed Tables." For now, I'll merely say that a row in a typed table *is* an instance of the structured type on which the table is defined and that gives the instance a unique identity.

Once an instance of a structured type has a unique identity, then it really behaves exactly as an object is expected to behave in an object-oriented environment. For all practical purposes, it *is* an object. The operations performed on that structured type instance by various procedures, functions, and methods (discussed in more detail in Chapter 4, "Routines and Routine Invocation") behave in the manner that an object system affects the objects in that system. In section 2.15, I explain SQL's object model and compare it to another well-known object model, Java's.

2.5 Major Characteristics of Structured UDTs

The two principle characteristics of structured types in SQL:1999 are these: they normally have stored data associated with them; and the operations that can be performed on them are implemented by code provided by the type definer. While distinct types can have operations on their instances enhanced by user-provided code, and they certainly have stored data associated with them, they behave much more like SQL's built-in types and thus don't really share with structured types all of the characteristics of object orientation discussed in this section. (On the other hand, it is certainly possible to define a distinct type based on SQL's BINARY LARGE OBJECT type and write functions to emulate many of the capabilities of structured types, which might provide a sort of poor man's structured type.)

However, there are other characteristics that we'll cover, including one very important one called *encapsulation,* which we'll discuss in some detail later on, primarily in section 2.6.1. But it's an important enough topic to introduce now and expand on later.

In SQL:1999, all structured types are *encapsulated,*[2] meaning that they are defined in a way that makes it difficult—though, as we'll see later in this chapter, not quite impossible—for applications to learn how various characteristics are actually implemented. The word *encapsulated* means that every component of the thing that is encapsulated is presented only through some interface. This interface permits the internal implementation details to be changed without affecting the applications using the type (as long, of course, as the interface remains the same and any changes to the resulting behavior don't cause incompatibilities in the behaviors seen by the applications).[3] In practice, encapsulation of structured types largely means that all access to instances of the types—including both its data and its behaviors—is through the use of various sorts of functions that are associated in some way with the types. These functions are mostly, but not exclusively, methods, which I'll contrast with ordinary functions in section 2.7 and in Chapter 4, "Routines and Routine Invocation."

As I go through the details of structured types in the next few sections of this chapter, I'll identify the ways in which encapsulation is provided.

2.5.1 Structured Type Attributes

The stored data associated with a structured type is actually stored in the various elements comprising the structure of the type (types built using Java being the exception). These elements are called the type's *attributes.* Each attribute has a single data type, although these data types are not limited to SQL's built-in *atomic*[4] types. The collection of attributes of a structured type is called the type's *represen-*

---

2 There are several different ways to define *encapsulation.* The definition that I give here is consistent with the SQL:1999 standard but is deficient according to some observers. For example, the fact that SQL:1999's object model doesn't allow for private attributes, but only public attributes, makes it impossible to completely hide the implementation details of types. In passing, I note that structured types defined as `Serializable` Java types are not even required to have methods defined on them, increasing the encapsulation characteristic considerably.

3 This principle is illustrated in section 2.7.6, especially in Example 2.17.

tation. In fact, in Syntax 2.1, you see the optional clause `AS representation`; it is that clause in which you would specify all of the attributes of a user-defined type.

Readers familiar with the Java language and object model will be comfortable with most of these concepts, but most likely use different terms to refer to them. In the Java programming language, objects may have *fields* or *instance variables,* each of which has a data type. Those variables may be simple values, such as short integers (`short`) or single characters (`char`), or they may be more complex values, such as Java objects like arrays (using notations like `int[]`) or strings (`String`). The fields of Java's objects correspond to the attributes of SQL's structured types (within reason—SQL:1999 doesn't support all of Java's features, such as `public/protected/private` attributes and `static` attributes).

2.5.2 Behaviors and Semantics

The other important characteristic of SQL:1999 structured types is their semantics, or behaviors. As in other object-oriented systems, the semantics/behaviors of these types are provided through *routines* (including methods, of course, as well as—in a limited sense, at least—functions and procedures). Unlike many other such systems, however, SQL:1999 allows type designers to provide the behaviors of its user-defined types through routines written in any of several languages, not only in SQL. In fact, Java is one of those languages, as you'll see when you get to Chapter 8, "SQL/OLB and SQL/JRT."

The terminology used in discussing objects and object models gets a bit confusing at times; this appears to be due to the use of different vocabularies to describe different object models. For example, some object models talk about objects as though they were independent entities that respond to external stimuli on their own (e.g., an application "sends a message" to an object and the object acts on that message), while other object models, including SQL:1999's, describe the same event by saying that an application "invokes a routine" and specifies the target object's identity as part of that invocation—so it's the routine that is active and the object is passive.

---

4 The word *atomic* is sometimes applied to most of SQL's *built-in* data types, such as INTEGER, CHARACTER VARYING, and TIMESTAMP, to distinguish them from SQL's *constructed* types, REF, ROW, and ARRAY.

Whichever way you like to think about these things, let's agree that—for the duration of this book, at least—we'll use the terminology that SQL:1999 uses (in part because it's compatible with Java's terminology, but mostly because this book is about SQL:1999).

Therefore, a type's behaviors (or, if you prefer, the behaviors of instances of that type) are supplied by the invocation of one or more routines, either directly by an application program or indirectly by some other routine, which may or may not be directly associated with that type. Now, by "behaviors," I mean actions that are performed by the system—in the case of SQL:1999 types, this will naturally be the SQL system—that either change the state of some type instance, return some value derived from the state of some type instance, or perform some other action involving the type or an instance of it.

Examples are naturally helpful in understanding what I mean: A type that represents rational numbers (numbers representable by fractions in which both the numerator and denominator are integers) might have actions like "add two rational values together" or "return the value of the numerator" or "send an e-mail message containing the real number resulting from the division of the numerator by the denominator and then turn on the lights at the Eiffel Tower." There are no limits to what these behaviors can be, other than those set by the environment in which you're operating. A type designer typically determines the behaviors supported by, or available to, the types being defined, but some systems permit applications to add new behaviors to existing types.

2.5.3 Inheritance and Type Hierarchies

Section 2.7.6 covers the subject of SQL:1999's type hierarchies in detail, and section 1.4.4, "Inheritance," gave you a brief overview of the topic. In this section, I'll illustrate the concepts to set the stage for the more detailed discussion later in this chapter.

In the narrow world of my music and video store, the notion of *movie* is quite important. In order to serve my customers well, I plan to give my users the ability to enquire about many aspects of movies in which they are interested—for example, the names of cast members, the running time, and information about other films by the same director. I also very much want to sell and rent videotapes and DVDs of movies to customers.

A little thought convinces me that I should *model* at least the following concepts:

- Movies—I cannot, of course, *sell* (or rent) a movie; I can only sell or rent some medium on which a movie has been recorded. Nonetheless, there is a great deal of information about each movie that I need to capture.
- Movies available on VHS
- Movies available on DVD

Now, it's probably obvious to you that the movie *Shrek* is (essentially) the same movie whether it's seen on VHS or on DVD (or, indeed, on older media like Beta or LaserDisc), but a description of a VHS tape release of *Shrek* will have additional characteristics, like its purchase price or rental price, number of units available for sale or rent, and so forth. Similarly, DVDs of *Shrek* are likely to have extra features, such as additional languages, Dolby Digital and/or DTS sound, and so on.

Therefore, an instance of "Movie available on VHS" has all of the characteristics of the "Movie" recorded on the VHS tape, and has additional characteristics as well. An instance of "Movie available on DVD" may not have all of the characteristics of an instance of "Movie available on VHS," but it certainly has all of the characteristics of the "Movie" itself, as well as its own additional characteristics.

SQL and other object-oriented systems use the word *subtype* to describe a data type that has all of the characteristics—including stored data and behaviors—of another type. The word *supertype* is used to describe the type whose characteristics are "had" by a subtype.

It is perfectly reasonable to model "Movies available on VHS" as a subtype of "Movies" and to model "Movies available on DVD" as a subtype of "Movies," but it is not reasonable to model "Movies available on DVD" as a subtype of "Movies available on VHS" (or vice versa), since those two types have different (although overlapping) sets of characteristics.

But, wait! There's more to consider: In their efforts to maximize return from distributing a film, studios often release more than one version of the DVD of a movie. The "original release" may be distributed a few months after the film hits the theaters, with a "special edition" or a "director's cut" following several months later. Studios also might release the DVD of a film in different markets with different sets of additional features, or they might release both a Dolby Digital DVD and a DTS DVD at the same time. Since I need to support my customers' demand for each of these variants, I should be prepared to model concepts like "Movies available on DVD in Dolby Digital sound" and "Movies available on DVD in DTS sound." Naturally, those are quite reasonably modeled as subtypes of "Movies available on DVD." Figure 2.2 on page 69 illustrates some of these relationships, but a real application—even one as simple as the one supporting my hypothetical music and video store—is likely to have many more structured types and a somewhat deeper type hierarchy.

2.6 Attributes in Detail

As I said in section 2.5.1, every instance of a structured type contains some stored data, and that data is stored in the type's attributes. (As we'll see later in this chapter, you can create structured types that are not instantiable, meaning that no instances of them will ever exist. Such types' attributes never have data stored in them, but the attributes are inherited by all subtypes of such types, and those subtypes might have instances that store data in the inherited attributes.) You'll also recall that each attribute has a single data type. The collection of data stored in all attributes of a specific instance of some structured type is often called the *state* of the type instance. However, since instances of SQL:1999's types are actually values (as you read in section 2.4.2), many object practitioners would reserve the use of the term *state* for structured type instances stored in rows of a typed table (which behave more like objects).

2.6.1 Encapsulation

As you saw in Chapter 1, "Introduction to SQL:1999," one of the observed values of object orientation is the ability to alter the internal details of your code and data without requiring applications that use it to be updated correspondingly. The characteristic of types that permits you to make such internal changes transparently is called *encapsulation*. As the word suggests, the physical composition of a structured type can be hidden from the view of the applications that make use of the type and of instances of the type. Perhaps rather less surprising, applications also remain unaware of the details of the code that implement the behaviors of the type.

SQL:1999 encapsulates each attribute of a structured type by providing a pair of built-in routines that are invoked whenever an application attempts to reference the type. One routine, called an *observer* (or *accessor* in some object systems), is used whenever an application retrieves the value of the attribute; the other, called a *mutator,* is invoked to change the value of the attribute. As discussed in section 2.6.3, applications use a variation of function invocation syntax—`function_name (argument...)`—to invoke the built-in observer and mutator associated with each attribute. The names that you use to invoke observers and mutators are the same as the names of the attributes to which they provide access; that is, an attribute named `movie_length` is encapsulated by provision of an observer named `movie_length` and a mutator also named `movie_length`. In Chapter 4, "Routines and Routine Invocation," I discuss how SQL:1999 supports the ability to have multiple functions that are invoked using the same name.

As stated in the preceding paragraph, applications use a variation of function invocation syntax (discussed in section 2.7.1 and again in Chapter 4, "Routines and Routine Invocation") to invoke every behavior of structured types that is performed by the special sort of function called a *method*.[5] This variant function invocation syntax is what allows a type definer to modify the implementation of a structured type, even replacing some attributes with new methods that emulate the former observer and mutator methods associated with those attributes.

It is through the requirement that applications access attributes *only* through methods that SQL:1999's structured types are encapsulated. Since every behavior of a structured type is provided only by routines of several sorts (primarily methods, although ordinary functions and even procedures can have an effect on type instances), applications can remain blissfully unaware of many sorts of changes in the type's definition.

2.6.2 Data Types

In SQL, there are very few limitations on where a given data type can be used. In fact, the primary limitation is that certain complex data types cannot be used to exchange data with the client programs that invoke the SQL statements of an application. For example, SQL-92 provided three datetime types (DATE, TIME, and TIMESTAMP) for which there were no mappings to host language types. Similarly, SQL:1999 provides an ARRAY type and a ROW type for which the SQL standard provides no mapping to host language data types (although such mappings are possible for most host languages and some vendors are expected to provide these mappings as product extensions). You may not be surprised to learn that SQL:1999 does not provide direct mappings from structured types to host language types,[6] either. However, as we'll see very shortly, there are straightforward ways of accessing structured types' values from client programs, as well as ways for type definers to provide user-defined routines to "map" structured type values to and from host program storage.

Each attribute of an SQL structured type can be specified to have a data type that is one of SQL's built-in scalar types, such as INTEGER, DECIMAL(7,2), CHARACTER VARYING(255), or TIMESTAMP(6). The type of an attribute can also be specified to be a distinct type. In addition, any attribute can be specified

5 For reasons that are difficult to explain, the SQL standard refers to observer and mutator methods using the phrases *observer function* and *mutator function*. This disparity of nomenclature extends to a very few other sorts of methods. I attempt to be more consistent in this volume, but I may sometimes slip up and use the standards' terminology.

6 Structured types defined using Java are mapped directly to Java objects and thus do not suffer from this limitation.

to have a data type that is one of SQL's built-in "constructed types," such as ARRAY or ROW (these types were covered in Volume 1 of this book). Finally, attributes can be specified to have a data type that is some other structured type—but, unfortunately, not the structured type in which the attribute is defined (more on this later).

There are no limits in the SQL:1999 standard on the relationships of all of these data types other than those appearing in the preceding paragraph. That is, a structured type can have attributes whose data types are ARRAYs of ROWs, some of whose fields are ARRAYs of some structured type, some of whose attributes are ROWs of ARRAYs of other types. For example, consider the following type that would be reasonable for representing street addresses in the United States (which the music and video store might use for shipping and billing Web-based purchases):

Example 2.7 *CREATE TYPE address*

```
CREATE TYPE address AS (
    number          CHARACTER(6),
    street          ROW (
       street_name     CHARACTER VARYING(35),
       street_type     CHARACTER VARYING(10) ),
    city            CHARACTER VARYING(35),
    state           CHARACTER(2),
    zip_code        ROW (
       base            CHARACTER(5),
       plus4           CHARACTER(4) ) )
    NOT FINAL
```

The address type contains within it two attributes whose data types are not scalar types. These two ROW types happen to have two fields each, but that is of course a coincidence, as is the fact that all non-ROW attributes and all fields are some variation of the CHARACTER type. I could just as easily have used INTEGERs and TIMESTAMPs if I had data of those types to record.

2.6.3 Accessing Attributes

You would be very surprised—and disappointed—if you were to learn that attributes of structured types couldn't be accessed fairly easily. In fact, they can be accessed quite easily, using more than one syntax notation. (To avoid any confusion, let me state clearly that *access* doesn't only mean *retrieve*. It means both retrieval and modification: accessing for whatever supported purpose.)

The most intuitive notation (for developers using most popular programming languages, at least) is what we call *dot notation*. To access a structured type attribute using dot notation, you simply specify the name of the "site" (as you learned in Volume 1 of this book, a *site* is a place where data can be stored, including columns of rows, SQL variables and host variables, and parameters of routines) whose data type is that structured type, followed by a period (the eponymous "dot"), followed by the name of the attribute.

Suppose we have a `customers` table with an associated correlation name `c`, one of whose columns, named `cust_addr`, has a data type of `address`—the very same structured type I defined earlier. The following notation would access the `number` attribute of that column:

```
c.cust_addr.number
```

Now, I find that notation to be intuitive simply because it follows the long-standing pattern in SQL—use a period (or dot) to separate the components of the name of some datum you want to access in your application. In fact, SQL takes this still further: dot notation is used to reach within a row:

```
c.cust_addr.zip_code.base
```

If, by some chance, the `customers` table had an array of addresses, perhaps to capture the fact that some customers have home addresses, vacation addresses, and business addresses, we could access the second of those using the notation

```
c.cust_addr[2].zip_code.base
```

Like I said, intuitive!

2.6.4 A Note about Table Names Versus Correlation Names

SQL programmers have long been accustomed to writing code like the following:

```
SELECT   name, city
FROM     customers
WHERE    cust_id = :hostvar1
```

This code, we've all learned, is equivalent to the fully qualified variation:

```
SELECT   customers.name, customers.city
FROM     customers
WHERE    customers.cust_id = :hostvar1
```

And, in turn, that is equivalent to the alternative that defines a *correlation name* to use in place of the table name:

```
SELECT   c.name, c.city
FROM     customers AS c
WHERE    c.cust_id = :hostvar1
```

When SQL:1999 added structured types to the data type mix, it would have been obvious to allow references to attributes of columns whose data type is some structured type by allowing a statement like this:

```
SELECT   name, city, cust_addr.street_name
FROM     customers
WHERE    cust_id = :hostvar1
```

or the *expected* equivalent:

```
SELECT   customers.name, customers.city, customers.cust_addr.street_name
FROM     customers
WHERE    customers.cust_id = :hostvar1
```

Unfortunately, the possibility of syntax ambiguities raises its ugly head and prevents that expected equivalent from being valid! Consider that you might happen to have in your database a schema named `customers` that holds a table named `cust_addr` that, in turn, has a column named `street_name`. How, then, in a query like this one

```
SELECT   customers.name, customers.city, customers.cust_addr.street_name
FROM     customers, customers.cust_addr
WHERE    customers.cust_id = :hostvar1
```

should the expression `customers.cust_addr.street_name` be resolved—as *schema.table.column* or as *table.column.attribute*? (Whether this specific example is likely or not is irrelevant to a language specification; the very possibility has to be taken into account and the possible ambiguity resolved.)

The solution chosen for SQL:1999 was to prohibit references to attributes that are qualified with table names and column names (or, for that matter, with column names alone). Instead, applications are required to create and use a correlation name in such instances.

Therefore, either of the following alternatives are valid in SQL:1999:

```
SELECT   name, city, c.cust_addr.street_name
FROM     customers AS c
WHERE    cust_id = :hostvar1
```

or

```
SELECT   c.name, c.city, c.cust_addr.street_name
FROM     customers AS c
WHERE    c.cust_id = :hostvar1
```

But SQL:1999 syntax prohibits the use of either `cust_addr.street_name` or `customers.cust_addr.street_name` as an expression. Any attempt to do so will cause a syntax error. Caveat programmer!

2.6.5 Attribute Characteristics

Attributes, as I've said several times, are where structured types store their data. Naturally, attributes have various characteristics, the most evident of which are their names and their data types. (In case it's not yet clear, *every* attribute of SQL:1999's user-defined types has both a name and a data type.)

But attributes have characteristics other than name and data type, as well. For example, attributes can be given a specified default value, like the default for `street_type` in this structured type definition:

Example 2.8 *CREATE TYPE with default values*

```
CREATE TYPE address AS (
    number          CHARACTER(6),
    street          ROW (
       street_name     CHARACTER VARYING(35),
       street_type     CHARACTER VARYING(10) DEFAULT 'Street' ),
    city            CHARACTER VARYING(35),
    state           CHARACTER(2),
```

```
zip_code        ROW (
   base            CHARACTER(5),
   plus4           CHARACTER(4) ) )
NOT FINAL
```

Like columns in SQL's tables, attributes have a "default default" value—the null value—that is used whenever the application designer doesn't provide a different default value.[7] And, perhaps obviously, you can explicitly make the null value an attribute's default value by using the keyword NULL, just as you can do for a column.

In addition, character string attributes, like character string columns, always have a known character set (that's a characteristic of the variants of the CHARACTER data type) and a known default collation, which you can either provide explicitly or permit to default to the character set's default collation.

However, unlike columns in tables, you cannot specify *constraints* on the attributes of a structured type—not even a NOT NULL constraint! When SQL:1999's definers were developing the structured type specifications, the ability to specify at least some sorts of constraints on attributes was considered. However, SQL has always distinguished between data stored in its tables and data in other, more transient, locations, such as in host variables, SQL variables, and the parameters to SQL routines. Only data that is stored in tables is affected by SQL's transaction semantics and by its constraints. The data found in variables, arguments, and other transient sites are outside the scope of those mechanisms.

Because structured types can be used as the data types of variables, arguments and parameters, and so forth, permitting constraints to be put on their attributes would imply that those constraints would be applied to such transient sites, violating that aspect of SQL's design. Instead, the designers concluded that constraints on columns whose data types are some structured type could be used to control the values allowed in the type's attributes, but only for instances stored in those columns.

Attributes have an additional characteristic, called a *reference scope check,* that I won't cover until section 2.8, "Defining Structured User-Defined Types." (I mention it here only for completeness.)

In section 2.6.1, you learned that all aspects of structured types are encapsulated; that particularly includes their attributes. Every attribute of an SQL:1999 structured type has two built-in, system-defined methods associated with it (see section 2.7.1 for details about methods and their invocation syntax). One of these methods is called an *observer method* and the other a *mutator method;* the

7 Attribute defaults are not permitted for structured types defined using Java.

observer method returns to its caller the value of its associated attribute in a structured type instance, while the mutator method allows the value of its associated attribute to be changed. In fact, one pair of methods (an observer and a mutator) is automatically created for each attribute by the database system when the structured type is created; you don't have to explicitly create them in any way other than defining the attributes of the type. In spite of the fact that these two methods provide access to the encapsulated attribute for which they're defined, you *always* use dot notation for invoking them; functional notation is reserved for (all) ordinary functions—that is, functions that are not methods.

The name of the observer method for an attribute is identical to the name of the attribute itself. The observer method takes no explicit argument, but it does have a single implicit argument: the name of some site (e.g., a column, parameter, or variable) whose data type is the structured type associated with the observer method; this argument is always provided *implicitly,* by using it to "qualify" the attribute (or method) name, rather than as an explicit argument. You *always* use the observer method to get the value of an attribute of a structured type instance. Using the `address` example from section 2.6.2 (including the use of `c` as a correlation name), you could write

```
c.cust_addr.number
```

or perhaps

```
c.cust_addr[2].zip_code.base
```

or even

```
c.cust_addr[2].zip_code.base()
```

Invocation of one of those methods *must be written* using the dot notation that I showed you in the previous section (note, however, that an empty pair of parentheses are permitted—but not required—to indicate that the invocation has no arguments other than the implicit one). The data type of the value returned by the observer method is the data type of the attribute, which of course is also the data type of the plain dot notation expression (without the parentheses that you might normally associate with functional notation).

The mutator method for an attribute isn't very different in appearance from the observer method—and, in fact, it has exactly the same name as the observer method (we'll see in Chapter 4, "Routines and Routine Invocation," exactly how this *overloading* works). There are two principle differences. First, the mutator method takes two arguments—one implicit and one explicit. As with the observer method, the implicit argument is the name of some site whose data type is the structured type. The explicit argument is an expression whose data type is the data type of the associated attribute and whose value is the value to which you want that attribute set. The second difference is perhaps unexpected: the data type returned by a mutator method has nothing to do with the data type of the attribute, but is the structured type itself! The reason for this is subtle, and a complete discussion will have to wait until section 2.10, but for now I'll just say that the mutator method actually returns a new instance (that is, a value) of the type whose attribute is being changed.

The observer method and the mutator method together *encapsulate* the attribute completely. If some future enhancement to the type were to change the internal representation (that is, the data type) of the `number` attribute from CHARACTER(6) to INTEGER, it would be possible to write a new function that contained a statement to CAST the INTEGER value retrieved to a CHARACTER(6) value before returning it to the invoker, thus protecting application programs from that change in the structured type's definition.

Unlike Java, SQL does not permit you to "protect" your types' observer and mutator methods. Java permits you to leave some observers and mutators `public`, and to limit others' uses only to subtypes (`protected`) and still others' uses only to the type being defined (`private`). SQL has no analog to this capability (although it may be added in a future version of the standard); all methods in SQL are effectively public methods. You can prevent their access by unauthorized users through the use of SQL's long-standing privilege mechanisms, such as denying EXECUTE privilege to some users on the methods.

At this point, let's stop talking about attributes and their pairs of methods. I say more (quite a lot more, in fact) about methods in Chapter 4, "Routines and Routine Invocation." But, for now, you've got the basics of attributes and are ready to tackle structured types' semantics.

2.7 Behavior and Methods

In section 2.5.2, you learned that the semantics of SQL's structured types is provided through the use of *routines* and that SQL:1999 allows the behaviors of its user-defined types to be provided through routines written in any of several languages, including Java.

Recall, too, that a type's behaviors are supplied by the invocation of one or more routines, either directly by an application program or indirectly by some other routine, which may or may not be closely associated with some structured type.

In SQL:1999, you can use any kind of routine supported by SQL to provide behavior for structured types, but the most important kind is known as a *method*. In SQL, a method is a special sort of function, invoked without the CALL statement used for procedure invocation. However, as you saw in section 2.6.5, the syntax for invoking a method differs slightly from that for invoking a function, since method invocation requires that the argument that identifies the structured type instance that you're accessing be specified as an implicit argument—the name of some site preceding the name of the method.

2.7.1 Procedures, Functions, and Methods

PSM-96[8] standardized for the first time the ability for SQL programmers to write functions and procedures (SQL-invoked routines) for use in their SQL code; those functions and procedures could be written in SQL or in any of several supported programming languages. SQL:1999 adds a third sort of routine to the mix: *methods*. Before we get into the details of methods, let's briefly review the broader subject of routines. (This material is covered in more detail in Chapter 4, "Routines and Routine Invocation," but a short introduction here makes other material in this chapter more accessible.)

SQL-invoked routines can be written in SQL, in which case they are called *SQL routines*. They can also be written in any of several other programming languages, and are then called *external routines*. The SQL standard specifies eight other languages in which SQL-invoked routines can be written—Ada, C, COBOL, Fortran, M (formerly known as MUMPS), Pascal, PL/I, and more recently Java. SQL products rarely support all eight alternatives (although C, COBOL, and Java seem to be especially popular) and frequently support languages not supported in the SQL standard.

SQL:1999's procedures, as you would expect from your familiarity with other programming languages, are routines that do not return a value in any way other than through an explicit parameter. Those of you who are Java programmers know that the closest analog in that language is its `void` methods. Procedures in SQL, as in most other languages, are permitted to have parameters that are used for output as well as parameters that are used for input (and, for that matter, parameters that are used for both).

While SQL procedures' parameters can have structured types as their data types, there is no special treatment of this, either in notation or in the handling of the parameter list. (External procedures are not allowed to use structured types for parameters, because the mapping between structured types and host lan-

8 ISO/IEC 9075-4:1996, *Information technology—Database languages—SQL—Part 4: Persistent Stored Modules (SQL/PSM)* (Geneva International Organization for Standardization, 1996).

guage types is not specified by the SQL standard. SQL:1999 does provide techniques with which external routines can be given access to structured types.) Consequently, procedures really don't affect the SQL object model very much and I do not discuss them in any depth in this chapter. (You can learn more about procedures in Chapter 4, "Routines and Routine Invocation.")

In the SQL world (and, with few exceptions, in most programming languages), the word *routine* generically applies to a variety of types of subprograms, including both functions and procedures. A function is a routine that has a value—in other words, that returns a value without using an explicit parameter to do so; functions are typically used in contexts such as value expressions. For example:

```
1+SQRT(2)
```

represents the concept "one plus the square root of two" in Fortran and many other languages. In that expression, "SQRT(2)" is the syntax for an invocation of the function SQRT to which a single argument, the number 2, is passed.

In SQL, functions have only input parameters; therefore, you cannot return more than a single value from a function. By contrast, procedures are routines that return values only through parameters.[9] Procedures are typically invoked using some form of "CALL" statement. In SQL, procedures can have both input parameters and output parameters (and parameters that are both at once).

In SQL:1999, a method is a special type of function. The most important differences between SQL's functions and its methods are summarized in Table 2.1.

In other words, an SQL:1999 method is a function that is closely associated with a single structured type[10] and is defined in the same schema as that type, that must be invoked using dot notation, and whose invocations might not be fully resolved when the containing program is compiled. I cover the invocation syntax and schema of residence issues and the routine resolution situation in Chapter 4, "Routines and Routine Invocation"; however, the notion of *associated type* is very central to understanding methods, so I'll address it right now.

2.7.2 Associated Type

SQL:1999 supports two types of method: *static methods* and *instance methods*. A static method operates on the user-defined *type* itself, while an instance method operates on an instance of the type. That has implications on the method's param-

9 Actually, SQL's procedures can also return data through the use of *dynamic result sets* that are not returned as a parameter value. Dynamic result sets are discussed in Volume 1 of this book.

10 Methods are inherited by all subtypes of the type with which they are closely associated (except when they are overridden by some subtype) and thus can be invoked on instances of the subtypes. Nonetheless, methods are tightly bound only to the type with which they are defined.

Table 2.1 *Differences between Functions and Methods*

Characteristic	*Functions*	*Methods*
Attached to a specific type?	No	Yes—tightly bound to exactly one type
Invocation syntax	Functional notation	Dot notation
Schema of residence	Any schema	Schema of its associated type
Routine resolution	Fully resolved at compilation time	Compilation resolves to set of candidate methods; final resolution at runtime

eter declarations and invocations. For the rest of this chapter, when I use the word *method,* I mean *instance method* unless I explicitly say otherwise. Static methods are addressed in Chapter 4, "Routines and Routine Invocation." (By the way, I recognize that you sometimes might not know exactly what I mean when I use the word *invocation* of a function or a method. That's because I often—if not usually—mean the source code that specifies the routine's name, using functional notation or dot notation, and that supplies any required arguments; in a few other situations, though, the word refers to the actual process of causing the code in the routine to be executed. I hope that the meaning in each case is clear from the context!)

As you saw in Table 2.1, in SQL:1999, an ordinary *function* (although methods are functions, too, I reserve the word *function* for those functions that are not methods) is not associated with, or bound to, a specific user-defined type. Instead, it may have one or more parameters whose data types are one or more user-defined types; alternatively, many functions in your database might have no user-defined type parameters at all; that is, all of their parameters are of built-in types.

By contrast, an SQL *method* is closely associated with—tightly bound to—exactly one user-defined type, called the method's *associated type*. The method might have several parameters whose data types are some structured type (even the same type as its associated type!), but only one of those parameters is treated specially. All methods that are closely associated with a given structured type are declared along with the type itself (well, to be thorough, their *signatures*[11] are declared as part of the structure type's definition, while their *implementations*

11 More precisely, SQL:1999 says that a *method specification* is provided in the structured type declaration for every method associated with that type. A method specification differs from a signature in that it contains more than just the method name and parameter declarations (it includes several additional characteristics of the method). In this volume, I generally use the word *signature* for convenience. In addition, it's worth pointing out that Java is an exception to this rule.

appear elsewhere). This is done as part of the CREATE TYPE statement. (In Syntax 2.1, this appears as the `method-specification-list`. Feel free to go back to that diagram and check it out now; we'll wait until you get back.) SQL:1999 allows type definers to add to the set of methods associated with a given type, as well as allowing them to disassociate existing associated methods from the type, through the ALTER TYPE statement.

The associated type of a method has several significant effects on the method's definition and invocation. Arguably, the most surprising effect to some is that the method's declaration does not specify an explicit parameter corresponding to the associated type! Similarly, the method's invocations don't use an explicit argument corresponding to that associated type. However, the SQL system effectively creates an implicit parameter for instance methods that precedes the first declared parameter; this implicit parameter is always named "SELF" and its data type is always the associated user-defined type of the method. Within those methods, you reference the instance of the UDT for which the invocation was intended by using the name SELF, just as though it were a user-assigned parameter name. (An obvious implication of this arrangement is that no explicit parameter can be named SELF.) But I'm getting a little ahead of myself. I'll cover this implicit parameter thoroughly in Chapter 4, "Routines and Routine Invocation," but you need to know something about it at a basic level now in order to fully understand structured user-defined types.

2.7.3 Methods: Definition and Invocation

The next two subsections, "Method Definition" and "Method Invocation," give you a fairly brief introduction to the way in which methods are defined and invoked, illustrating the relationship they have with their associated types.

Method Definition

Methods, other than Java method, in SQL are defined in two ways and in two places—and both are required. First, every method is declared as part of the definition of its associated structured type. That is, the method *signature* is coded within the structured type definition. (Well . . . that's true of methods known at the time the structured type is defined, but you can—except for types defined using Java—also use the ALTER TYPE statement to add the signatures of additional methods to the type definition later on, as well as removing methods—that is, their signatures—from type definitions.) It is because of this relationship (between the type definition that lists all its associated methods and the method definitions that identify the associated type) that the "association" between type and method comes into existence.

The second way, and place, in which methods are defined is independent of the structured type definition, although the end result must be that the method resides in the same schema as its associated type. This second way is the actual method declaration, including its *implementation*—either the SQL code comprising the method or the appropriate identification (e.g., filespec or URL) of some code written in a different programming language.

It is possible that some future version of SQL will remove the necessity of defining methods in two places, but I am not aware of any plans to modify the language to accomplish that goal.

To illustrate this, consider the following structured type definition:

Example 2.9 *Structured Type Definition*

```
CREATE TYPE movie AS (
  title            CHARACTER VARYING (100),
  description      CHARACTER VARYING (500),
  runs             INTEGER )
  NOT FINAL
```

This very simple structured type allows us to capture certain crucial information about movies: the name of the movie, a description of it, and the length in minutes. (Incidentally, the NOT FINAL is required syntax without an alternative; future editions of the SQL standard may change this situation.) But, suppose we really wanted to retrieve the length as an SQL INTERVAL type instead of as an INTEGER? We can build a method to perform this calculation for us, and the result would look like this:

Example 2.10 *Structured Type Definition with Method Signature*

```
CREATE TYPE movie AS (
  title            CHARACTER VARYING (100),
  description      CHARACTER VARYING (500),
  runs             INTEGER )
  NOT FINAL
  METHOD length_interval ( )
    RETURNS INTERVAL HOUR(2) TO MINUTE
```

The last two lines comprise the signature of our new method; it takes no parameters beyond the implicit parameter that I briefly mentioned earlier, and it returns an SQL INTERVAL (whose precision must be specified). Next, let's see the actual method definition:

Example 2.11 *Method Definition Associated with Method Signature*

```
CREATE INSTANCE METHOD length_interval ( )
    RETURNS INTERVAL HOUR(2) TO MINUTE
    FOR movie

  /* Allow for movies as long as 99 hours and 59 minutes */

  RETURN CAST ( CAST ( SELF.runs AS INTERVAL MINUTE(4) )
         AS INTERVAL HOUR(2) TO MINUTE )
```

Of course, you'll notice right away that the relationship is bidirectional: the type definition identifies the method by name, and the method definition identifies the name of the associated type.

Now, let's examine this example a little more closely. Recall from the earlier discussion of methods that both the signature and the actual definition of the method specify that the method has no parameters. But it is equally true that every method *always* has at least one implicit parameter, whose data type must be the associated type. Since that parameter is never absent and is always the implicit parameter, and since its data type is always known very precisely to be the associated type of the method, and since it must (by definition) always identify *the* instance of that type for which the method was invoked, that parameter need not be explicitly declared. (As you'll see in the following subsection, "Method Invocation," the corresponding argument must be provided to an invocation of the method, but it is not provided within the arguments that contain ordinary arguments.) You see from the body—that is, the implementation—of the method above that I use the keyword SELF within the method to identify the instance for which the method is invoked. (The SELF parameter is used only for instance methods and never for STATIC methods.)

The *unaugmented parameter list* of this method, therefore, has no parameters. But SQL builds an *augmented parameter list* for the method, which has to be used by the underlying function invocation mechanisms on any hardware/software platform. That augmented parameter list has one parameter. If we were allowed (we're not!) to specify that implicit parameter explicitly, the method declaration might have looked something like this:

```
CREATE INSTANCE METHOD length_interval ( SELF movie ) ...
```

Now, if a method has more than one parameter (that is, parameters other than the implicit parameter), then there are a few rules that have to be satisfied. Most importantly, the data type of each parameter declared in the method signature must be compatible with the data type of the corresponding parameter declared in the method definition. (*Compatible* means that the data types are essentially the same, even when considering things like length or precision.) The same goes for the data type specified as the RETURNS data type. Furthermore, if any parameter declaration in either the method signature or the method definition is given a name, then its corresponding parameter declaration must have the same name.

Method signatures—but not method definitions—can also contain a number of optional clauses that specify additional information about the method; the method definitions implicitly take on the characteristics that were specified along with their corresponding signatures. These optional characteristics may be written in any sequence and are as follows:

- The name of the programming language in which the method is written; the default is LANGUAGE SQL.
- Where the programming language is not SQL, the style of parameter list used for the method (an SQL-style list, in which indicator parameters and SQLSTATE parameters are implicit, or a general style, in which all parameters and arguments—other than the parameter and argument corresponding to SELF—are explicit); the default is PARAMETER STYLE SQL.[12]
- Whether the method does not contain SQL statements (NO SQL), may contain SQL statements but does not access the database (CONTAINS SQL), may retrieve data from the database but may not update the database (READS SQL DATA), or is permitted to update the database (MODIFIES SQL DATA); the default is CONTAINS SQL.
- Whether the method is deterministic (that is, for a given state of the database, it always returns the same result in response to a specific set of argument values) or not; the default is NOT DETERMINISTIC.
- Whether the method always returns the null value when any of its arguments is null, and thus need not be called in that situation; the default is CALLED ON NULL INPUT.

Methods written in a programming language other than SQL have one additional characteristic that participates in the signature:

- The name of the default transform group—a pair of functions used to transform instances of structured types to or from some host language represen-

12 The addition of support for a Java binding required the addition of PARAMETER STYLE JAVA, which is addressed in Jim Melton and Andrew Eisenberg, *Understanding SQL and Java Together: A Guide to SQLJ, JDBC, and Related Technologies* (San Francisco: Morgan Kaufmann Publishers, 2000).

tation; these are implicitly used whenever transferring a structured type instance between SQL and a host routine, such as an external method.[13] There is no default. Transform groups are discussed in section 2.11.8.

Method Invocation

A method invocation is, naturally, the mechanism by which a method is called, or invoked. While method definitions (and signatures) have *parameters,* method invocations have *arguments.* The number of arguments in a method invocation must be equal to the number of parameters in the definition of the method, and the data type of each argument must be compatible with the data type of its corresponding parameter (or there must be a conversion from the data type of the argument to the data type of the parameter that SQL can perform without the aid of a CAST expression).

Let's set up an example. First, let's assume I've defined the movie type shown in Example 2.10, including the length_interval method defined in Example 2.11. Next, we need a table that has a column whose data type is movie:

Example 2.12 *movie_table Definition*

```
CREATE TABLE movie_table (
    stock_number        CHARACTER(8),
    movie_info          movie,
    rental_quantity     INTEGER,
    rental_cost         DECIMAL(5,2) )
```

If we wanted to retrieve the length, in hours and minutes, of a particular film, we could write an SQL statement like the one seen in Example 2.13.

Example 2.13 *Retrieving from movie_table*

```
SELECT   mt.movie_info.length_interval
FROM     movie_table AS mt
WHERE    mt.movie_info.title = 'Ghosts of Mars'
```

In Example 2.13, I used dot notation, as required, to reference the title attribute (or, equivalently, to invoke the title observer method) in the WHERE clause; SQL:1999 also requires that we use dot notation to invoke the length_interval method. In both cases, mt.movie_info (the name of a column qualified by a correlation name—you might wish to review section 2.6.4 for a reminder of

13 Again, this does not apply to structured types defined using Java.

why a correlation name is required in this situation) is the implicit argument of the method; of course, the data type of that column is `movie`, the associated type of the methods.

Note that my code to invoke the `length_interval` method didn't even bother with the parentheses! If the only argument to a method invocation is the implicit argument—corresponding to the implicit SELF parameter—then you can't code an argument, and you don't have to code the parentheses surrounding that nonexistent implicit argument. However, if you prefer to code the empty parentheses, you're allowed to do so, as illustrated in Example 2.14.

Example 2.14 *Using Empty Argument Lists*

```
SELECT   mt.movie_info.length_interval()
FROM     movie_table AS mt
WHERE    mt.movie_info.title() = 'Ghosts of Mars'
```

2.7.4 Observers and Mutators

I've already told you that the only way that your applications can retrieve and update the attributes of UDT instances is through the use of the observer and mutator methods—which actually are methods—that the system automatically provides when a UDT is defined. (You cannot override the system-provided observers and mutators, either.) I also told you that all methods, including the observers and mutators, are invoked using "dot notation" instead of ordinary function syntax. In Example 2.13 and Example 2.14, you saw how an observer method is used in SQL code, using that dot notation.

Of course, SQL syntax is replete with the use of dot notation. For example, as you saw in section 2.6.3, when table names qualify column names, a period separates the two names; similarly, when a schema name qualifies a table name, the names are separated by a period: `schema_name.table_name.column_name`. SQL's designers observed that the most obvious choice for punctuation to separate, say, a column name from the name of an attribute (that is, an attribute of the UDT that is the column's type) is that old friend, the period, as in `column_name.attribute_name`. Dot notation was chosen instead of functional notation for method invocations simply because dot notation *is* comfortable to SQL programmers (along with the fact that other programming languages have made the same choice).

In Example 2.14, you see that an invocation of an explicitly defined method is permitted to supply an empty pair of parentheses:

```
mt.movie_info.length_interval()
```

The same, of course, is true of observer methods. If I wanted to retrieve the runtime of a movie as an integer (the data type of the runs attribute), I could write either

```
mt.movie_info.runs
```

or

```
mt.movie_info.runs()
```

As I told you in section 2.6.1, every attribute of a structured UDT has both an observer method and a mutator method provided by the system, and the names of both of those methods are the same as the name of the attribute. Thus, I can modify the value of the runs attribute in the row describing a movie by writing something like

```
mt.movie_info.runs(150)
```

That expression changes the runtime of the movie to 150—minutes, presumably. (Naturally, expressions like that must appear in an appropriate context; simply slipping it into the select list of a single-row SELECT statement isn't valid SQL syntax. You'll learn more about this subject, including why mutators can be invoked only in certain contexts, in section 2.11.2.) Even though the invocation syntax includes only the single numeric argument, the implicit SELF argument represented by the column name runs is effectively present.

2.7.5 Constructors

Of course, before you can retrieve or modify the value of an attribute of some UDT instance, that instance has to exist. In SQL:1999 (as in many object-oriented languages), the term *constructor* is used to describe the process of creating such an instance.

Since instances of structured user-defined types in SQL:1999 are values, rather than objects, the process of "constructing" an instance is a bit different from the analogous process in languages in which such instances are truly objects. If we were creating a new *object,* the process would have to allocate whatever resources the environment requires for objects, then cause the new object's attributes to take on the desired values.

By contrast, an SQL:1999 structured type is just that: a *type* that must be the data type of some site (see Volume 1 of this book for a detailed definition of *site*). A site, by definition, exists independently of the value stored in the site—for example, when an SQL variable whose data type is our `movie` type is allocated, the chunk of memory used for that variable exists regardless of the bits that are stored in it. Thus, the purpose of a constructor in SQL is to assign specific values to the components of a site corresponding to the attributes of the UDT that is the type of that site. Recognizing this fact, another term that is often applied to constructors is *initializer method.* SQL:1999 uses the latter phrase to mean something slightly different. I deal with constructors and initializers in more detail in section 2.10.

2.7.6 Encapsulation Redux

The behaviors of structured types are encapsulated by the routines—including, but not limited to, observers and mutators—that implement those behaviors. The purpose of encapsulation is to ensure that your applications won't be affected in any way if the routine implementing some behavior of a structured type is rewritten in a more efficient way, or even in another programming language, as long as the calling interface remains the same and the results of calling it remain the same.

Allow me to illustrate the nature of encapsulation through the following example (admittedly not directly related to selling music or movies): the position of a point in a 2-dimensional space can be specified in (at least) two different coordinate systems, the Cartesian coordinate system (sometimes known as the rectangular coordinate system) and the polar coordinate system. Figure 2.1 illustrates these two systems graphically.

In the two diagrams of Figure 2.1, we see a central point, usually called the *origin,* and a second point, the point in which we're interested. In the Cartesian coordinate system, the second point is located at a position measured by a distance along the horizontal *x*-axis and a distance measured along the vertical *y*-axis. In the polar coordinate system, the very same point—the same location in 2-dimensional space—is located at a specified distance, often called *rho,* from the origin and at a particular angle, called *theta,* from the *x*-axis. In trigonometry class, we learned that the two coordinate systems are equivalent because either can be used to identify precisely the same set of points. In fact, there is a well-known set of formulae to convert between the two systems.

If you have a point located at position (x, y) in Cartesian space, the same point is found at point (ρ, θ) in polar space, and you can determine the values of ρ and θ by applying these equations:

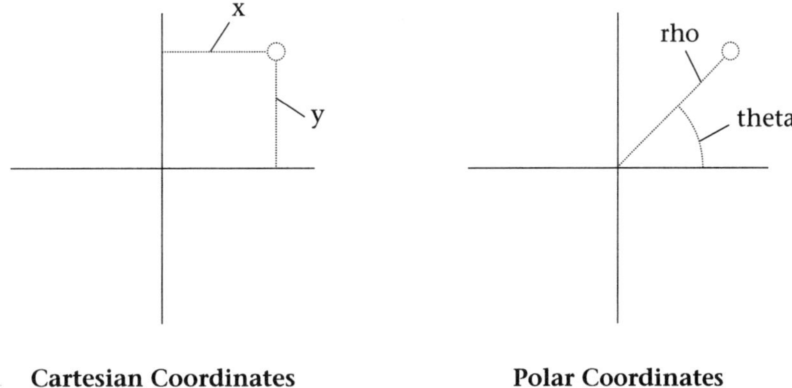

Figure 2.1 Cartesian and Polar Coordinate Systems

$$\rho = \sqrt{x^2 + y^2}$$

$$\theta = \arctan \frac{y}{x}$$

Conversely, if you have a point located in polar space at position (ρ, θ), you can find the same point in Cartesian space at position (x, y), computed by these equations:

$$x = \cos \theta \cdot \rho$$

$$y = \sin \theta \cdot \rho$$

As long as you keep the signs of your arguments properly coordinated, you can arbitrarily convert back and forth between the two systems without losing any information.

Now, suppose we need to build an application that deals with information about points in a 2-dimensional space. This application uses a structured user-defined type named `point`, whose definition includes two REAL attributes named `x_coord` and `y_coord`, as seen in Example 2.15.

Example 2.15 *Structured Type for Cartesian Coordinates*

```
CREATE TYPE point AS (
  x_coord     REAL,
  y_coord     REAL,
  ... )
NOT FINAL
```

We can happily write our application code to manipulate the *x* and *y* coordinates of points that we create using various values of x_coord and y_coord. We do so by invoking method invocations of methods named x_coord and y_coord, the observer and mutator methods provided automatically by the system when the type was defined.

Suppose that, for some reason, the designer of the point structured type redefines that type so that it manages points in polar space instead of Cartesian space. The natural result would be that the type's definition now includes two REAL attributes named rho and theta. (Perhaps obviously, any Cartesian point data in the database would have to be converted to polar coordinates, but that's not relevant to this example.)

But what about our application that invokes methods named x_coord and y_coord? Will it have to be rewritten, not merely to access methods named rho and theta, but also to perform radically different computations? Not if the type designer made the decision to explicitly create *new* methods named x_coord and y_coord, which compute and return the appropriate *x* coordinate and *y* coordinate values of points from the underlying ρ and θ values! Similarly, two additional methods, also named x_coord and y_coord, can be provided to accept *x* coordinate and *y* coordinate values and transform them into the corresponding ρ and θ values. If such methods are provided, then our application written to manipulate points in Cartesian space can continue to function without recoding or even recompilation (depending on implementation techniques, naturally). In fact, a clever type definer might have provided additional functions named rho and theta from the beginning, allowing applications that prefer the polar coordinate system to use the type alongside applications using the Cartesian system.

If I want to determine whether a particular point, defined using Cartesian coordinates as in Example 2.15, represented in an SQL variable I've declared happens to be at coordinates (10, 20), I might write a predicate like that seen in Example 2.16.

Example 2.16 *Accessing Attributes of a point*

```
...my_point.x_coord = 10 AND my_point.y_coord = 20...
```

Suppose, now, that I have determined that I prefer to represent my points using polar notation. Naturally, I must modify the definition of the point type so that it has rho and theta attributes instead of x_coord and y_coord attributes, but I must also take care to define methods that allow retrieval and modification of the *x* and *y* coordinates of each point so that my existing applications do not break. The statements in Example 2.17 illustrate what such definitions might be. (Please note that I have illustrated the situation by showing a new CREATE TYPE statement; in a real application, I would instead modify the existing structure type definition, but the example is probably easier to grasp using the CREATE TYPE approach.)

Example 2.17 *New point in Polar Coordinates with New Methods*

```
CREATE TYPE point AS (
  rho         REAL,
  theta       REAL,
  ... )
NOT FINAL
METHOD x_coord ( )
  RETURNS REAL
METHOD y_coord ( )
  RETURNS REAL

CREATE INSTANCE METHOD x_coord ( )
    RETURNS REAL
    FOR point
  RETURN cos(SELF.theta)*SELF.rho

CREATE INSTANCE METHOD y_coord ( )
    RETURNS REAL
    FOR point
  RETURN sin(SELF.theta)*SELF.rho
```

The two methods assume that there are additional routines available named `cos` and `sin` and that they respectively evaluate the cosine and the sine of the argument. Mutator methods for the *x* and *y* coordinates could be similarly provided, translating new positions to polar coordinates and updating the `rho` and `theta` attributes of the type.

Thus, through encapsulation of the internals of a structured user-defined type, applications using that type are allowed to be insensitive to changes in the type's internal details. Of course, with the change from Cartesian to polar conventions, `x_coord` and `y_coord` are no longer observer methods, but ordinary methods, while `rho` and `theta` are the names of new observer and mutator methods. But that change in the underlying nature of the methods does not affect how they are used by applications.

As will become more apparent when you get to Chapter 4, "Routines and Routine Invocation," the value of encapsulation is enhanced by other facilities provided by SQL:1999's structure types. For now, it's sufficient to emphasize that encapsulation of structured type behaviors protects your applications from changes in the internal implementations—the code—that provide those behaviors.

2.8 Defining Structured User-Defined Types

In Syntax 2.1, I introduced the fundamental syntax for defining structured user-defined types. It's time to delve into the details, covering each component of the statement. Syntax 2.2 repeats Syntax 2.1, using SQL:1999's more formal notation. After reviewing these components at a high level, I drill down into the more complex ones, showing their detailed syntax and explaining their purposes and results.

Syntax 2.2 *Detailed CREATE TYPE Syntax*

```
<user-defined type definition> ::= CREATE TYPE <user-defined type body>

<user-defined type body> ::=
    <user-defined type name>
    [ <subtype clause> ]
    [ <external Java type clause> ]
    [ AS <representation> ]
    [ <instantiable clause> ]
    <finality>
    [ <reference type specification> ]
    [ <ref cast option> ]
    [ <cast option> ]
    [ <method specification list> ]
```

As you would expect, <user-defined type name> is an ordinary 3-part SQL name. The structure is catalog_name.schema_name.type_name; of course, the first two components can be omitted and have defaults determined in the same manner as other SQL 3-part names (see Volume 1 of this book for details). The name specified by <user-defined type name> is, of course, the name of the structured user-defined type that is created by this statement.

The syntax of <subtype clause> is seen in Syntax 2.3.

Syntax 2.3 *<subtype clause> Syntax*

```
<subtype clause> ::=
    UNDER <supertype name>

<supertype name> ::=
    <user-defined type name>
```

<supertype name> is a <user-defined type name> and thus is also an ordinary 3-part SQL name. If specified, this clause identifies the structured user-defined type from which attributes and methods will be inherited by the type being defined. If this clause is omitted, then the type being defined has no supertype (such a type is often called a *maximal supertype*). The keyword UNDER was chosen to evoke the image of a type hierarchy diagram (like that in Figure 2.2 on page 69), in which a subtype is visualized as appearing beneath its supertype. I'll discuss subtypes in more detail in section 2.9.2.

A subtype can be defined in a schema other than the schema in which its direct supertype is defined. However, the schema in which the supertype is defined must be a schema that is located in the current *path.* (A path is a list of schemas that can be searched for user-defined types and routines. You'll read more about paths in Chapter 4, "Routines and Routine Invocation.") The methods defined for the supertype (and for its supertypes, if any) must be defined in the schemas in which their closely associated types are defined, as I told you in section 2.7.2. Those methods are inherited by the subtype being defined, but remain "closely associated" with the supertype on which they are originally defined. If you override an inherited method, the overriding method that you define must be defined in the same schema as the subtype for which it is being defined and is "closely associated" with that subtype.

In section 2.4, you learned that SQL:1999 provides both distinct user-defined types (covered in Volume 1 of this book) and structured user-defined types. Syntax 2.4 provides both alternatives, then expands the alternative concerning structured types.

Syntax 2.4 *<representation> Syntax*

```
<representation> ::=
    <predefined type>
  | <member list>

<member list> ::=
    <left paren> <member> [ { <comma> <member> }... ] <right paren>

<member> ::= <attribute definition>
```

The *representation* of a user-defined type determines whether it is a distinct type or a structured type. Specification of <predefined type> results in a distinct type, while <member list> produces a structured type. The representation of a structured type in SQL is a parenthesized, comma-separated list of attribute definitions. You should immediately recognize the similarity with SQL's `<table definition>`, which is a parenthesized, comma-separated list of column definitions. The syntax of attribute definitions appears in Syntax 2.5.

Syntax 2.5 *<attribute definition> Syntax*

```
<attribute definition> ::=
    <attribute name>
    <data type>
    [ <reference scope check> ]
    [ <attribute default> ]
    [ <collate clause> ]

<reference scope check> ::=
    REFERENCES ARE [ NOT ] CHECKED
    [ ON DELETE <reference scope check action> ]

<reference scope check action> ::=
    <referential action>

<attribute default> ::= <default clause>
```

Each attribute has a name, which must be unique among the names of attributes of the structured type being defined—including attributes that are inherited from a supertype, and a data type. The data type is permitted to be any SQL type other than the structured type being defined and its supertypes, including SQL's constructed types (such as ARRAY and ROW) and other user-defined types. If the data type is an SQL built-in type, then it may be given a default value using the same syntax that you would use to assign a default value to a column as part of a column definition in a table definition. If the data type is another user-defined type (structured or distinct), a REFERENCE type (see Chapter 3, "Typed Tables"), or a ROW type, then the only default value that you can assign to the attribute is the null value (using the keyword NULL). If the data type is an ARRAY type, the default value must be either the null value or an empty array value (specified by `ARRAY[]`).

For every `<attribute definition>` that you specify in a structured type's definition, the system automatically generates two method definitions: one that is the observer method associated with the attribute and one that is the mutator method associated with the attribute.

`<reference scope check>` is permitted only if the specified data type is a REFERENCE type (covered in Chapter 3, "Typed Tables"), in which case the clause is required. Briefly, this clause determines whether or not the system examines each value stored in the associated attribute to find out whether it references an existing instance of the specified structured type and whether a referential action is invoked whenever that referenced instance is deleted.

In section 2.6, I mentioned that structured types can be defined to be instantiable or not instantiable. Syntax 2.6 gives the syntax with which this definition is made. A type that is defined to be not instantiable is one for which no constructor method is defined and therefore you are not permitted to create a value of that type. Obviously, such types make no sense unless you are allowed to create subtypes that are instantiable. The purpose of creating noninstantiable types is to allow you to model abstract concepts on which more concrete concepts are based. Of course, if you define instance methods on a noninstantiable type, there are no instances of that type on which they can operate. However, the instantiable subtypes of noninstantiable types inherit attributes and methods from their noninstantiable supertypes, and the methods operate just fine on the instances of those subtypes.

You can specify noninstantiable types to be the types of attributes of other structured types or to be the types of columns, arguments, SQL variables, and so forth. However, you must ensure that either a value of an instantiable subtype or a null value is provided for each of those sites when they are populated.

Syntax 2.6 *<instantiable clause> and <finality> Syntax*

```
<instantiable clause> ::=
    INSTANTIABLE
  | NOT INSTANTIABLE

<finality> ::=
    FINAL
  | NOT FINAL
```

The mandatory `<finality>` clause seen in Syntax 2.6 specifies whether or not subtypes of the type being defined will be allowed. If you're defining a distinct type, you are required to specify FINAL. This pretty closely matches Java's use of `final` for methods and classes. If you're defining a structured type, SQL:1999 requires that you specify NOT FINAL; however, future versions of the SQL standard might relax this requirement, allowing you to define types that cannot be subtyped. Undoubtedly, types declared NOT INSTANTIABLE will never be allowed to be FINAL.

In Chapter 3, "Typed Tables," you'll learn how you can define tables whose rows are instances of a specific structured type; in this section, I merely introduce the syntax of `<reference type specification>` and summarize its intent. Rows of such tables have all the characteristics of objects in other object-oriented systems, including unique identities that can be referenced by other components of the environment. SQL:1999 provides three different mechanisms by which unique identities are given to instances of the structured types associated with such tables. All rows in all typed tables associated with a particular structured type use the same mechanism. You may infer from Syntax 2.7 that the unique identity given to instances of the type being defined can be

- values that the application requests the system to generate automatically (`<system-generated representation>`),
- values of some SQL built-in type (`<user-defined representation>`) that the application must generate whenever it stores an instance of the structured type as a row in a typed table, or
- values derived from one or more attributes of the structured type (`<derived representation>`).

Syntax 2.7 *<reference type specification> Syntax*

```
<reference type specification> ::=
    <system-generated representation>
  | <user-defined representation>
  | <derived representation>

<system-generated representation> ::= REF IS SYSTEM GENERATED

<user-defined representation> ::= REF USING <predefined type>

<derived representation> ::= REF FROM <list of attributes>

<list of attributes> ::=
    <left paren>
      <attribute name> [ { <comma> <attribute name> }... ]
    <right paren>
```

Syntax 2.8 holds the BNF of the clauses that are required when `<reference type specification>` is `<user-defined representation>`. These clauses are used to transform the built-in type values provided by the application to and from the REFERENCE type values that are actually required for referencing the rows in typed tables. As with `<reference type specification>`, this subject will be covered in more detail in Chapter 3, "Typed Tables."

Syntax 2.8 *<ref cast option> Syntax*

```
<ref cast option> ::=
    [ <cast to ref> ]
    [ <cast to type> ]

<cast to ref> ::=
    CAST <left paren> SOURCE AS REF <right paren>
      WITH <cast to ref identifier>

<cast to ref identifier> ::= <identifier>

<cast to type> ::=
    CAST <left paren> REF AS SOURCE <right paren>
      WITH <cast to type identifier>

<cast to type identifier> ::= <identifier>
```

By contrast with Syntax 2.8, Syntax 2.9 provides clauses that are used to cast instances of distinct types to their underlying built-in types (or any other built-in type), and vice versa. Since the `<cast option>` is not relevant for structured types, I do not discuss it further in this volume.

Syntax 2.9 *<cast option> Syntax*

```
<cast option> ::=
    [ <cast to distinct> ]
    [ <cast to source> ]

<cast to distinct> ::=
    CAST <left paren> SOURCE AS DISTINCT <right paren>
    WITH <cast to distinct identifier>

<cast to distinct identifier> ::= <identifier>

<cast to source> ::=
    CAST <left paren> DISTINCT AS SOURCE <right paren>
    WITH <cast to source identifier>

<cast to source identifier> ::= <identifier>
```

In Syntax 2.10, we find syntax for declaring the signatures of methods associated with the structured type being defined. As you see in this syntax, you can define *original methods,* which are methods that do not apply to any supertype of the structured type we're defining. If the type being defined is a subtype of some other type, you can also define *overriding methods.* An overriding method has the same name and argument list as a method defined on some supertype of the type being defined. You'll learn more about overriding methods in Chapter 4, "Routines and Routine Invocation"; in this chapter, I'll concentrate on original methods.

Syntax 2.10 *<method specification list> Syntax*

```
<method specification list> ::=
    <method specification> [ { <comma> <method specification> }... ]

<method specification> ::=
    <original method specification>
  | <overriding method specification>
  | <static field method spec>

<original method specification> ::=
    <partial method specification>
    [ SELF AS RESULT ]
    [ SELF AS LOCATOR ]
    [ <method characteristics> ]

<overriding method specification> ::=
    OVERRIDING <partial method specification>

<partial method specification> ::=
    [ INSTANCE | STATIC | CONSTRUCTOR ] METHOD <method name>
    <SQL parameter declaration list>
    <returns clause>
    [ SPECIFIC <specific method name> ]

<method characteristics> ::=
    <method characteristic>...

<method characteristic> ::=
    <language clause>
  | <parameter style clause>
  | <deterministic characteristic>
  | <SQL-data access indication>
  | <null-call clause>
```

```
<specific method name> ::=
    [ <schema name> <period> ] <qualified identifier>

<static field method spec> ::=
    STATIC METHOD <method name> <left paren> <right paren>
      <static method returns clause>
      [ SPECIFIC <specific method name> ]
      <external variable name clause>

<static method returns clause> ::= RETURNS <data type>

<external variable name clause> ::=
    EXTERNAL VARIABLE NAME <character string literal>
```

As you see in Syntax 2.10, an original method is defined by specifying whether it is an instance method (one that operates on instances of the type being defined), a static method (one that does not use or affect instances of the type, but operates on the type itself), or a constructor method (one that is used to construct—well, initialize—instances of the type); as you should infer, only static methods can be defined for noninstantiable types. If you don't specify one of these three choices, then the method is an instance method.

As you'd expect, you specify in a method's signature the name by which the method will be invoked (the *invocable name*); in addition, you may specify a *specific name* for a method that can be used to uniquely identify the method if its invocable name is overloaded (you'll read more about this subject shortly). As you saw in section 2.7.2, the methods associated with a structured type must be defined in the same schema as the type; therefore, if you specify the schema name component of the method, it must agree with the (explicit or implicit) schema name component of the structured type's name.

Of course, if the method whose signature you're declaring has any parameters other than the implicit SELF parameter, you declare the parameters as a parenthesized, comma-separated list of parameter names and data types. Parameter lists are specified fully in Chapter 4, "Routines and Routine Invocation."

Since methods are functions, you must specify the data type of the value that they return. Methods can return any SQL data type, including built-in types (even constructed types such as ROW and ARRAY), distinct types, and structured types—even the structured type associated with the method.

Each method has a *specific name* that is used to distinguish the method among all functions that have the same invocable name. If the schema containing a particular method contains more than one function with the same invocable name, such as overriding methods (which were mentioned a few paragraphs earlier), then your applications must have a way to uniquely identify each of those functions in order to manage them—to drop them, for example. As you'll learn in more detail in Chapter 4, "Routines and Routine Invocation," every method has a specific name that is used for that purpose.

Finally, each method has a set of `<method characteristics>`. Methods can be written in SQL or in any of several additional programming languages (your implementation determines which languages are supported; the SQL standards supports Ada, C, COBOL, Fortran, M (formerly known as MUMPS), Pascal, and PL/I, with Java receiving support in a slightly different manner than the other languages). In addition, a method's parameter list can be defined in a style most suitable for SQL routines (PARAMETER STYLE SQL) in which each parameter can naturally take a null value and in which a status parameter is not required because the status of the routine is handled in a natural SQL manner. Alternatively, the parameter list can be defined in a manner more suitable for routines written in a different programming language (PARAMETER STYLE GENERAL), in which each parameter that can acquire a null value must be given an explicit indicator parameter and in which an explicit status parameter must be specified. The parameter list can also be declared to be PARAMETER STYLE JAVA, which is not covered in this book (but is covered elsewhere).[14]

Each method is either DETERMINISTIC (that is, it always returns the same result in response to a specific set of argument values for a given state of the database) or NOT DETERMINISTIC (the default is NOT DETERMINISTIC). Each method has a characteristic that specifies its SQL language content: you can specify that a method does not contain SQL statements (NO SQL), may contain SQL statements but does not access the database (CONTAINS SQL), may retrieve data from the database but may not update the database (READS SQL DATA), or is permitted to update the database (MODIFIES SQL DATA); the default is CONTAINS SQL. Finally, you can determine for each method how it responds to arguments whose value is the SQL null value: if you specify RETURNS NULL ON NULL INPUT, then the method will always return a null value if the value of any of its arguments is the null value; if CALLED ON NULL INPUT is specified (or the default is taken), then the method will be explicitly executed whenever it is invoked, whether or not one or more arguments have the null value.

A `<static field method spec>` is used only for structured types defined using Java, which is covered in another book[15] and is included here only for completeness.

If, for any reason, you no longer need a particular structured type, you can destroy its definition by executing the DROP TYPE statement, whose syntax is shown in Syntax 2.11.

---

14 Jim Melton and Andrew Eisenberg, *Understanding SQL and Java Together: A Guide to SQLJ, JDBC, and Related Technologies* (San Francisco: Morgan Kaufmann Publishers, 2000).

15 Ibid.

Syntax 2.11 *<drop data type statement> Syntax*

```
<drop data type statement> ::=
    DROP TYPE <user-defined type name> <drop behavior>
```

where <drop behavior> is, as in all DROP statements, either CASCADE or RESTRICT. If you specify RESTRICT and there are any other schema objects (including subtypes, columns of the type or its subtypes, user-defined casts, and so forth) that depend on the specified type, the statement will fail. If you specify CASCADE, then the system not only drops the specified type, it drops all of those other schema objects that depend on the type.

You can also modify the definition of a structured type in several ways:

- You can add attributes to the type's definition, but only if the type is not currently the type of any site, the supertype of any other type, the element type of any collection type, or the referenced type of any reference types.
- You can drop attributes from the type's definition, but only if the type is not currently the type of any site, the supertype of any other type, the element type of any collection type, or the referenced type of any reference types.
- You can add new original methods and new overriding methods to the type's definition.
- You can drop methods from the type's definition, but only if there are no schema objects that depend on the method.

All of these are done by using the ALTER TYPE statement, whose syntax is seen in Syntax 2.12. I have not given the complete expansion of the method specifications, since you will encounter them in Chapter 4, "Routines and Routine Invocation."

Syntax 2.12 *<alter type statement> Syntax*

```
<alter type statement> ::=
    ALTER TYPE <user-defined type name> <alter type action>

<alter type action> ::=
    <add attribute definition>
  | <drop attribute definition>
  | <add original method specification>
  | <add overriding method specification>
  | <drop method specification>
```

```
<add attribute definition> ::=
    ADD ATTRIBUTE <attribute definition>

<drop attribute definition> ::=
    DROP ATTRIBUTE <attribute name> RESTRICT

<add original method specification> ::=
    ADD <original method specification>

<add overriding method specification> ::=
    ADD <overriding method specification>

<drop method specification> ::=
    DROP <specific routine designator> RESTRICT
```

In passing, I note that ALTER TYPE is not supported for structured types defined using Java.

2.9 Inheritance

In section 2.5.3, you were introduced to the concepts of inheritance and type hierarchies. In this section, I elaborate substantially on those notions.

2.9.1 What Is a Type Hierarchy?

A type hierarchy in SQL is a collection of user-defined types, some of which are "specializations" of other types. Again, this may best be illustrated by example.

In the music and video store example, I need to model a number of real-life objects, such as music (CDs and, no doubt, cassettes, vinyl LPs, and perhaps even MiniDiscs) and movies. Movies are available as VHS tapes, a few LaserDiscs, and DVDs, which now come with Dolby Digital 5.1 sound (sometimes called AC-3) and DTS 5.1 sound. In designing the applications and database, I observe that all of those movie formats have a lot in common, but there are differences among them, too.

For example, all movie formats include the title of the movie, the description, the studio, the director, the producer, and so forth; however, VHS tapes and DVDs have different stock numbers and quite often have different contents

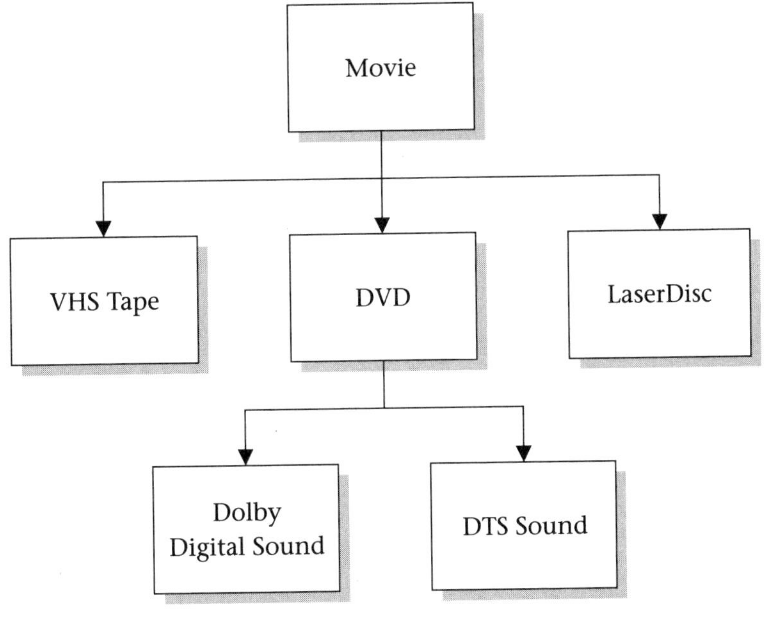

Figure 2.2 Sample Type Hierarchy

(DVDs usually have additional features, such as soundtracks in multiple languages, or even "featurettes" about the making of the movie). Therefore, I find it desirable to model "movie" as one concept and "DVD" as a different, but very closely related, concept. Figure 2.2 illustrates one possible relationship among the formats handled in this store.

In this figure, the box labeled "Movie" represents a structured type whose components capture information common to all movie formats that are stocked (e.g., title, description, running time), while the boxes labeled "VHS Tape," "DVD," and "LaserDisc" represent structured types whose components capture—*in addition to common information*—additional information specific to individual formats stocked. A specific instance of the VHS Tape type would contain components that identify the title of the movie on the tape, the description of the movie, the running time, the stock number of the VHS tape, the rental price of the VHS tape, and the number of VHS tapes of the specific movie that we have for rent. Similarly, a specific instance of the LaserDisc type for the same movie would contain components that identify the title of the movie, the description of the movie, the running time, the stock number of the LaserDisc, the LaserDisc rental price, the number of discs we have for rent, and whether the disc was recorded in CLV (constant linear velocity) or CAV (constant angular velocity) mode.

2.9.2 Subtypes and Supertypes

As you will recall from the discussion in section 2.5.3, the VHS Tape, DVD, and LaserDisc types are called *subtypes* of the Movie type; similarly, the Movie type is a *supertype* of each of those three other types. Type hierarchies can be as "deep" as desired; that is, the DVD type might have its own subtypes to represent, say, DVDs recorded with Dolby Digital Sound and DVDs recorded with the somewhat less common DTS sound. Dolby Digital Sound is also a subtype of Movie, but it is not a *direct subtype*. Analogously, Movie is a supertype of Dolby Digital Sound, but not a *direct supertype*.

Of course, attentive readers will immediately recognize that VHS tapes, DVDs, LaserDiscs, and so on, all share common attributes, such as a stock number, a sales price, and a list of stars; therefore, these attributes could (and probably *should*) be specified in the supertype Movie. The fact that the *values* of those attributes will differ, perhaps significantly, in various subtypes doesn't imply at all that they should be defined in the subtypes. Only those attributes that appear *only* in a subtype (and in its possible subtypes) should be defined in that subtype—such as whether CLV mode or CAV mode was used for a LaserDisc: since DVDs and VHS tapes don't have those characteristics, that attribute wouldn't be specified at all for those subtypes. However, let's avoid quasireligious discussions like data modeling for the moment—I'm trying to illustrate a point here, not fully design a system!

The idea of subtypes has to be distinguished from another sort of dependent relationship involving structured types, as illustrated in Figure 2.3. Any structured type can have attributes whose data type is another structured type (theoretically—although not in SQL:1999—the same structured type!). While that might seem to create a sort of "type hierarchy," the term is not applied to that concept; it's reserved for supertype/subtype relationships.

If the UNDER clause (see Syntax 2.3) is specified, the type being defined is a subtype of the type indicated by the `<supertype name>`. As you'll recall from earlier discussions in this chapter, this (sub)type inherits all of the attributes and methods that are defined for its supertype (including attributes and methods that the supertype might have inherited from its supertype, if any).

Now, let's consider the `AS representation` clause. You can see in Syntax 2.2 that this clause is optional, so you can define a new type to be a subtype of an existing type without being required to specify any additional attributes of the type. You might use that option, for example, to create a subtype with some new behaviors but without any additional stored data. On the other hand, if you're creating a type without any supertypes, then you will often find it appropriate to specify the `AS representation` clause; otherwise, the type won't have any attri-

```
movie (                                 studio (
  title    VARCHAR(100),                  name     VARCHAR(50),
  ...                                     ...
  owner    studio,   ----------->         founded  SMALLINT,
  ...                                     ...
  rating   CHAR(4) )                      Oscars   INTEGER )
```

Figure 2.3 Structured Type Dependency Relationship

butes at all! If you create a type without any supertypes and without any attributes, then the type should be defined as NOT INSTANTIABLE and NOT FINAL (SQL:1999 doesn't appear to require this specification, but the type will be rather useless otherwise!), in which case attributes will typically be defined for its subtypes.

Inclusion of the `AS representation` clause allows you to specify (enclosed in parentheses) a comma-separated list of type attributes that look a lot like column definitions inside a table definition—the principle difference being that attribute definitions can't contain constraints, while column definitions can. Attribute definitions comprise mostly an attribute name and a data type, and the data type can be a built-in type, a distinct type, or a structured type. (Attributes have other characteristics, as well, but they're not relevant to this discussion.)

A definition of our Movie type from Figure 2.2 might look like this:

Example 2.18 *A Supertype Definition*

```
CREATE TYPE movie AS (
  title         CHARACTER VARYING(50),
  description   CHARACTER VARYING(500),
  runs          INTEGER )
  NOT INSTANTIABLE
  NOT FINAL
```

We made this type NOT INSTANTIABLE because we don't stock any product that is just "Movie"; we stock only VHS tapes, DVDs, and so forth. Of course, it would be meaningless to make a NOT INSTANTIABLE type FINAL as well, so SQL:1999 prohibits that combination. (In fact, SQL:1999 completely prohibits specification of structured types that are FINAL, but a future version of the SQL standard may allow such types. However, structured types won't be allowed to be both FINAL and NOT INSTANTIABLE.)

Next, let's look at a type definition for the DVD type:

Example 2.19 *A Subtype Definition*

```
CREATE TYPE dvd UNDER movie AS (
  stock_number   INTEGER,
  rental_price   DECIMAL(5,2),
  extra_features feature_desc ARRAY[10] )
  INSTANTIABLE
  NOT FINAL
```

The dvd type, being a subtype of the movie type, contains all of the attributes that the movie type has, but it has three additional attributes: the stock number, the rental price, and an array of feature_desc values. We may guess that the feature_desc type is another structured type used to describe the extra features that DVDs often have, and we allow a maximum of 10 extra features on a single DVD (although we hasten to note that we rarely get that many features for our money!).

Since DVDs come in different formats—Dolby Digital DVDs and DTS DVDs—we would probably create a couple of additional subtypes to deal with that, but the information particular to each would probably be somewhat esoteric; for example, a Dolby Digital DVD is very likely to have an alternate sound track encoded in Dolby Surround sound, but that information might not be required on a DTS DVD.

In Figure 2.2, the DVD type is the *direct supertype* of the Dolby Digital Sound type; it is also a *direct subtype* of the Movie type. Every type hierarchy must have exactly one maximal supertype. In Figure 2.2, the maximal supertype is the Movie type. A type that does not have any subtypes is sometimes called a *leaf type.*

In SQL:1999, a structured type is a subtype of itself and, consequently, a supertype of itself; the phrase applied to a subtype other than the type itself is *proper subtype,* and the corresponding phrase for supertypes is *proper supertype.* The collection of subtypes of a particular type in a type hierarchy is called the *subtype family* of that particular type. (In fact, it's common usage to refer to the entire collection of types in a type hierarchy as the subtype family of any type in the hierarchy, but that's not the definition in the SQL standard.)

It's important to note that the feature_desc type is *not* likely to be a subtype of the movie type. In fact, it's unlikely that it's part of the same type hierarchy at all; it's more likely that it belongs to a different type hierarchy, possibly one with only the single type named feature_desc.

SQL:1999 doesn't allow you to define any structured type to be "based on" itself, directly or indirectly. Let's analyze that restriction, because there might be more than one way to interpret it.

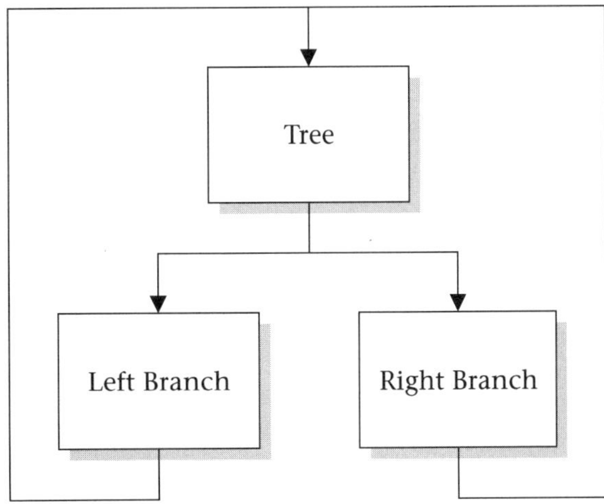

Figure 2.4 Invalid SQL:1999 Type Structure

You are allowed to define structured types having attributes whose data types are supertypes of the type being defined, but you cannot define a structured type with an attribute whose data type is the type you're defining, or an ARRAY type whose element type is the type you're defining, or a ROW type having a field whose type is the type you're defining. That second alternative would, if permitted, result in a type that is based on itself. Perhaps obviously, you cannot define a structured type having an attribute whose data type is a subtype of the type you're defining because the subtype cannot even be created until all of its supertypes (including the type you're defining) have been defined.

If you define a structured type having an attribute whose data type is some supertype of the type you're defining, then you can store in that attribute instances of that supertype and instances of any of its subtypes—including instances whose most specific type is the type you're defining! This might sound a little strange, but it works, as long as you don't try to store an instance of a type into one of its own attributes (which would be rather difficult to do, in any case).

This means, for example, that it would be invalid in SQL:1999 to define, say, a "tree" type recursively. In other words, the structure shown in Figure 2.4 would not be permitted if "Left Branch" and "Right Branch" were attributes of the "Tree" type and their data types were declared to be the "Tree" type. The structure in Figure 2.4 *would,* however, be permitted if "Left Branch" and "Right Branch" were subtypes of the "Tree" type and they each contained an attribute whose type was the "Tree" type.

It's true that there are other programming languages that allow type definers to define a type in terms of itself—to define types recursively. However, those languages don't have to deal with some of the concepts that SQL does, such as persistent storage of data, including type instances, type evolution (altering the definition of a type), and tables defined to be "of" a given type (see Chapter 3, "Typed Tables," for more information on this subject). Those problems make it somewhat more difficult—though not necessarily impossible—to define SQL:1999's structured types recursively. Perhaps some future revision of the SQL standard will offer that capability. (In SQL:1999, there are ways of working around this limitation through the creative use of typed tables and reference types. One possibility arises when the "Tree" type is the type of a typed table, "Left Branch" and "Right Branch" are attributes of the "Tree" type, and the data types of those attributes are reference types that reference values of the "Tree" type.)

2.9.3 Instantiable Types Versus Noninstantiable Types

As I told you when discussing Syntax 2.10, a structured type declared to be INSTANTIABLE is one for which instances can be created; that is, values in your applications can have that type as their data type. Once in awhile, though, a type designer may decide that she's creating a specific type for which values must never be created; instead, one or more (usually more!) subtypes of that type are defined and values in the system will be of one of those subtypes. This requirement is enforced by making the supertype NOT INSTANTIABLE. An `abstract` class in Java is roughly analogous to a NOT INSTANTIABLE structured type in SQL. Each attribute of an SQL:1999 NOT INSTANTIABLE structured type results in the creation of an observer method and a mutator method. Of course, those methods will never have instances of their closely associated structured type on which they can operate, but they are inherited by, and used to access their eponymous inherited attributes of, INSTANTIABLE subtypes of the NOT INSTANTIABLE type.

In the music and video application example, I have suggested that the `movie` type be made NOT INSTANTIABLE, since it's meaningless to talk about stocking, renting, and selling "movies," as opposed to DVDs and VHS tapes of those movies. Of course, it's possible that you might choose to model movies that you don't stock (perhaps they're out of print) but about which you wish to allow customers to ask questions; in that case, you would quite reasonably choose to make the `movie` type INSTANTIABLE. Making a type INSTANTIABLE imposes no requirement on your application to actually create any instances of the type; that's purely an application decision.

It's permitted in SQL:1999 to create NOT INSTANTIABLE subtypes of an INSTANTIABLE type. Of course, you cannot create instances of such noninstanti-

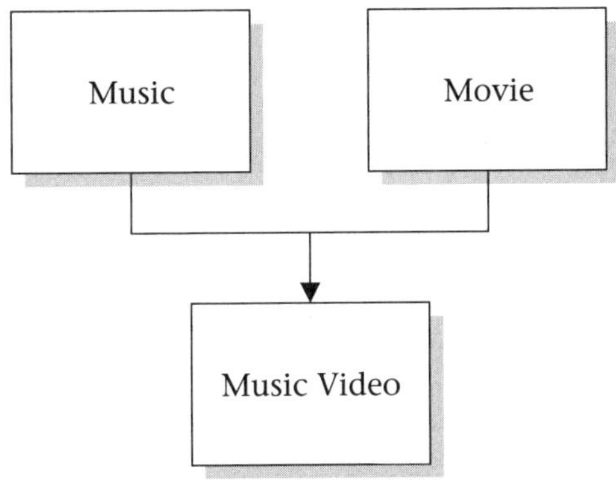

Figure 2.5 Multiple Inheritance Illustration

able types, but you can create INSTANTIABLE subtypes of those noninstantiable types, for which you can create instances.

2.9.4 Single Inheritance Versus Multiple Inheritance

If you're familiar with object-oriented systems and type hierarchies, you'll have already realized from Syntax 2.3 and related discussions that SQL:1999 provides a *single inheritance* type hierarchy. By this, I mean that a subtype is allowed to inherit attributes and methods from at most one direct supertype.

A few other programming languages, notably C++,[16] implement a *multiple inheritance* model for type hierarchies. Multiple inheritance permits the definition of types that inherit attributes and methods from more than one immediate supertype. This model makes the task of modeling certain real-world concepts somewhat easier, as illustrated in Figure 2.5, but significantly increases implementation difficulties for systems in which the applications and data may be widely distributed (e.g., in a wide-area network environment) and systems with persistent metadata, such as SQL.

If you're a fan of the rock group Queen, you may have encountered the concert video *Queen—We Will Rock You.* This videotape might be classified under "Music," because it contains performances of some 24 Queen songs, but it might also be reasonably classified as a "Movie," since it includes interviews, commentary, and other features of a documentary. Some applications might benefit from being able to simultaneously categorize this video as both "Music" and "Movie."

16 Bjarne Stroustrup, *The C++ Programming Language, Third Edition* (Reading, Mass: Addison-Wesley, 1997).

Unfortunately, SQL:1999 doesn't permit that approach, since it supports only single inheritance. SQL:1999 doesn't provide a good workaround for this issue, and it remains a problem for some applications to resolve in other ways.

2.9.5 Most Specific Type

Looking back at the Movie hierarchy (see Figure 2.2), you can infer that a movie distributed on a VHS tape is, at once, a Movie *and* a VHS Tape; similarly, one distributed on a Dolby Digital DVD is at once a Movie, a DVD, and a Dolby Digital DVD. This is, in fact, the essence of a subtype—that its instances are simultaneously of their own type as well as all of their supertypes.

Which leads to a terminology problem: if a specific structured type instance is a `dolby_dvd`, a `dvd`, and a `movie`, then what type is it really?

To resolve this (I don't want to overstate the problem) modest dilemma, SQL:1999 has chosen the term *most specific type* to mean "the structured type closest to the leaves of the type hierarchy of which the instance is a member." This is also the name of the constructor function that was used when the instance was created.

Therefore, if we have a structured type value whose data type is `dvd`, but that is (for whatever reason!) neither a `dolby_dvd` nor a `dts_dvd`, then its most specific type is `dvd`. Of course, one of its types (although not its most specific type) is `movie`. But none of its types are `dolby_dvd` or `dts_dvd`. Each site (e.g., column of a table, SQL variable, or parameter) has a *declared type* that is the data type used in its declaration; the type of the value stored at that site at any given moment is the most specific type of that value—and it must be the declared type or one of its subtypes, using the notion of substitutability discussed in the following section. You can never change the most specific type of a structured type instance to any type other than the one it had when it was created, not even to a proper supertype or a proper subtype. The only approach to use if you find yourself required to do something like that is to create a new instance of the desired most specific type and copy relevant attribute values from the existing instance to the new one.

2.9.6 Substitutability

The concept of "most specific type" is especially interesting because, if you have some site whose data type is some structured type, you can store into that location any value whose most specific type is that type—or any of its subtypes!

For example, if you declare an SQL variable whose type is `movie`:

```
DECLARE film movie;
```

you can store into that variable an instance that is a movie, a dvd, or a dolby_dvd:

```
SET film = NEW dolby_dvd(...);
```

The *declared type* of film is, of course, movie—you can see it right there on the page (that's what I mean by "the declared type"). But, after executing that SET statement, the *most specific type* stored in film is dolby_dvd.

The ability to provide an instance of a subtype at any location where an instance of a supertype is expected is called *substitutability*; that is, you can *substitute* a subtype instance for a supertype instance. The reverse, which may be surprising to some, is not true. Let's look very briefly at the reason why.

Recall that all declared attributes of structured types are encapsulated by means of that pair of methods described earlier (the observer and the mutator). If we wanted to assign the value that contains the title of a movie stored in our film variable to some other variable, we might write something like this:

```
SET newvar = film.title;
```

If there's a movie—that is, a value whose most specific type is movie—stored in film, then that statement will extract the value of the title attribute and store it into the variable named newvar. However, suppose that film actually has a dolby_dvd stored in it; since dolby_dvd instances are also, at the same time, movie instances, they have a title attribute, too. Therefore, the SET statement works as expected, assigning the value of the title attribute to newvar.

But what about doing things the other way around? Suppose we declared a variable

```
DECLARE cinema dvd;
```

As you will recall, dvds have a stock_number attribute, but movies do not. If we store a dvd instance into that variable

```
SET cinema = NEW dvd(...);
```

then we have a value stored there for which we can use six attributes: title, description, runs, stock_number, rental_price, and extra_features. However, suppose we decided to store a movie instance—not a vhs_tape or a dvd, just a movie—into that variable. The movie instance simply doesn't have a stock_number attribute, even though the variable inherently does. We can't just make up a value to put into that attribute! The only way to avoid problems that would be caused by attempting to invoke the stock_number observer method on a value that doesn't have the attribute is to prohibit storing a `movie` instance into a location declared as one of its subtypes.

As a result, substitutability works only in one direction!

2.9.7 Implementation Versus Interface

In section 2.9.4, you learned that SQL:1999 supports only single inheritance type hierarchies. Another well-known language that supports only single inheritance is Java; however, Java supports single inheritance of *implementation* (meaning stored data analogous to SQL's attributes, along with the code of methods), but multiple inheritance of *interface* (meaning the signatures of methods). SQL:1999 does not include the notion of interface in this sense, although future versions of the language might include that concept.

By contrast, C++ and a few other object-oriented programming languages do provide multiple inheritance. While there are a number of differences between C++ and Java, the significant difference for the purposes of this section is that Java was designed to work on the Web—an inherently distributed environment—while the design center for C++ is a single computer environment.

It is in a distributed environment that multiple inheritance becomes especially difficult to implement (at least to implement well). In particular, when instances of some subtype are permitted to be stored at any node in a network, the system must be able to invoke the type's methods on any of those instances—regardless of where in the network they reside. There are only a few ways to accomplish this: (1) The type instances can be transferred across the network to some node designated to be responsible for execution of that method, (2) the system can require that the method be stored at every node where it is possible to store an instance of the type so the method can be executed at the nodes where the instances exist, or (3) the methods can be transferred across the network to the appropriate node when its invocation is encountered (subject, of course, to the node being an appropriate platform for executing that code!). None of these are very satisfactory, as they involve both performance problems and management issues.

Consequently, Java, and SQL, provide only a single inheritance model of type hierarchies.

2.10 Creating Instances of Structured Types

By now, you should have a reasonable start on an understanding of SQL:1999's structured types, including how they are declared, how the data they contain is represented, and how their semantics are provided. But you still haven't seen how instances of these types are created, although I mentioned constructors in section 2.7.5. Before we can discuss the use of structured types in the database in any detail, we must first go over some important issues related to their nature and instantiation.

2.10.1 Instances Are Values

The most important characteristic of structured types, mentioned several times earlier, is this: their instances are *values,* not objects. (You may be getting tired of reading that, but it is so fundamental to the design of SQL's user-defined types that I feel it's worth emphasizing.)

Some readers—especially those of you with a strong Java background—are undoubtedly raising your eyebrows about now. After all, I've talked about object technology and implied that SQL's structured types have some characteristics in common with Java classes, and I've even used the term *SQL object model.* Furthermore, I've compared SQL's methods to Java methods. Why am I now saying that structured type instances are not objects?

Well, the fact is that instances of SQL's structured types have no object identity; there is no concept of some "other" value that uniquely identifies any structured type instance. The only "identity" that a structured type value has in SQL is its own value, just like an integer or character string value.

Still, don't despair! Structured type instances in SQL have many characteristics that would be considered "object-like" by many observers, including encapsulation and the ability to participate in type hierarchies. Even better, when you get to Chapter 3, "Typed Tables," you'll see exactly how SQL:1999 really does provide the remaining aspects of object orientation. But until we get there, let's focus on just how structured type *values* come into being and how they are used in the database.

2.10.2 A Little Mathematical Philosophy

Programmers in object-oriented programming languages use the term *constructor* to mean a routine that creates a new instance of an object class or type. As we'll see, the term has a slightly different meaning in SQL:1999. The difference is modest, and I'll let you judge for yourself whether it's an important one or not.

Mathematical purists will argue that nobody can ever "create" a value; all values simply *exist* and the most that can be done with them is to represent them at some location. For example, the number eight exists; there's nothing you or I can do that will make it go away or that will change anything at all about it. We can, of course, write it down on a piece of paper in any of several notations ("Eight," "ocho," "huit," "8," "viii," "VIII," "||||||||," "(2*3) + 2," and so forth). No matter what notation we use, no matter what national script or font we use, the meaning is still the number of fingers (excluding thumbs) on most people's hands.

So what?

Well, when you create a variable in some program you're writing, and you store into that variable a bit sequence that represents the number eight, you aren't "creating" the number eight, you're merely manifesting a representation of it in memory.

By contrast, a great many programmers use different terminology when they manifest a representation of a more complex value, such as a structure or an array. The word *construct* appears fairly often, as does the word *create,* as in "create an array with three elements in which the first element contains 1, the second 10, and the third 100." Of course, that array is a value, too, and already exists in the same sense that the number eight exists; but many (perhaps most!) of us think about it a little differently. So does SQL:1999, which uses the term *construct* to describe the process of manifesting a structured type value.

2.10.3 Constructors and the NEW Expression

An SQL:1999 constructor is a function (not, perhaps surprisingly, a method) that your applications use whenever a new value of a structured type is required. The SQL system always provides a default constructor function for you whenever you create a structured type. That system-provided constructor function returns a value of its associated structured type in which every attribute has its default value. (Incidentally, a structured type instance in which every attribute has the null value is *not* the same as a null structured type instance! Think about it and compare this with the notion of a "null integer.")

Constructor functions always have the same name as the structured type with which they're associated, in much the same way—and for much the same reason—that observer and mutator methods have the same name as the attributes with which they are associated. System-provided constructors have no parameters (we call them *niladic* methods).

Naturally, since the constructor function returns a value and not an object, it can be invoked over and over again, and a new instance of that value is produced each time. You can do what you wish with the value returned; you can store it into an SQL variable, put it into a column in a table, or simply throw it away—just as you can do with the number eight.

But, just how often will your application be satisfied with a "default" instance of a structured type? I believe that applications will often, perhaps usually, want to produce structured type instances in which some or all attributes have values other than their default values. While you are allowed to invoke the construction function of a structured type directly, you will probably do it most often in a context where you can provide attribute values appropriate to your application needs.

SQL:1999 responds to this requirement by supporting user-defined *constructor methods,* which I prefer to call *initializer methods*. An initializer method is one that takes a newly constructed instance of a structured type in which all attributes have been given their default values and replaces it with an instance in which some or all attributes have been given different values, based entirely on the semantics of the initializer method, which is written by the application builder or the type designer. Initializer methods are specified using the keyword CONSTRUCTOR in Syntax 2.10 (although I think that INITIALIZER might have been a better choice, given the usage of such methods). You can provide as many initializer methods as you wish for a given structured type. They are (normally) not niladic methods, but have whatever parameters you decide to be appropriate. Your user-written initializers always have the same name as the system-provided constructor (the name is thus overloaded). The parameter list of a user-defined initializer must differ in the number of parameters or in the data types of the parameters from the parameter list of all other initializers for that type.

Suppose we want to create a new instance of our `movie` structured type. We know that the system provides a niladic constructor function, also named `movie`. If we were allowed to invoke it ourselves (we're not!), the function invocation shown in Example 2.20 would construct a new, default instance of the `movie` type, which we might visualize as shown in Result 2.1.

Example 2.20 *Invalid Invocation of the System-Provided Constructor Function*

```
MOVIE()
```

Result 2.1 *Default MOVIE Instance*

Attribute Name	*Value*
TITLE	*(null)*
DESCRIPTION	*(null)*
RUNS	*(null)*

Of course, we probably don't need to represent very many movies with those characteristics, so we'll need an initializer method that we can use to put more reasonable values into our new `movie` instance. Such a method might be written something like that in Example 2.21.

Example 2.21 *Non-Default Initializer Method*

```
CREATE METHOD movie ( name        CHARACTER VARYING (50),
                      descr       CHARACTER VARYING (500),
                      len         INTEGER )
    RETURNS movie

  BEGIN
    SET SELF.title = name;
    SET SELF.description = descr;
    SET SELF.runs = len;
    RETURN SELF;
  END
```

This method takes the (presumably default) `movie` instance provided to it as its implicit parameter (remember: this is called SELF internally) and set its attributes to those values passed into it as explicit parameters. In this case, I've chosen to set all of the type instance's attributes, but I could have chosen as easily to set only some of them.

When we put all this together in an application that uses this type, we might write code like the SQL routine seen in Example 2.22, correctly using the NEW expression.

Example 2.22 *Sample Application Using Non-Default Initializer*

```
BEGIN           -- Some new block of code
  DECLARE film  movie;
  SET film =
     NEW movie(
       'The Game',
       'A chilling thriller in which Michael Douglas' ||
       'plays a man given a "gift" by his younger' ||
       'brother...a gift that threatens his life' ||
       'and his sanity.',
       128 );
  ...
END
```

That NEW expression is (effectively) syntactically transformed to the expression seen in Example 2.23. Remember: SQL:1999 prohibits the explicit invocation of the system-provided constructor function, but the NEW expression results in its invocation.

Example 2.23 *Transformation of the NEW Expression*

```
movie().movie(
        'The Game',
        'A chilling thriller in which Michael Douglas' ||
        'plays a man given a "gift" by his younger' ||
        'brother...a gift that threatens his life' ||
        'and his sanity.',
        128 )
```

In other words, the keyword NEW specifies that the constructor function, whose name is `movie`, is invoked, producing a new default value of the `movie` structured type, after which the initializer method, also named `movie`, is invoked; it receives the just-constructed default value as its implicit parameter and populates it with some new values. As we saw a few lines earlier, the initializer then returns the populated value to its caller, the SET statement, at which time it gets assigned to the SQL variable `film`.

One thing I don't want to forget to tell you is this: All methods (other than the system-provided constructor method) that are defined with names that are the same as the name of their associated structured type are presumed to be initializers for that type. This means that you can invoke those methods *only* in the context of the NEW expression. Such initializers must be defined using the SELF AS RESULT syntax that you saw in Syntax 2.10, because they always return an instance of the structured type being defined. Of course, the RETURNS clause must specify the name of the structured type being defined, as well.

Now, if you prefer to populate your type instances "manually," you can always use a niladic constructor method and then write statements that invoke mutator methods on the default instance that it returns, as illustrated in Example 2.24 (contrast this with the SET statements in Example 2.21, in which attributes are references as "`SELF.attribute-name`" and are therefore being directly modified; see also section 2.11.2 for information about updating structured type instances in the database).

Example 2.24 *An Alternative to User-Defined Initializers*

```
BEGIN
  DECLARE film    movie;
  SET film = NEW movie();    -- Invoke a niladic constructor method
  SET film.title = 'The Game';
  SET film.runs = 128;
END                          -- The description is still null!
```

2.11 Using Structured Types

Of course, creating and giving values to structured type instances is not really very interesting if you're not able to store them in your database, get them back out, and modify them. This section discusses actual use of structured types in your data.

2.11.1 Storing in the Database

If you want to store a structured type instance into a column of a table—let's use that `movie_table` that I declared earlier—then you'll naturally use SQL's INSERT statement, as you will see in Example 2.25.

Example 2.25 *Inserting a New MOVIE Instance Using a Constructor*

```
INSERT INTO movie_table
  VALUES ( '152208-A',           -- STOCK_NUMBER
           NEW movie(
           'The Game',
           'A chilling thriller in which Michael Douglas' ||
           'plays a man given a "gift" by his younger' ||
           'brother...a gift that threatens his life' ||
           'and his sanity.',
           128 ),                -- new MOVIE instance
           23,                   -- RENTAL_QUANTITY in stock
           2.99 )                -- RENTAL_COST
```

Yup, it's that easy. I just created, and populated, a new `movie` instance right in the middle of the VALUES clause of an INSERT statement. Of course, if I already had an SQL variable—perhaps the variable named `film` that I defined in Example 2.22—I could have used that in the INSERT statement as I've done in Example 2.26.

Example 2.26 *Inserting a New MOVIE Instance Using an Initialized Variable*

```
INSERT INTO movie_table
  VALUES ( '152208-A', -- STOCK_NUMBER
           film,       -- just a MOVIE instance
           23,         -- RENTAL_QUANTITY in stock
           2.99 )      -- RENTAL_COST
```

2.11.2 Updating in the Database

Updating structured type instances in the database isn't much more complicated than creating them. The additional complexity comes in because you're dealing with an existing value of which you often want to update only a part, not the entire value.

If you were to write something like the statement in Example 2.27, then you would correctly expect the value of the rental_cost column in the row for the specified film to be set to 1.99, regardless of what the cost was previously.

Example 2.27 *Updating the Price of a Movie*

```
UPDATE   movie_table
SET      rental_cost = 1.99
WHERE    stock_number = '152208-A'
```

Similarly, if you wrote a statement like the one in Example 2.28, you shouldn't be at all surprised when the entire movie value is replaced with something not terribly interesting—a film with no name or description. But we *do* know that it's a really long movie!

Example 2.28 *Creating an Uninteresting, but Lengthy, Movie*

```
UPDATE   movie_table
SET      movie = NEW movie('', '', 228 )
WHERE    stock_number = '152208-A'
```

How, then, can we change just the length (runs) of a movie without affecting the title or description? Well, we simply have to remember that all values we don't want to be affected must either be untouched or set to their original values. Example 2.29 illustrates one way to do that:

Example 2.29 *Updating the Length of a Movie*

```
UPDATE   movie_table
SET      movie = NEW movie( movie.title,
                            movie.description,
                            113 )
WHERE    stock_number = '152208-A'
```

I find that approach awkward; if I need to replace only one or two attributes of a type that has dozens of attributes, I must remember to copy every one of the attributes I don't want to change. That is certainly tedious and probably very error-prone. (Worse, using this approach requires that I have been granted appropriate privileges on the observer methods, which can be even more tedious in large enterprises.) Instead, I prefer a solution that uses a mutator method, like that in Example 2.30.

Example 2.30 *A Better Way to Update the Length of a Movie*

```
UPDATE   movie_table
SET      movie = movie.runs( 113 )
WHERE    stock_number = '152208-A'
```

You'll recall from reading section 2.7.4 that the mutator method for some attribute of a structured type has the name of the attribute (runs in this case) and takes one explicit parameter specifying the new value of the attribute. The implicit parameter mentioned earlier is represented by specifying the name of some site containing an instance of the type to the left of the "dot" (movie in this case). You may also recall that the mutator method returns a new instance of the type that is identical in all attributes to the "input" type *except* for the eponymous attribute, whose value is set to the value of the explicit parameter. Whew!

That's a long-winded way to say that the SET clause

```
SET movie = movie.runs ( 113 )
```

sets the value of the movie column to a new movie value in which the title and description are unchanged, but the runs value is now 113 (presumably minutes). If we wished to change two or more of the attributes for our movie instance, we could do so by stringing multiple mutator methods together:

```
SET movie = movie.runs ( 113 ).description( '...' )
```

An even more convenient way of (implicitly) invoking that mutator method is illustrated in Example 2.31.

Example 2.31 *An Even Better Way to Update the Length of a MOVIE*

```
UPDATE   movie_table
SET      movie.runs = 113
WHERE    stock_number = '152208-A'
```

This last alternative is certainly the most intuitive of the various choices. It's nothing more than a syntactic shorthand for the variation in Example 2.30, but it's surely a lot more comfortable for most programmers.

2.11.3 Retrieving from the Database

I've already introduced you (throughout various sections of this chapter) to the idea of retrieving structured type values, or parts thereof, from the database, so this will be quite painless.

If you wish to retrieve just the length of a movie, you might write

Example 2.32 *Retrieval into a Host Variable*

```
SELECT   mt.movie.runs
INTO     :length_var
FROM     movie_table mt
WHERE    mt.stock_number = '152208-A'
```

You can, of course, execute the first of those statements (in Example 2.32) from your application program written in C or COBOL (or any other programming language for which your SQL implementation has a language binding).

What you cannot do in a program written in a conventional programming language is to retrieve, without a little assistance, an entire structured type value at one time. In other words, the statement in Example 2.33, while perfectly valid if executed in an SQL/PSM stored routine, would be—well, not exactly invalid in a COBOL program, but not very useful without that assistance.

Example 2.33 *Invalid Retrieval into a Host Variable*

```
SELECT   mt.movie
INTO     :movie_var
FROM     movie_table mt
WHERE    mt.stock_number = '152208-A'
```

Can you quickly tell why Example 2.33 wouldn't normally be very useful in COBOL? Right—there's no way in COBOL to *meaningfully* declare a COBOL variable whose data type is an SQL structured type! Of course, you can imagine that you would be able to declare a COBOL structure like that shown in Example 2.34, and that would probably work just fine—if it were supported by SQL:1999.

Example 2.34 *Possible, but Useless, COBOL Declaration*

```
01 movie-var.
02   title           PIC X(100).
02   description     PIC X(500).
02   runs            PIC S9(9).
```

But it's very easy to define more complex structured types where the COBOL equivalent isn't as obvious, so the ability to retrieve structured type instances directly into host programs was deferred to a future edition of the SQL standard.

On the other hand, if you've declared an SQL variable whose data type is your structured type, you can easily retrieve into it. See Example 2.35.

Example 2.35 *Structured Type Retrieval into an SQL Variable*

```
BEGIN
  DECLARE film    movie;
  SELECT   movie
  INTO     film
  FROM     movie_table
  WHERE    stock_number = '152208-A';
END
```

The difference, of course, is that it *is* possible to declare SQL variables whose data type is a structured type.

SQL:1999 offers a facility called *transforms* that allows type definers to provide functions that can be used to map structured types to SQL built-in types, which can then be mapped to host language structures, and vice versa. Be patient; section 2.11.8 covers this issue.

2.11.4 CAST Functions

In section 2.11.3, I discussed retrieval of structured type instances from the database, but I also noted that SQL:1999 doesn't provide a way to retrieve such instances directly into an application program written in a conventional host programming language. SQL does provide facilities to help you with that problem, though, and it seems appropriate to discuss them here. In Syntax 2.2, you saw that the syntax for defining structured user-defined types includes a clause indicated by the BNF nonterminal symbol `<cast option>`; in section 2.8, though, I explained that `<cast option>` is used to specify the names of SQL-invoked routines that applications can use to cast instances of distinct types to and from their underlying SQL built-in types, as well as other SQL built-in types.

But SQL:1999 also provides you with a way of providing SQL-invoked routines that allow applications to cast instances of structured types to and from other SQL types, including both SQL's built-in types and other structured types. The mechanism for accomplishing this is called a *user-defined cast*. User-defined casts might have a number of potential uses, but one of the most interesting is in converting instances of structured types to and from SQL built-in types (including constructed types such as ROW) that can then be transferred between the SQL engine and an application program written in C, COBOL, or some other conventional programming language. See Example 2.34 for an illustration of the sort of host language structure that an application might use for this purpose.

Of course, use of user-defined casts is not limited to transferring to and from host programs; they're perfectly useful for transforming to and from various SQL types for use purely within SQL statements. Furthermore, in section 2.11.8, you'll learn about a related technique, transforms, that makes the job of exchanging structured type values between the SQL environment and the application environment even more straightforward.

The syntax to define a user-defined cast appears in Syntax 2.13. Either `<source data type>` or `<target data type>` must identify a structured user-defined type, which must of course already exist. If both `<source data type>` and `<target data type>` identify structured user-defined types, they must identify two different structured types and both types must already exist. Similarly, `<cast function>` must identify an SQL-invoked function that already exists; that function must have exactly one parameter whose data type is the type indicated by `<source data type>`, and its return type must be the type indicated by `<target data type>`. Observe that the `<cast function>` is specified by using the function's `<specific routine designator>` and not the invocable name of the function.

Syntax 2.13 *User-Defined Cast Syntax*

```
<user-defined cast definition> ::=
    CREATE CAST
      <left paren> <source data type> AS <target data type> <right paren>
      WITH <cast function>
      [ AS ASSIGNMENT ]

<cast function> ::= <specific routine designator>

<source data type> ::= <data type>

<target data type> ::= <data type>
```

The CREATE CAST statement associates the specified function with the structured type or types specified as the source and/or target of the user-defined cast. Once the user-defined cast has been created, "appropriate" invocation of the CAST expression will cause the specified function to be executed to actually perform the CAST. By "appropriate," I mean this: If a user-defined cast exists for casting instances of the movie type to CHARACTER VARYING(1000), then the expression

```
CAST (my_movie AS CHARACTER VARYING(1000))
```

will invoke the function specified in the user-defined cast. Consider Example 2.36, in which I repeat the definition of the movie type (to make it easy to see the relationship with the user-defined cast), followed by an SQL-invoked function and a user-defined cast that invokes that function.

Example 2.36 *Creating a User-Defined Cast*

```
CREATE TYPE movie (
  title              CHARACTER VARYING (100),
  description        CHARACTER VARYING (500),
  runs               INTEGER )
  NOT FINAL

CREATE FUNCTION movie_to_char ( my_movie movie )
    RETURNS CHARACTER (610)
    LANGUAGE SQL
    SPECIFIC sql_movie_to_char
    DETERMINISTIC
    CONTAINS SQL
    RETURNS NULL ON NULL INPUT
  BEGIN
    DECLARE n CHARACTER (100),
            d CHARACTER (500),
            r CHARACTER (10),
            return_value CHARACTER (610);
    SET n = my_movie.title;
    SET d = my_movie.description;
    SET r = CAST ( my_movie.runs AS CHARACTER (10) );
    SET return_value = n || d || r;
    RETURN return_value;
  END

CREATE CAST ( movie AS CHARACTER (610) )
            WITH movie_to_char
```

In Example 2.37, you see how that user-defined cast might be used by an embedded SQL program written in COBOL.

Example 2.37 *Using a User-Defined Cast*

```
...
01 movie-var.
02   title          PIC X(100).
02   description    PIC X(500).
02   runs           PIC X(10).
...
EXEC SQL SELECT CAST ( movie AS CHARACTER (610) )
         INTO     :movie_var
         FROM     movie_table
         WHERE    stock_number = '152208-A'
```

The CAST expression is recognized by the system to match the user-defined cast defined in Example 2.36, so the specified function is invoked to transform the `movie` value into a CHARACTER value that can be reasonably transferred to the COBOL program. (Of course, this example depends on COBOL actually implementing `movie_var` as the contiguous sequence of character items that it contains.)

Of course, if you've defined user-defined casts that you no longer need, you can destroy them with the DROP CAST statement whose syntax is shown in Syntax 2.14.

Syntax 2.14 *<drop user-defined cast statement> Syntax*

```
<drop user-defined cast statement> ::=
    DROP CAST
      <left paren> <source data type> AS <target data type> <right paren>
   <drop behavior>
```

As in other DROP statements, `<drop behavior>` is either RESTRICT or CASCADE. Executing a DROP CAST statement does not affect the existence of the SQL-invoked function that it references or either the source or target data types.

You should be aware that there are a few limitations on the user-defined casts:

- No more than a single user-defined cast can be specified for each combination of `<source data type>` and `<target data type>`.
- The specified function must be deterministic and cannot specify either POSSIBLY READS SQL DATA or POSSIBLY MODIFIES SQL DATA.
- The schema in which the function is defined must be owned by the same authorization identifier that owns the schema or schemas in which the source and/or target structured types are defined.

2.11.5 Deleting from the Database

You *delete* a structured type instance from the database in precisely the same manner that you delete a scalar value from the database: you can UPDATE the table and set the appropriate column to the null value, or you can DELETE the entire row containing the value from the table! Setting the value in some particular row of a column whose type is a structured type to SQL's null value has essentially the same effect as setting the value of a column whose type is a built-in type like INTEGER: it makes the value "go away," replaced by that special value meaning "ain't no value here." There are additional implications, though: attempts to retrieve the value of an attribute of a structured type site that has the null value will return the null value, but attempts to modify the value of an attribute at such a site results in an error.

Those of you that are approaching this material from a Java background may be wondering whether any sort of cleanup behavior can be built into structured types, similar to Java's `finalize` method. The answer is no—an instance value is simply destroyed. Of course, SQL's triggers may be useful for cleaning up after your programs delete (that is, set to the null value) instances of structured types that are stored in columns; referential actions might also prove useful.

2.11.6 Copying an Instance from One Site to Another

I've already talked about the fact that SQL variables and parameters of SQL routines can have a data type that is a structured type. But there's one additional point I'd like to emphasize related to using those variables and parameters.

Remember that instances of structured types are *values* and not objects! Therefore, when you assign an instance of a structured type to an SQL variable, it has a life of its own. Changing the value of some attribute of the instance in that SQL variable has no effect at all on the instance stored in the location from which you made the assignment.

Consider the following code snippet:

Example 2.38 *SET Statement Example*

```
BEGIN
  DECLARE v1, v2   movie;
  SET v1 = NEW movie('The Game',
      'A chilling thriller in which Michael Douglas ' ||
      'plays a man given a "gift" by his younger ' ||
      'brother...a gift that threatens his life ' ||
```

```
        'and his sanity.',
        128 );
    SET v2 = v1;
    SET v1 = v1.runs ( 135 );
END
```

The first SET statement, of course, creates a new instance of movie and assigns it to SQL variable v1. The second statement *copies* that movie value into SQL variable v2. The last SET statement changes the value of movie.runs in the value stored in v1, but that has *no effect at all* on the value stored in v2, which will continue to indicate the original movie length of 128 minutes. The same phenomenon holds when you pass a structured type value through an argument of a routine invocation.

2.11.7 User-Defined Type Locators

You saw in section 2.11.3 that SQL:1999 doesn't provide direct bindings for structured types in most host programming languages (Java is an important exception), but section 2.11.4 showed you a workaround using user-defined casts that depend on SQL-invoked functions. However, structured types do not necessarily have to be retrieved into your application program in order for you to manipulate them. Indeed, it's possible for some structured types to have attributes that are extremely large; we could conceivably define a movie type that includes the actual digitized movie! (I agree, that's not terribly likely, given the attitudes of the studios toward availability of movies in digital form.) Such a type might resemble the one shown in Example 2.39.

Example 2.39 *A movie Type That Contains a Movie*

```
CREATE TYPE movie (
  title              CHARACTER VARYING (100),
  description        CHARACTER VARYING (500),
  runs               INTEGER,
  the_film           BINARY LARGE OBJECT 125G )
  NOT FINAL
```

The fourth attribute, the_film, is specified to be (up to) 125 gigabytes in length! That's unlikely to be something you'd want to retrieve into your application program very often, particularly if all you're doing is performing a substring operation that grabs one particular frame. The designers of SQL:1999 recognized this problem and provided a special client-side data type to deal with it.[17]

SQL provides a facility called a *locator* that can be used to provide the application program code written in an ordinary programming language with a way to "get at" structured type values in the database. (Locators can be used to get at certain other values, including array instances and LOB instances, as described in Volume 1 of this book.)

A locator is a value that is meaningful only at the interface between the application program and the database system; it's meaningless in SQL/PSM routines, for example, and it cannot be the data type of a column in a table. But when passed to a host program, it can "represent" a structured type instance without actually having to move the value across the boundary. One use might be to INSERT a new row into some table in which one column of that row has a structured type value retrieved from some other table. If we have a table named `movie_table` that includes a column named `movie_info` whose data type is `movie`, then Example 2.40 suggests what a C program might look like when using a locator to manage the data in that column.

Example 2.40 *Using UDT Locators*

```
main() {
  EXEC SQL BEGIN SQL DECLARE SECTION
    SQL TYPE IS movie AS LOCATOR movie_loc;
  END SQL DECLARE SECTION

  EXEC SQL SELECT   movie_info
           INTO     :movie_loc
           FROM     movie_table
           WHERE    stock_number = '152208-A';
  EXEC SQL INSERT INTO other_table
           VALUES (..., :movie_loc, ...);
}
```

You can readily see that we were able to *reference* the value of the `movie` instance without actually having to retrieve it across the application/database interface, and then use it to create a new row for insertion into another table. The use of the column name `movie_info` in the select list did not have to be modified at all—the fact that the (host language) data type of the target of the retrieval,

17 In all fairness, this special data type is not of much use on the client side by itself; it might be more honest to say that the type is a client/server data type.

`:movie_loc`, was defined to be "`movie` AS LOCATOR" is sufficient to force the generation of a locator value instead of retrieval of the actual `movie` instance.

These locators have a relatively short maximum lifetime; they are usable until either the current transaction ends or the current session ends (each implementation decides which of those two lifetimes its locators have, which can be further limited by application use of the HOLD LOCATOR and FREE LOCATOR statements). Furthermore, locator values cannot be shared among different users or sessions; if you do try to use a locator value generated by one session in a different session, you'll almost certainly get an error saying that the value is meaningless.

2.11.8 Transforms and Transform Groups

Now that I've said, several times, that you cannot transfer instances of structured types across the application/database interface, I'll admit that statement is not entirely true (even for programming languages other than Java, which neither needs nor is allowed to use transforms). In fact, SQL:1999's transforms make it even easier than using the user-defined casts that I discussed in section 2.11.4.

SQL:1999 provides the ability to create sets of functions that permit transferring *representations* of structured type instances across the interface between the host language side and the SQL side, but the type designer (or application builder) has to provide those functions. Pairs of such *transform functions* are called *transform groups;* one of that pair of functions in a transform group, called the *to-sql function,* is invoked when transferring a structured type instance from the host language side of the interface to the SQL side, and the other, called the *from-sql function,* is used for transferring from the SQL side to the host language side. (Note that "host language side" does not necessarily mean "application program side," since user-defined functions, in the form of external functions, can be written in host programming languages. In fact, one of the primary motivations for providing transform groups is the need to support manipulation of structured type values by functions and methods written in a host programming language.) No structured type can have more than one transform group of the same name associated with it.

Although the application builder or type designer frequently has to define the transform functions and specify that they belong to the appropriate transform group, you don't have to invoke them explicitly; they are implicitly invoked whenever needed, as long as they have been defined and specified properly.

Let's take another look at the statement in section 2.11.3, in which I said that you'll need a little assistance to meaningfully declare a host language variable whose type is a structured type. Example 2.33 and Example 2.34 illustrate a couple of unsuccessful efforts to define COBOL variables to correspond to an SQL structured type. They are unsuccessful because COBOL doesn't support defining a host variable that maps to an SQL structured type, and SQL doesn't support mapping SQL structured types onto COBOL structures.

To help resolve this problem, SQL:1999 permits you to define a COBOL variable whose data type is an SQL structured type and specify that it is "represented" by some built-in SQL type, such as CHARACTER VARYING:

Example 2.41 *Useful COBOL Declaration*

```
01 movie-var USAGE IS SQL
     TYPE IS movie AS CHARACTER VARYING(610).
```

That declaration states that our new COBOL variable, movie_var, has the movie data type, but that its representation for the purposes of transferring to and from our application program is CHARACTER VARYING(610). (In Example 2.9, I defined the movie type to have three attributes; the first was up to 100 characters in length, the second up to 500, and the third was an INTEGER, which is (in most implementations, at least) no larger than 10 characters when cast to character format.)

With no more definition than that, I can't retrieve a movie instance into that host variable, because the database system has no way of knowing *how* I'd like the three-attribute movie instance to be mapped onto a CHARACTER VARYING (even though we humans might think it's fairly obvious). And that's where transforms come into play!

Briefly, a *transform* is an SQL-invoked function (possibly written by an application designer or a type designer, although it might be provided by the database vendor) whose job it is to map a structured type to and from the "representation" type (or, indeed, types). The application program's responsibility is to instruct the database system to use a specific *transform group* (which may comprise either one or two transform functions, one for converting from the host language environment into an SQL structured type and the other for converting in the other direction).

Transforms are created with (no surprises here) a CREATE TRANSFORM statement, in which you specify the name of the user-defined type (which can be either a structured type or a distinct type) and one or more transform group definitions. Each transform group definition names the transform group and then specifies either the to-sql transform function, the from-sql transform function, or both. The functions themselves must already exist, of course, before you can create a transform group naming them. The syntax of this statement appears in Syntax 2.15. In that syntax, the choice between using the keyword TRANSFORM and the keyword TRANSFORMS is a matter of taste; while native English speakers would tend to use the plural form when defining more than one `<transform group>`, the SQL processor treats the two keywords as equivalent.

Syntax 2.15 *<transform definition> Syntax*

```
<transform definition> ::=
    CREATE { TRANSFORM | TRANSFORMS } FOR <user-defined type>
      <transform group>...

<transform group> ::=
    <group name> <left paren> <transform element list> <right paren>

<group name> ::= <identifier>

<transform element list> ::=
    <to sql>
  | <from sql>
  | <to sql> <comma> <from sql>
  | <from sql> <comma> <to sql>

<to sql> ::= TO SQL WITH <to sql function>

<from sql> ::= FROM SQL WITH <from sql function>

<to sql function> ::= <specific routine designator>

<from sql function> ::= <specific routine designator>
```

It is the job of the from-sql function to transform an SQL user-defined type instance into some other, more host language–friendly form. In particular, you'd probably want to define a from-sql function in a transform group (that you might name something like `cobol_varchar_transforms`) to extract the values of each attribute of a `movie` instance and "cast" it into the "right format," positioned in the "right place" in a CHARACTER VARYING(610). You'd also probably want a to-sql function in the same transform group that populates a `movie` instance from a CHARACTER VARYING(610) value. The declarations of external methods associated with the user-defined type might specify the transform group or groups with which each such method is associated (the syntax that specifies this association appears in Chapter 4, "Routines and Routine Invocation"). The application must specify that the appropriate transform group to use is the `cobol_` varchar_transforms group. This is done by syntax in the embedded SQL COBOL program (the syntax shown in Syntax 2.16 is used for embedded SQL programs, as well as for SQL module language), specifying the name of the transform group to be used for each different user-defined type used in each such COBOL variable declaration. If you don't specify transform groups in your programs, SQL provides defaults for you, but specifying your own groups gives you much better control. Example 2.42 illustrates how you would create the cobol_varchar_transforms transform group and then use it.

Syntax 2.16 *<transform group specification> Syntax*

```
<transform group specification> ::=
    TRANSFORM GROUP
      { <single group specification> | <multiple group specification> }

<single group specification> ::= <group name>

<multiple group specification> ::=
    <group specification> [ { <comma> <group specification> }... ]

<group specification> ::=
    <group name> FOR TYPE <user-defined type>
```

Example 2.42 *Creating and Using a Transform Group*

```
/* Create the transform /*
CREATE TRANSFORM FOR movie
  cobol_varchar_transforms ( TO SQL WITH movie_to_char (movie),
                             FROM SQL WITH char_to_movie (CHARACTER(610) )
/* Specify its use */
TRANSFORM GROUP cobol_varchar_transforms FOR TYPE movie
```

Now, in order to actually make this information *useful* to your COBOL program, you've got to take one additional step: causing two COBOL names to refer to the same piece of storage. The first name is the one we declared in Example 2.41: movie-var. But that's going to "look like" a CHARACTER VARYING(610), and we don't really want to have to "unpack" the data it contains. Instead, we have to "know" (by reading the documentation—that's how!) what corresponding COBOL structure the from-sql function assumes. In COBOL, that requires the use of REDEFINES, as shown in Example 2.43.

Example 2.43 *Complete COBOL Declarations*

```
01 movie-var USAGE IS SQL
     TYPE IS movie AS CHARACTER(610).
01 movie-structure REDEFINES movie-var.
   02 title            PIC X(100).
   02 description      PIC X(500).
   02 length           PIC S9(9).
```

Assuming that we correctly read the definition (and the documentation) of the appropriate from-sql function in the `cobol_varchar_transforms` group, every time we retrieve an instance of the `movie` type into our `movie-var` variable, the fields of `movie-structure` will be populated with the attributes of that `movie` instance! (In Fortran, you'd use the `EQUIVALENCE` facility, and in C, you'd use the `union` capability; most programming languages allow this sort of duality of storage, although the specific syntax and limitations sometimes vary widely.)

If you're using Java and SQL together,[18] you will be pleased to know that JDBC 2.0 provides the ability for mapping tables to be defined that correlate Java classes with SQL's structured types courtesy of a USING clause. That capability, which transforms Java objects into SQL values and vice versa, is used by Java programs in lieu of transform groups, which are prohibited in SQL's Java support.

You can destroy transform groups (without affecting the associated function definitions or user-defined types) by using the DROP TRANSFORM statement seen in Syntax 2.17.

Syntax 2.17 *<drop transform statement> Syntax*

```
<drop transform statement> ::=
    DROP { TRANSFORM | TRANSFORMS } <transforms to be dropped>
    FOR <user-defined type> <drop behavior>

<transforms to be dropped> ::=
    ALL
  | <transform group element>

<transform group element> ::= <group name>
```

18 Jim Melton and Andrew Eisenberg, *Understanding SQL and Java Together: A Guide to SQLJ, JDBC, and Related Technologies* (San Francisco: Morgan Kaufmann Publishers, 2000).

Note that you can choose either to drop a specific transform group associated with a specified user-defined type, or to drop all transform groups associated with that type.

Some SQL implementations provide ways for applications to directly transfer UDT instances between the server and application programs. Providing such capabilities means finding ways to map the arbitrarily complex structures created by the attributes of a UDT (whose types might themselves be collection types or other structured types) onto the variable declaration facilities of ordinary programming languages. While it is certainly feasible to define such mappings, at least for the less complex cases, SQL:1999's designers felt that it was too difficult to do generally and thus decided that transforms provided an acceptable solution for all cases.

2.11.9 Comparison of UDTs

SQL:1999 naturally permits you to compare instances of structured types; certainly, you can compare `dvd` instances with other `dvd` instances, and you can even compare instances of multiple types in a type hierarchy under some circumstances. One reason that the comparison limitations are relatively minimal is that comparisons are done through user-defined functions, so you (as a type designer) can supply whatever semantics you need to your comparisons. Under certain conditions, SQL:1999 even provides a default comparison function that will be invoked for comparing instances of a given structured type. That default comparison function compares the type instances based on comparing each of their attributes, working from the first attribute to the last one ("left to right" is perhaps the best way to visualize it). It's important to realize, however, that the existence of a default comparison function doesn't necessarily make it possible to compare instances of every structured type; values of types that are declared to have an ordering form of NONE cannot be compared with values of any type.

Most comparison and casting functions can be either ordinary functions or methods; the exception to that rule is that "relative comparisons" (discussed shortly) can be done only using ordinary functions, not methods. Not to worry, though: the semantics of using a function and the semantics of using a method for the other forms of comparisons are identical, so the choice is up to you. (Actually, there's a single exception of which I'm aware: If you choose to use a method for "mapping comparisons," which are discussed below, it's possible to override the method, which can affect the semantics. But at least it's under your control!)

But you can define other comparison mechanisms for yourself. Among the variations supported are the ability to strictly limit comparisons to equality and inequality or to enable full comparisons, including equality and inequality as well as less-than and greater-than comparisons. You may have observed that Syntax 2.2 doesn't provide any syntax for defining how comparisons of a given type are to be performed. Instead, that specification is made through the use of the CREATE ORDERING statement, whose syntax is given in Syntax 2.18. Execution of this statement creates an association between the ordering form and category, the ordering function, and the structured type. After that, every attempt to compare instances of the specified type are automatically transformed into the appropriate function invocations and related program actions.

Syntax 2.18 *<user-defined ordering definition> Syntax*

```
<user-defined ordering definition> ::=
    CREATE ORDERING FOR <user-defined type> <ordering form>

<ordering form> ::=
    <equals ordering form>
  | <full ordering form>

<equals ordering form> ::= EQUALS ONLY BY <ordering category>

<full ordering form> ::= ORDER FULL BY <ordering category>

<ordering category> ::=
    <relative category>
  | <map category>
  | <state category>
  | <comparable category>

<relative category> ::= RELATIVE WITH <relative function specification>

<map category> ::= MAP WITH <map function specification>

<state category> ::= STATE [ <specific name> ]

<relative function specification> ::= <specific routine designator>

<map function specification> ::= <specific routine designator>

<comparable category> ::= RELATIVE WITH COMPARABLE INTERFACE
```

State Comparisons

You can instruct the system to do comparisons based on the values of the attributes, in which it is called a *state* comparison. A state comparison always implies that the SQL environment creates an equality comparison function that returns a Boolean value indicating whether or not the value of the first structured type instance is equal to the value of the second instance; this comparison is based on the values of the attributes alone (this is the default comparison mechanism that I mentioned a couple of paragraphs earlier). You can specify the state comparison approach only in the type definition for a maximal supertype (that is, a type that has no supertypes itself—a type whose definition does not have an UNDER clause), in which case this comparison mechanism is used for instances of the specified type and for all of its subtypes. What's more, you cannot specify a different sort of comparison for any subtypes; the decision to use state comparison for a maximal supertype applies to all subtypes of that supertype. This restriction makes state comparisons most useful for values of maximal supertypes and probably less valuable for comparing instances of subtypes. When instances of subtypes are compared, only the attributes that they inherit from their maximal supertypes participate in the comparison.

In Example 2.44, I've illustrated how to define a state comparison for the `movie` type; in this case, I've allowed only equality and inequality comparisons (*less than* and *greater than* are prohibited).

Example 2.44 *Specifying a State Function*

```
CREATE ORDERING FOR movie
   EQUALS ONLY BY STATE;
```

Mapping Comparisons

You can also choose to have the SQL engine compare two structured type instances by *mapping* them to some SQL built-in type and then comparing those two values. The conversion to the built-in types is performed by a *map* function, which returns a value of the selected built-in type. That function is implicitly invoked twice when constructing the comparison; you just write your normal comparison expression (`leftside > rightside`, for example), and SQL invokes the map functions for you. The comparison of the two built-in type values that result from invoking the map function is performed using ordinary SQL comparisons. You can specify mapping comparison for any type in a type hierarchy, but only if all other types in the hierarchy use mapping comparison. To provide greater flexibility in how the mapping from structured type instances to built-in types is performed, different types in a single type hierarchy can use different mapping functions. A mapping function is associated with a structured type, as shown in Example 2.45.

Example 2.45 *Specifying a Mapping Function*

```
CREATE ORDERING FOR movie
   ORDER FULL BY MAP WITH
      FUNCTION movie_mapping (movie);
```

Before associating the function with the type, I must create the mapping function as shown in Example 2.46:

Example 2.46 *Defining a Mapping Function*

```
CREATE FUNCTION movie_mapping (mv movie)
      RETURNS INTEGER
      STATIC DISPATCH
   RETURN length(mv.title)+mv.runs;
```

The function in Example 2.46 compares movies by adding their length in minutes to the length (in characters) of their titles. Whether this is a reasonable way to compare movies or not is an application decision! (Don't fret about my use of STATIC DISPATCH for now; you will learn about that clause in Chapter 4, "Routines and Routine Invocation").

Relative Comparisons

Finally, you can do the comparison by using the result returned by a *relative* function. A relative function returns an integer value in which –1 implies that the first structured type instance is less than the second, 0 implies that the two instances are equal, and +1 implies that the first instance is greater than the second. As with the state comparison, you can specify this only for a maximal supertype and the relative ordering will be used for all subtypes as well. (And, as with state comparisons, you cannot specify a different comparison capability for any subtypes. Consequently, as with state comparisons, relative comparisons are probably most appropriate for comparing values of maximal supertypes.)

With all three approaches, you write the function that determines the actual semantics used. If you're writing a state comparison function or a relative comparison function, you can apply any criteria you want to those comparisons. If you're writing a map function, then you can map the structured type instances to built-in types (such as INTEGER or CHARACTER) using whatever mechanisms you find appropriate. A relative function is associated with a structured type like this:

Example 2.47 *Specifying a RELATIVE Function*

```
CREATE ORDERING FOR movie
  ORDER FULL BY RELATIVE WITH
    FUNCTION movie_comp (movie, movie);
```

Naturally, you must first create the relative function like this:

Example 2.48 *Defining a RELATIVE Function*

```
CREATE FUNCTION movie_comp (mv1 movie, mv2 movie)
      RETURNS INTEGER
      STATIC DISPATCH

   IF (...)             /*Some application-relevant condition */
      THEN RETURN -1
      ELSEIF (...)      /*Some application-relevant condition */
      THEN RETURN 0
      ELSE RETURN 1
    END IF;
```

Example 2.48's function compares movies according to criteria that you choose and then returns –1 to indicate that the first movie is less than the second, 0 to indicate that they're equal, or +1 to indicate that the first is greater than the second.

The alternative `<comparable category>` is valid only for structured types defined using Java and signals dependence on the type's implementation of the `java.lang.Comparable` interface.

Once the structured types have had their comparison semantics defined, you actually compare instances using ordinary SQL comparison operators, such as = or >. These comparison semantics are also used by SQL's ORDER BY, GROUP BY, and DISTINCT. By comparison, one normally uses method invocations explicitly in Java for comparing class instances. Incidentally, you are syntactically prohibited from performing comparisons involving less-than and greater-than relationships (<, >, <=, and =) on values of structured types that are defined to have an ordering form of EQUALS ONLY.

Of course, if you decide you don't want the comparison semantics you've defined, you can destroy the user-defined comparison for a specific structured type using the DROP ORDERING statement shown in Syntax 2.19.

Syntax 2.19 *<drop user-defined ordering statement> Syntax*

```
<drop user-defined ordering statement> ::=
    DROP ORDERING FOR <user-defined type> <drop behavior>
```

2.11.10 The Type Predicate

SQL:1999 provides a predicate, called a *type predicate,* that can be used to test a structured type instance to determine its exact type. The type predicate is most useful when you have a site whose data type is some structured type that has one or more subtypes; the value stored in that site might be a value of the declared type or it might be a value of any one of the subtypes. Your application logic might depend on knowing the exact type of the value stored at that site, and that's where this predicate comes in.

The type predicate's syntax is shown in Syntax 2.20.

Syntax 2.20 *<type predicate> Syntax*

```
<type predicate> ::=
    <user-defined type value expression> IS [ NOT ] OF
      <left paren> <type list> <right paren>

<type list> ::=
    <user-defined type specification>
      [ { <comma> <user-defined type specification> }... ]

<user-defined type specification> ::=
    <inclusive user-defined type specification>
  | <exclusive user-defined type specification>

<inclusive user-defined type specification> ::= <user-defined type>

<exclusive user-defined type specification> ::= ONLY <user-defined type>
```

You can request the SQL system to tell you (by evaluating the predicate with a result of "true") whether the type of the expression you provide is (or is not) one of the types listed in the `<type list>` that you specify. If the `<type list>` does not contain any specification that uses the keyword ONLY, then a result of "true" means that the type of the expression was either one of the listed types or a subtype of one of the listed types. If one of the type specifications in the list uses the keyword ONLY, then a result of "true" means that the expression's type was one of the other types in the list or a subtype of one of those other types, or it was exactly the type specified using ONLY, but not one of its subtypes.

To determine whether a value stored in the `movie_info` column, whose type is `movie`, is some sort of DVD, I could express the predicate as shown in Example 2.49.

Example 2.49 *Use of Type Predicate*

```
...movie_info IS OF ( dvd )...
```

On the other hand, if I wanted to know if the value stored in the `movie_info` column was specifically an ordinary DVD, but not a Dolby Digital DVD or a DTS DVD, then I should express the predicate as shown in Example 2.50.

Example 2.50 *Use of Type Predicate with ONLY*

```
...movie_info IS OF ( ONLY dvd )...
```

2.12 Security for User-Defined Types

In some object-oriented programming languages, such as Java and C++, the environment allows you to protect some or all of your types' attributes from certain types of access; you may also be able to protect the methods associated with your types from certain sorts of uses. For example, in Java and C++, you provide *access control* for your attributes and methods by declaring them to be `private` (accessed only by methods of the type), `protected` (accessed by methods of the type and of subtypes of the type), or `public` (accessed by any method or function).

Although the designers of SQL:1999 experimented with those access control capabilities (private, protected, and public), they eventually concluded that a different sort of protection was required in the context of a language that has persistent data and persistent metadata—and that SQL already provided the foundation for the required protection: privileges.

Type definers in SQL, like the definers of any schema object in SQL, are granted all privileges on the types they define, as well as all privileges on all components of the type—specifically, all attributes, including the system-provided observer and mutator methods. Because all methods associated with a structured type must be defined in the same schema as the type itself, the owner of the type is also the owner of the methods and thus has all appropriate privileges on every method of the type. (Since ordinary functions are not closely associated with a single user-defined type, no such limitation is placed on them.) The privileges granted to the type definer include the USAGE privilege that allows the type to be used to define columns, routines, and other schema objects. They also include the UNDER privilege that permits subtypes of the type to be defined. These privileges are granted to the type definer with GRANT OPTION (see Volume 1 of this book for more information about privileges and the GRANT OPTION), so the type definer can then grant specific privileges to other users as required. Application of privileges to methods effectively provides protection at the attribute level, which accomplishes essentially the same result as the access control defined in Java and C++.

Whether or not future versions of the SQL standard augment the privilege mechanism for structured type security with access control analogous to Java's is yet to be determined. Frankly, I don't expect that enhancement to occur because it is unlikely to be required.

2.13 More Than One Way to Model Your Application

In most programming languages, especially those as rich and powerful as SQL:1999, there are usually several ways to accomplish almost any task.

SQL:1999 provides at least three different ways to approach the fundamental issue of how to model the real-world entities needed by your applications. The first approach is the traditional SQL mechanism of tables and columns; the second is the use of user-defined structured types whose instances are stored in columns of ordinary SQL tables; and the third is the use of user-defined structured types whose instances are rows in typed tables.

Deciding which approach to use in specific circumstances may not be trivial, but it is not necessarily difficult, either. In the following three sections, I briefly describe each approach and summarize the tradeoffs that will assist you in deciding which to use.

2.13.1 Traditional SQL Tables and Columns

SQL implementations have been on the market since roughly 1985, and there are many thousands of SQL programmers who are familiar and comfortable with the use of SQL's table-and-column model. In Volume 1 of this book, the music and video application shared with this volume was implemented using only SQL's conventional tables.

Countless applications, many of extreme complexity, have been written with that limitation. Clearly, ordinary SQL tables offer substantial modeling power. One simply defines one table per "object class" to be modeled and provides in that table one column for each attribute of the corresponding real-world entity that the application requires.

SQL's referential integrity facilities, including its referential actions, coupled with the triggers defined in SQL:1999, offer substantial capabilities for maintaining database integrity and enforcing complex business rules.

But there are increasing demands for applications to model data having semantics inherently more complex than SQL's traditional character, numeric, and datetime data types. User organizations are struggling with management of multimedia data, spatial data, data mining, and a host of other complex issues. To model the new data types required by those issues using SQL's traditional tables often requires application developers to express the model in syntactic terms that are cumbersome, awkward, and sometimes downright unnatural for the data needed by the applications. This awkwardness becomes especially apparent when the applications need to take advantage of the inherent semantics of that complex data.

2.13.2 Type Hierarchies and Columns

SQL:1999's structured user-defined types allow type definers and application developers to create new first-class data types—types that can be used as the type of any column in any SQL table, as the type of any SQL variable in an SQL routine, and as the type of any parameter of an SQL routine.

Those structured types can be, and normally are, defined along with a collection of routines that provide built-in semantics for the data associated with the types. For example, spatial data types can be provided with operators appropriate for spatial data. Such operators allow applications to determine whether a proposed highway crosses a wetland or whether two integrated circuits on a circuit board are too close to one another for adequate thermal dissipation; to represent municipal infrastructures and calculate taxation district boundaries; and to record physical information about the scene of a traffic accident.

Many applications require the ability to manage "traditional" data (such as character data, numeric data, datetimes, and even bit strings) concurrently with new, more complex and less traditional data like spatial and multimedia data. This requirement seems to occur rather often when existing application environments are enhanced with new data types and may involve modification of existing tables to add new columns whose type is some structured type.

If you choose to use this approach, then you will undoubtedly model *some,* but not *all,* of your real-world objects in the traditional SQL manner: as tables whose columns contain the values of attributes of those objects. Other objects that you must capture will be modeled as instances of structured types, the values of which are stored in columns of other tables. This is especially appropriate when the objects that you model as structured types are highly dependent on the objects modeled as tables, such as street addresses and the like.

Applications that use this approach—defining ordinary SQL tables having some columns of SQL's built-in types and other columns whose types are user-defined structured types—benefit from continuing to use long-standing SQL operations like joins, WHERE clauses, and so on to manipulate the data in their tables, while acquiring the ability to directly manage the complex data stored in structured type columns by invocation of the methods defined on those types.

2.13.3 Table Hierarchies

As you will learn in Chapter 3, "Typed Tables," it is possible in SQL:1999 to define a structured type and then to define one or more tables, called *typed tables,* each of whose rows is an instance of that structured type. Each row of a typed table has a unique identity that behaves in a manner that I find indistinguishable from the behaviors of the object identifiers found in object-oriented programming languages. Furthermore, each attribute of the structured type with which a typed table is associated results in a corresponding column in that typed table. Thus, a typed table is, in many ways, no different than an ordinary SQL table, but it has the important characteristic that its rows can be manipulated through method invocations in addition to ordinary SQL data manipulation statements.

SQL:1999 provides a *reference type* that can be the type of columns, variables, and parameters; the values of a reference type are the unique identifiers of rows in a typed table. That is, they provide the same behaviors that object identifier references provide in a more traditional object-oriented system.

When your applications use typed tables and reference types, they may then take advantage of many of the available object-oriented design methodologies and tools because the instances of the structured types associated with those typed tables are, for all practical purposes, truly objects. The similarities between SQL's object model and Java's may make it somewhat easier to use existing modeling tools and to find programmers sufficiently familiar with the approach so that your applications can be developed with relative ease.

2.14 Implementation Issues

While only a few readers of this book are likely to be database system implementors, it occurs to me that many of you might be interested in a paragraph or two about some of the challenges that vendors face in building the SQL:1999 structured type features.

Undoubtedly, the most complex part of the specification of SQL's structured types is the routine invocation algorithm; it goes on for several pages of the standard and is extremely dense. However, it is really rather simple and elegant when one pushes through the turgid prose and intricate rules. As a result, it should prove relatively easy to implement and quite stable once done. You will learn more about this algorithm in Chapter 4, "Routines and Routine Invocation."

By contrast, the concept of subtypes being "specializations" of their supertypes, simply containing a bit more data, seems awfully straightforward. But this may end up being the most difficult aspect of implementing this feature. The problem is caused in part by the very nature of a database management system and in part by the meaning of *subtype.*

As you are quite aware, a database system is used for *persistent* storage of data. The almost three decades of implementation experience that SQL vendors have accrued in developing their products has largely dealt with tables whose rows were (fairly predictably) all the same length, or at least they had some well-known maximum length. Of course, there were some minor exceptions, such as very long character string columns, that received special treatment, often by means of storing such data in a separate location and then "pointing" to it from the original row value. But, in general, rows in a table were usually approximately the same size.

However, if one or more columns of some table are of a structured type, and if that type participates in a type hierarchy, then different rows of the table may have values in those columns whose most specific type (that is, their actual runtime types, as opposed to the columns' declared types) have widely varying sizes! This poses some very interesting storage management challenges for SQL implementors. The problems escalate significantly when you consider the possibility of UPDATEing a row and replacing the value of some structured type column with a new value of a subtype that has significantly more data associated with it; the implementation can no longer be assured of updating a row "in place" but must be prepared to move the row to a new location that has adequate room.

While that is not necessarily very difficult, it becomes more complex if the row in question is actually a row of a typed table with an associated reference value. Reference values associated with specific rows are never allowed to change, *even if the location of the row must change*! If you're familiar with SQL implementations that use something like a "database key," which is often generated from a hardware-associated value like a disk address, you shouldn't expect reference values to be the same thing; rows are often relocated for various implementation reasons, which might (or might not) change the database key value, but the reference value will not change.

With that, we'll just leave the rest to your imagination (and perhaps you'll appreciate the efforts that database systems implementors have to put into building the products we take for granted).

2.15 The SQL Object Model

If you've been around the computer software business long enough, you've heard lots of buzzwords and phrases. One of the hottest such phrases in recent years seems to be *data model*. Regrettably, because of the confusion that it often causes, that phrase applies to a rather wide variety of concepts, ranging from a description of the data elements required by a specific application to the techniques and methodologies used to design very large systems. In the context of database systems, the phrase is often intended to identify the underlying concepts supported by those systems.

2.15.1 Why Does SQL Have an Object Model?

In 1989, I attended a seminar in which the inventor of the relational model, Dr. E. F. Codd, stated that object-oriented *approaches* (his word) are not needed in the database environment; he suggested that they're okay for programming languages, which don't "have the power to express complex ideas," but that "the relational model is more than adequate for data storage." Codd went on to acknowledge that the relational model is not necessarily appropriate for "*all* masses of data: for example, image data and voice- or fingerprinting, where the sequence of bits is important." Codd's rationale for this rejection of a need for object orientation in the database environment was straightforward: The relational model is a true model because it is based on a solid mathematical foundation and its principles are provable mathematically. By contrast, there are many different "approaches" that are called object models; none of them have mathematical foundations; their principles are entirely ad hoc and cannot be proven mathematically. In other words, Codd rejected the entire concept of "object model."

While I admit that I find the plethora of "object models" confusing and in many ways regrettable, I strongly disagree with Codd's rejection of the need for object orientation in the database environment. I have encountered many application problems that are difficult or impossible to solve *effectively* with the strict use of relational model principles, but that are addressed quite nicely using certain principles of object orientation. As object orientation has proved its worth in "programming languages," I find it ever more attractive to give access to those capabilities in the database environment, thus reducing the impedance mismatch between programming language concepts and database concepts. After all, any reduction of that impedance mismatch offers the promise of reducing semantic errors in applications and of reducing programming efforts—both very worthy goals.

Furthermore, the notion of encapsulation of behaviors and of the physical implementation of data offers database users increased hope that code to express the semantics of complex data will be written only once (more realistically, will be written much less often) and that the bugs and inconsistencies caused by multiple implementations of essentially "the same" code will be significantly reduced.

The problem, of course, is recognizing that different programming languages have different "object models" (indeed, *object oriented* is another one of those overused and inconsistent industry buzzwords) and deciding how to resolve those differences at points where they interface. Since SQL was designed to be used with several programming languages, it's unlikely in the extreme that any object model designed in SQL would map perfectly to object models of multiple programming languages. Indeed, the designers of SQL's object model encountered numerous difficulties in their efforts to minimize the impedance mismatch between SQL and Java.

As I wrap up this chapter, I'd like to outline what I consider the most important aspects of the SQL object model. If you happen to be a Java programmer, you probably know that language's object model fairly well, and that knowledge may help you become comfortable with SQL's object model a little more easily. But even if you're not a Java programmer, I think you'll find that the SQL object model is relatively straightforward and that it generally makes a lot of sense.

The rest of this section is a summary of the SQL object model. Many, even most, of the concepts and terms given here repeat material from earlier in the chapter; still, a concise summary may be useful.

2.15.2 SQL Object Model Summary

SQL's object model is at once simpler than and more complex than Java's. (I have chosen to compare and contrast SQL's object model with Java's for two reasons:

Java is arguably one of the most popular object-oriented programming languages today, and SQL's object facilities were quite consciously designed to be similar to Java's in many respects.) The reasons for the greater complexity deal entirely with the difficulties caused by the fact that SQL manages *persistent data* that is described by equally persistent *metadata*. The ability for applications to modify SQL's metadata—the data that describes the data under SQL's control—means that great care must be taken that such modifications neither impede correct and accurate access to the data itself, nor create enormous performance problems by requiring immediate and time-consuming restructuring of the data. The relative simplicity of SQL's object model, when compared to Java's, results principally from the observation that not all of Java's facilities are necessarily required in, nor even applicable to, a database environment.

SQL (perhaps obviously) does not assert that "everything is an object." In fact, the great majority, at least today, of data managed by SQL is nonobject data. Even after the addition of object-oriented capabilities to SQL, the language retains and enhances all of its "relational" capabilities, particularly the central design principle that all data is stored in tables—even object data! In fact, as will shortly become evident, it's somewhat unclear in the SQL standard exactly what an object *is*; I'll try to make that notion clear in this section, though.

As you've seen in this chapter, SQL provides two sorts of data in support of object orientation. The first is something called *user-defined types*. In fact, user-defined types come in two flavors, only one of which is relevant to this discussion. One flavor is the *distinct type,* which merely allows applications to give a new name to SQL's built-in primitive types while prohibiting indiscriminate mixing of the distinct type and its base type in expressions. The other is called the *structured user-defined type,* and it is that variant that relates most closely to object orientation. SQL's structured type is its closest analog to Java's classes. The other sort of data is SQL's *reference type,* the discussion of which I'll defer for a few paragraphs.

SQL's structured types are fully encapsulated in the sense that *all* access to them is through a functional (or method) interface. That is, there is no access permitted to the components (called *attributes* in SQL) of a value of a structured type except through system-provided observer methods (to retrieve the values of the attributes) and mutator methods (to change their values). While this would appear to imply that SQL's structured types are "more encapsulated" than Java's classes, the truth is a little more complicated. As the author of an SQL structured type, you are allowed to overload any user-defined functions that exist for the type, but you are not allowed to overload the two system-provided observer and mutator methods for any of the type's attributes.

SQL's structured types are permitted to contain attributes whose data types are primitive types (in SQL, called *predefined data types* or *built-in data types*), distinct types, constructed types, other structured types, and references to tables whose rows are actually values of structured types (called *typed tables*). A *constructed type* is a type that must be defined in terms of other types; the two primary examples are arrays and row types. A row type is very much like a `struct` in the C language because it allows nesting of values within other values. SQL's *reference type* (providing the ability to reference rows in tables of some structured type) is also a constructed type, though obviously less structured than arrays or row types.

SQL's structured types can participate in a type hierarchy. SQL supports only single inheritance, meaning that no type can have more than a single direct supertype. A subtype's attributes are therefore inherited only from a single direct supertype; the same is true of its methods. SQL does not currently support any notion of inheritance of interface from any source other than its supertype; in this respect, it is more limited than Java. (A future revision of the SQL standard may add this capability.) I must note, however, that SQL:1999 does not have an abstract, noninstantiable maximal supertype like Java does (in Java, all classes are defined to be subclasses of an abstract class named `object`).

SQL:1999 does not allow you to specify that a structured type is FINAL, meaning that no subtypes of the type can be defined (but the capability to do so is planned for the next generation of the SQL standard). It does permit structured types to be declared NOT INSTANTIABLE, which means that applications cannot create values of the type. These two characteristics (FINAL and NOT INSTANTIABLE) correspond with Java's `final` and `abstract` class characteristics.

SQL distinguishes between procedures, functions, and methods. Procedures are routines that are invoked by means of an SQL CALL statement and return values, if at all, through output parameters; they do not "return a value" as such (they are, however, allowed to return virtual tables in the form of dynamic result sets). By contrast, functions are invoked as a function invocation in a value expression, have only input parameters, and return a single value (although not necessarily an atomic value, like an integer) as the value of the function invocation.

Methods are special cases of functions that have several restrictions when compared to their more general-purpose origins:

1. A method is associated with a specific structured type by including in the type's definition the signature of the method. (Note: The SQL standard uses the term *specification* in place of *signature* for obscure reasons; I prefer to use *signature* in this book because it is the more widely recognized term for the intended concept, although the word is used in some other lan-

guages to mean only the name of a routine and the number and types of its parameters, possibly including the routine's return type.)

2. A method signature can be an "original method signature," meaning that the method declared in "this type" does not override a method defined in some supertype; alternatively, it can be an "overriding method signature," meaning that it does override some method inherited from a supertype. Original method signatures contain somewhat more information than overriding method signatures, because overriding methods are required to share certain characteristics with the methods they override. Those shared characteristics are not respecified in overriding method signatures.
3. While ordinary functions are allowed to be associated with any number of structured types, the association is "loose" because all arguments of that function's invocations are used equally to determine which of possibly several functions of the same name will be chosen for invocation; for all arguments whose declared type is a structured type, only that declared type is used to choose the specific function to be invoked. By contrast, methods are closely associated with a specific structured type. Instance methods have a distinguished parameter, always an implicit parameter, whose type is always the associated structured type, for which the most specific type of the invocation's corresponding argument is used; all other arguments of a method invocation are resolved using only their declared types.
4. Finally, the functions associated with various structured types may be defined anywhere in an SQL database—in any schema, to use the proper term. Methods, on the other hand, must be defined in the schema in which their associated structured type is defined.

In SQL, the functions and methods associated with a structured type (except for structured types defined using Java) are not written as part of the type definition, but are instead created separately (don't forget, though, that methods *are* declared as part of a type's definition). Like the structured type definitions, along with all persistent values of the types, the functions and methods are stored in the database itself; the type definitions, functions, and methods are stored in the database's metadata, and the values of the types are naturally stored in the database's actual data (called *SQL data* in the SQL standard).

It has been suggested that, in SQL, all arguments are passed by value. The SQL standard does not itself say anything explicit about the argument passing mechanism, but there is evidence to support this assertion: Arguments to invocations of SQL routines are permitted to be literals; if the code in an SQL routine were allowed to change the value of the argument, then that would have the effect of "changing" the value of the literal: for example, 3 could become 5, which is nonsense. However, SQL procedures can have output parameters, which cannot realistically be handled with arguments passed by value, in the ordinary sense of that phrase. Of course, SQL procedures also have input parameters—and SQL functions and methods have *only* input parameters—so pass-by-value works fine with them. Now, it would be confusing to have some parameters passed by reference and others by value, so it's reasonable to conclude that SQL routines use something else for their argument-passing semantics. The mechanism that I conclude is used (from a very careful reading of SQL:1999) is that SQL's procedures—which are the only sort of SQL-invoked routine that can have output parameters—use "pass-by-value, copy-in and copy-out" semantics. This implies that the values of input (and input–output) arguments are copied into the SQL routine from its invocation and the value of output (and input–output) arguments are set by copying the returned values out from the SQL routine. (Obviously, only "settable" arguments, such as host parameters or SQL variables, will be "set by copying," thus preserving literals.) SQL-invoked functions and methods, which do not have output parameters, can operate just fine with pure pass-by-value semantics.

SQL permits you to write procedures, functions, and methods associated with a structured type in several different languages, including SQL itself, as well as one of several more conventional programming languages (such as Java and C or even COBOL and Fortran).

While Java programs reference objects (instances of classes) by means of handles, which are really pointers to the storage occupied by those instances, SQL programs can only reference rows in tables. SQL originally allowed you to define a table and explicitly specify the columns of that table, giving their name and data type. When structured types were added to SQL's repertoire, the ability to define a table based on a structured type was also added. In order to reference specific rows in such a table, called a *typed table,* you use SQL's reference type. A given column (or variable or parameter) whose data type is a reference type is restricted to reference only rows of typed tables whose type is a specified structured type. There may be many such tables, and a given declaration of a reference type must specify a specific table to which its values refer. In this respect, you see that references are not free to reference just any value of any structured type, nor even any arbitrary value of a given structured type, but only those values of a specific structured type that are represented as rows in a specified table or tables. That excludes not only values of that structured type that are rows in other tables of that type, but also values of that type that are stored in columns of tables or in SQL variables or parameters. While this might appear limiting, in practice it seems to be sufficient for a great many applications.

2.16 Chapter Summary

In this, admittedly long, chapter, I have introduced you to SQL's structured user-defined types and shown you how to define such types and how to use them. I discussed the use of these types primarily as values (you'll see their use as objects in the very next chapter), but also called attention to the characteristics that such types have in common with object-oriented technologies.

Among other material, I showed you how instances of structured types can be compared with one another and how you can use SQL:1999's facilities to manipulate instances of those types from your application code, without transferring the structured type values back and forth between the application and the SQL engine. But, if you want to transfer such values across the client-server interface, this chapter revealed ways to accomplish that task as well.

Chapter 3

Typed Tables

3.1 Introduction

In Chapter 2, "User-Defined Types," you learned about SQL:1999's structured types—types that you and your applications (or some designated type definer) can define that include internal structure as well as behaviors appropriate to the types' requirements.

In this chapter, I'll show you how you can create a new type of SQL table, called a *typed table,* that is based on a structured type. You'll also learn how to create hierarchies of typed tables that are related to hierarchies of the types associated with those tables. I'll also tell you about creating instances of the structured types that are rows in typed tables and how referencing those rows behaves very much like referencing to objects in other object-oriented systems.

3.2 Typed Tables and Structured Types

During the presentation of structured user-defined types in Chapter 2, "User-Defined Types," I said a number of times that instances of such types are values that must be stored at some site; they have no notion of "existence" on their own (except in the sense that values, such as the number eight, always "exist" in an abstract sense). Throughout the examples in that chapter, the instances of structured types that I created were stored either in cells of a table or in SQL variables, or they were passed as argument values from an SQL statement into an SQL-invoked routine or returned from an SQL-invoked routine.

When you create a typed table, though, you are creating a table in which each row stored in the table *is* an instance, or a value, of the associated structured user-defined type.[1] A typed table has one column for each attribute of its associated structured type. The name and data type of that column is the same as the name and data type of the attribute. If the data type of an attribute is a complex attribute—an ARRAY, perhaps, or another structured type, then the column of the typed table has that same complex type.

Given our old friend, the `movie` type, reprised in Example 3.1, Figure 3.1 suggests how we might visualize the relationship between that structured type and a typed table associated with it.

Example 3.1 *The movie Type*

```
CREATE TYPE movie (
  title            CHARACTER VARYING (100),
  description      CHARACTER VARYING (500),
  runs             INTEGER )
  NOT FINAL
```

Notice that I said "we *might* visualize" the relationship in this way. There is one important difference between the relationship illustrated in Figure 3.1 and reality: every typed table has, in addition to the columns that correspond to the associated type's attributes, one additional column. That additional column is called a *self-referencing column,* and it contains in each row the value that uniquely identifies the row in which it is stored. I cover self-referencing columns in more detail in section 3.3, but you can look ahead to Figure 3.2 to see the proper way to visualize the relationship between a structured type and a typed table.

A typed table is, in many ways, an ordinary SQL table. That is, you can insert rows into the table, delete rows from the table, update rows in the table, retrieve rows from the table, and so forth. You can define referential constraints and triggers on the table, and the referential constraints can be given referential actions. In fact, the *only* way in which the data can be stored in typed tables is through ordinary INSERT, UPDATE, and DELETE statements. The use of the NEW expression and the consequent invocation of a constructor method for a structured type (see Chapter 2, "User-Defined Types," for more information) does not cause an instance of that type to be inserted as a row in a typed table. Why not? For two reasons: because there may be many typed tables associated with a given struc-

1 Structured types defined using Java SERIALIZABLE types cannot be used to define typed tables.

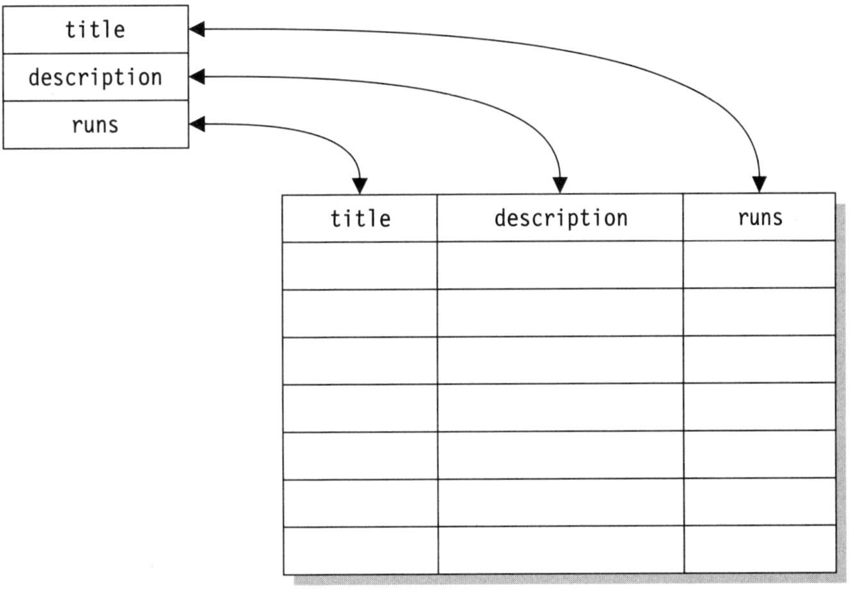

Figure 3.1 A Typed Table for the movie Type

tured type, and because you are permitted to create values of that type that are not managed as rows of a typed table. As a result, the simple act of constructing a value of a structured type does not signify its insertion into a typed table. You must explicitly execute an INSERT statement to make that insertion take place. Inserting structured type instances into typed tables, deleting instances from typed tables, and modifying instances within typed tables are all covered in section 3.8.

There may be many typed tables associated with a specific structured type; in addition, there is nothing to prevent you from creating ordinary values of the same structured type and manipulating them as described in Chapter 2, "User-Defined Types."

3.3 Self-Referencing Columns

The truly important characteristic of a typed table is that self-referencing column I mentioned in the previous section. Every row in a typed table contains a value of a structured type instance, one column per attribute of that instance. There is nothing to prevent you from creating two instances of a structured type in which

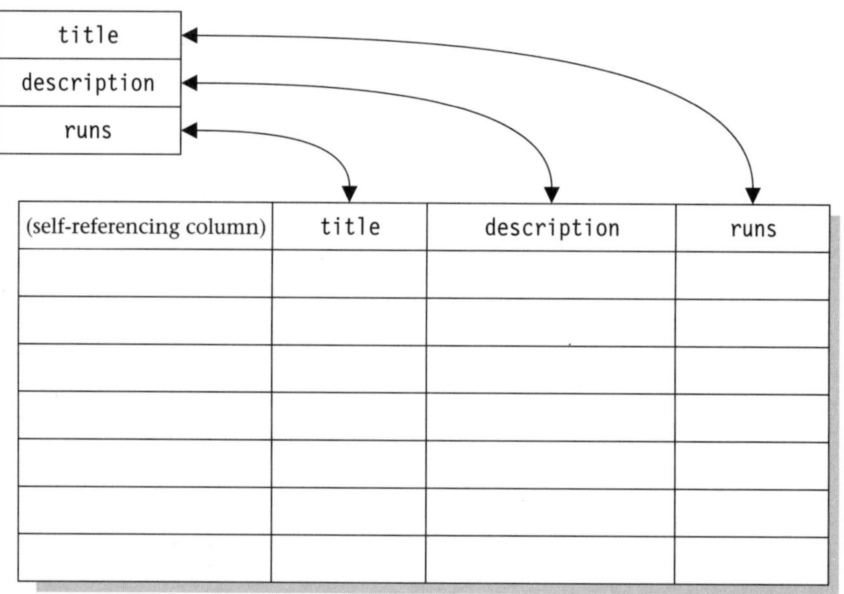

Figure 3.2 A More Complete Typed Table for the Movie Type

the value of every attribute in one instance is equal to the value of the corresponding attribute in the second instance. However, the value stored in the self-referencing column of the row corresponding to each instance is globally unique, allowing the two instances to be distinguished from one another. The phrase *globally unique* is intended to mean that no two rows that ever exist in a given typed table have the same value stored in the self-referencing column. (Rows in different typed tables may have equal values in their self-referencing columns, so it is fair to regard the self-referencing values as being "qualified" by the name of the typed table.) That rule should be applied to every row that occurs in the table from the time that the table is created until it is dropped. (As we'll see shortly, there are various mechanisms by which self-referencing column values are produced. Only those self-referencing column values that are generated by the system have the uniqueness characteristic over the lifetime of the table, while values generated by the application or that are derived from values stored in other columns of the table might not obey that stricture.) Figure 3.2 illustrates a self-referencing column in a typed table.

Your applications can use the values stored in the self-referencing columns as a sort of pointer to the rows containing those values in the typed tables; in fact, another phrase used to describe "typed table" is *referenceable table*. Those values can be stored wherever you like—even scribbled down onto the back of an envelope—and your applications are assured that the value never identifies any row other than the row with which it was first associated. (Of course, if that row is ever deleted, then the value scribbled on the back of your envelope might identify nothing at all, but at least it never identifies a different row!)

3.4 Table Hierarchies

In Chapter 2, "User-Defined Types," I discussed SQL's structured user-defined types, including the fact that they can participate in a single-inheritance type hierarchy. In section 3.2, you saw that SQL:1999 provides a new type of table, a typed table, that is closely associated with a user-defined type. It would undoubtedly violate the principle of least astonishment if SQL:1999 did not allow applications to combine those two features.

3.4.1 Relationship to Type Hierarchies

In fact, SQL:1999 does allow typed tables to participate in hierarchies analogous to those of their associated structured types. That is, you can define one table to be a subtable of another, called its *supertable*. You can only declare table hierarchies of typed tables, though, and all of the tables in a given table hierarchy have to have corresponding types that are in the same type hierarchy, and the tables in the table hierarchy must be in the same *relative positions* as the types in that type hierarchy. In fact, the relationships between the tables in a table hierarchy and the types in the corresponding type hierarchy must be one-to-one. That is, the associated structured type of the direct supertable of some typed table *must* be the direct supertype of the structured type associated with that subtable.

But—and this is just a little tricky—the complete table hierarchy does not have to have a one-to-one relationship with the complete type hierarchy. Recall our type hierarchy example from Chapter 2, "User-Defined Types" (see Figure 2.2, "Sample Type Hierarchy"). We can certainly define a table hierarchy like that shown in Figure 3.3, which has one typed table for each type in the type hierarchy. In fact, Figure 3.3 is identical to Figure 2.2, "Sample Type Hierarchy."

But you are not required to define your table hierarchy to support every type in a type hierarchy; you are permitted to "leave out" tables that would otherwise be used to store instances of types, as long as the range of types for which you define tables is contiguous. Consider the two table hierarchies illustrated in Figure 3.4 and Figure 3.5. In the first of those two figures, the table hierarchy stores

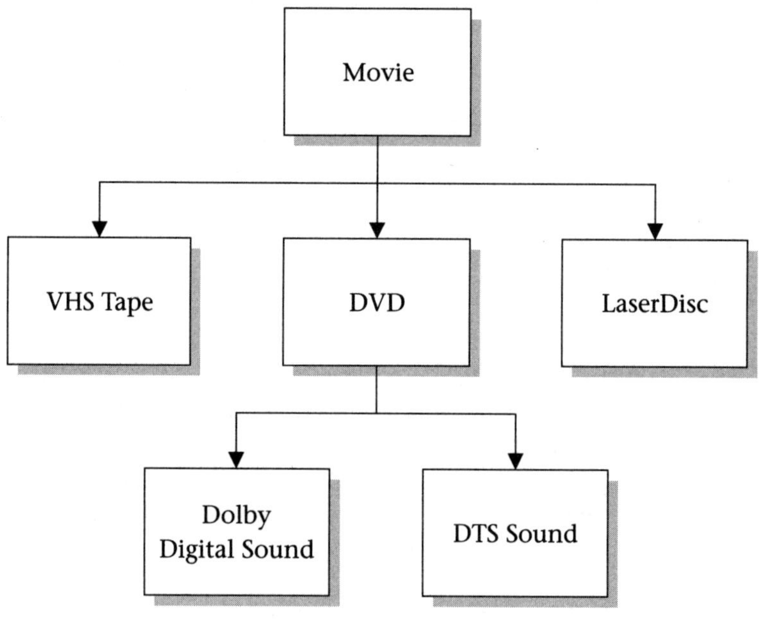

Figure 3.3 Movie Table Hierarchy

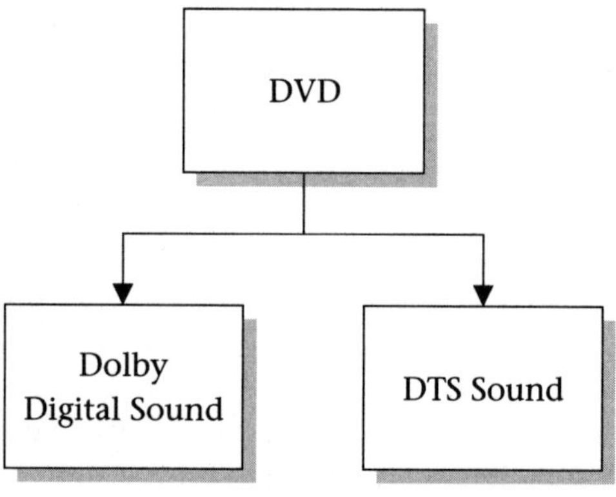

Figure 3.4 Movie Table Hierarchy for DVDs Only

only instances of our DVD type and its subtypes but does not store information about VHS tapes or LaserDiscs nor about movies that are not associated with a medium. In the second, the type hierarchy is able to store information about movies not associated with a medium, VHS tapes, LaserDiscs, and DVDs, but does not differentiate between DVDs without special sound, DVDs with Dolby Digital sound, and DVDs with DTS sound.

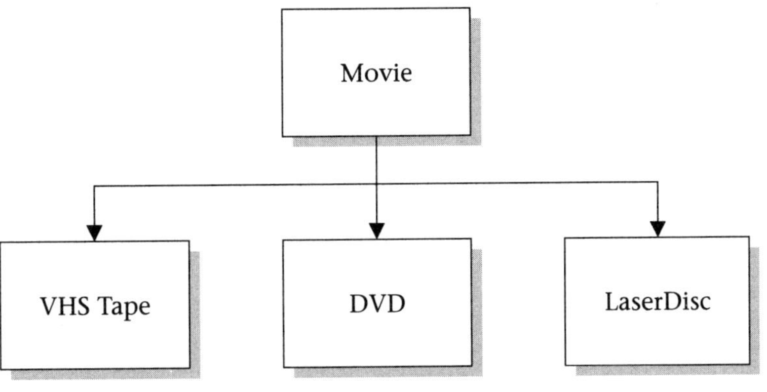

Figure 3.5 Table Hierarchy without Differentiation by Sound

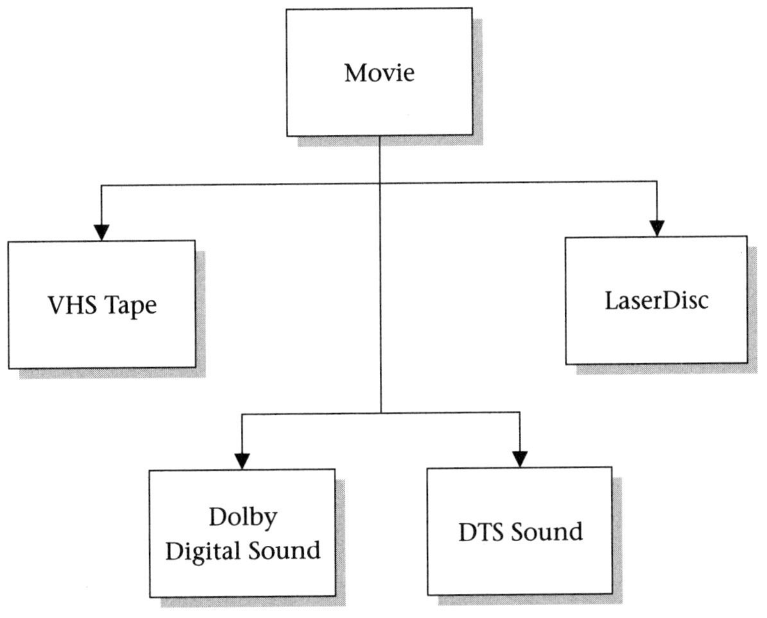

Figure 3.6 Invalid Table Hierarchy

By contrast, the type hierarchy suggested in Figure 3.6 is *not* valid, since it omits a table corresponding to a type "in the middle" of the corresponding type hierarchy.

In Figure 3.3 (which I'll use for the remainder of the discussion in this section), the DVD table is the *direct supertable* of the Dolby Digital Sound table; it is also a *direct subtable* of the Movie table. As you learned in Chapter 2, "User-

Defined Types," every type hierarchy must have exactly one maximal supertype. Similarly, every table hierarchy must have exactly one maximal supertable. In Figure 3.3, the maximal supertable is the Movie table. A table that does not have any subtables is called a *leaf table.*

In SQL:1999, a table is a subtable of itself and, consequently, a supertable of itself; the phrase applied to a subtable other than the table itself is *proper subtable* and the corresponding phrase for supertables is *proper supertable.* (While the distinction sounds a bit pedantic to some, it allows for cleaner definitions in the standard, as well as better alignment with the mathematical notion of sets and subsets.) The collection of subtables of a particular table in a table hierarchy is called the *subtable family* of that particular table. (In fact, it's common usage to refer to the entire collection of tables in a table hierarchy as the subtable family of any table in the hierarchy, but that's not the definition in the SQL standard.)

Because rows (ignoring the self-referencing column) in typed tables are instances of the associated structured type, those rows have a most specific type. As I said in section 2.9.5, "Most Specific Type," it is not possible to change the most specific type of a structured type instance once it has been created. That is especially important when the instance is a row in a typed table. If you have created a Dolby Digital Sound DVD and then discover that it was really recorded with DTS sound, you cannot somehow "migrate" the instance to become a DTS Sound instance, nor could you "promote" it to become an ordinary DVD instance. You *must* create a new instance of the proper most specific type (DTS Sound, say), copying (if desired) attributes from the existing (Dolby Digital Sound) instance, and then delete the row containing the existing (Dolby Digital Sound) instance. In doing those operations, the self-referencing column of the new DTS Sound instance receives a new value. As a result, all existing references to the Dolby Digital Sound instance become invalid! That is, they refer to nothing at all. Therefore, use caution when creating structured type instances to ensure that you choose the appropriate most specific type.

3.4.2 Table Hierarchy Model

There are several *mental models* (I've uncovered at least four or five, not all of which are obviously appropriate) that one could develop for the relationships between the tables in a table hierarchy and the rows in those tables. I recognize that the model I describe in this section might not be universally agreed to be the SQL:1999's model, but I'm confident that this model accurately describes the behavior of SQL:1999. Unfortunately, adherents to these various different models sometimes exhibit an almost religious fervor toward their preferred way of describing the languages' behavior, so I won't be too surprised if I'm criticized for selecting this model; indeed, I would expect criticism and disagreement with any model that I selected!

Using the table hierarchy shown in Figure 3.3, consider the actions taken when you create a new instance of the `dolby_dvd` type—that is, when you insert a new row into the `dolby_dvd` table: a row is inserted into the table. Similarly, when you insert a row into the `movie` table, a row is inserted into that table. Simple and obvious—and incomplete. It's incomplete because we also have to describe the effect that the insertions have on future retrievals of data from tables in the table hierarchy.

Suppose we inserted a row into the `dolby_dvd` table for director David Lynch's tour de confusion, *Eraserhead*. When we retrieve rows from that table, we expect to see *Eraserhead* among the movies retrieved (subject to restrictions such as those in a WHERE clause). What might surprise you is that retrieving rows from the `movie` table will also result in *Eraserhead* being retrieved!

Well, perhaps you shouldn't be surprised, because *Eraserhead* is an instance of the `dolby_dvd` type and, because `dolby_dvd` is a subtype of the `movie` type, it is simultaneously an instance of the `movie` type. So, you might ask, does the row for *Eraserhead* appear simultaneously in both tables? And that's where the religious fervor over the model comes into play: I assert that the retrieval operation effectively does a *union* of the table from which you're retrieving and all of its subtables (see section 3.7.2 for the exception to this rule). That way, the insert, update, and delete operations don't have to run around updating multiple tables in your database every time you perform one of those operations on some subtable.

Now, adherents to a different model description might argue that the effect is the same as if the insert, update, and delete operations did manipulate rows in all supertables of the subtable on which the operation is specified, and retrieval operations could retrieve only from the single table specified. I wouldn't argue (well, not *too* much!) with that view, since it also describes the behavior of SQL:1999. But that model is, in my viewpoint, needlessly complex and doesn't reflect the actual implementation of products of which I'm aware. (To be fair, adherents of this more complex model can point to text in SQL:1999 for justification, which does describe this sort of multitable behavior for insert, update, and delete, in spite of the fact that implementations using a simpler, more direct model get the same behavior in a different manner.)

I've illustrated three mental models that have been said to be reasonable implementation models for SQL:1999's table hierarchies (see section 2.14, "Implementation Issues," for additional discussion related to this issue). Figure 3.7 illustrates the model in which each row of a supertable has at most one corresponding row (but possibly none) in each subtable; each row of a subtable has exactly one corresponding row in each supertable. Figure 3.8 illustrates a model in which all rows contained in the tables of a table hierarchy are actually con-

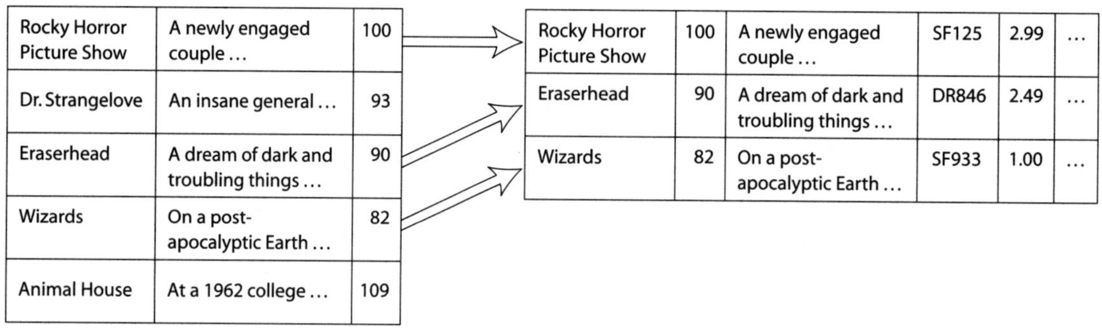

Rocky Horror Picture Show	A newly engaged couple ...	100
Dr. Strangelove	An insane general ...	93
Eraserhead	A dream of dark and troubling things ...	90
Wizards	On a post-apocalyptic Earth ...	82
Animal House	At a 1962 college ...	109

Rocky Horror Picture Show	100	A newly engaged couple ...	SF125	2.99	...
Eraserhead	90	A dream of dark and troubling things ...	DR846	2.49	...
Wizards	82	On a post-apocalyptic Earth ...	SF933	1.00	...

Figure 3.7 Duplicate-Row Model

DVD	Rocky Horror Picture Show	A newly engaged couple ...	100	SF125	2.99
movie	Dr. Strangelove	An insane general ...	93		
DVD	Eraserhead	A dream of dark and troubling things ...	90	DR846	2.49
DVD	Wizards	On a post-apocalyptic Earth ...	82	SF933	1.00
movie	Animal House	At a 1962 college ...	109		

Figure 3.8 Single-Table Model

tained in a single table; in this model, each row is "marked" with an indication of its most specific type and the columns in that row are "marked" to be valid or invalid based on the attributes of that most specific type. (In the figure, I have included an extra column to indicate the "marking" applied to each row; perhaps obviously, that column doesn't actually exist in any way that applications can detect.) Figure 3.9 shows the model that I believe most nearly corresponds to that defined by SQL:1999.

A few paragraphs of semantics could readily map each of the three models onto SQL:1999's specifications, but the simplest to describe is the model in Figure 3.9. Insert, update, and delete operations operate on precisely the table specified in the corresponding SQL statements, while retrieval operates either on the specified table or that table and all of its subtables, combined with an effective UNION operation (depending on syntactic alternatives). I describe the behaviors of these operations in sections 3.7 and 3.8.

Dr. Strangelove	93	An insane general . . .
Animal House	109	At a 1962 college . . .

Rocky Horror Picture Show	100	A newly engaged couple . . .	SF125	2.99	. . .
Eraserhead	90	A dream of dark and troubling things . . .	DR846	2.49	. . .
Wizards	82	On a post-apocalyptic Earth . . .	SF933	1.00	. . .

Figure 3.9 SQL:1999 "Union" Model

3.5 Defining Typed Tables

The syntax for creating tables was presented in Volume 1 of this book, but the details related to creating typed tables were omitted. The syntax of CREATE TABLE as it applies to typed tables starts in Syntax 3.1.

Syntax 3.1 *<table definition> Syntax*

```
<table definition> ::=
    CREATE TABLE <table name>
      OF <user-defined type name>
      [ <subtable clause> ]
      [ <table element list> ]
```

Using this variation of CREATE TABLE, you indicate that you're creating a typed table through the use of "`OF <user-defined type name>`," which specifies the structured type whose instances can be stored in the table. The `<user-defined type name>` used in this statement is a special sort of name, called a *path-resolved name*. Path-resolved names are contrasted with schema-resolved names. I address these two concepts in more detail in Chapter 4, "Routines and Routine Invocation." At this point, it is sufficient to observe that the `<user-defined type name>` that identifies the structured type associated with the typed table being created is not an SQL 3-part name that includes a schema name and catalog name (even implicitly). Instead, it is a 1-part name; the system will search a series of schemas (in the order in which their names appear in the SQL-path that is discussed in Chapter 4, "Routines and Routine Invocation") to locate a structured type with that name. When such a type is found, it is used as the associated type of the typed table; if there are multiple types (in different schemas, of course) with the same name, the one contained in the schema whose name appears earliest in the SQL-path is chosen.

If the table that you're creating is intended to be a subtable of another table, then you specify the UNDER clause, whose syntax appears in Syntax 3.2.

Syntax 3.2 *<subtable clause> Syntax*

```
<subtable clause> ::=
    UNDER <supertable clause>

<supertable clause> ::= <table name>
```

Observe that you can specify the table name of only a single supertable, which is consistent with single inheritance. The `<table name>` that you provide in the `<subtable clause>` must be the name of a typed table (a base table, not a view) whose associated structured type is the direct supertype of the type associated with the table you're creating. In addition, the supertable must be defined in the same schema as the table you're creating.

If you're defining a subtable, every column of the specified supertable is inherited by the subtable, along with the various characteristics of those columns (such as default values, column constraints, and collations). Naturally, such columns are known as *inherited columns*, and they correspond to the inherited attributes of the supertable's associated structured type. In addition to the inherited columns, if any, the table you're defining acquires one column corresponding to each originally defined attribute of the table's associated type; these columns are (big surprise) known as *originally defined columns* of the table. Just as the names of originally defined attributes cannot be the same as the names of inherited attributes, neither can the names of originally defined columns of typed tables be the same as the names of inherited columns.

The columns of the typed table being defined, like the columns of ordinary SQL tables, have an order to them. Inherited columns are ordered earlier in the table than originally defined columns and have the same order that they have in the supertable from which they are inherited. Originally defined columns have the same order as the colum definitions that define them.

The final component of Syntax 3.1 is the list of table elements, whose syntax is available in Syntax 3.3. Volume 1 of this book provides the syntax of CREATE TABLE as it applies to ordinary SQL tables (that is, not typed tables). In that syntax, the definition of `<table element list>` includes the ability to define columns of a table using a variation of `<table element>` known as `<column definition>`. I have omitted that alternative in Syntax 3.3 for the simple reason that it is not permitted to define arbitrary columns as part of a typed table definition. The only columns that can occur in typed tables are those corresponding to attributes of the associated structured type and the self-referencing column (which is defined using the `<self-referencing column specification>` whose definition is seen in Syntax 3.4).

Syntax 3.3 *<table element list> Syntax*

```
<table element list> ::=
    <left paren>
      <table element> [ { <comma> <table element> }... ]
    <right paren>

<table element> ::=
    <table constraint definition>
  | <self-referencing column specification>
  | <column options>
```

You might find it surprising at first to observe in Syntax 3.3 that you're permitted to specify table constraints as part of a typed table definition. You are *not* allowed to specify a PRIMARY KEY constraint for a subtable. However, as part of the definition of a maximal supertable, you are allowed to specify a PRIMARY KEY that identifies one or more columns; alternatively, you can specify a UNIQUE constraint that identifies one or more columns, each of which must also be specified to be NOT NULL (UNIQUE combined with NOT NULL is a reasonable facsimile of a PRIMARY KEY constraint).

You are also permitted to specify referential integrity constraints as part of a typed table's definition. This allows you to ensure that values of certain columns (which are, of course, derived from corresponding attributes of the associated structured type) appear as values in specified columns of particular tables. Those referenced tables can be other typed tables or they can be ordinary SQL tables. (See Volume 1 of this book for a comprehensive discussion of referential integrity constraints and referential actions.)

A self-referencing column (see Syntax 3.4) cannot be specified when you're defining a subtable, but one must be specified in the definition of a maximal supertable. The self-referencing column defined in a maximal supertable is inherited by every subtable of that maximal supertable.

Syntax 3.4 *<self-referencing column specification> Syntax*

```
<self-referencing column specification> ::=
    REF IS <self-referencing column name> <reference generation>
```

```
<self-referencing column name> ::= <column name>

<reference generation> ::=
    SYSTEM GENERATED
  | USER GENERATED
  | DERIVED
```

The subject of the values of self-referencing columns is covered in section 3.6.

The remaining type of `<table element>` that applies to typed tables is `<column options>`, whose syntax is seen in Syntax 3.5. You are not permitted to specify `<column options>` for any inherited column, but you may specify any or all of these optional clauses (in the order specified by the BNF) for originally defined columns.

Syntax 3.5 *<column options> Syntax*

```
<column options> ::=
    <column name> WITH OPTIONS <column option list>

<column option list> ::=
    [ <scope clause> ]
    [ <default clause> ]
    [ <column constraint definition>... ]
    [ <collate clause> ]
```

If an originally defined column's data type is a REF type, then you may specify the `<scope clause>` option; see section 3.6 for details about REF types and scoping. If the column's data type is some character string type, such as CHARACTER or CHARACTER LARGE OBJECT, then you can specify a `<collate clause>` to assign a specific collation other than the default collation of the column's character set.

If you'd like the column to have a default value other than the default value given to the corresponding attribute of the associated structured type, then you can specify the `<default clause>` option. The `<default clause>` specified in `<column options>` overrides the one in the associated structured type.

Finally, you are allowed to specify one or more `<column constraint definition>`s, of which NOT NULL may be the most often used; other constraint types, such as CHECK constraints, may also be useful.

In Example 3.2, I've provided a table definition for a typed table corresponding to my `movie` type, with a twist: This table can only contain movies that are shorter than one and one-half hours (catering to really busy people). I also define a subtable to represent DVDs of those movies, again with a limitation that allows only fairly inexpensive rentals. For clarity, I also include partial type definitions for the `movie` type and the `DVD` type.

Example 3.2 *Types and Typed Tables for Short Movies*

```
CREATE TYPE movie AS (
  title           CHARACTER VARYING (100),
  description     CHARACTER VARYING (500),
  runs            INTEGER )
  INSTANTIABLE
  NOT FINAL
  REF IS SYSTEM GENERATED

CREATE TYPE dvd UNDER movie AS (
  stock_number   INTEGER,
  rental_price   DECIMAL(5,2),
  extra_features feature_desc ARRAY[10] )
  INSTANTIABLE
  NOT FINAL

CREATE TABLE short_movies OF movie
  ( REF IS movie_id SYSTEM GENERATED,
    runs WITH OPTIONS
      CONSTRAINT short_movie_check_runs CHECK ( runs < 90 ) )

CREATE TABLE short_DVDs OF dvd
  UNDER short_movies
  ( rental_price WITH OPTIONS
      CONSTRAINT short_DVDs_check_price CHECK ( rental_price < 1.99 ) )
```

You'll recall from Chapter 2, "User-Defined Types," that the `dvd` type has six attributes, three inherited from the `movie` type and three defined exclusive to the `dvd` type. Similarly, as you've seen in this chapter, the `short_movies` table has four columns: three corresponding to the attributes of the `movie` type, plus the self-referencing column (`movie_id`). And, of course, the `short_DVDs` table has seven columns: the six columns that correspond to the inherited attributes and the originally defined attributes of the `dvd` type, plus the self-referencing column (again, `movie_id`).

3.6 Reference Values and REF Types

The concepts of reference values and REF types are essentially inseparable. A REF type is an SQL:1999 type that you can use as the data type of columns in ordinary SQL tables, of attributes of structured types, of SQL variables, and of parameters—any place you can use any other SQL data type. The values of sites whose type is some REF type are always the reference values of rows in typed tables (that is, the values of the self-referencing columns of those rows).

3.6.1 Providing Self-Referencing Column Values

In section 2.8, "Defining Structured User-Defined Types," specifically in Syntax 2.7, "<reference type specification> Syntax," you saw the BNF for `<reference type specification>`, which I repeat in Syntax 3.6 for your convenience. At that point in Chapter 2, "User-Defined Types," I referred you forward to this chapter for the discussion of that syntax. In this section, you'll see the three mechanisms by which the rows in your typed tables can be given values for the self-referencing columns, as well as how to define and use SQL:1999's data type for referencing rows of typed tables.

Syntax 3.6 *<reference type specification> Syntax (repeated)*

```
<reference type specification> ::=
    <user-defined representation>
  | <derived representation>
  | <system-generated representation>

<user-defined representation> ::= REF USING <predefined type>

<derived representation> ::= REF FROM <list of attributes>

<system-generated representation> ::= REF IS SYSTEM GENERATED

<list of attributes> ::=
    <left paren>
      <attribute name> [ { <comma> <attribute name> }... ]
    <right paren>
```

Notice that Syntax 3.4's `<reference generation>` production includes three alternatives and that Syntax 3.6's `<reference type specification>` production also includes three alternatives. There is a one-to-one correspondence between the three alternatives of each of those productions. Recall that rows of typed tables have most of the characteristics of objects in other object-oriented systems, including unique identities that can be referenced by other components in the environment.

SQL:1999 provides three different mechanisms by which unique identities are given to instances of the structured types associated with such tables. All typed tables associated with a particular structured type use the same mechanism. The three choices allow you to choose to have reference values that are

- values of some SQL built-in type (`<user-defined representation>`) that the application must generate whenever it stores an instance of the structured type as a row in a typed table,
- values derived from one or more attributes of the structured type, or
- values that the application requests the system to generate automatically.

When you define a structured type for which you intend to define one or more associated typed tables, you must specify the `<reference type specification>` attribute for the type. (You may specify the `<reference type specification>` attribute even if you don't intend to define any associated typed tables, which at least leaves your options open if you change your mind.) When you define the typed tables, you must specify (redundantly!) the corresponding choice for the tables' `<reference generation>`. Table 3.1 makes the relationships explicit. (The redundancy is required in SQL:1999, but doesn't seem, to me at least, to be necessary in theory. If it is truly redundant, a future generation of the SQL standard might relax this requirement.)

Table 3.1 *<reference generation> and <reference type specification>*

<reference type specification>	*<reference generation>*
`REF USING <predefined type>`	`USER GENERATED`
`REF FROM <list of attributes>`	`DERIVED`
`REF IS SYSTEM GENERATED`	`SYSTEM GENERATED`

If you choose user-generated reference values for a particular structured type, then it is the responsibility of your applications to choose the value stored in the self-referencing column of each row you insert into a typed table associated with that type. If you choose a value that is not globally unique, then you'll probably encounter significant application problems down the road. Of course, a PRIMARY KEY or UNIQUE predicate defined on the maximal supertable of the table family can ensure that the values you choose are unique at the time you define them, but SQL:1999 offers no facilities that prevent you from reusing values from deleted rows in the self-referencing columns of new rows. Doing so can mislead your applications when they use a reference value in an attempt to retrieve one of those deleted rows and instead get some unrelated row for which you reused the reference value.

If you choose to have derived reference values for a specified structured type, then the system uses the values of the specified columns (that is, of the attributes corresponding to the specified columns) to derive a reference value. Again, it is your applications' responsibility to ensure that the values of those columns, taken together, are globally unique; failure to do so will cause you the same problems as failure to ensure global uniqueness of user-generated reference values. In this case, however, you must specify either PRIMARY KEY or a UNIQUE constraint that covers precisely the columns from which the reference values are derived.

If you choose system-generated reference values for a given structured type, then every row that you insert into a typed table associated with that type is assigned a globally unique value (see section 3.3); that value is stored into the self-referencing column of that row and can then be used from any application to uniquely identify that row for the life of the table.

3.6.2 REF Types

In earlier material of this chapter, you learned that rows in typed tables always have one column in addition to the columns corresponding to the attributes of the tables' associated structured types; that additional column is called a *self-referencing column*, and its values are globally unique values that uniquely identify the rows in which they appear (subject to the caveats about your applications' responsibilities that I discussed in section 3.6.1). The data type of self-referencing columns is always a REF type. The specific REF type depends on two factors:

1. The structured type associated with the typed table: REF types are *always* specific to a particular structured type, so you cannot ever use a REF type defined for the `movie` type to access an instance of, say, an `employee` type.
2. The chosen `<reference generation>` of the typed table (equivalently, the `<reference type specification>` of the associated structured type): this information is inherent in the structured type, so it is not stated explicitly in the REF type.

The syntax for specifying a REF type is given in Syntax 3.7.

Syntax 3.7 *<reference type> Syntax*

```
<reference type> ::=
    REF <left paren> <referenced type> <right paren>
    [ <scope clause> ]

<scope clause> ::= SCOPE <table name>

<referenced type> ::= <user-defined type name>
```

The name of the type whose instances are referenced (called the *referenced type*) by values of the specified REF type must be specified, and you may optionally specify a SCOPE clause as well.

The REF type can be the type of an attribute of a structured type, in which case, the referenced type can be the same as the type being defined. Otherwise, the referenced type must be a structured type that already exists. (The sole exception to this limitation occurs when you define multiple structured types and associated typed tables in the context of a CREATE SCHEMA statement. Such statements frequently contain many definitions of schema objects, and those definitions are considered by the standard to—effectively—be executed simultaneously. It is in this context that you can create cycles of structured types and typed tables that reference one another.)

The SCOPE clause, if specified, must specify the name of a typed table whose associated structured type is the referenced type of the REF type in which that clause is contained. While one might expect that a REF type value should be allowed to reference rows in typed tables whose associated structured type is a proper subtype of the specified referenced type, SQL:1999 doesn't allow that sort of reference; the associated structured type of the REF type's referenced table must be *exactly* the REF type's specified referenced type. Of course, you can declare a REF type whose referenced type is the associated structured type of a subtable, even though the self-referencing column of the subtable is necessarily inherited from the maximal supertable in the table family.

In section 3.3, I said that each reference value never identifies any row other than the row with which it was first associated, but that, if that row is ever deleted, then the value might identify nothing at all—but it never identifies a different row. An implication of that statement is that the system somehow "knows" whether a given reference value identifies a row stored somewhere in the database or that it identifies nothing at all (a term given to the latter case is *dangling reference*). But how can the system know, without eating up enormous amounts of time, CPU cycles, and other resources, which of those two cases holds for a specific reference value, particularly when there could be hundreds of typed tables associated with any particular structured type? The secret lies partly in the SCOPE clause: That clause identifies one particular typed table in which the referenced row must exist for all values of a particular site whose data type is some REF type. (While SQL:1999 limits the scope of a REF value to a single typed table, future versions of the SQL standard might enhance the SCOPE clause to accept a list of typed table names, or even some syntax indicating "all tables of the specified type.")

When you define a column of a table, a field of a row type, or an attribute of a structured type and specify that its type is a REF type, you may specify a SCOPE clause. If you do specify a SCOPE clause, you must also specify whether or not reference values are checked, as shown in Syntax 3.8.

Syntax 3.8 *<references scope check> Syntax*

```
<reference scope check> ::=
    REFERENCES ARE [ NOT ] CHECKED
    [ ON DELETE <reference scope check action> ]

<reference scope check action> ::= <referential action>
```

If you specify REFERENCES ARE NOT CHECKED or if you omit the SCOPE clause entirely, then you can store any reference value—whether or not it is the value of the self-referencing column of any row in the referenced table—into the column, field, or attribute being defined. The system will not ensure that the value actually references a row (but, of course, the value has to be of the proper type: a REF type for the specified structured type).

If you specify REFERENCES ARE CHECKED, then every time that a value is stored into the column, field, or attribute being defined (whether by means of an INSERT operation or an UPDATE operation, including the invocation of a mutator method), the system examines the referenced table to ensure that there is a row in that table whose self-referencing column value is equal to the reference value you're storing.

When you specify REFERENCES ARE CHECKED, you can also specify a referential action to be invoked when the row identified by a reference value is deleted; SQL:1999 prohibits specification of that referential action if REFERENCES ARE NOT CHECKED is specified. Possible actions (these are covered in Volume 1 of this book) are RESTRICT, CASCADE, SET NULL, SET DEFAULT, and NO ACTION; if you omit the referential action, then NO ACTION is the default. All of the options are available when you specify REFERENCES ARE CHECKED, unless the clause is specified when defining a field of a row type or an attribute of a structured type, in which case the only choice is ON DELETE NO ACTION. The behavior of each of the choices is identical to an equivalent referential constraint that you could define yourself; in other words, the syntax is nothing but "syntactic sugar" for a referential constraint.

If you specify a SCOPE clause when defining an attribute of a structured type, then you cannot specify a SCOPE clause in the `<column options>` (see Syntax 3.5) for the column corresponding to that attribute. Attempting to do so is a syntax error.

3.6.3 <ref cast option>

In section 2.8, "Defining Structured User-Defined Types," I deferred discussion of `<ref cast option>` to this chapter. The syntax of that optional clause is repeated in Syntax 3.9 for your convenience. You are allowed to specify `<ref cast option>` only if the `<reference type specification>` of the structured type you're defining specified a user-defined representation (`REF USING <predefined type>`).

Syntax 3.9 *<ref cast option> Syntax (repeated)*

```
<ref cast option> ::=
    [ <cast to ref> ]
    [ <cast to type> ]

<cast to ref> ::=
    CAST <left paren> SOURCE AS REF <right paren>
      WITH <cast to ref identifier>

<cast to ref identifier> ::= <identifier>

<cast to type> ::=
    CAST <left paren> REF AS SOURCE <right paren>
      WITH <cast to type identifier>

<cast to type identifier> ::= <identifier>
```

For example, if your structured type definition specifies REF USING INTEGER, then it is the responsibility of your applications to provide a globally unique integer value to be stored in the self-referencing column of each row in every typed table associated with that structured type. But your application provides a value whose type is INTEGER, while the data type of the self-referencing column is some REF type, such as "`REF(movie)`." The `<ref cast option>` resolves that problem by identifying two SQL-invoked routines that are used to cast from the

INTEGER value provided by your application into the REF type as you insert a row into the typed table or update a row in the typed table (SOURCE AS REF) and cast from the REF type to an INTEGER value whenever you retrieve a row from the typed table (REF AS SOURCE). The system automatically generates the two SQL-invoked routines for you, so this clause merely allows you to choose their names; if you omit the clause entirely, then the system also chooses the names of the functions. The only advantage to your choosing the names is that you can then invoke the functions explicitly if you ever want to write an SQL statement in which you have expressions whose type is a REF type but whose desired type is the user-defined representation type. You cannot, by the way, write these two functions yourself, because the mapping between structured type instances and the representation type is strictly implementation-defined. That's why the SQL implementation must always provide the functions automatically.

3.7 Retrieving from Typed Tables

Now that you know how to create a typed table associated with a particular structured user-defined type, it's time to discuss how to retrieve information from such tables. In this section, you'll learn how retrieval from typed tables is affected by the existence of a table hierarchy and how to use the linkages provided by reference values.

3.7.1 Basic Retrieval

In section 3.2, I said that a typed table was, in many ways, just an ordinary table. That's certainly true when you're retrieving information from a typed table that doesn't participate in a type hierarchy.

If we've populated the tables that I defined in Example 3.2, then you could retrieve the name and running time of DVDs for movies whose titles contain the word *Rose* with the query expression in Example 3.3. (Please note that I identified the contents of Example 3.3 as a "query expression" and recall that, except in interactive SQL, a "SELECT statement" can return at most one row without giving an exception. Volume 1 of this book has information on this subject.)

Example 3.3 *Retrieving "Rose" DVDs*

```
SELECT title, runs
FROM short_DVDs
WHERE title LIKE '%Rose%'
```

There's absolutely nothing unusual about that query expression—an identical query expression would be used to retrieve information from an ordinary, non-typed table named short_DVDs that has columns named title and runs. Notice, however, that Example 3.3 references a leaf table—a table without subtables.

3.7.2 Type Hierarchies and ONLY

When the typed table of interest participates in a type hierarchy—particularly when it is not a leaf table in that hierarchy—then the situation becomes a little more interesting.

Suppose, again using Example 3.2, that we want to retrieve information about movies shorter than 60 minutes, regardless of whether or not they are available on DVD. A query expression much like that in Example 3.3 can be used, changing only the table name and the content of the WHERE clause, as shown in Example 3.4.

Example 3.4 *Retrieving Very Short Movies*

```
SELECT title, runs
FROM short_movies
WHERE runs < 60
```

SQL:1999 defines the semantics of the query expression in Example 3.4 to be equivalent to retrieving the title and run length columns from the short_movies table, then retrieving the title and run length columns from the short_DVDs table, then combining those two intermediate results with an SQL UNION operation. These semantics support the model of SQL:1999's table hierarchies that I presented in section 3.4.2 and illustrated in Figure 3.9. Recall that the so-called union model places each row in exactly one table of a table hierarchy, and the system effectively does a union of the table in a hierarchy "below" the specified table (that is, the subtables of the specified table) when determining the rows on which to operate.

But what if we wanted to retrieve information about only those really short movies that are *not* available on DVD? The query expression in Example 3.5 accomplishes that goal.

Example 3.5 *Retrieving Very Short Movies Not on DVD*

```
SELECT title, runs
FROM ONLY ( short_movies )
WHERE runs < 60
```

The insertion of the keyword ONLY (and the parentheses that surround the table name) instructs SQL to retrieve rows *only* from the specified table—only one table name is permitted—and not to perform that "effective union" with subtables of the specified table. Therefore, the query expression retrieves only those rows that appear in `short_movies`, but not in `short_DVDs`. The keyword ONLY acts as a sort of qualifier, or modifier, for table names that appear in FROM clauses and other related contexts.

Of course, even if your query expression uses "`SELECT *`" (which I normally do not recommend), only those columns that appear in the specified table will be retrieved. Additional originally defined columns that appear in subtables, but not in the specified table, are not retrieved when ONLY is specified. Queries using "`SELECT *`" that don't specify ONLY retrieve just the columns that are defined in the specified typed table (including the self-referencing column) while they retrieve rows from that table and from all of its subtables.

Incidentally, if in a query expression you use the ONLY keyword to qualify the name of a table that is not a typed table, or that is a typed table that has no subtables, then the effect is the same as though you had not used the keyword.

3.7.3 Reference Values: Follow the Pointer

The final complication involved in retrieving data from typed tables arises when reference values are considered. Recall from section 3.6 that you can declare any site (such as a column of a table, an SQL parameter, or an attribute of a structured type) to have a REF type as its data type. The values stored in such sites are, as you learned in section 3.6.1, reference values that identify rows in a specified typed table whose associated type is the structured type of the REF type (or else they identify nothing at all, that is, they are dangling references).

But what happens when you actually encounter a reference value, perhaps because you've retrieved it in the result of a query expression? Consider the types and tables in Example 3.6.

Example 3.6 *More Types and Typed Tables*

```
CREATE TYPE movie AS (
  title          CHARACTER VARYING (100),
  description    CHARACTER VARYING (500),
  runs           INTEGER )
  INSTANTIABLE
  NOT FINAL
  REF IS SYSTEM GENERATED
```

```
  INSTANCE METHOD rating()
    RETURNS DECIMAL(2,1)

CREATE TYPE player AS (
  player_name    name,
  role_played    name,
  film           REF(movie) )
  INSTANTIABLE
  NOT FINAL
  REF IS SYSTEM GENERATED

CREATE TABLE movies OF movie
  ( REF IS movie_id SYSTEM GENERATED )

CREATE TABLE actors OF player
  ( REF IS actor_id SYSTEM GENERATED,
    film WITH OPTIONS SCOPE movies )
```

The `player` type captures the name of an actor or actress and the name of the role played in a particular film; perhaps obviously, any particular actor can appear many times as an instance of this type, once per role played (even if, like Peter Sellers in *Dr. Strangelove,* he or she plays multiple characters in a single film). (I assume the existence of a type called `name` with attributes `first` and `last`.) The `player` type identifies the film in which the named actor plays the named role by means of a reference to instances of the `movie` type. In the definition of the `actors` table, I further clarify that the `film` column identifies only references to the `movie` type that appear as rows in the `movies` table.

If I'd like to learn the running time of a movie in which Peter Sellers played a character named Merkin Muffley, I would use a query expression like that in Example 3.7.

Example 3.7 *Retrieval Using Reference Value*

```
SELECT film -> runs
FROM actors
WHERE player_name.first = 'Peter' AND player_name.last = 'Sellers'
  AND role_played.first = 'Merkin' AND role_played.last = 'Muffley'
```

The notation `->` is called a *dereference operator* in SQL:1999, but I like to think of it as a "right arrow" or a "pointer," so I read the expression "`film -> runs`" as "film points to runs." And, in fact, that's a reasonable way to think of reference values:

as *pointers* to rows in typed tables. Of course, the result of the query expression in Example 3.7 is a virtual table with a single column whose name is runs and whose data type is INTEGER.

You might find it surprising that the statement in Example 3.7 retrieves a value from the movies table without even specifying that table in the FROM clause. The use of the dereference operator effectively causes a join between the actors table and the movies table, thus making the runs column "visible" to the query.

If I choose to invoke the ratings method on the movie in which Peter Sellers played that same character, I can use the rather similar query expression shown in Example 3.8.

Example 3.8 *Method Invocation Using Reference Value*

```
SELECT film -> ratings()
FROM actors
WHERE player_name.first = 'Peter' AND player_name.last = 'Sellers'
  AND role_played.first = 'Merkin' AND role_played.last = 'Muffley'
```

Again, the reference value retrieved from the films column "points to" an instance of the movie type stored as a row in the movies table; this time, however, the ratings method is invoked on that movie instance. In this case, the result of the query expression is a virtual table containing one column whose data type is DECIMAL(2,1) and whose name is ratings. I also note in passing that Example 3.7 implicitly invokes the observer function on the runs attribute and is therefore equivalent to the approach used in Example 3.8.

SQL:1999 offers one more possibility: you can even retrieve the entire instance of the structured type that a reference value identifies (SQL:1999 formally calls this a *reference resolution*). Should I decide that I wanted to retrieve the instance of the movie type in which Peter Sellers played that character, I could use an expression like the one in Example 3.9.

Example 3.9 *Retrieval of Structured Type Instance through Reference Type*

```
SELECT DEREF ( film )
FROM actors
WHERE player_name.first = 'Peter' AND player_name.last = 'Sellers'
  AND role_played.first = 'Merkin' AND role_played.last = 'Muffley'
```

Instead of retrieving an attribute of the referenced structured type instance, or the result of invoking a method on that instance, the entire instance itself is retrieved. Therefore, the result of the entire query expression is a virtual table with a single (unnamed) column whose data type is the structured type `movie`.

3.8 Inserting, Modifying, and Deleting in Typed Tables

Now that we've covered retrieval of data from typed tables, including the use of ONLY to cause subtable rows to be omitted and the various ways to use reference values, the subject of creating and destroying data in typed tables is simple. Arguably, modifying data already stored in a typed table is slightly more complex. Let's consider these operations one at a time.

3.8.1 INSERT

Creating a new instance of the `dvd` type as a row in the `short_DVDs` table from Example 3.2 is as simple as inserting a new row into that table, as shown in Example 3.10.

Example 3.10 *Creating a New dvd Instance in the short_DVDs Table*

```
INSERT INTO short_DVDs ( title, description, runs,
                         stock_number, rental_price )
  VALUES ( 'The Next Game',
           'Michael Douglas''s housekeeper's babysitter ' ||
           'arranges a birthday gift that "keeps on giving"...' ||
           'a subscription to "Housekeeping Monthly", ' ||
           'horrifying everyone in sight.',
           48,
           61992,
           0.49 )
```

There's nothing exceptional about that INSERT statement. It doesn't have (or need) a value for the self-referencing column of the table, `movie_id`, because the value is specified to be SYSTEM GENERATED. (Of course, the film that I used in the example, *The Next Game,* hasn't been purchased by the studios—yet.)

The row inserted into `short_DVDs` in Example 3.10 is not inserted into the `short_movies` table, but retrievals from the `short_movies` table that do not specify ONLY will retrieve this new `short_DVDs` row because of the effective UNION discussed in section 3.7.2. Similarly, if we had inserted a new row into the short_movies table, it would not be placed into the short_DVDs table. Insertions are made into the table specified in the INSERT statement and no others.

Surprisingly, it is not possible in SQL:1999 to create a new structured type instance with the NEW expression (see section 2.10.3, "Constructors and the NEW Expression") and then use the INSERT statement to insert the value as a row into a typed table. This omission might be corrected in some future version of the standard, if the rather complex syntax and semantic issues can be sufficiently resolved.

3.8.2 DELETE

What action is taken when we *delete* a row from the short_movies table?

There are two behaviors that we might want to support. First, we might want to ensure that all rows describing that incredibly famous (not!) film *The Lunch Lady: A Documentary,* whether or not the film is available on DVD, are removed from the database. In this case, the statement in Example 3.11 is appropriate.

Example 3.11 *Deleting from All Tables in a Subtable Family*

```
DELETE FROM short_movies
WHERE title = 'The Lunch Lady: A Documentary'
```

But, if we want to delete that film only if it happens to be unavailable in DVD format, Example 3.12 illustrates the approach to take. If the row in the short_movies table that describes the film has a corresponding subrow in any subtable of short_movies, including the short_DVDs table, the DELETE statement will retain (without signaling any sort of error) the row from short_movies or from any supertable or subtable of short_movies.

Example 3.12 *Deleting Only from a Specific Table and Its Supertables*

```
DELETE FROM ONLY ( short_movies )
WHERE title = 'The Lunch Lady: A Documentary'
```

The use of ONLY instructs the system to delete the row *only* from the specified table and from every supertable of the specified table. "What?" I can hear you ask, "Why would the supertables be involved?" Recall that the row describing a given film exists in only a single table, but the short_movies table could have had—it doesn't in Example 3.2—a supertable that contains, say, movies in general. The row for this particular movie might be found in that supertable or in the short_movies table, and the statement in Example 3.12 would delete it from either place. The use of ONLY instructs the SQL system not to delete the row if it also appears in any subtables (short_DVDs, for instance); the use of this modifier allows us to delete movies that are not available on DVD while retaining those that are available on DVD.

3.8.3 UPDATE

For the most part, updates are conceptually no different than deletions. This can be seen in Example 3.13 and Example 3.14, in which I correct the name of a short film whose title was initially entered incorrectly.

Example 3.13 *Updating a Row Wherever It Appears in a Subtable Family*

```
UPDATE short_movies
  SET title = 'The Lunch Lady: A Documentary'
WHERE title = 'The Cafeteria Lady: A Mockumentary'
```

In Example 3.13, all rows in the short_movies table that meet the criteria specified by the WHERE clause are updated, as are all such rows in every supertable of short_movies and every subtable of short_movies (such as short_DVDs). By contrast, in Example 3.14, the system updates only those rows in short_movies that meet the criteria and such rows in every supertable of short_movies (but not in subtables of short_movies).

Example 3.14 *Updating a Row in Only a Specific Table and Its Supertables*

```
UPDATE ONLY ( short_movies )
  SET title = 'The Lunch Lady: A Documentary'
WHERE title = 'The Cafeteria Lady: A Mockumentary'
```

The only relevant difference between deletions and updates arises in the modification of rows in supertables of the specified table. In either case (with or without the use of ONLY), when the rows in any supertable that match the criteria of the WHERE clause are updated, any SET clauses that modify columns that are not included in the supertable (that is, columns that are originally defined columns of some subtable of that supertable) are simply—and silently—ignored.

3.9 Typed Views

So far in this chapter, I've discussed typed tables that are base tables. SQL:1999 also supports *typed views,* also called *referenceable views* (also sometimes called *object views,* because the data visible in the view corresponds to rows in typed tables, which behave very much like objects in many object-oriented systems). As you might expect, there are many similarities between typed (base) tables and typed views, but there are a few differences caused by the inherent differences between base tables and views. SQL defines various (obvious) terms in conjunction with typed views: *superview, subview, direct superview, direct subview, proper superview,* and *proper subview.* Their meanings are direct analogs of the corresponding terms applied to typed base tables. The phrase *subtable family* applies equally to typed views and typed tables; after all, a view is a table, too!

The syntax for defining a typed view (omitting syntax elements used only for creating ordinary views) appears in Syntax 3.10.

Syntax 3.10 *<view definition> Syntax for Typed Views*

```
<view definition> ::=
  CREATE VIEW <table name>
      OF <user-defined type name>
      [ <subview clause> ]
      [ <view element list> ]
    AS <query expression>
    [ WITH [ <levels clause> ] CHECK OPTION ]

<subview clause> ::= UNDER <table name>

<view element list> ::=
  <left paren>
    <view element> [ { <comma> <view element> }... ]
  <right paren>

<view element> ::=
    <self-referencing column specification>
  | <view column option>

<view column option> ::= <column name> WITH OPTIONS <scope clause>
```

When you create a typed view, you must of course specify the name of the structured type with which the view is associated. The structured type is identified using the same mechanisms used for identifying the structured type on which a typed table is defined (see section 3.5).

The AS clause, as in ordinary view definitions, specifies the query expression by which rows from some underlying table are identified for inclusion in the view. For typed views, that query expression must identify a single underlying typed table (intuitively, a table from which a view's rows are derived is an underlying table of the view) or a single underlying typed view. That typed table or typed view must be associated with the same structured type as the view being defined. That underlying table is sometimes called the *basis table* of the typed view.

You may also define the typed view to be a subview of another typed view. In this case, the structured type associated with the view you're defining must be a direct subtype of the structured type associated with the superview you specify. Again, there is a close analogy with defining a subtable. In this case, the basis table must be a proper subtable or subview—not necessarily a *direct* subtable or subview—of the basis table of the direct superview of the view being created.

You may also specify one or more `<view column option>`s, where the analogy with subtable definition is quite accurate.

If you define your view to be a subview of another typed view, then you cannot specify `<self-referencing column specification>` (this is the same restriction that applies when you define a subtable). If you're defining a maximal superview (while SQL:1999 doesn't formally define the term, the meaning is obvious), you may—but you are *not* required to—define a `<self-referencing column specification>`. If you do, then you cannot specify SYSTEM GENERATED; you are limited to specifying USER GENERATED and DERIVED. If you specify USER GENERATED, then the degree of the view (that is, the number of columns in the view) is one greater than the number of attributes of the associated structured type; the additional column is (of course) the self-referencing column. If you specify DERIVED, then the degree of the view is equal to the number of attributes in the underlying UDT and no additional self-referencing column is included. It might seem strange at first that no additional self-referencing column is included when DERIVED is specified; the reasoning is that the value of the self-referencing column is derived from the same underlying columns that provide the values from which the *underlying* self-referencing column's value is derived.

An example of defining referenceable views is available in Example 3.15. (In Example 3.2, the definition of the `short_movies` typed table specifies that the self-referencing column has SYSTEM GENERATED values, which is not allowed for referenceable views; however, SQL:1999 requires that referenceable views' self-referencing columns use the same option as the corresponding self-referencing columns of their underlying base tables. Consequently, I have taken the liberty of presuming that the `short_movies` table was specified to have a DERIVED self-referencing column.)

Example 3.15 *A Referenceable View*

```
CREATE VIEW short_movies_with_long_titles
  OF movie ( REF IS movie_id DERIVED )
  AS SELECT title, description, runs
     FROM ONLY ( short_movies )
     WHERE CHAR_LENGTH ( title ) > 75

CREATE VIEW short_DVDs_with_long_titles
  OF DVD
  UNDER short_movies_with_long_titles
  AS SELECT title, description, runs, stock_number, rental_price
     FROM ONLY ( short_DVDs )
     WHERE CHAR_LENGTH ( title ) > 75
```

The CHECK OPTION clause is discussed in Volume 1 of this book and is not addressed in this volume.

3.10 Typed Tables and Privileges

It would be at least a little surprising if the addition of typed tables and typed views to SQL:1999 didn't result in some enhancements to the privilege model of the language. Indeed, some existing privileges (like USAGE and SELECT) have been adapted for use and some new ones have been added.

The USAGE privilege is required on a structured type before you can use the type as the type of any site in your applications or database, including host variables, SQL variables, columns, and parameters.

Prior to SQL:1999, the SELECT privilege applied only to columns of tables and views. In SQL:1999, it also applies to methods of structured types—but only when instances of those types are stored in typed tables. In Example 3.8, the authorization identifier causing the evaluation of the query expression must have the SELECT privilege on the `ratings` method or a privilege violation will be signaled. The SELECT privilege is required only when you use the -> syntax to "follow the reference" from a REF value to the referenced row and then invoke a method on that referenced row. When you're invoking a method on a structured type value that is stored in a column of an ordinary SQL table, you must have SELECT privilege on that column; if the method is a mutator method, you must also have UPDATE privilege on that column. As with all SQL-invoked routines, you must have the EXECUTE privilege on all methods that you invoke.

One new privilege is the UNDER privilege, which you must have before you can define a subtype of a structured type, a subtable of a typed table, or a subview of a typed view. Another new privilege is the SELECT WITH HIERARCHY OPTION privilege. This privilege can be granted only on (typed) tables, not on the individual columns of those tables. When you use a table reference (e.g., in a query expression), you must have SELECT WITH HIERARCHY OPTION on at least one supertable of the typed table identified in table reference (but don't forget that a typed table is a supertable of itself, so having the privilege on that specific table is sufficient to satisfy this requirement). The same requirement applies to evaluation of a `<reference resolution>` (see Example 3.9), where the table on which you must have the privilege is the one specified in the SCOPE clause associated with the REF type that you're dereferencing. Similarly, the requirement applies to typed tables from which you're deleting rows or in which you're modifying rows.

3.11 Chapter Summary

In this chapter, you've learned how to define typed tables and use them to store and manage instances of structured user-defined types. This facility offers significant possibilities for using SQL as an object-oriented database management system, particularly with the inclusion of object views (typed views). You've also learned about reference values and the associated REF types, including how to "follow the pointer" provided by a reference value to the row in a typed table that is the structured type instance.

Chapter 4

Routines and Routine Invocation

4.1 Introduction

In the preceding two chapters, I've talked about structured user-defined types and the fact that their behaviors are specified in the form of SQL-invoked routines. In this chapter, you'll learn about the three forms of SQL-invoked routines and how each form can be written either in SQL or in your choice of several more conventional application programming languages.

This chapter covers SQL:1999's routine invocation algorithm as it applies to each form of SQL-invoked routine, giving you both a "bird's-eye" view and the incredibly tedious details. Among other factors, you'll learn about SQL's *path,* how it affects selection of user-defined type for some contexts, and how it affects the routine invocation algorithm.

Naturally, I also provide the complete syntax for defining SQL-invoked routines of all flavors, for modifying certain characteristics of those routines, and for destroying them when you're done with them.

Much, *but not all,* of the material in this chapter has been adapted and extended from Chapter 17 in Volume 1 of this book.[1] The material is reiterated here, partly for your convenience, but primarily because the corresponding material in Volume 1 covers only two of the three classes of SQL-invoked rou-

1 Jim Melton and Alan R. Simon, *SQL:1999: Understanding Relational Language Components* (San Francisco: Morgan Kaufmann Publishers, 2001).

tines. The third class, methods, was omitted from that volume because it is relevant only in the context of user-defined types. The material in this volume emphasizes the definition and invocation of methods and goes more deeply into routine resolution in general than does Volume 1.

4.2 SQL-Invoked Routines

The most concise definition of an SQL-invoked routine is "a routine that is invoked from SQL code." I acknowledge that sounds a bit circular, but it's really the most accurate definition available.

The phrase *SQL-invoked routine* has two components. The second component, the word *routine*, identifies the concept of a "subprogram" that is executed on behalf of another program, usually through the use of some particular syntax that identifies that subprogram. Over the decades, programming languages have used a variety of terminology for different sorts of subprograms, but the programming community appears to have settled on consistent nomenclature, and SQL's terms are in agreement with those of other modern languages. The first component, "SQL-invoked," identifies subprograms that are executed in response to instructions issued from SQL statements or expressions.

As you'll see in this chapter, SQL-invoked routines have a variety of characteristics that allow them to be categorized in several important dimensions.

- An SQL-invoked routine is a routine that is invoked from SQL. The routine itself might be written in SQL, in which case it is also an *SQL routine*; alternatively, it might be written in some other programming language, in which case it is an *external routine*.
- External routines may have parameter sequences that are particularly oriented toward their use in an SQL environment, or they may have parameter sequences that allow their use in non-SQL environments as well.
- An SQL-invoked routine can be a *procedure,* a *function,* or a *method.*
- SQL-invoked routines might contain SQL statements (SQL routines necessarily do, but external routines need not); if they do, then those statements might read SQL data or update SQL data.
- SQL-invoked routines that are functions or methods might always return a null value when invoked with the null value as the value of any argument, or the code of the routine might be executed even in this situation.
- SQL-invoked routines are either *deterministic* or *nondeterministic.*

- SQL-invoked procedures are permitted to return dynamic result sets.
- External routines can be executed using various privilege mechanisms.

Before discussing the various dimensions of SQL-invoked routines in detail, I'd like to ensure that a sometimes-confusing bit of terminology is made clear: I use the word *parameter* to mean the mechanism declared as part of a routine by which the routine receives information passed from its invoker; by contrast, the word *argument* is reserved for the data that is transmitted by the code invoking a routine to that routine. In other words, a "parameter" occurs in and is used by a routine, while an "argument" occurs in and is used by the code that invokes a routine. There is normally exactly one argument in a routine invocation for every parameter in the routine being invoked (some programming languages—but not SQL—support optional parameters that need not be supplied with corresponding arguments), and the data types of arguments must "match" the data types of their corresponding parameters (SQL provides rules for certain data conversions when the data type match is not exact).

4.3 External Routines and SQL Routines

One dimension along which SQL-invoked routines are described is the implementation language of the routine. SQL-invoked routines can be written in SQL or in any of several more traditional programming languages. The choice of languages available in your SQL system is decided by the implementor of that product. The SQL standard provides specification for nine languages: SQL, of course, as well as Ada, C, COBOL, Fortran, MUMPS (now known as M), Pascal, PL/I, and (most recently) Java. I know of no vendor that supports external (that is, non-SQL) routines written in all eight of these languages, and there are several vendors that support languages other than these eight.

4.3.1 External Routines

An external routine is one written in a programming language other than SQL. Even though the routine itself is written in a language like C, Fortran, or Java, it is always declared in SQL so that information about it is recorded in the Information Schema (see Volume 1 of this book for more information). That information specifies the various characteristics of the routine and connects the SQL definition with the actual executable code of the routine (which is often stored as a file elsewhere in a computer system, rather than in the database along with its descriptive information).

There are, I believe, three compelling reasons to consider the use of external routines:

1. You may already own a number of routines written in some host language—a statistical package, for example. If you find that you need the capabilities provided by routines that you already own, then SQL's ability to provide access to those external routines saves you development time and other resources.
2. Furthermore, few SQL products implement SQL/PSM's procedural language, and the proprietary analogs of PSM (e.g., Oracle's PL/SQL and Sybase's Transact-SQL) aren't very portable among products. If you spend the resources to build a number of routines that require computational completeness, writing the routines in a host language may well mean that you can use them on several SQL database products. By contrast, if you develop them in the Microsoft SQL Server dialect of TSQL, you can't easily run them on an IBM database product.
3. Finally, you might discover that you have a need for certain functionality that is computationally intensive, such as time-series analysis of daily, weekly, monthly, and quarterly reports of DVD sales versus VHS tape sales. Writing such routines in SQL might not give you the performance that you need—after all, SQL is usually highly optimized for set-oriented database operations, not for computation-intensive math. Another language, like Fortran or C, might offer significant computational performance advantages for uses like this one.

External routines execute in a different *context* (you might be comfortable with the analogy between external routine execution contexts and the process contexts implemented in many operating systems). As you will learn in section 4.9, the privileges used during the execution of an external routine depend on how the routine is created—that is, whether its `<external security clause>` specifies DEFINER, INVOKER, or IMPLEMENTATION DEFINED. The privileges are part of the context in which an external routine is executed.

However, the context is more than just the authorization identifier (user identifier and/or role name) that is chosen. It includes other obvious items such as the temporary tables and cursors that are defined in the external routine.

But that raises an important question: Does the external routine itself contain SQL code in the form of embedded SQL statements? (Analogously, does it invoke

SQL statements that are contained in externally-invoked procedures collected into SQL client modules?)

Obviously, not all external routines will themselves execute SQL statements. If you've purchased a package of statistical routines, it's fairly unlikely that the routines in that package use SQL at all. On the other hand, your organization may have a large collection of routines that do use SQL code and that you are able to reuse for your applications.

External routines that do not contain SQL code or invocations of SQL code should be created using an `<SQL-data access indication>` that specifies NO SQL. Such routines can be treated generally as though they execute in the same process space as the SQL code that invokes them. (However, "process space" is a term highly dependent on specific implementation technologies and may not even apply to your environment. Furthermore, some implementations allow you to integrate such external routines into the database's process space for the performance advantages that ability offers, while others may force you to keep such external routines "fire-walled" off into a different process space for various reasons, including security of your database data, stability of the database environment, and so forth.)

External routines containing embedded SQL, or invocations of externally-invoked procedures (externally-invoked procedures are defined in Volume 1 of this book), are always given their own SQL session context in which to operate. This context includes all characteristics that any SQL session context includes. Perhaps the only important difference between this context and the one created when you first initiate an SQL session is how the authorization identifiers are determined.

There are advantages and disadvantages to the use of external routines. A summary of the principle advantages includes the following:

- You may already own routines written in a host language that were created for a different purpose.
- External routines may perform computationally intensive tasks more efficiently than SQL routines.
- External routines may be more portable among SQL database systems from different vendors.
- External routines provide the ability to invoke identical program code within the database and in other parts of your application.
- External routines support invokers' rights, which SQL routines do not support (in SQL:1999, at least—this might be enhanced in some future version of the SQL standard).

- External routines are usually able to access services provided by the underlying operating system, such as file systems, memory management, and the like.

However, there are disadvantages to be considered, too:

- Moving data between an external routine and your SQL code involves the famous impedance mismatch, both with data types and with set orientation versus single-datum orientation. (The impedance mismatch is often considerably less for Java routines than for routines written in other external languages.)
- Except for routines written in Java, it is not possible to transfer instances of structured types into external routines and retain their SQL behaviors.
- Creation of new SQL sessions for the execution of external routines that contain SQL code (if your implementation chooses this strategy) may be quite expensive, and changing between various session contexts is very likely to have a negative impact on your performance.
- Your application development process may suffer from having to consider development in yet another programming language. (This is somewhat offset by the fact that SQL's computational completeness capabilities require learning the procedural statements, block structuring conventions, etc.)

In short, don't be afraid of external routines, but think about the implications before you make the choice to use them in your database applications.

4.3.2 SQL Routines

By contrast, an SQL routine is, by definition, one that is written in SQL. As with external routines, SQL routines are declared in SQL so that metadata describing them is recorded in the Information Schema. Frequently, the actual code of the routine is also stored in the database, although not necessarily in the Information Schema; your applications may store the routines anywhere it's appropriate to do so.

SQL routines offer certain advantages over external routines:

- No impedance mismatch.
- No context switching overhead.

- No "special parameter lists" to be handled (see section 4.6.5).
- Reduced training and debugging costs—your database developers work only in SQL.

In many situations, those advantages will prove to be persuasive, and you would be right to make the choice to use SQL for your stored routines. But, even in an environment where that choice is appropriate for most stored routines, there may be cases where the disadvantages outweigh the advantages:

- If you already own a routine that performs a specific function, rewriting it in SQL costs you valuable development resources, especially if you expect the routine to be invoked relatively infrequently and it doesn't require the use of any SQL statements to do its job.
- If the routine must make extensive computations, SQL routines might not perform as well as your application requires.
- If the routine is expected to contain complex logic and you need the ability to run the routine on different database systems, you might not wish to lock yourself into either SQL/PSM's computationally complete statements or any one vendor's equivalent proprietary language.
- SQL routines are unable (without vendor extensions) to access operating system capabilities, such as file systems, memory management, and so forth.

In spite of these tradeoffs, I think that using SQL routines offers enough advantages in so many situations that many applications will use external routines only in specific circumstances and will use SQL routines for more (ahem) routine situations. The principle situation in which I observe the most external routine use arises when a database system supports the use of Java as a programming language in which external routines can be written. The availability of Java changes the situation so that I react much more favorably to the use of external routines, largely because of its ability to run in a variety of environments without change.

Because of the power available in SQL-invoked routines, triggers in your databases can invoke procedures that send e-mail messages, print documents, or activate robotic equipment to retrieve inventory to be shipped—but only if the language in which those routines are written supports such activities! Indeed, an external routine can do anything supported by the language in which it's written, as long as your database implementation supports the capability. (This caveat is important, because some implementations may prohibit external routines from performing nondatabase input/output operations in the interests of security or performance.)

By contrast, an SQL routine is limited to SQL statements and the operations that they provide; that is, they're pretty much restricted to database operations. If you need an SQL-invoked routine to send e-mail, that routine's going to have to be—or invoke—an external routine written in C, COBOL, or some other host language.

4.4 SQL-Paths

In many programming languages, all subprograms invoked from a given chunk of code are located in some well-defined repository, such as an object code library or a predefined file system directory. In other languages, you are required to somehow specify the precise location of the code that you're invoking.

Java, on the other hand, differs somewhat in how it locates its closest analog to "subprograms"—class definitions and the methods they contain. Java uses the concept of a *class path* that is used in locating class definitions required by a Java program. A class path is a list of "places" where the Java runtime system might find a class definition when it requires one—typically a list of file system directory names. When the Java runtime system encounters a command to use a class definition of which it is not yet aware (including an invocation of a method in such a class definition), it searches the file system directories in the order they appear in the class path. The first directory in that list that contains a class of the required name is then used as the source of the class definition being sought.

SQL's analog to a class path is called the *SQL-path.* An SQL-path is a list of database schemas in which functions may be located. In SQL:1999, an SQL-path is associated with each routine, which the routine inherits from the schema in which it is defined. (Each session also has a default SQL-path that is used when executing dynamic SQL statements.)

The SQL-path is also used to identify structured types. In Chapter 3, "Typed Tables," I told you that the name of the structured type on which a typed table is based is actually a special type of name, called a *path-resolved name,* and I contrasted that type of name with the more common schema-resolved name. Most SQL objects, like tables and views, are referenced by the use of schema-resolved names. That phrase means that the name of the object is an ordinary SQL 3-part name made up of a catalog name, a schema name, and a "local" name, separated by periods. Although the schema name is optional, there's always an implicit schema name that is used when you don't write one explicitly; the same is true of the catalog name. The object is located by finding the catalog whose name is explicitly or implicitly provided, then finding in that catalog the schema whose

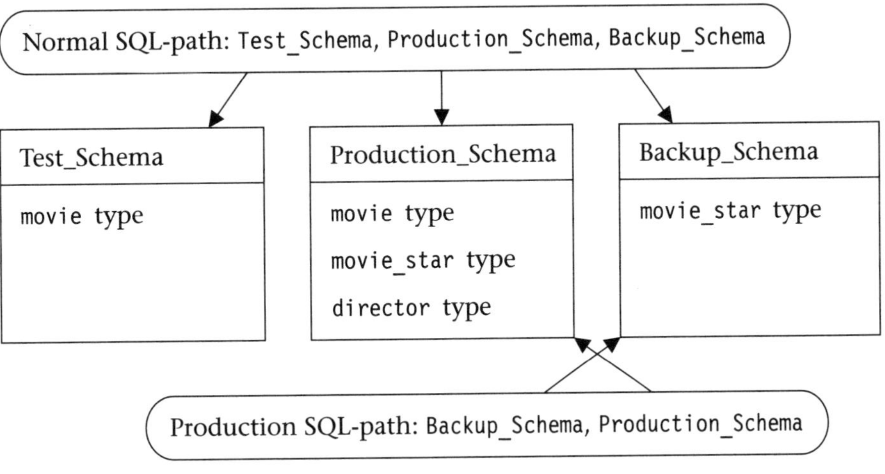

Figure 4.1 SQL-Paths

name is explicitly or implicitly provided, and finally locating in that schema the object whose name is given.

However, a path-resolved name works a little bit differently. When you specify only the "local" portion of the object's name, the system looks for an object with that name in a series of schemas, in the order in which those schemas' names are specified in the SQL-path. The first schema in which an object of the appropriate sort (e.g., structured type) with the specified local name is found is selected to be the schema from which the object is taken. Figure 4.1 illustrates a situation with three schemas, each containing one or more structured user-defined types (trust me—that's what they are), as well as two examples of SQL-paths. If the first SQL-path ("Normal SQL-path") is in effect and we try to create a typed table based on the movie type, the system would scan the schemas listed in the SQL-path in the order shown. Since a definition of the movie type is found in the first schema (Test_Schema), that definition would be used to create the typed table. On the other hand, if the second SQL-path ("Production SQL-path") were in effect, the definition of the movie type in Production_Schema would be used instead, because that schema is the first one listed in the SQL-path that contains a definition of the movie type.

In Example 4.1, you see how an SQL-path is specified for a particular schema. When a typed table is created in that schema, unless the SQL-path specified for that schema has been overridden in some manner, that SQL-path is used to find the specified structured type associated with the table.

Example 4.1 *Specifying an SQL-Path*

```
CREATE SCHEMA movie_db
  PATH movie_db, music_db, extra_routines

  CREATE TABLE OF movie ...
```

A similar policy applies to the resolution of invocations of ordinary functions. (However, as we'll see in this chapter, the special sort of functions called *methods* are always found in the same schema as the user-defined type with which they are closely associated, so the SQL-path is used to locate the type definition, from which the method can be located.)

When SQL encounters a function invocation, it searches the schemas in the SQL-path (in the order they appear in the SQL-path, of course) for a function with the required name and parameter list. (As we'll see in upcoming sections, procedures, functions, and methods are not always uniquely identified by their names in SQL, but by a combination of their names and their parameter lists.)

SQL metadata can continue to change long after SQL programs using that metadata have been compiled. In an environment this dynamic, it is quite possible that there may be many functions with the same name and parameter list (but no such duplication can occur within a single schema). If this should occur, the fact that schemas are searched in the order their names appear in the SQL-path means that a single user-defined type or routine is always unambiguously selected—the one in the schema appearing earlier in the SQL-path than any of the other competing functions. Later, in section 4.8, we'll see exactly how the SQL-path influences the selection of a specific function.

Whenever SQL expects a path-resolved name, you may choose to specify a name that includes an explicit schema name. In that case, the explicit schema name is used and the SQL-path is not used to locate the user-defined type or routine.

4.5 Procedures, Functions, and Methods

In SQL:1999, SQL-invoked routines fall into three principle classes: procedures, functions, and methods. Various implementations of SQL have long provided one or more of these classes of routine, and the distinctions among them in those implementations have not always been quite as clean as they are in the SQL standard. (A fairly detailed discussion of the treatment of SQL-invoked procedures and functions by various implementations can be found in another of my books.)[2]

As you'll learn in the following subsections, there are fundamental differences in the way SQL handles procedures and the way it handles functions, while functions and methods are much more closely related—in fact, methods are nothing more than special types of functions. To summarize the more important differences, I have prepared Table 4.1; after you've read the relevant subsections, you might wish to glance back to this table to review what you have learned about each type of SQL-invoked routine.

Table 4.1 *Relationship Between Procedures, Functions, and Methods*

Characteristic	*Procedures*	*Functions*	*Methods*
Invoked how?	CALL statement `CALL proc-name(args)`	Functional notation `func-name(args)`	Dot notation `site.method-name(args)`
Associated with specific type	No	No	Yes
Schema of residence	Any schema	Any schema	Schema of associated type
Routine resolution	Fully resolved at compilation time	Fully resolved at compilation time	Compilation resolves to set of candidate methods; final resolution at runtime
Input arguments	Yes	Yes	Yes; implicit argument of a static method is always a user-defined type instance
Output arguments	Yes (results can also be returned in dynamic result sets)	Only as return value of function	Only as return value of method

4.5.1 Procedures

A *procedure* is a subprogram that is executed in response to an explicit statement in the program on behalf of which it is used. That explicit statement is typically known as a *call statement,* and SQL, like many languages, uses the keyword "CALL" for this purpose. An SQL CALL statement causes an SQL-invoked procedure to be invoked. All information transferred from SQL code into an SQL-invoked procedure is passed through parameters of the procedure, as is all information—except for virtual tables returned in dynamic result sets—returned from

2 Jim Melton, *Understanding SQL's Stored Procedures: A Complete Guide to SQL/PSM* (San Francisco: Morgan Kaufmann Publishers, 1998).

the procedure to the SQL code. Throughout the remainder of this chapter, I use the word *procedure* to mean "SQL-invoked procedure." (The only other sort of procedure in SQL is the *externally-invoked procedures* that are used in SQL module language, described in Volume 1 of this book.)

SQL:1999's procedures are routines that do not return a value in any way other than through explicit parameters and dynamic result sets. By comparison, Java's closest analog is its `void` methods. Procedures are therefore permitted to have parameters that are used for output as well as parameters that are used for input (and, for that matter, parameters that are used for both).

While procedures' parameters can have structured types as their data types, there is no special treatment of this, either in terms of notation or in terms of the handling of the parameter list. (Of course, the locators and transform groups discussed in section 2.11.7, "User-Defined Type Locators," and section 2.11.8, "Transforms and Transform Groups," respectively, do provide forms of "special handling" of structured type values in procedures' parameters.) Consequently, procedures really don't affect the SQL object model very much and aren't very interesting in the context of structured types. They are, however, very useful for ordinary programming purposes, particularly for modularizing your code.

Procedure Definition

Procedures, being special cases of SQL-invoked routines, are defined with SQL's `<SQL-invoked routine>` syntax. Syntax 4.9 contains the complete syntax for defining all sorts of SQL-invoked routines, whereas I've captured just those parts relevant to procedures in Syntax 4.1.

Syntax 4.1 *Procedure Definition Syntax*

```
<SQL-invoked routine> ::=
    CREATE <SQL-invoked procedure>
  | ...

<SQL-invoked procedure> ::=
    PROCEDURE <schema qualified routine name>
      ( [ <SQL parameter declaration list> ] )
      [ <routine characteristic>... ]
      <routine body>

<schema qualified routine name> ::=
    3-part-name    (see Volume 1 of this book)

<SQL parameter declaration list> ::=
```

```
    <SQL parameter declaration>
      [ { <comma> <SQL parameter declaration> }... ]

<SQL parameter declaration> ::=
    [ <parameter mode> ] [ <SQL parameter name> ] <parameter type>

<parameter mode> ::=
    IN
  | OUT
  | INOUT

<SQL parameter name> ::= <identifier>

<parameter type> ::= <data type> [ AS LOCATOR ]

<routine characteristic> ::=
    LANGUAGE <language clause>
  | PARAMETER STYLE <parameter style>
  | SPECIFIC <specific name>
  | <deterministic characteristic>
  | <SQL-data access indication>
  | <dynamic result sets characteristic>

<language clause> ::=
    SQL
  | ADA | C | COBOL | FORTRAN | MUMPS | PASCAL | PLI
  | JAVA

<parameter style> ::=
    SQL
  | GENERAL
  | JAVA

<specific name> ::= 3-part-name    (see Volume 1 of this book)

<deterministic characteristic> ::=
    DETERMINISTIC
  | NOT DETERMINISTIC

<SQL-data access indication> ::=
    NO SQL
  | CONTAINS SQL
```

```
  | READS SQL DATA
  | MODIFIES SQL DATA

<dynamic result sets characteristic> ::=
    DYNAMIC RESULT SETS <maximum dynamic result sets>

<maximum dynamic result sets> ::= <unsigned integer>

<routine body> ::=
    <SQL routine body>
  | <external body reference>

<SQL routine body> ::= <SQL procedure statement>

<external body reference> ::=
    EXTERNAL [ NAME <external routine name> ]
    [ PARAMETER STYLE <parameter style > ]
    [ <transform group specification> ]
    [ <external security clause> ]

<external routine name> ::=
    <identifier>
  | <character string literal>

<external security clause> ::=
    EXTERNAL SECURITY DEFINER
  | EXTERNAL SECURITY INVOKER
  | EXTERNAL SECURITY IMPLEMENTATION DEFINED

<transform group specification> ::=
    TRANSFORM GROUP
      { <single group specification> | <multiple group specification> }

<single group specification> ::= <group name>

<multiple group specification> ::=
    <group specification> [ { <comma> <group specification> }... ]

<group specification> ::=
    <group name> FOR TYPE <user-defined type>
```

The syntax in Syntax 4.1 is long and might be intimidating at first glance, but it's actually fairly straightforward, so let me break it down into pieces.

You start with CREATE PROCEDURE, followed by the name (a 3-part schema-resolved name) by which you will invoke the procedure. The name must be followed by a pair of parentheses in which you may place one or more parameter declarations. Since a procedure might perform some activity that doesn't require specific input from your application (or return any data to your application), you are not required to define any parameters. Each parameter declaration must specify the data type of the parameter and may additionally specify the name of the parameter; parameters without names cannot be referenced by the code in an SQL routine, but might well be accessed by code in an external routine since the parameters are merely mapped to the parameters of the "real" procedure written in the external programming language. Parameter declarations may also specify whether the parameter is input only (IN), output only (OUT), or both (INOUT); if you do not specify the mode, then IN is assumed.

You are then allowed to specify one or more characteristics of the routine. Those were first discussed in section 2.7.3, "Methods: Definition and Invocation," but I summarize the information here to avoid the necessity of flipping pages too often. You may specify

- The name of the programming language in which the procedure is written; the default is LANGUAGE SQL.
- If the programming language is not SQL, then the style of parameter list used for the procedure (an SQL-style list, in which indicator parameters and SQLSTATE parameters are implicit, or a "general" style, in which all parameters, and arguments, are explicit); the default is PARAMETER STYLE SQL. (The third alternative, PARAMETER STYLE JAVA, is not discussed in this chapter.)
- Whether the procedure does not contain SQL statements (NO SQL), may contain SQL statements, but does not access the database (CONTAINS SQL), may retrieve data from the database, but may not update the database (READS SQL DATA), or is permitted to update the database (MODIFIES SQL DATA); the default is CONTAINS SQL.
- Whether the procedure is deterministic (that is, if it returns the same result in response to a specific set of argument values for a given state of the database) or not; the default is NOT DETERMINISTIC—naturally, the other possibility is DETERMINISTIC.
- The *specific name* of the procedure—that is, the name by which the procedure's definition can be modified and by which the procedure can be dropped, as distinguished from the routine's *invocable name* (the name used in a CALL statement).

- Whether or not the procedure returns dynamic result sets and, if so, how many it may return (dynamic result sets are discussed in Volume 1 of this book).

Finally, you specify the body of the routine. For SQL procedures, you actually specify the SQL statement that is executed when the procedure is called (if you need more than one statement, you use a BEGIN . . . END statement to encompass the other statements). For external procedures, the routine body may specify the name of the external routine (that is, the routine written in an ordinary programming language other than SQL) and may also (but not if you specified this in the routine's signature) specify that the parameter list must be in SQL's style or in the "general" style (or the Java style). Finally, the routine body can specify whether the external routine is invoked using the privileges assigned to the authorization identifier of the routine's definer, the privileges assigned to the authorization identifier that executes the CALL statement, or some implementation-defined set of privileges.

All of these characteristics are discussed in some detail in Volume 1 of this book (section 17.3, "SQL-Invoked Routines"), with one exception: Java routines. If the external routine is a Java routine, then the `<external routine name>` must be a character string literal whose structure is that defined in Syntax 4.2.

Syntax 4.2 *<external Java reference string> Syntax*

```
<external Java reference string> ::=
  <jar and class name> <period> <Java method name>
  [ <Java parameter declaration list> ]
```

In Example 4.2, I've illustrated the CREATE PROCEDURE statement by creating an external procedure, written in C, that can be invoked from SQL code with the apparent purpose of attempting to send e-mail to a specified recipient, with a specified subject, at a specified priority (the status of the attempt is returned as the value of the fourth parameter).

Example 4.2 *CREATE PROCEDURE*

```
CREATE PROCEDURE sendmail (
    IN   to     CHARACTER VARYING(32),
    IN   subj   CHARACTER VARYING(100),
    IN   prio   SMALLINT,
    OUT  status INTEGER )
  LANGUAGE C
  PARAMETER STYLE GENERAL
```

```
SPECIFIC sendmail_C
DETERMINISTIC
NO SQL
DYNAMIC RESULT SETS 0
EXTERNAL NAME '/usr/musicshop/bin/mailPackage/send'
  EXTERNAL SECURITY DEFINER
```

Procedure Invocation

You invoke an SQL-invoked procedure by using the SQL CALL statement, whose syntax is shown in Syntax 4.3.

Syntax 4.3 *<call statement> Syntax*

```
<call statement> ::= CALL <routine invocation>

<routine invocation> ::=
    <routine name> <SQL argument list>

<routine name> ::=
    [ <schema name> <period> ] <identifier>

<SQL argument list> ::=
    ( [ <SQL argument> [ { <comma> <SQL argument> }... ] ] )

<SQL argument> ::=
    <value expression>
  | <generalized expression>
  | <target specification>

<generalized expression> ::=
    <value expression> AS <user-defined type>
```

As you see in Syntax 4.3, the keyword CALL is followed by the name of the procedure you wish to invoke. You must supply a pair of parentheses, even if the procedure has no parameters. If you do supply arguments in the procedure invocation, then each input argument is either an ordinary SQL value expression whose data type corresponds to the data type of the corresponding parameter, or it's a `<generalized expression>`. A `<generalized expression>` forces SQL to treat the argument value as though it were actually a value of the specified type (which must be a supertype of the structured type of the corresponding parameter in the routine's declaration). Each output argument—even if that argument is also an input argument—must be a <target specification> (whose syntax is not given here, but appears in Volume 1 of this book) that identifies a site where you want the procedure to store the value returned in the corresponding parameter.

Example 4.3 demonstrates a CALL statement used to invoke the procedure defined in Example 4.2.

Example 4.3 *CALL*

```
CALL sendmail ( 'movie-customers@muvid.com',
                'Exciting sale for web customers only!',
                1,
                :mailStatus )
```

Complete details of invoking all types of routines, including procedures, appear in section 4.8, but I will mention here that the rules for procedure invocations for which there are multiple procedures with the same invocable name are rather simpler than the corresponding rules for functions and methods.

4.5.2 Functions

A *function* is a subprogram that is executed in response to function invocation syntax in the program on whose behalf it is used. Functions are routines that return a single datum as the "value" of a function invocation. In SQL:1999, functions are permitted only to have input parameters; they are not permitted to have output parameters or parameters that are used for both input and output. Functions can return data only as the value of the functions' invocations. For example, many languages include a built-in function that computes the square root of a number; the function is invoked with the number whose square root is desired, and the value of function invocation is that square root. Using that function, we would normally expect the value of the expression "`3*square_root(4)`" to be 6.

In Table 4.1, you saw some of the characteristics of functions compared with corresponding characteristics of procedures and methods.

Function Definition

Functions, like procedures, are special cases of SQL-invoked routines. Naturally, they are defined with SQL's <SQL-invoked routine> syntax detailed in Syntax 4.9. I have copied the parts of that syntax that are relevant to functions into Syntax

4.4. It's immediately obvious that Syntax 4.4 has a tremendous amount in common with Syntax 4.1, due to the fact that both define SQL-invoked routines.

Syntax 4.4 *Function Definition Syntax*

```
<SQL-invoked routine> ::=
    ...
  | CREATE <SQL-invoked function>

<SQL-invoked function> ::=
    FUNCTION <schema qualified routine name>
      ( [ <SQL parameter declaration list> ] )
      <returns clause>
      [ <routine characteristic>... ]
      [ <dispatch clause> ]
      <routine body>

<schema qualified routine name> ::=
    3-part-name    (see Volume 1 of this book)

<SQL parameter declaration list> ::=
    <SQL parameter declaration>
      [ { <comma> <SQL parameter declaration> }... ]

<SQL parameter declaration> ::=
    [ <parameter mode> ] [ <SQL parameter name> ] <parameter type>
    [ RESULT ]

<parameter mode> ::=
    IN
  | ...

<SQL parameter name> ::= <identifier>

<parameter type> ::= <data type> [ AS LOCATOR ]

<returns clause> ::= RETURNS <returns data type> [ <result cast> ]

<returns data type> ::= <data type> [ AS LOCATOR ]

<result cast> ::= CAST FROM <data type> [ AS LOCATOR ]
```

```
<routine characteristic> ::=
    <language clause>
  | PARAMETER STYLE <parameter style>
  | SPECIFIC <specific name>
  | <deterministic characteristic>
  | <SQL-data access indication>
  | <null-call clause>

<language clause> ::=
    SQL
  | ADA | C | COBOL | FORTRAN | MUMPS | PASCAL | PLI
  | JAVA

<parameter style> ::=
    SQL
  | GENERAL
  | JAVA

<specific name> ::= 3-part-name    (see Volume 1 of this book)

<deterministic characteristic> ::=
    DETERMINISTIC
  | NOT DETERMINISTIC

<SQL-data access indication> ::=
    NO SQL
  | CONTAINS SQL
  | READS SQL DATA
  | MODIFIES SQL DATA

<null-call clause> ::=
    RETURNS NULL ON NULL INPUT
  | CALLED ON NULL INPUT

<dispatch clause> ::= STATIC DISPATCH

<routine body> ::=
    <SQL routine body>
  | <external body reference>
```

```
<SQL routine body> ::= <SQL procedure statement>

<external body reference> ::=
    EXTERNAL [ NAME <external routine name> ]
    [ PARAMETER STYLE <parameter style > ]
    [ <external security clause> ]

<external routine name> ::=
    <identifier>
  | <character string literal>

<external security clause> ::=
    EXTERNAL SECURITY DEFINER
  | EXTERNAL SECURITY INVOKER
  | EXTERNAL SECURITY IMPLEMENTATION DEFINED
```

The syntax in Syntax 4.4 is as straightforward as the corresponding syntax for creating procedures. Creating a function requires a statement that starts with CREATE FUNCTION, followed by the 3-part schema-resolved name by which the function will be invoked. The name is followed by a pair of parentheses that may contain one or more parameter declarations; as with procedure definitions, the parentheses are required even if the function has no parameters. Parameter declarations for functions may specify the parameter mode IN, but that's the default and need not be specified. No other parameter mode (OUT or INOUT) is allowed, since functions cannot have parameters other than purely input parameters.

No more than a single parameter can be defined with the keyword RESULT. If you define a RESULT parameter, then the data type of that parameter must be the same structured user-defined type that is specified as the RETURNS type (see the next paragraph) of the function being defined. Functions with a RESULT parameter are called *type-preserving* functions, because they always return a value whose most specific type (that is, the actual runtime type) is the same as the most specific type of the RESULT parameter—not some subtype of that type. Mutator functions are always type-preserving functions, which is obviously necessary if they are to have the effect solely of changing the value of some attribute of a type instance. As you'll see in section 4.5.3, all methods are functions, so the notion of RESULT parameters and the concept of being type-preserving applies equally well to methods.

A function definition must always include a RETURNS clause that specifies the data type of the single value that is returned by the function. The RETURNS clause may also specify a CAST FROM clause that instructs the SQL environment to cast the value generated by the function itself into the data type specified in the RETURNS clause—particularly helpful when the function being declared is an external function.

Functions may be specified with one or more routine characteristics, first discussed in section 2.7.3, "Methods: Definition and Invocation." I reiterate the information here for convenience. You may specify

- The name of the programming language in which the function is written; the default is LANGUAGE SQL.
- If the programming language is not SQL, then the style of parameter list used for the function (an SQL-style list, in which indicator parameters and SQLSTATE parameters are implicit, or a "general" style, in which all parameters, and arguments, are explicit); the default is PARAMETER STYLE SQL. (Again, PARAMETER STYLE JAVA is supported, but not discussed in this chapter.)
- Whether the function does not contain SQL statements (NO SQL), may contain SQL statements, but does not access the database (CONTAINS SQL), may retrieve data from the database, but may not update the database (READS SQL DATA), or is permitted to update the database (MODIFIES SQL DATA); the default is CONTAINS SQL.
- Whether the function is deterministic (that is, if it returns the same result in response to a specific set of argument values for a given state of the database) or not; the default is NOT DETERMINISTIC, while the other possibility is DETERMINISTIC.
- Whether the function always returns the null value when any of its arguments is null and thus need not be called in that situation; the default is CALLED ON NULL INPUT, and the alternative is RETURNS NULL ON NULL INPUT.
- The *specific name* of the function—that is, the name by which the function's definition can be modified and by which the function can be dropped, as distinguished from the routine's *invocable name* (the name used in a function invocation).

There's one additional characteristic that you can specify: STATIC DISPATCH. If specified, it must follow all of the other characteristics in the function definition. (A future version of the SQL standard might add DYNAMIC DISPATCH as an alternative.) This clause, which is the default even if you don't code it explicitly, means that function invocations are fully resolved at compile time—without regard to subtypes of any arguments (see Chapter 2, "User-Defined Types," for information about subtypes). Note that, because SQL:1999 does not support dynamic dispatch for ordinary functions, this clause is redundant in function definitions.

Finally, you specify the body of the function. For SQL functions (those whose language clause specifies or defaults to SQL), you actually specify the SQL statement that is executed when the function is invoked (if you need more than one statement, you use a BEGIN . . . END statement to encompass the other statements). For external functions, the routine body may specify the name of the external routine (that is, the routine written in an ordinary programming language other than SQL) and may also choose to specify that the parameter list must be in SQL's style or in the "general" style (but only if you do not specify this information in the routine signature). Finally, the routine body can specify whether the external routine is executed using the privileges assigned to the authorization identifier of the routine's definer, the privileges assigned to the authorization identifier that executes the CALL statement, or some implementation-defined set of privileges. Again, these characteristics are discussed in some detail in Volume 1 of this book (section 17.3, "SQL-Invoked Routines").

During the course of the movie rental business, I may decide that it's important to easily discover whether there's a relationship between the length of a movie's title and the running time of the movie. In pursuit of this information, I first might want to know the ratio of title length (in characters, of course) to running time (in minutes).

Example 4.4 *CREATE FUNCTION*

```
CREATE FUNCTION ratio (
      IN       title_param      CHARACTER VARYING(100),
      IN       length_param     INTEGER )
    RETURNS REAL
    LANGUAGE SQL
    CONTAINS SQL
    RETURNS NULL ON NULL INPUT
    DETERMINISTIC
    STATIC DISPATCH
  RETURN CHAR_LENGTH(title_param)/length_param
```

Since, as you saw in Table 4.1, functions are not tightly bound to any associated structured type, this function could just as well have been defined in a schema other than the schema containing the `movie` type definition.

Function Invocation

By contrast with procedure invocation, there is no special SQL statement for invoking functions. Instead, functions are invoked using syntax that fits right into the syntax of expressions, as seen in Syntax 4.5.

Syntax 4.5 *Function Invocation Syntax*

```
<routine invocation> ::=
    <routine name> <SQL argument list>

<routine name> ::=
    [ <schema name> <period> ] <identifier>

<SQL argument list> ::=
    ( [ <SQL argument> [ { <comma> <SQL argument> }... ] ] )

<SQL argument> ::=
    <value expression>
  | <generalized expression>
  | <target specification>

<generalized expression> ::=
    <value expression> AS <user-defined type>
```

There's a remarkable similarity between this syntax and that shown in Syntax 4.3; the only bit missing is the CALL statement itself. Because a function invocation is a valid value expression all by itself, you can use a function invocation at any place in your SQL code where a value expression (of the appropriate type, of course) can be used. For example, the query expression in Example 4.5 contains a function invocation as part of an expression in a predicate contained in the WHERE clause.

Example 4.5 *Invoking a Function*

```
SELECT m.title
FROM movie_table m
WHERE ratio ( m.title, m.runs ) > 0.5
```

In that example, I've requested retrieval of the titles of each movie whose title has more than half as many characters as the film has minutes of length. A film such as *Dr. Strangelove,* whose full title is *Dr. Strangelove, or How I Learned to Stop Worrying and Love the Bomb,* would be identified by that query expression; its title is 68 characters in length, while the movie runs for 93 minutes, and 68/93 is 0.73 (and thus greater than 0.5).

4.5.3 Methods

In SQL:1999, a *method* is a special sort of function and, as such, is invoked using a variation of function invocation syntax. Methods and (ordinary) functions have much in common, but there are important differences between them, both in their definitions and in their uses. Some of the most important differences are

- As Table 4.1 implies, and I've said elsewhere in this volume, every method is closely associated with a single user-defined type.
- Each method must be defined in the same schema as its closely associated UDT.
- Every method associated with a UDT must be identified in that UDT's definition, and the method's definition must specify that UDT.
- The parameter list of instance and constructor methods (but not static methods) always includes one additional implicit parameter (a parameter that is not defined explicitly); that parameter, often called the *SELF parameter,* is effectively the first parameter in the list, and its data type is always the associated user-defined type.
- Invocations of instance and constructor methods also include one additional implicit argument (the *SELF argument*) that is not included in the parenthesized list of arguments; the value of that argument is provided using "dot notation."

There are three types of methods in SQL:1999. Instance methods are those that operate on specific instances of a user-defined type, and constructor methods give initial values to a newly created instance of a user-defined type. Both instance methods and constructor methods have the SELF parameter. Static methods (analogous to "class methods" in some object-oriented programming languages) are methods that are associated with a specific UDT, but that do not operate on specific instances of the type that are provided as the value of a distinguished parameter.

Method Definition

Methods in SQL are defined in two ways and in two places—and both are required. (That is, both are required for all current languages in which SQL-invoked methods can be written except Java. A future version of the SQL standard might relax this requirement for non-Java languages.) First, every method is declared as part of the definition of its associated user-defined type. Another way to say this requirement is that the method *signature* is specified as part of the user-defined type definition. (To be complete, that's true of methods known at the time the structured type is defined; in addition, you can use the ALTER TYPE statement to add the signatures of additional methods to the type definition later on, as well as to remove methods—that is, their signatures—from type definitions. ALTER TYPE does not apply to structured types defined using Java.) It is because of this relationship (between the type definition that lists all its associated methods and the method definitions that identify the associated type) that the "association" between type and method comes into existence.

The second way, and place, in which methods are defined is independent of user-defined type definitions, although the end result must be that the method resides in the same schema as its associated type. This second way is the actual method declaration, including its *implementation,* either the SQL code comprising the method or the appropriate identification (e.g., file specification or URL) of some code written in a different programming language.

The syntax used to declare a method signature in a UDT definition can be seen in Syntax 2.10, "<method specification list> Syntax," in Chapter 2, "User-Defined Types." I won't repeat it here, since it is more relevant to user-defined types than to routine definitions.

The BNF for method definition is found in Syntax 4.6.

Syntax 4.6 *Method Definition Syntax*

```
<SQL-invoked routine> ::=
      ...
    | CREATE <method specification designator>

<method specification designator> ::=
      [ INSTANCE | STATIC | CONSTRUCTOR ] METHOD <method name>
        ( <SQL parameter declaration list> )
      [ <returns clause> ]
      FOR <user-defined type>
    <routine body>
```

```
<SQL parameter declaration list> ::=
    [ <SQL parameter declaration>
      [ { <comma> <SQL parameter declaration> }... ]

<SQL parameter declaration> ::=
    [ <parameter mode> ] [ <SQL parameter name> ] <parameter type>
    [ RESULT ]

<parameter mode> ::=
    IN
  | ...

<SQL parameter name> ::= <identifier>

<parameter type> ::= <data type> [ AS LOCATOR ]

<returns clause> ::= RETURNS <returns data type> [ <result cast> ]

<returns data type> ::= <data type> [ AS LOCATOR ]

<result cast> ::= CAST FROM <data type> [ AS LOCATOR ]

<routine body> ::=
    <SQL routine body>
  | <external body reference>

<SQL routine body> ::= <SQL procedure statement>

<external body reference> ::=
    EXTERNAL [ NAME <external routine name> ]
    [ PARAMETER STYLE <parameter style > ]
    [ <external security clause> ]

<external routine name> ::=
    <identifier>
  | <character string literal>

<external security clause> ::=
    EXTERNAL SECURITY DEFINER
  | EXTERNAL SECURITY INVOKER
  | EXTERNAL SECURITY IMPLEMENTATION DEFINED
```

You don't have to look too hard to see a couple of differences between this syntax and that for function definition seen in Syntax 4.4. Perhaps the most obvious is the absence of the ability to specify `<routine characteristics>` in method definitions. As you read in Chapter 2, "User-Defined Types," the `<routine characteristics>` of a method are specified as part of the method's signature in the definition of the associated UDT and *not* in the actual method definition.

The other difference is the specification of a method as STATIC, INSTANCE, or CONSTRUCTOR, which are characteristics that do not apply to ordinary functions. INSTANCE methods are methods that operate on (obviously) a specific instance of the associated user-defined type. For example, a method that returns the running time of a movie as an INTERVAL value necessarily operates on a particular instance of the `movie` type.

By contrast, STATIC methods are those that do not manipulate instances of the associated UDT, but might be visualized as being defined for the type itself. Static methods are allowed to have parameters whose data type is the method's associated UDT, but they are not invoked by providing an instance of the type as an implicit (SELF) parameter—in fact, static methods do not have that implicit parameter at all.

CONSTRUCTOR methods, contrary to the implications of the name, are methods used to initialize a newly constructed instance of the associated type. You will recall from section 2.10.3, "Constructors and the NEW Expression," that constructor functions create new, default values of structured types, and constructor methods can be used to assign values to the attributes of those default structured type instances. A constructor method may take no arguments at all, or it can be defined to take as many arguments as your application requires. It is an ordinary instance method and is always used in conjunction with a constructor function. Constructor methods are invoked with the NEW statement.

The syntax in Syntax 4.6 is no less straightforward than the corresponding syntax for creating procedures and ordinary functions. Creating a method requires one of CREATE INSTANCE METHOD (which is implied if you specify CREATE METHOD by itself), CREATE STATIC METHOD, or CREATE CONSTRUCTOR METHOD, followed by the 3-part schema-resolved name by which the method will be invoked. The name is followed by a pair of parentheses that may contain zero or more parameter declarations; as with procedure and function definitions, the parentheses are required even if the method takes no parameters. Parameter declarations for methods, like those for functions, may specify the parameter mode IN, which is the default if not specified; however, no other parameter mode (OUT or INOUT) is allowed, since methods cannot have parameters other than purely input parameters.

A method definition may include a RETURNS clause to specify the data type of the value returned by the method. If the RETURNS clause is present, then the type that is specified must be compatible with the type specified in the RETURNS clause in the corresponding method signature included in the associated structured type definition. If you don't use a RETURNS clause, then the type specified in that method signature is assumed. A CAST FROM clause (instructing the SQL environment to cast the value generated by the function itself into the data type specified in the RETURNS clause) is optional. As with ordinary functions, this clause is particularly helpful when the method being declared is an external method.

Unlike ordinary functions, you do not specify STATIC DISPATCH for methods. All instance methods in SQL:1999 are, by definition, dynamically dispatched (always on the implicit SELF parameter, as we'll see shortly). Static methods are—you guessed it—always statically dispatched, because they don't have that implicit parameter. Unfortunately, SQL does not have keywords, such as DYNAMIC DISPATCH, to explicitly state this characteristic of methods.

As with functions and procedures, you must also specify the body of the function. For SQL methods (those written in SQL), you actually specify the SQL statement that is executed when the method is invoked (if you need more than one statement, you use a BEGIN . . . END statement to encompass the other statements). For external methods, the routine body may specify the name of the external routine (that is, the routine written in an ordinary programming language other than SQL) and may also specify that the parameter list must be in SQL's style or in the "general" style (but only if you do not provide this information in the routine signature). Finally, the routine body can specify whether the external routine is executed using the privileges assigned to the authorization identifier of the routine's definer, the privileges assigned to the authorization identifier that executes the CALL statement, or some implementation-defined set of privileges.

To illustrate this, consider the following structured type definition (our old friend, the `movie` type):

Example 4.6 *Structured Type Definition*

```
CREATE TYPE movie (
  title            CHARACTER VARYING (100),
  description      CHARACTER VARYING (500),
  runs             INTEGER )
  NOT FINAL
```

This very simple structured type allows us to capture certain critical information about movies: the name of the movie, a description of it, and the length in minutes. But, suppose I really wanted to retrieve the length as an SQL INTERVAL type instead of as an INTEGER? I can use an instance method to perform this calculation, and I include its signature in the type definition, as seen in Example 4.7.

Example 4.7 *Structured Type Definition with Method Signature*

```
CREATE TYPE movie (
  title           CHARACTER VARYING (100),
  description     CHARACTER VARYING (500),
  runs            INTEGER )
  NOT FINAL
  METHOD length_interval ( )
    RETURNS INTERVAL HOUR(2) TO MINUTE
```

The last two lines comprise the *signature* of my new method (see Chapter 2, "User-Defined Types," for more information). It takes no parameters beyond the implicit SELF parameter mentioned earlier, and it returns an SQL INTERVAL. The actual method *definition* appears in Example 4.8.

Example 4.8 *Method Definition Associated with Method Signature*

```
CREATE INSTANCE METHOD length_interval ( )
    RETURNS INTERVAL HOUR(2) TO MINUTE
    FOR movie
  /* Allow for movies as long as 99 hours and 59 minutes */

  RETURN CAST ( CAST ( SELF.runs AS INTERVAL MINUTE(4) )
         AS INTERVAL HOUR(2) TO MINUTE )
```

Of course, you'll notice right away that the relationship is bidirectional: the type definition identifies the method by name, and the method definition identifies the name of the associated type.

Now, let's examine this example a little more closely. Neither the signature nor the actual definition of the method specifies any parameters. However, every method *always* has at least the implicit parameter, whose data type is the associated type. Since that parameter is never absent and is always implicit, since its data type is always known very precisely, and since it must (by definition) always be "the" instance of that type for which the method was invoked, it is not explicitly declared. You see from the body (that is, the implementation) of the method above that we use the keyword "SELF" within the method to identify the instance for which the method is invoked.

The *unaugmented parameter list* of this method, therefore, has no parameters. But SQL builds an *augmented parameter list* for the method, which naturally has to be used by the underlying function invocation mechanisms on any hardware/software platform. (See section 4.6.5 for details about augmented and unaugmented parameter lists.) That augmented parameter list has one parameter. If we were allowed (but we're not!) to specify that implicit parameter explicitly, the method declaration might look something like this:

```
CREATE INSTANCE METHOD length_interval ( SELF movie ) ...
```

If a method has parameters other than the implicit SELF parameter, there are a few rules that have to be satisfied. Most importantly, the data type of the parameter declared in the method signature must be compatible with the data type of the parameter declared in the method definition. ("Compatible" means that the data types are essentially the same, even when considering things like length or precision.) The same goes for the data type specified as the RETURNS data type, by the way! Furthermore, if any parameter declaration in the method signature is given a name, then its corresponding parameter declaration must have the same name (and vice versa).

Method signatures—but not method definitions—can also contain a number of optional clauses that specify additional information about the method. The method definitions themselves are simply assigned the same characteristics that were specified with their corresponding signatures.

Method Invocation

Superficially, the syntax for method invocation is very similar to the syntax for function invocation. However, there are important, although sometimes subtle, differences, so it is most definitely worth spending additional time on method invocations. Syntax 4.7 contains the syntax for method invocation. Note that there are three different forms of method invocations. The first sort, simply called `<method invocation>`, is used to invoke instance methods when a site containing an instance of the associated type is used. The second, called `<method reference>`, is used to invoke instance methods when you have a REF value that identifies an instance of the type. The third form, `<static method invocation>`, is used to invoke static methods.

Syntax 4.7 *Method Invocation Syntax*

```
<method invocation> ::=
    <direct invocation>
  | <generalized invocation>
```

```
<direct invocation> ::=
    <value expression primary> <period>
      <method name> [ <SQL argument list> ]

<generalized invocation> ::=
    ( <value expression primary> AS <data type> ) <period>
        <method name> [ <SQL argument list> ]

<method reference> ::=
    <value expression primary> <right arrow>
      <method name> [ <SQL argument list> ]

<static method invocation> ::=
    <user-defined type> <double colon>
      <method name> [ <SQL argument list> ]

<SQL argument list> ::=
    ( [ <SQL argument> [ { <comma> <SQL argument> }... ] ] )

<SQL argument> ::=
    <value expression>
  | <generalized expression>
  | <target specification>

<generalized expression> ::=
    <value expression> AS <user-defined type>

<right arrow> ::= ->

<double colon> ::= ::
```

In Syntax 4.7, you will find three approaches to invoking methods in SQL:1999. The first, identified as `<method invocation>`, uses SQL's familiar dot notation. The `<value expression primary>` in both alternatives of `<method invocation>` is an expression whose data type (specifically, its declared type, as discussed in Chapter 2, "User-Defined Types") is some UDT, and `<method name>` identifies a method associated with that UDT.

You will recall from Chapter 2, "User-Defined Types," that all attributes of a structured type are encapsulated and that the system automatically provides two methods (the observer function and the mutator function) that are implicitly invoked whenever you reference an attribute of that type. When you retrieve the value of an attribute, the observer method is implicitly invoked and you normally do not provide the empty parentheses following the attribute (and method) name; you are, however, permitted to do so if you wish.

The value (at execution time, of course) of the <value expression primary> must be a value of the appropriate type, but it does not have to be exactly the declared type of that value expression—its most specific type might be some subtype of the declared type. Therefore, if I invoke the runs method (corresponding to the runs attribute) of the movie type on some value whose most specific type is dvd (a subtype of movie), there is no need for a syntax error or a runtime error.

There may be situations, however, when I have a site (such as an SQL variable or a column) whose declared type is dvd, but my application semantics require that I invoke a method that is originally defined in the movie type and overridden in the dvd type. That is, for application reasons, I want to execute the movie version of the method instead of the dvd version. The solution to this dilemma is found in the second alternative of <method invocation> in Syntax 4.7. By specifying "(movie_var AS movie).length_interval()," I can force the system to act as though the dvd value found in the SQL variable movie_var is a movie instance for the purposes of invoking the length_interval method.

The second approach is seen in Syntax 4.7 as <method reference>. In that approach, the declared type of the <value expression primary> must be a REF type that references instances of some structured type, and those instances must be rows in a typed table associated with that type. At runtime, the value of the <value expression primary> is treated as a sort of pointer that can be followed to access a row of the referenced type, and the specified method is applied to the instance of that type found in that row.

The third approach in Syntax 4.7 is used to invoke static methods of UDTs. Instead of specifying a value (as the other two approaches do in their <value expression primary>s), static methods are invoked by qualifying the name of the method with the name of the associated UDT. In addition, a new syntactic construct, the double colon (::), is used to separate the qualifier from the method name. (The double colon was chosen instead of a period so you don't have to worry so much about the names of your SQL variables, columns, and so forth clashing with the names of structured types.)

Example 4.9 *Invoking Methods*

```
movie_col . runs

( movie_col AS movie ) . length_interval()

movie :: longest ( column1, column2 )
```

The third example in Example 4.9 depends on the existence of a static method named `longest` that takes two arguments. We may infer that each of the arguments is of the `movie` type and that the method returns a value that indicates which of the two specified movies has the longest running time.

The NEW Expression

One possibly unexpected aspect of invoking constructor methods is that they are typically invoked only through the use of SQL's NEW expression. (You may often see this called a *NEW statement*—I sometimes use that terminology myself—but it is actually an expression whose data type is the specified structured type.)

Syntax 4.8 *<new specification> Syntax*

```
NEW <routine invocation>
```

The `<new specification>` is nothing more than a convenient syntactic shorthand for a `<routine invocation>` of a constructor function coupled with a `<method invocation>` of a constructor method. Therefore, I can construct a new instance of the `movie` type by writing the expression in Example 4.10.

Example 4.10 *Creating a New movie Instance*

```
NEW movie ( 'Animal House',
            'At a 1962 college...'
            109 )
```

That NEW expression has the same effect as the `<routine invocation>` in Example 4.11, which SQL:1999 forbids us from writing directly. In SQL:1999, a constructor function cannot be invoked directly but can only be implicitly invoked through the use of the NEW expression. Still, examining the equivalent, though invalid, explicit invocation is helpful in understanding how the NEW expression does its job.

Example 4.11 *Syntactic Equivalent Creation of a New movie Instance*

```
movie().movie('Animal House',
              'At a 1962 college...'
              109 )
```

Example 4.11 might seem a bit confusing upon first encountering it, so it's worth decomposing. The first expression, `movie()`, is a function invocation of the constructor function for the `movie` type. The constructor function for a type always has the same name as the type itself and it always has no parameters. As you will recall from Chapter 2, "User-Defined Types," the constructor function returns an instance of its associated type in which each attribute has its default value. The second expression (the `movie` method invocation with the three arguments) is an invocation of a constructor method to populate the new `movie` instance created by the first expression. Constructor methods are instance methods, so they always operate on an instance of the associated type. I should point out that the constructor function and the constructor method (or methods—you may define any number of constructor methods that are distinguished by the number and declared types of parameters) will have the same name, but the constructor function is not overloaded (although the constructor methods may be). As I said earlier, it seems unfortunate that SQL:1999 chose the keyword CONSTRUCTOR to identify constructor methods that might better be considered initializer methods; this choice adds to the confusion, while the use of a keyword such as INITIALIZER might have been better.

4.5.4 Complete Syntax to Define SQL-Invoked Routines

In this section, I have brought together the syntax components found in Syntax 4.1, Syntax 4.4, and Syntax 4.6 so you can see the entire syntax used to define `<SQL-invoked routine>`s in one place. Some of these items (`<transform group specification>`, for example) are covered in Chapter 2, "User-Defined Types," and Chapter 3, "Typed Tables."

Syntax 4.9 *<SQL-invoked routine> Syntax*

```
<SQL-invoked routine> ::=
    CREATE <SQL-invoked procedure>
  | CREATE <SQL-invoked function>
  | CREATE <SQL-invoked method>

<SQL-invoked procedure> ::=
    PROCEDURE <schema qualified routine name>
      ( [ <SQL parameter declaration list> ] )
      [ <routine characteristic>... ]
      <routine body>
```

```
<SQL-invoked function> ::=
    FUNCTION <schema qualified routine name>
      ( [ <SQL parameter declaration list> ] )
      <returns clause>
      [ <routine characteristic>... ]
      [ <dispatch clause> ]
      <routine body>

<SQL-invoked method> ::=
    [ INSTANCE | STATIC | CONSTRUCTOR ] <method name>
    ( [ <SQL parameter declaration list> ] )
    [ <returns clause> ]
    FOR <user-defined type>
    <routine body>

<schema qualified routine name> ::=
    3-part-name
(see Volume 1 of this book)

<SQL parameter declaration list> ::=
    <SQL parameter declaration>
      [ { <comma> <SQL parameter declaration> }... ]

<SQL parameter declaration> ::=
    [ <parameter mode> ] [ <SQL parameter name> ] <parameter type>
    [ RESULT ]

<parameter mode> ::=
    IN
  | OUT
  | INOUT

<SQL parameter name> ::= <identifier>

<parameter type> ::= <data type> [ AS LOCATOR ]

<returns clause> ::= RETURNS <returns data type> [ <result cast> ]

<returns data type> ::= <data type> [ AS LOCATOR ]
```

```
<result cast> ::= CAST FROM <data type> [ AS LOCATOR ]

<routine characteristic> ::=
    <language clause>
  | PARAMETER STYLE <parameter style>
  | SPECIFIC <specific name>
  | <deterministic characteristic>
  | <SQL-data access indication>
  | <null-call clause>
  | <dynamic result sets characteristic>

<language clause> ::=
    SQL
  | ADA | C | COBOL | FORTRAN | MUMPS | PASCAL | PLI
  | JAVA

<parameter style> ::=
    SQL
  | GENERAL
  | JAVA

<specific name> ::= 3-part-name    (see Volume 1 of this book)

<deterministic characteristic> ::=
    DETERMINISTIC
  | NOT DETERMINISTIC

<SQL-data access indication> ::=
    NO SQL
  | CONTAINS SQL
  | READS SQL DATA
  | MODIFIES SQL DATA

<null-call clause> ::=
    RETURNS NULL ON NULL INPUT
  | CALLED ON NULL INPUT

<dynamic result sets characteristic> ::=
    DYNAMIC RESULT SETS <maximum dynamic result sets>
```

```
<maximum dynamic result sets> ::= <unsigned integer>

<dispatch clause> ::= STATIC DISPATCH

<routine body> ::=
    <SQL routine body>
  | <external body reference>

<SQL routine body> ::= <SQL procedure statement>

<external body reference> ::=
    EXTERNAL [ NAME <external routine name> ]
    [ PARAMETER STYLE <parameter style > ]
    [ <transform group specification> ]
    [ <external security clause> ]

<external routine name> ::=
    <identifier>
  | <character string literal>

<transform group specification> ::=
    TRANSFORM GROUP
      { <single group specification> | <multiple group specification> }

<single group specification> ::= <group name>

<multiple group specification> ::=
    <group specification> [ { <comma> <group specification> }... ]

<group specification> ::=
    <group name> FOR TYPE <user-defined type>

<external security clause> ::=
    EXTERNAL SECURITY DEFINER
  | EXTERNAL SECURITY INVOKER
  | EXTERNAL SECURITY IMPLEMENTATION DEFINED

<external Java reference string> ::=
  <jar and class name> <period> <Java method name>
  [ <Java parameter declaration list> ]
```

4.6 Routine Invocation—In Brief

Routine invocation involves a number of steps. In very broad terms, you can view it as involving two phases: syntax analysis and runtime execution. In many computer languages, both phrases are very simple because all routines that can be invoked have very precise names and locations. The algorithms get more complex in object-oriented languages, and SQL:1999 is no exception. The two factors that contribute the most to this complication are (1) routine *overloading* and (2) the availability of a type hierarchy that allows routine *overriding*. Those topics are discussed in greater detail in section 4.7, so I'll content myself with these two brief definitions for the purposes of this section:

- *Overloading:* The ability to define multiple routines with the same (invocable) name, but with different numbers of parameters and/or different declared data types of the parameters, then to choose among them based on the number of arguments in a routine invocation and on the particular declared data types of those arguments.
- *Overriding:* The ability to define multiple routines with the same (invocable) name, with the same numbers of parameters or different numbers of parameters, and with different declared data types of one or more parameters, choosing among them based on the number of arguments, the declared data types of arguments, and the most specific type of one or more argument values.

In SQL:1999, overriding applies only to methods, and then only based on the runtime value of the implicit (SELF) argument. By contrast, overloading applies to ordinary functions (based on all arguments) and to methods (based on arguments other than the implicit argument).

In this section, you have the opportunity to look at SQL:1999's routine invocation from the 10,000-meter level; the detailed algorithm is found in section 4.8.

4.6.1 Procedure Invocation Summary

In SQL:1999, as you learned in section 4.5.1, SQL-invoked procedures are invoked only by an SQL CALL statement, they have no optional parameters, and parameters can be used to transfer data to the procedure, returned from the procedure, or both. Furthermore, procedures are not closely associated with any specific user-defined type, although the data types of their parameters can be user-defined types as well as built-in types.

SQL-invoked procedures are never involved in routine invocations that involve overriding. They can be overloaded, but only on the number of parameters and not on the particular data types of parameters. For example, you can create two procedures whose signatures are `transmit(INTEGER)` and `transmit(INTEGER, REAL)`, since their signatures declare a different number of parameters. SQL:1999 prohibits defining two procedures whose signatures are `transmit(INTEGER)` and `transmit(REAL)`, because they have the same number of parameters—even though the declared data types of the parameters are different. The reason for this limitation is quite obscure and arises from the principle of substitution in which a site (including a parameter) whose data type is some structured type must be able to hold an instance of any subtype of that type, but not an instance of a supertype of that type.

This characteristic means that it is not feasible to define, say, a number of specialized `print` procedures, each printing instances of different structured types in customized formats. (Well, this could be done by having a different number of parameters declared for each variant of the `print` procedure, but that's not usually very practical.)

Here's a simplified version of SQL:1999's routine invocation algorithm as it applies to procedures. Each of the first four steps applies to "compile time," or "syntax evaluation time," because they can typically be evaluated statically, knowing only the source text of the SQL statements and not knowing the values of any data being processed. (Of course, in an SQL environment, new privileges can be granted or existing privileges revoked, new procedures can be defined, and so forth, so SQL systems must ensure that all syntax checks remain valid at execution time.)

- First, all routines of the particular invocable name are identified. All routines contained in schemas that are not part of the current SQL-path are eliminated from consideration.
- All of the remaining routines that are ordinary functions or methods are eliminated.
- Then, all remaining routines—which are procedures—for which the invoker does not have EXECUTE privilege are eliminated (see section 4.9).
- All procedures whose number of parameters is not equal to the number of arguments in the CALL statement are eliminated.
- If there are two or more procedures remaining after all this elimination, then the algorithm selects the one contained in the schema that appears earlier in the SQL-path than any other schema containing a remaining procedure. If there are no procedures remaining, then a syntax error is raised.

The last step must be performed at runtime, because it depends on the specific values being processed by the routine invocation.

- Finally, if a procedure has been selected, the argument values are converted to the parameter data types as required and the code of the procedure is actually executed with those parameter values.

Example 4.12 illustrates the creation of two procedures (adapted from Example 4.2) with the same (invocable) name and shows how they can be invoked unambiguously.

Example 4.12 *Creating and Invoking Procedures*

```
CREATE PROCEDURE sendmail (
    IN   to     CHARACTER VARYING(32),
    IN   subj   CHARACTER VARYING(100),
    IN   prio   SMALLINT,
    OUT  status INTEGER )
  LANGUAGE C
  PARAMETER STYLE GENERAL
  SPECIFIC sendmail_C
  DETERMINISTIC
  NO SQL
  DYNAMIC RESULT SETS 0
  EXTERNAL NAME '/usr/musicshop/bin/mailPackage/send1'
    EXTERNAL SECURITY DEFINER

CREATE PROCEDURE sendmail (
    IN   to     CHARACTER VARYING(32),
    IN   subj   CHARACTER VARYING(100),
    OUT  status INTEGER )
  LANGUAGE C
  SPECIFIC sendmail_C
  DETERMINISTIC
  NO SQL
  DYNAMIC RESULT SETS 0
  EXTERNAL NAME '/usr/musicshop/bin/mailPackage/send2'
    PARAMETER STYLE GENERAL
    EXTERNAL SECURITY DEFINER
```

```
CALL sendmail ( 'movie-customers@muvid.com',
                'Exciting sale for web customers only!',
                1,
                :mailStatus )

CALL sendmail ( 'movie-customers@muvid.com',
                'Exciting sale for web customers only!',
                :mailStatus )
```

The two procedures differ in the number of parameters and in the particular external function that provides their implementations. Otherwise, their definitions are identical. (We might guess that some default priority is used by the second procedure.) The two procedure CALLs are unambiguous because the number of arguments differs in the two statements.

4.6.2 Function Invocation Summary

Function invocations are rather more complex than procedure invocations. There are several factors that contribute to the increased complication, and the most important of these is the existence of routine overloading based on parameter and argument declared types.

When there are multiple functions with the same name, SQL uses several criteria to choose the particular function to execute in response to a specific function invocation. Here's the simplified version of the function invocation algorithm. As with the procedure invocation algorithm outlined in section 4.6.1, the first steps can be performed statically at syntax analysis time:

- First, all routines of the particular invocable name are identified. All routines contained in schemas that are not part of the current SQL-path are eliminated from consideration.
- All of the remaining routines that are procedures or methods are eliminated.
- Then, all remaining routines, which are ordinary functions, for which the invoker does not have EXECUTE privilege are eliminated (see section 4.9).
- All functions whose number of parameters is not equal to the number of arguments in the function invocation are eliminated.
- For every remaining function, the data type of each parameter is checked against the data type of the corresponding argument; if some parameter's

data type is not in the type precedence list (see section 4.6.6) of the argument's data type, then the function is eliminated.

- If there are two or more functions remaining after all this elimination, then the algorithm selects the one contained in the schema that appears earlier in the SQL-path than any other schema containing some other remaining function. If there are no functions remaining, then a syntax error is raised.

The final step can be performed only at runtime when the argument values are known.

- If a function has been selected, then at runtime the argument values are converted to the parameter data types as required and the code of the function is actually executed with those parameter values.

In Example 4.4, I defined a function named `ratio` that allows me to perform a specific type of analysis on my data. In Example 4.13, you can see how I can invoke that function (assuming, of course, that there is an ordinary SQL table, such as the one defined in Example 4.14, named `movie_table` that has a column named `movie_info` whose type is `movie`).

Example 4.13 *Invoking a Function*

```
SELECT   mt.movie_info.title, mt.movie_info.length,
         ratio(movie_info.title, movie_info.length)
FROM     movie_table AS mt
WHERE    mt.movie_info.title = 'Titanic'
```

Note particularly that I used *functional notation* when we invoked the `ratio` function; by contrast, I used *dot notation* when we invoked the `title` and `length` observer methods.

4.6.3 Instance Method Invocation Summary

A method invocation is, naturally, the mechanism by which a method is called, or invoked. While method definitions (and signatures) have *parameters*, method invocations have *arguments*. The number of arguments in a method invocation must be equal to the number of parameters in the definition of the method, and the data type of each argument must be compatible with the data type of its corresponding parameter (or there must be a conversion from the data type of the argument to the data type of the parameter that SQL can perform without the aid of a `CAST` expression).

Method invocation differs from invocation of ordinary functions in a couple of important ways. First, methods are not only capable of overloading, they are capable of overriding based on the most specific (runtime) type of the implicit argument corresponding to the implicit SELF parameter. Second, the SQL-path is not used for method resolution, since all methods share a schema with the user-defined type with which they are closely associated. Here's the simplified version of SQL:1999's method resolution algorithm:

- First, all routines of the particular invocable name are identified.
- All of the remaining routines that are procedures or ordinary functions are eliminated.
- Then, all remaining routines, which are methods, for which the invoker does not have EXECUTE privilege are eliminated (see section 4.9).
- Every method that is not associated with the declared type of the implicit argument corresponding to the implicit SELF parameter or with some sub-type of that declared type is eliminated.
- All methods whose number of parameters is not equal to the number of arguments in the method invocation are eliminated.
- For every remaining method, the data type of each parameter is checked against the data type of the corresponding argument; if some parameter's data type is not in the type precedence list (see section 4.6.6) of the argument's data type, then the method is eliminated.
- If there are no methods remaining in the collection, then the method invocation results in a syntax error.

That ends the processing of method invocations until the invocation is executed at runtime. At that time, the algorithm continues as follows:

- If the most specific type of the actual runtime value of the implicit argument to the method invocation has a type definition that includes one of the methods remaining in the collection, then that method is chosen for execution.
- If the most specific type of the actual runtime value of the implicit argument to the method invocation has a type definition that does not include one of the methods remaining in the collection, then the method chosen

for execution is the method in the collection whose associated type is the "nearest" supertype of all supertypes having such methods.

- The argument values are converted to the parameter data types as required, and the code of the function is actually executed with those parameter values.

I emphasize that this is a naive look at method invocation. The complete algorithm, which is considerably more complex, is discussed in section 4.8.

Let's set up a method invocation example. First, assume that I've defined the `movie` type in Example 4.7, including the `length_interval` method from Example 4.8. Next, I define a table that has a column whose data type is `movie`, as in Example 4.14.

Example 4.14 *`movie_table` Definition*

```
CREATE TABLE movie_table (
    stock_number          CHARACTER(8),
    movie_info            movie,
    rental_quantity       INTEGER,
    rental_cost           DECIMAL(5,2) )
```

If I want to retrieve the length, in hours and minutes, of a particular film, I might write an SQL statement like the one in Example 4.15.

Example 4.15 *Retrieving from `movie_table`*

```
SELECT   mt.movie_info.length_interval
FROM     movie_table AS mt
WHERE    mt.movie_info.title = 'The Matrix'
```

In this example, I use dot notation, as required, to reference the `title` attribute (or, equivalently, to invoke the `title` observer function) in the WHERE clause, and SQL:1999 requires that we use dot notation to invoke the `length_interval` method.

Note that the `length_interval` method invocation doesn't even bother with the parentheses! If the only argument to a method invocation is the implicit argument—corresponding to the implicit SELF parameter—then you aren't permitted to code an argument and you don't have to code the parentheses surrounding that nonexistent implicit argument. However, if you prefer to code the empty parentheses, you're allowed to do so, as Example 4.16 illustrates.

Example 4.16 *Using Empty Argument Lists*

```
SELECT   mt.movie_info.length_interval()
FROM     movie_table AS mt
WHERE    mt.movie_info.title = 'The Matrix'
```

4.6.4 Effects of Null Parameters

Two variants of SQL-invoked routine, functions and methods, can specify a <routine characteristic> that indicates whether or not the routine is executed when it is invoked with one or more arguments that are null values. Most (but not all) of SQL's built-in functions behave as though they had been declared RETURNS NULL ON NULL INPUT, because the rules in the standard require that they return a null value whenever they are invoked with an argument that is the null value. The description of the <routine characteristic> included a bullet that reads

- Whether the method always returns the null value when any of its arguments is null, and thus need not be called in that situation; the default is CALLED ON NULL INPUT.

When you write a method (or a function or procedure), you have many choices regarding its behaviors. One choice that you make—perhaps in the name of runtime efficiency—is to choose whether the method should actually be invoked in the case that any of the arguments of a method invocation have the null value. For instance, a method that returns the title of a movie concatenated with a string indicating its running time in hours and minutes would never return a meaningful value if the column containing the movie's data were missing.

As a result, you might choose to bypass the otherwise inevitable runtime costs associated with that method invocation whenever the value of the movie_table.movie_info column is null. To implement this decision, you could revise the function definition to look like Example 4.17.

Example 4.17 *Defining a Method with RETURNS NULL ON NULL INPUT*

```
CREATE METHOD another_schema.title_and_length
                (movie_param movie)
    RETURNS REAL
    RETURNS NULL ON NULL INPUT
  RETURN ...
```

On the other hand, you might choose to return some actual value—perhaps some numeric value such as zero—in this situation. If you wanted to do that, then you could revise the function to look like the method in Example 4.18.

Example 4.18 *Defining a Method with CALLED ON NULL INPUT*

```
CREATE METHOD another_schema.title_and_length
                    (movie_param movie)
    RETURNS REAL
    CALLED ON NULL INPUT

  IF movie_param.title IS NULL OR
     movie_param.runs IS NULL
    THEN RETURN 0
    ELSE RETURN ...
  END IF
```

Now, there's an important "exception" to the rule that says, "Whether the method always returns the null value when any of its arguments is null . . ." quoted at the start of this section. The exception occurs only if the routine being invoked is a method and that method is a type-preserving method (such as a mutator for some attribute of a structured type). Even in this case, the exception is only relevant to the implicit parameter of the method: if the implicit argument of an invocation of a type-preserving method is the null value, then the method doesn't *return* a null value—instead, you'll *always* (regardless of whether the method was declared CALLED ON NULL INPUT or RETURNS NULL ON NULL INPUT) get a runtime exception indicating that the operation you attempted is prohibited.

4.6.5 Augmented and Unaugmented Parameter Lists

Recall that an SQL routine is defined using an SQL routine body. An SQL routine body is trivial (from a syntactic viewpoint, at least); it is simply a single SQL statement. Of course, if SQL/PSM (or a proprietary analog) is supported in your implementation, then that SQL statement can be a compound statement: BEGIN . . . END.

By contrast, an external routine is defined by providing an external body reference. The use of the word *reference* in this phrase implies that the actual code of the external routine is not provided at this point—it is *referenced* and resides elsewhere. Unlike an SQL routine, it doesn't make sense to provide an SQL processor with, say, your C code. Instead, you provide the name of the routine and the system locates the routine in some manner specified by your implementation. If you leave off the external routine name clause, then the name is presumed to be the same as the third part of the 3-part `<schema qualified routine name>`. You can specify either an identifier or a character string literal as the name. Although SQL:1999 isn't specific about this, it's usually safe to presume that the character string literal should specify a fully qualified filename identifying the object code for your external routine. And, lest you forget, an external routine is one that is written in one of several host languages (which you must specify in the `<language clause>`).

Part of an external body reference is the `<external security clause>`, which was discussed in sections 4.3.1 and 4.5. I won't repeat that discussion here, but you might wish to take a quick look at those sections now to refresh your memory of the three alternatives and their meanings. It would also be beneficial for you to be sure that you understand the concepts surrounding SQL-session authorization stacks that are covered in Volume 1 of this book.

Now, you are undoubtedly aware (if not, Volume 1 of this book covers the issue) that none of the various host languages support SQL's null values (this is one of the contributors to that infamous impedance mismatch discussed in several places). Therefore, if you want your external routines, written in a host language, to deal with null values, you have to use an appropriate style of parameter for that external routine. You can specify PARAMETER STYLE SQL or PARAMETER STYLE GENERAL;[3] if you don't specify, then the default is PARAMETER STYLE SQL. (Incidentally, you are not allowed to specify this clause at all for SQL routines, since their parameters are inherently PARAMETER STYLE SQL.)

PARAMETER STYLE GENERAL means that each parameter in the routine declaration corresponds to one argument in invocations of the routine. That's it. You write your external routine with one parameter for each argument that you want your users to code in their routine invocations. Each parameter has the data type that you specify in the declaration (well, to be compulsively complete, you must ensure that the host language type of the parameter is compatible, according to SQL's rules, with the SQL data type that you declared in the parameter declarations). When the routine is invoked, the input arguments provided in the routine invocation are simply passed to the routine as the values of the corresponding parameters and any output arguments are returned from the routine as the values of the corresponding parameters. Of course, you cannot ever pass null values in either direction when you use PARAMETER STYLE GENERAL, because the host language's types do not support that concept. (Naturally, if you're writ-

---

3 PARAMETER STYLE JAVA is also supported, but this chapter does not discuss Java routines in any detail.

ing both the routines and the code invoking them, you could invent a convention to signal that you're passing a null value, such as using the character string '`**null value**`' or using a numeric –1 if that's not a normally valid value for a parameter, to avoid using PARAMETER STYLE SQL. However, I don't recommend that approach since it is likely to cause confusion among the programmers who maintain your code in the future.) If you want to use external routines that were not written specifically to be used in SQL code—such as routines written for a different purpose that you already happen to own—then PARAMETER STYLE GENERAL is your choice. While this choice doesn't allow you to exchange SQL-specific information, like null values, between your SQL code and your external routines, it does allow the use of routines that know nothing about SQL's conventions.

PARAMETER STYLE SQL is a little more complicated, primarily because it allows—actually, it requires—you to account for null values. If you're writing external routines specifically for use with your SQL code, this is a better choice. For every argument, input or output, or both, that you declare in the definition of an external routine, the external routine itself must be coded to have two parameters—one to exchange non-null values and the other to exchange an indicator parameter (see Volume 1 of this book, Chapter 12, "Accessing SQL from the Real World," for a discussion of indicators). If the external routine is an SQL-invoked function or method, then you must provide two additional parameters: one is for the value returned from the function, and the other is the indicator parameter associated with that return value (in case it's a null value). Finally, you provide either four or six additional parameters (six only if you're defining a function that is an *array-returning external function,* discussed in Volume 1 of this book). The parameter meanings are given in Table 4.2 for external procedures and in Table 4.3 for external functions and methods.

Table 4.2 *PARAMETER STYLE SQL Parameter Meanings for External Procedures*

Effective Parameter Number	*Meaning or Use*
1 through N	Values of actual parameters 1 – N from invoker to routine
N + 1 through 2N	Values of indicator parameters for parameters 1 – N to routine
2N + 1	SQLSTATE value returned to invoker
2N + 2	Routine's "invocable" name
2N + 3	Routine's specific name
2N + 4	Message text from routine returned to invoker

Table 4.3 *PARAMETER STYLE SQL Parameter Meanings for External Functions*

Effective Parameter Number	*Meaning or Use*
1 through *N*	Values of actual parameters 1 – *N* from invoker to routine
N + 1	Value of function result returned to invoker
N + 2 through 2*N* + 1	Values of indicator parameters for parameters 1 – *N* to routine
2*N* + 2	Indicator for function result returned to invoker
2*N* + 3	SQLSTATE value returned to invoker
2*N* + 4	Routine's "invocable" name
2*N* + 5	Routine's specific name
2*N* + 6	Message text from routine returned to invoker
2*N* + 5 through 2*N* + 6	Used only for array-returning external functions (and not present for other external functions)

Therefore, if you're writing an external function in, say, C or PL/I that has three input parameters (from SQL's viewpoint), and you want this function to deal with null values, then the actual C or PL/I code requires a function definition with 12 parameters: ((3 + 1)*2) + 4. We draw your attention to the fact that Table 4.3 states that some parameters are used to return information to the invoker. This does not invalidate my earlier statement that SQL-invoked functions and methods have only input parameters. From SQL's point of view, that remains true even in Table 4.3, since all of the external function's parameters that correspond directly to an SQL argument are input-only. Only the "supplementary" parameters ever return values—and those parameters reflect information about the execution of the routine, never data resulting from that execution!

4.6.6 Type Precedence Lists

As you saw in sections 4.6.2 and 4.6.3, routine resolution depends in part on something called a *type precedence list,* which is a list of data types indicating preferred type conversions from one type to the various types in the list. In a type precedence list for some type A, we might find types A, B, and C. If the types appear in that sequence, then we would say that type A has precedence over type B and that type B has precedence over type C. The implication of one type having precedence over another is this: When there are two possible routines that might be selected for a routine invocation—the routines having the same invocable name and the same number of parameters—then SQL must choose the routine whose parameter data types have the "best match" with the data types of the corresponding arguments in the routine invocation. If the data type of an argument in the routine invocation is, say, type A, and the data type of the corresponding parameter in one routine is B and the data type of the corresponding parameter in the other routine is C, then the first routine would be chosen. Why? Because its parameter's data type *precedes* the data type of the other routine's parameter in the relevant precedence list.

Every data type in SQL has an associated type precedence list that is defined by the SQL standard (and, undoubtedly, refined by various implementations), so this doesn't have to be computed for every specific routine resolution attempt. Products typically have the lists built into their code, since the answers are going to be the same every time a type precedence list is required.

Before I actually give you the precedence lists for each of SQL's data types, let me give you some rules that will allow you to generalize these relationships so that they can be applied to any combination of data types, including more than two data types. Those rules are

1. If data type A has precedence over data type B and data type B either has precedence over data type C or has equal precedence to data type C, then data type A has precedence over data type C.
2. If data type A has the same precedence as data type B and data type B has the same precedence as data type C, then data type A has the same precedence as data type C, too.
3. If data type A has the same precedence as data type B and data type B has precedence over data type C, then data type A has precedence over data type C, too.

Now, here are the precedence lists for various SQL data types. They're not quite as simple as I would like them to be, but that's because SQL:1999 permits implementations to make certain decisions about the precision of some of the numeric types, and individual implementations might make different decisions.

- For the fixed-length character string data type, the type precedence list is

  CHARACTER, CHARACTER VARYING, CHARACTER LARGE OBJECT

  This means that CHARACTER has precedence over CHARACTER VARYING, which has precedence in turn over CHARACTER LARGE OBJECT.
- For the varying-length character string data type, the type precedence list is

  CHARACTER VARYING, CHARACTER LARGE OBJECT

(I clearly hear you asking, "Huh? Why isn't CHARACTER in the type precedence list for the varying-length character string type? Well, it has to do with the need to order all types in a "type family"—an informal term not directly related to the subtype family in a type hierarchy, but its meaning is intuitive—in such a way that there are no "cycles" in the ordering. The same argument holds for BIT and BIT VARYING as well as REAL and DOUBLE PRECISION.)

- For the fixed-length bit string data type, the type precedence list is

  BIT, BIT VARYING

  This means that BIT has precedence over BIT VARYING.

- For the varying-length bit string data type, the type precedence list is

  BIT VARYING

- For the binary string data type (also known as the BLOB type), the type precedence list is

  BINARY LARGE OBJECT

- For numeric types, it gets a bit more complicated. To "normalize" numeric types that are implemented using different radixes (some decimal and some binary), this algorithm requires that the precisions effectively be converted to decimal radix for comparison.
  - If the implementation-defined precision of INTEGER is greater than the implementation-defined precision of SMALLINT, then SMALLINT has precedence over INTEGER; otherwise, SMALLINT has the same precedence as INTEGER.
  - If the implementation-defined maximum precision of DECIMAL is greater than the implementation-defined precision of INTEGER, then INTEGER has precedence over DECIMAL. If those precisions are equal, then INTEGER has the same precedence as DECIMAL. Otherwise, DECIMAL has precedence over INTEGER *and* we then apply the same relationship comparisons to DECIMAL and SMALLINT to determine whether one has precedence over the other or their precedences are equal.
  - If the implementation-defined maximum precision of NUMERIC is greater than the implementation-defined precision of INTEGER, then INTEGER has precedence over NUMERIC. If those precisions are equal, then INTEGER has the same precedence as NUMERIC. Otherwise, NUMERIC has precedence over INTEGER *and* we then apply the same relationship comparisons to NUMERIC and SMALLINT to determine whether one has precedence over the other or their precedences are equal.

  - If the implementation-defined maximum precision of NUMERIC is greater than the implementation-defined maximum precision of DECIMAL, then DECIMAL has precedence over NUMERIC. If those precisions are equal, then DECIMAL has the same precedence as NUMERIC. Otherwise, NUMERIC has precedence over DECIMAL.
  - REAL has precedence over DOUBLE PRECISION.
  - If the implementation-defined maximum precision of FLOAT is greater than the implementation-defined precision of REAL, then REAL has precedence over FLOAT. If those precisions are equal, then REAL has the same precedence as FLOAT. Otherwise, FLOAT has precedence over REAL.
  - If the implementation-defined maximum precision of FLOAT is greater than the implementation-defined precision of DOUBLE PRECISION, then DOUBLE PRECISION has precedence over FLOAT. If those precisions are equal, then DOUBLE PRECISION has the same precedence as FLOAT. Otherwise, FLOAT has precedence over DOUBLE PRECISION.
  - Whichever of INTEGER, NUMERIC, and DECIMAL that has the greatest precedence has precedence over whichever of REAL and FLOAT that has the least precedence.
  - The precedence list for numeric data types is then constructed from the precedence relationships that we've just computed. One possible example of such a precedence list is

    ```
    SMALLINT, INTEGER, DECIMAL, NUMERIC, REAL, FLOAT, DOUBLE
    PRECISION
    ```

- For an interval data type, the type precedence list depends on the specific interval type. Intervals containing only the YEAR and MONTH fields have a type precedence list containing only the type INTERVAL YEAR; intervals containing any combination of DAY, HOUR, MINUTE, and SECONDS fields have a type precedence list containing only the type INTERVAL DAY.
- For a datetime data type, the type precedence list depends on the specific datetime type. The datetime type DATE has a precedence list containing only the type DATE. The datetime type TIME (with or without a fractional seconds precision) has a precedence list containing only the type TIME. The datetime type TIMESTAMP (with or without a fractional seconds precision) has a precedence list containing only the type TIMESTAMP.
- For the Boolean data type, the type precedence list contains only the type BOOLEAN.
- For the ARRAY data type, the type precedence list is patterned after the type precedence list for the element type of the ARRAY type. It is formed by

making a precedence list of ARRAY types whose element types are the types in the type precedence list of the specified ARRAY type's element type. For example, the type precedence list for CHARACTER(10) ARRAY[50] is

```
CHARACTER(10) ARRAY[50], CHARACTER VARYING(10) ARRAY[50],
CHARACTER LARGE OBJECT(10) ARRAY[50]
```

The entries in the two lists are in corresponding order.

- For a user-defined type *UDT* that is a maximal supertype, the type precedence list is

  UDT

- For a user-defined type that is not a maximal supertype, the type precedence list is constructed by inserting the type itself, its direct supertype, that type's direct supertype, and so on until the maximal supertype has been inserted.
- For a REF type, the type precedence list is patterned after the type precedence list of the type referenced by the REF type. Each entry in the type precedence list is REF(*T*), where *T* is a type taken from the type precedence list of the referenced type. The entries in the two lists are in corresponding order.
- For the ROW data type, the type precedence list is

  ROW

  Note, however, that a ROW type can never be the type of an SQL parameter in SQL:1999 (this might be relaxed in a future version of the SQL standard). Therefore, the ROW type doesn't actually participate in type precedence decisions; I have included it here only to ensure that you don't assume that I overlooked it!

The notion of type precedence lists might not seem intuitive at first, but they are designed to prevent loss of data. That's why the relative precedence of, say, INTEGER and NUMERIC is determined by their precisions—whichever has the lower precision can be converted to the other without loss of data, but the reverse isn't always true.

You'll notice that, as well, INTEGER and TIMESTAMP are not in one another's type precedence lists. That means that the parts of the algorithm that require the data type of a parameter to be in the type precedence list of the data type of a corresponding argument will not be satisfied by a combination of those two data types, or any other combination that involves data types with this sort of relationship. Now, it might have been possible for SQL:1999 to have had rules that put CHARACTER and/or CHARACTER VARYING into the precedence lists of all other data types, since any other data type can be *cast* to those data types; however, SQL's designers chose not to do that since that behavior is not common in SQL database management systems and the value added for users and applications would have been minimal.

SQL's overloading rules prohibit the definition of two or more functions that have the same number of parameters and for which every parameter of one function has a data type that is in the type precedence list of the corresponding parameter of the other function or functions.

4.7 Polymorphism

As you've already read, the SQL-invoked routine facility was designed so that those routines are *polymorphic,* meaning that they have the characteristic of *polymorphism.* The word *polymorphism* comes from the Greek word πολιμορφοσ (in Latin characters, that's *polimorphos*) meaning "many forms." Webster's Third New International Dictionary defines the related word *polymorphic* to mean "having or assuming various forms, characters, styles, or functions."

I particularly like Webster's use of "various . . . functions," since that is extremely appropriate for SQL's purposes. After all, the word here is used to indicate that multiple SQL-invoked routines share a routine name. Strictly speaking, it's really the *routine name* that's polymorphic. After all, the routine name is what you would see as "having . . . various . . . functions" associated with it. And, as you saw earlier in this chapter, SQL-invoked routines each have unique (non-polymorphic—or is that monomorphic? or unimorphic?) "specific names" that can be used to identify them when, for example, you want to drop them.

In this context, then, the word implies that a single name, the `<schema qualified routine name>`, which is sometimes called the *invocable name,* can be given to more than one routine. The actual behavior that occurs in response to a routine invocation using that name is determined by other factors, such as the number of arguments provided in the routine invocation, the data types of those arguments, and the SQL-path that governs which schemas are "searched" to locate routines to be considered.

4.7.1 Polymorphism and Overloading

In this chapter, you've encountered the term *overloading* as it applies to SQL's procedures, methods, and functions. In fact, I defined the term in section 4.6. I've also told you that SQL-invoked procedures can be overloaded only using the number of parameters. (I should note that it's theoretically possible for some future edition of the SQL standard to enhance that capability, but nothing of the sort is being discussed at the time this volume goes to press.)

In SQL, as in Java and other programming languages with this capability, the word *overload* implies the creation of multiple routines that have the same name. Now, obviously, there has to be some way for any system—whether it's a compiler, a linker, or a runtime system—to choose exactly one routine to invoke in response to a given routine invocation. In SQL, one could argue that routines with the same name that are stored in different schemas can be distinguished by using the schema name. That's true, of course, but irrelevant, since SQL considers the routine name to include the schema name (and, where supported, the catalog name as well).

Well, then, you might ask: How can there be more than one routine with the same name, since SQL doesn't permit us to store multiple objects (of the same kind) with the same name into a single schema? The answer is that SQL's routines each have two names! One of these names, called the "specific name" is an ordinary schema-qualified name. It is this name that is used to ensure that we don't store two routines with the same identifier into a given schema. The specific name is thus always completely unique in a database.

The other name of a routine is just called its "routine name," but I often call it the "invocable name." This second name is the one that is used when you want to invoke a method or function (or call a procedure), and it is the name that can be duplicated among many routines in the database. Now, it's relevant to explore just how SQL decides which routine to actually invoke among those having the same invocable name. As I suggested earlier, the argument list of the routine invocation is used (along with the SQL-path, in the case of functions, but not methods).

I gave you a simplified look at the routine invocation algorithm in sections 4.6.1, 4.6.2, and 4.6.3, and you can read the detailed algorithm in section 4.8. In this section, I specifically discuss the influence that overloading has on the algorithm.

Methods and ordinary functions in SQL:1999 are *polymorphic* (a fancier name for *overloadable*),[4] and all routines with the same invocable name are candidates for execution of some particular function or method invocation using that name—as long as there are sufficient differences in the parameter declarations to allow the system to resolve that function or method invocation to a single specific routine with the specified name. In the absence of a type hierarchy (see Chapter 2, "User-Defined Types," for more on this topic), functions and methods are resolved using almost identical algorithms. Invocations of ordinary functions have an additional factor not used to resolve invocations of methods: the SQL-path.

---

4 In recent years, it has become common to reserve the word *polymorphic* to identify routines whose invocation behaviors can change at runtime based solely on the most specific runtime type of one (or more) arguments (see section 4.7.2). I use the more traditional (original) definition of the word here.

When you write an invocation for a method or for an ordinary function, the system can often resolve that invocation to a single routine at the time the code containing the invocation is compiled. The number of arguments in the routine invocation is used to limit the routines examined; only those routines declared with the same number of parameters are considered. After that, the *declared type* of each argument, including the first implicit argument of methods, is used by the system to discover the specific routine with the best match between each argument and the corresponding declared parameter of the various possible functions or methods. If the invocation being resolved is for an ordinary function, then the function contained in the schema whose name appears first in the SQL-path is chosen; if the invocation is for a method, then the selection of a single routine is deferred until runtime, when the actual most-specific runtime type of the distinguished argument can be used to make the proper selection choice.

This means that the system can either find a single best-match routine to execute for the routine invocation, or else it will determine that there are two or more routines with equivalent matches of arguments and parameters, in which case a syntax error will be given at compile time. (Of course, the presence of multiple methods differing only by the most specific type of the implicit SELF parameter is an exception to this rule.)

To illustrate this, I've postulated two sorts of ratio I might like to examine. One of them operates on a value of the `movie` type and computes the ratio between the length of the movie's title (in characters) and the movie's running time (in minutes). The second computes the ratio between the running time of a movie (in minutes) and its rental cost (in whatever currency units we're using). The first `ratio` function takes one parameter whose type is `movie`; the other has two parameters, a `movie` instance and a decimal number, as seen in Example 4.19.

Example 4.19 *Overloading a Function Name*

```
CREATE FUNCTION
            another_schema.ratio ( movie_param movie )
    RETURNS REAL
    SPECIFIC another_schema.ratio_1
  RETURN CHAR_LENGTH ( movie_param.title ) / movie_param.runs

CREATE FUNCTION
            another_schema.ratio ( movie_param movie,
                                   cost_param  DECIMAL(5,2) )
    RETURNS REAL
    SPECIFIC another_schema.ratio_2
  RETURN movie_param.runs / cost_param
```

Note that I've added clauses to specify the "specific name" of these functions; the default specific name of a function is implementation-defined, but I generally prefer to assign a specific name that helps me identify the routine when I need to get to *that* specific routine for some reason. In the second of these functions, the first parameter has the same data type (`movie`) that the first `ratio` function's parameter has. However, the fact that it has a second parameter means that the SQL system can easily distinguish between invocations of the two functions, as seen in Example 4.20.

Example 4.20 *Using Overloaded Functions*

```
SELECT   mt.movie_info.title, mt.movie_info.runs,
         another_schema.ratio(mt.movie_info),
         another_schema.ratio(mt.movie_info, mt.rental_cost)
FROM     movie_table mt
WHERE    mt.movie_info.title = 'Titanic'
```

As you'll see in section 4.7.2, the existence of a type hierarchy makes this slightly—but only slightly—more complex.

4.7.2 Method Overriding

Since SQL:1999's structured types can participate in type hierarchies, and since SQL:1999 supports only single inheritance, I need to slightly modify the description of method overloading in section 4.7.1.

Recall from the earlier discussion of this subject that you are allowed to have more than one method or function (or, in a more limited way, procedures) in your database with the same invocable name; they are distinguished by having unique specific names, as well as in having distinct parameter lists. Such routines with the same invocable name are said to be overloaded, or polymorphic. The SQL environment identifies exactly one routine for each routine invocation based on the number of arguments provided and (except for procedures) their data types.

Once we add subtypes to the mix, the situation gets a little more complicated—but only a little. Adding support for type hierarchies means that we now have to distinguish between the sort of overloading I've already described and a new type of overloading: specifying a method in a subtype that has the same name and same parameter list as a method in one of its supertypes. Java programmers will know this phenomenon as *overriding,* and SQL:1999 makes the same terminological distinction.

The principle new complication arises with "overriding methods." As you will quickly appreciate, once you spend a few minutes thinking about it, there is a high probability that you'll want methods defined on some subtype to be different—if only slightly—than the methods of the same name (and the same conceptual functionality) defined on its supertypes. An SQL:1999 enhancement to method overloading is the key to taking care of this requirement. But let's be clear: The availability of subtypes has no effect on *function* overloading, only method overloading, and the new term, *overriding*, is used to emphasize the capability.

Method Resolution Redux

Let's look at a typical situation: You've defined a type hierarchy like the one I've been using in this volume, including a `movie` type, its three subtypes (`vhs_tape`, `dvd`, and `laser_disc`), and the two `dvd` subtypes (`dolby_dvd` and `dts_dvd`). Now, you want to have methods that will format the attributes of instances of these types in preparation for displaying them on users' screens; let's call this method `display`.

To nobody's surprise, because `vhs_tape` instances have different attributes than `dolby_dvd` instances, the formatting won't be identical for all types in the type hierarchy. Now, you *could* define several methods, such as `display_vhs_tapes` and `display_dolby_dvds`, but that loses some of the advantages of having subtypes—including the use of substitution. Happily, SQL:1999 lets you use overriding methods to resolve this problem (thus providing one of the principle benefits of object-oriented languages).

In SQL:1999, method invocations (but not invocations of ordinary functions) are not completely resolved at compile time, in spite of the impression you may have gotten in section 4.7.1. Instead, at compile time, method invocations are narrowed down to just those methods for which all parameters other than the implicit parameter are an appropriate match, and for which the implicit parameters' specified data types are all in the same type hierarchy.

Therefore, you might define six methods named `display`, each having only the implicit parameter. The data type of the implicit parameter for one of these `display` methods would be `movie`; for another one, it would be `vhs_tape`; and for yet another it would be `dolby_dvd`. All six of these methods would be candidates for resolving a routine resolution like

```
...movie_info.display...
```

At runtime, the *most specific type* of the `movie` instance passed to that method invocation would be used to determine which of the six methods named `display` is actually invoked.

Overriding Methods

The display method defined on the movie type is called an *original method,* and the methods with the same name that are defined on the subtypes are called *overriding methods.* You may wish to refer back to Chapter 2, "User-Defined Types," (section 2.8, "Defining Structured User-Defined Types"), to refresh your memory of how such methods are defined. As a reminder, the term *overload* applies to functions or methods in which the parameter list differs in some way other than with respect to methods' implicit, distinguished, parameter. By contrast, *override* applies to methods within a type hierarchy in which the parameter lists differ only in the declared type of the implicit, distinguished, parameter. SQL:1999 does not permit overloading (or overriding) the observer and mutator methods associated with a type's attributes, so there can never be overriding methods with the same names as the attributes of any type in the type hierarchy. (Although the observer and mutator methods associated with a type's attributes cannot be overridden, they can be overloaded. SQL:199 allows you to define methods having the same name as an attribute, provided that its parameters differ in number or in data type from those of the observer and mutator methods.) All other methods defined on a supertype can be overridden in any (or all!) of its subtypes, as illustrated in Example 4.21. (The original method definition for length_interval can be found in Example 4.8.)

Example 4.21 *Overriding a Method in a Subtype*

```
CREATE TYPE dvd UNDER movie AS (
   stock_number   INTEGER,
   rental_price   DECIMAL(5,2),
   extra_features feature_desc ARRAY[5] )
   INSTANTIABLE
   NOT FINAL;

CREATE TYPE dolby_dvd UNDER dvd AS (
   alt_language   BOOLEAN )
   INSTANTIABLE
   NOT FINAL

   OVERRIDING METHOD length_interval ( )
      RETURNS INTERVAL HOUR(2) TO MINUTE;

CREATE INSTANCE METHOD length_interval ( )
  RETURNS INTERVAL HOUR(2) TO MINUTE
  FOR dolby_dvd
```

```
/* Allow for movies as long as 99 hours and 59 minutes */
/* Estimate 10 minutes additional for second language */

RETURN CAST ( CAST ( SELF.runs AS INTERVAL MINUTE(4) )
                 + INTERVAL '10' MINUTE(4)
              AS INTERVAL HOUR(2) TO MINUTE );
```

This new method, with the same name as a method of one of its supertypes (movie), has the same signature and thus overrides that other method, but has somewhat different behavior.

To see how the existence of an overriding method affects routine invocation, consider the sequence of events in Example 4.22, which uses two SQL variables to hold two values created in the example (one dvd instance and one dolby_dvd instance), then invokes the length_interval method on the instance in each of the variables.

Example 4.22 *Invocation of Overriding Methods*

```
DECLARE dvd1, dvd2     dvd;
DECLARE len1, len2,
        len3, len4     INTERVAL HOUR TO MINUTE;
DECLARE lang1, lang2   BOOLEAN;

SET dvd1 = NEW dvd ('Seven',
                    '...a serial killer using the seven deadly sins...',
                    123,
                    299369,
                    1.89,
                    ARRAY[] );

SET dvd2 = NEW dolby_dvd ('Seven',
                    '...a serial killer using the seven deadly sins...',
                    123,
                    299369,
                    1.89,
                    ARRAY[],
                    TRUE );

SET len1 = dvd1.length_interval;
SET len2 = dvd2.length_interval;
SET len3 = (dvd1 AS dvd).length_interval;
SET len4 = (dvd2 AS dvd).length_interval;
```

```
SET lang1 = dvd1.alt_language;
SET lang2 = (dvd1 AS dolby_dvd).alt_language;
```

Please observe that both variables dvd1 and dvd2 are declared to be of type dvd, even though the second such variable is actually used to hold an instance of the dolby_dvd type. Because of SQL's use of the principle of substitutability, every site that can hold a value of a supertype can also hold a value of that supertype's subtypes. In this case, variable dvd1 has declared type dvd, and it is allowed to store any value whose most specific (runtime) type is dvd, as well as any value whose most specific type is any subtype of dvd, such as dolby_dvd. Similarly, every *expression* whose declared type (that is, the type determined statically at syntax analysis time) is some supertype, such as dvd, is capable of returning a value whose most specific type (the actual runtime type of that value) is some subtype, like dolby_dvd, of that supertype. In this case, variable dvd2 also has declared type dvd, but it has been assigned a value whose most specific type is dolby_dvd, a subtype of type dvd.

Also, note that the first two SET statements that assign values to variables len1 and len2 do so in identical ways. But, while the first of those two statements returns an INTERVAL value equivalent to 02:03 (two hours and three minutes), the second returns an INTERVAL value that is ten minutes longer (02:13, or two hours and thirteen minutes) because the SQL system actually executes the overriding method named length_interval instead of the original method of the same name.

The SET statement that assigns a value to len3 operates identically to the SET statement that assigns a value to len1, since the value stored in dvd1 is already known to be an ordinary dvd instance.

But what about the SET statement that assigns a value to len4? The value stored in dvd2 is not an ordinary dvd; it's a dolby_dvd instance. Will the statement execute properly? Of course—a dolby_dvd instance is also a dvd instance, so the invocation is valid. In fact, the dvd version of length_interval (that is, the originally defined method) is chosen for execution in this case. The expression (dvd2 AS dvd) instructs the SQL system to treat the dolby_dvd instance as though it were an ordinary dvd instance.

Now, let's consider the two SET statements that assign values to lang1 and lang2. The first of those two statements will fail with a syntax error, because dvd1 is of declared type dvd, and the dvd type does not have an attribute named alt_language. The second also fails, but for a slightly different reason: SQL:1999 requires that the declared type of the expression preceding the keyword AS (the expression is simply the variable name dvd1) be a *subtype* of the type named after the AS keyword (dolby_dvd). But, in this statement, the declared type of dvd1 is dvd, which is a *supertype* of dolby_dvd. Because this syntax (expression AS type) allows us to force invocation of a method defined on a supertype, we can view it as casting the value of the expression to one of its supertypes. As a result, the operation is often called an *upcast* (casting "up" the type hierarchy). That last SET statement represents an attempt to cast the dvd value in dvd1 "down" the type hierarchy to the subtype dolby_dvd, which is not permitted. The next subsection, "Direct Invocation and General Invocation," addresses this subject in a little more detail.

To accomplish what that last SET statement attempts, I must use a *downcast*, which SQL:1999 provides in the form of the TREAT expression, also known as <subtype treatment>, the syntax of which is shown in Syntax 4.10.

Syntax 4.10 *<subtype treatment> Syntax*

```
<subtype treatment> ::=
    TREAT ( <value expression> AS <user-defined type> )
```

The TREAT expression does not actually change the data type of the value of the <value expression>, but it allows the SQL system to treat that value as though it had been declared to be the subtype specified as <user-defined type>. Therefore, I would be successful if I used the statement found in Example 4.23.

Example 4.23 *Using a Subtype's Method*

```
SET lang2 = TREAT (dvd2 AS dolby_dvd).alt_language;
```

The use of TREAT allows me to recognize the fact that the most specific (runtime) type of the value stored in the variable dvd2 (whose declared type is dvd) is actually dolby_dvd and thus to access an attribute that is defined only for dolby_dvd instances.

Direct Invocation and General Invocation

Now, the designers of SQL:1999 recognized that there are exceptions to just about every situation. If you've built a type hierarchy and provided some overriding methods defined on subtypes in that hierarchy (a more complete example can be found in Example 4.21), there may still be times when you *really* want to invoke the original method defined on the supertype, even when a subtype instance is provided to the method invocation.

Case in point: You're likely to encounter the need to display only dvd attributes, even if you happen to retrieve a dolby_dvd from the database. If you've defined an overriding display method associated with the most specific type dolby_dvd, you normally would find that the overriding method is the one that's invoked, regardless of your needs. SQL:1999 calls this *direct invocation.* However, SQL:1999 provides us with a slightly different facility, called *general invocation,* that allows us to tell SQL that we want to use the dvd version of the display method instead:

```
...(movie_info AS dvd).display...
```

While that might seem like a strange notation, all you have to do to analyze it is to recall that the text to the left of the .display is an expression whose type is some type in the appropriate type hierarchy. The expression "(movie_info as dvd)" is such an expression, whose type is dvd—even if the value returned in the movie_info column happens to be a dolby_dvd. But this isn't a cure-all: remember that this syntax only lets you do this for *subtypes* of the specified type—that is, the declared type of movie_info has to be dvd or some proper subtype of dvd (naturally, if it's dvd, then the syntax won't be very useful). Note that this does *not* convert or cast the movie_info value into a dvd value; it merely instructs the system to use the display method that is closely associated with the dvd type.

SQL:1999 provides a different facility that (temporarily) converts instances of one type to an instance of a specified *sub*type:

```
TREAT(movie_info AS dvd).display
```

When this TREAT expression is evaluated, the value retrieved from movie_info is actually converted into a new value whose most-specific (runtime) type is dvd, which would also force the use of the display method defined for the dvd type. However, in this case, it's possible that you might get, at runtime, a subtype of the declared type of movie_info that isn't a subtype of dvd, such as vhs_tape, in which case you'll get a runtime exception. Use with caution!

Static Method Invocation

I introduced static methods in section 4.5.3, but it seems appropriate to review it nearer the discussion of polymorphism. If you're comfortable with the notion, you can skip this subsection without losing any information.

Java has the notion of *static methods,* methods that don't operate on instances of a class, but are conceptually associated with the class itself. Several other object-oriented programming languages have analogous capabilities, although other names, like *class method,* are sometimes used. SQL:1999 has a similar notion, also called *static methods.* SQL:1999's static methods do not have an implicit (SELF) parameter, simply because they don't operate on (implicit) instances of the associated structured type. Instead, all their parameters must be explicit. For example, if you wanted to compare the lengths of two movies available on LaserDisc, you might choose to provide a static method on that subtype with two parameters, each of that type. Such a method might be invoked like this:

```
...laserdisc::length(v1.movie_info, v2.movie_info)...
```

The double-colon notation (`::`) is used in SQL:1999 to specify that a static method associated with the `laserdisc` structured type is being invoked.

4.7.3 Classical Dispatch Versus Generalized Dispatch

In Chapter 2, "User-Defined Types," I discussed SQL:1999's object model, including the capability to define type hierarchies of your structured types. You learned in that chapter that SQL:1999 supports a model of type hierarchy known as *single inheritance*. Some other languages (C++ being one of them) support a model of type hierarchy that allows *multiple inheritance*. Let's quickly review the two models to refresh your memory about the differences, after which we'll see how the inheritance model affects routine invocation in SQL.

In a single inheritance hierarchy, each subtype inherits attributes and methods from exactly one direct supertype (which may, of course, have inherited attributes and methods from its single direct supertype). In a multiple inheritance hierarchy, a subtype may inherit attributes and methods from more than one direct supertype (each of which can inherit attributes and methods from multiple direct supertypes).

In both models, subtypes are normally free to add new attributes, to add new methods, and to override methods inherited from their supertypes. In some object-oriented programming languages, subtypes can also override, or redefine, attributes inherited from supertypes. However, that is not allowed in SQL's type system.

In SQL:1999, the existence of a type hierarchy that does not support multiple inheritance means that methods (and, of course, attributes) can be inherited from only a single supertype, not from multiple supertypes. That offers considerable simplification of the routine invocation algorithm, at least in part because it is now impossible to encounter the situation where each of two or more supertypes might have methods of the same invocable name. That latter situation would lead to such possible undesirable consequences as having more than one inherited method with the same name, arbitrarily choosing between the two inherited methods (does the first-listed supertype have precedence, or is the last-listed supertype allowed to "override" the first?), or omitting the method entirely because of the redundant names.

Unfortunately, there are interesting application problems that are nicely addressed by multiple inheritance. For example, a music and video store almost certainly sells some of its products to some of its employees, making those employees customers as well. It's usually desirable to model an individual person only once in an environment, and multiple inheritance allows the creation of a class of persons that are both employees (with a salary, for example) and customers (with a credit rating, perhaps). Without multiple inheritance, applications may have to model a single person twice, once as an employee and another time as a customer, with possible pitfalls that include different information about some aspects of the person, such as the spelling of her name or the details of her street address.

Java's solution to this problem is to support only single inheritance of *implementation* (including both attributes and the code of methods), but multiple inheritance of *interface* (that is, the signatures of methods). Class definitions in Java are allowed to inherit interfaces from many superclasses, but the implementations of the methods in those interfaces must be provided in the subclass definition. SQL:1999 has no concept corresponding to Java's interfaces, but a future version of the SQL standard might include that notion.

Routine resolution in a single inheritance environment is thus somewhat simpler than routine resolution in a multiple inheritance environment. When single inheritance algorithms are used, specific routines are selected for invocation ("dispatched") based on the most specific type of an argument whose type can have no more than a single supertype. Because such algorithms were the first to be designed and implemented, they have become known as *classical dispatch* algorithms. Routine resolution in a multiple inheritance environment are more complex, but also more powerful and more generalized. As a result, they have become known as *generalized dispatch* algorithms.

4.8 Routine Invocation—The Details

Now that I've covered the basics of the routine resolution algorithm that SQL:1999 uses to implement polymorphism of routines, it's time to dig into the details. (Actually, as I suggested earlier, it's really routine *names* (invocable names, in particular) for which polymorphism is provided, but you'll find that most people will not be so rigorous and will simply say that SQL provides polymorphic routines.) As I go through these details, you'll notice that the precise sequence of the algorithm doesn't always quite match up with the naive looks given earlier in this chapter; that's a byproduct of the fact that the actual algorithm develops certain concepts in a different sequence for purposes that have little to do with clarity to a casual reader. Still, the effects are essentially the same.

When I was planning this chapter, one alternative that I considered was to actually quote the rules in SQL:1999 and annotate them one by one. I finally rejected that approach because so much of the detailed wording would have to be supported by quoting material from other parts of the SQL standard and, even with all that extra text, there would still have to be considerable explanation of the notation and language used. Instead of unnecessarily burdening you (and undoubtedly boring you!) with such soporific material, I decided to attempt to explain the algorithm in plain English—at least to the degree that such material lends itself to natural language.

The algorithm actually has two major components. First, there is the main part of the algorithm—the part that finds routines with the appropriate name. You'll recall from section 4.6 that one step of this takes into account the type precedence list of the data types of arguments; this determination comprises the second component of the algorithm. (Type precedence lists are addressed in section 4.6.6.)

Here's the approach I'm going to take to make this as clear as I can: I'm going to set up an example in which there are two schemas in a catalog (plus the Information Schema, of course) and several routines of a given name; after that, I'll give the algorithm, step by step, using the example schemas to illustrate the effect and meaning of each step as I go along. Of course, the routines in the example are going to be shown only as "signatures," since the body of the routines—the part that specifies what work they accomplish—has nothing to do with the routine resolution algorithm's actions.

4.8.1 Example Setup

Let's assume that there's already a catalog in existence (in any case, since there are no SQL statements for creating a catalog, that action is performed using implementation-defined mechanisms) and that its name is `videostore`. The CREATE SCHEMA statements in Example 4.24 populate that catalog sufficiently for purposes of explaining the routine resolution algorithm. As you examine the example, notice that a subtype, `dvd`, is defined in a different schema than its supertype, `movie`. SQL:1999's designers realized that type definers whose types reside in a schema they own will benefit from the ability to leverage types defined by other type definers whose types reside in their schemas.

Example 4.24 *Creating Schemas and Other Objects*

```
--
-- Main schema for the rental aspect of the business
--
CREATE SCHEMA videostore.rentals
    AUTHORIZATION melton          -- Well, it is my store ;^)
    PATH rentals, sales

  CREATE MODULE specials          -- Some routines in modules
      PATH rentals                -- Note omission of SALES

    FUNCTION compute_discount (
          title                   CHARACTER VARYING (50),
          regular_rental_price    DECIMAL (5,2),
          vhs_owned               INTEGER )
        RETURNS DECIMAL (5,2)
        SPECIFIC rentals_specials_compute_discount_func
      -- (some statements to perform the computation)

    PROCEDURE compute_discount (
          title                   CHARACTER VARYING (50),
          regular_rental_price    DECIMAL (5,2),
          vhs_owned               INTEGER )
        SPECIFIC rentals_specials_compute_discount_proc
      -- (some statements to perform the computation)

  END MODULE

  CREATE FUNCTION compute_discount (
        title                   CHARACTER VARYING (50),
        regular_rental_price    DECIMAL (5,2),
        vhs_owned               DECIMAL (3,0) )
      RETURNS DECIMAL (5,2)
      SPECIFIC rentals_compute_discount_func_dec

  CREATE TYPE movie AS (
      title            CHARACTER VARYING (100),
      description      CHARACTER VARYING (500),
      runs             INTEGER )
```

```
    NOT FINAL
    INSTANCE METHOD length_interval ( )
      RETURNS INTERVAL HOUR(2) TO MINUTE

  CREATE INSTANCE METHOD length_interval ( )
      RETURNS INTERVAL HOUR(2) TO MINUTE
      FOR movie
    SPECIFIC lenint1

    /* Allow for movies as long as 99 hours and 59 minutes */
    RETURN CAST ( CAST ( SELF.runs AS INTERVAL MINUTE(4) )
          AS INTERVAL HOUR(2) TO MINUTE )


--
-- Main schema for the sales side of the business
--
CREATE SCHEMA videostore.sales
    AUTHORIZATION melton        -- It's still my store

  CREATE FUNCTION compute_discount (
        title                 CHARACTER VARYING (50),
        regular_rental_price  DECIMAL (5,2),
        vhs_owned             DECIMAL (3,0) )
      RETURNS DECIMAL (5,2)
      SPECIFIC sales_compute_discount_func_dec

  CREATE FUNCTION compute_discount (
        title                 CHARACTER VARYING (50),
        regular_rental_price  DECIMAL (5,2) )
      RETURNS DECIMAL (5,2)
      SPECIFIC sales_compute_discount_func_none

  CREATE FUNCTION compute_discount (
        title                 CHARACTER VARYING (50),
        regular_rental_price  DECIMAL (5,2),
        vhs_owned             INTEGER )
      RETURNS DECIMAL (5,2)
      SPECIFIC sales_compute_discount_func_int
```

```
CREATE PROCEDURE compute_discount (
      title                   CHARACTER VARYING (50),
      regular_rental_price    DECIMAL (5,2),
      vhs_owned               DECIMAL (3,0) )
    SPECIFIC sales_compute_discount_proc

CREATE TYPE dvd UNDER rentals.movie AS (
    stock_number   INTEGER,
    rental_price   DECIMAL(5,2),
    extra_features feature_desc ARRAY[10] )
  INSTANTIABLE
  NOT FINAL
  OVERRIDING INSTANCE METHOD length_interval ( )
    RETURNS INTERVAL HOUR(2) TO MINUTE

CREATE INSTANCE METHOD length_interval ( )
  RETURNS INTERVAL HOUR(2) TO MINUTE
  FOR dvd
  SPECIFIC lenint2

  /* Allow for movies as long as 99 hours and 59 minutes */
  /* Estimate 10 minutes additional for second language */
  RETURN CAST ( CAST ( SELF.runs AS INTERVAL MINUTE(4) )
                  + INTERVAL '10' MINUTE(4)
               AS INTERVAL HOUR(2) TO MINUTE );

GRANT EXECUTE ON specials TO horowitz
GRANT EXECUTE ON rentals_compute_discount_func_dec TO horowitz
GRANT EXECUTE ON sales_compute_discount_func_dec TO horowitz
GRANT EXECUTE ON sales_compute_discount_func_int TO horowitz
GRANT EXECUTE ON sales_compute_discount_proc TO horowitz
GRANT EXECUTE ON sales_compute_discount_func_none TO horowitz
GRANT USAGE ON movie TO horowitz
GRANT USAGE ON dvd TO horowitz
GRANT EXECUTE ON lenint1 TO horowitz
GRANT EXECUTE ON lenint2 TO horowitz
```

"Wow," you might well say, "Why would anybody define seven different routines to compute discounts—some of them procedures, some functions, some in modules, some in schemas?" Well, the most obvious reason is because it helps to demonstrate the algorithm! But a more practical reason is that discounts must be computed sometimes on rentals and sometimes on sales, using different approaches; sometimes they are computed as part of a larger expression and a function provides the best mechanism, but other times they are computed "standalone," and a procedure works best. Don't quibble—the purpose of the schemas (would you prefer *schemata*?) is for use in explaining the algorithm, which is next.

4.8.2 The Algorithm

I'm going to take you through the algorithm more than once to illustrate different scenarios. The first trip through uses just one scenario along with the details of the algorithm itself. Subsequent trips don't repeat the algorithm, but merely follow the steps that are used.

For our first trip, I'm going to use a procedure invocation (a `CALL` statement):

```
CALL compute_discount ('Priscilla, Queen of the Desert',
                        19.95, 30)
```

For clarity, I'll identify routines by their specific names (since that's the easiest way to distinguish among many routines with the same routine name). Let's also assume that this routine invocation (and the others considered in this section) are executed by authorization identifier `horowitz` and that our SQL-path is identical to the path specified in the first CREATE SCHEMA statement in Example 4.24, `PATH rentals, sales`.

Before getting started on the algorithm, I should remind you that instance methods and constructor methods always have that implicit SELF parameter, which implies that instance and constructor methods have augmented parameter lists that have one parameter more than their explicit, unaugmented parameter lists (see section 4.6.5). The algorithm uses the complete, augmented argument lists and augmented parameter lists for resolving routine invocations.

1. The first step taken by the routine invocation algorithm identifies all routines that fit into the category called *possibly candidate routine* (yes, I realize that's not very good English, but that's what SQL:1999 calls the category).
   a. If the routine invocation with which we're working is a CALL statement, then the possibly candidate routines are all SQL-invoked procedures whose routine names (without the schema name and catalog name components) are the same as the routine name used in the CALL statement.

b. If the routine invocation is a static method invocation, then the possibly candidate routines are all SQL-invoked methods that are closely associated with a supertype of the type specified in the static method invocation (including that type itself), that are defined to be STATIC methods and that have routine names (without the schema name and catalog name components) that are the same as the routine name used in the static method invocation.

c. If the routine invocation is a constructor method invocation, then the possibly candidate routines are all SQL-invoked constructor methods whose routine names (without the schema name and catalog name components) are the same as the routine name used in the method invocation.

d. If the routine invocation is a method invocation other than a static method invocation, then the possibly candidate routines are all SQL-invoked methods that are not defined to be STATIC methods whose routine names (without the schema name and catalog name components) are the same as the routine name used in the method invocation.

e. If the routine invocation is a function invocation, then the possibly candidate routines are all SQL-invoked functions whose routine names (without the schema name and catalog name components) are the same as the routine name used in the function invocation.

> Since our example is a CALL statement, then the first alternative is the one chosen, so we eliminate all of the functions, including all methods, in our example schemas. This leaves the two routines `rentals_specials_compute_discount_proc` and `sales_compute_discount_proc` as our possibly candidate routines.

2. Next, the algorithm identifies all routines in the category that SQL:1999 calls *executable routines* by eliminating some routines from the possibly candidate routines. In order for a possibly candidate routine to be an executable routine,

   a. If the possibly candidate routine is contained in an SQL server module, then the authorization identifier associated with the invoking context must have EXECUTE privilege on that SQL server module.

   b. Otherwise, the possibly candidate routine is directly contained in a schema and the authorization identifier must have EXECUTE privilege on the routine itself.

> Our example schemas contain two procedures, one in an SQL server module and one directly in a schema; since the authorization identifier invoking the CALL statement—`horowitz`—has EXECUTE privilege for both, our executable routines are `rentals_specials_compute_discount_proc` and `sales_compute_discount_proc`.

3. The algorithm then derives the "invocable routines" from the executable routines by eliminating executable routines that have the wrong number of parameters for the routine invocation.
   a. If the routine invocation has no arguments, then the possibly invocable routines are those executable routines that have no parameters.
   b. Otherwise, if the routine invocation has one or more arguments, it gets a little bit more complicated.
      i. The algorithm eliminates all executable routines that have a number of parameters different than the number of arguments in the routine invocation.
      ii. Then, for function and method invocations only, it further eliminates SQL-invoked functions or SQL-invoked methods for which the data type of some parameter isn't in the type precedence list of the corresponding argument's data type.
      iii. Note: SQL:1999 doesn't support overloading for SQL-invoked procedures based on the data types of arguments, so the type precedence list has no effect here; a later step in the algorithm will require that the procedure invocation's arguments and the procedure definition's parameters have data types that are "assignable" and that there be exactly one such procedure definition (this recognizes that there is never procedure overloading under any circumstances).

> Both of our executable procedures have the same number of parameters as the CALL statement, so our invocable routines are `rentals_specials_compute_discount_proc` and `sales_compute_discount_proc`.

4. If the routine invocation supplies no arguments, then the algorithm identifies the *subject routine* (the routine that is selected for execution) of the routine invocation as the invocable routine contained in the schema that is listed earlier in the SQL-path than any other schema containing an invocable routine. If this condition is satisfied, then we have the subject routine and the algorithm terminates.

a. If the routine invocation is a static method invocation, then the subject routine is the invocable routine defined in the "nearest" supertype (of the specified type) in which such an invocable routine is defined.
b. If the routine invocation specifies a schema name, then the subject routine is the routine contained in that schema. If the routine invocation specifies the schema name INFORMATION_SCHEMA, then the subject routine is an SQL built-in function. (Note that SQL:1999 has no built-in functions with no parameters; however, some future version of the SQL standard might define some such functions.)
c. If there is more than one such routine or no such routine, then you'll get a syntax error.
d. If a subject routine is identified and it is not a procedure, then the effective return type of the routine invocation is defined to be the result data type of the subject routine (function or method).

> Because our CALL statement does have arguments, this rule doesn't apply; therefore, we have not yet defined the subject routine.

5. If the routine invocation supplies one or more arguments, then the algorithm identifies the *candidate routines* of the routine invocation.
   a. If the routine invocation specifies a schema name, then the candidate routine is the routine contained in that schema. If the routine invocation specifies the schema name INFORMATION_SCHEMA, then the candidate routine is an SQL built-in function, such as LENGTH or SUBSTRING.
   b. Otherwise, the candidate routines of the routine invocation are the invocable routines contained in the schemas listed in the SQL-path. If the routine invocation is a static method invocation, then the candidate routines are the invocable routines defined in the supertypes (of the specified type) in which such an invocable routine is defined.

> Our CALL statement didn't provide a schema name, so our candidate routines are the invocable routines that lie in the current path; if we assume that the relevant path for the CALL statement includes both of our sample schemas, then our candidate routines are `rentals_specials_compute_discount_proc` and `sales_compute_discount_proc`.

6. If the routine invocation supplies one or more arguments and the previous step identified two or more candidate routines, the algorithm next identifies the *subject routine* of the routine invocation.

a. If the routine invocation is a CALL statement, then the candidate routine is the subject routine contained in the schema that appears earlier in the SQL-path than any other schema that contains a subject routine. If any of the parameters (input, output, or input/output) of the subject routine are not assignment-compatible with any of the arguments of the CALL statement, then we'll get a syntax error.

b. If the routine invocation is a function invocation or method invocation, then the algorithm eliminates from the set of candidate routines all routines other than those for which every parameter has the highest precedence in the type precedence list of the data type of the corresponding argument in the routine invocation. Again, this uses the notion of a type precedence list and has the intent of retaining only those routines for which every parameter has the highest precedence among all candidate routines. (Don't forget that this step starts with the first—"left-most"—parameter and eliminates routines whose parameter's data type isn't the "best match," moves on to the second parameter, and so forth to the last—"right-most"—parameter. Also, note that this rule supports internationalization where multiple character sets are required by an application; it may not apply to your environment, in which case all possibly invocable routines are invocable routines.)

c. If the routine invocation is a function invocation and there is more than one candidate routine remaining, then the algorithm must choose between two (or more) candidate routines that have identical signatures. The seemingly arbitrary choice is made to select the routine contained in the schema whose name appears earlier in the path than the name of any other schema containing a remaining candidate routine.

d. If the routine invocation is a method invocation, then there must be at least one candidate routine or you'll get a syntax error. If there are two or more candidate routines, then the system will defer the choice among those candidate routines until execution time. At execution time, the choice will be made based on the most specific type of the implicit argument (the one corresponding to the implicit SELF parameter).

> We have two candidate routines: `rentals_specials_compute_discount_proc` and `sales_compute_discount_proc`, and our routine invocation was a CALL statement, so we must determine which of those appear in a schema appearing earliest in the SQL-path. Our path is made of two schemas, first `rentals`, followed by `sales`, so the `rentals_specials_compute_discount_proc` is the subject routine of the routine invocation.

Whew! We're done!

That, I admit freely, is a complex algorithm. However, it does achieve the critical goal of selecting the one unique routine that has the best possible match for the routine invocation. I believe that the only possibly nonintuitive assumption made by the algorithm is that the "best match" for parameters is made starting with the first parameter and moving ("left to right") to the last parameter, eliminating potential routines based on type precedence list membership. This was clearly an arbitrary decision made for SQL:1999, and a different approach might have been chosen; for example, the parameters could have been taken starting with the last one and progressing to the first. However, *some* ordering of parameters was inherently going to be required to avoid a deadlock situation where one parameter/argument pair had some particular precedence relationship and a different parameter/argument pair had exactly the inverse precedence relationship—thus making it impossible to choose between them. By ordering the parameters and then using the sequence of schemas in the path, SQL's designers have virtually eliminated situations where there can be more than one routine satisfying all the requirements, therefore causing ambiguities (which SQL:1999 reports as syntax errors).

Another aspect of the algorithm that might catch you by surprise, since it has no analog in other programming languages, is the consideration of the EXECUTE privilege in selection of routines. Step 2 of the algorithm eliminates all routines for which the invoking user does not have that privilege, which is a concept that doesn't apply to languages like C++ or Java that don't deal with persistent data like SQL does.

Now, let's try a different routine invocation and check out the steps that it takes through the algorithm:

```
... + compute_discount ('Priscilla, Queen of the Desert',
                        19.95, 30) + 0.50 + ...
```

- Since the routine invocation is a function invocation, the possibly candidate routines are all functions. They are
  - `rentals_specials_compute_discount_func`
  - `rentals_compute_discount_func_dec`
  - `sales_compute_discount_func_dec`
  - `sales_compute_discount_func_int`
  - `sales_compute_discount_func_none`
- Because authorization identifier `horowitz` has EXECUTE privilege on all of those routines, the executable routines are

  - `rentals_specials_compute_discount_func`
  - `rentals_compute_discount_func_dec`
  - `sales_compute_discount_func_dec`
  - `sales_compute_discount_func_int`
  - `sales_compute_discount_func_none`
- The invocable routines are those that have the appropriate number of parameters, three in this case, and those for which all parameters' data types are in the type precedence list of the data type of its corresponding argument. This rule eliminates `sales_compute_discount_func_none`, because it only has two parameters. Therefore, our possibly invocable routines are
  - `rentals_specials_compute_discount_func`
  - `rentals_compute_discount_func_dec`
  - `sales_compute_discount_func_dec`
  - `sales_compute_discount_func_int`

(In the example I'm using, no routines will be eliminated because of parameter data types not being in the type precedence list of argument data types, so we're safe on that point.)

- The function invocation supplied one or more arguments, so we have to determine the candidate routines. Since we aren't using any specific character sets anywhere, we can assume that the same (default) character set is used for both the parameters of the routines and the arguments of the routine invocation. If we assume that our current path includes both of our sample schemas, then the fact that our routine invocation didn't specify a schema name means that the candidate routines include all of the invocable routines:
  - `rentals_specials_compute_discount_func`
  - `rentals_compute_discount_func_dec`
  - `sales_compute_discount_func_dec`
  - `sales_compute_discount_func_int`
- The subject routines are derived next. First, we use the type precedence list to eliminate routines other than those having the highest available precedence for each parameter (working left to right). That eliminates `rentals_compute_discount_func_dec` because, for the argument value 30 (an exact numeric literal), the data type INTEGER has higher precedence than does the data type DECIMAL (3,0). Then, the algorithm eliminates `sales_`

`compute_discount_func_dec` for the same reason. We are thus left with `rentals_specials_compute_discount_func` and `sales_compute_discount_func_int` as our potential compatible candidate routines. By taking the one contained in the schema appearing earliest in the path, we have `rentals_specials_compute_discount_func` as our single remaining candidate routine. Since the data type returned is a numeric type—DECIMAL (5,2)—and in the context where we're invoking the function (addition to the numeric literal value 0.50) we're expecting a numeric type, we have our answer!

- Therefore, our subject routine is `rentals_specials_compute_discount_func`.

Finally, let's try a method invocation:

```
...movie_variable.length_interval()...
```

- Since the routine invocation is a method invocation, the possibly candidate routines are all methods. They are
  - `lenint1`
  - `lenint2`
- Because authorization identifier `horowitz` has EXECUTE privilege on all of those routines, the executable routines are
  - `lenint1`
  - `lenint2`
- The invocable routines are those that have the appropriate number of parameters, none in this case. Therefore, our invocable routines are
  - `lenint1`
  - `lenint2`
- The method invocation supplied zero arguments, so we can determine the subject routines without having to determine the candidate routines first. If we assume that our current path includes both of our sample schemas, then the fact that our routine invocation didn't specify a schema name means that our subject routines are identical to our invocable routines:
  - `lenint1`
  - `lenint2`
- Therefore, our subject routines are `lenint1` and `lenint2`. The choice between them will be made at runtime based on the most specific type of the value found in `movie_variable` (either `movie` or `dvd`).

Another consequence of SQL's orientation toward persistent data and the persistent metadata that describes its databases is that schema manipulation statements can modify the definitions of the schema objects in your database—including creation of new SQL-invoked routines. To minimize the probable confusion and unexpected behaviors that would otherwise result, SQL "freezes" the list of SQL-invoked routines that are considered for each routine invocation at the time that your code is compiled. This decision extends to views (at the time the view is defined), constraints and assertions (at the time they're defined), and all other uses of routine invocations that SQL:1999 allows. If the list of routines wasn't frozen at compile time, then addition of new routines to some schema in your path—possibly done by a user unaware of your application needs—could cause the behavior of your applications to change (if the new routine were a better match for one of your routine invocations than any of the routines available when you compiled your code).

4.9 Security and Rights in Routine Invocation

It would be surprising if SQL failed to require appropriate privileges for the definition and invocation of SQL-invoked routines. As with all schema objects, the SQL standard (though not all implementations!) permits only the owner of a schema to define schema objects in that schema. That limitation applies to user-defined types, including subtypes of structured types defined in other schemas, to typed tables, and to SQL-invoked routines, including methods associated with user-defined types.

In order to create a subtype of some existing structured user-defined type, you must have the UNDER privilege on the existing supertype. If you have been given the UNDER privilege on some existing structured type WITH GRANT OPTION, then you may grant the UNDER privilege on the subtypes you create to other authorization identifiers. If your UNDER privilege on an existing structured type is WITHOUT GRANT OPTION, then you are not permitted to grant the UNDER privilege on your subtypes to anybody else.

Because you can create user-defined types only in schemas that you own, you can create all the methods you wish to create on those user-defined types, including subtypes. Remember that methods of user-defined types must be defined in the schemas that contain the UDTs, and you must be the owner of those schemas in order to create the UDTs themselves.

But what about methods that are overriding methods of some inherited method? Some observers might expect that some special privilege is required on those inherited methods before you're allowed to override them. SQL:1999 does not have such a restriction, although you must have USAGE privilege on the associated user-defined type before you can create any routine that uses the type as the type of a parameter, the return type (for a function or method), or in a declaration within the routine.

You must also have EXECUTE privilege on every SQL-invoked routine that you wish to invoke, including procedures, functions, and methods. When you invoke an SQL routine, the SQL statement contained in that routine executes under the authorization of the routine's definer. Such routines are commonly called *definer's rights* routines. Therefore, if your application happens to be executing under one authorization identifier (`store_clerk`, perhaps) and it invokes an SQL routine stored in a schema owned by a different authorization identifier (`store_manager`, let's say), then the routine execution context created upon invocation of the SQL routine[5] uses that different authorization identifier (`store_manager`) as the source of all privileges used to execute the SQL statement contained in the routine.

SQL:1999 does not support execution of SQL routines using the privileges associated with the authorization identifier that executes the invocation of the routine (e.g., a CALL statement). Such routines would be known as *invokers' rights* routines and might be supported in a future edition of the SQL standard.

External routines are treated slightly differently in this respect than SQL routines. In Syntax 4.9, you will see a production for a BNF nonterminal symbol named `<external security clause>`. That clause offers three alternatives: EXTERNAL SECURITY DEFINER, EXTERNAL SECURITY INVOKER, and EXTERNAL SECURITY IMPLEMENTATION DEFINED. If DEFINER was chosen when an external routine was created, then all SQL statements that might be contained in that routine are executed using the privileges of the owner of the schema containing the routine. If INVOKER was chosen, then those contained SQL statements are executed using the privileges of the authorization identifier under whose privileges the routine invocation was executed. Finally, if IMPLEMENTATION DEFINED was selected, then the SQL implementation chooses some authorization identifier (not *necessarily* either the routine's definer or the routine's invoker, although those are the most obvious choices) under whose privileges contained SQL statements will be executed.

5 See Volume 1 of this book, particularly Chapter 17, "Routines and Routine Invocation (Functions and Procedures)," for more information about routine invocation contexts.

4.10 Chapter Summary

In this lengthy chapter, you've been exposed to SQL's SQL-invoked routines and the several ways in which such routines are invoked. You learned how to define and invoke procedures, ordinary functions, and methods, as well as how SQL routines and external routines differ from one another.

Through annotated examples, I showed you the details of SQL:1999's routine invocation algorithm. A good understanding of that algorithm makes it easier for you to design application architectures including type hierarchies that effectively respond to the needs of your users.

Chapter

5

Foreign Servers and Foreign-Data Wrappers

5.1 Introduction

Very few readers will be unaware that not all data is managed by SQL engines. The quantity of data stored in non-SQL repositories greatly exceeds the quantity of data managed by SQL servers. However, there are significant advantages in managing all of your data in a single language, instead of having to use one language for one sort of data, another API for a second sort of data, and so on.

In this chapter, I switch gears a bit to discuss a subject that influences database product implementers at least as much as application writers.[1] That subject is the part of SQL:1999 known as Management of External Data, or SQL/MED.[2] (Even though SQL/MED did not emerge as a published standard until 2001, it is written to align with the other parts of SQL:1999 and is thus properly characterized as a part of the 1999 standard.) SQL/MED addresses two aspects of managing non-SQL data: data that is *accessed* through the services of the SQL interface, and data that must be *coordinated* with SQL data but is still accessed through its native

1 Some material in this chapter was inspired by Jim Melton et al., "SQL and Management of External Data," *SIGMOD Record*, 30, No. 1, pp. 70–77.

2 ISO/IEC 9075-9:2001, *Information technology—Database languages—SQL—Part 9: Management of External Data (SQL/MED)* (Geneva: International Organization for Standardization, 2001).

API. This chapter addresses the access of non-SQL data through the SQL server. Chapter 6, "Datalinks," covers the coordination of non-SQL data that is accessed using its native interface. (SQL/MED also provides facilities through which SQL data managed by one SQL server can be coordinated with SQL data managed by a different SQL server, usually one provided by a different vendor than the first server.)

SQL/MED provides a standardized interface by which SQL servers can access data managed by other servers—including non-SQL data. Such data is *external* to the SQL server and is thus *foreign data*. The strategic goal of this standardized interface is support for an open, third-party marketplace in which developers can publish shrink-wrapped software (called *foreign-data wrappers*) that accesses specific data sources (called *foreign servers*) without requiring separate releases for different SQL servers. In other words, the interface allows a single wrapper that supports a particular foreign server to be accessed from all SQL engines that conform to SQL/MED.

Other goals, discussed later in the chapter, include support of integrating access to non-SQL data into an SQL environment and ease of developing software components that support that integration.

Several commercial SQL products available today have interfaces that are analogous to the SQL/MED interface. Oracle's Open Transparent Gateway provides a well-documented API that can be used to build software components to access other SQL servers as well as non-SQL data sources. Sybase's OmniConnect serves much the same purpose, as does IBM's former DataJoiner product (now part of DB2 Universal Database). Other vendors—both major database companies and smaller niche-market businesses—offer products that operate in this space. More recently, IBM's *Garlic* research project included the development of an API to which third-party developers can build foreign-data wrappers that allow SQL servers to easily access a wide variety of non-SQL data sources and SQL servers other than those built by IBM.

5.2 Overview of Distributed Databases

Before I describe the specifics of SQL/MED in any detail, it is useful to summarize the notions of *distributed database* that the standard may be considered to address. The subject of distributed database is quite large; indeed, there are undoubtedly a great many definitions of just what the term means.

For the purposes of this book, however, I use this definition: A distributed database is a database that is physically decentralized and managed by a database management system in a way that provides a logically centralized view of the database to the user.[3] While not particularly specific, that definition is intuitively meaningful and is a good place for this discussion to begin.

There are several ways of looking at distributed database systems. One of the dimensions that can be considered is whether or not each separate component (some people might call this a *subdatabase* or a *node* of a distributed database, but I prefer to think of it as a *partition* of the larger database and use that latter term in this chapter) must be managed by the same kind of database manager. Another dimension is the degree to which separate components, nodes, or partitions operate autonomously or to which their management is centralized.

5.2.1 Homogeneous Distributed Databases

Some distributed database environments require that every partition of the distributed database be managed by the same type of database manager. For example, if one partition happens to be managed by IBM's DB2, then all partitions must be managed by DB2. In some cases, all partitions must be managed by the same major version of the software, while other environments add the further restriction that all partitions be managed by the exact same minor version. If any of these restrictions exists, the distributed database is usually called a *homogeneous* distributed database.

Homogeneous distributed database systems are often easier to implement, since a single database system implementer has great control over the details of interpartition communication and coordination. Because all partitions are controlled by software well known to the implementer, all of that implementation's tricks and features can be applied to query analysis, partitioning, optimization, and execution.

Of course, the disadvantage to a customer wishing to use such a system is that every partition of a distributed database must be controlled by software acquired from a single source, which may be appropriate for new application systems, but is often not possible when existing data is being integrated.

5.2.2 Heterogeneous Distributed Databases

On the other hand, some distributed database environments allow a mixture of partitions controlled by different database managers. For example, if some com-

3 From ISO/IEC 2382-17:1996, *Information technology—Vocabulary—Part 17: Databases,* definition 17.08.02 (Geneva: International Organization for Standardization, 1996).

ponents are managed by DB2, others by Oracle, and still others by Sybase, then the distributed database is sometimes called a *heterogeneous* distributed database.[4]

Heterogeneous distributed database systems offer both advantages and disadvantages when compared to homogeneous systems. When one enterprise merges with another (including, of course, acquisition of one by the other), the business data of the two, formerly separate, enterprises must be made available to the new, merged enterprise. Quite often, the data owned by one of the merging enterprises is managed by software of one brand, while the data owned by the other enterprise is managed by software of another brand. Frequently, that data must be completely integrated, at least from the perspective of application programs. But migrating all of the data managed by one brand of database manager so that it is managed by newly purchased copies of the other brand is not generally economical. Consequently, a heterogeneous environment is often a business reality.

But heterogeneous environments are, by definition, not managed by software whose implementer is the implementer of all of the components. The result is that the coordination between partitions is limited by the knowledge available to the implementer of the distributed database management software. Although commercially successful distributed database management software is generally good at providing such coordination, it is limited by the fact that many aspects of database management systems are controlled by mechanisms that are highly proprietary to their implementers (i.e., trade secrets) and are rarely public knowledge. The result is that queries in such environments may not be fully optimized or even divided among partitions in optimal ways.

5.2.3 Distributed Databases That Include Non-SQL Data

Some heterogeneous database environments are sufficiently flexible to support the inclusion of components that manage non-SQL data in addition to various SQL data managers. If you're familiar with SQL database systems, this might seem like an extreme form of heterogeneity.

But enterprises today increasingly find it necessary to query SQL data and non-SQL data together, in the same query, as well as in the same application. The SQL language, of course, is designed to access SQL data; however, if a way can be found to make non-SQL data *look like* SQL data, then the SQL language can be used to access that data, too. In some situations, non-SQL data can be sufficiently coerced into an SQL shape so that it can be retrieved and updated using

4 Some observers claim that all SQL database systems are essentially similar enough that a collection of components managed by a variety of implementations are properly viewed as a homogeneous distributed database. I disagree, in part because no two implementations of SQL are truly compatible with one another.

SQL; in other cases, the use of SQL is practical only for retrieval, while updates have to be performed using some interface native to the non-SQL data source.

One of the principle goals of SQL/MED is the support of integrating access to non-SQL data into an SQL environment. As implied earlier in this chapter, satisfying that goal requires the ability to coerce non-SQL data into tabular form—a sort of simulated table—and supplying to the SQL server that accesses such data with metadata that describes the simulated table. Throughout the remainder of this chapter, I assume that SQL/MED is used specifically to provide an SQL interface to heterogeneous data.

5.2.4 Managing a Distributed Database

There are many approaches to distributed database management, and SQL/MED selects one approach as its design center. I won't discuss alternative approaches in this book, but there are numerous resources available that cover the subject in great detail.[5]

In its current version, SQL/MED does not pretend to provide a general solution to the overall problem of *distributed database*. It merely provides tools by which application programs using a specific SQL database system can (more or less) seamlessly access data managed by other data managers. The design center chosen by SQL/MED's architects designates the SQL server to which an application program submits its queries (the "local SQL server") as the overall manager of the application's queries. That means that all data accessed by an application program using an SQL query—including "local" SQL data, data managed by other SQL servers, and non-SQL data—must be described by metadata under the control of the local SQL server. The local SQL server is responsible for

1. Analyzing and compiling the queries, using metadata available to the local SQL server;
2. Decomposing those queries into smaller sets of operations that might be executed by various other data managers;
3. Negotiating with and communicating with those other data managers as required;
4. Dealing with different physical representations of data, including differing character set encodings (such as ASCII versus Unicode versus EBCDIC) and different floating point representations (IEEE versus proprietary formats);

5 A good place to start is Ahmed Elmagarmid et al., eds., *Management of Heterogeneous and Autonomous Database Systems* (San Francisco: Morgan Kaufmann Publishers, 1998).

5. Providing the appropriate security mechanisms to govern the SQL use of the external data;
6. Integrating the results returned from those other data managers with the results of any query segment executed by the local SQL server; and
7. Returning the final integrated results to the application that made the initial query.

SQL/MED presumes that all data sources are managed independently of the local SQL server. That is, those data sources remain autonomous and can be queried (as well as updated) independently of the local SQL server. Those data sources may (subject to their own limitations) independently participate in SQL/MED-style distributed behavior initiated by more than one "local" SQL server, even though those multiple participations are not mutually coordinated in any way by any of those local SQL servers. The possible participation of a foreign server in multiple such SQL/MED environments is not specified by the SQL/MED standard.

See Figure 5.1 for an illustration of the possible relationships. Notice that Client 1 accesses SQL Server 1 directly and that SQL Server 1 then accesses both SQL Server 2 and Flat File Server 2 on behalf of Client 1. (This sort of access is represented in the figure by the "lightening bolt" connections, while the straight-line connections represent actual network connections.) Similarly, Client 2 accesses SQL Server 3 directly, while SQL Server 3 accesses SQL Server 2 and the Hierarchical Database Server on behalf of Client 2. The fact that SQL Server 2 participates concurrently in operations on behalf of both Client 1 and Client 2 is not addressed in any way by SQL/MED, since it is presumed that SQL Server 2 is autonomous from both SQL Server 1 and SQL Server 3. Of course, it's possible that the implementation of SQL Server 2 might not allow it to participate concurrently in more than one SQL/MED-style situation, but that merely results in Client 2 having to wait until Client 1's query is completed (or vice versa).

Henceforth, I'll refer to the local SQL server as simply the "SQL server" unless I need to distinguish between it and an SQL server that manages foreign data.

5.3 Foreign Tables, Foreign Servers, and Foreign-Data Wrappers

SQL is, of course, based on the relational model of data. Consequently, all of SQL's primary tasks operate on tables and produce tables as their results. Thus, all collections of data accessed by an SQL server (other than parameters supplied to

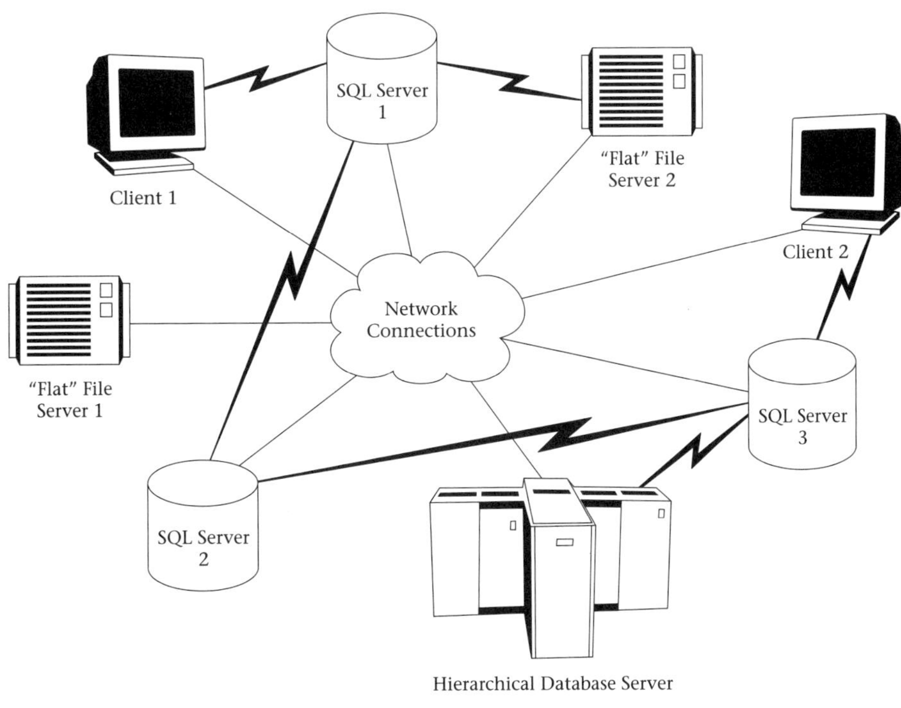

Figure 5.1 Autonomous Data Sources and SQL/MED

it by application programs) must be organized as an SQL table—or appear as though they are organized as one.

When the data managed by those other servers (*foreign data*) is to be accessed through the facilities of SQL/MED, it must be provided to the local server as though it were in tabular form. Of course, in some cases, when the foreign data is managed by another SQL server, the data *is* already in tabular form. In other cases—ordinary "flat" files, for example—the data must be manipulated into tabular form before the SQL server receives it.

In both situations, the collection of foreign data that the SQL server "sees" as a table is called a *foreign table*. Some foreign tables really are tables, while others are mere phantoms created by a software layer called a *foreign-data wrapper* from data provided by the manager of that data, called a *foreign server*. The foreign-data wrapper *mediates* (or negotiates, or manages) the SQL server's access to the foreign server. In many situations, a single foreign server makes several collections of data available for access as foreign tables, all of which can be accessed through a single network (or other) connection. In general, each category of foreign server (such as Linux file systems, IMS hierarchical database systems, or Oracle SQL database systems) presents a single interface. Thus, each category is mediated by a single foreign-data wrapper that is designed to communicate through that interface. That is, a single foreign-data wrapper can normally be used to mediate access to any number of foreign servers of the type that it is designed to access. Some foreign-data wrappers may even be able to mediate access to more than one type of foreign server, but SQL/MED makes no statement about this capability.

Each foreign server to be accessed by a foreign-data wrapper is typically characterized by some sort of configuration information, such as a host name and port number, that differentiates it from other foreign servers accessed via the same foreign-data wrapper. Because the sorts of information required are likely to vary from wrapper to wrapper, SQL/MED does not specify a specific, fixed set of attributes. Instead, the concept of *generic options* (attribute/value pairs used by foreign-data wrappers for configuration purposes) is used. Generic options can be associated with each of the foreign data modeling concepts introduced by SQL/MED, including foreign servers, foreign tables, and even the columns of foreign tables. These generic options are created as part of the metadata of each of those concepts and are stored in the SQL server's catalog where they are made available upon request by the foreign-data wrapper. The SQL server does not interpret them, but delivers their values whenever requested by the foreign-data wrappers. For example, a foreign-data wrapper that represents data stored in ordinary files as foreign tables can associate an option with each table that specifies some character that is to be used to delimit fields in the corresponding file.

Figure 5.2 illustrates the relationships between the SQL server, the foreign-data wrapper, and the foreign server. Although the figure implies that the foreign-data wrapper is somehow contained within the same "box" (e.g., computer, process space) as the SQL server, SQL/MED makes no such requirement. Conforming SQL/MED implementations might well choose to permit some sort of network protocol as part of the implementation of the SQL/MED API. Similarly, the foreign-data wrapper and the foreign server may be located in different computer systems or within a single process space. However, I believe that the SQL/MED API operates much more efficiently when the foreign-data wrapper and the SQL server are located in a single computer system, if not a single process space.

When an application program submits a query to the SQL server, that query is examined by the SQL server to determine whether it references only data that the SQL server manages. If so, the SQL server executes the query without assistance from any foreign server.

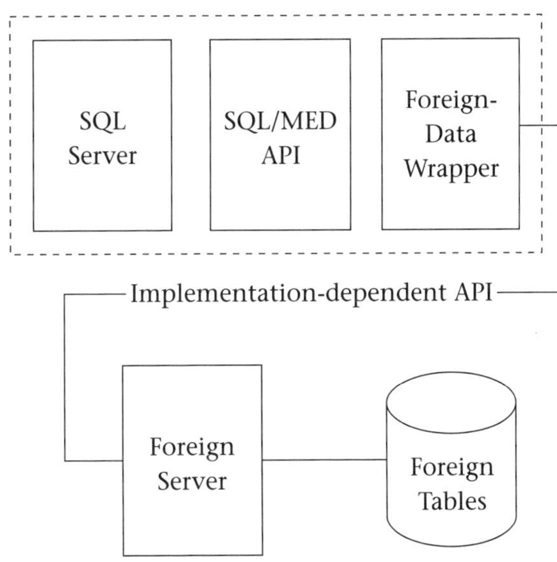

Figure 5.2 Components Defined by SQL/MED

However, if the query references one or more foreign tables, then the SQL server must determine where those foreign tables are located and what foreign servers manage them. Most importantly, the SQL server must identify the specific foreign-data wrappers that mediate access to the relevant foreign servers.

Once the SQL server has identified the foreign servers that manage each of the foreign tables referenced in a query, that query is *decomposed* into smaller queries (called *query fragments*) that access each of those foreign tables. In the first version of SQL/MED, each query fragment can access only a single foreign table; future versions may allow query fragments that reference multiple foreign tables managed by a single foreign server to be submitted as a single request to that foreign server. If the query also references tables local to the SQL server, a smaller query that accesses those tables is also generated.

The SQL server then begins the process of communicating—through the appropriate foreign-data wrappers—with each of the foreign servers for which a query fragment has been produced. When the result of each of those query fragments is available, the SQL server combines them as appropriate for the initial query and produces a unified query result. I'll discuss the processes of query planning and execution in section 5.5.

Before going into that level of detail, however, please look closely at Figure 5.3. This figure illustrates the overall architecture of SQL/MED (and, in fact, the

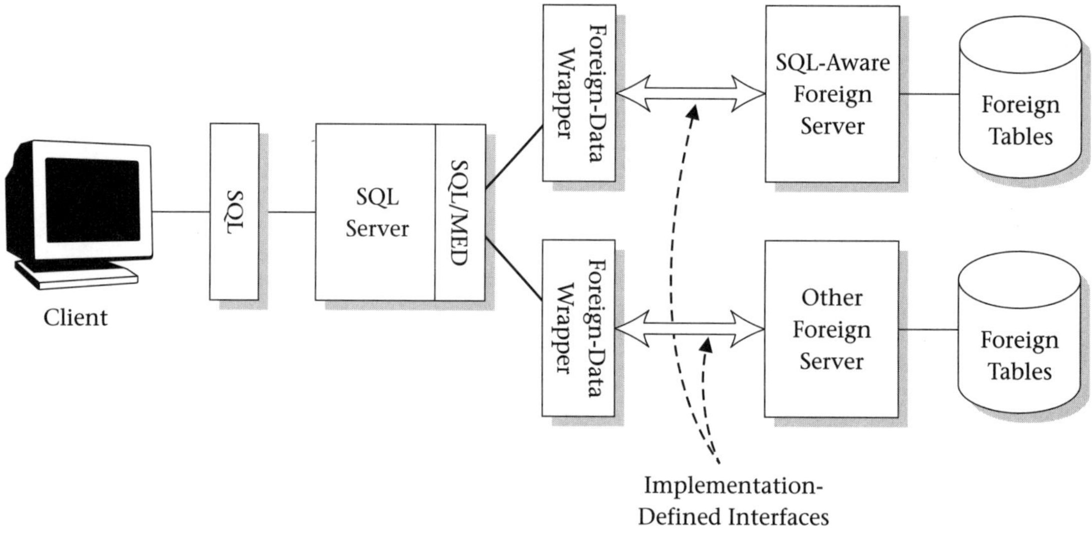

Figure 5.3 SQL/MED Architecture

figure is modeled closely after one that appears in the SQL/MED standard). Although neither Figure 5.2 nor Figure 5.3 explicitly indicates that a single foreign-data wrapper can mediate more than one foreign server, SQL/MED readily supports that configuration.

5.4 Metadata Associated with Management of External Data

Earlier in the chapter, I said that metadata had to be available to the SQL server for every foreign table that it can access on behalf of its client programs. In fact, the SQL server must have access to information that describes not only the foreign tables, but also the foreign servers themselves, the foreign-data wrappers, and the users that are permitted to access the foreign tables and the privileges that they have on those foreign tables.

In a typical environment, some user—often a database administrator—creates the metadata that describes every foreign table that can be accessed by the SQL server, every foreign server that manages one of those foreign tables, and every foreign-data wrapper available to the SQL server, as well as metadata that defines a mapping between users of the SQL server and the corresponding security mechanisms at those foreign servers. In some cases (see section 5.4.4), foreign servers may allow some of its metadata to be exported in a form suitable for direct import on the SQL server, possibly saving some poor overworked database administrator a lot of work.

5.4.1 Foreign-Data Wrappers

Foreign-data wrappers are usually implemented as code that is not tightly bound with the SQL server. In most environments, the typical implementation is a shared library of functions that are invoked by the SQL server through the SQL/MED API (see section 5.5). For example, on Windows systems, the most likely implementation is a DLL.

Foreign-data wrappers are made known to an SQL server by successful execution of a CREATE FOREIGN DATA WRAPPER statement, the syntax for which is shown in Syntax 5.1.

Syntax 5.1 *<foreign-data wrapper definition> Syntax*

```
<foreign-data wrapper definition> ::=
    CREATE FOREIGN DATA WRAPPER <foreign-data wrapper name>
    [ AUTHORIZATION <authorization identifier> ]
    [ <library name specification> ]
    <language clause>
    [ <generic options> ]

<library name specification> ::= LIBRARY <library name>

<library name> ::= <character string literal>
```

Every foreign-data wrapper known to an SQL server has a unique name when qualified by the name of the catalog in which it has been created. A foreign-data wrapper is *not* a schema object, as are tables, views, triggers, and assertions. Instead, it is a *catalog* object and is thus a kind of peer to schemas.

Like schemas, foreign-data wrappers are assigned an owner at the time they are created. The optional AUTHORIZATION clause specifies the owner of the foreign-data wrapper; if the clause is omitted, then the authorization identifier executing the statement is used. (As this volume goes to press, a correction to SQL:1999 is being considered that would remove the AUTHORIZATION clause so that the owner of a foreign-data wrapper is always the authorization identifier executing the statement.)

The LIBRARY clause provides the mechanism by which the actual code that implements the foreign-data wrapper is identified. It is an optional clause, but its omission means that the SQL server determines the library name in some implementation-defined manner. In most cases, I suspect that you'll want to specify this clause yourself. It requires a character string literal, because ordinary SQL identifiers are unlikely to identify a library adequately in very many environments. In most cases, the literal will provide something like a full directory path to a shared library or to a directory containing the routines that implement the foreign-data wrapper.

The `<language clause>` (which is required) identifies the language whose function invocation mechanism is used to invoke the foreign-data wrapper's library routines. The most common choices today seem to be C and Java, but others are certainly possible.

If the specific foreign-data wrapper for which you're creating metadata requires one or more generic options to be specified, you should do so when you execute the CREATE FOREIGN DATA WRAPPER statement. Neither I nor the SQL/MED standard can give additional guidance about the generic options; only your foreign-data wrapper's documentation can do that. However, I can tell you the syntax for specifying generic options: it appears in Syntax 5.2, and `<option name>`s are SQL identifiers.

Syntax 5.2 *<generic options> Syntax*

```
<generic options> ::=
    OPTIONS <left paren> <generic option list> <right paren>

<generic option list> ::=
    <generic option> [ { <comma> <generic option> }... ]

<generic option> ::= <option name> [ <option value> ]

<option value> ::= <character string literal>
```

I can create the metadata for a foreign-data wrapper with a statement like that shown in Example 5.1. In that example, I create a foreign-data wrapper that I call `UNIX_FILES` (presumably because its purpose is to access Unix files); its owner is some authorization identifier `JIM` and it depends on a library with C language calling conventions located at `/usr/bin/sharelibs/filmgr.shr`. The wrapper is given two generic options: the first, `protocol`, is given the value `"TCP/IP"`, and the second, `recordsep`, is given the value `"LF"`.

Example 5.1 *Creating a Foreign-Data Wrapper*

```
CREATE FOREIGN DATA WRAPPER unix_files
  AUTHORIZATION jim
  LIBRARY '/usr/bin/sharelibs/filmgr.shr'
  LANGUAGE C
  OPTIONS ( protocol 'TCP/IP', recordsep 'LF' )
```

When a foreign-data wrapper is no longer required—if, for example, your applications no longer need access to the type of data it mediates—then you can remove it from your environment by using the DROP FOREIGN DATA WRAPPER statement whose syntax is shown in Syntax 5.3.

Syntax 5.3 *<drop foreign-data wrapper statement> Syntax*

```
<drop foreign-data wrapper statement> ::=
    DROP FOREIGN DATA WRAPPER <foreign-data wrapper name>
    <drop behavior>
```

As with all DROP statements, the `<drop behavior>` is either RESTRICT or CASCADE. RESTRICT means that the DROP will fail if there remains any foreign server definition in your system that is mediated by the foreign-data wrapper that you're trying to drop. CASCADE means that any such foreign server definitions will also be dropped, as will all foreign table definitions of foreign tables managed by those foreign servers. Only the owner of a foreign-data wrapper can drop its definition.

In addition to merely creating and dropping foreign-data wrappers, SQL/MED permits you to modify the definitions of existing foreign-data wrappers in two ways. First, you can replace the specified library with a different library, perhaps because you have installed a new version of the software (but you cannot change the specification of the programming language in which the library is written; to make that change requires dropping the wrapper and creating a new one). Second, you can alter the generic options, by adding to them, deleting one or more of them, or modifying the definition of one or more of them. The syntax for altering a foreign-data wrapper definition appears in Syntax 5.4. At least one of the two optional clauses must be specified in order for there to be any effect; you are free to specify both of them. Only the owner of a foreign-data wrapper can alter its definition.

Syntax 5.4 *<alter foreign-data wrapper statement> Syntax*

```
<alter foreign-data wrapper statement> ::=
    ALTER FOREIGN DATA WRAPPER <foreign-data wrapper name>
    [ <library name specification> ]
    [ <alter generic options> ]
```

The syntax for altering generic options appears in Syntax 5.5. If you don't specify the optional `<alter operation>`, then ADD is implicit. If you specify SET, then the value of the specified option is modified (if there is no such option, then you'll get an error). And, of course, if you specify DROP, the specified option is removed from the set of generic options for this foreign-data wrapper (again, if there is no such option, you'll get an error).

Syntax 5.5 *<alter generic options> Syntax*

```
<alter generic options> ::=
    OPTIONS <left paren> <alter generic option list> <right paren>

<alter generic option list> ::=
    <alter generic option> [ { <comma> <alter generic option> }... ]

<alter generic option> ::=
    [ <alter operation> ] <option name> [ <option value> ]

<alter operation> ::=
    ADD
  | SET
  | DROP
```

Example 5.2 illustrates how I might alter my foreign-data wrapper to use a different library and to change its generic options.

Example 5.2 *Altering a Foreign-Data Wrapper's Definition*

```
ALTER FOREIGN DATA WRAPPER unix_files
  LIBRARY '/usr/bin/sharelibs/filmgr.v2.shr'
  OPTIONS ( DROP protocol, SET recordsep 'CRLF', fieldsep '\t' )
```

In that ALTER FOREIGN DATA WRAPPER statement, I've removed the generic option for `protocol`, changed the value of the `recordsep` option, and added a `fieldsep` option.

5.4.2 Foreign Servers

Once I have defined a foreign-data wrapper that has the capability of mediating access to foreign servers of a particular type, I can now create definitions for one or more foreign servers of that type. As you would expect, a CREATE SERVER statement (for reasons that escape me, the keyword FOREIGN is not permitted in this statement) is used for this purpose. The syntax for this statement is seen in Syntax 5.6.

Syntax 5.6 *<foreign server definition> Syntax*

```
<foreign server definition> ::=
    CREATE SERVER <foreign server name>
    [ TYPE <server type> ]
    [ VERSION <server version> ]
    [ AUTHORIZATION <authorization identifier> ]
    FOREIGN DATA WRAPPER <foreign-data wrapper name>
    [ <generic options> ]
```

In the CREATE SERVER statement, the optional TYPE and VERSION clauses respectively specify `<server type>` and `<server version>` values; if one or both of these values are omitted, then it is presumed that there are no meaningful values for the clauses. The formats and acceptable values of those items are left completely up to each foreign-server implementation. (I happen to believe that the SQL/MED standard should have required both of those values to be character string literals whose *content* remained implementation-defined, so this might be considered to be a bug in the SQL/MED standard.)

As with foreign-data wrapper creation, if the AUTHORIZATION clause is omitted, then the owner of the foreign server is the user executing the CREATE SERVER statement. Also, foreign servers are catalog objects (as are foreign-data wrappers) and not schema objects such as tables, and the like. (In another similarity with foreign-data wrapper creation, at the time this volume goes to press, a correction to SQL:1999 is being considered that would remove the AUTHORIZATION clause so that the owner of a foreign server is always the authorization identifier executing the statement.)

While most of the clauses of this statement are optional, it is mandatory that every foreign server definition provides the name of the foreign-data wrapper that will mediate access to the foreign server. That, perhaps obviously, means that the foreign-data wrapper must always be created before the foreign servers that depend on its services. In Example 5.3, you can see how a foreign server might be created.

Example 5.3 *Creating a Foreign Server*

```
CREATE SERVER new_dvd_files
  TYPE 'Ultrix' VERSION '3.5'
  AUTHORIZATION jim
  FOREIGN DATA WRAPPER unix_files
  OPTIONS ( node '128.0.0.12', port '1258' )
```

In addition to creating foreign server descriptions, it is also possible to drop them and to alter them. The syntax for dropping a foreign server is seen in Syntax 5.7, and the syntax for altering the definition of a foreign server is found in Syntax 5.8.

Syntax 5.7 *<drop foreign server statement> Syntax*

```
<drop foreign server statement> ::=
    DROP SERVER <foreign server name>
    <drop behavior>
```

As with other DROP statements, a DROP SERVER statement that specifies RESTRICT will fail if there are any other SQL schema objects that depend on the object being dropped; if CASCADE is specified, then it will drop those dependent objects. For example, if there are one or more foreign tables defined that are associated with the foreign server, the statement will fail or drop those foreign tables. Only the owner of a foreign server can drop it.

Syntax 5.8 *<alter foreign server statement> Syntax*

```
<alter foreign server statement> ::=
    ALTER SERVER <foreign server name>
    [ VERSION <server version> ]
    [ <alter generic options> ]
```

The only attributes of a foreign server that can be changed are the generic options and the server version (again, I believe that the `<server version>` value should always be a character string literal, but the SQL/MED standard leaves that entirely up to the implementation). Note particularly that it is not possible to change the foreign-data wrapper associated with a foreign server; if you find that you need to do something like this, then you should plan to drop the foreign server entirely (which, of course, means dropping all of the foreign tables that it manages) and recreating it with the association to the new foreign-data wrapper. And, finally, only the owner of a foreign server is allowed to alter its definition.

You can see an example of modifying the definition of a foreign server in Example 5.4.

Example 5.4 *Altering a Foreign Server Definition*

```
ALTER SERVER new_dvd_files
  OPTIONS ( SET node '128.0.0.101' )
```

5.4.3 Foreign Tables

Once I have created the definition of a foreign server (and, before that, the foreign-data wrapper that mediates access to the foreign server), I can start defining the foreign tables that are managed by that foreign server.

Defining a foreign table is a lot like defining an ordinary SQL table, which is described in the first volume of this book.[6] The most obvious differences, which you see in Syntax 5.9, are the specification of the foreign server that manages the foreign table and the possibility to define generic options associated with the foreign table as well as generic options associated with the columns of the foreign table. Foreign tables' names, when fully qualified, cannot duplicate the names of other SQL tables or views.

Syntax 5.9 *<foreign table definition> Syntax*

```
<foreign table definition> ::=
    CREATE FOREIGN TABLE <table name>
      [ <left paren> <basic column definition list> <right paren> ]
      SERVER <foreign server name> [ <table generic options> ]

<table generic options> ::= <generic options>

<basic column definition list> ::=
    <basic column definition> [ <comma> <basic column definition>... ]

<basic column definition> ::=
    <column name> <data type> [ <column generic options> ]

<column generic options> ::= <generic options>
```

6 Jim Melton and Alan R. Simon, *SQL:1999—Understanding Relational Language Components* (San Francisco: Morgan Kaufmann Publishers, 2000).

An additional difference that is worth emphasizing is the use of `<basic column definition>`s to define columns of the foreign table (by contrast, the columns of ordinary SQL tables are defined using `<column definition>`s).

A `<basic column definition>` allows only a column name and data type (plus generic options), while a `<column definition>` allows additional options like a default value and column constraints. A little thought reveals the reason for this difference. When you define columns of ordinary tables, you're creating both the table and its columns and the metadata that describes them, and you're doing so on your local SQL server where you presumably have the privileges to create such objects. But when you define a foreign table and its columns, all you're doing is creating a local metadata description of an object that exists elsewhere, under the control of another server. You're not actually creating the object on the remote site, merely describing it at your local server. Therefore, it's inappropriate to specify characteristics like default values or column constraints (or, for that matter, table constraints) for such foreign objects.

Writing a CREATE FOREIGN TABLE statement requires understanding the data that the foreign table is supposed to represent, along with the manner in which that foreign table is to be presented to the application programs. These matters are governed entirely by the nature of the foreign-data wrapper that you have chosen to mediate access to the foreign server that manages the foreign tables you're establishing.

Let's consider a flat file that contains data about recent DVD releases. In that file, each record (a concept appropriate for files, though not an SQL term) contains information about one DVD. Each record contains several fields (also appropriate for files, while used in SQL for the ROW type): DVD title, release date, and studio name. Records are separated by carriage-return/line-feed pairs, and fields are separated by tab characters. The foreign-data wrapper that you saw created in Example 5.1 and modified in Example 5.2 contains generic options named `recordsep`, whose value is "`CRLF`," and `fieldsep`, whose value is "`\t`." The `recordsep` value is some code that the foreign-data wrapper interprets (using information inherent to the wrapper) and uses to identify the separation between records in the file. Similarly, the `fieldsep` value is interpreted and used to identify boundaries between fields of a single record. We may assume, for the purposes of this discussion, that the character string "`CRLF`" is meant to inform the wrapper that a carriage return followed by a line feed make up the record separator, and that the string "`\t`" implies that a tab character delineates fields. Obviously, I planned this relationship so that the foreign-data wrapper definition suits the actual data in the file. Example 5.5 shows what some of this data might look like; I've used a convention in which each record appears on a new line (therefore, the end of a line is meant to represent the carriage return and line feed combination) and two or more spaces indicate the tabs that separate fields. ("More" is meant to simulate the common practice of having tab stops at fixed increments of display columns; the result is usually not very aesthetic, but it accurately reflects how a file like this is typically displayed.)

Example 5.5 *Sample File Containing DVD Release Information*

```
Seven                1995  New Line Cinema
Copycat              1995  Warner Bros.
The Bone Collector   1999  Columbia Pictures
From Hell            2001  20th Century Fox
Serial Mom           1994  Polar Entertainment
```

My preferred foreign-data wrapper, named `unix_files`, is capable (it had better be!) of transforming each record into a row of a table and each field of a record into a column of the corresponding row. Therefore, I want to create a foreign table like the one shown in Example 5.6, which defines the columns of the foreign table and identifies the foreign server that manages the data from which the rows of the foreign table are derived.

Example 5.6 *Sample Foreign Table Definition*

```
CREATE FOREIGN TABLE dvd_releases (
  title           CHARACTER VARYING(50),
  year            INTEGER,
  released_by     CHARACTER VARYING(50) )
  SERVER new_dvd_files
  OPTIONS ( filename '/usr/mvstore/new-releases.txt' )
```

Note that the CREATE FOREIGN TABLE statement does not have any standardized way to indicate the specific "file" (or other external data source) that corresponds to the foreign table being defined. In Example 5.6, I used a generic option, `filename`, to provide that information. In some cases, a generic option will be used (although the name will probably be different), while other foreign servers will be "hard-wired" to a particular data source.

The combination of the data in Example 5.5 and the foreign table definition in Example 5.6 is going to behave a lot like Table 5.1. (I say "a lot like," because the current version of SQL/MED doesn't support modification of foreign tables, so you cannot execute INSERT, UPDATE, or DELETE statements that specify this table.)

Table 5.1 *Foreign Table dvd_releases*

TITLE	*YEAR*	*RELEASED_BY*
Seven	1995	New Line Cinema
Copycat	1995	Warner Bros.
The Bone Collector	1999	Columbia Pictures
From Hell	2001	20th Century Fox
Serial Mom	1994	Polar Entertainment

Unlike foreign-data wrappers and foreign servers, foreign tables are schema objects. Therefore, the foreign table's table name is an ordinary SQL 3-part name (`catalog.schema.table`). This fact implies that the owner of the table is the owner of the schema in which it is defined.

By now, you've come to expect that foreign objects can be dropped as well as altered, and foreign tables are no exception. The syntax used to drop a foreign table is given in Syntax 5.10, while the syntax used for altering a foreign table's definition is given in Syntax 5.11.

Syntax 5.10 *<drop foreign table statement> Syntax*

```
<drop foreign table statement> ::=
    DROP FOREIGN TABLE <table name>
    <drop behavior>
```

As with previous DROP statements, a `<drop behavior>` of RESTRICT means that the DROP statement fails if there are any schema objects (such as views) that depend on the object being dropped; similarly, specifying CASCADE means that those dependent objects will be dropped, too.

Syntax 5.11 *<alter foreign table statement> Syntax*

```
<alter foreign table statement> ::=
    ALTER FOREIGN TABLE <table name>
    <alter foreign table action>

<alter foreign table action> ::=
    <add basic column definition>
  | <alter basic column definition>
  | <drop basic column definition>
  | <alter generic options>
```

```
<add basic column definition> ::=
    ADD [ COLUMN ] <basic column definition>

<alter basic column definition> ::=
    ALTER [ COLUMN ] <column name>
      <alter basic column action>

<alter basic column action> ::=
    <alter generic options>

<drop basic column definition> ::=
    DROP [ COLUMN ] <column name> <drop behavior>
```

As you can see in Syntax 5.11, there are several ways in which you can alter the definition of a foreign table: you can add columns to the table and drop columns from the table; you can alter the generic options of a column of the table; and you can alter the generic options of the table itself. Unfortunately, only one of these actions can be performed with each ALTER FOREIGN TABLE statement; I suspect that a future version of SQL/MED will extend this to allow multiple actions to be specified in a single statement. Suppose I learned that I was supposed to identify the field associated with each column using a generic option that specifies the field's relative position in each record. The ALTER FOREIGN TABLE statements in Example 5.7 would make the necessary changes.

Example 5.7 *Altering a Foreign Table Definition*

```
ALTER FOREIGN TABLE dvd_releases
  ALTER COLUMN title OPTIONS ( ADD position '1' )
ALTER FOREIGN TABLE dvd_releases
  ALTER COLUMN year OPTIONS ( ADD position '2' )
ALTER FOREIGN TABLE dvd_releases
  ALTER COLUMN released_by OPTIONS ( ADD position '3' )
```

Naturally, only the owner of a foreign table is permitted to drop it or alter its definition.

Happily, using a foreign table is very much like using an ordinary table, with only a few restrictions. In SQL:1999, foreign tables cannot be updated (at least not through the use of SQL statements), so they are effectively read-only tables. Future versions of the SQL standard are expected to relax that restriction.

After you create a foreign table, you use SQL's GRANT and REVOKE statements to control access to the table and to its columns.

5.4.4 Foreign Schemas

The CREATE FOREIGN TABLE statement described in section 5.4.3 is obviously quite useful. But it's rather inconvenient when a particular foreign server has a very large number of data sources for which you'd like to create foreign table definitions. In many situations, you really don't have much of a choice, especially if the foreign server manages data for which there is no inherent metadata and for which "obvious" metadata isn't readily deduced. Even a sophisticated foreign-data wrapper will rarely be able to infer meaningful metadata in such situations, so manually generating copious numbers of foreign tables is your only option.

However, particularly if the foreign server happens to be some kind of database manager, the foreign data sources might have inherent metadata associated with them. In fact, foreign SQL servers (which SQL/MED calls *SQL-aware foreign servers*) will have SQL metadata available for your use. Clever foreign-data wrappers can often manipulate non-SQL metadata (or SQL metadata provided by a database system in a nonstandard format) into conforming SQL table and column definitions that you can use to create your foreign table definitions. But how?

The answer lies in a statement designed just for this purpose, as seen in Syntax 5.12.

Syntax 5.12 *<import foreign schema statement> Syntax*

```
<import foreign schema statement> ::=
    IMPORT FOREIGN SCHEMA <foreign schema name>
    [ <import qualifications> ]
    FROM SERVER <foreign server name>
    INTO <local schema name>

<import qualifications> ::=
    LIMIT TO <left paren> <table name list> <right paren>
  | EXCEPT <left paren> <table name list> <right paren>

<table name list> ::=
    <table name> [ { <comma> <table name> }... ]

<foreign schema name> ::= <schema name>

<local schema name> ::= <schema name>
```

The IMPORT FOREIGN SCHEMA statement does precisely what its name suggests: it imports a schema definition from a foreign server and converts it into appropriate foreign table definitions in a selected schema on your local SQL server. You specify the name of the local schema into which you wish the foreign table definitions to be created, as well as the name of the schema (or the closest corresponding concept!) at the foreign server. Of course, you must also specify the foreign server from which you wish to import these table definitions.

The optional `<import qualifications>` clause allows you to modify the selection of tables whose definitions you wish to import. The foreign schema might contain scores of tables, of which you might wish to import only a few. In this case, you'd use the LIMIT TO clause to specify a list of table names identifying the tables whose definitions you want imported. Alternatively, you might wish to import most of the tables, but a relatively small number are of no interest. This latter case calls for the EXCEPT clause, which takes a list of table names identifying the tables to be omitted from the import operation.

If the specified foreign server is unable to export schema information—perhaps because it has no concept analogous to schemas or because the associated foreign-data wrapper doesn't support the capability to import schemas—then the statement fails with an exception condition. A different exception is raised if you specify a schema name that the foreign server does not recognize; similarly, if you identify tables to be imported using table names that the foreign server does not recognize, an exception condition is raised.

If you provided correct information, however, the statement generates and executes the appropriate CREATE FOREIGN TABLE statements, just as though you had entered them yourself. Example 5.8 illustrates the use of IMPORT FOREIGN SCHEMA.

Example 5.8 *Importing a Foreign Schema*

```
IMPORT FOREIGN SCHEMA movie_material
  EXCEPT ( press_releases )
  FROM SERVER new_dvd_files
  INTO movies_schema
```

In Example 5.8, I've imported from the `new_dvd_files` foreign server all of the foreign tables in the foreign schema named `movie_material`, except for the table known as `press_releases`. (Of course, it's somewhat unlikely that a Unix file server will have SQL-relevant metadata for the files that it manages, so this example is merely illustrative of the syntax of the IMPORT FOREIGN SCHEMA statement.)

5.4.5 User Mappings

Users of SQL database products and readers of the first volume of this book[7] will be familiar with the notions of authorization identifiers and of privileges. Every schema and every schema object in an SQL environment has an owner, represented by an authorization identifier. The owners of those schema objects have all possible privileges on the objects (in the case of views, the range of possible privileges is sometimes limited because of the owners' lack of certain privileges on underlying tables) and are able to grant their privileges to other authorization identifiers.

As you read in sections 5.4.1 and 5.4.2, SQL/MED adds foreign-data wrappers and foreign servers to the objects in SQL environments that have owners. Every foreign-data wrapper and every foreign server has a particular owner; since the metadata for those objects is not contained in a schema, their ownership is independent of the ownership of any schema. The owner of one of those objects can grant USAGE privilege on the object to other authorization identifiers, who are otherwise unable to perform any operation using the object. Users who have not been granted USAGE privilege on a foreign-data wrapper are not able to create foreign servers that depend on that wrapper, and users who have not been granted USAGE privilege on a foreign server cannot create foreign tables that are managed by that server.

By contrast, as you learned in section 5.4.3, the definition of a foreign table is contained in some schema and is thus owned by the owner of the schema that contains it—and privileges to access a foreign table must be granted by the schema's owner or by some authorization identifier to whom the owner has granted the privilege WITH GRANT OPTION.

But what about the data in the external data source from which the foreign table's data is derived? How is that data protected from unauthorized use?

Some foreign servers do not recognize the notion of authorized users or of privilege requirements. Data managed by such servers are generally unprotected, except perhaps by facilities of the operating systems under which they operate. Connecting to such a server requires only the ability to negotiate permission to connect to the server, after which there are no limitations on data access. Negotiating such permission often consists of nothing more than providing a user name and a password to the foreign server, perhaps in the form of a couple of generic options.

However, many foreign servers, particularly SQL servers, recognize the concept of *ownership* of the data that they manage. Individual data collections (such as SQL tables) may be owned by particular users who are known to the foreign

7 Ibid.

server by some identifier. That identifier likely has little relationship to the authorization identifier under which some (other) user submits a query at his local SQL server. The obvious question is: How are privileges determined at a foreign server based on authorization information available at the local SQL server? SQL/MED provides the solution in the form of *user mappings*. A user mapping is a mechanism that specifies the information necessary to authorize access to specific data managed by a foreign server based completely on the authorization identifier making the access requests from a local SQL server. When an SQL statement involving a foreign table is executed by the local SQL server, the relevant security information is obtained from the user mapping and provided to the appropriate foreign-data wrapper, which will presumably use it in negotiations with the foreign server that manages the foreign table.

Syntax 5.13 provides the syntax of the CREATE USER MAPPING statement.

Syntax 5.13 *<user mapping definition> Syntax*

```
<user mapping definition> ::=
    CREATE USER MAPPING FOR <specific or generic authorization identifier>
    SERVER <foreign server name>
    [ <generic options> ]

<specific or generic authorization identifier> ::=
    <authorization identifier>
  | USER
  | CURRENT_USER
  | PUBLIC
```

The CREATE USER MAPPING statement requires that you specify an authorization identifier that is valid at the local SQL server and that you identify the foreign server for which the mapping applies. But please observe that the statement does not specify any particular way to identify corresponding identifying information that is relevant to that foreign server. The reason is easy to deduce: some foreign servers will require merely an authorization identifier, while others might require user names, passwords, and encrypted certificates. Because of the tremendous variability that is possible, SQL/MED depends on generic options to specify this information.

The authorization identifier at the local SQL server can be either a specific authorization identifier explicitly provided, USER or its synonym CURRENT_USER (to indicate the authorization identifier in control when the CREATE USER MAPPING statement was executed), or PUBLIC (meaning "every user on the local SQL server"). To ensure that I have the relevant privileges at the foreign server that I defined in Example 5.3, I might execute a statement like the one seen in Example 5.9.

Example 5.9 *Mapping Some Users*

```
CREATE USER MAPPING FOR CURRENT_USER
  SERVER unix_files
  OPTIONS ( user 'jim.melton', password 'Xdk103Bo' )
```

The presence of a visible password in the generic options clause of that statement might seem like a terrible breach of security, leading one to demand that generic options be enhanced to permit value expressions instead of mere character string literals. However, the contents of that character string are meaningful only to the foreign-data wrapper. That means that I could have encoded some information that allowed the foreign-data wrapper to retrieve a security certificate from some repository, or perhaps to initiate a dialog through a user interface during which I would enter a password dynamically.

When the foreign server is an SQL server or some other data source with analogous authorization concepts, the relationships between authorization identifiers on the local SQL server and the foreign server's analogs can get rather complex. Some application environments might require "1:1" mappings, in which each local SQL server authorization identifier is mapped to exactly one analogous entity on the foreign server. Others might encourage "n:m" mappings, in which system administrators must maintain separate sets of privileges for every combination of user and foreign server. Some users report that mapping several local authorization identifiers to a single set of privileges at a foreign server ("m:1" mapping) offers a reasonable compromise of complexity and flexibility.

By now, none of us are surprised to learn that user mappings can be dropped and altered. The syntax for accomplishing these tasks is given in Syntax 5.14 and Syntax 5.15, respectively.

Syntax 5.14 *<drop user mapping statement> Syntax*

```
<drop user mapping statement> ::=
    DROP USER MAPPING FOR <specific or generic authorization identifier>
    SERVER <foreign server name>
```

Note that the usual `<drop behavior>` clause is not present. Because there are no objects whose existence depends wholly on a user mapping (as opposed to objects whose semantics are influenced by a user mapping) there is (arguably) no need to RESTRICT or CASCADE the DROP.

Syntax 5.15 *<alter user mapping statement> Syntax*

```
<alter user mapping statement> ::=
    ALTER USER MAPPING <specific or generic authorization identifier>
    SERVER <foreign server name>
    <alter generic options>
```

Execution of an ALTER USER MAPPING statement can change only the generic options associated with the user mapping. I've provided examples of changing generic options earlier in this chapter, in Example 5.4, for example.

5.4.6 Capabilities Information

Foreign servers, as stated earlier in this chapter, range greatly in the abilities that they have. Some foreign servers are capable of executing entire SQL statements (and might thus take advantage of a special mode defined for foreign servers, called *passthrough mode,* which is covered in section 5.5). Other foreign servers might be able to access only a single field of a single record per request.

To allow an SQL server to include all sorts of foreign servers in the queries its users submit, the capabilities of those foreign servers must somehow be made known to the SQL server. This need is satisfied in SQL/MED by a routine that the SQL server can invoke to retrieve information about the capabilities and supported options of a foreign-data wrapper or a foreign server. That routine, `getOpts()`,[8] returns information about the specified object in either a format defined by the foreign-data wrapper or in a valid XML document (the DTD for which is specified in SQL/MED). The kind of information returned by that routine is determined entirely by the implementations and is not in any way specified by the SQL/MED standard.

5.4.7 Generic Options

As you have seen throughout this chapter, generic options are specified in an OPTIONS clause used when you create foreign-data wrappers, foreign servers, foreign tables, columns of foreign tables, and user mappings. In addition, they can be modified once the objects with which they are associated have been created. A generic option is a generic option name paired with a character string literal specifying the value of the named generic option.

---

8 I use the notation `identifier()` to specify the name of, or an invocation of, a particular routine without having to specify the particular arguments for that routine.

The SQL/MED standard does not specify any generic option names, much less any values associated with any generic options. The generic option names, and their permissible values, are defined completely by foreign-data wrappers and the foreign servers whose access they mediate. The only way to find out what generic options you can—or must—specify when you create a foreign object is to consult the products that you're using, probably by reading the documentation.

5.5 The SQL/MED API

The SQL/MED API is an interface between SQL servers and foreign-data wrappers. Although it bears some (deliberate) resemblence to SQL/CLI—discussed in Volume 1 of this book—it is not an interface that is used by application programs. Nor is it an interface between foreign-data wrappers and foreign servers; that interface is entirely defined by authors of the foreign-data wrappers.

The SQL/MED API includes a large number of functions, generically called *foreign-data wrapper interface routines*. Some foreign-data wrapper interface routines are implemented by the foreign-data wrapper and are invoked from the SQL server; these routines are called *foreign-data wrapper interface wrapper routines,* or just *wrapper routines*. Others are implemented by the SQL server and are invoked from the foreign-data wrapper; these are known as *foreign-data wrapper interface SQL-server routines,* or just *SQL-server routines*. One routine, `GetDiagnostics()`, is called a *foreign-data wrapper interface general routine*. That routine must be implemented in both the SQL server and in the foreign-data wrapper, so it can be invoked from either side of the SQL/MED interface.

Before you see the names of all of these routines, it will be helpful if I explain a bit of terminology and outline some of the relationships among the components used by the routines. You'll see how some of these components and routines are used in section 5.7.

5.5.1 SQL/MED Components

The SQL/MED interface utilizes a number of different components for which resources must be allocated when required and deallocated when they are no longer needed. SQL/MED tracks these components through the use of *handles,* which might be visualized as "pointers" to the memory data structures that provide storage for the components. Of course, handles are not necessarily implemented as memory addresses; that level of detail is left entirely up to the implementation.

The components used by SQL/MED, including the names applied to the handles associated with them, and a brief explanation of their purpose, are listed here:

- Foreign-data wrapper environment (WrapperEnv handle): Allocated by a call from the SQL server to the foreign-data wrapper; used as the context for all other interactions between the SQL server and the foreign-data wrapper.
- Foreign server connection (FSConnection handle): Allocated by a call from the SQL server to the foreign-data wrapper; used as the context for all requests to be handled by the foreign server.
- Foreign server (Server handle): Allocated by a call from the foreign-data wrapper to the SQL server; used by the foreign-data wrapper to obtain information about the foreign server to which a connection is made.
- Foreign-data wrapper (Wrapper handle): Allocated by the SQL server; used to obtain information about the foreign-data wrapper with which the SQL server is communicating.
- User (User handle): Allocated by the SQL server; used to obtain information about the user on whose behalf a connection to a foreign server is being made.
- Request (Request handle): Allocated by the SQL server to reference the SQL statement fragment that is to be executed by the foreign-data wrapper and foreign server; used by the foreign-data wrapper to obtain information about the names of foreign tables referenced in the FROM clause, names of columns referenced in the SELECT list, and so on.
- Table reference (Table Reference handle): Allocated by the SQL server to reference foreign tables cited in the FROM clause of a request.
- Value expression (Value Expression handle): Allocated by the SQL server to reference value expressions appearing in the SELECT list of a request. (In the current version of SQL/MED, such value expressions are restricted to simple column references.)
- Reply (Reply handle): Allocated by a foreign-data wrapper to represent the subset of SQL statements that it is capable of handling.
- Execution (Execution handle): Allocated by a foreign-data wrapper to provide the context needed to process a Request and a Reply.
- Wrapper Parameter Descriptor (WPDHandle): Allocated by a foreign-data wrapper to represent parameters used in the execution of SQL statement

fragments; contains one descriptor area for each parameter, describing its data type and related information.

- Wrapper Row Descriptor (WRDHandle): Allocated by a foreign-data wrapper to represent the row returned by an execution of SQL statement fragments; contains one descriptor area for each column of the result row, describing its data type and related information.
- Server Parameter Descriptor (SPDHandle): Allocated by an SQL server to represent parameters used in the execution of SQL statement fragments; contains one descriptor area for each parameter, describing its data type and related information.
- Server Row Descriptor (SRDHandle): Allocated by an SQL server to represent the row returned by an execution of SQL statement fragments; contains one descriptor area for each column of the result row, describing its data type and related information.

5.5.2 SQL/MED Routines

The SQL/MED interface makes use of a significant number of functions, each of which plays a strategic role in communication between an SQL server and a foreign-data wrapper. As you read in section 5.5, the foreign-data wrapper is composed of a number of routines that are invoked by the SQL server, while the SQL server provides a number of additional routines that are invoked by the foreign-data wrapper. The routines that make up the SQL/MED API fall into several major categories:

- Allocate and deallocate resources.
- Control connections to foreign servers.
- Receive data from the SQL server about the SQL statement to be executed at the foreign server.
- Send data from the foreign server to the SQL server about the SQL statement that the foreign server is willing to execute.
- Initiate and terminate the execution of SQL statements by the foreign server.

The complete list of wrapper routines can be seen in Table 5.2, along with a brief explanation of their purposes; similarly, Table 5.3 contains a list of SQL server routines and brief explanations. Table 5.4 summarizes the only foreign-data wrapper interface general routine, `GetDiagnostics()`. The routines are given in alphabetic order by their routine names, rather than some "typical" order in which they might be invoked.[9] I have not documented the routines' parameters, since it is unlikely that SQL application programmers will need the information. If you find yourself needing to write a foreign-data wrapper, it would be a very good idea for you to acquire a copy of the SQL/MED standard (Appendix C, "Relevant Standards Bodies," contains the information necessary to do this).

Table 5.2 *Foreign-Data Wrapper Interface Wrapper Routines*

Wrapper Routine	*Purpose*
`AllocWrapperEnv`	Allocate a foreign-data wrapper environment and assign a handle to it.
`Close`	Close a foreign-data wrapper execution.
`ConnectServer`	Establish a connection to a foreign server and assign a handle to it.
`FreeExecutionHandle`	Deallocate resources associated with a foreign-data wrapper execution.
`FreeFSConnection`	Deallocate resources associated with a connection to a foreign server.
`FreeReplyHandle`	Deallocate resources associated with a reply to a query.
`FreeWrapperEnv`	Deallocate resources associated with a foreign-data wrapper environment.
`GetNumReplySelectElems`	Get the number of value expressions in the SELECT list of a query that the foreign-data wrapper is capable of handling.
`GetNumReplyTableRefs`	Get the number of table references in the FROM clause of a query that can be processed by the foreign-data wrapper.
`GetOpts`	Request the foreign-data wrapper to supply information about the capabilities and other information of the requested object.
`GetReplySelectElem`	Get the number of a value expression element from the select list of a query that the foreign-data wrapper is capable of handling.

(continued)

9 In ISO/IEC 9075-9:1999, *Information technology—Database Language—SQL—Part 9: Management of External Data (SQL/MED),* Table 3, "Sequence of actions during foreign server request executions," provides typical routine invocation sequences.

Table 5.2 *(Continued)*

Wrapper Routine	*Purpose*
GetReplyTableRef	Get the number of a table reference element from the FROM clause of a query that the foreign-data wrapper is capable of handling.
GetSPDHandle	Get the descriptor handle of the server parameter descriptor associated with an ExecutionHandle.
GetSRDHandle	Get the descriptor handle of the server row descriptor associated with an ExecutionHandle.
GetStatistics	Retrieve implementation-defined statistics associated with a specified SQL statement.
GetWPDHandle	Get the descriptor handle of the wrapper parameter descriptor associated with an ExecutionHandle.
GetWRDHandle	Get the descriptor handle of the wrapper row descriptor associated with an ExecutionHandle.
InitRequest	Determine whether a foreign-data wrapper can execute an SQL statement.
Iterate	Retrieve the next row from a foreign-data wrapper execution.
Open	Open a foreign-data wrapper execution.
ReOpen	Reopen a foreign-data wrapper execution (often used for subqueries in a loop implied by a join).
TransmitRequest	Supply a statement to be analyzed by the foreign server.

Table 5.3 *Foreign-Data Wrapper Interface SQL Server Routines*

Wrapper Routine	*Purpose*
AllocDescriptor	Allocate a foreign-data wrapper descriptor area and assign a handle to it.
FreeDescriptor	Release resources associated with a foreign-data wrapper descriptor area.
GetAuthorizationID	Get the authorization identifier associated with a user mapping.
GetDescriptor	Get a field from a foreign-data wrapper descriptor area.
GetNumSelectElems	Get the number of value expressions in the SELECT list of a query.

Table 5.3 *(Continued)*

Wrapper Routine	*Purpose*
GetNumServerOpts	Get the number of generic options associated with the foreign server.
GetNumTableColOpts	Get the number of generic options associated with a column of a foreign table.
GetNumTableOpts	Get the number of generic options associated with a foreign table.
GetNumTableRefElems	Get the number of table references contained in the FROM clause of a query.
GetNumUserOpts	Get the number of generic options associated with a user mapping.
GetNumWrapperOpts	Get the number of generic options associated with a foreign-data wrapper.
GetSelectElem	Get a value expression element from the SELECT list of a query.
GetSelectElemType	Get the type of a value expression.
GetServerName	Get the name of a foreign server.
GetServerOpt	Get the value of a generic option associated with a foreign server.
GetServerOptByName	Get the value of a generic option associated with a foreign server.
GetServerType	Get the type of a foreign server.
GetServerVersion	Get the version of a foreign server.
GetSQLString	Get a character string representation of the query that is associated with the request handle.
GetTableColOpt	Get the name and value of a generic option associated with a column of a foreign table, given an option number.
GetTableColOptByName	Get the name and value of a generic option associated with a column of a foreign table, given the option name.
GetTableOpt	Get the name and value of a generic option associated with a foreign table, given an option number.
GetTableOptByName	Get the name and value of a generic option associated with a foreign table, given the option name.

(continued)

Table 5.3 *(Continued)*

Wrapper Routine	*Purpose*
GetTableRefElem	Get a table reference element from the FROM clause of a query.
GetTableRefElemName	Get the table name of a table reference.
GetTableRefElemType	Get the type of a table reference.
GetTRDHandle	Get the descriptor handle of the table reference descriptor associated with a TableReferenceHandle.
GetUserOpt	Get the name and value of a generic option associated with a user mapping, given an option number.
GetUserOptByName	Get the name and value of a generic option associated with a user mapping, given the option name.
GetValExprColName	Get the column name associated with a value expression.
GetWrapperLibraryName	Get the library name of the library associated with a foreign-data wrapper.
GetWrapperName	Get the name of a foreign-data wrapper.
GetWrapperOpt	Get the name and value of a generic option associated with a foreign-data wrapper, given an option number.
GetWrapperOptByName	Get the name and value of a generic option associated with a foreign-data wrapper, given the option name.
SetDescriptor	Set a field in a foreign-data wrapper descriptor area.

Table 5.4 *Foreign-Data Wrapper Interface General Routine*

General Routine	*Purpose*
GetDiagnostics	Retrieves information from a foreign-data wrapper diagnostics area.

5.6 Processing Queries

As you have read in this chapter, foreign servers come in a wide array of types and capabilities. Some foreign servers (probably SQL servers themselves) understand the SQL language. Others might be handled by foreign-data wrappers that communicate with the local SQL server using SQL that they translate into sequences of actions appropriate for the foreign server.

When an SQL server is given an SQL statement that includes references to foreign tables, SQL/MED's query processing algorithms are invoked.

5.6.1 Decomposition Mode and Pass-Through Mode

Foreign servers that have no SQL capabilities of their own and are mediated by foreign-data wrappers that don't have SQL language facilities must communicate with the local SQL server in *decomposition mode*. Foreign servers that understand SQL, or that are mediated by foreign-data wrappers that understand SQL, may use *pass-through mode* instead. The design center of SQL/MED is decomposition mode, and most of this chapter addresses that subject. However, a few words about pass-through mode will be useful before I change the focus to decomposition mode.

While it is probably more common for pass-through mode to be used with SQL-aware foreign servers, SQL/MED certainly supports the use of pass-through mode to communicate with non-SQL-aware servers using whatever their "native language" might be. Similarly, decomposition mode is useful both with SQL-aware and non-SQL-aware foreign servers.

In pass-through mode, the SQL server transfers a query, as is, to the foreign-data wrapper. (The query is quite likely to be an SQL query but may be any query that the foreign-data wrapper and/or the foreign server understand.) The SQL server does not analyze the query at all, so the query must be handled by a single wrapper (which might require that a single foreign server execute it). The wrapper and the foreign server are then responsible for analyzing and executing the query. If the SQL statement cannot be executed at the foreign server—perhaps because the statement specified operations on tables unknown to the foreign server—then the foreign server must raise an appropriate error. Although implementation of pass-through mode by a foreign-data wrapper is optional, it is especially useful when the foreign server is also an SQL engine. Of course, using pass-through mode has disadvantages, too. Among other things, a query that is invoked using pass-through mode cannot combine data from multiple sources, since the query is entirely processed by a single foreign-data server.

Every SQL session has a characteristic called a *pass-through flag*. When you first start using SQL/MED facilities during an SQL session, the pass-through flag is set to *false*—meaning that communication with all foreign-data wrappers is done in decomposition mode. You can explicitly change your SQL session's pass-through flag by executing a SET PASSTHROUGH statement, whose syntax is shown in Syntax 5.16.

Syntax 5.16 *<set passthrough statement> Syntax*

```
<set passthrough statement> ::=
    SET PASSTHROUGH <passthrough specification>

<passthrough specification> ::=
    <value specification>
  | OFF
```

When you execute the SET PASSTHROUGH statement, you can turn the pass-through mode off by specifying OFF, or you can turn it on for a particular foreign server by specifying its name as part of the `<value specification>` (perhaps as a character string literal, or as the value of a host language variable passed to the statement). If pass-through mode is set for any foreign server, then the session pass-through flag is *true*; if passthrough mode is not set for any foreign server, then the session pass-through flag is *false*.

Decomposition mode requires that the SQL server analyze each SQL query for possible foreign table references. If a query includes a reference to a foreign table, then the SQL server must *decompose* the query into fragments. One or more of those fragments are often handled by the SQL server itself, but portions of the query that deal with the foreign table must be processed in cooperation with the foreign-data wrapper associated with the foreign server that manages that foreign table. Depending on the capabilities of the foreign-data wrapper (and, of course, of the foreign server), the steps required to initiate, execute, and complete that part of a query dealing with a particular foreign server can be quite extensive.

The interaction between the SQL server and the foreign-data wrapper can be divided into two phases:

- A *query planning* phase, in which the foreign-data wrapper and the SQL server cooperatively produce an execution plan for the fragment. Section 5.6.2 covers query planning in decomposition mode.
- A *query execution* phase, in which the agreed-upon plan is executed and foreign data is returned to the SQL server. Section 5.6.3 describes execution of queries in decomposition mode.

In both the query planning and query execution phases, the foreign-data wrapper and the SQL server exchange information. The SQL/MED API is based on the common programming concept of *handles*—values that identify (during the course of a query or of a session) some component or piece of information required by the SQL server or the foreign-data wrapper. The use of handles tends to make conforming implementations simpler by providing an easy mechanism to preserve the "state" of a query and to pass that state back and forth between the cooperating processes. Handles also make it easier to write the cooperating programs in different programming languages.

For example, suppose information managed by a foreign-data wrapper is to be passed to the SQL server. If the API required an explicit data structure to be passed from the foreign-data wrapper to the SQL server, then both would have to be written in the same programming language, or the authors would have to go to some effort to ensure that the components of the data structure were mapped properly between the programming language constructs of each language.

Instead of using such a data structure for this purpose, the SQL server passes an integer value—the handle—*representing* such a structure to the foreign-data wrapper. For each type of handle that can be exchanged, SQL/MED specifies a set of functions that are invoked with a handle as one argument and returns the requested value from the corresponding data structure.

In the two sections that follow, I generally avoid explicit discussion of the handles in an effort to keep the discussion at the conceptual level. However, you may assume that whenever a data structure is passed from the SQL server to a foreign-data wrapper or vice versa, the exchange is done by means of a handle.

5.6.2 Query Planning—Decomposition Mode

When a query is submitted to the SQL server in decomposition mode, the SQL server examines the query to determine whether it references any foreign tables. If it does, then the SQL server "rewrites" the query into query fragments. Each fragment represents some component of the query that can be fulfilled by the foreign-data wrapper (and, by implication, the foreign server) associated with a foreign table. The specific nature of each query fragment depends very heavily on the capabilities of the foreign-data wrapper and of the foreign server (as indicated in section 5.4.6).

During the query planning process, the interaction between the SQL server and the foreign-data wrapper is based on a request/reply dialog. The SQL server builds a request that represents the query fragment to be handled by the specific foreign server and notifies the foreign-data wrapper of the request. The foreign-data wrapper analyzes the request and returns a reply that describes that portion of the request that can be handled by the foreign server. The SQL server must then compensate for any part of the query fragment that cannot be executed by the foreign server. For example, the foreign-data wrapper (which, of course, has intimate knowledge of the foreign server's capabilities) might respond that it is capable only of retrieving a single column of a single table, even though the request asked for multiple selected columns of a single table to be retrieved. In this case, the SQL server must be prepared to retrieve the required columns one at a time from the data returned by the foreign-data wrapper when the request is executed.

The flexibility of this dialog-based approach is essential, since the query-processing capabilities of data sources may vary widely. Experience in research and industry has shown that a purely declarative approach to describing the capabilities of data sources is not as practical as one might like. Unfortunately, there are so many possible variations in the features of data managers that a strictly declarative approach often leads to unmanageable numbers of descriptive attributes. Consequently, the full power of this paradigm is not exploited in the first version of the SQL/MED standard. However, ongoing evolution of the standard will continue to exploit the wide array of data sources that should be accessible using SQL/MED.

Before the SQL server can begin planning the execution for a query fragment, it must first identify the foreign server that manages the foreign table accessed by the fragment and create a *connection* to the foreign server. Foreign-data wrappers may concurrently have multiple connections open to various foreign servers, so the connection provides a context for subsequent interaction between the SQL server and a particular foreign server. Creation of a connection does not imply that the foreign-data wrapper actually connects to the data source at this time; the timing of making a physical (e.g., network) connection from the foreign-data wrapper to the data source is highly dependent on the implementation of the particular foreign-data wrapper. To create a connection (more accurately, to create the context for a connection) to a foreign server, the SQL server invokes the `ConnectServer()` routine provided by the appropriate foreign-data wrapper, supplying (via a handle) information that identifies the foreign server, including the names and values of any generic options that were supplied when the foreign server was defined with the CREATE FOREIGN SERVER statement. The SQL server also supplies a second handle identifying information that describes the user on whose behalf the query is to be executed, as specified in a CREATE USER MAPPING statement. The user mapping information is used, if and when needed, by the foreign-data wrapper to authenticate the user at the foreign server. The `ConnectServer()` function returns to the SQL server a handle associated with the newly established connection. Once a connection has been created, it is not necessarily destroyed after processing each query fragment; the SQL server can preserve the handle for reuse later with other requests.

Once a connection is established, the SQL server invokes the foreign-data wrapper's `InitRequest()` routine, passing the query fragment to the foreign-data wrapper in the form of an SQL/MED *request*. A request is a data structure that describes, in an abstract fashion, the effective SQL statement that corresponds to the query fragment, rather than an explicit (e.g., character string) representation of that statement. The use of an abstract representation of the request, rather than an SQL statement in source language form, is a crucial aspect of SQL/MED. Parsing native SQL text is sometimes quite complex, and parsers to perform that task tend to be large, complex, and awkward to use. Since SQL/MED's goals include ease of developing foreign-data wrappers, it was quickly decided to avoid requiring them to be able to parse SQL. The components of the abstract request are subordinate data structures representing the individual clauses of an SQL statement, such as the SELECT clause, FROM clause, and so on.

Each element of the SELECT list is represented by a *value expression* that describes a result column of the fragment. In the first version of SQL/MED, each value expression must denote exactly one simple column name; future versions will support more complex expressions. Each element of the FROM clause is represented by a *table reference* that identifies a foreign table. The initial version of the SQL/MED standard allows only a single table reference in the part of the query fragment corresponding to SQL's FROM clause. Other clauses, such as WHERE, ORDER BY, and the like, are also not currently supported. While future versions of SQL/MED will undoubtedly allow for more complex requests, the effect of the current limitations is that the only query fragments that can be described are of the form "`SELECT <column_list> FROM` *FTN*," where *FTN* is the name of a foreign table and each element of `<column_list>` refers to a column of that table. Since all of the columns in the request are needed for the SQL server to produce the complete query result, the foreign-data wrapper must be able to process the entire request.

However, once SQL/MED supports transmission of more complex requests to a foreign server, a foreign-data wrapper might find itself unable to process the entire request. For example, a request might include a predicate that cannot be evaluated by the foreign server. In a case such as this, the foreign-data wrapper might be able to return only the basic data values, requiring that the SQL server compensate by applying the predicate and filtering the result. When a foreign-data wrapper receives a request via the `InitRequest()` routine, it examines the request by invoking routines implemented by the SQL server (called "foreign-data wrapper interface SQL server routines"). Routines are provided to extract table references from the FROM clause (`GetTableRefElem()`, `GetTableRefElemName()`), as well as the values of generic options associated with a referenced table (`GetTableOpts()`). Other routines supply information about the columns in the SELECT list (`GetSelectElem()`, `GetValExprColName()`) and their generic option values (`GetTableColOpt()`).

Once the foreign-data wrapper has analyzed the request, it constructs an SQL/MED *reply*. The structure of a reply is similar to that of a request, but the corresponding routines for examining the reply (`GetReplyTableRef()`, `GetReply-SelectElem()`, etc.) are implemented by the foreign-data wrapper (i.e., they are "foreign-data wrapper interface wrapper routines"). The reply is returned to the

SQL server from `InitRequest()`, along with a second data structure, an *execution plan*. The content of this second data structure is determined solely by the foreign-data wrapper, and it is not interpreted by the SQL server. (That is, it is an execution plan for the foreign-data wrapper, and not a plan for the SQL server.) Its purpose is to encapsulate all the information that is needed by the foreign-data wrapper to execute the portion of the query fragment represented by the reply. The SQL server merely records the execution plan given it by the foreign-data wrapper, then gives it back to the foreign-data wrapper at the start of the query execution phase. The execution plan is the wrapper's means of preserving information between the planning and execution phases of query processing. By contrast, the SQL server can discard the reply when query planning is complete.

5.6.3 Query Execution—Decomposition Mode

During the execution phase, the portion of the query fragment that is described by the reply is executed by the foreign-data wrapper and the foreign server. To initiate query execution, the SQL server invokes the `Open()` routine in the foreign-data wrapper, passing the execution plan as an argument. To fetch a row of the result, the SQL server invokes the `Iterate()` routine. Once all rows have been fetched, the SQL server invokes the `Close()` routine to allow the foreign-data wrapper to clean up after the execution. The execution plan may be reused if, for example, the query fragment represents the inner table of a nested-loop join. When it is no longer needed, the SQL server can release the resources associated with the execution plan by invoking the `FreeExecutionHandle()` routine.

SQL/CLI (described in the first volume of this book)[10] uses *descriptors* to exchange data between an SQL server and the application program invoking that server. Similarly, SQL/MED makes use of descriptors to exchange data between the SQL server and a foreign-data wrapper. These descriptors are, in fact, adapted from those used in SQL/CLI. SQL/MED uses five sorts of descriptor:

- Server Row Descriptors (SRD): Used by the SQL server to describe the type and location of data to be provided by a foreign-data wrapper.
- Server Parameter Descriptors (SPD): Used by the SQL server to describe the type and location of input values to be provided by the SQL server.
- Wrapper Row Descriptors (WRD): Describe the results of an SQL statement to be executed by a foreign-data wrapper in pass-through mode.

10 Jim Melton and Alan R. Simon, *SQL:1999: Understanding Relational Language Components* (San Francisco: Morgan Kaufmann Publishers, 2001).

- Wrapper Parameter Descriptors (WPD): Describe the input values required for the execution of an SQL statement by a foreign-data wrapper in pass-through mode.
- Table Reference Descriptors (TRD): Describe foreign tables that are referenced in SQL statements.

Descriptors are implemented by the SQL server; that is, they are presumed to be physically part of the SQL server and not part of the foreign-data wrapper, but they are allocated and deallocated by request of the foreign-data wrapper. They are used to encapsulate both the types and the values of rows of data. Depending on the SQL server implementation environment, the information (especially data values) may be stored in the descriptor itself, or the descriptor may point to a buffer. Use of pointers is generally more efficient, but they are difficult to support in some languages that are popular for implementing foreign-data wrappers (e.g., Java).

SQL/MED defines only the fields that make up the descriptors; it does not define the actual programming language data structures that implement them. As with other data structures discussed in this chapter, SQL/MED provides a number of functions that the SQL server and the foreign-data wrapper use to get and set the values of descriptor fields when given a handle identifying a specific descriptor and the identity of some field in the descriptor.

A descriptor consists of zero or more *descriptor areas*. Each descriptor area describes one column, which can be an instance of any SQL data type, including types like ROW and ARRAY as well as basic types like INTEGER, CHARACTER VARYING, and so forth. If the programming language in which the foreign-data wrapper is implemented supports a data type that corresponds directly to the SQL data type in the descriptor (using the same correspondence rules that are defined for SQL/CLI), then the SQL server is allowed to convert this standard representation to whatever internal representation it requires. If no such correspondence exists (for example, the SQL standard's DATE data type cannot be directly mapped into any programming language that SQL/MED supports other than Java), then the foreign-data wrapper should use the *canonical* character string representation of the type as described in SQL/Foundation.

5.7 An Example

Let's consider an example to illustrate the principles outlined in the preceding sections. Consider a Unix text file containing records that represent new movie DVDs whose release is scheduled for the near future. Each record of the file represents one such DVD, and the fields of the records are separated by a colon (':'). Assuming that an appropriate foreign-data wrapper and foreign server have already been declared, the data definition language (DDL) statement in Example 5.10 could be employed to declare this file as a foreign table:

Example 5.10 *Creating a Foreign Table for DVD Releases*

```
CREATE FOREIGN TABLE upcoming_DVDs (
  mpaa_id          INTEGER,
  title            CHARACTER VARYING(50),
  studio           CHARACTER VARYING(30),
  release_date     DATE,
  ... )
  SERVER myForeignServer
    OPTIONS ( Filename '/usr/data/releases.txt',
      Delimiter ':' ) ;
```

Since the foreign-data wrapper that will be used to access this file supports access to any file of this general type, each foreign table definition specifies the appropriate filename and delimiter using generic options. A user who would like to know how many upcoming DVDs released through 20th Century Fox are stored in the table could submit the query in Example 5.11 (note that the user does not need to be aware that `upcoming_DVDs` is a foreign table):

Example 5.11 *Counting Upcoming Fox Movies*

```
SELECT COUNT (studio)
FROM upcoming_DVDs
WHERE studio = '20th Century Fox';
```

The SQL server first parses and validates this query, ensuring that it is syntactically and semantically correct and that the user has all necessary privileges. Next, it examines the FROM clause and discovers that it contains a reference to a foreign table. Therefore, the SQL server establishes a connection to `myForeignServer` and formulates a request equivalent to the SQL statement "`SELECT studio FROM upcoming_DVDs`." The request does not include the predicate from the WHERE clause or the aggregate function COUNT in the SELECT list, but future versions of the standard are expected to allow such requests.

The foreign-data wrapper examines the request using the foreign-data wrapper interface SQL server routines (see Table 5.3) to obtain the name of the referenced table, its associated options, the columns to be retrieved and their types, and so forth. In this example, the wrapper returns a reply indicating that the request can be completely satisfied, as well as an execution plan (optimized to whatever degree is appropriate for the Unix file system and the foreign-data wrapper). A simple implementation of the foreign-data wrapper might use Unix shell commands to extract the requested columns from the file. In this case, the execution plan would contain the relevant commands, such as

```
cut -d: -f2 /usr/data/releases.txt
```

The SQL server examines the reply handle and discovers that the foreign-data wrapper can completely handle the request. It incorporates the execution plan for the fragment into its overall execution plan, which must include extra processing steps to filter and aggregate the result set that will be returned by the foreign-data wrapper.

Table 5.5 contains (in a very informal style) a highly simplified sample dialog between an SQL server and a foreign-data wrapper to illustrate the communication that occurs.

Table 5.5 *Simplified Dialog Between SQL Server and Foreign-Data Wrapper*

SQL Server	*Foreign-Data Wrapper*
Wrapper, please initialize yourself; here's some information that you need.	
	What information do I need to know about myself?
Here's some information you need to know about the current user and about the foreign server. Go ahead and connect to that foreign server.	
	Okay, let me see what you're telling me about the foreign server and the user.
	I'm connecting now, and here is the handle that you must use when discussing this connection with me.
Here's the query fragment that I need for you to execute.	
	That's interesting. Here is what I am able to handle in that query fragment.
Okay, I'll revise my plan to accommodate your capabilities.	

(continued)

Table 5.5 *(Continued)*

SQL Server	*Foreign-Data Wrapper*
Get ready to execute the query fragment. Go!	
	Okay, I'll send you data, one row at a time, until the last row has been sent.
Okay, give me a row of data . . .	
Okay, give me a row of data.	Okay . . . here's a row of data.
Thanks! Free your resources.	That was the last row.
	Okay, I'm finished.

5.8 Chapter Summary

In this chapter, you've learned what external data is and how it fits into the context of database language SQL. You've also learned about foreign tables, the foreign servers that manage them, and the foreign-data wrappers that mediate access between your local SQL server and a foreign server. I provided the syntax of all of the statements involved in using SQL/MED's facilities and then explained, at a high level, how a foreign-data wrapper and an SQL server cooperate to plan and execute a query that involves a foreign table. While the contents of this chapter will not enable you to write a foreign-data wrapper for your favorite non-SQL data sources (and SQL servers supplied by "other" vendors), it provides you with a good overview of the necessary components, which will allow you to make use of the actual SQL/MED standard when you're ready to write that wrapper.

Chapter 6

Datalinks

6.1 Introduction

In Chapter 5, "Foreign Servers and Foreign-Data Wrappers," I examined SQL/MED's facilities that allow you to access non-SQL data (as well as SQL data managed by other SQL servers) through the SQL language.

In this chapter, I discuss a new SQL facility, called *datalinks* (including a new data type, DATALINK), that allows you substantial control over the security, consistency, and even recoverability of your non-SQL data—even when you don't want to access that data using SQL statements.

At the time this volume goes to press, I am aware of only one implementation of this facility, IBM's DB2 Universal Database. By the time you read these words, there may be others.

6.2 Two Sides of a Coin

When you read Chapter 5, "Foreign Servers and Foreign-Data Wrappers," you learned how you can use SQL to access foreign data that is managed by a server other than your local SQL server, as long as you have access to a foreign-data wrapper to mediate access to that foreign server.

But SQL is hardly the only interface that applications use to access data. Even today, there is probably more data stored in ordinary files, hierarchical database systems, and network (CODASYL) database systems than in SQL database systems. Your application environment undoubtedly includes many programs that access such data using some API other than SQL, which I refer to as the *native API* of the data.

Regardless of whether your data is stored within an SQL database system or in some other repository, you need to control access to the data, ensure its consistency, and protect it from unauthorized deletion and modification. In short, you need the ability to control your non-SQL data as closely as you do your SQL data.

SQL/MED provides a facility, called *datalinks,* that gives you the ability to bring your non-SQL data under the control of an SQL database management system without requiring that you move your data into the SQL databases. Using datalinks permits you to exercise control over certain aspects of your non-SQL data through a cooperative relationship between your SQL server and your external data's native manager; that cooperative relationship is provided through the services of a *datalinker,* which I'll discuss in section 6.3.3.

Table 6.1 illustrates the relationships between the interface with which you access your data and the manner in which access to that data is controlled.

Table 6.1 *API Versus Control*

	Native Access	*SQL Access*
Other Control	*(not relevant to SQL)*	Foreign servers and foreign-data wrappers
SQL Control	Datalinks	Foreign servers, foreign-data wrappers, and datalinks

As you readily observe in that matrix, SQL/MED provides two complementary facilities, foreign-data wrappers and datalinks, that can be used separately or together. They each have advantages, and using them together offers a particularly powerful way to integrate your non-SQL data into your SQL application environment without having to migrate the data itself.

6.3 Datalinkers and External Data Managers

Before I go into the details of SQL's new DATALINK data type and the role of the datalinker, I'd like to motivate the new facilities a bit more and establish additional context for discussing them.

There are, as you probably know, many computer-based facilities that are used to store data. Almost every computer system user has data stashed away in the native file system; while a great deal of that data is likely to be in the form of documents of one type or another, most of us also have nontextual data stashed away on various systems. Enterprises of all varieties, particularly those more than four or five years old, have probably used a variety of data managers during the course of their activities. IBM mainframe shops are likely to have used IMS (a manager of hierarchical databases) and may have tremendous amounts of business-critical data stored under control of that system.

Users of relational systems may well have versions of Digital Equipment Corporation's Rdb/VMS system (now Oracle's RDB) with applications written in the RDMS language, or versions of Ingres with applications written in Quel. Long-time users of database systems may well have one or more network database systems, such as Cincom's TOTAL, or even an inverted index database system like Adabas.

Advanced technologies that you might want to integrate with your SQL applications include so-called native XML databases and even transactional file systems available now on several operating system platforms.

Non-SQL data that might be used in conjunction with SQL data come in many forms and from many sources. Some examples[1] include

- Medical applications where X-ray images are stored in a file server and the attributes of the images, plus related patient information, are stored in the database.
- Entertainment industry application of management of video clips. The video clips may be stored in a file server, but the attributes about the clips may be stored in a database. Access control is required for accessing the video clips based on database privileges that were needed to access the meta information about the clips.
- World Wide Web applications to manage millions of files and allow access control based on database privileges.
- A bank's requirement for the distributed capture of check images, but a central location search for retrieval of those images.
- CAD/CAM applications with design documents stored as files and with meta information about the content of those files.
- Version control for document management systems.

1 Taken from an SQL standards discussion paper, X3H2-96-586, "DATALINK," by Frank Pellow.

In each of those applications, one might be tempted to conclude that the external data should be stored in the database, along with the associated attributes, but there are often compelling reasons not to make that decision (see section 6.3.2 for additional reasons).

One reason is the existence of other, nondatabase applications that create or otherwise use the non-SQL data. In many cases, your application environment includes large numbers of legacy applications and shrink-wrapped applications that deal with non-SQL data through some "native" interface, such as file-handling commands issued through a scripting language. Those applications often cannot be readily rewritten to access SQL database storage of the data they use. In many cases, the sources of the applications are simply not available. In other cases, the predominant access to the data is best performed using some API designed especially for use with that data, and SQL would be a less desirable choice.

Regardless of the underlying cause, there are often inviolate reasons for retaining native API access to non-SQL data. The use of datalinks permits you to gain many of the advantages of an SQL data management environment for non-SQL data that continues to be accessed through its native API.

6.3.1 Control and Integrity

When an application environment encounters the need to use non-SQL data and SQL data together, a host of questions arise about the relationships between the two categories of data. For example:

- The application writer must understand whether SQL data references the non-SQL data. If such references exist, how is the SQL data to be protected from changes to the non-SQL data that would invalidate those references? This question is obviously related to the referential integrity issue that relational databases solve through FOREIGN KEY constraints—but those constraints are inherently restricted to define relationships between rows of SQL data.
- Applications that access SQL data are run under the privileges that have been granted to some authorization identifier. Every attempt to access SQL data is checked against the privileges granted to the initiater of the attempt. In this way, the data are protected from unauthorized access. But what about data referenced by the SQL data that happen to be stored in some other repository—should those data be granted the same protection from unauthorized access?

- Database management systems typically protect against errors and inconsistencies that can be caused by concurrent updates from multiple applications. Transaction isolation facilities are the primary mechanism used to detect and prevent such problems. Should non-SQL data referenced from SQL data be similarly protected?

As you'll learn in detail in this chapter, SQL/MED's DATALINK data type supports a number of optional behaviors related to these questions. You can acquire the ability to enforce firm constraints against changes to the non-SQL data referenced by your SQL data, or you can relax those constraints when they are not needed by your application's semantics.

A datalink value is essentially a reference to an external data source that is parameterized in ways that allow you to enforce referential integrity between your SQL data and the referenced external data, to coordinate access control to both your SQL data and your referenced non-SQL data, and even to assist in the coordination of backup and recovery of non-SQL data along with the SQL data that references it.

6.3.2 Don't Move It—Link It

Many of the applications mentioned in section 6.3 involve non-SQL data that are quite substantial in size. Digitized video clips—particularly complete movies—are downright huge, often many gigabytes in size. The network costs, both in terms of elapsed time and in terms of resource unavailability for other applications, can be substantial if data are gathered in one form and copied or moved to a database.

Some data are not only large, but are used in applications where predicatable data rates are mandatory, implying that they should be maintained close to their users rather than in a central data repository.

In short, it is not uncommon for the size or other nature of data to mandate that they be maintained in some non-SQL form. Replicating the data in two forms—SQL and non-SQL—is rarely appropriate, due to the inherent cost of storage and conversions, as well as consistency issues. Linking to the non-SQL data is frequently the best choice for many reasons, particularly if concerns related to security and consistency are resolved.

Datalinks provide a solution to those issues, permitting you to maintain your non-SQL data in their native form, while allowing your applications to use them closely with your SQL data and gain many of the advantages of your SQL database system when using the external data.

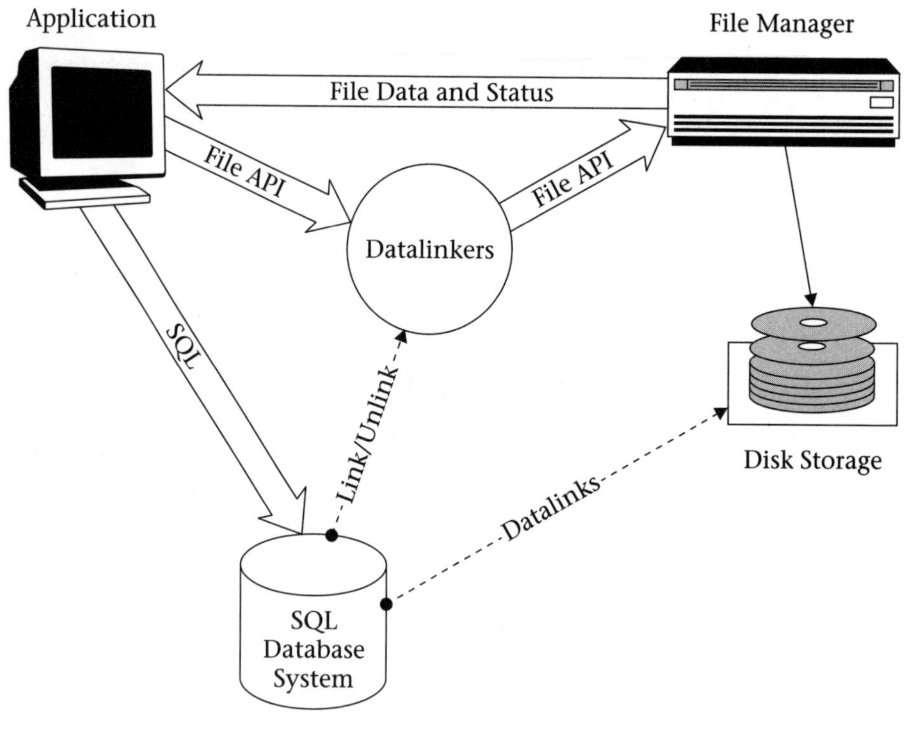

Figure 6.1 Where the Datalinker Fits

6.3.3 Functionality of the Datalinker

As you saw in section 6.2, SQL/MED defines a new facility, called a *datalink*, that gives you the ability to reference non-SQL data from within SQL data. SQL/MED also defines a new component in the application environment that mediates the access between your application programs, your SQL server, and the native manager of your non-SQL data. This new component is called a *datalinker.*

The datalinker, illustrated in Figure 6.1, serves two purposes, both of which involve cooperation with the native manager of the non-SQL data referenced by a datalink value.

In some implementations, the code performing one or both purposes of the datalinker is physically integrated with the file system or other non-SQL data manager. In other implementations, the datalinker is a completely separate unit of code. (Let's agree that I will commonly use the term *file manager* in this chapter, and you'll understand that it extends generally to any non-SQL data manager.) Whichever approach is taken, the datalinker and the file data manager must work together cohesively—even if the datalinker and the file data manager reside on separate network nodes. In many cases, the SQL server and the file manager will be on separate nodes.

The two roles that the datalinker plays are often called the *datalinker file manager* and the *datalinker filter.* (In IBM's DB2 Universal Database, these roles are known respectively as the "Data Links File Manager" and the "Data Links Filesystem Filter." Other implementations of SQL/MED may have similar variations on the terminology used.)

The datalinker file manager registers, for a particular file manager, every file that is linked from any datalink value stored in any SQL server. This, in effect, comprises the metadata for the linked files. The datalinker file manager is the facility that receives and processes the "link file" and "unlink file" commands that arise from SQL INSERT, UPDATE, and DELETE statements that create, modify, or remove datalink values in the database. For every linked file, this facility tracks the specific SQL server that holds the datalink value referencing the file, along with the fully qualified name of the table and the column in which the reference occurs. The datalinker file manager can also maintain files that were at one time linked but later unlinked in case the link needs to be restored as part of some database recovery operation. Part of the responsibility of the datalinker file manager is often to schedule backup operations on the linked files to correspond to backups of the references to those files in datalink columns of the database.

The other aspect of the datalinker, the datalinker filter, performs the complementary jobs of "intercepting" native file access commands that might threaten the integrity of the references contained in datalink values in the database. For example, instructions to delete or rename a file that was registered with the datalinker file manager are normally blocked, since either operation would cause a datalink reference to become invalid. Depending on the kinds of protection specified in the datalink reference (recall that I said in section 6.3.1 that the datalink values can include parameters), the datalinker filter facility might ensure that proper access authority has been granted even for read-only access of linked files.

Let's consider how we might create a linkage between some SQL data and a file:

1. The application program executes an SQL INSERT statement that provides values for several columns of a table. One of the columns is of the DATALINK data type, and the value provided for that column is a valid datalink value, specifying at least a complete reference to the desired file—including some way to identify the file manager.

2. The SQL server contacts the datalinker associated with the identified file manager to determine whether the specified file exists. If the file does exist, the datalinker is now aware that the file is "controlled" by the SQL server. That is, the file is now *linked.*
3. If the file does exist, the SQL server reports success to the application; otherwise, the SQL server reports the appropriate error condition back to the application.

Using the linkage thus created,

1. When the application needs to access the file through its native API, it first contacts the SQL server to request an *access token* for the file.
2. Once the access token that authorizes access to the file has been produced, the application can invoke the `OPEN()` function (using the proper syntax for the file manager, of course) to begin accessing the file.
3. The datalinker intercepts that `OPEN()` function invocation and verifies that the application has been granted the proper access token for the requested type of access. Since, in this case, the proper token was provided, the datalinker forwards the `OPEN()` function invocation onward to the file manager.

When an SQL DELETE statement is executed that deletes the row containing the datalink value linking to a particular file, the datalinker is notified that the link to the file has been terminated. The datalinker deletes its record of the linkage and returns control of the file to the file server, at which time "normal" access to the file is once again permitted.

Datalinkers are typically aware of transaction boundaries, including transaction initiation and commit or rollback, just like the SQL systems with which they are used. SQL/MED does not specify the interface with which datalinkers and SQL systems are coordinated, but the XA interface[2] is a popular choice.

6.4 DATALINK Data Type

A datalink value is a value of the DATALINK type, just as a value of the INTEGER type is an integer. A datalink value is a reference to some external data source that

2 ISO/IEC 14834, *Information technology—Distributed Transaction Processing—The XA Specification* (Geneva: International Organization for Standardization, 1996).

is not part of the data directly managed by the SQL server. It is, conceptually, a *file reference,* a *control definition,* and a Boolean value (called the *SQL-mediated access indication*) that indicates whether or not the referenced file is accessible only through certain specially provided operations (discussed in this section). Only the file reference is directly available to an application using this data type. Datalink values can, of course, be stored in columns whose data types are DATALINK. They can also be stored in SQL variables of the DATALINK type, passed as the value of parameters of the DATALINK type, stored in DATALINK attributes of structured user-defined types, stored in DATALINK fields of ROW types, and so forth.

The file reference is, in effect, a character string value whose format is *normally* that of a Universal Resource Identifier (URI); implementations are required to support datalink file references using URIs, but they are free to support additional formats for the file references as well. SQL/MED specifies two URI formats: HTTP URLs and file URLs, both using the standardized structure defined by the Internet Engineering Task Force (IETF); I do not duplicate the syntax of those URI formats in this book, because they are readily available.[3] You are probably familiar with URLs such as *http://sqlstandards.org* or *file:///userdata/myfile.* In general, a URI contains sequences of characters indicating the protocol, followed by a colon, followed by two slashes, followed by a host name (or IP number), followed by a file path. The only unusual aspect of the URIs applicable to datalinks is that the `localhost:` variant is not supported, due to difficulties with determining its precise meaning in the SQL environment—that is, is the "local host" the network node hosting the SQL client or the node hosting the SQL server?

The control definition is arguably part of the definition of the *site* at which a datalink value is stored, instead of a part of the datalink value itself. That is, as you'll see in section 6.4.1, you specify the control characteristics when you define a column, and not as part of the URI comprising the file reference. (Please note that you cannot specify control definitions when declaring an SQL variable whose data type is DATALINK or any other type—such as a ROW type or a structured type—that has some component that is a DATALINK.) In most cases, you will be unable to distinguish between the datalink value and the characteristics defined for a site whose data type is DATALINK, which is why I include the control definition as a characteristic of datalink values. However, it is possible to assign a datalink value stored in one site to another site for which different control characteristics have been specified; by doing so, the relationship between the control characteristics and the datalink value has been altered.

---

3 *http://www.ietf.org:* RFC 1738, T. Berners-Lee, L. Masinter, and M. McCahill, *Uniform Resource Locators (URL),* December 1994, and RFC 1808, R. Fielding, *Relative Uniform Resource Locators,* June 1995.

The DATALINK data type can be specified with a control definition that specifies NO LINK CONTROL, which is the default if no control definition is specified; this alternative means that there is no file linked to the SQL database, even when the site being defined has a file reference stored in it. That is, you may reference a file from some DATALINK column but *not link the file*. By making this choice, you have effectively given instructions that the datalinker, the file manager, and the SQL server should not provide the specified file with the protections discussed in section 6.3.1.

If you specify FILE LINK CONTROL, additional file control options can be associated with the DATALINK data type. They are

- INTEGRITY (ALL or SELECTIVE)
- READ PERMISSION (FS or DB)
- WRITE PERMISSION (FS or BLOCKED)
- RECOVERY (NO or YES)
- ON UNLINK (RESTORE or DELETE)

Not all combinations of these additional definitions are allowed. Table 6.2 specifies the valid combinations. Any other combination will give you a syntax error.

Table 6.2 *Valid Combinations of DATALINK Control Definitions*

Integrity	*Read Permission*	*Write Permission*	*Recovery*	*Unlink*
ALL	FS	FS	NO	NONE
ALL	FS	BLOCKED	NO	RESTORE
ALL	FS	BLOCKED	YES	RESTORE
ALL	DB	BLOCKED	NO	RESTORE
ALL	DB	BLOCKED	NO	DELETE
ALL	DB	BLOCKED	YES	RESTORE
ALL	DB	BLOCKED	YES	DELETE
SELECTIVE	FS	FS	NO	NONE

The meanings of the various control definitions are

- NO LINK CONTROL: Although every file reference must have the format of a URI, specifying this option means that there does not necessarily have to be a file referenced by that file reference. This option implies that the integrity control option is NONE, the read permission option is FS, the write permission option is FS, the recovery option is NO, and the unlink option is NONE. There is no explicit syntax to specify these options except for NO LINK CONTROL.

- FILE LINK CONTROL: Specification of this option means that every file reference must reference an existing file. Further file control depends on the link control options.
- INTEGRITY ALL: This option means that files identified by file references cannot be deleted or renamed, except possibly through the use of SQL statements that operate on the datalink column in question.
- INTEGRITY SELECTIVE: If you choose this option, then files referenced by file references can be deleted or renamed using operators provided by the file manager (that is, through the native API for the external data source), unless a datalinker has been installed in connection with that file manager.
- INTEGRITY NONE: When this option is in effect, files referenced by file references can *only* be deleted or renamed using operators provided by the file manager. That is, executing SQL statements that affect the column in question have no effect on the referenced file. (This option cannot be specified explicitly but it's the default if NO LINK CONTROL is specified.)
- READ PERMISSION FS: Permission to read files referenced by datalink values is determined by the file manager. (The characters "FS" imply "File Server" or "Foreign Server.")
- READ PERMISSION DB: Permission to read files referenced by datalink values is determined by the SQL implementation. (The characters "DB" imply "Database.") When you've specified this option, the referenced file is said to be *SQL-mediated,* meaning that the SQL environment determines whether a request to access the file is permitted or prohibited.
- WRITE PERMISSION FS: Permission to write files referenced by datalink values is determined by the file manager.
- WRITE PERMISSION BLOCKED: Write access to files referenced by datalink values is not available through any direct action. However, updates can occur indirectly through the use of some implementation-defined mechanism, but that's obviously not defined by SQL/MED.
- RECOVERY YES: This option means that *point in time recovery* of files referenced by datalink values is desired. ("Point in time recovery" provides the ability to restore a database or other data repository by using a backed-up copy and reapplying from a log all completed transactions that occurred after the backup was made.)
- RECOVERY NO: Choosing this option means that point in time recovery of files referenced by datalink values is disabled.

- ON UNLINK RESTORE: When a file referenced by a datalink value is unlinked, the external file manager attempts to reinstate the ownership and permissions that existed just before that file was linked to the SQL server.
- ON UNLINK DELETE: A file referenced by a datalink value is deleted when it is unlinked.
- ON UNLINK NONE: When a file referenced by a datalink value is unlinked, no changes are made to the ownership and permissions as a result of the unlinking operation.

With these options, it can be determined how completely the SQL server controls the referenced file. The possibilities range from no control at all (the file does not even have to exist) to total control, where removal of the datalink value from the database leads to deletion of the physical file.

6.4.1 Defining Datalinks

The syntax for defining a DATALINK data type is given in Syntax 6.1.

Syntax 6.1 *<datalink type> Syntax*

```
<datalink type> ::=
    DATALINK [ <datalink control definition> ]

<datalink control definition> ::=
    NO LINK CONTROL
  | FILE LINK CONTROL <datalink file control option>

<datalink file control option> ::=
    <integrity option> <read permission> <write permission>
    <recovery option> [ <unlink option> ]

<integrity option> ::=
    INTEGRITY ALL
  | INTEGRITY SELECTIVE

<read permission> ::=
    READ PERMISSION FS
  | READ PERMISSION DB
```

```
<write permission> ::=
    WRITE PERMISSION FS
  | WRITE PERMISSION BLOCKED

<recovery option> ::=
    RECOVERY NO
  | RECOVERY YES

<unlink option> ::=
    ON UNLINK RESTORE
  | ON UNLINK DELETE
```

SQL/MED includes rules that limit the combinations that you can choose to those indicated in Table 6.2. If you attempt to choose combinations other than the ones allowed, you will get a syntax error (or else you have taken advantage of some implementation extension to the SQL/MED standard).

In Syntax 6.1, `<unlink option>` is shown as optional. You must specify that syntax element except in situations where the Unlink column in Table 6.2 contains the word NONE, in which case you must omit the `<unlink option>` syntax.

Example 6.1 illustrates the creation of a column whose data type is DATALINK. In my hypothetical music and video store, I like to keep a digitized image of the front of the package in which my DVDs are sold. For various reasons, I've found it easier to keep those images in separate files (rather than in, say, a BINARY LARGE OBJECT, or BLOB, column in my database). But, naturally, I want those images to be secured right along with the database data that references them. The DATALINK type defined below gives me the protection that I need.

Example 6.1 *Creating a DATALINK Column*

```
CREATE TABLE movies (
  title           CHARACTER VARYING ( 30 ),
  year_released   INTEGER,
  jewelbox_photo  DATALINK FILE LINK CONTROL
                    INTEGRITY ALL
                    READ PERMISSION DB
                    WRITE PERMISSION BLOCKED
                    RECOVERY YES
                    ON UNLINK RESTORE,
  our_cost        DECIMAL (4,2),
  ...
)
```

Once I have created a table containing a datalink column, as in Example 6.1, I can store values in that column to describe the movies I'm tracking. Although I said in section 6.4 that the file reference is, *in effect,* a character string value whose format is that of a URI, I can't just store a character string in the `jewelbox_photo` column. After all, its data type is not one of the variations of CHARACTER; its data type is DATALINK, so I have to store a datalink value in the column. SQL/MED provides a special constructor that creates a datalink value from a character string representation of a URI; see Syntax 6.2 for the syntax of this constructor.

Syntax 6.2 *<datalink value constructor> Syntax*

```
<datalink value constructor> ::=
    DLVALUE <left paren> <data location> <right paren>

<data location> ::= <character value expression>
```

The `<character value expression>` can be a character string literal or any character expression whose value has the form of a valid URI. Since my datalink column was specified with FILE LINK CONTROL, the file must actually exist when I insert the row containing its datalink reference.

Example 6.2 *Inserting a Row Containing a Datalink*

```
INSERT INTO movies
  VALUES ( 'Monsters, Inc.', 2001,
           DLVALUE ( 'file://auxfiles/usr/movie/photos/Monsters.jpg' ),
           19.95, ... )
```

The DLVALUE constructor creates a datalink value from the FILE URI that I provided. If the image were stored on a Web server somewhere, accessed using the HTTP protocol, I could have specified that, but most Web servers wouldn't have the ability to exercise the FILE LINK CONTROL options that I chose.

Once I've inserted that row, any effort (from my application or any other) to directly access the file is prohibited unless a valid file access token has been granted (see section 6.4.2).

6.4.2 Accessing Datalinks

SQL/MED provides several functions that you can invoke from SQL statements to determine various characteristics of datalink values. The most important of these functions are those that return the URI by which the linked file can be located, with or without the access token that is required to access the file's contents.

The syntax of these functions can be seen in Syntax 6.3. All of the functions return character string values that contain information derived from the datalink value supplied as an argument to the function.

Syntax 6.3 *Syntax of Datalink Functions*

```
<url complete expression> ::=
    DLURLCOMPLETE ( <datalink value expression> )

<url path expression> ::=
    DLURLPATH ( <datalink value expression> )

<url path only expression> ::=
    DLURLPATHONLY ( <datalink value expression> )

<url scheme expression> ::=
    DLURLSCHEME ( <datalink value expression> )

<url server expression> ::=
    DLURLSERVER ( <datalink value expression> )
```

The first of those functions, `<url complete expression>`, returns (as a character string value, of course) the complete URI associated with the file referenced by the supplied datalink value. If the file is SQL-mediated (that is, the datalink reference specified READ PERMISSION DB), then the URI will be augmented—in an implementation-defined manner—with an encrypted value that serves as the file access token. When you supply the augmented URI to some native API routine that accesses the file, that access is intercepted by the datalinker (as discussed in section 6.3.3) and the access token is validated. If it's valid, then the datalinker forwards your native API invocation to the file manager; otherwise, you get an error directly from the datalinker and your access to the file is prohibited.

Similarly, the `<url path expression>` function returns the path of the URI associated with the referenced file. Again, if the file is SQL-mediated, then the path is augmented with the encrypted access token. The difference between the `<url complete expression>` and the `<url path expression>` is that the `<url complete expression>` returns the entire URI, while the `<url path expression>` strips off the leading "scheme" information along with the name of the "host" (the file server). If `<url path expression>` evaluated the URL I wrote in Example 6.2, the characters "`file://auxfiles/`" ("`file:`" is the schema, and "`//auxfiles/`" identifies the host) would be stripped off, after which the function would return the remaining string: `usr/movie/photos/Monsters.jpg`. If you used an implementation-defined format (that is, not a standard URI format) for the file reference, then `<url path expression>` returns a zero-length string.

The `<url path only expression>` function returns exactly the same value as the `<url path expression>` except that the file access token is never included, regardless of the READ PERMISSION characteristic.

The `<url scheme expression>` function returns either `http` or `file`, depending on which format of URI was used in your file reference. Unlike the `<url path expression>`, the `<url scheme expression>` does not include the name of the host. If the URI is not in a standard format, then a zero-length string is returned.

Finally, the `<url server expression>` function returns just the server name (or host name) component of the URI. In Example 6.2, this would be the string `auxfiles`. Again, if the URI is not in a standard format, then a zero-length string is returned.

6.4.3 Using Datalinks

Now, let's put the pieces together into a single example. Example 6.3 illustrates the creation and use of datalinks. The example is written in a sort of pseudocode so I don't get sidetracked with the details of specific programming language syntax; I've also made up a file system function, called `fileopen()`, whose parameters are explained in comments in the example.

Example 6.3 *Using Datalinks*

```
...
/* Create a table that has a datalink column                          */
EXEC SQL CREATE TABLE movies (
            title           CHARACTER VARYING ( 50 ),
            year_released   INTEGER,
            jewelbox_photo  DATALINK FILE LINK CONTROL
                              INTEGRITY ALL
                              READ PERMISSION DB
                              WRITE PERMISSION BLOCKED
                              RECOVERY YES
                              ON UNLINK RESTORE,
            our_cost        DECIMAL (4,2),
            ...
        );
...
```

```
/* Many SQL implementations do not allow DDL and DML statements
   in the same transaction, so commit the CREATE TABLE.         */
EXEC SQL COMMIT;
...
/* Insert a few rows of data with links to DVD jewel box images */
EXEC SQL INSERT INTO movies
  VALUES ( 'Monsters, Inc.', 2001,
           DLVALUE ( 'file://auxfiles/usr/movie/photos/MonstersInc.jpg' ),
           19.95, ... );
EXEC SQL INSERT INTO movies
  VALUES ( 'The Haunting', 1999,
           DLVALUE ( 'file://auxfiles/usr/movie/photos/TheHaunting2.jpg' ),
           12.50, ... );
EXEC SQL INSERT INTO movies
  VALUES ( '13 Ghosts', 2001,
           DLVALUE ( 'file://auxfiles/usr/movie/photos/13Ghosts.jpg' ),
           9.95, ... );
EXEC SQL INSERT INTO movies
  VALUES ( 'Star Wars: Episode I, The Phantom Menace', 1999,
           DLVALUE ( 'file://auxfiles/usr/movie/photos/StarWars1.jpg' ),
           20.99, ... );
...
/* Commit the insertion of those rows                            */
EXEC SQL COMMIT;
...
/* Let's get a link and valid access token for one of the images */
/*  Our datalinkvar variable is a character string               */
EXEC SQL SELECT title, DLURLCOMPLETE ( jewelbox_photo )
         INTO :titlevar, :datalinkvar
         FROM movies
         WHERE title LIKE '%Haunting%';
/* The contents of the host variable :datalinkvar should be
   something like:
      file://auxfiles/usr/movie/photos/TheHaunting2.jpg\Je$9@nd^}
   under the premise that a backslash (\) separates the URI value
   from the encrypted access token.                              */
...
/* The fileopen() function opens a file identified by the value
   of the second argument and places a file handle into the
   first argument.  It returns a negative number if it fails.    */
```

```
status = fileopen ( imagehandle, datalinkvar );
if ( status < 0) message ("fileopen() failed!");
...
/* Let's try a few other functions                                    */
EXEC SQL SELECT DLURLPATHONLY ( jewelbox_photo ),
                DLURLSCHEME ( jewelbox_photo ),
                DLURLSERVER ( jewelbox_photo ),
         INTO :pathvar, :schemevar, :servervar
         FROM movies
         WHERE title LIKE '%Haunting%';
/* The contents of the three host variables should be:
     pathvar:   usr/movie/photos/TheHaunting2.jpg
     schemevar: file
     servervar: auxfiles                                              */
...
```

As I said in section 6.2, the DATALINK type represents one aspect of the use of external data in your SQL applications. Foreign tables (see Chapter 5, "Foreign Servers and Foreign-Data Wrappers") represent another aspect. Although this book does not contain an example of the two facilities used together, I think that it would be very natural to use a foreign-data wrapper that interfaces with the file system and to define a foreign table that corresponds to the collection of images. In that way, the images are protected through the datalink facilities, but accessible using SQL language through the foreign table.

6.5 The Future

The current SQL/MED standard[4] has one important limitation on the use of datalinks: If you find a need to change the contents of a linked file—for example, if a new jewel box image is released for the examples in this chapter—you must perform several steps in order to make the change. First, you have to unlink the file, which may be done either by deleting the row that references the file or by modifying the DATALINK column of that row so that it no longer references the file. Next, you delete the referenced file and replace it with the new image. Finally, you relink the file, either by reinserting the referencing row or by re-modifying the DATALINK column so that it once again references the file.

4 ISO/IEC 9075-9:2001, *Information technology—Database languages—SQL—Part 9: Management of External Data (SQL/MED)* (Geneva: International Organization for Standardization, 2001).

At best, that operation is clumsy, but it may also be dangerous. Deleting rows in your database is not something to be done lightly, and even "temporarily" changing the value of some column can have undesirable effects. For example, you might have UPDATE triggers on the table that would be executed as a result of the modification of the datalink column, or you might have cascading referential actions defined on `FOREIGN KEY` constraints associated with the table.

A much better approach would be to permit the file to be "updated in place," so that the datalink value that references the file does not have to be disturbed, but the datalinker would allow you to replace the data in the file without affecting the reference in your database. The next generation of the SQL/MED standard (expected in early 2003) will provide this capability.

6.6 Chapter Summary

In this chapter, you've learned about the DATALINK data type and how it is used to reference files that are outside of the SQL environment, but for which access is to be controlled by the SQL server. I told you about the datalinker, a new software component that mediates between your applications, the SQL server, and the file manager to protect the contents of your referenced files. You also learned how to create datalink columns and the datalink values that are stored in them, as well as how to use the values stored in datalink columns.

Chapter 7

OLAP

7.1 Introduction

SQL was from its beginning a very powerful language for managing traditional business data. More recently, it has been enhanced to address the needs of less traditional data via the object-relational features of SQL:1999. These enhancements were discussed in Chapter 2, "User-Defined Types," Chapter 3, "Typed Tables," and Chapter 4, "Routines and Routine Invocation."

However, earlier versions of SQL were not particularly good at one important job: complex data analysis. If your requirements included the sort of analysis that has often been called *on-line analytical processing* (and sometimes called *business intelligence*), most SQL systems required that you retrieve your data from the database into your client application environment and perform the analyses there. A principal disadvantage of that approach is the overhead caused by retrieval of sometimes huge amounts of data into a client system. Client systems capable of handling such quantities of data are typically somewhat costly, and the elapsed time required to transfer the data can be significant. Because of the overhead involved in preparing the data for client-side analysis, users often chose to perform their analyses on data that was not updated for days, weeks, or even months at a time. In addition, the software itself is rarely cheap, making it expensive to acquire licenses for more than a few clients.

In spite of the disadvantages, businesses everywhere have acquired the necessary software to perform vital analysis of their data in the client environment; there are few viable alternatives.

The SQL standard provided a solution to this dilemma in 2000 by adopting an amendment to SQL:1999, called SQL/OLAP.[1] By *amending* the SQL:1999 standard, SQL's designers managed to make the OLAP material formally a part of SQL:1999 but were not forced to delay publication of the 1999 version of the standard for another year while the OLAP material was completed.

In this chapter, I discuss all of the features defined by SQL/OLAP, including both the underlying concepts and the actual SQL syntax used to accomplish the goals meant to be satisfied by the standard. I do *not,* however, attempt to teach you all about business data analysis or statistical methods. I must assume that you know the basics of those fields, or that you have other resources that you can consult to acquire that knowledge.

7.2 Facilities for Data Analysis without OLAP

Even before SQL/OLAP was published, the SQL standard provided a few basic data analysis facilities. From the beginning, the SQL standard provided several so-called set functions (often known as *aggregate functions* or sometimes simply *aggregates*) that could be used to compute primitive summary data, like the sum and average of a column of numbers, the maximum and minimum values in a column, or the number of rows in a table (all discussed in detail in the first volume of this book).[2] All versions of SQL also included the GROUP BY and HAVING clauses that offer considerable help in partitioning your data when computing those sums, averages, maxima, minima, and cardinalities.

SQL:1999 added a few more facilities that support data analysis: CUBE and ROLLUP. It also offered the ability for you to define new functions of your own to assist in such analysis; admittedly, writing user-defined functions to do statistical operations remains quite a challenge—so much so that I don't even bother covering this possibility! In fact, early drafts of this third edition of the SQL standard experimented with support for user-defined aggregates. However, the only way a user-defined routine could do analysis of a data set would be for the routine to

1 *Information technology—Database languages—SQL—Part 1: Framework (SQL/Framework), Part 2: Foundation (SQL/Foundation), Part 5: Host Language Bindings (SQL/Bindings)—AMENDMENT 1: On-Line Analytical Processing (SQL/OLAP)* (Geneva: International Organization for Standardization, 2000).

2 Jim Melton and Alan R. Simon, *SQL:1999: Understanding Relational Language Components* (San Francisco: Morgan Kaufmann Publishers, 2001).

fetch the data itself and analyze the rows. That approach clearly doesn't provide the same division of labor between specifying a set of rows to analyze and performing the calculation on those rows that is provided by true set functions in SQL.

Before I launch into the details of SQL/OLAP, a short review of the earlier analysis features will be useful.

7.2.1 Set Functions

All versions of SQL have offered five so-called set functions—functions that operate on collections of data to produce a value derived from the values in the collections. Those functions are

- COUNT: Return the number of rows in a virtual table, or the number of different values (when DISTINCT is specified) in a column of a virtual table.
- MAX: Return the largest value in a column of a virtual table.
- MIN: Return the smallest value in a column of a virtual table.
- SUM: Return the sum of the values in a column of a virtual table; the data type of the column must be some numeric type or an interval type.
- AVG: Return the average of the values in a column of a virtual table; the data type of the column must be some numeric type or an interval type.

For example, I could compute some interesting information about my video sales by using the SQL statement in Example 7.1.

Example 7.1 *Using Basic Set Functions*

```
SELECT COUNT(*),                  -- Total number of DVD titles stocked
       MAX(total_dvd_units_sold), -- Maximum DVDs sold of any single title
       MIN(total_dvd_units_sold), -- Minimum DVDs sold of any single title
       SUM(total_dvd_units_sold), -- Total number of DVDs sold (all titles)
       AVG(total_dvd_units_sold)  -- Average number of DVDs among titles
FROM movie_titles
```

In addition to those five functions, SQL:1999 added three more set functions that operate on Boolean values:

- EVERY: Returns *true* if and only if the value of its argument is *true* for every row in the virtual table; otherwise, returns *false*.

- ANY: Returns *true* if and only if the value of its argument is *true* for at least one row in the virtual table; otherwise, returns *false*.
- SOME: Synonymous with ANY.

EVERY and ANY/SOME are more likely to be used in a WHERE clause than in the SELECT list of an SQL statement. If I wanted the values that Example 7.1 calculates only when I have sold at least 10 units of every DVD carried by each of my stores, I could use the modified statement seen in Example 7.2.

Example 7.2 *Using Boolean Set Functions*

```
SELECT COUNT(*),                   -- Total number of DVD titles stocked
       MAX(total_dvd_units_sold), -- Maximum DVDs sold of any single title
       MIN(total_dvd_units_sold), -- Minimum DVDs sold of any single title
       SUM(total_dvd_units_sold), -- Total number of DVDs sold (all titles)
       AVG(total_dvd_units_sold)  -- Average number of DVDs among titles
FROM movie_titles
GROUP BY store
HAVING EVERY ( total_dvd_units_sold >= 10 )
```

For every store for which the total number of DVDs sold exceeds 10, a summary row is generated; stores selling 10 or fewer DVDs are not represented in the result.

7.2.2 GROUP BY and HAVING

Even the most basic statistical operations benefit greatly from the ability to partition data into collections of rows that share a characteristic. In my case, I may well want to compute the values from Example 7.1 for each of several movie categories, such as action, romance, horror, and so forth. SQL's GROUP BY and HAVING clauses provide this capability. The GROUP BY clause separates a virtual table into one or more groups in which the value of a specified column (you can specify multiple columns, in which case it is the combined values of all columns) are equal; for the purpose of grouping, all null values are considered to be in the same group—even though null values are not equal to one another. The HAVING clause acts as a filter (much like the WHERE clause) on the result of the GROUP BY clause. Example 7.3 illustrates this process by retrieving the summary information about no more than three types of movie, but only those types that include at least 10 different titles.

Example 7.3 *Set Functions and Partitioned Data*

```
SELECT movie_type,                  -- The type of movie in each group
       COUNT(*),                    -- Total number of DVD titles stocked
       MAX(total_dvd_units_sold),   -- Maximum DVDs sold of any single title
       MIN(total_dvd_units_sold),   -- Minimum DVDs sold of any single title
       SUM(total_dvd_units_sold),   -- Total number of DVDs sold (all titles)
       AVG(total_dvd_units_sold)    -- Average number of DVDs among titles
FROM movie_titles
GROUP BY movie_type
HAVING movie_type IN ('Horror', 'Romance', 'Action')
   AND COUNT(DISTINCT title) >= 10
```

7.2.3 CUBE and ROLLUP

SQL:1999 added a couple of significant new features to the GROUP BY clause, providing a sort of preview to the capabilities that SQL/OLAP provides. These features, invoked with the keywords CUBE and ROLLUP, provide multidimensional summaries and "control breaks" for grouped data.

Suppose that I'd like to know how many DVDs I have in stock for each type of movie, broken down by the year in which the films were released, then summarized by year and by type. Using SQL's GROUP BY facilities alone, there is no convenient way to write a single statement that would return all of that information. However, the ROLLUP clause shown in Example 7.4 provides the information in a single, easy-to-write (and easy-to-read!) statement.[3]

Example 7.4 *Example of ROLLUP*

```
SELECT movie_type, year_released, SUM(dvds_in_stock) AS sum_of_dvds
FROM movie_titles
GROUP BY ROLLUP ( movie_type, year_released )
```

That statement returns a result that looks something like the output shown in Result 7.1.

3 Ibid., pp. 330–331.

Result 7.1 *Result of ROLLUP Grouping*

MOVIE_TYPE	*YEAR_RELEASED*	*SUM_OF_DVDS*
Action	1990	250
Action	1991	374
Action	1992	288
|	|	|
Action	*(null)*	912
Romance	1990	195
Romance	1991	439
Romance	1992	221
|	|	|
Romance	*(null)*	855
Comedy	1990	347
Comedy	1991	122
Comedy	1992	201
|	|	|
Comedy	*(null)*	670
(null)	*(null)*	2437

As you see in Result 7.1, The `sum_of_dvds` column contains the total number of DVDs sold in each year for each movie type, as well as a "sum of sums" value for each movie type for all years—those are the lines with *"(null)"* in the `year_released` column. The `sum_of_dvds` column also contains a "final sum" value on the very last row, capturing the sum of those sum of sum rows. The ROLLUP grouping provides the same sort of "control break" that COBOL programmers will be used to coding.

If the query in Example 7.4 were to be augmented by appending the HAVING clause, as seen in Example 7.5, then the results would be considerably different, since only those rows for which the total number of DVDs in stock is less than 300 would be retained.

Example 7.5 *Example of ROLLUP with HAVING Clause*

```
SELECT movie_type, year_released, SUM(dvds_in_stock) AS sum_of_dvds
FROM movie_titles
GROUP BY ROLLUP ( movie_type, year_released )
HAVING SUM(dvds_in_stock) < 300
```

Result 7.2 *Result of ROLLUP Grouping with HAVING Clause*

MOVIE_TYPE	*YEAR_RELEASED*	*SUM_OF_DVDS*
Action	1990	250
|	|	|
Action	*(null)*	250
Romance	1990	195
Romance	1992	221
|	|	|
Romance	*(null)*	416
Comedy	1991	122
Comedy	1992	201
|	|	|
Comedy	*(null)*	323
(null)	*(null)*	989

If I want to have summaries by year as well as by movie type, I need to use something a little more sophisticated than ROLLUP, and the CUBE clause is the solution, as you can see in Example 7.6.

Example 7.6 *Example of CUBE*

```
SELECT movie_type, year_released, SUM(dvds_in_stock) AS sum_of_dvds
FROM movie_titles
GROUP BY CUBE ( movie_type, year_released )
```

That statement returns a result that looks something like the output shown in Result 7.3.

Result 7.3 *Result of CUBE Grouping*

MOVIE_TYPE	*YEAR_RELEASED*	*SUM_OF_DVDS*
Action	1990	250
Action	1991	374
Action	1992	288
|	|	|
Action	*(null)*	912
Romance	1990	195
Romance	1991	439
Romance	1992	221
|	|	|
Romance	*(null)*	855
Comedy	1990	347
Comedy	1991	122
Comedy	1992	201
|	|	|
Comedy	*(null)*	670
(null)	1990	792
(null)	1991	935
(null)	1992	710
|	|	|
(null)	*(null)*	2437

In Result 7.3, you will observe that the result is almost identical to that in Result 7.1 but that there are new rows near the end of the result in which the values of the `movie_type` column is "*(null)*." Those rows contain the summary data (sum of sums) for each year appearing in other rows of the result. CUBE can be used for multidimensional analysis for any number of dimensions, not merely the two used in this example.

7.3 What More Do We Need?

It's quite reasonable to ask what sorts of queries one might want to ask that cannot be satisfied by the statistical and grouping capabilities described in section 7.2. In fact, there are a wide variety of questions that business analysis requires to be answered that are very difficult to do with no more capabilities than those offered by pre-OLAP SQL:1999.

Consider the following examples (which are by no means comprehensive):

- My music and video organization has several stores, and I've captured sales data for a number of months. For every month recorded, I'd like to see the sales of each store averaged over that month and the two preceding months. By averaging over three months, spikes caused by unusual conditions can be smoothed out, giving a more accurate picture of sales trends.
- For every store, I'd like to see the cumulative sales for every month of last year, ordered by month.
- To watch how sales are growing, or shrinking, in each store, I need to compare each month's actual sales with the average sales at that store in the previous three months.
- At the end of each year, I would like to give special recognition to the top 10 salespeople based on their total annual sales, and also to the 10 salespeople who were rated highest on customer satisfaction questionnaires.
- To evaluate the relative importance to my business of each store and of each DVD title, I want to see the percentage contribution to my company's total sales last year from each combination of DVD title and store, showing also the percentage contribution of each title for all stores together and the percentage contribution of each store considering all sales.

Some of those questions cannot be answered easily using SQL:1999's capabilities without the features of SQL/OLAP.

7.4 SQL Does Windows

The most fundamental enhancement that SQL/OLAP adds to the SQL language is the notion of a *window*—a user-specified selection of rows within a query (or a logical partition of a query) that determines the set of rows used to perform certain calculations with respect to the current row under examination. Figure 7.1 suggests a way to visualize the SQL/OLAP concept of "window." In this case, I have a selection of rows (presumably from an SQL query that retrieves the title, quantity in stock, and type of film), and I've placed a window around seven of the rows retrieved from that query. (Don't place too much importance on the exact nature of the window or the rows visible through the window—this figure is not meant to demonstrate specific features of SQL's windows.)

In SQL/OLAP, window sizes can be specified in terms of individual rows (for example, you can specify that a window extends for four rows on either side of

```
Title                 Qty  Type
===================   ===  =========
Wizards                 1  Animation
Heavy Traffic           3  Animation
Liquid Sky              3  Sci-Fi
Get Shorty              5  Action
Apocalypse Now          9  Action
Blow                    9  Action
Spy Game               11  Action
Toy Story              12  Animation
Apocalypse Now Redux   17  Action
Pulp Fiction           18  Action
Vanilla Sky            19  Action
Name of the Rose       20  Mystery
Cast Away              22  Action
Spy Kids               28  Comedy
The Heist              31  Action
Traffic                35  Action
Chicken Run            37  Animation
Shrek                  41  Animation
High Fidelity          45  Action
Domestic Disturbance   46  Action
Planet of the Apes     58  Action
Monsters, Inc.        104  Animation
```

Figure 7.1 Visualizing Windows

the current row), or it can be specified that a window extends to all rows on either side of the current row in which the value of some column is within a certain range of the value of that column in the current row. In Figure 7.1, there is no obvious relationship between the values in any columns of the rows within the window, so we might presume that the window is specified to extend four rows on either side of some row of interest, which I have indicated by underlining the text.

Okay, many of you must be muttering, so we can define windows around portions of queries—what new capability does that give? In the same way that grouping operations (GROUP BY and HAVING) allow you to develop rows in a query that summarize groups of other rows, "windowing" operations allow you to ascertain information such as the ranking of each row within its partition, the distribution of values in rows within a partition, and similar operations. Windowing also allows you to compute values such as moving averages and sums on your data, enhancing the ability to evaluate your data and its impact on your operations.

SQL/OLAP windows have three essential aspects: *window partitioning, window ordering,* and *window framing.* Each of these aspects has a significant impact on the specific rows of data visible in a window at any point in time. Let's look at each aspect in turn.

A window partitioning is a bit like the result of forming a grouped table with the GROUP BY clause. A grouped table contains only the rows that result from "collapsing," or summarizing, groups of rows (in which every row in each group has equal values on the specified set of grouping columns) into single rows representing each group. In a window partition, each row of the partition has equal values on the specified set of partitioning columns, but the partition retains the individual rows instead of collapsing them into a single representative, or summary, row. For some specific row of a table, the window partition of that row is the set of all rows that have (in the partitioning columns) values that are equal to the values in the specified row. In Figure 7.1, there are a fairly large number of partitions, if we partition by the `qty` column; in fact, the only partitions with more than one row in them are the partition for `qty = 3` and `qty = 9`. (Please note, however, that a window does not extend beyond a specific window partition, so a partitioning by the `qty` column would not permit a window of the size shown in Figure 7.1. Instead, the windowing illustrated in that figure would result from a partitioning in which the entire table comprised a single partition, which is quite permissible in SQL/OLAP.)

A window ordering is the ordering of rows within each partition. Because all rows in a partition have equal values in their partitioning columns, you might order rows within a partition by the values of other columns. In Figure 7.1, the rows in each partition (evidenced by the only two partitions that happen to have equal values in the `qty` column) are ordered by the movie `title`. For particular purposes, you may need to control how your queries deal with null values when each partition is ordered; SQL/OLAP provides new syntax (which can now be applied to ordinary cursors, too) that allow you to specify whether all null values are ordered before or after all non-null values.

A window framing defines the size of the window within a window partition; it can be expressed in physical terms (the number of rows) or logical terms (a range of values). Window frames expressed in logical terms are likely to vary in physical size, as your data is likely to contain different numbers of rows sharing specific values. Window framing is sometimes called *window aggregation grouping,* since it defines the selection of rows within a partition that participates in the calculation of some aggregating function (such as AVG to compute a moving average).

7.4.1 Windows: Explicit and InLine

SQL/OLAP provides two ways of specifying a window in a query. One of these involves the use of a new high-level clause in an SQL query block (an informal term sometimes applied to the more formal `<query specification>`), following the HAVING clause. This approach is called an *explicit window clause.*

The alternative, called an *inline window clause,* allows you to define a window in the SELECT list of a query expression. An inline window clause is functionally equivalent to an explicit window clause but imposes some restrictions on the capabilities that explicit window clauses offer. I cover the explicit window clause first and explain the inline window clause a bit later.

In Syntax 7.1, you see the `<table expression>` component of SQL's query expression. The first volume of this book discussed this series of clauses in detail.[4] Here, the clause of greatest interest is the last one, the `<window clause>`.

Syntax 7.1 *Extended <table expression> Syntax*

```
<table expression> ::=
    <from clause>
    [ <where clause> ]
    [ <group by clause> ]
    [ <having clause> ]
    [ <window clause> ]

<window clause> ::=
    WINDOW <window definition list>

<window definition list> ::=
    <window definition> [ { <comma> <window definition> }... ]

<window definition> ::=
    <new window name> AS <window specification>

<new window name> ::= <window name>

<window specification> ::=
    <left paren> <window specification details> <right paren>
```

4 Ibid., Chapter 9.

The keyword WINDOW is followed by at least one `<window definition>` (and possibly more, each subsequent one following a comma). A `<window definition>` includes a name by which the window will be known in the query and the details of the window's specification (the syntax for which I'll cover shortly).

From section 7.4, you know that a window has three components: its partitioning, its ordering, and its framing (or aggregate grouping). The next sections cover each of these components, one at a time. The detailed discussion will benefit from a concrete example to illustrate the three components, so please examine Example 7.7 and the corresponding Result 7.4. The query returns, for each store and for each month in the last third of 2001, the total DVD sales during the month at the store, plus the running average of DVD sales for that month averaged with at most two months preceding that month (all months included in the running average must be in the last third of 2001).

Example 7.7 *Querying for Moving Average of Sales over Previous Three Months*

```
SELECT h.store_id, h.month, h.total_dvd_sales,
       AVG (h.total_dvd_sales) OVER w AS moving_avg
FROM sales_history AS h
WHERE h.month BETWEEN 200109 AND 200112
WINDOW w AS ( PARTITION BY h.store_id
              ORDER BY h.month
              ROWS 2 PRECEDING )
```

This example illustrates an interesting difference between grouped queries and windowed queries. The SELECT list of a grouped query is permitted to contain only set functions or grouping columns (or columns that are functionally dependent on grouping columns). However, as this example illustrates, the SELECT list of a windowed query is permitted to contain columns other than those used to define the window; `total_dvd_sales` is such a column.

That PARTITION clause says that the rows resulting from the WHERE clause (which is all rows from the `sales_history` table that have `month` values in the specified range) will be assigned to partitions based on the value of the `store_id` column. The ORDER BY clause (which behaves much like the ORDER BY clause of cursors but operates on the rows of a partition and is not limited to use in cursor declarations) rearranges the rows in each partition so that they are in order by `month` value. Finally, the ROWS 2 PRECEDING clause determines that the AVG . . . OVER clause in the SELECT list will operate on each row and up to two rows that precede that row in the ordered partition.

Result 7.4 *Moving Average of Sales over Previous Three Months*

store_id	*month*	*total_dvd_sales*	*moving_avg*	
City	200109	46936.75	46936.75	*—This month only*
City	200110	22842.41	34889.58	*—Average of Sept. and Oct.*
City	200111	30927.90	33569.02	*—Average of Sept., Oct., and Nov.*
City	200112	51751.03	35173.78	*—Average of Oct., Nov., and Dec.*
South	200109	20554.16	20554.16	*(repeat)*
South	200110	9418.14	14986.15	
South	200111	13600.54	14524.28	
South	200112	24977.81	15998.83	
Web	200109	23157.55	23157.55	*(repeat)*
Web	200110	26591.08	24874.32	
Web	200111	31565.37	27104.67	
Web	200112	48153.39	35466.95	

Result 7.4 gives the results in sequence by store ID and by date for each store. Of course, rows are included in the result of a query in no particular order (unless you're using an ordered cursor), but it's convenient for us to see related rows adjacent to one another, so I habitually present things in whatever order seems most reasonable to illustrate the query being discussed.

Before I start breaking down the window components, let's see the syntax for specifying those `<window specification details>`, which appears in Syntax 7.2.

Syntax 7.2 *<window specification details> Syntax*

```
<window specification details> ::=
    [ <existing window name> ]
    [ <window partition clause> ]
    [ <window order clause> ]
    [ <window frame clause> ]

<existing window name> ::= <window name>
```

As you see, all of its four components are optional. (I'll get to the meaning of the `<existing window name>` in section 7.4.5; for now, I'll just say that you can define windows that inherit one or more characteristics from windows defined earlier in the query.) If you specify none of the clauses (that is, if you specify "`WINDOW` name AS ()"), then the effect is that the entire set of rows is the partition and aggregation is performed over that entire set of rows.

7.4.2 Window Partitioning

The first of three components of a window is the window's partitioning. As you learned earlier in this chapter, windows can be divided into partitions so that the values of selected columns are equal for all rows in a given partition. Windows for which a partitioning has not been specified are considered to have a single partition.

The syntax for a `<window partition clause>` is given in Syntax 7.3. One or more columns can be named, and you can specify an explicit collation for any column whose data type is CHARACTER or one of its variants.

Syntax 7.3 *<window partition clause> Syntax*

```
<window partition clause> ::=
    PARTITION BY <window partition column reference list>

<window partition column reference list> ::=
    <window partition column reference>
      [ { <comma> <window partition column reference> }... ]

<window partition column reference> ::=
    <column reference> [ <collate clause> ]
```

As you saw in Syntax 7.1, the `<window clause>` lexically follows the other clauses of a `<table expression>`; it also follows those other clauses semantically, meaning that the virtual table on which the `<window clause>` operates is the virtual table that results from the HAVING clause (if the query doesn't contain a HAVING clause, then the result of the GROUP BY clause; if there is no GROUP BY clause, then the WHERE clause; if there is no WHERE clause, then the FROM clause). That virtual table is partitioned by the WINDOW clause into partitions—as few as one, as many as there are rows in the input virtual table—based on the values of the one or more columns referenced in the `<window partition column reference list>` (which are called the *partitioning columns*). Each partition has one or more rows, and the values of those columns are equal among all the rows of the partition. (Technically, the rows are "not distinct," which means that all rows for which a particular partitioning column has the null value are considered equal for the purposes of partitioning.)

Looking at Result 7.4 one more time, you will observe that the output illustrated there has three partitions, one for each distinct value of the `store_id` column; however, each partition still retains the original rows from which the partition is derived. Contrast this with the result of a similar GROUP BY clause, which would have caused each of the partitions to have been "collapsed" into a single row representing the entire group.

7.4.3 Window Ordering

The second component of a window is its ordering. The ordering of a window is really the ordering of each of its partitions, because the sorts of analysis for which SQL/OLAP has been defined require that users be able to control the sequence in which rows are considered within each partition. Syntax 7.4 gives the syntax of the `<window order clause>`, including the syntax of the `<sort specification list>` that is also used by cursor declarations.

Syntax 7.4 *<window order clause> Syntax*

```
<window order clause> ::=
    ORDER BY <sort specification list>

<sort specification list> ::=
    <sort specification> [ { <comma> <sort specification> }... ]

<sort specification> ::=
    <sort key>
    [ <ordering specification> ] [ <null ordering> ]

<sort key> ::= <value expression>

<ordering specification> ::=
    ASC
  | DESC

<null ordering> ::=
    NULLS FIRST
  | NULLS LAST
```

I repeat the syntax for `<sort specification list>` here (it was discussed in detail in the first volume of this book) because of one new feature that it has acquired because of SQL/OLAP requirements: the `<null ordering>` clause.

From past experience with SQL or from reading the first volume of this book, you know that ORDER BY is not used with ordinary SELECT expressions (that is, query expressions) because SQL's semantics, based on the relational model's semantics, do not depend on any ordering of rows in virtual or physical tables. The ORDER BY clause is used in cursors because that is how data is retrieved into your application programs, which must deal with those rows one at a time, and because the order in which rows are retrieved into applications might be important.

However, SQL/OLAP allows you to sequence the rows within each window partition based on the values of columns other than the partitioning columns. (In fact, you can ORDER BY the values of partitioning columns, but that accomplishes nothing, since all partitioning columns are equal within a partition.) The columns specified in the ORDER BY clause of a window are known as the window's *ordering columns*. An illustration of this capability can be seen in Example 7.7, where I requested that my data be partitioned according to the values in the `store_id` column, then for each partition to be sorted by the values in the `month` column.

Ordering within a Window: NULLS FIRST or LAST

The `<null ordering>` clause allows you to control where null values are placed within each partition of a window. For some analysis operations, such as the computation of moving averages and cumulative sums, it may be preferable to ensure that all non-null values are processed first. By doing so, you can ensure that the meaningful data is not "nullified" (pun intended!) by inclusion of unknown or missing data in the computations. In other cases, you may wish to dispose of the null values as early as possible in your running computations so that later values have greater meaning.

Before the advent of SQL/OLAP, ordering of rows that included one or more null values in the ordering columns was performed so that all null values were sorted as though they were less than all non-null values, or so that all null values were sorted as though they were greater than all non-null values. The choice of which was left implementation-defined. This choice remains valid whenever you specify an ORDER BY clause without a `<null ordering>` clause, although implementations must make the same choice (greater than or less than) for cursors and for windows.

However, if you specify ORDER BY and include a `<null ordering>` clause, you instruct the SQL engine that all null values are placed first in each partition (or cursor) or last in each partition (or cursor)—regardless of whether you specify ASC or DESC. That is, NULLS FIRST in an ASC order makes nulls sort greater than the highest non-null value, while NULLS FIRST in a DESC order makes nulls sort lower than the lowest non-null value. Either way, the null values appear first in the ordering. This is a subtle, but important difference from the default behavior.

The `<null ordering>` clause does not allow you to specify whether nulls are treated greater than or less than non-null values—only whether they are sorted at the beginning of a set of rows or at the end. I agree that this is confusing, but the designers of SQL/OLAP had received considerable input from data analysts that justified the first-versus-last semantics, and it was far too late to change the default null-ordering semantics of the ORDER BY clause for cursors.

Ordering and Its Relationship to Ordinary Cursors

In spite of the fact that the `<sort specification list>` is used in both a window ordering clause and in a cursor declaration, specifying ORDER BY in a window specification has no influence on the order of rows that are returned when you FETCH from a cursor whose declaration includes that window specification.

The ORDER BY that you use in your `<window order clause>` controls only the sequence in which rows belonging to each window partition are produced when the partition's rows are being processed within the query. SQL's normal rules that govern the order in which rows are returned from a query expression—that is, in no particular order—remain in effect unless you apply an ORDER BY to your cursor declarations, too.

Example 7.8 repeats the query in Example 7.7 in the form of a cursor declaration with its own ORDER BY clause. An application that declares this cursor, opens it, and FETCHes rows from it would actually encounter the rows in the order in which they appear in Result 7.4. Without the cursor's ORDER BY clause, however, the rows that appear in Result 7.4 could appear in any order at all—including potentially different orders upon successive executions of the application. The cursor's ORDER BY clause controls the sequence in which rows are retrieved through the cursor, while the window's ORDER BY clause determines the ordering of rows within a window partition. The two orders really have nothing to do with one another.

Example 7.8 *Cursor to Query Moving Average of Sales over Previous Three Months*

```
DECLARE CURSOR c1 AS
  SELECT h.store_id, h.month, h.total_dvd_sales,
         AVG (h.total_dvd_sales) OVER w AS moving_avg
  FROM sales_history AS h
  WHERE h.month BETWEEN 200109 AND 200112
  WINDOW w AS ( PARTITION BY h.store_id
                ORDER BY h.month
                ROWS 2 PRECEDING )
  ORDER BY h.store_id, h.month
```

SQL/OLAP provides the additional rather useful capability of allowing your cursor's ORDER BY clause to specify expressions that include OLAP functions themselves. For example, the cursor shown in Example 7.8 could have been written to return rows sorted according to the computed moving average (`ORDER BY moving_avg`), or even by an OLAP function that doesn't appear in the SELECT list of the query.

7.4.4 Window Framing: Aggregations Groups

And so we come to the third and final component of window definitions: the window framing, or the window aggregation grouping. The phrase *window framing* is not inappropriate, since the characteristic does put a sort of "frame" or bound around the section of a window partition for which some computation is being done. Many people prefer calling this characteristic *aggregation group* because it defines the group of rows to which some aggregate operation is applied. Personally, I'm neutral on the choice of terminology.

The SQL/OLAP specification prefers the word *frame,* so that's what I use in most of the following material; however, the phrases *physical frame* and *logical frame* sound inferior to *physical aggregation group* and *logical aggregation group,* so those terms do show up.

SQL/OLAP defines the window frame associated with a given row as a collection of rows that, in the ordering of that row's partition, lie within some neighborhood of that given row. It is this collection of rows on which the aggregate functions of the query are applied. The syntax used to specify window framing appears in Syntax 7.5.

Syntax 7.5 *<window frame clause> Syntax*

```
<window frame clause> ::=
    <window frame units>
    <window frame extent>
    [ <window frame exclusion> ]

<window frame units> ::=
    ROWS
  | RANGE

<window frame extent> ::=
    <window frame start>
  | <window frame between>
```

```
<window frame start> ::=
    UNBOUNDED PRECEDING
  | <unsigned value specification> PRECEDING
  | CURRENT ROW

<window frame between> ::=
    BETWEEN <window frame bound 1> AND <window frame bound 2>

<window frame bound 1> ::= <window frame bound>

<window frame bound 2> ::= <window frame bound>

<window frame bound> ::=
    <window frame start>
  | UNBOUNDED FOLLOWING
  | <unsigned value specification> FOLLOWING

<window frame exclusion> ::=
    EXCLUDE CURRENT ROW
  | EXCLUDE GROUP
  | EXCLUDE TIES
  | EXCLUDE NO OTHERS
```

Syntax 7.5 is somewhat longer than the syntax of the other windowing clauses, but it's not really complicated, as you'll see in the following paragraphs.

RANGE and ROWS

Window frames can be defined in terms of actual numbers of rows, or in terms of ranges of values. If you define your window frames in terms of a number of rows preceding and/or following each "current" row, we might say that such frames define *physical* aggregation groups (less common is the term *physical frames*). On the other hand, if you define them in terms of ranges of values relative to a value in each "current" row, the frames define *logical* aggregation groups.

In Syntax 7.5, the syntax element `<window frame units>` lets you choose between ROWS and RANGE. Specification of ROWS defines a window frame whose content is determined by including a specified number of rows before and/or after the "current" row. Specification of RANGE defines a window frame whose content is determined by finding rows in which the ordering column (or columns) have values within the specified range of values relative to the "current" row.

To compute a moving average that includes the current month (that is, the month for which the computation is being performed), the prior month, and the subsequent month, I could write a query that includes the `<window clause>` shown in Example 7.9.

Example 7.9 *Window Frame Using ROWS*

```
...
WINDOW w2 AS ( PARTITION BY store_id
               ORDER BY month
               ROWS BETWEEN 1 PRECEDING AND 1 FOLLOWING )
```

Of course, that `<window frame clause>` depends on there being exactly one row for each store in every month. If some stores were closed during one or more of the months in question and no rows exist for those months, the computation will be performed on a different selection of months for those stores than for the others. Similarly, if through some data entry misadventure, two or more rows had been created for a single month at a single store, the computations will give inaccurate results.

The only way to avoid such problems when your data might have gaps or the kind of duplication mentioned in the previous paragraph is to use logical aggregation groups, as shown by the `<window clause>` in Example 7.10.

Example 7.10 *Window Frame Using RANGE*

```
...
WINDOW w2 AS ( PARTITION BY store_id
               ORDER BY month
               RANGE BETWEEN INTERVAL '1' MONTH PRECEDING
                         AND INTERVAL '1' MONTH FOLLOWING )
```

(Let's assume for the purposes of this example that the `month` column has a data type of INTERVAL YEAR TO MONTH.) By using RANGE instead of ROWS, the query is protected against gaps or duplication in the data.

Physical aggregation (that is, the use of ROWS) is appropriate under some conditions, but logical aggregation (the use of RANGE) is better under others. In fact, the two alternatives have precisely opposite strengths and weaknesses!

You can use ROWS only if the input data is "dense" (that is, there are no gaps in the sequence of ordering column values) but not "too dense" (such as having multiple rows for a given month—this is often called a *tie* and can result in non-deterministic results; ties are discussed later in this section). When using ROWS, you can have more than one ordering column, because counting physical rows readily crosses the boundaries between the "sort group" formed by ordering one of those columns. In addition, there doesn't have to be a simple formula (like "add or subtract one month") for computing preceding and succeeding ordering column values.

By contrast, you can use RANGE only when there is a very simple formula that involves nothing more than adding or subtracting a value from the ordering column value. Among other things, this means that your ordering column has to have a data type that is a numeric type, a datetime type, or an interval type, since those are the only data types for which addition and subtraction are defined. Because of this, it's prohibited to use more than one ordering column when you use RANGE. However, when you use RANGE, your queries are not limited to dense data and the existence of ties does not lead to nondeterminism.

Bounded and Unbounded

So far, the window frames that I've discussed have involved specific criteria for choosing a set of rows to include in the OLAP computations for the "current" row. We call these window frames *bounded* frames, since they have a boundary determined by a specified number of rows or by a range of values. Sometimes, however, your business analysis needs require that your computations use all of the data available. For example, I can compute the running sum of DVD sales throughout the entire history of each store's sales by specifying that the window frame is ROWS 100000 PRECEDING. Any maintenance programmer reading the query a few years hence would probably be bewildered by that number; how likely is it that any store (in the New World, at least) has been in business for 100,000 months?

What such queries really require is the ability to specify *unbounded* frames. Window frames in SQL/OLAP can be unbounded preceding the current row and bounded following the current row, they can be bounded preceding the current row and unbounded following the current row, or they can be unbounded on both sides of the current row. The word *unbounded* means that the frame extends all the way to the partition boundary in the given direction; the frame is, of course, "bounded" by the partition boundary.

When you specify a `<window frame extent>` that doesn't specify UNBOUNDED, the resulting frame is a bounded frame. Conversely, if you use UNBOUNDED (PRECEDING or FOLLOWING), the resulting frame is an unbounded frame. SQL/OLAP does not specify terminology to distinguish between frames that are unbounded preceding the current row, following it, or both. We might say that a window frame that specifies RANGE UNBOUNDED PRECEDING is unbounded in the preceding direction and bounded in the following direction. Similarly, specification of RANGE UNBOUNDED FOLLOWING implies unbounded in the following direction and bounded in the preceding direction.

When a `<window frame extent>` specifies BETWEEN, it explicitly provides an indication of the beginning and end of the frame (even if one or both of those are unbounded). However, `<window frame extent>`s are valid even if they specify only one of the two values; in that case, the other value defaults to CURRENT ROW.

In Example 7.11, I've coded several examples of `<window frame extent>`s to illustrate the combinations of syntax that are valid—and a few that are invalid, too. The comment preceding each example explains the example's meaning.

Example 7.11 *Examples of Bounded and Unbounded Window Frames*

```
/* Valid <window frame extent> definitions */

/* Preceding row, current row, and following row */
...ROWS BETWEEN 1 PRECEDING AND 1 FOLLOWING

/* Preceding 3 rows, current row, and 2 following rows */
...ROWS BETWEEN 3 PRECEDING AND 2 FOLLOWING

/* Preceding 5 rows and current row */
...ROWS BETWEEN 5 PRECEDING AND CURRENT ROW

/* Preceding 5 rows and current row (another alternative) */
...ROWS 5 PRECEDING

/* All preceding rows and current row */
...ROWS BETWEEN UNBOUNDED PRECEDING AND CURRENT ROW

/* All preceding rows and current row (another alternative) */
...ROWS UNBOUNDED PRECEDING

/* Current row and all following rows */
...ROWS BETWEEN CURRENT ROW AND UNBOUNDED FOLLOWING

/* The 3 rows starting 6 rows before the current row */
/* This is called an "uncentered" frame, as it excludes the current row */
...ROWS BETWEEN 6 PRECEDING AND 3 PRECEDING
```

```
/* The 4 rows starting with the next row */
/* This is another "uncentered" frame */
...ROWS BETWEEN 1 FOLLOWING AND 5 FOLLOWING

/* Invalid <window frame extent> definitions */

/* "Earlier" rows must be specified before "later" rows */
...ROWS BETWEEN UNBOUNDED FOLLOWING AND CURRENT ROW

/* "Earlier" rows must be specified before "later" rows; this
   example is syntactically equivalent to
   ...ROWS BETWEEN UNBOUNDED FOLLOWING AND CURRENT ROW */
...ROWS UNBOUNDED FOLLOWING

/* "Earlier" rows must be specified before "later" rows */
/* This syntax is not actually invalid, but results in empty frames */
...ROWS BETWEEN 3 PRECEDING AND 5 PRECEDING
```

If no window framing is specified at all and no window ordering is specified, then the effect is as though you had specified BETWEEN UNBOUNDED PRECEDING AND UNBOUNDED FOLLOWING. If you don't specify a window framing, but you do specify a window ordering, then the implicit window framing is RANGE UNBOUNDED PRECEDING.

Incomplete Aggregation Groups

In Example 7.7 and Result 7.4, you can see that the moving average for the City store in September 2001 (`month` value 200109) is identical to the `total_dvd_sales` value for that store in that month. That value results from the fact that there are no preceding months in the data (after all, the query includes a WHERE clause that limits the data to the months of September through December) to average into the computation. Similarly, the moving average for the City store in October is the average of the September and October `total_dvd_sales` values—a two-month average. The South and Web stores suffer from the same limitations. When this situation is encountered, we say that we're using *incomplete aggregation groups,* because the query was unable to satisfy the specified `<window frame extent>`.

Since September data cannot be averaged with previous months (those previous months don't exist for the purposes of the query), the computation is performed on a smaller selection of rows than the query's WINDOW clause requested: ROWS 2 PRECEDING. Since there is always a limit to the amount of data available, many queries will encounter situations where they are unable to acquire the specified number of rows preceding and/or following the "current" row. SQL/OLAP responds to that situation by using rows up to the relevant partition boundary.

However, some applications cannot tolerate incomplete aggregation groups. Such applications might choose to return some predetermined value, such as the null value, whenever an incomplete aggregation group is encountered. Example 7.12 does just that by using SQL's CASE expression to test the size of each frame.

Example 7.12 *Incomplete Aggregation Groups*

```
SELECT h.store_id, h.month, h.total_dvd_sales,
       CASE
         WHEN COUNT(*) OVER w < 3 THEN NULL
         ELSE AVG (h.total_dvd_sales) OVER w
       END AS moving_avg
FROM sales_history AS h
WHERE h.month BETWEEN 200109 AND 200112
WINDOW w AS ( PARTITION BY h.store_id
              ORDER BY h.month
              ROWS 2 PRECEDING )
```

Null Values and Ties

When your queries use physical aggregation (ROWS), the existence of null values in your ordering columns doesn't cause any unusual issues to arise. After all, the OLAP operators are operating on rows that have been obtained by counting a specific number of rows relative to the current row.

However, when you use logical aggregation (RANGE), the rows to be used in a given frame are determined by adding and subtracting a particular value from the value of the ordering column in the current row. What value should be added to or subtracted from, say, 125 in order to get the null value? In other words, how can a RANGE be specified in such a manner that rows with null values in the ordering column will be included in the frame? Obviously, no (non-null) value can be added to or subtracted from 125 to get the null value (although SQL's semantics do cause the result of adding 125 and a null value, as well as subtracting one from the other, to be the null value). I've heard it said that the null-valued rows in a partition are separated from the non-null-valued rows by "infinity," because no number can be identified that will bridge the gap between the two types of rows, but we cannot add infinity to anything else in SQL; SQL doesn't support that particular notion. The solution lies in syntax that we've already seen.

SQL/OLAP, as you saw in section 7.4.3, allows you to control where null values sort in a window partition—either at the very beginning of the partition or at the very end; even if you don't specify NULLS FIRST or NULLS LAST, your implementation is required to collect all such rows together and sort them greater than or less than (the choice is implementation-defined) all rows with non-null values in the ordering columns. In either case, the null-valued rows will be at one end or the other end of each partition.

Consequently, you can take advantage of the ability to control where those null-valued rows sort in each partition by using the UNBOUNDED PRECEDING or UNBOUNDED FOLLOWING clauses in the window frame definition. Doing so automatically includes all rows to the beginning of the partition or the end of the partition, depending on which clause you specify, and the null-valued rows will be included at whichever end of the partition they have been sorted.

When your window frames are based on ROWS, there is a different semantic problem that requires attention. While you don't have semantic issues caused by rows with null values in the ordering columns, you may encounter difficulties caused by rows having equal values in the ordering columns.

Recall that SQL's rows are ordered only when, and to the degree that, you specify their ordering. In a table like the one illustrated in Figure 7.1, there are several rows whose `type` column contains the value `Action`. An SQL statement to retrieve just those rows from that table would return only rows whose `type` column contains the value `Action`, but those rows might be returned in any order, and a second execution of the retrieval statement might return the rows in a different order.

Similarly, a cursor declaration that retrieves all of the rows in the table might order the rows by using `ORDER BY type`. All rows for `Action` movies would appear before all rows for `Animated` movies, but the `Action` movies could still appear in any order within the cluster of `Action` movies. If I wanted the `Action` movies to be returned in, say, alphabetical order by title, I must be prepared to `ORDER BY type, title`. We say that SQL returns rows in a *non-deterministic order* when the order is not specified or when it is only partially specified.

The question of determinism becomes most important when you have two or more OLAP functions invoked in the same query, the window on which they are defined uses physical aggregation, and the rows have ties in the ordering column. It may not matter for a single OLAP query whether the tied rows are returned in one sequence when the query is run once and in a different sequence when the query is run a second time. However, it is vital that the rows all be returned in the same order when computing the two OLAP functions during a single invocation of the query. Otherwise, you could find the results quite counterintuitive, such as having a running sum and a running average that could not possibly have resulted from the same data. Determinism is especially important when using in-line windows, which are discussed in section 7.4.6, "In-Line Window Specifications," and you will read about determinism and its benefits, particularly in the face of multiple moving aggregates, in section 7.5.

Exclusions

Once in a while, it may be desirable to perform your OLAP computations without including some particular segment of data. For example, you might wish to compare the "current" row with the average of all other rows in a partition, or you might want to perform the computation without including all of the ties (discussed in the previous section).

The `<window frame exclusion>` clause provides the ability to exclude the current row (EXCLUDE CURRENT ROW), to exclude the current row and all rows that are tied with it (EXCLUDE GROUP), to exclude all rows that are tied with the current row but retain the current row (EXCLUDE TIES), or not to exclude any rows at all (EXCLUDE NO OTHERS). If you omit the `<window frame exclusion>` clause, then you get the same effect as if you had specified EXCLUDE NO OTHERS.

7.4.5 Multiple Windows and Building on Previous Windows

In Syntax 7.1, you observe that a `<window clause>` can contain multiple `<window definition>`s (separated by commas). This permits queries that define more than one window, which in turn allows you to write a single query that presents your data from several angles at once without you having to write complicated joins or unions in the query.

When doing a business analysis of my music and video store, I need good information about the contribution that every store and every title makes to my sales. It's frequently useful to know what percentage of each title's sales come from each store, as well as what percentage of each store's sales come from each title. It's also good to know what percentage contribution to my overall gross sales come from each title at each store. The facilities discussed so far in this chapter allow these facts to be determined, but only by writing multiple queries (or a complicated query that involves multiple subqueries combined with a UNION). We can answer all three questions with a single query by defining multiple windows, as indicated in Example 7.13.

Example 7.13 *Multiple Windows in a Single Query*

```
SELECT title, store_id,
  total_dvd_sales / SUM (total_dvd_sales) OVER everything,
  total_dvd_sales / SUM (total_dvd_sales) OVER by_title,
  total_dvd_sales / SUM (total_dvd_sales) OVER by_store,
FROM sales_by_store_and_product
WINDOW everything AS (),
       by_title AS ( PARTITION BY title ),
       by_store AS ( PARTITION BY store_id )
```

That query returns, for each product sold in each store, the fraction of overall sales contributed by a specific title at a given store, the fraction of sales of the specific title that were made at a given store, and the fraction of the given store's sales that were contributed by a specific title. In this case, the three windows are independent of one another, but the three invocations of the SUM function in the SELECT list use the three windows concurrently.

It might be interesting to observe that the query shown in Example 7.13 can be accomplished without using OLAP, but it gets rather messy and substantially more complicated. For contrast, see the alternative solution in Example 7.14.

Example 7.14 *Simulating Multiple Windows in a Single Query*

```
SELECT title, store_id,
       total_dvd_sales / ( SELECT SUM ( total_dvd_sales )
                           FROM sales_by_store_and_product ),
       total_dvd_sales / t.s,
       total_dvd_sales / s.s
FROM sales_by_store_and_product AS s
     ( SELECT title, SUM ( total_dvd_sales ) AS s
       FROM sales_by_store_and_product
       GROUP BY title ) AS byt,
     ( SELECT store_id, SUM ( total_dvd_sales ) AS s
       FROM sales_by_store_and_product
       GROUP BY store_id ) AS bys
WHERE s.title = byt.title
  AND s.store_id = bys.store_id
```

Not only is the alternative query considerably longer than the OLAP version in Example 7.13, the number of partial results and intermediate concepts adds too much complexity for my taste.

However, you can define multiple windows in a query that are not independent of one another. That is, one window can be defined in terms of a window that was defined earlier in the query. For example, I could rewrite Example 7.7 using window definitions that extend other window definitions as illustrated in Example 7.15, which uses the optional `<existing window name>` from Syntax 7.2 that I promised to cover in this section.

Example 7.15 *Moving Average of Sales Using Cumulative Windows*

```
SELECT h.store_id, h.month, h.total_dvd_sales,
       AVG (h.total_dvd_sales) OVER w3 AS moving_avg
FROM sales_history AS h
WHERE h.month BETWEEN 200109 AND 200112
WINDOW w1 AS ( PARTITION BY h.store_id ),
       w2 AS ( w1 ORDER BY h.month ),
       w3 AS ( w2 ROWS 2 PRECEDING )
```

In Example 7.15, window w3, which is the only window actually used in the output, adds a window framing to window w2, which adds a windows ordering to window w1. Window w1 by itself defines only a partitioning.

SQL/OLAP windows that build on one another must define window characteristics in this order: partitioning, ordering, and framing. If window w2 had been defined by itself (that is, not building on window w1), then window w3 would have been prohibited from adding a PARITIONING to the window definition that it inherited from window w2. One implication of this requirement is that the maximum length of a series of windows that build on one another is three—there are only three clauses in a window definition, and each must define at least one of those characteristics.

The query in Example 7.15 doesn't derive any benefit from defining the three separate windows. The real advantage comes when one window definition provides one or two window characteristics and additional windows specify different variations of the remaining characteristics. For example, suppose that in my business analysis I need to know the cumulative sum of sales for each month as well as a *centered average* of sales for the same months. The cumulative sum would undoubtedly use a window frame defined using something like "BETWEEN UNBOUNDED PRECEDING AND CURRENT ROW," while the centered average might use "BETWEEN 1 PRECEDING AND 1 FOLLOWING." Obviously, those two framings require two separate windows, but it's tedious to define every window from scratch (particularly when there might be several such variations involved). I could satisfy these requirements with a query like the one in Example 7.16.

Example 7.16 *Using Cumulative Windows More Effectively*

```
SELECT h.store_id, h.month, h.total_dvd_sales,
       SUM (h.total_dvd_sales) OVER w2a AS cum_sum,
       AVG (h.total_dvd_sales) OVER w3b AS cen_avg,
FROM sales_history AS h
WHERE h.month BETWEEN 200109 AND 200112
WINDOW w1 AS ( PARTITION BY h.store_id
               ORDER BY h.month ),
       w2a AS ( w1 ROWS BETWEEN UNBOUNDED PRECEDING AND CURRENT ROW ),
       w2b AS ( w1 ROWS BETWEEN 1 PRECEDING AND 1 FOLLOWING )
```

In that query, window w2a and window w2b each inherit window w1's partitioning and ordering, but add their own framing.

7.4.6 In-Line Window Specifications

So far in this chapter, you've learned how to define windows in the new WINDOW clause that follows the HAVING clause. As you have seen in several examples, you reference the windows defined with those WINDOW clauses by specifying their names when you invoke an OLAP function (such as "SUM (...) OVER w2").

Sometimes, however, you may feel that queries would be simpler to write if you only had the ability to specify a window at the same time you write the OLAP function invocation. SQL/OLAP responds to this need by providing the ability to define a window "in line" in the SELECT list of your query. See Syntax 7.6 for the definition of syntax that allows definition of in-line windows. (The window functions themselves are discussed in section 7.6.2.)

Syntax 7.6 *<window function> Syntax*

```
<window function> ::=
    <window function type> OVER <window name or specification>

<window function type> ::=
    <rank function type> <left paren> <right paren>
  | ROW_NUMBER <left paren> <right paren>
  | <aggregate function>

<rank function type> ::=
    RANK
```

```
    | DENSE_RANK
    | PERCENT_RANK
    | CUME_DIST

<window name or specification> ::=
      <window name>
    | <in-line window specification>

<in-line window specification> ::= <window specification>
```

This capability allows you to choose whether to define your windows in a WINDOW clause that follows the HAVING clause and then reference them by name from your window function invocations, or to define them along with the function invocations. If you choose to use an in-line window definition, then you cannot give the window a name. Two or more window function invocations in a single SELECT list that use identical windows must either reference a named window defined in a WINDOW clause or they must define their in-line windows redundantly.

Example 7.16 could be rewritten with in-line window specifications as shown in Example 7.17.

Example 7.17 *Using Cumulative Windows More Effectively*

```
SELECT h.store_id, h.month, h.total_dvd_sales,
       SUM (h.total_dvd_sales)
            OVER ( PARTITION BY h.store_id
                   ORDER BY h.month
                   ROWS BETWEEN UNBOUNDED PRECEDING AND CURRENT ROW )
         AS cum_sum,
       AVG (h.total_dvd_sales)
            OVER ( PARTITION BY h.store_id
                   ORDER BY h.month
                   ROWS BETWEEN 1 PRECEDING AND 1 FOLLOWING )
         AS cen_avg,
FROM sales_history AS h
WHERE h.month BETWEEN 200109 AND 200112
```

In-line window specifications can be built on top of windows that are defined in WINDOW clauses, simply by starting the in-line specification with the name of the other window.

7.5 Coordinated Nondeterminism

When you have more than one moving aggregate computed over the same ordered data, it is frequently important to have the same ordering used in each moving aggregate. For example, suppose you have a set of transactions posted to the sales account for a customer. Each transaction records its date and the amount, either positive (for a credit to the account) or negative (for a debit). You want to produce a report ordered by transaction date, showing the transaction amount, the cumulative balance, cumulative maximum, and cumulative minimum amounts. Suppose we have the data illustrated in Table 7.1.

Table 7.1 *Sample Data for Coordinated Moving Aggregates*

trans_date	*amount*
DATE '2001-12-07'	100.00
DATE '2001-12-07'	50.00
DATE '2001-12-07'	25.00

Note that the dates are the same, so that it would be equally valid to order these rows in some other fashion, such as "25, 100, 50" or "50, 25, 100." Now consider the SQL query in Example 7.18.

Example 7.18 *Retrieving Coordinated Moving Aggregates*

```
SELECT trans_date, amount,
  SUM (amount) OVER (ORDER BY trans_date ROWS UNBOUNDED PRECEDING),
  MAX (amount) OVER (ORDER BY trans_date ROWS UNBOUNDED PRECEDING),
  MIN (amount) OVER (ORDER BY trans_date ROWS UNBOUNDED PRECEDING)
FROM ...
```

Let's analyze this query as it fetches the first row of the result (not the first row of the source data in Table 7.1, but the first—and, with no more data than shown here, the only—row of the result of the grouped table produced by the query). In this first row, suppose that the window for the SUM has used the order "100, 50, 25," so the sum is computed to be 100. Meanwhile, the window for the MAX might have used the order "25, 100, 50," so the maximum is found to be 25. And the window for the `MIN` could have used the order "50, 25, 100," so the minimum is calculated as 50. Thus, the first row of output contains the values shown in Result 7.5.

Result 7.5 *Moving Aggregates without Coordinated Nondeterminism*

trans_date	*amount*	*(sum)*	*(max)*	*(min)*
DATE '2001-12-07'	100.00	100	25	50

The user of this report is not likely to find it acceptable. On the very first row, with only one row processed, how can the maximum be less than the minimum? How can the sum be different from either of these?

The solution to this problem is called *coordinated nondeterminism*. This means that even though the ordering of a window is nondetermininistic when there are ties, all windows must use the same ordering under certain conditions. Two windows W1 and W2 are said to be *order-equivalent* if the following two conditions are met:

- Both windows have the same number of partition columns, and corresponding partition columns are the same (the first partition column of W1 is the same as the first partition column of W2, etc.)
- Both windows have the same number of sort keys, every sort key is a column reference, and corresponding sort columns are the same (the first sort column of W1 is the same as the first sort column of W2, etc.)

In Example 7.18, all three in-line window specifications have the same partitioning (none) and the same list of columns in the ORDER BY clause. Consequently, all three windows are order-equivalent and must use the same ordering. This assures the coordinated nondeterminism that the user wants. Because SQL:1999 provides coordinated nondeterminism, we can depend instead on seeing results such as those shown in Result 7.6 in which an aggregate column has been computed using the same ordering of its respective window. (In this case, the ordering used was apparently "100, 25, 50" or "100, 50, 25" for all three windows.)

Result 7.6 *Moving Aggregates with Coordinated Nondeterminism*

trans_date	*amount*	*(sum)*	*(max)*	*(min)*
DATE '2001-12-07'	100.00	100	100	100

Using explicit window specifications, there is another way to coordinate the ordering across windows. If W1 is defined using W2, and W2 has an ORDER BY clause, then W1 must use the same ordering as W2. If W3 is also defined using W2, then W3's ordering is the same as W2's, which makes it the same as W1's ordering.

7.6 Query Functions

Almost all of the content of the chapter up to this point has been devoted to the specification of windows on which OLAP functions can operate. The explanation of the WINDOW clause and its components is lengthy and sometimes a bit complicated. But with that behind us, we can examine each of the OLAP functions.

As I said in the introduction to this chapter, the purposes of this book do not include teaching statistics or business analysis. Consequently, each function is introduced briefly and its syntax is provided; some functions are the subject of an example, but not all of the functions appear in examples.

7.6.1 Grouped Table Functions

In the first volume of this book, the discussion of CUBE and ROLLUP included coverage of a new function called the GROUPING function.[5] The GROUPING function is used to help distinguish the summary rows that are inserted into result tables as a result of grouping operations.

Result 7.3 illustrates the result of a CUBE grouping. In that table, you will find several rows in which the `year_released` column contains a null value, indicated by *"(null)."* The input data from which that result was derived may or may not have contained rows in which the `year_released` column was null—indicating, perhaps, that the year the corresponding movie was released is unknown or was not entered into the database for some reason.

When the data already includes rows in which null values appear, the system must provide some way for us to distinguish between rows corresponding to those input rows and the generated "super-aggregate" rows in which null values identify the column for which the summary was created. SQL:1999 provides a special function, GROUPING, that you can use in your SELECT lists to make this distinction in your query results. The GROUPING function has a single parameter, the name of another column in the SELECT list. When the value returned for that other column is the null value because it appears in a super-aggregate row, the value of the GROUPING function is 1; in all other cases, the value of the GROUPING function is 0. You can see how this works in Example 7.19 and Result 7.7.

5 Ibid., Chapter 9.

Example 7.19 *Example of CUBE with GROUPING*

```
SELECT movie_type, year_released, SUM(dvds_in_stock) AS sum_of_dvds,
       GROUPING ( movie_type ) AS gm,
       GROUPING ( year_released ) AS gy
FROM movie_titles
GROUP BY CUBE ( movie_type, year_released )
```

Result 7.7 *Result of CUBE Grouping Using the GROUPING Function*

MOVIE_TYPE	*YEAR_RELEASED*	*SUM_OF_DVDS*	*GM*	*GY*
Action	1990	250	0	0
Action	1991	374	0	0
Action	1992	288	0	0
Action	*(null)*	20	0	0
|	|	|	|	|
Action	*(null)*	932	0	1
Romance	1990	195	0	0
Romance	1991	439	0	0
Romance	1992	221	0	0
|	|	|	|	|
Romance	*(null)*	855	0	1
Comedy	1990	347	0	0
Comedy	1991	122	0	0
Comedy	1992	201	0	0
|	|	|	|	|
Comedy	*(null)*	670	0	1
(null)	1990	792	1	0
(null)	1991	935	1	0
(null)	1992	710	1	0
(null)	*(null)*	20	1	0
|	|	|	|	|
(null)	*(null)*	2457	1	1

More information on the GROUPING function is available in the first volume of this book.

7.6.2 OLAP Functions

The purpose of the `<window clause>` specified by SQL/OLAP is to provide collections of data on which analysis functions can be performed. In the SQL/OLAP amendment to SQL:1999, the analysis functions are provided in three categories.

One of these categories adds several functions to SQL:1999's `<numeric value function>` syntax. In SQL:1999, the `<numeric value function>`s include such functions as POSITION, CHARACTER_LENGTH, and EXTRACT. SQL/OLAP adds seven additional functions, which are all discussed in section 7.6.3. These new numeric value functions are named LN, EXP, POWER, SQRT, FLOOR, CEILING (and its synonym CEIL), and WIDTH_BUCKET.

Another category adds several functions, plus an optional feature called FILTER, to SQL:1999's `<set function specification>` syntax. As part of the change, SQL/OLAP changed the name of the BNF nonterminal from `<set function specification>` to `<aggregate function>`; of course, that change has no effect on application programs, but it does make the purpose a bit more apparent to readers of the SQL standard. Like the existing aggregate functions (COUNT, SUM, AVG, MAX, and MIN), the new aggregate functions can be applied to grouped tables as well as to windows; when they are applied to windows as `<window function type>`, they are specified using the syntax shown in Syntax 7.6. These new aggregate functions are covered in the subsection entitled "Window Aggregate Functions" below. The new aggregate functions are named STDDEV_POP, STDDEV_SAMP, VAR_SAMP, VAR_POP, COVAR_POP, COVAR_SAMP, CORR, REGR_SLOPE, REGR_INTERCEPT, REGR_COUNT, REGR_R2, REGR_AVGX, REGR_AVGY, REGR_SXX, REGR_SYY, REGR_SXY, PERCENTILE_CONT, and PERCENTILE_DISC.

The final category includes the true OLAP functions, which are specified by the `<window function>` syntax. This collection of functions includes several functions that determine the ranking of rows within window partitions, as well as a function (ROW_NUMBER) that can be used to assign a unique number to each row of a partition. These functions are all discussed in this section. The ranking functions can also be used as aggregate functions under certain circumstances; this ability is described in section 7.6.3, under the subsection entitled "Hypothetical Set Functions." The ranking functions are named RANK, DENSE_RANK, PERCENT_RANK, and CUME_DIST.

Rank Functions

SQL/OLAP defines four functions that are categorized as *rank functions*; three of these functions use the word *rank* as part of their function name. The syntax for the four rank functions appears in Syntax 7.7. (Unlike most syntax presentations, Syntax 7.7 does not directly copy the BNF from the SQL standard. Instead, I have adapted some of the BNF nonterminal symbol names and sequencing for use in this section. You may be comfortable that the syntax is completely faithful from an application program viewpoint. Because a rank function is a window function, you may wish to compare this syntax with that shown in Syntax 7.6.)

Syntax 7.7 *Syntax of Rank Functions*

```
<rank function> ::=
    <rank function name> () OVER <window name or specification>

<rank function name> ::=
    RANK
  | DENSE_RANK
  | PERCENT_RANK
  | CUME_DIST
```

The RANK function returns a number that indicates the rank of the "current" row among the rows in the row's partition. The first row in the partition has a rank of 1, and the last rank in a partition containing 35 rows is, naturally, 35. RANK is specified as a syntax transformation, which means that an implementation can choose to actually transform `RANK()` into its equivalent, or it can merely return a result equivalent to the result that the transformation would return. Example 7.20 shows the transformation (I use the symbol `ws1`, in italics, to indicate the `<window specification>` that defines the window named `w1`).

Example 7.20 *Transformation of RANK Function*

```
RANK() OVER ws
```

is equivalent to

```
( COUNT (*) OVER ( ws RANGE UNBOUNDED PRECEDING )
- COUNT (*) OVER ( ws RANGE CURRENT ROW ) + 1 )
```

Note that the transformation of the RANK function uses logical aggregation (RANGE). As a result, two or more records that are tied—that is, that have equal values in the ordering column—will have the same rank. The next group in the partition that has a different value will have a rank that is more than one greater than the rank of the tied rows. For example, if there are rows whose ordering column values are 10, 20, 20, 20, 30, the rank of the first row is 1 and the rank of the second row is 2. The rank of the third and fourth rows is also 2, but the rank of the fifth row is 5. There are no rows whose rank is 3 or 4. This algorithm is sometimes known as *sparse ranking.*

By contrast, the DENSE_RANK function returns ranking values without such gaps. The values for rows with ties are still equal, but the ranking of the rows represents the positions of the clusters of rows having equal values in the ordering column, rather than the positions of the individual rows. In the example having rows whose ordering column values are 10, 20, 20, 20, 30, the rank of the first row is still 1 and the rank of the second row is still 2, as are the ranks of the third and fourth rows. So far, this function returns the same values as the RANK function. However, the DENSE_RANK function returns a rank of 3 for the last row. DENSE_RANK is computed through a syntax transformation, too, as seen in Example 7.21.

Example 7.21 *Transformation of DENSE_RANK Function*

```
DENSE_RANK() OVER ws
```

is equivalent to

```
COUNT ( DISTINCT ROW ( VE1, ..., VEN ) )
  OVER ( ws RANGE UNBOUNDED PRECEDING )
```

where *"VE1"* through *"VEN"* represent the list of `<value expression>`s in the `<sort specification list>` of window `w1`.

The PERCENT_RANK function returns the *relative rank* of a row, which is a number that indicates the relative position of the current row within the window partition in which it appears. For example, in a partition that contains 10 rows having different values in the ordering columns, the third row would be given a PERCENT_RANK value of 0.222 . . . , because you have covered 2/9 (22.222 . . . %) of the rows following the first row of the partition. More precisely, PERCENT_RANK of a row is defined as one less than the RANK (not the DENSE_RANK!) of the row divided by one less than the number of rows in the partition, as seen in the syntax transformation found in Example 7.22. (In that transformation, *"ANT"* stands for "some approximate numeric type, such as REAL or DOUBLE PRECISION"; SQL/OLAP leaves the precise choice up to the implementation.)

Example 7.22 *Transformation of PERCENT_RANK Function*

```
PERCENT_RANK() OVER ws
```

is equivalent to

```
CASE
  WHEN COUNT(*) OVER ( ws RANGE BETWEEN UNBOUNDED PRECEDING
                                  AND UNBOUNDED FOLLOWING ) = 1
  THEN CAST (0 AS ANT)
  ELSE
    ( CAST ( RANK () OVER ( ws ) AS ANT ) - 1) /
    ( COUNT (*) OVER ( ws RANGE BETWEEN UNBOUNDED PRECEDING
                                  AND UNBOUNDED FOLLOWING ) – 1 )
END
```

One seemingly arbitrary decision illustrated by that transformation is this: If a window partition contains exactly one row, the PERCENT_RANK of that row is 0.00. Another choice would have been 1.00, but feedback from people who use such functions in their business suggested that 0.00 was a more useful result.

The fourth ranking function, CUME_DIST, also reflects the relative rank of a row within its partition. However, where PERCENT_RANK used the actual RANK of a row, CUME_DIST uses the actual position of the row within its partition; when a row has *peers* (that is, rows with tied values in the ordering columns), the CUME_DIST value of that row is determined by the position of the "last" such peer within the partition (due to the nondeterminism discussed in section 7.4.4, using the position of the "current" row could lead to different results when the query is executed another time). The CUME_DIST value of the third row in a partition of 10 rows is 0.30, but if the third and fourth rows are tied, then the CUME_DIST value would be 0.40. The CUME_DIST value is defined to be the number of rows preceding *or peers with* the row being examined divided by the total number of rows in the partition. The format transformation can be seen in Example 7.23.

Example 7.23 *Tranformation of CUME_DIST Function*

```
CUME_DIST() OVER ws
```

is equivalent to

```
( CAST ( COUNT (*) OVER ws RANGE UNBOUNDED PRECEDING ) AS ANT ) /
         COUNT (*) OVER ( ws RANGE BETWEEN UNBOUNDED PRECEDING
                                     AND UNBOUNDED FOLLOWING ) )
```

Row Number Function

The ROW_NUMBER function has syntax similar to that of the ranking functions; the details are seen in Syntax 7.8.

Syntax 7.8 *Syntax of ROW_NUMBER Function*

```
<row number function> ::=
    ROW_NUMBER () OVER <window name or specification>
```

The ROW_NUMBER function assigns a number to each row, based on its position within its window partition. Because of the nondeterminism discussed in section 7.4.4, you might get different ROW_NUMBER values for a particular row among its peers when you execute the query another time. Like the other ranking functions, ROW_NUMBER is defined using a syntax transformation, as seen in Example 7.24. ROW_NUMBER differs from RANK and DENSE_RANK by ignoring the presence of ties (peer rows).

Example 7.24 *Transformation of ROW_NUMBER Function*

```
ROW_NUMBER() OVER ws
```

is equivalent to

```
COUNT (*) OVER ws RANGE UNBOUNDED PRECEDING
```

Window Aggregate Functions

As you read in the introductory paragraphs of section 7.6.2, SQL's existing set functions, or aggregate functions, can be used as window aggregate functions in addition to their use as grouped table aggregate functions. SQL/OLAP augments the list of aggregate functions with several new functions that are typically used in statistical analysis.

I also mentioned briefly that SQL/OLAP adds a new optional feature to the syntax of all of the aggregate functions. This new features allows you to specify that the rows of each window partition (or grouped table, if that is the context in which you use the aggregate functions) are filtered by a `<search condition>` *before* the specified aggregate function is computed; all rows of the partition (or group) for which the `<search condition>` is not true (that is, the result is false or unknown) are discarded before applying the aggregate function. The syntax of aggregate function invocation, with the optional FILTER clause, is shown in Syntax 7.9.

Syntax 7.9 *Aggregate Functions and the FILTER Clause*

```
<aggregate function> ::=
    <function name> <left paren> [ <arguments> ] <right paren>
      [ FILTER <left paren> WHERE <search condition> <right paren> ]
```

For example, I might wish to determine how many different movie titles my business has in stock as DVDs, how many of those titles belong to a series, and how many of those titles cost more than $50.00 in the DVD format. The FILTER clause makes such queries easy to write, as illustrated in Example 7.25.

Example 7.25 *Using the FILTER clause*

```
SELECT COUNT(*),
       COUNT(*) FILTER ( WHERE part_of_series = 'Yes' ),
       COUNT(*) FILTER ( WHERE our_dvd_cost > 50.00 ),
FROM movies
WHERE dvds_in_stock > 0 ;
```

In the remainder of this section, I provide the syntax of each of the new functions, but not of the SQL:1999 aggregate functions, since you can read about those in the first volume of this book. I also give a brief summary of the meaning of each of the new functions.

The complete syntax of all aggregate functions is given in Syntax 7.10.

Syntax 7.10 *Complete Aggregate Function Syntax*

```
<aggregate function> ::=
    COUNT <left paren> <asterisk> <right paren> [ <filter clause> ]
  | <general set function> [ <filter clause> ]
  | <binary set function> [ <filter clause> ]
  | <ordered set function> [ <filter clause> ]

<general set function> ::=
    <set function type>
        <left paren> [ <set quantifier> ] <value expression> <right paren>

<set function type> ::= <computational operation>

<computational operation> ::=
    AVG | MAX | MIN | SUM
  | EVERY | ANY | SOME
```

```
  | COUNT
  | STDDEV_POP | STDDEV_SAMP | VAR_SAMP | VAR_POP

<set quantifier> ::=
    DISTINCT
  | ALL

<filter clause> ::=
    FILTER <left paren> WHERE <search condition> <right paren>

<binary set function> ::=
    <binary set function type> <left paren>
        <dependent variable expression> <comma>
        <independent variable expression> <right paren>

<binary set function type> ::=
    COVAR_POP | COVAR_SAMP | CORR | REGR_SLOPE
  | REGR_INTERCEPT | REGR_COUNT | REGR_R2 | REGR_AVGX | REGR_AVGY
  | REGR_SXX | REGR_SYY | REGR_SXY

<dependent variable expression> ::= <numeric value expression>

<independent variable expression> ::= <numeric value expression>

<ordered set function> ::=
    <hypothetical set function>
  | <inverse distribution function>

<hypothetical set function> ::=
    <rank function name> <left paren>
        <hypothetical set function value expression list> <right paren>
        <within group specification>

<within group specification> ::=
    WITHIN GROUP
        <left paren> ORDER BY <sort specification list> <right paren>

<hypothetical set function value expression list> ::=
    <value expression> [ { <comma> <value expression> }... ]
```

```
<inverse distribution function> ::=
    <inverse distribution function type> <left paren>
        <inverse distribution function argument> <right paren>
        <within group specification>

<inverse distribution function argument> ::= <numeric value expression>

<inverse distribution function type> ::=
    PERCENTILE_CONT
  | PERCENTILE_DISC
```

The first alternative for `<aggregate function>` is COUNT(*), which has not changed its meaning from SQL:1999; it counts all rows in the group of the grouped table or in the partition (after applying the FILTER clause, if one is specified).

The next alternative, `<general set function>`, includes several functions that take a single argument, optionally with duplicate values eliminated before applying the function, and with an optional FILTER clause. Some of these general functions are old friends from the first version of the SQL standard: SUM, AVG, MAX, and MIN, as well as COUNT (with an expression instead of "*"). Those five respectively return the sum of the values of the argument expression across all rows of the group or window partition, the average of those values, the maximum of the values, the minimum of the values, and the number of such values. In most cases, `COUNT(*)` and `COUNT(`*expression*`)` return the same value, but `COUNT(DISTINCT` *expression*`)` counts unique values of the specified expression.

`<general set function>` also includes three Boolean functions new to SQL:1999, named EVERY, ANY, and SOME (again, these are discussed in Volume 1 of this book). They return the Boolean value "true" when, respectively, the specified expression evaluates to "true" for every row or any (ANY and SOME are synonyms) row of the group or partition.

New SQL/OLAP `<general set function>`s that take one argument include

- STDDEV_POP: Computes the population standard deviation of the provided `<value expression>` evaluated for each row of the group or partition (if DISTINCT was specified, then each row that remains after duplicates have been eliminated), defined as the square root of the population variance.
- STDDEV_SAMP: Computes the sample standard deviation of the provided `<value expression>` evaluated for each row of the group or partition (if DISTINCT was specified, then each row that remains after duplicates have been eliminated), defined as the square root of the sample variance.

- VAR_POP: Computes the population variance of <value expression> evaluated for each row of the group or partition (if DISTINCT was specified, then each row that remains after duplicates have been eliminated), defined as the sum of squares of the difference of <value expression> from the mean of <value expression>, divided by the number of rows (remaining) in the group or partition.
- VAR_SAMP: Computes the sample variance of <value expression> evaluated for each row of the group or partition (if DISTINCT was specified, then each row that remains after duplicates have been eliminated), defined as the sum of squares of the difference of <value expression> from the mean of <value expression>, divided by one less than the number of rows (remaining) in the group or partition.

SQL/OLAP also specifies a number of functions that take two arguments, as seen in Syntax 7.10. These functions include

- COVAR_POP: Computes the population covariance, defined as the sum of products of the difference of <independent variable expression> (the second argument) from its mean times the difference of <dependent variable expression> (the first argument) from its mean, divided by the number of rows (remaining) in the group or partition.
- COVAR_SAMP: Computes the sample covariance, defined as the sum of products of the difference of <independent variable expression> (the second argument) from its mean times the difference of <dependent variable expression> (the first argument) from its mean, divided by one less than the number of rows (remaining) in the group or partition.
- CORR: Computes the correlation coefficient, defined as the ratio of the population covariance divided by the product of the population standard deviation of <independent variable expression> (the second argument) and the population standard deviation of <dependent variable expression> (the first argument).
- REGR_SLOPE: Computes the slope of the least-squares-fit linear equation determined by the (<independent variable expression>, <dependent variable expression>) pairs.
- REGR_INTERCEPT: Computes the y-intercept of the least-squares-fit linear equation determined by the (<independent variable expression>, <dependent variable expression>) pairs.
- REGR_COUNT: Computes the number of rows remaining in the group or partition.

- REGR_R2: Computes the square of the correlation coefficient.
- REGR_AVGX: Computes the average of `<independent variable expression>` (the second argument) for all rows in the group or partition.
- REGR_AVGY: Computes the average of `<dependent variable expression>` (the first argument) for all rows in the group or partition.
- REGR_SXX: Computes the sum of squares of `<independent variable expression>` (the second argument) for all rows in the group or partition.
- REGR_SYY: Computes the sum of squares of `<dependent variable expression>` (the first argument) for all rows in the group or partition.
- REGR_SXY: Computes the sum of products of `<independent variable expression>` (the second argument) times `<dependent variable expression>` (the first argument) for all rows in the group or partition.

Finally, SQL/OLAP defines several functions that deal with ordered sets, called (logically enough) *ordered set functions*. Two of these are called *inverse distribution functions* and are covered here; the remainder are called *hypothetical set functions* and are covered in section 7.6.3.

The two inverse distribution functions are named PERCENTILE_CONT (implying "continuous") and PERCENTILE_DISC (implying "discrete"). Both inverse distribution functions specify an argument and an ordering of a value expression. The value of the argument must be between 0 and 1 (inclusive), representing the "percent rank" of each row among the rows in the group or window partition. The expression is evaluated for each row of the group, null values are discarded, and the remaining rows are sorted by the value of the expression.

- PERCENTILE_DISC: The value of the expression for the row whose CUME_DIST value is the first value in the ordering of the value expression whose CUME_DIST value is greater than or equal to the value of the argument. PERCENTILE_DISC is sometimes called a "one-sided inverse" of CUME_DIST.
- PERCENTILE_CONT: Locates the pair of rows whose PERCENT_RANK values are respectively the greatest such PERCENT_RANK value that is no greater than the value of the ("percent rank") argument and the least such PERCENT_RANK value that is no less than the value of the ("percent rank") argument; returns the value computed by adding the values of the ordering column in those two rows and multiplying that sum by the value of the ("percent rank") argument. PERCENTILE_CONT is sometimes called a *one-sided inverse* of PERCENT_RANK.

To visualize the behavior of PERCENTILE_DISC, consider the expression `PERCENTILE_DISC (X) WITHIN GROUP (Y)`, where the values of Y are 1, 3, 3, 6, and 7. The corresponding CUME_DIST values will be 0.20, 0.60, 0.60, 0.80, and 1.00. The PERCENTILE_DISC values for various illustrative values of X are shown in Result 7.8.

Result 7.8 *Result of PERCENTILE_DISC*

X	*PERCENTILE_DISC (X)*
0.00	1
0.19	1
0.20	1
0.21	3
0.50	3
0.50	3
0.61	6
0.80	6
0.81	7
1.00	7

Notice that PERCENTILE_DISC is a *discontinuous step function* with discontinuities at each value that CUME_DIST attains. No result is ever a value that is not in the original data set. The boundaries between the values have a position determined by the expression 1/N, where N is the number of values in the collection. Since we have five values (1, 3, 3, 6, and 7), each position represents 1/5, or 0.20. The first range, 0.00 through 0.20, contains the value 1; the second, 0.20 through 0.40, contains 3, and so does the third range, 0.40 through 0.60. The complete set of relationships is

- If $0.00 \le X \le 0.20$, then the result is 1.
- If $0.20 < X \le 0.60$, then the result is 3.
- If $0.00 < X \le 0.80$, then the result is 6.
- If $0.00 < X \le 1.00$, then the result is 7.

By contrast, PERCENTILE_CONT is better explained as an *interpolation,* or a *continuous function*. Consider the expression `PERCENTILE_CONT (X) WITHIN GROUP (Y)`, where the values of Y are again 1, 3, 3, 6, and 7. In performing this computation, we use the expression 1/(N – 1), so our five values are partitioned into ranges defined by boundaries at intervals of 1/4, or 0.25. The PERCENTILE_CONT values for various illustrative values of X are shown in Result 7.9.

Result 7.9 *Result of PERCENTILE_CONT*

X	*PERCENTILE_CONT (X)*
0.00	1
0.50	3
0.75	6
1.00	7

Suppose we wanted to determine the 90th percentile for the sample data set, using continuous interpolation. That is, we want to compute `PERCENTILE_CONT (0.9) WITHIN GROUP (Y)`. From Result 7.9, it's apparent that the result will lie between 6 and 7, so we use linear interpolation to find the value, using the formula

$$\frac{(X-6)}{(7-6)} = \frac{(0.9-0.75)}{(1.00-0.75)}$$

Then, use ordinary algebra to solve for X. In this case

$$X = \left((7-6) \times \frac{(0.9-0.75)}{(1.00-0.75)}\right) + 6 = \left(1 \times \frac{0.15}{0.25}\right) + 6 = (1 \times 0.6) + 6 = 6.6$$

Thus, the final interpolated value of `PERCENTILE_CONT (0.9) WITHIN GROUP (Y)` is 6.6.

7.6.3 Additional Analysis Facilities

As indicated in the introduction to section 7.6.2, SQL/OLAP introduces a number of functions that are used like other `<numeric value function>`s such as POSITION, CHARACTER_LENGTH, and EXTRACT. The next subsection, entitled "Numeric Value Functions," summarizes these functions. The final subsection, entitled "Hypothetical Set Functions," discusses the use of SQL's aggregate set functions for a new purpose.

Numeric Value Functions

The `<numeric value function>`s introduced by SQL/OLAP are specified in Syntax 7.11.

Syntax 7.11 *New <numeric value function> Syntax*

```
<numeric value function> ::=
    <natural logarithm>
  | <exponential function>
  | <power function>
  | <square root>
  | <floor function>
  | <ceiling function>
  | <width bucket function>

<natural logarithm> ::=
    LN <left paren> <numeric value expression> <right paren>

<exponential function> ::=
    EXP <left paren> <numeric value expression> <right paren>

<power function> ::=
    POWER <left paren> <numeric value expression base>
        <comma> <numeric value expression exponent> <right paren>

<numeric value expression base> ::= <numeric value expression>

<numeric value expression exponent> ::= <numeric value expression>

<square root> ::=
    SQRT <left paren> <numeric value expression> <right paren>

<floor function> ::=
    FLOOR <left paren> <numeric value expression> <right paren>

<ceiling function> ::=
    CEILING <left paren> <numeric value expression> <right paren>

<width bucket function> ::=
    WIDTH_BUCKET <left paren> <width bucket operand> <comma>
        <width bucket bound 1> <comma> <width bucket bound 2>
        <comma> <width bucket count> <right paren>

<width bucket operand> ::= <numeric value expression>
```

```
<width bucket bound 1> ::= <numeric value expression>

<width bucket bound 2> ::= <numeric value expression>

<width bucket count> ::= <numeric value expression>
```

The semantics of these new `<numeric value function>`s are

- LN: Returns the natural logarithm of the argument value. (Raises an exception condition if the argument value is zero or negative.)
- EXP: Returns the value computed by raising the value of *e* (the base of natural logarithms) to the power specified by the value of the argument.
- POWER: Returns the value computed by raising the value of the first argument to the power specified by the value of the second argument. If the first argument is zero and the second is zero, returns one. If the first argument is zero and the second is positive, returns zero. If the first argument is zero and the second is negative, raises an exception. If the first argument is negative and the second is not an integer, raises an exception.
- SQRT: Returns the square root of the argument value, defined by syntax transformation to "`POWER (expression, 0.5)`."
- FLOOR: Returns the integer value nearest to positive infinity that is not greater than the value of the argument.
- CEILING: Returns the integer value nearest to negative infinity that is not less than the value of the argument. (CEIL is a synonym for CEILING.)

The WIDTH_BUCKET function is a bit more complicated than the other `<numeric value function>`s. It accepts four arguments: a "live value," two range boundaries, and the number of equal-sized (or as nearly so as possible) partitions into which the range indicated by the boundaries is to be divided. The function returns a number indicating the partition into which the live value should be placed, based on its value as a percentage of the difference between the higher range boundary and the lower boundary. The first partition is partition number one.

In order to avoid errors when the live value is outside of the range boundaries, live values that are less than the smaller range boundary are placed into an additional first bucket, bucket zero, and live values that are greater than the larger range boundary are placed into an additional last bucket, bucket N+1.

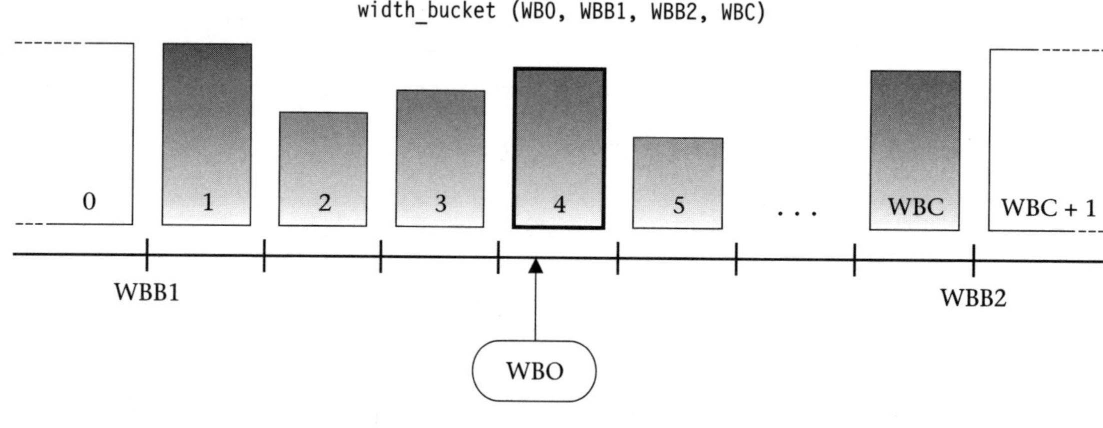

Figure 7.2 Visualizing the Meaning of WIDTH_BUCKET

For example, "`WIDTH_BUCKET (14, 5, 30, 5)`" returns 2, because

- (30-5)/5 is 5, so the range is divided into 5 partitions, each 5 units wide.
- The first bucket represents values from 0.00% to 19.999 . . . %; the second represents values from 20.00% to 39.999 . . . %; and the fifth bucket represents values from 80.00% to 100.00%.
- The bucket chosen is determined by computing (5*(14 – 5)/(30 – 5)) + 1—one more than the number of buckets times the ratio of the offset of the specified value from the lower value to the range of possible values, which is (5*9/25) + 1, which is 2.8. This value is in the range of values for bucket number 2 (2.0 through 2.999 . . .), so bucket number 2 is chosen.

The SQL standard illustrates the function of WIDTH_BUCKET with a diagram from which Figure 7.2 was taken.

Hypothetical Set Functions

SQL/OLAP also provides four functions known as *hypothetical set functions,* or *what-if* functions. Their purpose is, in essence, to return the value that would be returned from a window function if the value provided as an argument were to be inserted in a new row in the proper window partition. In other words, they allow the application to ask the question, "What if a row with this value existed?"

The four hypothetical set functions are closely related to the window functions with the same names: RANK, DENSE_RANK, PERCENT_RANK, and CUME_DIST, although they use a slightly different syntax, as seen in Syntax 7.10. These functions take an argument and specify a window ordering, specifying a second value expression. The second value expression is evaluated for all rows of the group or window partition, and the multiset of values that results is augmented by adding a row for which the ordering column has the value of the first argument (the values of the remaining columns are irrelevant). The resulting collection is treated like it was a window partition of the corresponding window function (RANK, etc.) whose window ordering is the ordering of the second value expression. The result of the hypothetical set function is the value that would have been returned by the window function of the same name for the hypothetical "row" that contributes the value of the first value expression to the collection.

7.7 Chapter Summary

In this chapter, you have learned that "SQL does windows," as well as how to specify windows and their three characteristics: window partitioning, window ordering, and window framing (or aggregate grouping). You have also learned about the various OLAP functions that operate on the windows and that can be specified and how you can specify in-line windows along with some of those functions.

Chapter 8

SQL/OLB and SQL/JRT

8.1 Introduction

An earlier book[1] detailed several technologies that have been devised to ease the task of bringing together the power of two important languages: SQL and Java. Among those technologies are three that were developed by a group of engineers who are called the SQLJ Group.

The three technologies that were developed by the SQLJ Group involve embedding SQL static statements in Java programs, invoking Java methods from SQL statements, and defining SQL structured user-defined types that are actually Java classes used from within the database.

This short chapter contains a rather brief review of the information presented in the book mentioned at the start of this section. However, that book was published before some of the specifications discussed in this chapter had been finalized. Consequently, some of the information published in that book is now slightly out of date, a situation that this chapter rectifies by updating that information based on ISO's adoption—and adaptation—of the ANSI standards discussed in that book for publication as a new part of SQL:1999. For more extensive details about the three technologies described briefly in this chapter, that book is the most complete resource of which I am aware (except, perhaps, for the actual ISO standards).

1 Jim Melton and Andrew Eisenberg, *Understanding SQL and Java Together: A Guide to SQLJ, JDBC, and Related Technologies* (San Francisco: Morgan Kaufmann Publishers, 2000).

8.2 The SQLJ Group

In mid-1997, engineers from Oracle, IBM, and Tandem (now Compaq) formed a group whose stated goal was the development of a specification for embedding SQL statements in Java programs and the establishment of a reference implementation of that specification. Rather than forming a formal consortium, which requires significant effort and expenditure of resources better spent on technical work, an informal group, eventually known as the SQLJ Group, was created, and engineers from other companies interested in the subject were invited to participate. During the lifetime of the SQLJ Group, it also included participants from Sun Microsystems, Sybase, Informix (now part of IBM), Cloudscape (later acquired by Informix), Microfocus, and even Microsoft. The SQLJ Group's Web site can be found at *http://sqlj.org*.

The very earliest work of the SQLJ Group used technology contributed by Oracle, including an implementation of a translator that accepted Java programs containing embedded SQL statements, and produced corresponding Java programs that used the JDBC interface for execution of those SQL statements. IBM and Tandem (at least) submitted significant technology to enhance those initial contributions, including technology related to profiles (discussed in section 8.4.1), test suites, and other technical proposals. The other members contributed technical proposals, prototype experiences, and considerable review of the specifications.

It didn't take long for Group members to start work on two additional specifications, for which Sybase drafted the initial documents. One of these new specifications allowed methods written in Java to be invoked from SQL statements. The other permitted users to define new SQL structured user-defined types that were, in fact, Java classes. Both were actively implemented by several companies while the specifications were being written, so they were known to be on very solid ground.

The SQLJ Group approached NCITS (the National Committee for Information Technology Standards, an organization accredited by ANSI in the United States for developing American National Standards) about the possibility of publishing the three specifications as ANSI standards. At NCITS's urging, the SQLJ Group chose to submit the specification for embedding SQL statements in Java code (by then commonly called "SQLJ Part 0") to the NCITS Technical Committee responsible for SQL, NCITS H2, but to submit the other two specifications (called "SQLJ Part 1" and "SQLJ Part 2") for processing under a new NCITS fast-track procedure that allowed their publication as ANSI standards in a matter of months. Indeed, SQLJ Part 0 was quickly published as Part 10 of the ANSI SQL standard under the name SQL/OLB,[2] and Parts 1 and 2 were published in due course as two parts of a new multipart ANSI standard.[3]

Although the SQLJ Group was never formally disbanded, its activities have virtually ceased, since all of its specifications have been published. While this chapter was being written, work continued to update and formalize the reference implementation of SQLJ Part 0 (that is, SQL/OLB) with hopes that it might be submitted to the Java Community Process for possible inclusion in some version of J2EE (Java 2 Enterprise Edition). Regrettably, at the time that this volume goes to press, that outcome, apparently, is not being actively pursued.

8.3 The Joys of Java

Readers of Volume 1 of this book and experienced SQL programmers know about the "impedance mismatch" that causes difficulties for application developers who use SQL together with programming languages such as C or COBOL. As Java surged in popularity during the 1990s, it was naturally used along with SQL for building applications. But the impedance mismatch between SQL and Java was no better than between SQL and other languages. In fact, it was arguably more severe because of Java's inherent object-oriented nature.

The members of the SQLJ Group resolved to develop specifications that would reduce the impedance mismatch between SQL and Java as much as possible. SQLJ Part 1 includes facilities for *iterators* that provide Java facilities that are closely tied to SQL cursors, reducing that aspect of the impedance mismatch. SQL Parts 1 and 2, when both are implemented, allow the use of Java classes, along with their (Java) methods, as first-class types in the database. Data created as instances of those classes *are* Java objects. When such types are in use, the data type component of the impedance mismatch between the SQL environment and the Java applications that depend on that environment simply vanishes.

Of course, it is rare to achieve such benefits without some costs. SQLJ Part 2 facilities that allow you to create SQL structured types that are Java classes introduce some syntactic and semantic differences relative to the SQL user-defined type capabilities defined in Chapter 2, "User-Defined Types," and Chapter 3, "Typed Tables." Some of the most important differences are

---

2 ANSI X3.135.10-1998, *Information Systems—Database Language—SQL—Part 10: Object Language Bindings (SQL/OLB)* (New York, NY: American National Standards Institute, 1998).

3 ANSI NCITS 331.1-1999, *SQLJ—Part 1: SQL Routines using the Java Programming Language* (American National Standards Institute, 1999), and ANSI NCITS 331.2-2000, *SQLJ—Part 2: SQL Types using the Java Programming Language* (American National Standards Institute, 2000).

- For ordinary SQL user-defined types, there is no association with an underlying class in any object-oriented programming language. Naturally, there is such an association for Java types.
- Each method of a structured type that is not defined using Java can be written in a different language (for example, one method could be written in SQL and another written in Fortran)—however, such user-defined types cannot have methods written in Java. By contrast, all methods of a structured type defined using Java must be written in Java, (implicitly) have a parameter style of JAVA, and be defined in the associated Java class or in one of its superclasses.
- There is no explicit association between a non-Java structured type's attributes and any external representation of their content. In addition, the mapping between such a type's methods and external methods is made by subsequent CREATE METHOD statements. By contrast, for types defined using Java, the association between the structured type's attributes and methods and the public attributes and methods of a subject Java class is specified by the CREATE TYPE statement.
- For types defined using Java, the mechanism used to convert the SQL environment's representation of an instance of a structured type into an instance of a Java class is specified in the `USING <interface specification>` clause. Such conversions are performed, for example, when a Java type is specified as a (subject) parameter in a method or function invocation, or when a Java object returned from a method or function invocation is stored in a column declared to be a Java type. `<interface specification>` can be either SERIALIZABLE, specifying the Java-defined interface `java.io.Serializable` (not to be confused with the isolation level of SERIALIZABLE), or SQLDATA, specifying the JDBC-defined interface `java.sql.SQLData`.
- For non-Java types, there is no explicit support of static attributes. For Java types, the CREATE TYPE is allowed to include static field method specifications that define observer methods for specified static attributes of the subject Java class.
- For non-Java types, the implementation of every method that isn't an SQL routine exists externally to the SQL environment. For external Java data types, the implementation of the methods is provided by a specified subject Java class that exists within the SQL environment in an *installed JAR*.
- Support for the specification of overriding methods is not provided for methods that are external Java routines.

- The definitions of Java types, once created, cannot be changed. The definitions of non-Java types can be modified through use of the ALTER TYPE statement.

8.4 Embedding SQL in Java

Those of you who have written Java programs that access SQL databases using JDBC are vividly aware of the pros and cons of that interface. Of course, JDBC bears a strong resemblance to the very popular ODBC interface used for SQL access from other programming languages—indeed, JDBC's design was largely based on ODBC. The resemblance often helps developers make the transition from ODBC use in C to programming in Java with JDBC.

On the other hand, JDBC can be difficult to write, particularly if you're more used to writing static embedded SQL in other programming languages. Furthermore, most JDBC programs are highly dynamic, preparing and optimizing the SQL statements at runtime, even if those statements are completely known at the time that the containing programs are written. Such unnecessary dynamic interaction with the database often introduces numerous performance problems.

8.4.1 SQL/OLB (SQLJ Part 0)

A new part[4] of the SQL:1999 standard offers an arrangement that resolves most of the difficulties posed by writing programs using JDBC while retaining all of its benefits. This new part of the SQL standard, known as SQL/OLB (Object Language Bindings) provides a way for you to write Java programs in which you embed SQL statements similarly to the embedded SQL capabilities provided for other programming languages. (A number of database vendors refer to their SQL/OLB implementations as "SQLJ." That occasionally causes confusion, since the SQLJ Group defined three specifications, of which SQLJ Part 0 defines the embedded SQL facilities. I prefer to use "OLB" or "SQL/OLB" for this specification.)

Undoubtedly the two most important motivations for SQL/OLB are support for *static* SQL statements and ease of programming. Compare the program frag-

4 ISO/IEC 9075-10:2000, *Information technology—Database languages—SQL—Part 10: Object Language Bindings (SQL/OLB)* (Geneva: International Organization for Standardization, 2000). This standard was derived from the earlier ANSI standard X3.135.10-1998 but was modified to correct several errors as well as to add support for several JDBC 2.0 capabilities, such as batch updates, scrollable cursors, and others.

ment written using JDBC in Example 8.1 with the program in Example 8.2 that uses the embedded capabilities provided by SQL/OLB. Note that the two programs accomplish precisely the same task: insertion of a row defining a movie (one that doesn't really exist, for which we may be thankful). I have highlighted the differences in boldface type to make them more readily visible.

Example 8.1 *Sample JDBC Program*

```
import java.sql.*;

public class Sample {

public static void main (String [] argv) {

    try {
      // Set driver name
      String driverName="oracle.jdbc.driver.OracleDriver";
      // Load driver
      Driver d=(Driver) Class.forName(driverName).newInstance();
      // Register the JDBC driver
      DriverManager.registerDriver(d);
      // Use the JDBC/OCI driver to connect to an Oracle database
      String url="jdbc:oracle:oci9:@";
      // Specify the database user id and password
      String user="jim";
      String pwd="mypassword";
      // Connect to the database
      Connection conn = DriverManager.getConnection ( url, user, pwd );

      // Execute an INSERT statement
      // First, establish the text of the statement; the values to
      //  be inserted are not hard-coded into the statement
      String insertstmt =
             "INSERT INTO
              movie_stars ( movie_title, year_released, actor_last_name )
              VALUES   ( ?, ?, ? )";

      // Prepare the statement for execution
      PreparedStatement pstmt = conn.prepareStatement ( insertstmt );
```

```
        // Establish the values of the columns for the row being inserted
        pstmt.setString (1, "Dumb, Dumber, and Dumbest");
        pstmt.setInt (2, 2002);
        pstmt.setString (3, "Atkinson");

        // Execute the INSERT statement
        int count = insertstmt.executeUpdate ();
      }
      catch (SQLException sqlex) {
        System.out.println (sqlex.getMessage());
      }
      catch (Exception ex) {
        System.out.println (ex.getMessage());
      }
    }
  }
```

Example 8.2 *Sample SQL/OLB Program*

```
import java.sql.*;
import sqlj.runtime.*;
import sqlj.runtime.ref.DefaultContext;

public class Sample {

  public static void main (String [] argv) {

    try {
      // Set driver name
      String driverName="oracle.jdbc.driver.OracleDriver";
      // Load driver
      Driver d=(Driver) Class.forName(driverName).newInstance();
      // Register the JDBC driver
      DriverManager.registerDriver(d);
      // Using JDBC/OCI driver to connect to an Oracle database
      String url="jdbc:oracle:oci9:@";
      // Specify the database user id and password
      String user="jim";
      String pwd="mypassword";
```

```
      // Initialize SQLJ default context
      DefaultContext.setDefaultContext (
        new DefaultContext (DriverManager.getConnection (url, user, pwd)));
      // Set up host variables containing data to be inserted
      String title = "Dumb, Dumber, and Dumbest";
      Integer year = 2002;
      String lname = "Atkinson";
      // Execute an INSERT statement using the host variables
      #sql { INSERT INTO
              movie_stars ( movie_title, year_released, actor_last_name )
              VALUES   ( :title, :year, :lname )
           };
    }
    catch (SQLException sqlex) {
      System.out.println (sqlex.getMessage());
    }
    catch (Exception ex) {
      System.out.println (ex.getMessage());
    }
  }
}
```

Most people find that the SQL/OLB approach—embedding SQL statements in their Java programs—produces programs that are somewhat more intuitive to write and easier to read than the corresponding JDBC programs.

SQL/OLB implementations actually generate JDBC method invocations under the covers. In fact, an SQL/OLB implementation provides two primary components:

- A set of extensions to the Java core classes that support embedding SQL in Java programs.
- A translator that converts Java programs containing embedded SQL statements into equivalent programs that typically invoke JDBC methods to execute the embedded SQL statements. (In fact, the invoked API is defined by SQL/OLB, but the default implementation is defined in terms of JDBC.)

The translator produces Java programs in which every embedded SQL statement has been replaced by an invocation of a "stub" method. (The default implementations of the stub methods are defined in terms of JDBC methods, but other implementations are permitted.) The translator also produces one or more Java objects, called *serialized profiles,* that represent the SQL statements and descriptions of the host variables that supply values to those statements or that receive values returned by the statements. The Java program is an ordinary, standard Java program that is compiled with a normal Java compiler to produce Java byte code (`.class` files).

The serialized profiles must be run through a *customizer* that produces code specific to your database management system. For example, an Oracle customizer translates a serialized profile into code that can be used in an Oracle environment, while a DB2 customizer produces code that is used in a DB2 environment. Most customizers produce code that reflects the SQL statements after they have been optimized for execution on a particular database. However, some customizers produce "raw" JDBC code, and their output can be used on almost any database system, although they behave like the dynamic SQL programs that they are.

SQL/OLB allows you to "mix and match" the two styles of coding. Because SQL/OLB is defined in terms of JDBC, you can write Java methods that contain use of SQL/OLB operations and explicit JDBC operations on the same JDBC connections. In addition, should it ever be necessary to do so (which should be quite rare), the ability exists to refer to and manipulate the JDBC objects that underlie the SQL/OLB runtime implementations. For example, you can write embedded SQL statements in your programs, then use JDBC methods to perform some of the operations on the objects corresponding to those statements. SQL/OLB also allows you to invoke stored SQL routines (including those defined using the facilities specified in SQL/PSM[5] and proprietary languages such as Oracle's PL/SQL and Microsoft's Transact-SQL).

In short, SQL/OLB gives you capabilities that are very similar to those provided by the SQL standard for other programming languages,[6] but using slightly different syntax (particularly the use of `#sql{...}` instead of `EXEC SQL...END-EXEC` to delineate the embedded SQL statements). There are other differences as well, mostly caused by the fact that Java is an object-oriented programming language and object programming techniques are required for creating and using database connections and other facilities. While JDBC is inherently dynamic in its use of SQL, SQL/OLB provides both static and dynamic SQL capabilities.

5 ISO/IEC 9075-4:1999, *Information technology—Database languages—SQL—Part 4: Persistent Stored Modules (SQL/PSM)* (Geneva: International Organization for Standardization, 2000).

6 ISO/IEC 9075-5:1999, *Information technology—Database languages—SQL—Part 5: Host Language Bindings (SQL/Bindings)* (Geneva: International Organization for Standardization, 1999).

8.4.2 The Reference Implementation

As it happens, Oracle was the original source for the SQLJ Part 0 (SQL/OLB) specification, which it contributed to the SQLJ Group for standardization. As part of Oracle's initial development of that specification, it developed a *reference implementation,* including the translator cited in section 8.4.1, a collection of class definitions that form a runtime environment for SQL/OLB programs, and a default customization that uses JDBC (instead of, for example, Oracle-specific customizations). A reference implementation of a specification is (typically) a collection of software that implements some or all of the specification, usually without particular consideration to performance or elegance. It frequently serves as a demonstration of the specification's features and often includes a number of examples of code that uses the implementation.

The SQL/OLB reference implementation is reasonably well documented and implements the full complement of SQL/OLB features. It is written in Java, which makes it portable to any hardware and operating system platform for which a Java Virtual Machine is available. It provides both an *on-line syntax checker* that uses JDBC to connect to a specified SQL database to validate the syntax of SQL statements, and an *off-line syntax checker* that can be used if no JDBC connection is available at the time that Java programs containing embedded SQL are translated. The off-line checker uses a Java class that can be customized by SQL database vendors to provide off-line syntax checking for their dialects of SQL.

You can acquire the reference implementation at the SQLJ Group's Web site: *http://sqlj.org*. However, you can get commercial implementations of the technology from any of several SQL database system vendors—but those implementations are almost certain to be customized for use with the selected vendor's SQL system.

8.5 Java Routines

As the SQLJ Group worked to complete its specifications for embedding SQL statements in Java, it became apparent to its participants that significant advantages would arise if it were possible to invoke Java code from within SQL statements. Since 1996, the part of the SQL standard known as SQL/PSM has provided the ability to write procedures and functions, either in SQL or in some other programming language, store those routines (or at least a definition of their interfaces) in the database, and invoke them from your SQL code. Adding the ability for such routines to be written in Java was a natural enhancement. However, defining and invoking Java routines for use in SQL is sufficiently different from providing those facilities in C, Fortran, and other languages supported by the SQL standard that SQL's designers decided that a new part of the standard was justified (as opposed to, for example, a new version of SQL/PSM).

8.5.1 Technical Overview

SQLJ Part 1 was developed in response to the observation that developers should be free to use Java routines within their database applications, even when those Java routines were originally developed for use in other environments. The approach taken in that specification was clearly inspired by the specifications for SQL-invoked routines originally published in SQL/PSM and more recently included in SQL:1999s Part 2, SQL/Foundation. That is, Java routines could be stored in SQL databases through the use of CREATE PROCEDURE or CREATE FUNCTION statements and removed with DROP PROCEDURE and DROP FUNCTION statements. In addition, privileges to invoke the routines were granted and revoked using SQL's GRANT and REVOKE statements.

However, because of the nature of the Java programming language and the Java virtual machine environment, it is uncommon for Java routines to exist independently of one another—and impossible for them to exist independently of a class definition. Consequently, SQLJ Part 1 defined additional SQL facilities that supported the management of Java archives (commonly called *JAR files* or *JARs,* because their filenames typically use the extension `.jar`) and the class paths used to resolve Java routine invocations. Rather than define new SQL statements for these purposes, SQLJ Part 1 provides several new built-in procedures that application programs can invoke:

- `SQLJ.INSTALL_JAR`: Used to load a set of Java classes, including their associated routines, into an SQL system.
- `SQLJ.REPLACE_JAR`: Used to supersede (replace) an installed set of Java classes, including their associated routines, that exist in an SQL system.
- `SQLJ.REMOVE_JAR`: Used to delete an installed set of Java classes, including their associated routines, from an SQL system.
- `SQLJ.ALTER_JAVA_PATH`: Used to specify a path for name resolution within Java classes that are installed in an SQL system.

In addition, SQLJ Part 1 defined a new SQL schema, named `SQLJ`, that is used to contain the metadata associated with the built-in procedures defined by this specification. This schema, which exists in every catalog that implements the

SQLJ facilities, is analogous to SQL's INFORMATION_SCHEMA. The names of the four built-in procedures contain the string `sqlj.` because they are found in the schema by that name. These four procedures are invoked using the SQL CALL statement.

When creating the JAR to contain one or more Java routines that you want to install in your SQL database, you must (because Java requires it) create at least one Java class. However, that class need not contain any fields; it is allowed to contain only methods. Java methods that are declared using the Java keyword `void` do not return data as the value of the routine invocation; any values returned by `void` methods must be returned as the values of one or more parameters. Such methods correspond to SQL's SQL-invoked procedures and are, in fact, the way that SQL-invoked procedures are created using Java routines.

Java routines that are not declared to be `void` do return data as the value of the routine invocation—that is, they are declared to have a return type that is some Java data type (e.g., `int` or `float`) or some Java class (e.g., `java.lang.String` or `java.lang.BigDecimal`). Such routines correspond to SQL's SQL-invoked functions and are the way in which SQL-invoked functions are created using Java routines.

When creating an SQL-invoked procedure or function that is a Java routine, you must perform the following steps in this sequence:

1. Create a JAR file containing the class file whose definition includes the Java routine.
2. Install the JAR file by using CALL SQLJ.INSTALL_JAR, specifying the name of the JAR file as a parameter and specifying a name by which the JAR is to be known within the SQL environment. Note that the names of JARs are fully qualified SQL names and that omission of the catalog name or schema name components means that the JAR is installed in the default catalog or schema, respectively.
3. Create SQL metadata for the SQL-invoked procedure or function by using CREATE PROCEDURE or CREATE FUNCTION, specifying the SQL name of the routine and its parameters, as well as the name of the Java routine that you want to be executed when you code an SQL-invoked routine invocation using that SQL name. When specifying the name of the Java routine, it must be qualified with the JAR name and the name of its containing class.
4. Grant privileges on the SQL-invoked routine to the authorization identifiers that you wish to be able to use the routine.

When you install a JAR file, it is possible that some of the contained Java methods cannot be used for the creation of SQL-invoked routines. You can create an SQL-invoked routine that uses a Java method only if that Java method is *visible*. A Java method is visible if the method is declared to be `public` and `static`, and if the data type of each parameter has a corresponding SQL data type (alternatively, if the data type is a Java `array` used for output parameters or for result sets) and either the method is declared `void` or the return type has a corresponding SQL data type. Methods that do not satisfy these requirements are not visible and, from the viewpoint of the SQL environment, simply do not exist. However, such methods can be referenced from other Java methods, including methods that implement SQL-invoked routines.

JAR files are permitted to contain one or more *deployment descriptors* in addition to the class definitions. A deployment descriptor is a text file that allows you to specify the CREATE PROCEDURE and/or FUNCTION statements and the GRANT statements that you want to be invoked when you install a JAR, as well as the DROP PROCEDURE and/or FUNCTION statements and the REVOKE statements that you want to be invoked when you remove a JAR. The `SQLJ.INSTALL_JAR` and `SQLJ.REMOVE_JAR` procedures execute the statements of a deployment descriptor contained in the specified JAR whenever those procedures are invoked. Because the name of a JAR within an SQL environment is often not known until the `SQLJ.INSTALL_JAR` procedure has been executed, you may qualify the names of the routines with the name `thisjar`.

8.5.2 NCITS 331.1 and SQL/JRT

After SQLJ Part 1's specification was completed, it was submitted in 1999 to NCITS for progression under then-experimental procedures for rapid adoption of completed specifications. These fast-track procedures avoid the sometimes lengthy process of development within a Technical Committee, but encourage the designation of an NCITS Technical Committee as the organization responsible for future maintenance of the resulting standard. In this case, H2 (the so-called SQL committee in the United States) was quite appropriately named as the responsible maintenance authority.

With the knowledge that the SQLJ Group planned to submit another specification (see section 8.6.2) for fast-track progression, NCITS elected to create a new multipart standard that incorporated both specifications. The first part of this new standard was known as NCITS 331.1-1999 and was (after extensive negotiations with Sun Microsystems, the owner of the Java trademark) given the formal title *SQLJ—Part 1: SQL Routines Using the Java Programming Language*.

After SQLJ Part 1 had been submitted to NCITS for fast-track processing, the ISO committee responsible for the international SQL standard (formally known as ISO/IEC JTC1/SC32/WG3) was asked to consider its adoption as an international standard. That group concluded that the technology would best progress after merging the Java Routines specification with the anticipated Java Types specification (section 8.6.2) and updating them both to be fully aligned with SQL:1999, which was then nearing completion. Once the Java Types specification was completed, H2 undertook the merger of the two specifications along with a complete rewrite into the more formal language of the SQL standard, after which H2 submitted the merged specification to ISO for consideration as a new part of the SQL:1999 standard.[7] This new part of SQL, published in early 2002, is legitimately part of SQL:1999 and is currently being revised as a part of the emerging next generation of the SQL standard.

As the Java Routines specification was merged with the Java Types specification and updated to align with SQL:1999, several changes—including a few incompatibilities—crept into the document. The book mentioned in section 8.1 includes a thorough discussion of NCITS 331.1 (that is, SQLJ Part 1), which I do not repeat here. Instead, I bring that earlier book's information up to date by summarizing the more important changes made while SQL/JRT was being produced. In this section, I have included only those changes that affect Java Routines; for changes that affect Java Types, see section 8.6.2.

1. More formal specification: The text of NCITS 331.1 was written in a style that many characterize as "user manual style," which is very appropriate for use by application programmers but was eventually concluded to be insufficiently precise for implementers of the specification. SQL/JRT was rewritten to use the more precise, but arguably less intuitive, style of other parts of the SQL standard.
2. More complete conformance requirements: NCITS 331.1 required that conforming products implement the entire specification except for the items specifically listed as optional, and that such products state which of the optional items are implemented. SQL/JRT uses the more formal SQL:1999 technique of assigning explicit Feature ID values to every feature, optional and required, and stating the conformance requirement in terms of those Feature ID values. More particularly, SQL/JRT requires that conforming implementations specify whether or not they provide Java routines that can be installed using explicit CREATE PROCEDURE or CREATE FUNCTION statements, and whether or not such statements can be executed in the context of a deployment descriptor file. In addition, implementations must specify whether or not they support output parameters in Java routines.

7 ISO/IEC 9075-13:1999, *Information technology—Database languages—SQL—Part 13: SQL Routines and Types Using the Java Programming Language (SQL/JRT)* (Geneva: International Organization for Standardization, 2002).

3. The following incompatibilities with and extensions to NCITS 331.1 were introduced:
   a. The rules for determining the values of implicit catalog and schema names to be used in a JAR name that did not specify them were changed to align with the rules used in other parts of the SQL standard.
   b. CREATE PROCEDURE and CREATE FUNCTION statements are allowed to specify the SPECIFIC NAME clause, the EXTERNAL SECURITY clause, the CAST FROM clause, and the STATIC DISPATCH clause for Java routines.
   c. In the CREATE PROCEDURE and CREATE FUNCTION statements, the position of the routine's external name, the LANGUAGE JAVA clause, and the PARAMETER STYLE JAVA clause have been moved to different positions.
   d. In SQL/JRT, the SQL data-access option (see Chapter 4, "Routines and Routine Invocation") is required, while it was optional in NCITS 331.1.

8.5.3 Updated Syntax for Java Routines

As I told you in section 8.1, the specifications for SQLJ Part 1, now part of SQL/JRT, were not finalized when the earlier book on using SQL and Java together was published. To ensure that the picture is complete, Syntax 8.1 contains the complete, final syntax for defining SQL-invoked routines written in Java. (This syntax reiterates Syntax 4.9, "<SQL-invoked routine> Syntax," from Chapter 4, "Routines and Routine Invocation.") Material specific to SQL/JRT is in boldface for easy identification.

Syntax 8.1 *<SQL-invoked routine> Syntax for Java Routines*

```
<SQL-invoked routine> ::=
    CREATE <SQL-invoked procedure>
  | CREATE <SQL-invoked function>
  | CREATE <SQL-invoked method>

<SQL-invoked procedure> ::=
    PROCEDURE <schema qualified routine name>
      ( [ <SQL parameter declaration list> ] )
      [ <routine characteristic>... ]
      <routine body>
```

```
<SQL-invoked function> ::=
    FUNCTION <schema qualified routine name>
      ( [ <SQL parameter declaration list> ] )
      <returns clause>
      [ <routine characteristic>... ]
      [ <dispatch clause> ]
      <routine body>

<SQL-invoked method> ::=
    [ INSTANCE | STATIC | CONSTRUCTOR ] <method name>
    ( [ <SQL parameter declaration list> ] )
    [ <returns clause> ]
    FOR <user-defined type>
    <routine body>

<schema qualified routine name> ::=
    3-part-name    (see Volume 1 of this book)

<SQL parameter declaration list> ::=
    <SQL parameter declaration>
      [ { <comma> <SQL parameter declaration> }... ]

<SQL parameter declaration> ::=
    [ <parameter mode> ] [ <SQL parameter name> ] <parameter type>
    [ RESULT ]

<parameter mode> ::=
    IN
  | OUT
  | INOUT

<SQL parameter name> ::= <identifier>

<parameter type> ::= <data type> [ AS LOCATOR ]

<returns clause> ::= RETURNS <returns data type> [ <result cast> ]

<returns data type> ::= <data type> [ AS LOCATOR ]

<result cast> ::= CAST FROM <data type> [ AS LOCATOR ]
```

```
<routine characteristic> ::=
    <language clause>
  | PARAMETER STYLE <parameter style>
  | SPECIFIC <specific name>
  | <deterministic characteristic>
  | <SQL data access indication>
  | <null-call clause>
  | <dynamic result sets characteristic>

<language clause> ::=
    SQL
  | ADA | C | COBOL | FORTRAN | MUMPS | PASCAL | PLI
  | JAVA

<parameter style> ::=
    SQL
  | GENERAL
  | JAVA

<specific name> ::= 3-part-name    (see Volume 1 of this book)

<deterministic characteristic> ::=
    DETERMINISTIC
  | NOT DETERMINISTIC

<SQL data access indication> ::=
    NO SQL
  | CONTAINS SQL
  | READS SQL DATA
  | MODIFIES SQL DATA

<null-call clause> ::=
    RETURNS NULL ON NULL INPUT
  | CALLED ON NULL INPUT

<dynamic result sets characteristic> ::=
    DYNAMIC RESULT SETS <maximum dynamic result sets>

<maximum dynamic result sets> ::= <unsigned integer>

<dispatch clause> ::= STATIC DISPATCH
```

```
<routine body> ::=
    <SQL routine body>
  | <external body reference>

<SQL routine body> ::= <SQL procedure statement>

<external body reference> ::=
    EXTERNAL [ NAME <external routine name> ]
    [ PARAMETER STYLE <parameter style > ]
    [ <transform group specification> ]
    [ <external security clause> ]

<external routine name> ::=
    <identifier>
  | <character string literal>  !! For Java, the value must match
                                !!  <external Java reference string>

<transform group specification> ::=
    TRANSFORM GROUP
      { <single group specification> | <multiple group specification>
}

<single group specification> ::= <group name>

<multiple group specification> ::=
    <group specification> [ { <comma> <group specification> }... ]

<group specification> ::=
    <group name> FOR TYPE <user-defined type>

<external security clause> ::=
    EXTERNAL SECURITY DEFINER
  | EXTERNAL SECURITY INVOKER
  | EXTERNAL SECURITY IMPLEMENTATION DEFINED

<external Java reference string> ::=
  <jar and class name> <period> <Java method name>
  [ <Java parameter declaration list> ]
```

8.6 Java Types

As the development of SQL:1999 progressed, SQLJ Group participants recognized that SQL's structured user-defined types (see Chapter 2, "User-Defined Types") have much in common with Java classes. Users would benefit greatly if they were able to use the Java classes they define inside their SQL systems, as well as in other components of their application environments. As with the design of the Java Routines specification, however, the details of defining and using SQL types that are based on Java classes differs sufficiently from doing so for "pure SQL" structured types that SQL's designers felt that a new part was justified (as opposed to, for example, modifying the structured user-defined type facilities in SQL/Foundation).

8.6.1 Technical Overview

SQLJ Part 2 was developed to allow developers to use their Java classes in their database applications, even when those classes were originally developed for use in other environments. The approach taken in the specification was based on the specifications for structured user-defined types in SQL:1999 Part 2, SQL/Foundation; Java classes could be stored in SQL databases through the use of CREATE TYPE statements and removed with DROP TYPE statements. In addition, privileges to use the types were granted and revoked using SQL's GRANT and REVOKE statements.

In section 8.5.1, you learned that Java routines that are used as SQL routines must first be placed into Java archives (JAR files, or JARs) and that those JAR files are then installed into an SQL database. Similarly, Java classes that are to become SQL user-defined types are first placed into JAR files, which are then installed. The procedures for installing Java classes as SQL user-defined structured types are the same as those used for installing Java routines:

- `SQLJ.INSTALL_JAR` : Used to load a set of Java classes, including their associated routines, into an SQL system.
- `SQLJ.REPLACE_JAR` : Used to supersede (replace) an installed set of Java classes, including their associated routines, that exist in an SQL system.
- `SQLJ.REMOVE_JAR` : Used to delete an installed set of Java classes, including their associated routines, from an SQL system.
- `SQLJ.ALTER_JAVA_PATH` : Used to specify a path for name resolution within Java classes that are installed in an SQL system.

The new SQL schema that was defined in SQLJ Part 1 (named `SQLJ`) is also defined by SQLJ Part 2. It continues to provide a container for the four procedures listed above.

The classes defined in the JAR files being installed to correspond to SQL user-defined types are quite likely to include field definitions (unlike classes being installed specifically to create SQL-invoked routines). SQLJ Part 2 carefully specifies the ways in which Java classes' fields corresponded to SQL user-defined types' attributes. Once a set of Java classes are loaded into an SQL system, they can be used in most of the same ways that ordinary SQL structured types can be used; a principle exception is the prohibition against defining a typed table based on a Java class whose definition includes an interface specification of SERIALIZABLE.

Although SQLJ Part 1 did not depend in any way on SQLJ Part 2, the reverse is not true. SQLJ Part 2 assumes the existence of SQLJ Part 1—and an implementation of SQLJ Part 2 requires that SQLJ Part 1 also be implemented. When the two parts are used (and implemented) together, it becomes possible to define a complete SQL environment containing SQL-invoked routines and structured types that are written entirely in Java, using the following steps:

1. Create a JAR file containing the class file whose definition includes the classes to be used as SQL structured user-defined types.
2. Install the JAR file by using CALL SQLJ.INSTALL_JAR, specifying the name of the JAR file as a parameter and specifying a name by which the JAR is to be known within the SQL environment. Note that the names of JARs are fully qualified SQL names and that omission of the catalog name or schema name components means that the JAR is installed in the default catalog or schema, respectively.
3. Create SQL metadata for the SQL structured user-defined types by using CREATE TYPE, specifying the SQL name of the type, as well as the name of the Java class that you want to use as the definition of the SQL type. In addition, for each method and each attribute of the type, specify the name of the corresponding Java field and method. When specifying the name of the Java type and the names of Java methods, they must be qualified with the JAR name. (Java fields are implicitly qualified by their class name.)
4. Grant privileges on the SQL user-defined type to the authorization identifiers that you wish to be able to use the type.

JAR files used to create SQL user-defined types are permitted to contain one or more *deployment descriptors* in addition to class definitions. A deployment descriptor is a text file that allows you to specify the CREATE TYPE statements and the GRANT statements that you want to be invoked when you install a JAR, as well as the DROP TYPE statements and the REVOKE statements that you want to be invoked when you remove a JAR. Invocating the `SQLJ.INSTALL_JAR` and `SQLJ.REMOVE_JAR` procedures cause the execution of the statements of a deployment descriptor contained in the specified JAR. Because the name of a JAR within an SQL environment is often not known until the `SQLJ.INSTALL_JAR` procedure has been executed, you may qualify the names of the routines with the name "`thisjar`."

8.6.2 NCITS 331.2 and SQL/JRT

The SQLJ Group completed SQLJ Part 2 early in 2000 and submitted it to NCITS for progression using the same fast-track procedures that were used for SQLJ Part 1. Since this specification was intended to be the second part of the multipart SQLJ standard, H2 was again selected as the responsible maintenance authority. This second part was designated NCITS 331.2-2000 and was formally titled *SQLJ—Part 2: SQL Types using the Java Programming Language.*

As you read in section 8.5.2, this specification was merged with NCITS 331.1 and restated in the more formal language of the SQL standard, after which the combined document was submitted to NCITS H2, which, in turn, submitted it to the ISO SQL group for consideration as an international standard.

As with the Java Routines specification, the Java Types specification was updated to align with SQL:1999. Again, several changes—including a few incompatibilities—crept into the document. While that "earlier book" mentioned in section 8.1 contains a thorough discussion of NCITS 331.2 (that is, SQLJ Part 2), I bring the information up to date by summarizing the more important changes made while SQL/JRT was being produced. In this section, I have included only those changes that affect Java Types; for changes that affect Java Routines, see section 8.5.2.

1. More formal specification: The text of NCITS 331.2 was written in a style that many characterize as "user manual style," which is very appropriate for use by application programmers but was eventually concluded to be insufficiently precise for implementers of the specification. SQL/JRT has been rewritten to use the more precise, but arguably less intuitive, style of other parts of the SQL standard.
2. More complete conformance requirements: NCITS 331.2 required that conforming products implement the entire specification except for the items specifically listed as optional, and that such products state which of the optional items are implemented. SQL/JRT uses the more formal SQL:1999

technique of assigning explicit Feature ID values to every feature, optional and required, and stating the conformance requirement in terms of those Feature ID values. More particularly, SQL/JRT requires that conforming implementations specify whether or not they provide Java classes that can be installed using explicit CREATE TYPE statements, and whether or not such statements can be executed in the context of a deployment descriptor file.

3. The following incompatibilities with, and extensions to, NCITS 331.2 were introduced:

   a. SQL/JRT places additional restrictions on the ORDERING clause of user-defined types that were not placed by NCITS 331.2.
   b. SQL/JRT supports a DROP ORDERING statement that was not supported by NCITS 331.2.
   c. SQL/JRT supports DROP with the CASCADE option, which NCITS 331.2 did not support.
   d. Some exception condition values have changed in SQL/JRT.
   e. In SQL/JRT, additional checks are made when the `SQLJ.REPLACE_JAR` and `SQLJ.REMOVE_JAR` procedures are invoked to ensure that no external Java routines are adversely affected by the actions of those procedures.

8.6.3 Updated Syntax for Java Types

Section 8.1 observed that the specifications for SQLJ Part 2, now part of SQL/JRT, were not yet final when the earlier book discussing the use of SQL and Java together went to press. To ensure that the picture is complete, Syntax 8.2 contains the complete, final syntax for defining structured user-defined types written in Java. Material specific to SQL/JRT is in boldface for easy identification.

Syntax 8.2 *<SQL-invoked routine> Syntax for Java Types*

```
<user-defined type body> ::=
    <user-defined type name>
    [ <subtype clause> ]
    [ <external Java type clause> ]
    [ AS <representation> ]
    [ <instantiable clause> ]
    <finality>
    [ <reference type specification> ]
    [ <ref cast option> ]
    [ <cast option> ]
    [ <method specification list> ]
```

```
<external Java type clause> ::=
    <external Java class clause>
    LANGUAGE JAVA
    <interface using clause>

<interface using clause> ::= [ USING <interface specification> ]

<interface specification> ::=
    SQLDATA
  | SERIALIZABLE

<method specification> ::=
    ...
  | <static field method spec>

<method characteristic> ::=
    ...
  | <external Java method clause>

<static field method spec> ::=
    STATIC METHOD <method name> <left paren> <right paren>
    <static method returns clause>
    [ SPECIFIC <specific method name> ]
    <external variable name clause>

<static method returns clause> ::= RETURNS <data type>

<external variable name clause> ::=
    EXTERNAL VARIABLE NAME <character string literal>

<external Java class clause> ::= EXTERNAL NAME <character string literal>

<external Java method clause> ::= EXTERNAL NAME <character string literal>

<Java method and parameter declarations> ::=
    <Java method name> [ <Java parameter declaration list> ]

<attribute definition> ::=
    <attribute name>
    <data type>
    [ <reference scope check> ]
    [ <attribute default> ]
```

```
    [ <collate clause> ]
    [ <external Java attribute clause> ]

<external Java attribute clause> ::=
    EXTERNAL NAME <character string literal>

<ordering category> ::=
    ...
  | <comparable category>

<comparable category> ::=
    RELATIVE WITH COMPARABLE INTERFACE
```

8.7 Chapter Summary

In this chapter, the focus was on reviewing material that is covered more extensively in an earlier book, bringing that material up to date to reflect changes made in the corresponding technical specifications as they progressed toward standardization.

Chapter 9

SQL/XML

9.1 Introduction

The material presented in this chapter is not part of SQL:1999, but is currently under development for inclusion in the next generation of the SQL standard (expected in 2003). Even though this book is supposed to present the more advanced aspects of SQL:1999, the use of XML with SQL is such an important subject that I have chosen to include an overview of the material currently under consideration.

Please don't rely too heavily on the contents of this chapter. Until the specifications that I discuss herein have been submitted for ballot in the ISO arena and the results of the ballot reflected back into the document (or documents), what you read here is rather speculative. I have fairly high confidence that some of the material presented in this chapter will become part of the eventual standard, while other aspects are considerably less certain—especially with regard to the details available now. During the course of the chapter, I indicate the portions that are (in my opinion) reasonably likely to be included and those that are more tentative.

XML's enormous popularity has already resulted in the implementation of various XML-related facilities by several SQL database vendors, as well as promotion of "pure XML" databases by other vendors. Many of the language features described in this chapter have already been implemented in one or more SQL databases, although sometimes in a slightly different form.

9.2 The SQLX Group

In the last half of 2000, NCITS Technical Committee H2 (the SQL committee in the United States) began discussing the increasingly obvious fact that XML was becoming an important technology for data management in business and industry. H2 invited its membership to consider whether the SQL standard should be directly affected by XML and, if so, what effects there should be. In short order, the members concluded that there are significant opportunities for combining the power of SQL and the power of XML to benefit application developers. Several of the most interested parties worked together to establish an informal group, not directly associated with H2, called the SQLX Group.

The SQLX Group, analogous to the SQLJ Group discussed in Chapter 8, "SQL/OLB and SQL/JRT," is not a formal consortium with all of the legal implications associated with that style of organization. Instead, it is a group of interested software engineers who have the support and backing of their employers. Members of the group include most of the relational database vendors, as well as a good representation from the user community, including large aerospace contractors, private consultants, and third-party software developers.

The stated goals of the SQLX Group include development of specifications that are driven by concurrent implementation efforts, thus ensuring that they are solidly grounded in reality and experience. The goals explicitly exclude publication of "standards" or, indeed, public documents of any sort; instead, the SQLX Group agreed to submit its specifications to other organizations for consideration and possible publication.

So far, the technologies developed by the group have been submitted directly to NCITS H2, which has in turn submitted them to the corresponding ISO group (ISO/IEC JTC1/SC32) for consideration. ISO has established a project for a new part of the SQL standard. That new part will be commonly called "SQL/XML." At the time this volume goes to press, the first formal ISO ballot on the SQL/XML specification is in progress, suggesting that publication as an International Standard may occur in mid-2003.[1]

Readers interested in the SQLX Group will find their Web site at *http://sqlx.org*.

9.3 Brief Overview of XML

It would be surprising if most readers of this book were not aware of XML by now. XML is certainly one of the fastest growing phenomena in information technol-

1 The current project plans anticipate publication of ISO/IEC 9075-14, *Information Technology—Database Languages—SQL—Part 14: XML-Related Specifications (SQL/XML)* sometime in 2003.

ogy today and is widely viewed as a principle component in business-to-business (B2B) communication, in Web services, and in data management in general.

While it is beyond the scope of this book to cover XML in detail (and there are many resources to which you can turn, starting with the World Wide Web Consortium, or W3C),[2] a quick review of some of the concepts underlying XML will assist in understanding some of the discussion later in this chapter.

XML (the eXtended Markup Language) is a markup language—a language used to "mark up" documents for various purposes. XML is a subset of another markup language, known as SGML,[3] and is intended to be compatible with SGML, but simpler and easier both to implement and to use.

Many readers will be familiar with other markup languages that are used to indicate how the text in a document should appear when printed or displayed on a computer monitor. HTML (HyperText Markup Language) is a well-known example of a markup language that is (largely) oriented toward formatting issues. The Unix text processing system troff is another, as is Knuth's $\TeX$.

By contrast, XML is intended for use in marking up the content of documents to readily identify the information they contain. Instead of, for example, specifying that a certain text component should be displayed in italics, in red ink, or centered on a page, XML markup might specify that a piece of text is actually an employee name or a final budget figure. Of course, XML can be used for traditional appearance-based document markup, but that is not where its strengths lie.

Contrasted with HTML and most other markup languages, XML shares several important characteristics with its ancestor, SGML. By definition, an XML document is *well formed,* which means that

- There is exactly one element, called the *root element,* that does not appear in the context of any other element.
- Every element, including the root element, is explicitly terminated. An element begins with an "opening tag" and is terminated with a "closing tag." The spelling of the opening and closing tags are identical except that the closing tag includes a slash (/) preceding the tag name. (An element without any content can be presented as a single tag in which a slash follows the tag name.) Example 9.1 illustrates valid empty elements.
- Every element other than the root element is wholly (and directly) contained in exactly one other element; this can be more simply stated by saying that the elements are "properly nested."

---

2 *http://www.w3.org*

3 ISO 8879:1986, *Information processing—Text and Office Systems—Standard Generalized Markup Language (SGML)* (Geneva: International Organization for Standardization, 1986).

The implication of those three aspects of XML is that every XML document forms a *tree* structure. (For the mathematically inclined: A tree is a directed acyclic graph, or DAG, in which no node is entered by more than one arc.) Therefore, every element is a node and every element (except the root element) has exactly one parent element.

Example 9.1 contains some text that has been marked up consistently with the three points given above. You will observe in the example that XML elements are formed by tags that are enclosed in angle brackets (< and >) and that the tag that terminates an element includes a slash (/).

By contrast, Example 9.2 contains examples that violate the rules, along with explanations of why they are invalid. It's worth saying that "invalid XML" is not, strictly speaking, XML at all.

Example 9.1 *Properly Constructed XML Instances*

```
<movie>
  <title>The Thirteenth Floor</title>
  <ourCost>12.50</ourCost>
  <qty>31</qty>
</movie>
```

Valid example of an empty element.

```
<movie></movie>
```

Another valid way to represent an empty element.

```
<movie/>
```

Example 9.2 *Invalid XML Instances*

Invalid because there is no single root element.

```
<movie>
  <title>The Terminator</title>
  <ourCost>11.00</ourCost>
  <qty>22</qty>
</movie>
<movie>
  <title>Die Hard</title>
  <ourCost>7.50</ourCost>
  <qty>43</qty>
</movie>
```

Invalid because the root element is not terminated.

```
<movie>
  <title>The Cell</title>
  <ourCost>9.00</ourCost>
  <qty>12</qty>
```

Invalid because elements are not properly nested.

```
<movie>
  <title><italics>The <boldface>Fifth</italics> Element</boldface></title>
  <ourCost>9.00</ourCost>
  <qty>12</qty>
</movie>
```

Tree structures are quite well understood in computer science, but XML (and SGML) adds some complications. The most significant complication is the presence of *attributes* that appear within the tag that begins an element, as seen in Example 9.3.

Example 9.3 *XML Attributes*

```
<movie year="1956">
  <title>Night of the Living Dead</title>
  <ourCost>4.50</ourCost>
  <qty>7</qty>
</movie>
```

Attributes are a natural way to express some concepts, but they are rather awkward in the context of XML's otherwise strict tree organization. The awkwardness arises in part from the fact that the branch of an XML document's tree that represents an attribute can never be anything other than a leaf of the tree—that is, the content of an attribute is always a simple value and nothing else can be nested within it. This seemingly simple extension to XML's attribute syntax adds surprisingly many complications to specifications based on XML. It is not within the scope of this chapter, however, to cover those complications.

9.3.1 The XML Data Models

Because XML is widely viewed as a data representation language, its definition and use demand that there be a data model that describes the organization of data and the operations that can be performed on that data. The various documents that have been, or are in the process of being, published by the W3C actually define multiple data models for XML. Each of the data models is appropriate for particular uses of XML (and I am skeptical that they will soon be merged into a single encompassing model).

The most basic of the W3C's data models for XML is called the Information Set, or Infoset.[4] Every (well-formed) XML document that satisfies certain *namespace* constraints (I don't discuss namespaces in this book and suggest that you turn to XML-specific resources for information about them) has an Infoset. The Infoset of a document describes every node of the document's corresponding tree: every element, every element's value, every attribute, every attribute's value, and other document components (such as comments and processing instructions). An Infoset is tree-structured, and each node of the tree can be made available to a program through one or more accessor functions—functions that retrieve values associated with a node.

XML Schema[5] provides a mechanism to define metadata for XML documents, including the ability to specify the data types of element and attribute values much more precisely than "plain" XML. XML documents that have been partially or wholly validated by a schema processor have a Post-Schema Validation Infoset, or PSVI. Like an Infoset, a PSVI is tree-structured. In fact, as the name suggests, a PSVI is an Infoset that has been enhanced with additional information that is determined during the process of validating a document against a particular XML schema.

The emerging XML Query (XQuery) specification[6] defines yet another data model,[7] this one oriented toward the requirements of a query language. This data model is founded on the PSVI but adds still more information about XML documents—and collections of documents—while ignoring some aspects of the PSVI that are not required by XQuery or XPath.[8]

One more popular XML data model is known as the Document Object Model, or DOM.[9] The DOM is not quite a data model, nor even an object model, because it is a definition of an API (application program interface) that *implies* a data

---

4 *XML Information Set W3C Recommendation,* 2001 (*http://www.w3.org/TR/xml-infoset*).

5 *XML Schema Part 1: Structures W3C Recommendation,* 2001 (*http://www.w3.org/TR/xmlschema-2*), and *XML Schema Part 2: Datatypes W3C Recommendation,* 2001 (*http://www.w3.org/TR/xmlschema-1*).

6 *XQuery 1.0: An XML Query Language, W3C Working Draft,* 2001 (*http://www.w3.org/TR/xquery*).

7 *XQuery 1.0 and XPath 2.0 Data Model, W3C Working Draft,* 2001 (*http://www.w3.org/TR/query-datamodel/*).

8 *XML Path Language (XPath), W3C Recommendation,* 1999 (*http://www.w3.org/TR/xpath*).

9 *Document Object Model (DOM) Level 1 Specification, W3C Recommendation,* 1998 (*http://www.w3.org/TR/REC-DOM-Level-1*).

model. That implication is enough, though, for the DOM to be included in the menagerie of data models for XML that the W3C specifies.

All of these data models support the essential characteristics of XML documents. For example, they all define XML to be a language that can represent *semistructured data*—data that is "self-defining" in that the markup tags themselves can be construed as providing metadata within the document. Of course, we humans can look at a document like the one in Example 9.1 and "know" that the element `<title>...</title>` is intended to identify the title of a movie. But a computer program doesn't have the context that humans do, because the semantics of the elements is not specified in XML documents themselves.

Furthermore, XML is, quite deliberately, ordinary text. Without metadata, such as that provided by XML Schema, the values of elements and attributes are "just strings," although certain programs might interpret a string of digits as a number if the context in which that string appears justifies that interpretation. XML documents are often encoded in Unicode[10] and are always modeled in terms of Unicode. The presumption of Unicode offers tremendous benefits, but at the possible expense of making data occupy more physical storage (e.g., disks) than, say, binary data would occupy.

Thus, XML data models specify a tree-structured environment in which metadata may or may not be available and in which specific pieces of data may be supplied or absent.

9.3.2 Related SQL Concepts

While SQL is also used as a data management language, there are several significant differences between it and XML when used for storing and manipulating data.

For one thing, SQL data *always* has metadata associated with it. In fact, SQL database systems virtually always store the metadata that describes a database in the same database. Furthermore, SQL metadata describes itself in the same manner that it describes other data. In an XML environment, there may or may not be explicit metadata that describes the XML documents found in that environment, and XML metadata may take several forms, of which XML Schema is the only one that is also represented in XML.

In addition, SQL data is completely regular in structure, not semistructured in the sense that some data may be entirely absent. In an SQL environment, unknown or missing data is always represented in the database, since every row of a table must have cells corresponding to every column of the table. Such

10 *The Unicode Standard* (various versions), The Unicode Consortium (*http://www.unicode.org*).

unknown or missing data is typically represented in SQL databases by the null value. XML doesn't provide anything directly analogous to SQL's null value. Instead, unknown or missing information can be reflected in XML by an empty element (an element with no content), with the absence of an element, or (when an XML schema that supports this alternative is available) the use of a particular attribute, `xsi:nil="true"`.

The most important difference between XML and SQL lies in the fact that XML documents are, by definition, tree structures, while SQL databases are, by definition, flat tabular structures. The implications of this difference go very deep and form the root of many significant diferences in approach to issues such as querying the data found in each of the two universes.

Of course there are other differences that are less sweeping but important in detail. The following sections examine several of those areas and discuss the ways in which SQL/XML addresses them.

9.4 Mapping SQL and XML Concepts

The first material specified by the SQLX Group for inclusion into SQL/XML dealt with some of those narrower and more subtle issues, such as mapping between SQL's identifiers and XML's QNames (qualified names), as well as mapping between SQL data types and XML data types. SQL/XML also deals with mapping SQL tables onto XML documents and XML schema types.

Compare and contrast the XML document in Example 9.4 with a possible corresponding SQL table in Table 9.1. The QName of the XML document's root element is rather long—41 characters. That's longer than most SQL implementations support for identifiers, but popular XML products have no difficulty with such lengthy identifiers. By contrast, the name of the SQL table contains characters—the ampersand (&) and surrounding spaces—that are prohibited in XML QNames. The data type of the `<runs>` element in the XML document can be inferred to be the XML Schema type `duration`. The data type of the corresponding SQL column, `RUNS`, is the SQL type INTERVAL. The root element of the XML document contains five instances of another element, `movie`—one per movie being described, and one per row of the SQL table; a different style of XML omits the `<movie>` and `</movie>` tags in favor of repeating the `<moviesAndTitlesThat-CauseFearInManyViewers>` element once per movie. Each of these aspects of the two mechanisms relates to the difficulties encountered when mapping XML and SQL to one another.

Example 9.4 *A Sample XML Document*

```
<moviesAndTitlesThatCauseFearInManyViewers>
  <movie>
    <title>Seven</title>
    <description>Police drama about two cops, one new and one about to
retire, after a serial killer using the seven deadly sins as his MO.
</description>
    <runs>PT2H3M</runs>
  </movie>
  <movie>
    <title>Copycat</title>
    <description>A psychiatrist who specializes in serial killers
suffers from agoraphobia and her only link to the outside world is her
computer. A serial killer who copies the methods of famous serial
killers threatens her on-line. </description>
    <runs>PT2H3M</runs>
  </movie>
  <movie>
    <title>The Bone Collector</title>
    <description>Denzel Washington plays a quadriplegic homicide
detective. He and his female partner track down a serial killer.
</description>
    <runs>PT1H58M</runs>
  </movie>
  <movie>
    <title>Bone Daddy</title>
    <description>A pathologist's book about his work is a good recipe
for sick people.</description>
    <runs>PT1H30M</runs>
  </movie>
  <movie>
    <title>Serial Mom</title>
    <description>She's a fabulous, loving, caring mother, who happens
to be a serial killer!</description>
    <runs>PT1H35M</runs>
  </movie>
</moviesAndTitlesThatCauseFearInManyViewers>
```

Table 9.1 *A Sample SQL Table*

Movies and Titles

TITLE	*DESCRIPTION*	*RUNS*
Seven	Police drama about two cops, one new and one about to retire, after a serial killer using the seven deadly sins as his MO.	2:03
Copycat	A psychiatrist who specializes in serial killers suffers from agoraphobia and her only link to the outside world is her computer. A serial killer who copies the methods of famous serial killers threatens her on-line.	2:03
The Bone Collector	Denzel Washington plays a quadriplegic homicide detective. He and his female partner track down a serial killer.	1:58
Bone Daddy	A pathologist's book about his work is a good recipe for sick people.	1:30
Serial Mom	She's a fabulous, loving, caring mother, who happens to be a serial killer!	1:35

9.4.1 Mapping Identifiers

The SQL standard specifies two forms of identifier. The older and probably more familiar form is the *regular identifier.* Examples of regular identifiers are: MOVIE, TITLE, and FIRST_NAME. SQL requires that regular identifiers begin with a letter, syllabic character (such as those found in Japanese Hiragana or the Indic languages), or ideographic character (such as those used in those Japanese and Chinese languages), and that it contain only those characters plus digits and underscores (_). While lowercase letters are allowed in regular identifiers, SQL automatically translates them into their uppercase forms; therefore, the regular identifier that you write in your application program as '`description`' is recorded by SQL as '`DESCRIPTION`'.

SQL-92 introduced the form called *delimited identifier,* which requires that double quotes surround the identifier's characters but permits arbitrary characters to be used at any point in the identifier: `"My Favorite Films® & other [strange] things = $$$"`. The SQL standard specifies that no transformations, such as changing lowercase letters to their uppercase equivalents, are performed on delimited identifiers.

SQL limits the length of identifiers at two levels. Core SQL:1999 limits the length to 18 characters, while a higher-level feature of SQL:1999 extends that to

128 characters. Many SQL products support identifiers with a maximum length of 31 or 32 characters.

By contrast, XML specifies no maximum length for QNames, although XML products may apply some reasonable limit. But XML strictly prohibits the use of many characters in QNames. Names in XML must always start with a letter, syllabic character, or ideographic character, and can contain only those characters, digits, underscores, and colons (`:`). The XML Namespace recommendation strongly recommends that colons be used only to separate the namespace component of a QName from the local component. XML provides no analog to SQL's delimited identifiers, so there is no ability to use other characters such as spaces, ampersands, and such. Furthermore, XML's "special characters," such as ampersand (`&`) and left angle bracket (`<`) are prohibited from appearing (to represent themselves, at least) in XML documents under most conditions and must usually be expressed as "character entities," such as "`&`" or "`<`".

These differences make it challenging to devise rules that map between SQL identifiers and XML QNames. SQL/XML approaches the mapping by using the following principles:

- Mapping SQL regular identifiers to XML QNames poses only one possible problem (names starting with "`XML`" are treated specially, as indicated in the third bullet). The SQL identifier "`employee`" is automatically converted to upper case as "`EMPLOYEE`" and the corresponding XML QName is "`EMPLOYEE`"; as an element tag, this would be "`<EMPLOYEE>`".
- Mapping SQL delimited identifiers to XML QNames introduces problems related to characters that are prohibited by XML.
- Mapping SQL identifiers of either form that begin with the letters X, M, and L (in either upper- or lowercase) requires special handling to avoid invalid XML QNames.

The approach chosen by the SQLX Group to resolve these problems relies on using an *escape notation* that transforms characters that are not acceptable in XML QNames into a sequence of allowable characters derived from the unacceptable characters' Unicode values.

For example, the SQL delimited identifier that names my table in Table 9.1 contains two spaces and an ampersand, all prohibited in XML QNames. The Unicode value for a space is U+0040 (the notation "U+xyzw" is used to identify the Unicode character at the position whose number, in hexadecimal notation, is "xyzw"), and the Unicode value for an ampersand is U+0026. The SQL/XML convention is to prefix the hexadecimal digits of the Unicode value of a disallowed character with an underscore and a lowercase letter x and to suffix the digits with another underscore: _x0040_ or _x0026_. Thus, the SQL table name can become the valid XML element tag "<Movies_x0040__x0026__x0040_Titles>". (Note that there are two consecutive underscores following the "0040" and the "0026.") Incidentally, the length of that XML element tag is 35 characters, including the opening and closing angle brackets.

SQL identifiers that begin with the letters X, M, and L (in any combination of uppercase and lowercase) are handled with a slightly different technique. Because XML prohibits the use of names starting with that sequence of letters, all SQL identifiers starting with those characters must be modified as they are mapped to XML names. The technique chosen is to escape the leading "x" or "X" using the escaping mechanism described above. Therefore, the SQL identifier XMLdocs maps to the XML name _x0058_MLDOCS. Similarly, the SQL delimited identifier "xmldocs" maps to the XML name _x0078_MLDOCS. Of course, there are possible situations when an application doesn't want such identifiers to be escaped in that way. The need to distinguish between such cases requires that the SQL/XML rules be *parameterized* so that their use in particular circumstances (determined by the application causing the transformations) determines whether the identifiers are *fully escaped* or *partially escaped.*

The collection of characters that can be represented using no more than four hexadecimal digits is known as the Basic Multilingual Plane (BMP). Recent versions of the Unicode standard encode more characters than can be represented using four hexadecimal digits, and the Unicode standard encourages the use of exactly six hexadecimal digits to represent characters defined outside of the BMP. SQL/XML's notation extends to the use of six hexadecimal digits, too: _x012345_ is a valid notation (although I am unaware of a Unicode character defined at that position). It is partly because of the two possible lengths that the trailing underscore is needed in this transformation.

The existence of colons in an XML delimited identifier is treated as a special case in SQL/XML's identifier mapping rules. An XML-aware SQL database might well use identifiers in which a namespace prefix and colon have already been provided, in which case the XML QName derived from such identifiers should retain the colon. Non-XML-aware SQL databases might use the colon for other purposes entirely (such as a column named "Sales:2001"), so corresponding SQL QNames must have the colon replaced with the corresponding escape sequence (_x003A_). Colons thus provide a second situation in which applications must be allowed to choose whether identifier transformations are fully or partially escaped.

Transforming XML QNames to SQL identifiers is somewhat easier:

- If there is a leading sequence of the form _x0058_ or _x0078_, then it is replaced by X or x, respectively.

- All sequences of the form _xnnnn_, where "nnnn" is a sequence of four hexadecimal digits, are translated to the corresponding Unicode character.

There are only two possible difficulties:

- The XML QName might be longer than SQL identifier is allowed to be. In this case, the implementation might truncate the name (in which case it is possible that duplicate SQL identifiers will be created) or the implementation might raise an exception condition.
- The XML QName might contain a sequence of the form _xnnnn_ (or the form _xnnnnnn_), where "nnnn" represents one of the several *not-a-character* values in Unicode. In this situation, the implementation is free to substitute its choice of character (including omission of the character entirely).

One more possible issue is raised by SQL identifiers that include a string of characters that mimics an escape sequence. If the SQL identifier contains a sequence of characters starting with "_x", followed by four characters that correspond to hexadecimal digits, followed by an underscore (such as Fooled_x00A0_you), the corresponding XML QName would be identical: Fooled_x00A0_you. However, reversing this mapping would result in the SQL delimited identifier "Fooled you", which is not the same identifier at all! To avoid this problem, SQL identifiers that include an underscore followed by a lowercase letter "x" are transformed by mapping the underscore to its Unicode escape sequence: _x005F_.

Of course, it is possible that an XML QName can be transformed to a valid SQL regular identifier, in which case transforming it to a delimited identifier is overkill. The SQLX Group decided that this case wasn't worth writing special rules to handle, since delimited identifiers are valid everywhere in SQL code that regular identifiers are allowed.

A few examples of identifier mapping can be seen in Example 9.5.

Example 9.5 *Identifier Mapping Examples*

SQL Identifier	*XML QName*
"Sales:FY2001" *(fully escaped)*	Sales_x003A_FY2001
"Work@home"	Work_0040_home
"Work_x0040_home"	Work_x005F_0040_home
"Work_home"	Work_home
XmlText	_xFFFF_XMLTEXT

9.4.2 Mapping Data Types

SQL has a number of well-defined built-in data types, in addition to the user-defined data types discussed in Chapter 2, "User-Defined Types." SQL's built-in types are divided into *predefined types* and *constructed types*. The predefined types include exact numeric types (INTEGER, SMALLINT, DECIMAL, and NUMERIC), approximate numeric types (REAL, FLOAT, and DOUBLE PRECISION), a logical type (BOOLEAN), character string types (CHARACTER, CHARACTER VARYING, and CHARACTER LARGE OBJECT), a binary type (BINARY LARGE OBJECT), and datetime types (DATE, TIME, TIMESTAMP, and INTERVAL). The constructed types are ARRAY and ROW (and, coming in the next generation of SQL, MULTISET). SQL:1999 has two bit string types, BIT and BIT VARYING, that have been removed from the next generation of the SQL standard, of which SQL/XML will be a part; as a result, SQL/XML does not (and cannot) provide support for those two data types.

XML also has—if XML Schema is considered—a number of built-in data types, called *primitive types*. XML Schema also accommodates types that are derived from those primitive types and are known as *derived types*. XML Schema defines a number of such derived types, which are derived from primitive types by application of one or more *facets*—aspects of a type that characterize properties of the type's value space or its lexical representation. (An example of a facet is the length of a `string` type.) Primitive types and derived types are collectively known as *simple types*, which are contrasted with *complex types* that can be defined in XML schemas. XML Schema defines the primitive type `decimal` from which built-in derived types `integer`, `nonPositiveInteger`, `negativeInteger`, `long`, `int`, `short`, `byte`, `nonNegativeInteger`, `positiveInteger`, `unsignedLong`, `unsignedInt`, `unsignedShort`, and `unsignedByte` are derived (many by derivation from other derived types in the list). It also defines numeric primitive types named `float` and `double`, as well as a logical primitive type named `boolean`. In addition, XML Schema defines two binary primitive types, named `hexBinary` and `base64Binary` and three specialized XML-related primitive types, named `anyURI`, `QName`, and `NOTATION`. There is a primitive type named `string`, from which come derived types named `normalizedString`, `token`, `language`, `Name`, `NCName`, `NMTOKEN`, `ID`, `IDREF`, and `ENTITY`. There are three additional `string`-derived types that are lists of derived types: `NMTOKENS`, `IDREFS`, and `ENTITIES`. Finally, XML Schema defines several datetime-related types: `duration`, `date`, `time`, `dateTime`, `gYearMonth`, `gYear`, `gMonth`, `gMonthDay`, and `gDay`.

As you quickly recognize from the two lists of data types, there are similarities between the types of SQL and the types of XML at a high level of abstraction, but the details are quite different. This naturally raises challenges in mapping SQL types and XML types.

The approach taken by the SQLX Group is straightforward: Map each SQL type to its closest analog among XML Schema types, using XML Schema type facets to capture as much of the semantics of the SQL type as possible. An XML Schema facility known as an *annotation* may optionally be used to capture the exact SQL data type information, as well. In Example 9.6, you will see examples of mapping from SQL types to XML Schema types.

Example 9.6 *Mapping SQL Types to XML Schema Types*

SQL Type	*XML Schema Type*

`CHARACTER(10) CHARACTER SET LATIN1 COLLATION ESPAÑOL`

```
<xsd:simpleType>
 <xsd:restriction base="xsd:string">
  <xsd:length value="10"/>
  <xsd:annotation>
   <sqlxml:sqltype name="CHAR" length="10"
                   characterSetName="LATIN1"
                   collation="ESPAÑOL"/>
  </xsd:annotation>
 </xsd:restriction>
</xsd:simpleType>
```

`DECIMAL(8,2)` *(where the implementation uses the next highest odd number for decimal precision)*

```
<xsd:simpleType>
 <xsd:restriction base="xsd:decimal">
  <xsd:precision value="9"/>
  <xsd:scale value="2"/>
  <xsd:annotation>
   <sqlxml:sqltype name="DECIMAL"
       userPrecision="8" scale="2"/>
  </xsd:annotation>
 </xsd:restriction>
</xsd:simpleType>
```

`SMALLINT` *(where the implementation uses 16-bit twos-complement integers)*

```
<xsd:simpleType>
 <xsd:restriction base="xsd:integer">
  <xsd:maxInclusive value="32767"/>
  <xsd:minInclusive value="-32768"/>
  <xsd:annotation>
   <sqlxml:sqltype name="SMALLINT"/>
```

```
                                 </xsd:annotation>
                                </xsd:restriction>
                               </xsd:simpleType>

INTERVAL YEAR(4) TO MONTH      <xsd:simpleType>
                                <xsd:restriction
                                    base="xsd:duration">
                                 <xsd:pattern value=
                                    "-?P\p{Nd}{1,4}Y\p{Nd}{2}M"/>
                                 <xsd:annotation>
                                  <sqlxml:sqltype
                                    name="INTERVAL YEAR TO MONTH"
                                    leadingPrecision="4"/>
                                 </xsd:annotation>
                                </xsd:restriction>
                               </xsd:simpleType>
```

The mapping between SQL types and corresponding XML types is given in Table 9.2. Not yet defined, but (as I write this chapter) being discussed, are SQL:1999's structured and distinct user-defined types, its reference types, and its ARRAY and ROW types.

Table 9.2 *SQL Data Type Mapping to XML Schema Types*

SQL Data Type	*Analogous XML Schema Type*
CHARACTER	`xsd:string`, using facet `xsd:length` or `xsd:maxLength`
CHARACTER VARYING	`xsd:string`, using facet `xsd:length` or `xsd:maxLength`
CHARACTER LARGE OBJECT	`xsd:string`, using facet `xsd:length` or `xsd:maxLength`
BINARY LARGE OBJECT	`xsd:nexBinary` or `xsd:base64Binary`, using facet `xsd:maxLength`
NUMERIC	`xsd:decimal`, using facets `xsd:precision` and `xsd:scale`
DECIMAL	`xsd:decimal`, using facets `xsd:precision` and `xsd:scale`
INTEGER	`xsd:integer`, using facets `xsd:minInclusive` and `xsd:maxInclusive`

Table 9.2 *(Continued)*

SQL Data Type	*Analogous XML Schema Type*
SMALLINT	xsd:integer, using facets xsd:minInclusive and xsd:maxInclusive
BIGINT (next generation of the SQL standard)	xsd:integer, using facets xsd:minInclusive and xsd:maxInclusive
FLOAT	xsd:float or xsd:double (depending on the precision)
REAL	xsd:float
DOUBLE PRECISION	xsd:double
BOOLEAN	xsd:boolean
DATE	xsd:date, using facet xsd:pattern
TIME WITHOUT TIME ZONE	xsd:time, using facet xsd:pattern
TIME WITH TIME ZONE	xsd:time, using facet xsd:pattern
TIMESTAMP WITHOUT TIME ZONE	xsd:dateTime, using facet xsd:pattern
TIMESTAMP WITH TIME ZONE	xsd:dateTime, using facet xsd:pattern
INTERVAL	xsd:duration, using facet xsd:pattern

In addition to the facets cited in the second column of Table 9.2, annotations can always be used to more readily capture precise SQL type information.

SQL/XML does not currently address the mapping of XML Schema types onto SQL types, except as a reverse mapping from XML Schema types that were initially mapped from SQL types. Whether or not such mappings will be defined is not yet decided, but it seems somewhat unlikely that the first version of SQL/XML will contain specifications to perform them. Future versions might support mapping from XML Schema types to SQL types as a way of assisting applications that require the ability to automatically transfer XML data into SQL databases.

9.4.3 Mapping Data Values

Mapping between SQL values and corresponding XML values is relatively easy, once the data type mappings have been specified. The degenerate rule is quite simply stated: Every value of an SQL type has a corresponding value of the closest analogous XML Schema type, so map the SQL value to that corresponding XML Schema type value.

Of course, life isn't always quite that simple. In fact, there are a couple of rather minor complications. The first such complication arises when converting

SQL numeric values to their corresponding XML values; if the SQL value is representable as an integer (that is, it has no fractional component), should the corresponding XML value include a trailing decimal point or not? The SQLX Group concluded that SQL's rules for CASTing to CHARACTER string provided a reasonable precedent by choosing to use "the shortest literal," implying that a trailing decimal point is both redundant and undesirable. (When there are two possible values of the same length that are equivalent, then neither the SQL:1999 standard nor the SQL/XML specification currently provide a way to choose between them, so I am forced to assume that each implementation is free to choose based on its own criteria.)

The other complication arises when an XML `xsd:string` value is produced that contains one of XML's special characters (ampersand and left angle bracket). Those values are never permitted to appear in an XML document except in their special-case uses (ampersand to introduce an entity and left angle bracket to start a tag) or when embedded in a CDATA section. The conversion of SQL character string values to XML values must be able to convert instances of those two special characters to their entity representations (`&` and `<`, respectively) when required, but to leave them unchanged in other cases (e.g., when a CDATA section is the target of the mapping). As with some of the identifier mapping rules, this determination is made through the use of a parameter.

9.4.4 Mapping SQL Tables

As you might expect, mapping SQL tables to XML is somewhat more complex than mapping identifiers, data types, and simple values. In fact, there are a number of approaches that have been adopted by the SQLX Group, which implies further parameterization of the mapping facilities.

Consider the SQL table in Table 9.1. It contains three columns and several rows. Since the data type of each column is one of SQL's predefined types, there are (at least!) two ways in which that table could be represented in XML, as seen in Example 9.7 and Example 9.8.

Example 9.7 *Corresponding XML Document, Alternative 1*

```
<Movies_x0040__x0026__x0040_Titles>
  <movie>
    <TITLE>Seven</TITLE>
    <DESCRIPTION>Police drama about two cops, one new and one about to
retire, after a serial killer using the seven deadly sins as his MO.
</DESCRIPTION>
```

```
    <RUNS>PT2H3M</RUNS>
  </movie>
  <movie>
    <TITLE>Copycat</TITLE>
    <DESCRIPTION>A psychiatrist who specializes in serial killers
suffers from agoraphobia and her only link to the outside world is her
computer. A serial killer who copies the methods of famous serial
killers threatens her on-line. </DESCRIPTION>
    <RUNS>PT2H3M</RUNS>
  </movie>
  <movie>
    <TITLE>The Bone Collector</TITLE>
    <DESCRIPTION>Denzel Washington plays a quadriplegic homicide
detective. He and his female partner track down a serial killer.
</DESCRIPTION>
    <RUNS>PT1H58M</RUNS>
  </movie>
  <movie>
    <TITLE>Bone Daddy</TITLE>
    <DESCRIPTION>A pathologist's book about his work is a good recipe
for sick people.</DESCRIPTION>
    <RUNS>PT1H30M</RUNS>
  </movie>
  <movie>
    <TITLE>Serial Mom</TITLE>
    <DESCRIPTION>She's a fabulous, loving, caring mother, who happens
to be a serial killer!</DESCRIPTION>
    <RUNS>PT1H35M</RUNS>
  </movie>
</Movies_x0040__x0026__x0040_Titles>
```

Example 9.8 *Corresponding XML Document, Alternative 2*

```
<Movies_x0040__x0026__x0040_Titles>
  <movie TITLE="Seven" RUNS="PT2H3M">
    <DESCRIPTION>Police drama about two cops, one new and one about to
retire, after a serial killer using the seven deadly sins as his MO.
</DESCRIPTION>
  </movie>
  <movie TITLE="Copycat" RUNS="PT2H3M">
```

```
    <DESCRIPTION>A psychiatrist who specializes in serial killers
suffers from agoraphobia and her only link to the outside world is her
computer. A serial killer who copies the methods of famous serial
killers threatens her on-line. </DESCRIPTION>
  </movie>
  <movie TITLE="The Bone Collector" RUNS="PT1H58M">
    <DESCRIPTION>Denzel Washington plays a quadriplegic homicide
detective. He and his female partner track down a serial killer.
</DESCRIPTION>
  </movie>
  <movie TITLE="Bone Daddy" RUNS="PT1H30M">
    <DESCRIPTION>A pathologist's book about his work is a good recipe
for sick people.</DESCRIPTION>
  </movie>
  <movie TITLE="Serial Mom" RUNS="PT1H35M">
    <DESCRIPTION>She's a fabulous, loving, caring mother, who happens
to be a serial killer!</DESCRIPTION>
  </movie>
</Movies_x0040__x0026__x0040_Titles>
```

In Example 9.7, each column is represented by a separate element contained within the movie element. Those contained elements have names that are obviously mapped from the names of the columns. In fact, the name of the root element and the all-capitalized names of the contained elements are the only differences between this example and its initial form seen in Example 9.4.

By contrast, in Example 9.8, the TITLE and RUNS columns have both been represented as XML *attributes* instead of XML elements. In many situations, the use of attributes to represent values of SQL columns is quite natural. In this example, representing the DESCRIPTION column as an attribute would result in valid XML, but it doesn't seem very natural (to me, at least) to have attributes with such lengthy values. SQL/XML provides yet another parameter that allows applications to choose whether columns should be represented as elements or as attributes.

Mapping an SQL column to an XML attribute is infeasible when the data type of the column is an SQL structured type or an SQL constructed type like ARRAY or ROW.

Another dimension of variability in mapping SQL tables to XML comes from an issue that I mentioned very briefly in section 9.4: the use of a separate element to highlight each row of an SQL table. In Example 9.9 and Example 9.10, you can see the two approaches that SQL/XML allows.

Example 9.9 *Corresponding XML Document, Alternative A*

```
<moviestore>
  <Movies_x0040__x0026__x0040_Titles>
    <row>
      <TITLE>Seven</TITLE>
      <DESCRIPTION>Police drama about two cops, one new and one about
to retire, after a serial killer using the seven deadly sins as his
MO.</DESCRIPTION>
       <RUNS>PT2H3M</RUNS>
    </row>
    <row>
      <TITLE>Copycat</TITLE>
      <DESCRIPTION>A psychiatrist who specializes in serial killers
suffers from agoraphobia and her only link to the outside world is her
computer. A serial killer who copies the methods of famous serial
killers threatens her on-line. </DESCRIPTION>
       <RUNS>PT2H3M</RUNS>
    </row>
    <row>
      <TITLE>The Bone Collector</TITLE>
      <DESCRIPTION>Denzel Washington plays a quadriplegic homicide
detective. He and his female partner track down a serial killer.
</DESCRIPTION>
       <RUNS>PT1H58M</RUNS>
    </row>
    <row>
      <TITLE>Bone Daddy</TITLE>
      <DESCRIPTION>A pathologist's book about his work is a good
recipe for sick people.</DESCRIPTION>
       <RUNS>PT1H30M</RUNS>
    </row>
    <row>
      <TITLE>Serial Mom</TITLE>
      <DESCRIPTION>She's a fabulous, loving, caring mother, who
happens to be a serial killer!</DESCRIPTION>
       <RUNS>PT1H35M</RUNS>
    </row>
  </Movies_x0040__x0026__x0040_Titles>
  <special_movies>
  </special_movies>
</moviestore>
```

Example 9.10 *Corresponding XML Document, Alternative B*

```
<moviestore>
  <Movies_x0040__x0026__x0040_Titles>
    <TITLE>Seven</TITLE>
    <DESCRIPTION>Police drama about two cops, one new and one about to
retire, after a serial killer using the seven deadly sins as his MO.
</DESCRIPTION>
     <RUNS>PT2H3M</RUNS>
  </Movies_x0040__x0026__x0040_Titles>
  <Movies_x0040__x0026__x0040_Titles>
    <TITLE>Copycat</TITLE>
    <DESCRIPTION>A psychiatrist who specializes in serial killers
suffers from agoraphobia and her only link to the outside world is her
computer. A serial killer who copies the methods of famous serial
killers threatens her on-line. </DESCRIPTION>
     <RUNS>PT2H3M</RUNS>
  </Movies_x0040__x0026__x0040_Titles>
  <Movies_x0040__x0026__x0040_Titles>
    <TITLE>The Bone Collector</TITLE>
    <DESCRIPTION>Denzel Washington plays a quadriplegic homicide
detective. He and his female partner track down a serial killer.
</DESCRIPTION>
     <RUNS>PT1H58M</RUNS>
  </Movies_x0040__x0026__x0040_Titles>
  <Movies_x0040__x0026__x0040_Titles>
    <TITLE>Bone Daddy</TITLE>
    <DESCRIPTION>A pathologist's book about his work is a good recipe
for sick people.</DESCRIPTION>
     <RUNS>PT1H30M</RUNS>
  </Movies_x0040__x0026__x0040_Titles>
  <Movies_x0040__x0026__x0040_Titles>
    <TITLE>Serial Mom</TITLE>
    <DESCRIPTION>She's a fabulous, loving, caring mother, who happens
to be a serial killer!</DESCRIPTION>
     <RUNS>PT1H35M</RUNS>
  </Movies_x0040__x0026__x0040_Titles>
</moviestore>
```

In Example 9.9, the table whose SQL name is "Movies & Titles" is represented by an XML element `<Movies_x0040__x0026__x0040_Titles>`, and each row of that table is represented by an XML element `<row>`, which contains one element for each of the columns of the SQL table. At the end of Example 9.9, I've included an *empty* element `<special_movies>` to illustrate how this approach would represent an SQL table that contained no rows at all.

By contrast, in Example 9.10, every row of the SQL table ("`Movies & Titles`") is represented by an instance of the XML element `<Movies_x0040__x0026__x0040_Titles>`, but the table itself does not have a corresponding XML element. In fact, there is no indication at all in Example 9.10 that the table `special_movies` even exists.

Both approaches have their adherents—and different applications will no doubt require different approaches. SQL/XML will almost certainly support both of these alternatives, determined by still another parameter.

It's worth mentioning that SQL tables can be mapped directly to XML elements, but it is more likely that applications will map them to XML Schema complex types from which XML elements are then defined. While this seemingly increases the complexity (by introducing a level of indirection), experience strongly suggests that the resulting XML schemas and documents are much easier to maintain and to be processed by other programs.

Yet another issue arises when SQL's null values are considered. What is the "proper" representation of an SQL null value in XML? In fact, as I said in section 9.3.2, there are several reasonable ways to represent a null value stored in an SQL column when expressing the containing table in an XML document: an empty element, the absence of the corresponding element, and an element containing the attribute `xsi:nil="true"`. It's too soon for me to predict with confidence just how this will be specified in the published SQL/XML standard, but discussions in the SQLX Group suggest that still another parameter will be provided that allows the application (quite reasonably, in my opinion) to choose the proper representation.

In fact, SQL/XML is likely to map SQL tables to XML documents by simultaneously mapping the schema information describing the tables to XML schemas that describe the XML documents. This is, as you might expect, done by mapping the data types of the columns of the tables onto XML Schema types, then mapping the tables onto XML Schema complex types, then generating XML elements defined on those complex types, and so forth. In the same manner, an entire SQL schema can be mapped into an XML document and an XML schema. An SQL catalog can similarly be mapped to XML.

9.5 Publishing SQL Data Using XML

Application environments that involve the use of SQL data (environments that don't use SQL are somewhat rare) are beginning to find increasing need for integrating XML data into their operations. Naturally, SQL database system implementers, as well as the SQL standard, are responding to this requirement by developing ways to store XML documents in SQL databases and to locate and retrieve those documents, or parts of them, when needed by applications.

9.5.1 Storing XML in SQL Databases

The issue of storing SQL documents in SQL databases is not necessarily as obvious as one might like and thus deserves a brief discussion of its own. In very broad terms, there are three general approaches that I have seen used:

- Store XML text in character string form. This alternative almost always involves the definition of a column whose data type is CHARACTER LARGE OBJECT (or CLOB). Raw XML documents are stored in their character string, or serialized, form, which makes it quite efficient to insert them into the database and very easy to retrieve them in their original form. This approach also makes it fairly easy to build full-text indexing to the documents, so that full-text retrieval algorithms can be readily applied for contextual and relevance retrieval.
- Store XML in fully or partially "shredded" form. The word *shred,* when applied to an XML document, implies that the document has been broken into pieces corresponding to elements within the document. Some applications might benefit from placing the values associated with particular elements into separate database columns—or even separate tables. Storing shredded documents makes it much easier to index the values of particular elements, as long as those elements are placed into their own columns, which in turn makes it much more efficient to retrieve documents based on the values of those elements using ordinary relational database technology.
- Store XML in a completely parsed form (that is, converted to some internal format, such as an Infoset or PSVI representation). This variation is often used by so-called native XML database systems, but it is also used by relational systems under certain circumstances. This approach makes it straightforward to identify and retrieve information based on the structure of the XML document in addition to its contents, and often provides good performance for indexing based on element values. Reconstructing the identical form of the original XML document from the completely parsed form remains somewhat challenging, in part because this process rarely retains detailed information about the white space (blanks, newlines, and so forth) in documents except when it occurs within quoted strings.

Each of these approaches has advantages and disadvantages. The relational database community, as well as the object-oriented database community, remain somewhat divided in their expressed opinions about the "best" way to support XML, although I see signs that the relational vendors are likely to support a combination of approaches, based on specific application requirements.

9.5.2 XMLType

More recently (in fact, concurrent with the writing of this chapter), the SQLX Group has been wrestling with the specifications for a new SQL data type that will be used to natively store and manage XML documents. Called XMLType, this new built-in SQL type would be accompanied by a number of pseudo-functions used to "publish" SQL data in an XML format. (The term *pseudo-functions* implies that they are invoked using syntax that resembles function invocation syntax, but that they are not defined or implemented as true SQL functions. In some cases, it is possible to define them as ordinary SQL functions, but that's not true in all cases. For example, in some cases, the parameter list has a variable number of parameters or a repeating list of the final parameter. In other cases, one or more parameters include an SQL keyword as part of the definition.)

When the SQLX Group first began to consider how XML might be best stored in an SQL database, they found themselves tempted to specify an SQL:1999 structured user-defined type and a set of methods to represent and manipulate XML. After all, that technique was being successfully used to represent full-text, spatial, image, and other data in a related standard (discussed in Chapter 10, "SQL Multimedia and Application Packages"). However, a closer analysis of the details of the requirements convinced the Group that a built-in SQL type would offer improved ease of specification at no cost to application ease of use.

At the time that I write this chapter, proposals for an XMLType are still being developed and discussed by the SQLX Group, so the information contained in this chapter is very speculative. Be sure that you determine the details as published in the final SQL/XML standard before you depend on anything you learn here about this new type!

The XMLType is very likely to permit storage of several types of XML, including well-formed XML elements and full XML documents (that is, well-formed elements accompanied by an XML prolog), XML fragments (that might not be well-formed), and even "forests" of XML (multiple well-formed elements without a common root element).

Access to instances of the XMLType is likely to be available only through a number of pseudo-functions—invoked using a notation that resembles function invocation syntax but with several enhancements for usability that would prevent their definition as actual functions. You will read about two of these pseudo-functions, XMLEXISTS and XMLEXTRACT. These functions are used to extract information from XML data stored in an SQL database. In sections 9.5.3 and 9.5.4, I cover several other pseudo-functions that deal with conversion of SQL data into XML values within an SQL statement—that is, publication of SQL data in an XML form.

In this section, I cite several new predicates that the SQLX Group is considering for testing XMLType values:

- To test whether an XMLType value is a complete XML document, you may be able to use `expression HAS XML PROLOG`.
- To test whether an XMLType value is an XML element (but not a document with a prolog), you may be able to use `expression IS XML ELEMENT`.
- To test whether an XMLType value is, in fact, XML, you may be able to use `expression IS XML TEXT`.
- To test whether an XMLType value is actually an XML schema, you may be able to use `expression IS XML SCHEMA`.
- To test whether an XMLType value is an XML document whose prolog identifies an XML schema and whether the document can be validated against that schema, you may be able to use `expression IS VALID`.
- To test whether an XMLType value contains an instance of a specified XML schema, you may be able to use `doc-expression IS VALID INSTANCE OF schema-expression`.

Another predicate is being considered (but does not yet have proposed syntax) to test whether an XMLType value is a forest of XML elements. Current drafts provide only the positive forms of these predicates, but I would find it surprising if negative forms (such as "`expression IS NOT VALID`") were not included in the expected SQL/XML standard.

9.5.3 Querying XML within SQL Databases

Two of the pseudo-functions being considered for inclusion in SQL/XML provide the capability of querying XML documents in SQL databases using a combination of SQL and XPath expressions. XPath defines a non-XML syntax that permits navigation within an XML document. It is a terse notation that will immediately seem, in some ways, familiar to anyone who uses a modern operating system, because part of its syntax is similar to the path notation used for file system navigation. Of course, it is not my intent in this book to present the details of XPath, so the discussion and examples of this section presume knowledge of the notation.

One of the two XPath-using pseudo-functions, XMLEXISTS, behaves like a predicate, since it returns a Boolean value. The syntax being proposed for this pseudo-function can be seen in Syntax 9.1.

Syntax 9.1 *<xml exists predicate> Syntax*

```
<xml exists predicate> ::=
    XMLEXISTS <left paren> <xml instance> <comma> <xpath expression>
              [ <comma> <namespaces> ] <right paren>

<xml instance> ::= <xml value expression>

<xpath expression> ::= <string value expression>

<namespaces> ::= <string value expression>
```

XMLEXISTS returns *true* if the XPath expression specified in the string value of `<xpath expression>` identifies a node in the tree corresponding to the value of the XMLType expression associated with `<xml instance>`. If either the first or second of the arguments are the null value, then this pseudo-function returns *unknown*. Otherwise, it returns *false*. If the optional argument `<namespaces>` is specified, then it is used to specify the XML namespaces that may be present in the XPath expression; its structure is the same as the syntax used to define namespaces in an XML document.

The other pseudo-function that uses XPath is XMLEXTRACT, whose syntax is shown in Syntax 9.2. Its parameters have the same definitions as the parameters using the same BNF nonterminal symbols in Syntax 9.1.

Syntax 9.2 *<xml extract expression> Syntax*

```
<xml exists predicate> ::=
    XMLEXTRACT <left paren> <xml instance> <comma>
               <xpath expression> [ <comma> <namespaces> ] <right paren>
```

The syntax of XMLEXTRACT is identical to that of XMLEXISTS except for the keyword. This pseudo-function uses the XPath expression specified in the string value of `<xpath expression>` to identify a node in the tree corresponding to the value of the XMLType expression associated with `<xml instance>` and actually extracts and returns that node.

Consider the SQL table shown in Example 9.11 and assume that the XML document given in Example 9.10 is stored in the column named `movie`. The SQL statement in Example 9.12 returns the description of the movie *Seven* as indicated in Result 9.1.

Example 9.11 *An SQL Table Containing an XML Column*

```
CREATE TABLE moviesInXML (
  ( stock_number       CHARACTER(10),
    rental_price       DECIMAL(3,2),
    movie              XMLTYPE )
```

Example 9.12 *Extracting XML from an XMLType Column*

```
SELECT stock_number AS SN,
       XMLEXTRACT ( B.movie,
         '/moviestore/Movies_x0040__x0026__x0040_Titles/DESCRIPTION' )
         AS movie_desc
FROM moviesInXML AS B
WHERE  XMLEXISTS ( B.movie,
         '/moviestore/Movies_x0040__x0026__x0040_Titles/TITLE[.="Seven"]' )
```

Result 9.1 *The Extracted Result*

SN	*MOVIE_DESC*
T2301-19SK	Police drama about two cops, one new and one about to retire, after a serial killer using the seven deadly sins as his MO.

9.5.4 XML Publishing Functions

One of the most interesting problems being addressed by the SQLX Group is publication of SQL data in an XML format. (I like to call this operation "viewing SQL data through an XML lens.") There are many different ways in which data extracted from an SQL database can be represented in XML. You saw some of the differences in approach in section 9.4.4. Indeed, among the liveliest of the discussions in which members of the group participate are those dealing with the details of the pseudo-functions used to construct XML from retrieved SQL data. As a result, the material in this section is especially subject to radical change before the final SQL/XML standard is published.

While XML defines several "basic" syntax components—the root node, element nodes, attribute nodes, processing instruction nodes, comment nodes, namespace nodes, and text nodes—most of them are not used to represent data that might be extracted from an SQL database. In fact, only element nodes, attribute nodes, and the text nodes that element nodes contain are used to represent SQL data. Therefore, *publication* principally means "construction of elements, attributes, and their values." Several pseudo-functions to accomplish this are being discussed.

The first of these pseudo-functions, XMLELEMENT, is used to construct an XML element. Construction of an XML element frequently involves construction of attributes as well, so the XMLELEMENT pseudo-function permits the invocation of the XMLATTRIBUTES function as an optional argument to XMLELEMENT. The syntax of these two pseudo-functions can be seen in Syntax 9.3.

Syntax 9.3 *<XML element> Syntax*

```
<XML element> ::=
    XMLELEMENT <left paren> NAME <element name> [ , <XML attributes> ]
      [ { <comma> <element content> }... ] <right paren>

<element name> ::= <identifier>

<XML attributes> ::=
    XMLATTRIBUTES <left paren> <attribute list> <right paren>

<attribute list> ::=
    <attribute> [ { <comma> <attribute> }... ]

<attribute> ::= <attribute value> [ AS <attribute name> ]

<attribute value> ::= <value expression>

<attribute name> ::= <identifier>

<element content> ::= <value expression>
```

When used in an SQL statement that retrieves values from your database, XMLELEMENT constructs an XML element whose QName is given by the `<element name>` argument (which, you may have observed, is an SQL identifier and not a character string expression). If no other arguments are specified, then the constructed element has neither content nor attributes.

If the XMLATTRIBUTES argument is present, then the constructed element gets one or more attributes. The names of the attributes—like the name of the element—are provided as identifiers. Naturally, the values of those attributes are generated, usually by retrieval of values from the database. Similarly, the element content, if specified, is generated from retrieval of database values.

Consider the SQL table in Example 9.13 (adapted from the first volume of this book).

Example 9.13 *The Simplified movie_titles Table*

```
CREATE TABLE movie_titles (
    title                       CHARACTER ( 30 ),
    year_released               DATE,
    our_dvd_cost                DECIMAL ( 5,2 ),
    regular_dvd_sale_price      DECIMAL ( 5,2 ),
    current_dvd_sale_price      DECIMAL ( 5,2 ),
    movie_type                  CHARACTER ( 10 ),
    dvds_owned                  INTEGER,
    dvds_in_stock               INTEGER,
    total_dvd_units_sold        INTEGER,
    total_dvd_sales_revenue     DECIMAL ( 9,2 )
) ;
```

A query to generate an XML element having an attribute representing the year that the movie was released and whose content is the title of the movie is illustrated in Example 9.14.

Example 9.14 *Use of XMLELEMENT*

```
SELECT XMLELEMENT ( NAME "movieTitle",
                    XMLATTRIBUTES ( B.year_released AS "movieYear" ),
                    B.title ) AS xmldata
FROM movie_titles
WHERE B.title LIKE '%Rose%'
```

The results of that query are postulated (because I haven't shown the contents of the table from which the data is being retrieved) in Table 9.3.

Table 9.3 *Result of Query Using XMLELEMENT*

XMLDATA
<movieTitle movieYear="1979">The Rose</movieTitle>
<movieYear="1980">Honeysuckle Rose</movieTitle>
<movieTitle movieYear="1986">The Name of the Rose</movieTitle>
<movieTitle movieYear="1989">War of the Roses</movieTitle>

Sometimes you may wish to create an "outer" element for each row of data retrieved from a table, then create a sequence of "inner" elements, one per column of interest. For example, the query in Example 9.14 returns several rows in the virtual table that SQL retrieval statements produce. The use of XMLELEMENT in the SELECT list results in an XML element in each such row. You might wish that element to contain multiple nested elements. Such sequences of elements are often called a *forest* in the XML world. The XMLFOREST pseudo-function, whose syntax is seen in Syntax 9.4, is designed to be used within the XMLELEMENT pseudo-function for that purpose (analogous in some ways to XMLATTRIBUTES).

Syntax 9.4 *<XML forest> Syntax*

```
<XML forest> ::=
    XMLFOREST <left paren> <forest element list> <right paren>

<forest element list> ::=
    <forest element> [ { <comma> <forest element> }... ]

<forest element> ::=
    <forest element value> [ AS <forest element name> ]

<forest element value> ::= <value expression>

<forest element name> ::= <identifier>
```

Given the table definition in Example 9.13, the query in Example 9.15 returns a result like that shown in Table 9.4.

Example 9.15 *Use of XMLFOREST*

```
SELECT ELEMENT ( NAME "movieData",
                 XMLATTRIBUTES ( B.year_released AS "movieYear" ),
                 XMLFOREST ( B.title,
                             B.movie_type AS "type" ) AS xmldata
FROM movie_titles
WHERE B.title LIKE '%Rose%'
```

The results of that query are postulated (because I haven't shown the contents of the table from which the data is being retrieved) in Table 9.3.

Table 9.4 *Result of Query Using XMLFOREST*

XMLDATA
<movieData movieYear="1979">   <TITLE>The Rose</TITLE>   <type>Musical drama</type> </movieData> <movieData movieYear="1980">   <TITLE>Honeysuckle Rose</TITLE>   <type>Romance</type> </movieData> <movieData movieYear="1986">   <TITLE>The Name of the Rose</TITLE>   <type>Historical drama</type> </movieData> <movieData movieYear="1989">   <TITLE>War of the Roses</TITLE>   <type>Comedy</type> </movieData>

A more complex, perhaps more controversial, XML publishing pseudo-function is XMLGEN, seen in Syntax 9.5 (where the syntax doesn't capture the complexity of the pseudo-function). XMLGEN produces an XML value that is created by an XQuery constructor. At the time this volume goes to press, the XQuery specifications are not yet finalized. As a result, the portion of the SQL/

XML specifications that depend on XQuery are subject to change, and some of those changes might well render obsolete some of the following.

Syntax 9.5 *<XML gen> Syntax*

```
<XML gen> ::=
    XMLGEN <left paren> <XML constructor>
                        [ <XML gen variable list> ] <right paren>

<XML constructor> ::= <character string literal>

<XML gen variable list> ::=
    <XML gen variable> { <comma> <XML gen variable> }...

<XML gen variable> ::=
    <XML gen variable value> [ AS <XML gen variable name> ]

<XML gen variable value> ::= <value expression>

<XML gen variable name> ::= <identifier>
```

The XMLGEN pseudo-function allows an XML element to be created by specifying a sort of template that contains specified locations in which either variable names or the values of expressions will be substituted as determined by other arguments. The first argument to XMLGEN is a character string value that defines the template, which must be a valid XQuery element constructor. (XQuery provides two syntaxes for element constructors, and either can be used. It is beyond the scope of this book to provide the details of XML element constructors.) In that character string value, sequences that begin with a left curly brace ({) and end with a right curly brace (}) must contain nothing other than an SQL identifier—prefixed with a dollar sign ($)—between the braces. Each SQL identifier contained within such sequences must be the name of a column or the alias of an expression used in one of the other arguments to the pseudo-function. The value of the named column or aliased expression is substituted at each appearance of the corresponding name appearing within curly braces.

Using the by now familiar table from Example 9.13, the query in Example 9.16 will return results like those shown in Table 9.5.

Example 9.16 *Use of XMLGEN*

```
SELECT XMLGEN ( '<movieData type="{$MOVIE_TYPE}">
                   {$MOVIE_TITLE}{$YEAR)
                 </movieData>',
                 mt.movie_type,
                 ( 'The movie titled "' || mt.title ) AS movie_title,
                 ( '" was released in ' || mt.year_released || '.' )
                   AS year ) AS xmldata
FROM movie_titles AS mt
WHERE B.title LIKE '%Rose%'
```

Table 9.5 *Result of Query Using XMLGEN*

XMLDATA
<movieData type="Musical drama">The movie titled "The Rose" was released in 1979.</movieData>
<movieData type="Romance">The movie titled "Honeysuckle Rose" was released in 1980.</movieData>
<movieData type="Historical drama">The movie titled "The Name of the Rose" was released in 1986.</movieData>
<movieData type="Comedy">The movie titled "War of the Roses" was released in 1989.</movieData>

Several additional XML publishing pseudo-functions are being discussed, including one named XMLAGG that, like other SQL aggregate functions, combines values from each row in a table into a group (based on equality of values of one or more columns) and converts the aggregated column into a single value. In the case of XMLAGG, the aggregated column would essentially be the concatenation of the XMLType values in each of the individual rows that have been grouped together.

Another function that is likely to be included in SQL/XML is named XMLCONCAT. XMLCONCAT differs from ordinary SQL concatenation (whose syntax uses two consecutive vertical bars: ||) in its treatment of null values. When concatenating a non-null string with the null value using ordinary SQL concatenation, the result is the null value. That is often not appropriate for concatenating XML elements to produce forests. The XMLCONCAT pseudo-function treats null values as though they were zero-length strings.

9.6 Chapter Summary

This chapter is unconventional in that it presents material that was not standardized as part of SQL:1999 but that is in preparation for the next generation of the SQL standard. However, interest in XML-related matters runs quite high, and it seemed appropriate to give you a preview—admittedly speculative—of what the SQL standard was likely to do with regard to XML. I must remind you, however, that the material in this chapter is based strictly on my knowledge of the current status of the work being done in the SQLX Group, and there is no guarantee that any of it (much less all of it) will survive for publication in any part of the SQL standard.

Chapter 10

SQL Multimedia and Application Packages

10.1 Introduction

Even though the topic of this book is the SQL:1999 standard, you may be interested in another standard that uses facilities defined by SQL. The structured user-defined types provided by SQL:1999 (see Chapter 2, "User-Defined Types," Chapter 3, "Typed Tables," and Chapter 4, "Routines and Routine Invocation") form the foundation for a different, but related, standard called SQL Multimedia and Application Packages, or SQL/MM. In this chapter, the various components of SQL/MM are surveyed, but the chapter does not contain the level of detail that you can get from the standard itself.

10.2 What Is SQL/MM?

Like SQL:1999, SQL/MM is a multipart standard. Unlike SQL:1999, the various parts of SQL/MM are quite independent from one another (with one exception, about which you will read in section 10.3). The origins of SQL/MM help explain how its various parts were developed.[1]

1 Some material in this section is adapted from Jim Melton and Andrew Eisenberg, "SQL Multimedia and Application Packages (SQL/MM)," *SIGMOD Record,* 30, No. 4, pp. 97–102.

In late 1991 or early 1992, a specification for a language called SFQL (Structured Full-text Query Language) was issued by a group of vendors of text search engines. Their work was being done under the auspices of the IEEE. SFQL's stated goal was the definition of extensions to standard SQL to make that popular language more suitable for performing full-text searches of document repositories. The immediate target marketplace was the aviation industry, which uses full-text systems for the management and retrieval of aircraft manufacturing and maintenance data.

The full-text community gave significant attention to the proposal, but the specification was criticized by several other data management communities on the grounds that SFQL "hijacked" many useful keywords that were in common use by those other communities. For example, the keyword CONTAINS was proposed by SFQL to mean "the indicated unit of text *contains* the supplied word or phrase," but the spatial data community used the same keyword to mean "one spatial entity *contains* a second spatial entity." While the high-level semantics of the word may seem to be quite similar in each case, the actual code required to implement it is dramatically different. That is, the word was already significantly overloaded in practice, but SFQL reserved it for use only in a single data domain: full-text retrieval.

The problem illustrated by the controversy related to CONTAINS turned out to be much broader and more significant than initially imagined. As a result, the ANSI and ISO SQL standards groups recognized that many incompatible extensions to SQL were being considered by various data management communities. The end result of the competing efforts would inevitably be a situation in which no one SQL product could possibly implement all of the extensions, if for no other reason than conflicting keywords.

The SFQL community organized a "summit meeting" in Tokyo later in 1992 to seek a solution to the problem of mutually exclusive SQL extensions. By the time that meeting was held, the SQL standards committees had already begun the process of adding object-oriented extensions to SQL, and several SQL vendors had expressed interest in what is often called the *object-relational model.* Based on input from those vendors, the recommendation that resulted from the Tokyo meeting suggested that a second standard defining several "class libraries" of SQL object types, one for each significant category of complex data, might successfully address the conflicts.

The data types defined in such libraries would be first-class types that could be accessed through ordinary facilities of the SQL language, including expressions that invoke SQL-invoked routines associated with such types (that is, methods).

The proposed standard was soon to become known as SQL/MM, and the letters "MM" were understood to imply "MultiMedia." Several candidate data domains were suggested, including full-text data, spatial data, image data (both still and moving), and several others. Responsibility for SQL/MM's development was given to the same ISO subcommittee as SQL (at that time, JTC1/SC21, now JTC1/SC32), with the hope that domain experts would attend to develop the specifications for each data domain.

Unfortunately, domain experts for only a few of the proposed categories of data have ever participated in the development of SQL/MM, which has resulted in a standard that has not covered as many subject areas as was once hoped. It may also be true that the late-20th-century consolidation in the database industry resulted in fewer implementations of SQL's structured types than expected. Nonetheless, it appears that SQL/MM provides interesting solutions to several significant problem areas.

SQL/MM currently includes five parts, as shown in Table 10.1. Most of these parts address a specific data domain. The major exception to that characteristic is Part 6, Data Mining.

Table 10.1 *The Parts of the SQL/MM Standard*

Part Number	*Part Subject*
1	Framework
2	Full Text
3	Spatial
5	Still Image
6	Data Mining

There is no Part 4; at one time, a draft of Part 4 was being developed under the title "General Purpose Facilities," with the intent of standardizing a library of mathematical routines and related material. However, support for this work failed to materialize among the data management community, and the project was cancelled. Not all of the work put into Part 4 has gone to waste—happily, specifications for angles, which are in the draft of the next generation of SQL/MM Spatial, were adapted from Part 4.

When SQL/MM was initially proposed, several additional data domains were suggested for consideration. These include Moving Image, Sonar and Radar, Seismographic, and Music. Because the participants in the SQL/MM development group (ISO/IEC JTC1/SC32/WG4) do not include experts in any of those fields, no projects to define a part of SQL/MM related to those domains have been proposed.

As with SQL:1999, SQL/MM's Framework document contains material that is common to all other parts of the language. While SQL:1999's Framework defines a number of concepts and terms that are used widely throughout SQL:1999, the focus of SQL/MM's Framework is specification of the definitional technique used in that standard's other parts.

Each of the parts of SQL/MM (other than the Framework) define one or more structured user-defined types and the methods required to support those types, using the features and syntax specified in SQL:1999. The various data domains addressed by current SQL/MM parts vary widely in their requirements. As a result, the style in which the various structured types and their methods are defined varies considerably between parts.

Discussions of SQL/MM are complicated a bit by the absence of informal project names that reflect the year of progression. For example, the first version of the SQL standard is now commonly called "SQL-86" or "SQL-87" to reflect the year of publication (in ANSI and in ISO, respectively). Similarly, while SQL:1999 was under development, it was often called "SQL3," since it was the third major generation of the standard. By contrast, there are no widely known names applied to the parts of SQL/MM that reflect the revision or the date of final publication. Partly in response to the absence of such names, I caution you that the versions of SQL/MM parts discussed in this chapter are the first versions published, but observe that some parts are already nearing publication of revised versions.

The next several sections survey each part of SQL/MM in turn.

10.3 Framework

SQL/MM Framework[2] was initially published in August 2000 (several months after the appearance of the first-published, substantive part, Spatial). This document identifies no fewer than 31 concepts from the SQL:1999 standard on which the various parts of SQL/MM depend. In addition, it defines three terms used throughout the other parts of SQL/MM. The most interesting term whose definition is included in SQL/MM Framework is *multimedia,* which is defined to be "any kind of data other than conventional data, examples being graphic, audio, and visual data."

Framework identifies the benefits of SQL/MM to include a shared understanding of multimedia data, exchange of such data, and provision of common facilities to manipulate such data. It specifies that the routines that implement the behaviors of the various structured types defined in each part of SQL/MM are sometimes specified explicitly using SQL statements contained in SQL routines

2 ISO/IEC 13249-1:2000, *Information technology—Database languages—SQL Multimedia and Application Packages—Part 1: Framework* (Geneva: International Organization for Standardization, 2000).

(see Chapter 4, "Routines and Routine Invocation") and sometimes specified less formally by supplying English-language text that describes those semantics.

SQL/MM Framework clearly anticipates that the structured types defined in the other parts of the standard will be used to define columns in ordinary SQL tables. (The alternative not chosen would be to define typed tables, as discussed in Chapter 3, "Typed Tables.") In practice, however, some implementations of SQL/MM data domains don't literally specify the structured user-defined types. Instead, they use the signatures of the methods as an API (application programming interface) to access underlying technology that is sometimes quite different in detail than the user-defined types.

10.4 Full-Text

Part 2 of SQL/MM specifies SQL:1999 structured types, including methods, in support of full-text data.[3] The term *full-text* (SQL/MM defines the term with the hyphen separating the two words, but many people spell the phrase *full text*) is normally applied to textual data that often differs from ordinary character string data in its length, but also in database-specific operations that can be applied to it. SQL database systems typically support a facility (not defined in or used by the SQL standard) called an *index*. Indexes are data structures used by the database system to quickly and efficiently locate rows of data based on the values stored in their columns.

Ordinary character string columns are usually indexed by the entire value of each string stored in rows of the columns. However, special types of indexes can be defined for full-text data. Such indexes might record information about the proximity of words and phrases to one another or about words that appear in a document and related words that also appear in the same document. Full-text data is data to which you can apply search operations that are normally not applied to ordinary character strings. This sort of "full-text operation" is quite different from the kind of relatively simple, character-based pattern matches with which most computer software people are intimately familiar (such as SQL's LIKE predicate and the regular expressions that are used in SQL's SIMILAR predicate).

Full-text operations tend to involve linguistic concepts and are thus sensitive to the natural (human) language represented by the textual data. For example, linguistic concepts such as *word, sentence,* and *paragraph* can be used to control aspects of searches. Queries may also use a concept known as *stemming* in which queries can search for words that are linguistically related to specified words;

3 ISO/IEC 13249-2:2000, *Information technology—Database languages—SQL Multimedia and Application Packages—Part 2: Full-Text* (Geneva: International Organization for Standardization, 2000).

application of stemming might find plural forms of singular nouns, past-tense forms of verbs, or even verbs that are derived from specified nouns. Similarly, full-text queries are frequently used to locate documents containing certain *concepts,* even if the specified words or phrases do not themselves appear in the documents. Another common requirement on full-text systems is the ability to *rank* the documents identified by queries so applications can retrieve or perform additional searches on documents that have the most relevance to search terms.

The SQL/MM Full-Text standard defines a number of structured user-defined types (UDTs) to support the storage of textual data. One of these types—arguably the most important—is named `FullText`; this type supports the construction and storage of full-text data values. It also supports testing whether instances of the type contains specified patterns, as well as conversion of that data to ordinary SQL character strings. The `FullText` type provides a constructor that prepares the value associated with an instance of the type for the application of full-text searches, as well as several Boolean methods that perform the searches themselves.

In addition to the `FullText` type, SQL/MM Full-Text defines a number of additional types—used internally by the `FullText` type and not publicly visible—that represent various sorts of patterns that can be used in full-text searches. Search patterns can be quite complex, including searching for text that includes specific words, words stemmed from specified words, words with similar definitions, and even words that *sound like* a given word.

Any linguists reading this book will know that some natural languages are more amenable than others to automatic identification of the various components of text. For example, most Western languages use some form of "white space" (blank space, line endings, and so forth) to separate words from one another and use special punctuation (such as a period, or full stop) to separate sentences. Other languages, such as Japanese, do not separate words from one another through the use of spaces, depending primarily on context to distinguish words. SQL/MM Full-Text is often perceived to have better support for languages for which automatic distinction of language tokens (such as words) is relatively easy. However, the standard leaves the identification of such language tokens up to the implementation, and there are products today that apply a wide variety of approaches to identification of tokens in a great many languages.

To illustrate how SQL/MM Full-Text is used to identify full-text documents by searching their contents, let's first consider the SQL table defined in Example 10.1 containing data as indicated in Table 10.2.

Example 10.1 *Table Definition Including a Full-Text Column*

```
CREATE TABLE DVD_information (
  stock_number   INTEGER,
  liner_notes    FULLTEXT )
```

Table 10.2 *Table Including Full-Text Data*

STOCK_NUMBER	*LINER_NOTES*
1339	The Dude. One cool guy. Who one day comes home to find two thugs have broken in and ruined his favorite carpet—the one that made the room "hang together." Thing is, they did it because he's got the same name as one of the richest men in town. Lebowski. But, hey, no problem. He'll get even. At least he'll get someone to pay for the carpet.
...	
1023	For four years, the courageous crew of the NSEA Protector—"Commander Peter Quincy Taggart" (TIM ALLEN), "Lt. Tawny Madison" (SIGOURNEY WEAVER) and "Dr. Lazarus" (ALAN RICKMAN)—set off on thrilling and often dangerous missions in space . . . and then their series was canceled! Now, 20 years later, aliens under attack have mistaken the *Galaxy Quest* television transmissions for "historical documents" and beamed up the crew of has-been actors to save the universe. With no script, no director and no clue, the actors must turn in the performances of their lives in this hilarious adventure Jeffrey Lyons (NBC-TV) calls "the funniest, wittiest comedy of the year."

The `DVD_information` table includes one column, `stock_number`, whose data type is INTEGER and whose values hold some sort of document identifier. The table also includes a second column, `liner_notes`, whose values are full-text documents. This table can be populated through the use of SQL's INSERT statement as shown in Example 10.2, which uses an SQL:1999 NEW expression and a constructor method.

Example 10.2 *Populating a Table Containing a Full-Text Column*

```
INSERT INTO DVD_information
  VALUES ( 1339,
           NEW FullText ( 'The Dude. One cool guy. Who one day comes home '
                       || 'to find two thugs have broken in and ruined '
                       || 'his favorite carpet - the one that made the '
                       || 'room "hang together." Thing is, they did it '
                       || 'because he's got the same name as one of the '
                       || 'richest men in town. Lebowski. But, hey, no '
                       || 'problem. He'll get even. At least he'll get '
                       || 'someone to pay for the carpet.' ) ) ;
```

When you use SQL/MM Full-Text against documents like those found in the documents in Table 10.2, you can search for documents using the following sorts of Boolean predicates:

- Searching for individual words
- Searching for specific phrases
- Searching based on context
- Searching based on linguistic characteristics
- Masking facilities
- Expansion of search patterns, including sound expansion (sometimes known as *sounds like*), broader or narrower term expansion ("movie" is broader than "documentary"), and synonym expansion ("movie" is a synonym for "film").

We could retrieve from that table the identifier of movies in which the liner notes contain words closely related to "funny" in the same paragraph as words that sound like "lions" by using a query like the one seen in Example 10.3. Note the syntax that invokes the CONTAINS method on the `FullText` instances in the `liner_notes` column: `liner_notes.CONTAINS(...)`. This syntax is explained in Chapter 4, "Routines and Routine Invocation." Note, too, that the single argument passed to the CONTAINS method is a character string literal in which I have embedded SQL/MM Full-Text keywords and phrases such as "STEMMED FORM OF." Within that character string literal, I have used two "embedded" literal values, "funny" and "lions"; SQL/MM Full-Text's conventions require that double quotes be used to embed words or phrases within the character string literal argument values.

Example 10.3 *Locating Documents Using Full-Text Facilities*

```
SELECT stock_number
FROM DVD_information
WHERE liner_notes.CONTAINS
      ('STEMMED FORM OF "funny"
       IN SAME PARAGRAPH AS
       SOUNDS LIKE "lions"') = 1
```

The query in Example 10.3 retrieves the `stock_number` column from the `DVD_information` table for every document for which the value returned by the CONTAINS method applied to the `liner_notes` column is 1, meaning *true*. The parameter passed to that method uses three different full-text operations:

STEMMED FORM OF will find any of several words derived from *funny,* such as *funnier* and *funniest;* IN SAME PARAGRAPH AS requires that a second word (or phrase) appear in the same paragraph as the stemmed word; and SOUNDS LIKE finds words that are pronounced (presumably in English, since I didn't specify a different language) like *lions* (of which Jeffrey Lyons's name is a case). The value retrieved is, of course, 1023.

Example 10.4 illustrates several of SQL/MM Full-Text's facilities.

Example 10.4 *Example Full-Text Queries*

```
/* Example of single-word search */
SELECT stock_number
FROM DVD_information
WHERE liner_notes.CONTAINS
      ('"thugs"') = 1

/* Example of phrase search */
SELECT stock_number
FROM DVD_information
WHERE liner_notes.CONTAINS
      ('"historical documents"') = 1

/* Example of context search */
SELECT stock_number
FROM DVD_information
WHERE liner_notes.CONTAINS
      ('"attacked" IN SAME SENTENCE AS "crew"') = 1

/* Example of linguistic search */
SELECT stock_number
FROM DVD_information
WHERE liner_notes.CONTAINS
      ('STEMMED FORM OF "funny"
       IN SAME PARAGRAPH AS
       SOUNDS LIKE "lions"') = 1

/* Example of ranking search */
SELECT stock_number
FROM DVD_information
WHERE 1.2 < liner_notes.RANK ('"carpet"')
```

```
/* Another example of ranking search, used with a cursor */
SELECT stock_number, liner_notes.RANK ('"carpet"') AS score
FROM DVD_information
WHERE score > 0
ORDER BY score DESCENDING

/* Example of conceptual search */
SELECT stock_number
FROM DVD_information
WHERE liner_notes.CONTAINS ('IS ABOUT "science fiction"') = 1
```

In Example 10.4, the code fragments that deserve further explanation are the ranking and conceptual search examples. The RANK function uses implementation-defined criteria, such as the number of times the specified word or phrase appears in a document, to rank documents by their relevance to the query; higher numbers imply that a document is ranked higher among all documents considered. The IS ABOUT function uses implementation-defined rules, specific to the language of the document, to determine whether the subject of a document is sufficiently related to the word or phrase specified in the query.

Some readers may be concerned with the apparently large number of details of SQL/MM Full-Text that are left implementation-defined. The reason behind this seeming carelessness with semantics is that the SQL/MM Full-Text standard's chances of success are increased if the standard doesn't completely invalidate the existing implementations of full-text capabilities. There were already several full-text products whose technology was incorporated into the SQL/MM specifications, but many of the finer details of how those various products performed certain functions varied, sometimes considerably. Worse, it turns out to be exceedingly difficult—perhaps impossible, using current technology—to describe precisely what a function like IS ABOUT does when analyzing documents. For example, should a document describing the living conditions of the common flea be returned in response to a query requesting documents using IS ABOUT 'dogs'? Such a document might well describe the conditions under which dogs acquire fleas and how the flea benefits from the relationship, but not all interested parties would agree that the document *is about* dogs. As a result, the semantics of such queries are probably best left in the category of features on which products compete.

SQL/MM Full-Text functions allow queries that respond to individual words or phrases, or any of a set of words or phrases. When you want to search for documents using functions whose results are based on the relationships between words or phrases, you may specify a thesaurus for use by the facility. Use of a thesaurus is particularly helpful when your queries involve subject matter that is highly specialized or technical.

The patterns used in query functions can also be single patterns or sets of patterns. Patterns are nothing more than words or phrases that include one or more wildcard characters, such as the underscore ("_") and percent ("%") used in SQL:1999's LIKE predicate. Patterns can also include Boolean operators such as "|" (or), "&" (and), and "NOT" (negation).

SQL/MM Full-Text defines two categories of structured types and routines. One of these categories comprises the *public* types and routines—the ones that you can use in your applications. The other category is made up of types and routines that are used for definitional purposes within the Full-Text standard.

The public types include the `FullText` type mentioned and used earlier in this section, as well as another type named `FT_Pattern`. (SQL/MM Full-Text prefixes the names of most of its types and routines with the sequence "`FT_`" to capture the fact that they are defined by the Full-Text standard. Other parts of SQL/MM follow this convention but use other letters that are associated with the specific part of the standard.)

The `FullText` type contains only two attributes: `Contents` and `Language`, each of which is defined as CHARACTER VARYING with an implementation-defined maximum length (the methods listed below use the symbol "*maxlength*" to reference this implementation-defined maximum length). In real implementations, the `Contents` attribute is probably implemented as a CLOB type to permit very large values. The type definition includes signatures of several methods. In the list below, I indicate the name of each method and the name and data type of its parameter or parameters. As you read in Chapter 4, "Routines and Routine Invocation," each method has an additional, implicit parameter that identifies a value of the structured type associated with the method.

- `Contents (pattern FT_Pattern)`
- `Contains (pattern CHARACTER VARYING(`*maxlength*`))`
- `Rank (pattern FT_Pattern)`
- `Rank (pattern CHARACTER VARYING(`*maxlength*`))`
- `Tokenize ()`
- `TokenizePosition (unit FullText_token)`
- `Segmentize (unit FullText_token)`
- `TokenizeAndStem ()`
- `TokenizePositionAndStem ()`

- `FullText (string CHARACTER VARYING(`*`maxlength`*`))`
- `FullText (string CHARACTER VARYING(`*`maxlength`*`),`
  `language CHARACTER VARYING(`*`maxlength`*`))`

The `Language` attribute is public and can be accessed by application programs; the `Contents` attribute is usable only within the methods associated with the `FullText` type.

The public methods include both versions of `Contains()`, both versions of `Rank()`, and both versions of `FullText()` (which initializes a `FullText` value). The other methods listed above are used only within the definition of the `FullText` type's semantics. In addition, the type defines an ordinary function named `FullText_to_Character()` that is used for casting `FullText` values to CHARACTER VARYING values.

The `FT_Pattern` type is a distinct type based on CHARACTER VARYING (and thus not a structured type). As you saw earlier in this section, the value of an `FT_Pattern` instance is essentially a character string whose contents obey a particular structure. SQL/MM Full-Text defines the required structure of `FT_Pattern` values through roughly three pages of BNF specified in the standard. The standard defines approximately 20 additional types that are used internally (that is, they are not public types) to construct search patterns from `FT_Pattern` values. The bulk of SQL/MM Full-Text is the definition of those additional types and the methods associated with them.

The standard also defines three SQL schemas and a variety of views and base tables used to capture metadata associated with the various facilities defined by the standard. The `FT_THESAURUS` schema includes four base tables: `TERM_DICTIONARY`, `TERM_HIERARCHY`, `TERM_SYNONYM`, and `TERM_RELATED`. These tables are populated with rows that provide information for use in stemming operations, determining related words, and so forth.

The `FT_INFORMATION_SCHEMA` and `FT_DEFINITION_SCHEMA` contain, respectively, two views and two base tables. One view and base table, each named `FT_FEATURES`, identify optional features and implementation-defined user-visible constants (like the maximum length of the `Contents` attribute of a `FullText` value). The other view and base table, each named `FT_SCHEMATA`, identify other SQL schemas that include definitions of user-defined types, methods, and functions necessary to support the functionality of SQL/MM Full-Text.

As with all standards, SQL/MM Full-Text includes a specification of how implementations can claim conformance to the standard. In this case, implementations must provide both the `FullText` type and the `FT_Pattern` type, including their public attributes and methods, as well as the casting function `FullText_to_Character()`. A conforming implementation must also provide the views of `FT_INFORMATION_SCHEMA`.

10.5 Spatial

SQL/MM provides support for Spatial data in its Part 3,[4] which specifies several SQL:1999 structured types, along with their associated methods.

Many enterprises need the ability to store, manage, and retrieve information based on aspects of spatial data, such as geometry, location, and topology. Applications making use of spatial data include automated mapping, facilities management, geographic systems, graphics, multimedia, and even integrated circuit design. The SQL/MM Spatial standard provides the interface and semantics to support such applications.

Spatial data are most often data that represent 2-dimensional and 3-dimensional concepts and real-world objects; 0-dimensional and 1-dimensional data can also be properly categorized as spatial data but often exhibit less dramatic challenges for applications. The current SQL/MM Spatial standard supports 0-dimensional (point), 1-dimensional (line, or curve), and 2-dimensional (plane, or surface) data; future revisions are expected to support 3-dimensional (volumetric shapes) and possibly data of even higher dimensions (there is significant interest in including 2- and 3-dimensional data that include a time component, commonly known as spatio-temporal data).

Spatial data typically represent real-world objects, or hypothetical objects that are expected to map to the real world. Such data can range from the microscopic—such as integrated circuit layout—to geographic—such as mapping national boundaries or continental structures. Small-scale spatial data, whether microscopic or scaled large enough to deal with municipal government data, are almost always used to represent data whose reference system is a purely flat 2-dimensional plane. Such data may have 3-dimensional aspects (the structures of integrated circuits usually have many layers, and municipal data may require representation of hilly terrain), but the data assume an underlying flat surface. By contrast, large-scale spatial data must take into account the curvature of the earth, which provides a spheroidal surface. The specific nature of the applications that use the data determines the way in which the precise nature of that surface is modeled—called the *spatial reference system*. The current version of SQL/MM Spatial provides support for a "flat world" but deals with curved surfaces through spatial reference systems.

There are, somewhat to my surprise, an astonishingly large number of spatial reference systems in common use. The vast majority of spatial reference systems are used for data that describe geographic entities and concepts on the surface of our relatively spherical planet. Some of them may treat the surface of the planet

---

4 ISO/IEC 13249-3:1999, *Information technology—Database languages—SQL Multimedia and Application Packages—Part 3: Spatial* (Geneva: International Organization for Standardization, 1999).

as a perfect sphere, which significantly reduces modeling complexities at the cost of reduced accuracy over long distances. Others recognize the fact that the earth is not a perfect sphere, but is a *spheroid*. Many spatial reference systems deal with large structures for which the curvature of the planet is significant. Consequently, various systems have evolved to describe structures in particular regions (e.g., countries, states, and provinces, etc.) for which the impacts of planet curvature vary from the impacts in other regions. For example, lines of longitude converge toward one another as one moves close to the poles—seemingly parallel lines of longitude are in fact not parallel. Spatial reference systems used in nations whose territory extends far from the equator must take into account that convergence.

In SQL/MM Spatial, spatial reference systems control such aspects of spatial data as the units used (e.g., microns, miles, kilometers), the location of the prime meridian (for geographic systems), and the specific coordinate system in use. The reference systems supported by Spatial are all defined by other authorities, including other standards bodies and governmental agencies.

Support for a wide variety of spatial reference systems is quite important to the design of SQL/MM Spatial in order for the standard to have any value to the customers of conforming products. The largest users of spatial data management systems are often governmental bodies and very large (frequently multinational) commercial enterprises that must deal with large-scale geographic data. Such users include local municipal governments (whose requirements include city planning, traffic management, and accident investigation), state and provincial governments (whose applications are highway planning, design and construction, natural resource management, economic resource allocation, etc.), national governments (which handle defense, border control, and national parks, among other activities), extractive industries (including mineral, petroleum, and water location), and farming (including plot allocation and crop yield management). Because of the economic implications of such large customers, SQL/MM Spatial's design seems to more naturally support geospatial data than smaller-scale data such as integrated circuit design and computer graphics. This appearance is confirmed by the fact that its most active designers were employed in the geospatial industry.

SQL/MM Spatial defines several structured types, including one moderately large type hierarchy (you learned about type hierarchies in Chapter 2, "User-Defined Types"). One of those hierarchies has as its most generalized type (that is, its maximal supertype) a type called `ST_Geometry` (SQL/MM Spatial prefixes the names of all of its types with "`ST_`"). That type is defined to be *not instantiable* (meaning that no instances of it can be created; Spatial defines about a half-dozen such types), but it has a number of (about a dozen) subtypes that are instantiable, such as `ST_Point`, `ST_LineString`, and `ST_MultiPolygon`.

A type (not a subtype of `ST_Geometry`, but a type in a different type hierarchy) called `ST_SpatialRefSys` is used to describe spatial reference systems. All geometric calculations that occur as part of a given query are done in the same spatial reference system (the reference system of the first `ST_Geometry` value), although a future version of the Spatial standard might relax that restriction.

The SQL/MM Spatial standard partitions the types that it defines into several categories: 0-dimensional geometry types (usually known as *point types*), 1-dimensional geometry types (which Spatial calls *curve types*), 2-dimensional geometry types (called *surface types* in the standard), geometry collection types, and spatial reference system types. Some categories include several types, as you can see in Table 10.3.

Table 10.3 *Spatial Types*

Type	*Subtype of . . .*	*Used for . . .*
ST_Geometry	*(none: maximal supertype)*	*(not instantiable)*
ST_Point	ST_Geometry	Represents points (0-dimensional objects) in 2-dimensional space.
ST_Curve	ST_Geometry	*(not instantiable)* Curves whose starting point and ending point are the same point are *closed*. Curves that do not pass through the same point more than once are *simple*. A simple closed curve is called a *ring*.
ST_LineString	ST_Curve	Represents linear interpolation between a sequence of points (that is, straight lines between consecutive points).
ST_CircularString	ST_Curve	Represents circular interpolation between points (the first circular arc is defined by the first three points—start, intermediate, and end points; subsequent arcs are defined by two points each—intermediate and end points—starting at the end point of the preceding arc).
ST_CompoundCurve	ST_Curve	Represents curves composed from straight-line segments and circular-line segments.
ST_Surface	ST_Geometry	*(not instantiable)* *Simple* surfaces are planes. *Polyhedral* surfaces are simple surfaces that adjoin other simple surfaces; in 3-dimensional space, polyhedral surfaces need not form a plane.

(continued)

Table 10.3 *(Continued)*

Type	*Subtype of . . .*	*Used for . . .*
ST_CurvePolygon	ST_Surface	Represents simple (planar) surfaces, possibly with one or more interior rings (*holes*); the boundaries may include circular arcs.
ST_Polygon	ST_CurvePolygon	Represents polygons whose boundaries contain only straight-line segments.
ST_GeomCollection	ST_Geometry	Represents a collection of zero or more ST_Geometry values (values of its subtypes, since that type is noninstantiable); all members of a collection are in the same spatial reference system.
ST_MultiPoint	ST_GeomCollection	Represents an unordered and unconnected collection of points (0-dimensional values).
ST_MultiCurve	ST_GeomCollection	Represents a collection of lines, including curves (1-dimensional values).
ST_MultiLineString	ST_MultiCurve	Represents a collection of straight lines.
ST_MultiSurface	ST_GeomCollection	Represents a collection of planes and polyhedral surfaces (2-dimensional values).
ST_MultiPolygon	ST_MultiSurface	Represents a collection of planes and polyhedral surfaces whose boundaries are formed by straight-line segments.
ST_SpatialRefSys	*(none: maximal supertype)*	Encapsulates all aspects of spatial reference system; spatial reference systems are characterized by *well-known* text representations.

Every subtype of `ST_Geometry` (including itself) includes an attribute that specifies the dimension (0, 1, or 2) of the values of that type. The definition of `ST_Geometry` includes no fewer than 31 methods, even though the type is not instantiable. Of course, all of its subtypes inherit those methods, which saves the trouble of having to define the methods in all of those subtypes. In addition, other types define additional methods of their own.

The methods defined for the `ST_Geometry` type are listed in Table 10.4. Other types are defined with appropriate methods, including constructor methods (to create new instances of the type), observer and mutator methods (to retrieve and modify the values of type instance attributes), and sometimes additional methods (to convert and transform type instances). In addition, the standard defines a number of ordinary functions (that is, functions that are not methods) to perform various tasks required by most of the types. I have omitted the methods for the types other than `ST_Geometry`, as well as the ordinary functions, in the interests of (relative) brevity, but you can learn all their details from a copy of the SQL/MM Spatial standard.

Table 10.4 *Methods Defined for ST_Geometry Type*

Method Name	*Returns . . .*
ST_Dimension()	The dimension of the specified (SELF) value
ST_CoordDim()	The coordinate dimension of the specified (SELF) value
ST_GeometryType()	The geometry type of the specified (SELF) value (e.g., 'ST_Point' is returned for values of the ST_Point type)
ST_SRID()	The Spatial Reference System Identifier of the specified (SELF) value's spatial reference system
ST_SRID (asrid INTEGER)	The specified (SELF) value modified to contain a new Spatial Reference System Identifier
ST_Transform (asrid INTEGER)	A new value that is the specified (SELF) value transformed to the (presumably different) spatial reference system identified by the provided Spatial Reference System Identifier
ST_IsEmpty()	1 (one) if and only if the specified (SELF) value corresponds to the empty set; otherwise, 0 (zero)
ST_IsSimple()	1 (one) if and only if the specified (SELF) value contains no *anomalous points* (self-intersection or self-tangency); otherwise, 0 (zero)
ST_IsValid()	1 (one) if and only if the specified (SELF) value is well-formed; otherwise, 0 (zero)
ST_Boundary()	An ST_Geometry value indicating the boundary of the specified (SELF) value
ST_Envelope()	The bounding rectangle of the (SELF) specified value
ST_ConvexHull()	The convex hull of the specified (SELF) value
ST_Buffer (adistance DOUBLE PRECISION)	A buffer, whose width is specified in the coordinate units of the associated Spatial Reference System, surrounding the specified (SELF) value
ST_Intersection (ageometry ST_Geometry)	The point set intersection of the specified (SELF) value and the argument value
ST_Union (ageometry ST_Geometry)	The point set union of the specified (SELF) value and the argument value
ST_Difference (ageometry ST_Geometry)	The point set difference of the specified (SELF) value and the argument value

(continued)

Table 10.4 *(Continued)*

Method Name	*Returns . . .*
ST_SymDifference (ageometry ST_Geometry)	The point set symmetric difference of the specified (SELF) value and the argument value
ST_Distance (ageometry ST_Geometry)	The minimum (shortest) distance between any two points in the specified (SELF) value and the argument value
ST_Equals (ageometry ST_Geometry)	1 (one) if the specified (SELF) value and the argument value are spatially equal (contain the same point set); otherwise, 0 (zero)
ST_Relate (ageometry ST_Geometry, amatrix CHARACTER(9))	1 (one) if the specified (SELF) value and the first argument value are spatially related; otherwise 0 (zero). The second argument value specifies the criteria for "spatially related" determination for each of nine possible types of intersection (such as the interior of one ST_Geometry value intersecting the boundary of the other)
ST_Disjoint (ageometry ST_Geometry)	1 (one) if the specified (SELF) value and the first argument value are spatially disjoint; otherwise 0 (zero)
ST_Intersects (ageometry ST_Geometry)	1 (one) if the specified (SELF) value and the first argument value spatially intersect; otherwise 0 (zero)
ST_Touches (ageometry ST_Geometry)	1 (one) if the specified (SELF) value touches the first argument value; otherwise 0 (zero)
ST_Crosses (ageometry ST_Geometry)	1 (one) if the specified (SELF) value crosses the first argument value; otherwise 0 (zero)
ST_Within (ageometry ST_Geometry)	1 (one) if the specified (SELF) value is spatially within the first argument value; otherwise 0 (zero)
ST_Contains (ageometry ST_Geometry)	1 (one) if the specified (SELF) value spatially contains the first argument value; otherwise 0 (zero)
ST_Overlaps (ageometry ST_Geometry)	1 (one) if the specified (SELF) value overlaps the first argument value; otherwise 0 (zero)
ST_WKTToSQL (CHARACTER LARGE OBJECT (size))	An ST_Geometry value constructed from the well-known textual representation of spatial objects (specified in the standard)
ST_AsText()	The well-known textual representation of the specified (SELF) value
ST_WKBToSQL (BINARY LARGE OBJECT (size))	An ST_Geometry value constructed from the well-known binary representation of spatial objects (specified in the standard)
ST_AsBinary()	The well-known binary representation of the specified (SELF) value

Figure 10.1 illustrates several of the SQL/MM Spatial types, which may improve your ability to visualize the various concepts involved. In the figure, I've provided a point (`ST_Point`), a collection of points (`ST_MultiPoint`), a straight line

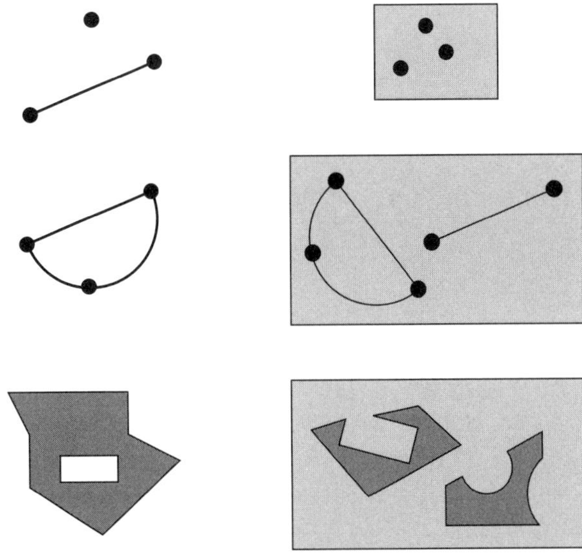

Figure 10.1 Visualization of Spatial Types

(ST_LineString), a ring made up of one straight-line segment and a circular arc (ST_CompoundCurve), a collection of curves (ST_MultiCurve), a planar surface with straight-line boundaries and a "hole" (ST_Polygon), and a collection of surfaces (ST_MultiSurface).

Many operations can be performed on Spatial data. The most common—and obvious—operations include construction of a straight line between two points and construction of a polygon from several lines or from several points. Other important operations are detection of whether two lines intersect and whether two areas overlap or are adjacent to one another.

Most Spatial types have publicly visible accessor methods (which SQL:1999 calls *observer methods*) that permit applications to extract fundamental information about instances of the type, such as determining the values of the *X* and *Y* coordinates of a point type.

Example 10.5 contains a table definition in which one column's data type is Spatial's ST_Geometry type.

Example 10.5 *A Table Containing Spatial Data*

```
CREATE TABLE CITY (
  NAME        CHARACTER VARYING(30),
  POPULATION  INTEGER,
  CITY_PARKS  CHARACTER VARYING(200) ARRAY[100],
  LOCATION    ST_GEOMETRY )
```

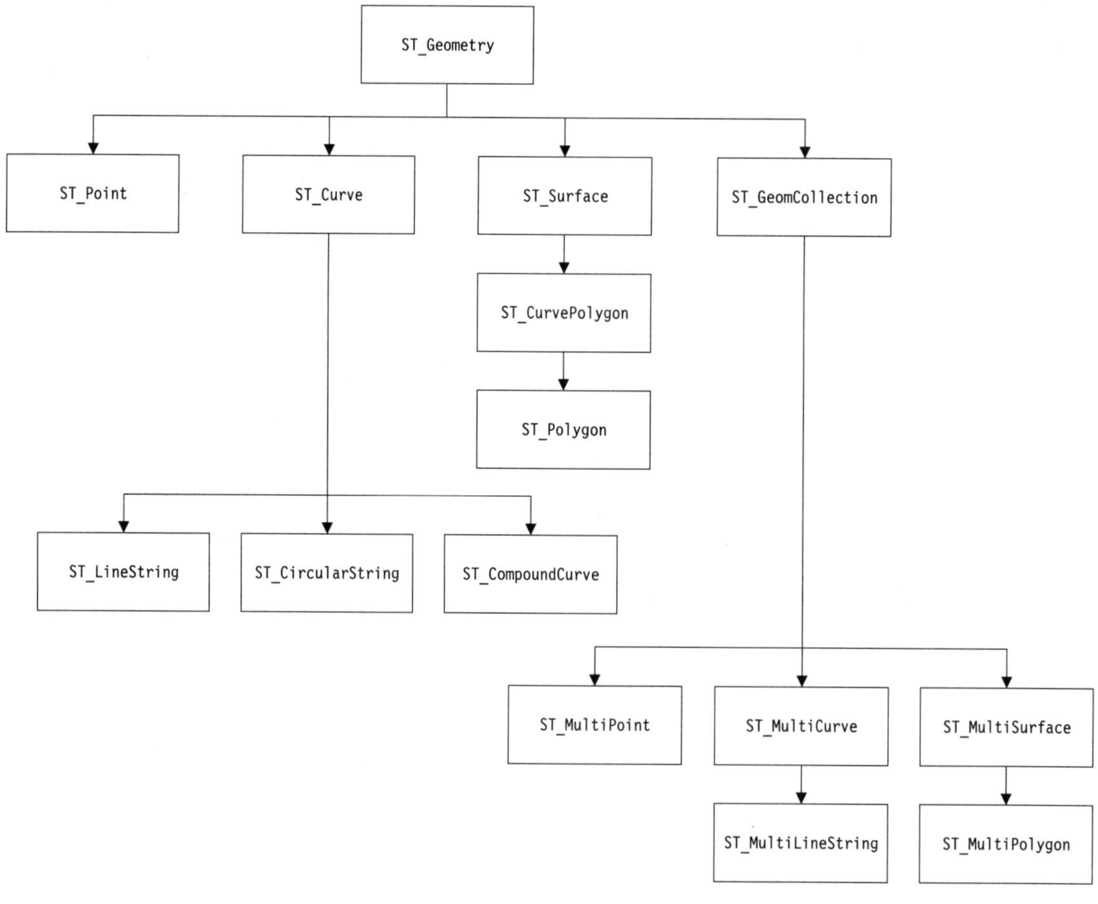

Figure 10.2 Type Hierarchy Defined by SQL/MM Spatial

Assuming the table contains the relevant data, we might determine the population and area of the city of San Francisco by executing a query like the one in Example 10.6.

Example 10.6 *Querying Spatial Data*

```
SELECT population, location.area
FROM CITY
WHERE name = 'San Francisco'
```

The expression `location.area` retrieves the `area` attribute (by invoking the observer method of the same name) of the `ST_Geometry` structured type value stored in the `location` column of the row corresponding to San Francisco.

Figure 10.2 (adapted from a figure that appears in the SQL/MM standard) captures the type hierarchy defined by SQL/MM Spatial. It gives a visual representation of the type relationships provided in Table 10.3.

I find it a bit surprising that SQL/MM Spatial does not specify an Information Schema containing views that allow applications to determine the specific types available for use. This part of SQL/MM is unique in this respect, as the other parts all define the views and underlying base tables for the part's metadata. The next generation of SQL/MM Spatial is expected to include an Information Schema. In fairness, I should point out that all of SQL/MM Spatial's types are represented in the views of the SQL:1999 Information Schema, so the metadata information is certainly available, just not in a Spatial-specific organization.

SQL/MM Spatial does include a specification of how implementations can claim conformance to the standard. The conformance clause of this standard is fairly complex, but it can be summarized in the following points:

1. Which of the following two groups of structured types are supported.
   a. `ST_Point`, `ST_LineString`, `ST_Polygon`, and `ST_GeomCollection` with noninstantiable types `ST_Geometry`, `ST_Curve`, and `ST_Surface`
   b. `ST_Point`, `ST_LineString`, `ST_Polygon`, `ST_MultiPoint`, `ST_MultiLineString`, `ST_MultiPolygon`, and `ST_GeomCollection` with noninstantiable types `ST_Geometry`, `ST_Curve`, `ST_Surface`, `ST_MultiCurve`, and `ST_MultiSurface`
2. Whether or not the SQL:1999 facility that allows method parameters and return clauses to be declared with an ARRAY type.
3. Whether or not the `ST_CircularString` and `ST_CompoundCurve` types are supported.
4. Whether or not the `ST_MultiCurve` type is instantiable.
5. Whether or not the `ST_MultiSurface` type is instantiable.
6. Whether or not the `ST_Curve` method `ST_CurveToLine()` is supported.

SQL/MM Spatial is closely related to, and essentially aligned with, other important spatial data standards being developed by another ISO Technical Committee, TC 211 (Geomatics) and by OGC, the Open GIS Consortium (*GIS* stands for *Geographic Information Systems*). Keeping standards being developed in all three forums aligned has proved politically challenging, but all participants seem committed to doing so. As a result, SQL/MM Spatial is possibly the most effective part of SQL/MM—at least in terms of having visibility and influence in the broader community.

A future version of SQL/MM Spatial currently under development may provide another pair of types, `ST_Angle` and `ST_Direction`, so applications can capture information about angles and directions. The future of Spatial likely includes support for GML 2.0, an OGC specification for representing geographic data in XML.

10.6 Still Image

Part 5 of the SQL/MM standard[5] specifies structured user-defined types for use in managing still-image data. The concept of "still image" is to be distinguished from the concept of "moving image." The latter term refers to data made up of a sequence of images that are displayed one after the other, usually in rapid succession, to create the illusion of motion or continual change; in many cases, some of those *frames* (individual images) are incomplete when considered alone, since they are formed as the difference between a preceding frame and the image they are intended to represent. By contrast, the former term implies a single frame that is entirely self-contained, and thus does not represent any implied motion. Common examples are photographs, paintings, and caricature sketches.

Still images can be represented in digital form for storage and management in computer environments in a mind-numbing number of manners. There are quite a few standards—both *de jure* and *de facto*—that specify ways to encode still images. Table 10.5 lists some of the most common of these. All of these are, in essence, 2-dimensional arrays of picture elements (often called *pixels*). All of these formats represent *raster* images made up of multiple *lines* (often hundreds or thousands of them), each containing multiple *columns* (again, hundreds or thousands of them); every column on every line is *digitized* (converted to a numeric value that represents the associated picture element).

There is another way in which digital images can be formed, commonly called *vector images*. Vector graphic images are typically made up of lines drawn from one point directly to another point (thus the term *vector*). Thus, they are commonly used to generate "line drawings" rather than "pictures," but that characterization is undoubtedly an overgeneralization of the differences between the two approaches. Vector images are typically digitized by specifying the start and end points of each line in the image, along with a specification of the characteristics of the line (e.g., its width, color, etc.).

5 ISO/IEC 13249-5:2001, *Information technology—Database languages—SQL Multimedia and Application Packages—Part 5: Still Image* (Geneva: International Organization for Standardization, 2001).

Table 10.5 *Some Common Still-Image Encoding Formats*

Format Name	*Meaning*
BMP	Bitmap
CGM	Computer Graphics Metafile
GIF	Graphics Interchange Format
JPEG (or JPG)	Joint Photographic Experts Group
PCD	Photo Compact Disc
PNG	Portable Network Graphics
TIFF (or TIF)	Tagged Image File Format
WMF	Windows Metafile Format

SQL/MM Still Image is designed specifically to deal with raster images rather than vector images. The goal of SQL/MM Still Image is to provide a way to store the images that enterprises increasingly need to conduct business and, more importantly, to allow applications and users to efficiently and effectively find those images when they are needed. (If you've ever found yourself staring in dismay at a box filled with uncataloged photographs, wondering how you'll manage to locate that picture of you when you just started school, you'll appreciate the value of computerized image searching.)

Since the technology required to effectively search digitized images is rapidly advancing, SQL/MM Still Image is designed to be readily extensible to accommodate that technology as it evolves. This standard has adopted the convention that the names of the types, methods, and functions that it defines all begin with the characters `SI_`.

The principle structured type used by Still Image is the `SI_StillImage` type. For every `SI_StillImage` value, image attributes include the raw digitized image, the length in octets of that raw image, an indication of the format (such as the formats cited in Table 10.5) in which the image is encoded, and the dimensions ("horizontal" and "vertical" sizes) of the image. The `SI_StillImage` type definition includes two constructors, one whose only argument is a BINARY LARGE OBJECT value containing the digitized image, and another whose first argument is a BINARY LARGE OBJECT value and whose second argument is a character string specifying the format of the digitized image explicitly.

`SI_StillImage` also defines four methods in addition to the default observer and mutator methods that are always provided for each attribute of the type. These methods are used to set the content of the `SI_StillImage` value (`SI_changeContent`), to set the format of the value (`SI_setFormat`), and to compute a *thumbnail* (a smaller, lower-resolution version) of the `SI_StillImage` value, either at a default size or at the size specified in arguments to the method invocation (SI_Thumbnail). The type definition further includes a number of methods that are used internally by the public methods of the type and are not available for application use.

Images have quite a few possible characteristics that are not inherent in the digitized SI_StillImage values, and SQL/MM Still Image provides five additional types to represent those characteristics.

- SI_AverageColor: A color value that represents the "average color" of an image.
- SI_ColorHistogram: A list of the relative frequencies of each color in an image.
- SI_PositionalColor: An array of the average colors of each rectangle within an image. (The number of rectangles into which an image is partitioned is implementation-defined.)
- SI_Texture: A characterization of an image by the size of repeating items (known as the image's *coarseness*), brightness variations (the image's *contrast*), and predominant direction of features (*directionality*).
- SI_FeatureList: A list containing one value each of one, two, three, or all four of the preceding types.

Images can be compared according to the values associated with their additional image characteristics. Colors are represented by values of the type SI_Color.

Each of the four structured types used to represent image characteristics have a method named SI_Score. When SI_Score is invoked on an SI_AverageColor value and an SI_StillImage value provided as an argument, it returns a non-negative number that represents how closely the average color of the SI_StillImage value matches the SI_AverageColor value. Lower numbers are returned for better matches, and 0.0 is returned for a perfect match. The average color of an SI_StillImage value can be obtained by invoking the SI_AverageColor constructor method with that image as the argument.

The SI_ColorHistogram type defines both an SI_Score method and an SI_Append method. SI_Append extends an existing histogram by appending a new pair of values that include an SI_Color value and a value that indicates the frequency with which that color is represented. The SI_Score method, when invoked on an SI_ColorHistogram value and an SI_StillImage value provided as an argument, returns a non-negative number that represents how closely the color histogram of the SI_StillImage value matches the SI_ColorHistogram value. Lower numbers are returned for better matches, and 0.0 is returned for a perfect match. The color histogram of an SI_StillImage value can be obtained by invoking the SI_ColorHistogram constructor method with that image as the argument.

The SI_PositionalColor type defines an SI_Score method that returns a value that represents how closely the specified SI_PositionalColor value matches the SI_PositionalColor value computed from the SI_StillImage value provided as the argument to the method. Lower numbers are returned for better matches, and 0.0 is returned for a perfect match. The positional color information of an SI_StillImage value can be obtained by invoking the SI_PositionalColor constructor method with that image as the argument.

The SI_Texture type stores (as an attribute) a character string value that represents the texture information of an image. While that character string value represents image characteristics such as coarseness, contrast, and directionality, it does so in an implementation-defined manner. The SI_Texture type's SI_Score method, when invoked on an SI_Texture value and an SI_StillImage value provided as an argument, returns a non-negative number that represents how closely the texture of the SI_StillImage value matches the SI_Texture value. Lower numbers are returned for better matches, and 0.0 is returned for a perfect match. The texture of an SI_StillImage value can be obtained by invoking the SI_Texture constructor method with that image as the argument.

The SI_FeatureList type captures values of the SI_AverageColor, SI_ColorHistogram, SI_PositionalColor, and SI_Texture types, along with a weight value for each of those characteristics. The SI_Score method, when invoked on an SI_FeatureList value and an SI_StillImage value provided as an argument, returns a non-negative number that represents how closely the various features captured in the SI_FeatureList value, adjusted by their weights, match the values of the corresponding characteristics of the specified SI_StillImage value. Lower numbers are returned for better matches, and 0.0 is returned for a perfect match. An SI_FeatureList value for an SI_StillImage value can be obtained by invoking the SI_ColorHistogram constructor method with that image as the argument.

Instances of the SI_Color type capture the red, blue, and green information that represents a particular color in the SQL/MM Still Image environment. It's worth noting that there are other systems for representing specific colors—known as *color spaces*—that are not currently supported by SQL/MM. Those other color spaces (including CMYK—cyan, magenta, yellow, and black—frequently used to describe printer colors) might be considered in some future version of SQL/MM Still Image, but the RGB (red, green, blue) color space is the only one supported at present.

Typical uses of SQL/MM Still Image include retrieval of images that have certain characteristics and identification (and retrieval) of images that are similar to specified images. For example, my music and video operation's new record label might want to determine whether a logo being designed for the label is overly similar to some existing label's logo. An application can test the new logo against a database of logos using a query like that in Example 10.7.

Example 10.7 *Screening an Image Against an Image Database*

```
SELECT label_name
FROM label_logos_table
WHERE 0.7 > SI_InitFeatureList ( SI_findTexture ( my_logo ), 0.75 ) .
            SI_Append ( SI_findPositionalColor ( my_logo ), 0.25 ) .
            SI_Score ( label_logo )
```

A short explanation of that query will be helpful. It specifies retrieval of the name of record labels (SELECT label_name) from a table of logos I've scanned for all other labels of which I'm aware (FROM label_logos_table). The statement retrieves only those rows for which the similarity of the label's logo (SI_Score (label_logo)) to the logo I'm considering adopting (my_logo) is less than 0.7 (a value that probably indicates that the logos are quite similar, no doubt determined by some highly competent legal source that specializes in intellectual property issues). The similarities are evaluated using a feature list created from the texture information for my new logo (SI_findTexture (my_logo)), with a weight of 0.75, and appending the positional colors (SI_findPositionalColor (my_logo)), with a weight of 0.25—implying that the texture of the image is three times as important as the color distribution.

The standard defines two SQL schemas and a variety of views and base tables used to capture metadata associated with the various facilities defined by the standard. The SI_INFORMTN_SCHEMA (no, that's not a typographical error—but I am unaware of the reason for the unusual spelling) and SI_DEFINITION_SCHEMA contain, respectively, five views and five base tables. One view and base table, each named SI_IMAGE_FORMATS, identify the various image formats supported by an implementation. Another view and base table, each named SI_IMAGE_FORMAT_CONVERSION, identify the format-to-format conversions supported by an implementation. A third view and base table, each named SI_IMAGE_FORMAT_FEATURES, identify the image formats for which specific basic features (such as SI_AverageColor or SI_Texture) are supported by an implementation. The fourth pair of view and base tables, named SI_THUMBNAIL_FORMATS, identifies the image formats from which an implementation can derive thumbnail images. The fifth and final pair, named SI_VALUES, contains rows identifying all of the implementation-defined values associated with Still Image.

Like the other parts of SQL/MM, the Still Image part includes a conformance clause. Still Image implementations must provide a number of types, including their public attributes and methods:

- `SI_StillImage`
- `SI_AverageColor`
- `SI_ColorHistogram`
- `SI_PositionalColor`
- `SI_Texture` type
- `SI_FeatureList`

A conforming implementation must also provide access to the views of `SI_INFORMTN_SCHEMA`.

10.7 Data Mining

As you have seen, the full name of the multipart standard known as *SQL/MM* is *SQL Multimedia and Application Packages*. The three parts (other than Framework) of SQL/MM described earlier in this chapter specify user-defined types that are used to manipulate data (arguably "multimedia" data) of different sorts: full-text documents, spatial data, and still images. Part 6 of SQL/MM[6] falls into the "application package" classification because it does not address "multimedia" data but deals with models and algorithms on data through the use of SQL:1999 user-defined types, rather than the direct storage of data.

Data mining is a process by which hidden information—patterns—are discovered in data, usually massive amounts of data that have been gathered for other purposes during the course of doing business. Data mining is not a process in which some (human) user guesses that some particular pattern exists in the data and then tries to prove it through analysis of that data—that process is more properly categorized as *statistics*. Instead, data mining requires that the user describe the kinds of patterns that are interesting, and the data mining algorithms find the patterns.

6 ISO/IEC 13249-6:2002 (publication expected late in 2002), *Information technology—Database languages—SQL Multimedia and Application Packages—Part 5: Data Mining* (Geneva: International Organization for Standardization, 2002).

Data mining is not a new concept. Enterprises have long wanted to use the data that they accumulate while conducting their business to learn more about their customers, their marketplace, their supply chain, and all of the various factors that affect their business. A number of approaches were taken, including On-Line Analytical Processing (OLAP) tools (see Chapter 7, "OLAP") and data mining tools. During the 1990s, a number of companies supplied data mining products that provided many of the capabilities needed by businesses. Some of these products were based on relational database systems, but the majority were dedicated applications that required users to import the data stored in another repository (often a relational database) into the data mining repository, reorganizing it into structures advantageous to the algorithms of the particular data mining product.

The designers of the SQL/MM Data Mining standard took a different approach. They specified a standardized interface to data mining algorithms that can be layered on any object-relational database system (e.g., Oracle 9i and DB2 v7.2) and even deployed as middleware when required. This interface is being deployed by database vendors concurrently with final development of the Data Mining standard. The advantages of integrating both OLAP and data mining with the database engine are many: improved performance, the ability to analyze data that is truly current, the ability to analyze ever larger amounts of data, and so forth.

In most data management environments, applications submit queries that are intended to retrieve information based on specific criteria. By contrast, in a data mining environment, applications are much more likely to ask the repository to discover what criteria are most important.

For example, a data mining engine might discover that (to use a famous, if apocryphal, example) about half of a convenience store's customers who buy both disposable diapers and beer also buy an air freshener product. This is not the sort of question that typical users would dream up by themselves—it certainly doesn't come unbidden to *my* mind—but it is precisely the kind of relationship that a data mining product is designed to discover.

Typical questions that a data mining product might be asked are, Who are my most important customers? What are the most significant attributes of those customers? and What are the trends in the values of those attributes? The first question doesn't pose much of a challenge. It's usually fairly straightforward to find out which customers have bought significant quantities of your products or services recently. However, the phrase *most important* might well have other meanings than *recent purchases*. For example, profits are not always directly related to purchases, since growth rates, service demands, and other factors can significantly affect the meaning of *importance*.

Data mining tools are also used for predictive purposes. Insurance companies must mine the data they've accumulated about their existing customers to help evaluate the risks associated with new customers. Retailers learn from mining their sales data whether they would benefit from mailing expensive color catalogs to certain classes of customer. Petrochemical companies use data mining to evaluate the probability of finding new crude oil reserves in certain types of rock formations.

The kinds of patterns that can be discovered using the facilities defined by SQL/MM Data Mining include

- Frequent combinations of values (either similar values or identical values), such as the purchases made by the apocryphal convenience shopper I mentioned above. This sort of pattern is called a *group*.
- Frequent sequences of values (again, either similar or identical) over a particular period of time. This sort of pattern is based on *time*.
- Groups of similar records based on the overall content of the records (rather than just one or two columns or fields).
- Patterns that predict the value of some particular attribute.
- Patterns that identify *deviations* from predicted values.

SQL/MM Data Mining supports four different data mining techniques. One technique, the *rule model,* allows you to search for patterns (*rules*) in the relationships between different parts of your data. A second technique, the *clustering model* (sometimes called the *segmentation model*), helps you group together data records that share common characteristics and identify the most important of those characteristics. The third technique, the *regression model,* helps you predict the ranking of new data based on an analysis of existing data. The final technique, the *classification model,* shares many concepts with the regression model but is oriented toward predicting the group or class into which new data will fit based on its relationship to existing data.

For each of those techniques, as with most data mining products, there are distinct stages through which you can mine your data. First, you have to *train* a model. Training a model involves choosing the technique most appropriate to your goals, setting some parameters that orient the model, and training the model by applying it to some data set that is of a more manageable size than your entire data warehouse. The model may be applied to your training data several times for improved validity. SQL/MM Data Mining refers to this process as the *training phase.* The training phase applies to all four data mining model techniques.

Second, if you're using the classification or regression techniques, you will usually *test* the model by applying it to known data sets. By comparing the model's predictions with the classification or ranking of that known data, you are able to evaluate how well the model has been trained. This process is called the *testing phase* in the standard. The testing phase is not used with the rule model or the clustering model.

Finally, you *apply* the model to your business data, allowing the data mining algorithms to discover the desired patterns in that data. After the model has been applied, you can use the results to improve your enterprise. The standard calls this process the *application phase*. The application phase does not apply to the rule model technique, since the rules are discovered during the training phase.

The models are supported through the use of several groups of structured user-defined types. Like the other parts of SQL/MM, data mining adopts the convention of prefixing the name of its user-defined types and routines with a particular character sequence; in this part of SQL/MM, the sequence is "DM_."

If you want to use a rule model, then the type used to define the model is named DM_RuleModel. If you prefer a classification model, then the type used to define the model is named DM_ClasModel. To create a regression model, the type used to define the model is named DM_RegressionModel. Creation of a clustering model results in definition of a type named DM_ClusteringModel.

The models are parameterized using instances of types DM_RuleSettings, DM_ClasSettings, DM_RegSettings, or DM_ClusSettings, augmented by instances of DM_RuleTask, DM_ClasTask, DM_RegTask, or DM_ClusTask, depending on the type of model being developed. The DM_RuleSettings, DM_ClasSettings, DM_RegSettings, or DM_ClusSettings type instances allow various parameters of a data mining model, such as the depth of a decision tree, to be set. The models are trained using instances of the DM_ClassificationData type.

Once a model has been created and trained, it can be tested by building instances of the DM_MiningData type that identifies test data stored in SQL tables. Instances of the DM_LogicalDataSpec type identify the columns in an SQL table that are to be used as a data source. DM_MiningData instances identify SQL tables (base tables and views are both permitted), specify the columns from that table that are to be used in the data mining model, assign aliases (names) to columns if required, and classify the columns depending on how they are to be used by the algorithms. Instances of the DM_LogicalDataSpec type map the fields of the data source (as defined by the DM_MiningData type) to fields specified by the consumer of the model (the application). This mapping is based on the aliases assigned to columns by the DM_MiningData type.

The result of testing a model is one or more instances of the DM_ClasTestResult or DM_RegTestResult type. When you invoke your model with real production data, the results are supplied as values of the `DM_ClasResult`, `DM_RegResult`, or `DM_ClusResult` type. The `DM_RuleTask`, `DM_ClasTask`, `DM_RegTask`, and `DM_ClusTask` types are used to control the actual testing and running of your models.

Table 10.6 lists the SQL/MM Data Mining user-defined types and summarizes the purpose of each type.

Table 10.6 *Data Mining Types*

Type	*Category*	*Purpose*
DM_RuleModel	Data mining models	Represents models that are the result of a search for association rules in data
DM_ClusteringModel	Data mining models	Represents models that are the result of a segmentation of data
DM_RegressionModel	Data mining models	Represents regression models
DM_ClasModel	Data mining models	Represents classification models
DM_RuleSettings	Data mining settings	Describes the settings that are used to generate an association rule model
DM_ClusSettings	Data mining settings	Describes the settings that are used to generate a segmentation model
DM_RegSettings	Data mining settings	Describes the settings that are used to generate a regression model by defining a target field and the parameters that guide the algorithms
DM_ClasSettings	Data mining settings	Describes the settings that are used to generate a classification model by defining a target field and the parameters that guide the algorithms
DM_RuleTask	Data mining settings	Represents the information about a search for classification rules, including the input data and the parameter settings; provides a method that computes an association rule model
DM_ClusTask	Data mining settings	Represents the information about a clustering task, including the input data and the parameter settings; provides a method that computes a clustering model
DM_RegTask	Data mining settings	Represents the information required to invoke the training of a regression model, including representations of the input data and the parameter settings

(continued)

Table 10.6 *(Continued)*

Type	*Category*	*Purpose*
DM_ClasTask	Data mining settings	Represents the information comprising a classification task, including the input data and the classification settings; provides a method that computes a classification model
DM_ClusResult	Data mining application results	Describes the result of an application run of a clustering model
DM_RegResult	Data mining application results	Describes the result of an application run of a regression model
DM_ClasResult	Data mining application results	Describes the result of an application run of a classification model
DM_RegTestResult	Data mining test results	Describes the result of a test run of a regression model
DM_ClasTestResult	Data mining test results	Describes the result of a test run of a classification model
DM_LogicalDataSpec	Data mining data	Abstracts the set of data mining fields, identified by their names, including their associated data mining field type ("usage"); used to represent the input data used for training a model and for testing it
DM_MiningData	Data mining data	Provides an abstraction of the input data used for training a model and for testing it
DM_ApplicationData	Data mining data	Describes the data used by an application of a model

SQL/MM Data Mining, like the other parts of this standard, specifies requirements that must be met by conforming implementations. All implementations must provide the `DM_LogicalDataSpec` and `DM_MiningData` types, as well as the group of types that implement at least one of the four modeling techniques.

Each of the modeling types can be exported from an SQL/MM Data Mining implementation into an XML format known as Predictive Model Markup Language (PMML).[7] Models represented in PMML can be imported into a Data Mining implementation, too.

As this volume goes to press, it seems likely that final progression of the SQL/MM Data Mining specification to International Standard status might be deliber-

7 Predictive Model Markup Language (PMML) 1.1 (available at *http://www.dmg.org/html/pmml_v1_1.html*).

ately delayed to ensure that it is fully compatible with a related data mining API being developed for the Java environment by a working group of the Java Community Process.

10.8 Chapter Summary

In this chapter, you read about the several parts of the SQL/MM standard. This standard is, like the SQL standard, a multipart standard including a Framework part that describes the conventions used by the other parts. Unlike SQL, however, the other parts of SQL/MM are independent of one another. All parts of SQL/MM except the Data Mining part have already been published and are currently being revised for publication as new editions. The first edition of the Data Mining part is expected to be finalized during 2002.

Chapter 11

A Look to the Future

11.1 Introduction

The earlier chapters in this volume have examined the more advanced features of SQL:1999 in considerable detail, including a review of some aspects of SQL:1999 that are covered more thoroughly in another book.[1] In addition, you've seen a "sneak preview" of a brand-new part of SQL, SQL/XML, that is not even part of the SQL:1999 edition of the standard, as well as a short examination of a related standard, SQL/MM. No doubt you will be interested in an update of what the next generation of SQL will bring. The first volume of this book gave you a late-2000 snapshot of the status, and this volume brings that information up to date.

The democratic nature of the standardization process makes it impossible to know with certainty what the future may bring for the SQL standard, but I'm willing to hazard a guess based on my participation in the various groups involved in its development. Both the ISO group and the ANSI group have, since late 1999, been busy working on the next generation of the SQL standard, which was initially given the working title "SQL:200*n*." The name SQL:200*n* was chosen to help encourage republication of the standard about three years after SQL:1999, thus avoiding the extremely long seven-year cycle between SQL-92 and SQL:1999. In recent months, the schedule has become a bit firmer, and I predict that "200*n*" will actually be "2003." One important implication of the use of date-based project nomenclature is that the standards organizations have adopted

1 Jim Melton and Andrew Eisenberg, *Understanding SQL and Java Together: A Guide to SQLJ, JDBC, and Related Technologies* (San Francisco: Morgan Kaufmann Publishers, 2000).

the goal of becoming more schedule-driven and less feature-driven. Whether this attitude will result in more-timely publication of less-ambitious editions of the standard remains to be seen, but I find the change quite promising.

11.2 Additional Parts of SQL:1999

In Chapter 8, "SQL/OLB and SQL/JRT," you learned that a new part of the SQL standard, Part 13 (SQL/JRT), has just (as of the publication date of this volume) been published as an International Standard. Like all other parts of SQL, SQL/JRT immediately became the subject of revision; it is already being updated as part of the next generation of the standard.

In Chapter 9, "SQL/XML," I told you about another new part of SQL, Part 14 (SQL/XML), which started its first formal steps toward publication as a standard only in mid-2002. SQL/XML has excited the interest of every SQL database vendor of which I am aware and has attracted attention from the user community as well. Will SQL/XML serve as a bridge between the relational world of SQL and the semistructured world of XML? Or will it begin the transition of an industry from SQL into a new and different data management paradigm? While there is no shortage of observers who argue that SQL's day is done and a new day awaits us, I observe that relational systems have repeatedly risen to meet serious challenges before this one, and I don't expect them to give up without a fight. In fact, I am inclined to believe that the enormous investment that has been made in making SQL systems faster, more robust, more reliable, and more powerful than any previous data management system will prove impossible to overcome.

Finally, in complete candor, I have to admit that I had hoped to tell you about yet another part of SQL that would be progressing toward standardization by now. The academic and user communities have shown interest in "temporal SQL" for several years, and the SQL vendors have struggled to find a true business justification for implementing temporal facilities into their products. Unfortunately, the economic conditions that prevailed in late 2000 and throughout 2001 have made it impossible for the resources to be allocated to build temporal extensions to SQL without significantly greater demand from major customers in the marketplace. It was with some regret that the ANSI and ISO SQL groups withdrew the SQL/Temporal project from further development in late 2001, but some of us hope that interest in the technology might be revived and that standardization might continue in the future.

11.3 SQL:2003 and Beyond

It seems quite likely that the fourth major generation of the SQL standard will be published as both an International Standard and an American National Standard sometime in 2003.

In the first volume of this book, several new features were mentioned as having a high probability of being part of SQL:2003. An update on those features should be interesting.

- New data types: It now seems probable that the only new collection type that will be included in SQL:2003 is MULTISET, since LIST can be characterized as a sequenced MULTISET and SET as a MULTISET without duplicates. As you read in Chapter 9, "SQL/XML," a new XMLType seems likely, too.
- Enhancements to triggers: After the first formal round of ballots on the SQL:2003 documents, it no longer seems likely that SQL:2003 will specify a facility to define triggers on views.
- SQL-invoked routines: It remains likely that SQL-invoked routines will be able to return MULTISETs of ROWs to their invokers.
- Improved security features: The current drafts of SQL:2003 already contain support for execution of SQL-invoked routines using invoker's rights, so standardization of the capability seems likely.
- Object capabilities: Must to my surprise, there has been little work done on adding the Java-like notion of *interface* to SQL:2003, but interest continues among some participants. The probability of this item is lower than I would have thought, but certainly not zero.

It would be fair to conclude from this update that the differences between SQL:1999 and SQL:2003 are likely to be fairly modest, certainly by comparison with the rather dramatic increase in size and functionality between SQL-92 and SQL:1999. I don't believe that absence of massive change is in any way "bad." It reflects both the much shorter development cycle of SQL:2003 and (more important, I think) the increasing maturity of SQL as a data management sublanguage. While SQL's evolution is likely to continue for a while yet, it has definitely reached a stage in its life where its current facilities satisfy the great majority of its users (and offer sufficient challenges to its implementers).

Readers should not consider SQL standardization "done" in any sense of the word. While it may be true that no great extensions of the language are currently on the drawing board, SQL's designers will continue to find and correct errors that are discovered in the various parts of the standard. It also seems likely that, for the foreseeable future, implementers will find and propose new features as their markets request them, and that new parts or new editions of the SQL standard will include them. SQL is likely to remain a vibrant and popular data management standard for more than a few additional years.

11.4 Chapter Summary

In this brief chapter, I have given you my thoughts about where the SQL standard is likely to go in its next edition. As you read, it seems unlikely that dramatic changes should be anticipated, but minor evolution—and, most definitely, bug fixing—will continue for the foreseeable future.

Appendix A

An SQL:1999 Example Using UDTs

A.1 Introduction

In the first volume of this book, the corresponding appendix (Appendix B, "An SQL:1999 Application Example") contained an application example using the features of SQL:1999 that were discussed in that volume. In this appendix, you will see a variation of the other volume's example adapted to use structured user-defined types. While the code examples here don't form a complete application in every detail, they do capture in one place many of the features discussed in this volume. Naturally, the examples in this appendix are based on the music and video store used in the rest of the book.

A.2 The Schema Definition

The following schema definition creates the application schema along with several base tables, views, user-defined types, and routines, some of which are used in the remainder of the appendix. The choices in this appendix of whether to model some piece of information as a user-defined type versus modeling it as colums of SQL built-in types, as well as the choices of creating typed tables versus ordinary SQL base tables, were made primarily on the basis of demonstrating various language features. If I were building a real application, greater consistency of choice would be appropriate.

```
CREATE SCHEMA video_and_music
    AUTHORIZATION m_s_enterprises
    DEFAULT CHARACTER SET "Latin-1"

-- The definition of the schema for the company includes definitions
--   of base tables, views, privileges, referential constraints,
--   integrity constraints, assertions, and domains.
-- It also includes definitions of user-defined types and
--   their associated methods and other routines.
-- Next, we create the base tables required for the application.

/* A distinct type for money is defined; the precision is unnecessarily
   large for many purposes, but not harmful */

CREATE DISTINCT TYPE money AS DECIMAL ( 9,2 ) ;
/* The movie type includes several attributes that are associated
   with a film, as opposed to the DVD or VHS tape on which the film
   might be distributed.  Its definition includes two methods. */

CREATE TYPE movie
  AS (
    movie_ID                      INTEGER,
    title                         CHARACTER VARYING ( 100 ),
    year_released                 SMALLINT,
    genre                         CHARACTER VARYING ( 20 ) ARRAY [ 10 ],
    description                   CHARACTER VARYING ( 300 ),
    long_description              CHARACTER LARGE OBJECT ( 2500 ),
    run_time                      INTEGER,
    MPAA_rating                   CHARACTER ( 4 )
  )
  INSTANTIABLE
  NOT FINAL
  METHOD length_interval ( )
    RETURNS INTERVAL HOUR ( 2 ) TO MINUTE
  METHOD family_fare ( )
    RETURNS BOOLEAN ;
```

```
CREATE INSTANCE METHOD length_interval ( )
    RETURNS INTERVAL HOUR ( 2 ) TO MINUTE
    FOR movie
  /* Allow for movies as long as 99 hours and 59 minutes */
  RETURN CAST ( CAST ( SELF.run_time AS INTERVAL ( 4 ) )
           AS INTERVAL HOUR ( 2 ) TO MINUTE ) ;

CREATE INSTANCE METHOD family_fare ( )
    RETURNS BOOLEAN
    FOR movie
  /* Movies rated G and PG return True; movies without a rating
     return Unknown; others return False */
  RETURN CASE
           WHEN SELF.MPAA_rating = 'G' THEN TRUE
           WHEN SELF.MPAA_rating = 'PG' THEN TRUE
           WHEN SELF.MPAA_rating = ' ' THEN UNKNOWN
           WHEN SELF.MPAA_rating IS NULL THEN UNKNOWN
           ELSE FALSE
         END ;

/* The movies table specifies information about media that our shop
   carries for various films, tracking costs, sales information, and
   rental information about both DVDs and VHS tapes. */

CREATE TABLE movies (
    stock_number                 CHARACTER ( 10 )
        CONSTRAINT movies_stock_number_not_null NOT NULL,
    movie                        movie,
    part_of_series               CHARACTER ( 3 ),
    our_tape_cost                money,
    regular_tape_sale_price      money,
    current_tape_sale_price      money,
    tapes_in_stock               INTEGER,
    total_tape_units_sold        INTEGER,
    total_tape_sales_revenue     money,
    our_dvd_cost                 money,
    regular_dvd_sale_price       money,
    current_dvd_sale_price       money,
    dvds_in_stock                INTEGER,
    total_dvd_units_sold         INTEGER,
    total_dvd_sales_revenue      money,
```

```
    CONSTRAINT movies_primary_key
      PRIMARY KEY ( stock_number )
);

/* The movie_stars table associates actors and actresses with the films
   in which they have appeared. */

CREATE TABLE movie_stars (
    movie_title                 CHARACTER VARYING ( 100 ),
        CONSTRAINT movie_stars_movie_title_not_null NOT NULL,
    year_released               SMALLINT,
    actor_last_name             CHARACTER VARYING ( 35 ),
        CONSTRAINT movies_star_actor_last_name_not_null NOT NULL,
    actor_first_name            CHARACTER VARYING ( 25 ),
    actor_middle_name           CHARACTER VARYING ( 25 ),
    CONSTRAINT movie_stars_unique
      UNIQUE ( movie_title, year_released,
               actor_last_name, actor_first_name, actor_middle_name )
        NOT DEFERRABLE,
    CONSTRAINT movie_stars_fk_movie_titles
      CHECK ( ( movie_title, year_released )
            = SOME ( SELECT movie.title, movie.year_released
                       FROM movies ) )
);

/* The music_titles table captures information about the media carried
   by our shop for various music titles */

CREATE TABLE music_titles (
    music_id                    CHARACTER ( 10 )
      CONSTRAINT music_titles_music_id_primary_key PRIMARY KEY,
    title                       CHARACTER ( 50 )
      CONSTRAINT music_titles_title_not_null NOT NULL,
    artist                      CHARACTER ( 40 ),
    artist_more                 CHARACTER ( 50 ),
    record_label                CHARACTER ( 25 ),
    greatest_hits_collection    BOOLEAN,
    category                    CHARACTER ( 20 ),
    date_released               DATE,
```

```
    cd_list_price              money,
    cd_current_price           money,
    cassette_list_price        money,
    cassette_current_price     money
) ;

/* The music_distributors structured type defines attributes for
   information we must know about each of the distributors from which
   we buy music media. */

CREATE TYPE music_distributors AS (
    distributor_id             CHARACTER ( 15 ),
    distributor_name           CHARACTER ( 25 ),
    distributor_address        CHARACTER ( 40 ),
    distributor_city           CHARACTER ( 30 ),
    distributor_state          CHARACTER ( 2 ),
    distributor_zip_code_full  CHARACTER ( 10 ),
    distributor_phone_1        CHARACTER ( 10 ),
    distributor_phone_2        CHARACTER ( 10 ),
    distributor_fax_number_1   CHARACTER ( 10 ),
    distributor_fax_number_2   CHARACTER ( 10 ),
    distributor_web_site_addr  CHARACTER ( 40 )
) ;

/* The music_distributors table is a typed table of music_distributor
   type instances. */

CREATE TABLE music_distributors
  OF music_distributors (
    REF IS dist_ref SYSTEM GENERATED,
    distributor_id WITH OPTIONS
      CONSTRAINT music_distributors_distributor_id_not_null NOT NULL,
    distributor_name WITH OPTIONS
      CONSTRAINT music_distributors_distributor_name_not_null NOT NULL
) ;

/* The music_inventory table captures current inventory about music
   media that we stock, but (naturally) only for music that we track,
   which is enforced through a foreign key constraint */
```

```
CREATE TABLE music_inventory (
    music_id                      CHARACTER ( 10 )
      CONSTRAINT music_inventory_music_id NOT NULL
      CONSTRAINT music_inventory_fk_music_titles
        REFERENCES music_titles,
    number_cd_now_in_stock        INTEGER,
    number_cassette_now_in_stock  INTEGER,
    total_cd_sold                 INTEGER,
    total_cassette_sold           INTEGER,
    total_cd_returned             INTEGER,
    total_cassette_returned       INTEGER
) ;

/* The current_distributor_costs table references music_distributors
   instances by means of a REF type */

CREATE TABLE current_distributor_costs (
    music_id                      CHARACTER ( 10 )
      CONSTRAINT current_distributor_costs_music_id_not_null NOT NULL
      CONSTRAINT current_distributor_costs_fk_music_titles
        REFERENCES music_titles,
    distributor                   REF(music_distributors)
      SCOPE music_distributors,
    our_cd_cost                   money,
    our_cassette_cost             money
) ;

/* The address type captures the basics of mail addresses */

CREATE TYPE address
  AS (
    street                        CHARACTER VARYING ( 35 ),
    city                          CHARACTER VARYING ( 40 ),
    country                       CHARACTER ( 3 )
  ) ;

/* An ordering function is needed to allow comparisons of addresses */

CREATE ORDERING FOR address EQUALS ONLY BY STATE ;

/* The US_address type extends the address type for US-style addresses */
```

```
CREATE TYPE US_address
  UNDER address AS (
    state                   CHARACTER ( 2 ),
    zip                     ROW (
                              basic   INTEGER,
                              plus4   SMALLINT )
  )
    METHOD zipcode ( )
      RETURNS CHARACTER VARYING ( 10 );

CREATE INSTANCE METHOD zipcode ( )
    RETURNS CHARACTER VARYING ( 10 )
    FOR US_address
  BEGIN
    IF SELF.zip.plus4 IS NULL
      THEN RETURN CAST ( SELF.zip.basic AS CHARACTER VARYING ( 5 ) );
      ELSE RETURN CAST ( SELF.zip.basic AS CHARACTER VARYING ( 5 ) )
              || '-'
              || CAST ( SELF.zip.plus4 AS CHARACTER VARYING ( 4 ) );
    ENDIF;
  END ;

/* The customers table assumes US-style addresses, as we are not yet
   able to process international orders */

CREATE TABLE customers (
    cust_last_name          CHARACTER ( 35 )
       CONSTRAINT customers_cust_last_name_not_null NOT NULL,
    cust_first_name         name
       CONSTRAINT customers_cust_first_name_not_null NOT NULL,
    cust_address            US_address,
    cust_phone              CHARACTER ( 10 ),
    cust_fax                CHARACTER ( 10 ),
    cust_e_mail_address     CHARACTER ( 30 ),
    cust_credit_card        CHARACTER VARYING ( 20 )
      CONSTRAINT customers_cust_credit_card_not_null NOT NULL,
    cust_current_charges    money,
    cust_total_charges      money,
    number_of_problems      SMALLINT,
    last_access             TIMESTAMP
) ;
```

```
/* Similarly, all employees are currently US residents */

CREATE TABLE employees (
    emp_id                  INTEGER
        CONSTRAINT employees_emp_id_pk PRIMARY KEY,
    emp_last_name           CHARACTER ( 35 ),
        CONSTRAINT employees_emp_last_name_not_null NOT NULL,
    emp_first_name          CHARACTER ( 25 ),
        CONSTRAINT employees_emp_first_name_not_null NOT NULL,
    emp_address             US_address,
    emp_phone               CHARACTER ( 10 ),
    emp_start_date          DATE,
    emp_hourly_rate         money
) ;

-- Third, we create a few views that help us manage some aspects
--  of our business.

CREATE VIEW problem_customers ( last, first, addr, city, state, email )
  AS
    SELECT cust_last_name, cust_first_name, cust_address.street,
           cust_address.city, cust_address.state,
           cust_e_mail_address
      FROM customers
      WHERE number_of_problems
          > 0.8 * ( SELECT MAX ( number_of_problems )
                     FROM customers ) ;

CREATE VIEW employee_customers AS
    SELECT emp_id, cust_current_charges
    FROM customers INNER JOIN employees
      ON cust_last_name = emp_last_name AND
         cust_first_name = emp_first_name AND
         cust_address = emp_address AND
         cust_phone = emp_phone
    WHERE cust_total_charges > 1000.00 AND
          emp_hourly_rate < 5.00 ;

CREATE VIEW emp_view AS
    SELECT emp_id, emp_last_name, emp_first_name, emp_address.street,
           emp_address.city, emp_address.state, emp_address.zip,
           emp_phone, emp_start_date, emp_hourly_rate
```

```
    FROM employees
    WHERE emp_id = SESSION_USER ;

-- The next thing we do is define the various privileges required
--  by our employees, managers, auditors, etc., to do their jobs.

GRANT USAGE ON TYPE movie
    TO store_manager WITH GRANT OPTION ;

GRANT EXECUTE ON INSTANCE METHOD movie_ID FOR movie
    TO store_manager WITH GRANT OPTION ;

GRANT EXECUTE ON INSTANCE METHOD movie_ID(INTEGER) FOR movie
    TO store_manager WITH GRANT OPTION ;

GRANT EXECUTE ON INSTANCE METHOD title FOR movie
    TO store_manager WITH GRANT OPTION ;

GRANT EXECUTE ON INSTANCE METHOD title(CHARACTER VARYING(100)) FOR movie
    TO store_manager WITH GRANT OPTION ;

GRANT EXECUTE ON INSTANCE METHOD year_released FOR movie
    TO store_manager WITH GRANT OPTION ;

GRANT EXECUTE ON INSTANCE METHOD year_released(SMALLINT) FOR movie
    TO store_manager WITH GRANT OPTION ;

GRANT EXECUTE ON INSTANCE METHOD genre FOR movie
    TO store_manager WITH GRANT OPTION ;

GRANT EXECUTE ON INSTANCE METHOD genre(CHARACTER VARYING(20) ARRAY[10])
    FOR movie
    TO store_manager WITH GRANT OPTION ;

GRANT EXECUTE ON INSTANCE METHOD description FOR movie
    TO store_manager WITH GRANT OPTION ;

GRANT EXECUTE ON INSTANCE METHOD description(CHARACTER VARYING(300))
    FOR movie
 TO store_manager WITH GRANT OPTION ;
```

```
GRANT EXECUTE ON INSTANCE METHOD long_description FOR movie
    TO store_manager WITH GRANT OPTION ;

GRANT EXECUTE ON INSTANCE METHOD
    long_description(CHARACTER LARGE OBJECT(2500)) FOR movie
    TO store_manager WITH GRANT OPTION ;

GRANT EXECUTE ON INSTANCE METHOD run_time FOR movie
    TO store_manager WITH GRANT OPTION ;

GRANT EXECUTE ON INSTANCE METHOD run_time(INTEGER) FOR movie
    TO store_manager WITH GRANT OPTION ;

GRANT EXECUTE ON INSTANCE METHOD MPAA_rating FOR movie
    TO store_manager WITH GRANT OPTION ;

GRANT EXECUTE ON INSTANCE METHOD MPAA_rating(CHARACTER(4)) FOR movie
    TO store_manager WITH GRANT OPTION ;

GRANT EXECUTE ON INSTANCE METHOD length_interval FOR movie
    TO store_manager WITH GRANT OPTION ;

GRANT EXECUTE ON INSTANCE METHOD family_fare FOR movie
    TO store_manager WITH GRANT OPTION ;

GRANT USAGE ON TYPE money
    TO store_manager WITH GRANT OPTION ;

GRANT ALL PRIVILEGES ON TABLE movies
    TO store_manager WITH GRANT OPTION ;

GRANT ALL PRIVILEGES ON TABLE movie_stars
    TO store_manager WITH GRANT OPTION ;

GRANT ALL PRIVILEGES ON TABLE music_titles
    TO store_manager WITH GRANT OPTION ;

GRANT USAGE ON TYPE music_distributors
    TO store_manager WITH GRANT OPTION ;
```

```
GRANT EXECUTE ON INSTANCE METHOD distributor_id FOR music_distributors
    TO store_manager WITH GRANT OPTION ;

GRANT EXECUTE ON INSTANCE METHOD distributor_id(CHARACTER(15))
    FOR music_distributors
    TO store_manager WITH GRANT OPTION ;

GRANT EXECUTE ON INSTANCE METHOD distributor_name FOR music_distributors
    TO store_manager WITH GRANT OPTION ;

GRANT EXECUTE ON INSTANCE METHOD distributor_name(CHARACTER(25))
    FOR music_distributors
    TO store_manager WITH GRANT OPTION ;

GRANT EXECUTE ON INSTANCE METHOD distributor_address
    FOR music_distributors
    TO store_manager WITH GRANT OPTION ;

GRANT EXECUTE ON INSTANCE METHOD distributor_address(CHARACTER(40))
    FOR music_distributors
    TO store_manager WITH GRANT OPTION ;

GRANT EXECUTE ON INSTANCE METHOD distributor_city
    FOR music_distributors
    TO store_manager WITH GRANT OPTION ;

GRANT EXECUTE ON INSTANCE METHOD distributor_city(CHARACTER(30))
    FOR music_distributors
    TO store_manager WITH GRANT OPTION ;

GRANT EXECUTE ON INSTANCE METHOD distributor_state
    FOR music_distributors
    TO store_manager WITH GRANT OPTION ;

GRANT EXECUTE ON INSTANCE METHOD distributor_state(CHARACTER(2))
    FOR music_distributors
    TO store_manager WITH GRANT OPTION ;

GRANT EXECUTE ON INSTANCE METHOD distributor_zip_code_full
    FOR music_distributors
    TO store_manager WITH GRANT OPTION ;
```

```
GRANT EXECUTE ON INSTANCE METHOD distributor_zip_code_full(CHARACTER(10))
    FOR music_distributors
    TO store_manager WITH GRANT OPTION ;

GRANT EXECUTE ON INSTANCE METHOD distributor_phone_1
    FOR music_distributors
    TO store_manager WITH GRANT OPTION ;

GRANT EXECUTE ON INSTANCE METHOD distributor_phone_1(CHARACTER(10))
    FOR music_distributors
    TO store_manager WITH GRANT OPTION ;

GRANT EXECUTE ON INSTANCE METHOD distributor_phone_2
    FOR music_distributors
    TO store_manager WITH GRANT OPTION ;

GRANT EXECUTE ON INSTANCE METHOD distributor_phone_2(CHARACTER(10))
    FOR music_distributors
    TO store_manager WITH GRANT OPTION ;

GRANT EXECUTE ON INSTANCE METHOD distributor_fax_number_1
    FOR music_distributors
    TO store_manager WITH GRANT OPTION ;

GRANT EXECUTE ON INSTANCE METHOD distributor_fax_number_1(CHARACTER(10))
    FOR music_distributors
    TO store_manager WITH GRANT OPTION ;

GRANT EXECUTE ON INSTANCE METHOD distributor_fax_number_2
    FOR music_distributors
    TO store_manager WITH GRANT OPTION ;

GRANT EXECUTE ON INSTANCE METHOD distributor_fax_number_2(CHARACTER(10))
    FOR music_distributors
    TO store_manager WITH GRANT OPTION ;

GRANT EXECUTE ON INSTANCE METHOD web_site_addr
    FOR music_distributors
    TO store_manager WITH GRANT OPTION ;
```

```
GRANT EXECUTE ON INSTANCE METHOD web_site_addr(CHARACTER(40))
    FOR music_distributors
    TO store_manager WITH GRANT OPTION ;

GRANT ALL PRIVILEGES ON TABLE music_distributors
    TO store_manager WITH GRANT OPTION ;

GRANT ALL PRIVILEGES ON TABLE music_inventory
    TO store_manager WITH GRANT OPTION ;

GRANT ALL PRIVILEGES ON TABLE current_distributor_costs
    TO store_manager WITH GRANT OPTION ;

GRANT USAGE ON TYPE address
    TO store_manager WITH GRANT OPTION ;

GRANT EXECUTE ON INSTANCE METHOD street FOR address
    TO store_manager WITH GRANT OPTION ;

GRANT EXECUTE ON INSTANCE METHOD street(CHARACTER VARYING(35))
    FOR address
    TO store_manager WITH GRANT OPTION ;

GRANT EXECUTE ON INSTANCE METHOD city FOR address
    TO store_manager WITH GRANT OPTION ;

GRANT EXECUTE ON INSTANCE METHOD city (CHARACTER VARYING(40))
    FOR address
    TO store_manager WITH GRANT OPTION ;

GRANT EXECUTE ON INSTANCE METHOD country FOR address
    TO store_manager WITH GRANT OPTION ;

GRANT EXECUTE ON INSTANCE METHOD country(CHARACTER(3)) FOR address
    TO store_manager WITH GRANT OPTION ;

GRANT USAGE ON TYPE US_address
    TO store_manager WITH GRANT OPTION ;

GRANT EXECUTE ON INSTANCE METHOD state FOR US_address
    TO store_manager WITH GRANT OPTION ;
```

```
GRANT EXECUTE ON INSTANCE METHOD state(CHARACTER(2)) FOR US_address
    TO store_manager WITH GRANT OPTION ;

GRANT EXECUTE ON INSTANCE METHOD zip FOR US_address
    TO store_manager WITH GRANT OPTION ;

GRANT EXECUTE ON INSTANCE METHOD zip(ROW(basic INTEGER,
                                          plus4 SMALLINT)) FOR US_address
    TO store_manager WITH GRANT OPTION ;

GRANT EXECUTE ON INSTANCE METHOD zipcode FOR US_address
    TO store_manager WITH GRANT OPTION ;

GRANT ALL PRIVILEGES ON TABLE customers
    TO store_manager WITH GRANT OPTION ;

GRANT ALL PRIVILEGES ON TABLE employees
    TO store_manager WITH GRANT OPTION ;

GRANT ALL PRIVILEGES ON TABLE problem_customers
    TO store_manager WITH GRANT OPTION ;

GRANT ALL PRIVILEGES ON TABLE employee_customers
    TO store_manager WITH GRANT OPTION ;

GRANT ALL PRIVILEGES ON TABLE emp_view
    TO store_manager WITH GRANT OPTION ;

GRANT SELECT ( movie,
               regular_tape_sale_price, current_tape_sale_price,
               regular_dvd_sale_price, current_dvd_sale_price,
               part_of_series ) ON TABLE movies
    TO PUBLIC ;

GRANT EXECUTE ON INSTANCE METHOD title() FOR movie
    TO PUBLIC ;

GRANT EXECUTE ON INSTANCE METHOD year_released() FOR movie
    TO PUBLIC ;
```

```
GRANT EXECUTE ON INSTANCE METHOD genre() FOR movie
    TO PUBLIC ;

GRANT SELECT ON TABLE movies
    TO movie_clerk ;

GRANT UPDATE ( tapes_in_stock, dvds_in_stock,
               total_tape_units_sold, total_dvd_units_sold,
               total_tape_sales_revenue, total_dvd_sales_revenue )
            ON TABLE movies
    TO movie_clerk ;

GRANT INSERT ON TABLE movies
    TO movie_clerk ;

GRANT DELETE ON TABLE movies
    TO movie_clerk ;

GRANT INSERT ON TABLE movie_stars
    TO movie_clerk ;

GRANT SELECT ON TABLE movie_stars
    TO PUBLIC ;

GRANT SELECT ( title, artist, artist_more, record_label,
               greatest_hits_collection, category, date_released,
               cd_list_price, cd_current_price, cassette_list_price,
               cassette_current_price )
            ON TABLE music_titles
    TO PUBLIC ;

GRANT SELECT ON TABLE music_titles
    TO music_clerk ;

GRANT UPDATE ( number_cd_now_in_stock, number_cassette_now_in_stock,
               total_cd_sold, total_cassette_sold,
               total_cd_returned, total_cassette_returned )
            ON TABLE music_inventory
    TO music_clerk ;
```

```
GRANT INSERT ON TABLE music_titles
   TO music_clerk ;

GRANT DELETE ON TABLE music_titles
   TO music_clerk ;

GRANT REFERENCES ON TABLE music_titles
   TO music_clerk ;

GRANT SELECT ( cust_last_name, cust_first_name, cust_address,
               cust_phone, cust_fax,
               cust_e_mail_address, cust_credit_card )
            ON TABLE customers
   TO register_clerk ;

GRANT UPDATE ( cust_current_charges, cust_total_charges,
               number_of_problems, last_access )
            ON TABLE customers
   TO register_clerk ;

GRANT INSERT ON TABLE customers
   TO register_clerk ;

/* Finally, we create a couple of assertions that will implement
     rules placed on us by our bank. */

/* First, the bank doesn't allow us to stock more than one million
     dollars' worth of CDs and cassettes */

CREATE ASSERTION limit_total_movie_stock_value
   CHECK ( ( SELECT SUM ( ( our_tape_cost * tapes_in_stock ) +
                          ( our_dvd_cost * dvds_in_stock ) )
             FROM movies )
        < 1000000.00 ) ;

/* In addition, once we have 10 problem customers, we are required
     to stop sales until we figure out how to reduce that number */

CREATE ASSERTION do_not_sell_to_many_problem_customers
   CHECK ( ( SELECT COUNT(*)
             FROM customers
```

```
        WHERE cust_total_charges > 150.00 AND
              cust_total_charges < 1000.00 AND
              number_of_problems > 5 )
  < 10 ) ;
```

A.3 Application Code

Instead of including complete SQL modules or embedded host programs, which you can learn about in the first volume of this book, the examples in this volume are made up of a series of individual SQL statements.

A.3.1 Data Input

1. Insert a new movie title, including information about the movie's stars

```
INSERT INTO movies
  VALUES (
    'SF139-486C',         -- Our stock number
    NEW movie (           -- Create a new movie instance
      86856,              -- The unique movie identifier
      'The Adventures of Buckaroo Banzai Across the 8th Dimension',
      1984,               -- The year the film was released
                          -- An array of genre names
      ARRAY [ 'Science Fiction', 'Comedy', 'Adventure' ],
      'Beings from Another Dimension have invaded your world. ' ||
        'You can''t see them...but they can see you. ' ||
        'Your only hope is Buckaroo Banzai.',
      'Buckaroo Banzai is a rock-star/brain-surgeon/' ||
        'comic-book-hero/samurai/ etc who along with his ' ||
        'group, the Hong Kong Cavaliers, must stop evil ' ||
        'creatures from the 8th dimension (all named John) ' ||
        'who are trying to conquer our dimension. He is ' ||
        'helped by Penny Pretty, who is a dead ringer for his ' ||
        'ex-wife, and some good extra-dimensional beings who ' ||
        'look and talk like they are from Jamaica.',
      116,                -- Runtime in minutes
      'PG'                -- Parental Guidance suggested
    ),
```

```
    'No',                     -- Not part of a series
    CAST (5.00 AS money),     -- VHS tape information
    CAST (9.99 AS money),     -- These values are exact numeric, but
    CAST (7.49 AS money),     --   we must coerce them to the money type
    17, 0,                    -- (No sales yet; we just started stocking)
    CAST (0.00 AS money),
    CAST (11.00 AS money), -- DVD information
    CAST (19.99 AS money),
    CAST (12.99 AS money),
    15, 0,                    -- (No sales yet; we just started stocking)
    CAST (0.00 AS money),
  ) ;

INSERT INTO movie_stars
  VALUES (
    'The Adventures of Buckaroo Banzai Across the 8th Dimension',
    1984,
    'Weller', 'Peter', NULL          -- Actor name information
  ) ;

INSERT INTO movie_stars
  VALUES (
    'The Adventures of Buckaroo Banzai Across the 8th Dimension',
    1984,
    'Lithgow', 'John', NULL          -- Actor name information
  ) ;

INSERT INTO movie_stars
  VALUES (
    'The Adventures of Buckaroo Banzai Across the 8th Dimension',
    1984,
    'Barkin', 'Ellen', NULL          -- Actor name information
  ) ;

INSERT INTO movie_stars
  VALUES (
    'The Adventures of Buckaroo Banzai Across the 8th Dimension',
    1984,
    'Goldblum', 'Jeff', 'Lynn',      -- Actor name information
  ) ;
```

```
INSERT INTO movie_stars
  VALUES (
    'The Adventures of Buckaroo Banzai Across the 8th Dimension',
    1984,
    'Lloyd', 'Christopher', NULL     -- Actor name information
  ) ;
```

2. Insert information about a music title, along with information about the distributor from which we acquire the title

```
INSERT INTO music_titles
  VALUES (
    'J516-14LIT',                   -- Our identifier
    'Singin'' in the Bathtub',      -- The title
    'Lithgow', 'John',              -- The artist
    'Sony/Wonder',                  -- The label
    CAST('FALSE' AS BOOLEAN)        -- Not a best-hits collection
    'Kids/Family',                  -- No kidding!
    DATE'1999-03-09',               -- Release date
    CAST (13.97 AS money),          -- CD list and current prices
    CAST (11.50 AS money),
    CAST (NULL AS money),           -- Not available on cassette
    CAST (NULL AS money)
) ;

/* Note that inserting a row into the music_distributors table implicitly
   creates a new instance of the music_distributors type with a
   system-generated value inserted into the self-referencing column */

INSERT INTO music_distributors
  VALUES (
    'NJ456/12/XDB',                 -- Our identifier
    'Soapy Wet Music',              -- The distributor's name,
    '3909 Yale Blvd.',              --   address, and phone numbers
    'Musicville', 'CA', '99909',
    '9199919190', NULL, NULL, NULL,
    'www.soapywetmusic.com.yu'      -- Web address
) ;
```

```
INSERT INTO music_distributors
  VALUES (
    'BV581/94/BRP',                -- Our identifier
    'Fine Acoustics',              -- The distributor's name,
    '256 Bitbucket St.',           --   address, and phone numbers
    'Ordervale', 'MN', '41980',
    '7774440000', NULL, '7775551234', NULL,
    'www.music-with-echoes.com'  -- Web address
) ;

/* Inserting a row into current_distributor_costs requires that we
   have, or acquire, the REF value corresponding to the distributor */

INSERT INTO current_distributor_costs
  VALUES (
    'J516-14LIT',                  -- Our identifier for the music
    ( SELECT DISTINCT dist_ref     -- Get the self-referencing column
      FROM music_distributors      --   value for our favorite distributor
      WHERE distributor_id
          = 'NJ456/12/XDB' ),
    CAST (4.50 AS money),          -- CD cost; not available on cassette
    CAST (NULL AS money)
) ;
```

3. Create a customer record

```
INSERT INTO customers
  VALUES (
    'Solomon', 'Thomas',           -- Customer's name
    NEW US_address (               -- Customer lives in USA
      '417 Pensdale Road',
      'Rutherford',
      'USA',
      'OH',
      ( 45499, 1983 ) ),           -- Zipcode is a row type
      '9375559163', NULL,          -- No fax number
      'tommie@jgl.com',
      '99991111888',
      CAST (116.00 AS money),
      CAST (931.00 AS money),
      0,
      TIMESTAMP'2001-12-15'
) ;
```

A.3.2 Data Retrieval and Manipulation

1. We've been given a new long description of *Buckaroo Banzai.*

```
UPDATE movies AS m
  SET m.movie.long_description =
        'Neurosurgeon/Rock Star/Superhero Buckaroo has perfected ' ||
        'the oscillation overthruster, which allows him to ' ||
        'travel through solid matter by using the eighth dimension. ' ||
        'The Red Lectroids from Planet 10 are after this device ' ||
        'for their own evil ends, and it''s up to Buckaroo ' ||
        'and his band and crime-fighting team "The ' ||
        'Hong Kong Cavaliers" to stop them. '
WHERE m.movie.title =
        'The Adventures of Buckaroo Banzai Across the 8th Dimension' ;
```

2. Do we have any CDs in stock that were recorded by an actor who stars in a science fiction movie suitable for family viewing? If so, what are their titles and their current prices?

```
SELECT title, cd_current_price
FROM music_titles AS mt, movies AS m, movie_stars AS ms
WHERE mt.artist = ms.actor_last_name
  AND mt.artist_more = ms.actor_first_name || ' ' || ms.actor_middle_name
  AND ms.movie_title = m.movie.title
  AND m.movie.family_fare( )     -- Invoke a method on the movie instance
  AND 'Science Fiction' IN       -- Use collection-derived table to check
      ( SELECT genre             --   the movie's genre in the array
        FROM UNNEST ( m.movie.genre ) AS mg ( genre ) ) ;
```

3. What are the Web site URLs of the distributors of those CDs?

```
SELECT cdc.distributor -> distributor_web_site_addr
FROM music_titles AS mt, movies AS m, movie_stars AS ms,
     current_distributor_costs AS cdc
WHERE mt.artist = ms.actor_last_name
  AND mt.artist_more = ms.actor_first_name || ' ' || ms.actor_middle_name
  AND ms.movie_title = m.movie.title
  AND m.movie.family_fare( )     -- Invoke a method on the movie instance
  AND 'Science Fiction' IN       -- Use collection-derived table to check
      ( SELECT genre             --   the movie's genre in the array
        FROM UNNEST ( m.movie.genre ) AS mg ( genre ) )
  AND cdc.music_id = mt.music_id ;
```

4. Out of curiosity, do we have any customers whose extended ZIP code happens to be equal to the last four digits of their phone numbers?

```
SELECT cust_last_name, cust_first_name
FROM customers
WHERE SUBSTRING ( cust_phone FROM 7 FOR 4 )
    = CAST ( cust_address.zip.plus4 AS CHARACTER ( 4 ) ) ;
```

5. How much profit would we make if we sold every DVD copy of every movie starring Jeff Goldblum?

```
SELECT SUM ( m.dvds_in_stock *
             ( CAST ( m.current_dvd_sale_price AS DECIMAL ( 9, 2 ) )
             - CAST ( m.our_dvd_cost AS DECIMAL ( 9, 2 ) ) ) ) AS profit
FROM movies AS m, movie_stars AS ms
WHERE m.movie.title = ms.movie_title
  AND m.movie.year_released = ms.year_released
  AND ms.actor_first_name || ' ' || ms.actor_last_name
    = 'Jeff Goldblum' ;
```

6. Produce an XML document that contains selected information about all movies that we have in stock, along with the names of their stars.

```
SELECT m.stock_number,
       XMLELEMENT ( "movie",
                    XMLATTRIBUTES ( m.movie.year_released AS "year" ),
                    XMLELEMENT ( "summary", m.movie.description ),
                    XMLELEMENT ( "length",
                                 CAST ( m.movie.run_time AS
                                        INTERVAL HOUR TO MINUTE )
                               ),
                    XMLELEMENT ( "stars",
                          XMLAGG ( XMLELEMENT ( "name",
                                                ms.actor_first_name ||
                                                ' ' ||
                                                ms.actor_last_name
                                              )
                                 )
                               ),
                    XMLELEMENT ( "price", m.current_dvd_sale_price )
                  ) AS "Movie_Data"
FROM movies AS m, movie_stars AS ms
GROUP BY m.stock_number ;
```

Appendix B

The SQL:1999 Annexes

B.1 Introduction

Most parts of the SQL:1999 standard contain several Annexes. These Annexes are not *normative* parts of the standard to which implementations can claim conformance, but are *informative* in nature. In fact, most of the Annexes in each part merely summarize information that is available in other places in the standard. In some parts, one or two Annexes offer material that might be difficult to ascertain in other ways. In addition, both SQL/OLB and SQL/JRT have Annexes that offer significant tutorial material. In this appendix, I try to capture the essence of the Annexes, without actually going into the detail that is inevitably present in the standard. The corresponding appendix in the first volume of this book covered the contents of SQL:1999's Annexes as they related to the material in the chapters of that volume. Accordingly, this appendix covers the contents of the SQL:1999 Annexes as they relate to user-defined types, typed tables, routines and routine invocations, management of external data, Java routines and types, and XML-related specifications.

B.2 Implementation-Defined and Implementation-Dependent

It would have been very nice, indeed, if the SQL standard had completely defined every aspect of every language feature. However, there are a number of elements of the language for which the standard's specifications are, for one reason or another, not complete. In many cases, the standard has left some specifications incomplete because the variations among existing implementations is too great for compromises to be reached; in other cases, the standard's designers felt that application programmers would not benefit significantly from achieving complete specification. The precise definition of these aspects of the language will, of course, be determined in one way or another by each implementation.

The standard uses the phrase *implementation-defined* to indicate one of these areas. This is meant to imply that the implementation *must* document the syntax, value, or behavior of the element. For example, the standard leaves the exact precision of the `INTEGER` data type as implementation-defined, and in order to claim conformance to the standard, the implementation *must* document the precision.

The other phrase the standard uses is *implementation-dependent*. This phrase means that the implementation need not document the syntax, value, or behavior of some element and that application programs certainly must never depend on it. (In fact, interpretations of the SQL standard have indicated that implementors are actually *discouraged* from documenting items that are specified to be implementation-dependent.) For example, the physical representation of a value of any given data type is implementation-dependent. Implementation-dependent information is typically the sort that may change from version to version of a product, that is unusually difficult to describe, or is of no (logical) use to applications.

SQL:1999, including corrections that are applied in the recently approved Technical Corrigendum,[1] identifies no fewer than 563 items that are implementation-defined (17 in SQL/Framework, 134 in SQL/Foundation, 200 in SQL/CLI, 5 in SQL/PSM, 28 in SQL/Bindings, 90 in SQL/MED, 40 in SQL/OLB, and 44 in SQL/JRT, plus 5 in the SQL/OLAP amendment) and 191 that are implementation-dependent (11 in SQL/Framework, 52 in SQL/Foundation, 50 in SQL/CLI, 11 in SQL/PSM, 15 in SQL/Bindings, 23 in SQL/MED, 22 in SQL/OLB, and 7 in SQL/JRT, but none in the SQL/OLAP amendment). While that may sound like the standard is left wide open for almost anything, many of these items are closely related to others, many are so obvious that they may be overlooked by a more casual specification, and others are descriptive of realistic behaviors in any situation. (It

1 ISO/IEC 9075:1999/Cor.1:2002, *Information technology—Database Languages—SQL—Technical Corrigendum 2* (Geneva: International Organization for Standardization, 2002).

may also be worth observing that the eight parts of SQL:1999 occupy a total of 3094 pages, so the density of implementation-defined and implementation-dependent items isn't particularly high.)

B.2.1 Implementation-Defined

The following lists contain a large selection of the implementation-defined items of SQL:1999 that are related to the material in the chapters of this volume.

User-Defined Types, Typed Tables, and Routines

1. In a host variable, a reference type is materialized as an *N*-octet value, where *N* is implementation-defined.
2. The `<entry name>` of an entry point to an SQL-invoked function defined as part of a user-defined type is implementation-defined.
3. If an SQL-invoked routine does not contain SQL, does not possibly read SQL data, and does not possibly modify SQL data, then the SQL session module of the new SQL session context *RSC* is set to be an implementation-defined module.
4. If a parameter P_i of an SQL-invoked routine is an output SQL parameter, then the effective value CPV_i if that parameter is referenced in the routine is an implementation-defined value of the parameter's declared type T_i.
5. If the syntax for invoking a built-in function is not defined in ISO/IEC 9075, then the result of `<routine invocation>` is implementation-defined.
6. When a new SQL-session context *RSC* is created, the current default catalog name, current default unqualified schema name, the current character set name substitution value, the SQL-path of the current SQL session, the current default time zone, and the contents of all SQL dynamic descriptor areas are set to implementation-defined values.
7. If *R* is an external routine, then it is implementation-defined whether the identities of all instances of created local temporary tables that are referenced in the `<SQL-client module definition>` of *P*, declared local temporary tables that are defined by <temporary table declaration>s that are contained in the `<SQL-client module definition>` of *P*, and the cursor position of all open cursors that are defined by <declare cursor>s that are contained in the `<SQL-client module definition>` of *P* are removed from *RSC*.

8. After the completion of *P*, it is implementation-defined whether open cursors declared in the `<SQL-client module definition>` of *P* are closed and destroyed, whether local temporary tables associated with *RCS* are destroyed, and whether prepared statements prepared by *P* are deallocated.
9. If *R* is an SQL-invoked procedure, then for each SQL parameter that is an output SQL parameter or both an input and output SQL parameter whose corresponding argument was not assigned a value, that corresponding argument is set to an implementation-defined value of the appropriate type.
10. If the external security characteristic of an external SQL-invoked routine is IMPLEMENTATION DEFINED, then the user identifier and role name in the first cell of the authorization stack of the new SQL-session context are implementation-defined.

Management of External Data

1. The possible values of server type and server version, and their meanings, are implementation-defined.
2. Both the option name and the option value of a generic option are implementation-defined.
3. The time at which a valid access token ceases to be valid is implementation-defined.
4. The datalink character set is implementation-defined.
5. The implementation-defined *maximum datalink length* determines the amount of space, in octets, that is allocated for a host variable of data type DATALINK, an argument of declared type DATALINK to an invocation of an external routine, the value returned by an invocation of an external function whose result type is DATALINK. The maximum datalink length constrains the values of expressions whose declared type is DATALINK such that every such value can be assigned to a host variable, substituted for a parameter to an external routine, or returned by an invocation of an external function.
6. The validity of a handle in a compilation unit other than the one in which the identified resource was allocated is implementation-defined.
7. If the routine's return code indicates **No data found**, then no status record is generated corresponding to SQLSTATE value '02000' but there may be status records generated corresponding to SQLSTATE value '02*nnn*', where '*nnn*' is an implementation-defined subclass value.

8. Equivalence of two `<option name>`s is determined using an implementation-defined collation that is sensitive to case.

9. If `<url complete expression>` is specified, then the data type of the result is a variable-length character string with an implementation-defined maximal length.

10. If `<url path expression>` is specified, then the data type of the result is a variable-length character string with an implementation-defined maximal length.

11. If `<url path only expression>` is specified, then the data type of the result is a variable-length character string with an implementation-defined maximal length.

12. If `<url scheme expression>` is specified, then the data type of the result is a variable-length character string with an implementation-defined maximal length.

13. If `<url server expression>` is specified, then the data type of the result is a variable-length character string with an implementation-defined maximal length.

14. The format of the DLVALUE expression may be implementation-defined.

15. The scheme of a datalink value, the host of a datalink value, and the path of a datalink value may be implementation-defined.

16. If `<basic column definition list>` is specified, then the nullability characteristic and `<default option>` of each column specified by `<basic column definition>` is implementation-defined.

17. If `<basic column definition list>` is not specified, then column descriptors included in a foreign table descriptor are implementation-defined.

18. Additional privileges, if any, necessary to execute `<foreign table definition>` are implementation-defined.

19. If `<alter generic options>` is specified, then any effect on the foreign table descriptor, apart from its generic options descriptor, is implementation-defined.

20. The nullability characteristic and `<default option>` included in the column descriptor specified by `<basic column definition>` is implementation-defined.

21. The permissible Format and values for `<server type>`, `<server version>`, and `<password>` are implementation-defined.

22. Additional privileges, if any, necessary to execute <foreign server definition> are implementation-defined.
23. The privileges necessary to execute <foreign-data wrapper definition> are implementation-defined.
24. Additional privileges, if any, necessary to execute <user-mapping definition> are implementation-defined.
25. The privileges necessary to execute <alter user mapping statement> are implementation-defined.
26. The privileges necessary to execute <drop user mapping statement> are implementation-defined.
27. If TYPE indicates DATALINK, then LENGTH is set to the length of maximum length in characters of the character string; OCTET_LENGTH is set to the maximum possible length in octets of the character string; CHARACTER_SET_CATALOG, CHARACTER_SET_SCHEMA, and CHARACTER_SET_NAME are set to the <character set name> of the character string's character set; and COLLATION_CATALOG, COLLATION_SCHEMA, and COLLATION_NAME are set to the <collation name> of the character string's collation. If the subject <language clause> specifies C, then the lengths specified in LENGTH and OCTET_LENGTH do not include the implementation-defined null character that terminates a C character string.
28. The maximum length of a datalink is implementation-defined.
29. Let *IDA* be an item descriptor area in a wrapper parameter descriptor. One condition that allows *IDA* to be valid is if TYPE indicates an implementation-defined data type.
30. One condition that allows a foreign-data wrapper item descriptor area in a foreign-data wrapper descriptor area that is not a wrapper row descriptor to be consistent is if TYPE indicates an implementation-defined data type.
31. Let *IDA* be an item descriptor area in a server parameter descriptor. One condition that allows *IDA* to be valid is if TYPE indicates an implementation-defined data type.
32. One condition that allows a foreign-data wrapper item descriptor area in a server row descriptor to be valid is if TYPE indicates an implementation-defined data type.

33. If the result is a zero-length character string, then it is implementation-defined whether or not an exception condition is raised: *data exception—zero-length character string.*
34. It is implementation-defined which of the invocation of wrapper procedures or wrapper functions is supported.
35. If the value of any input argument provided by *CP* falls outside the set of allowed values of the data type of the parameter, or if the value of any output argument resulting from the execution of the `<foreign-data wrapper interface routine>` falls outside the set of values supported by *CP* for that parameter, then the effect is implementation-defined.
36. If *RN* did not execute successfully, then one or more exception conditions may be raised as determined by implementation-defined rules.
37. If the resources to manage a foreign-data wrapper environment cannot be allocated for implementation-defined reasons, then an implementation-defined exception condition is raised.
38. If the resources to manage an FS-connection cannot be allocated for implementation-defined reasons, then an implementation-defined exception condition is raised.
39. The CDATA values of the SQLMEDOptionName attribute and the PCDATA text of the SQLMEDGenericOption tag are implementation-defined.
40. The way in which the foreign-data wrapper knows the URI to specify in the XML document is implementation-defined.
41. The CDATA values of the SQLMEDStatisticName attribute and the PCDATA text of the SQLMEDStatistics tag are implementation-defined.
42. If the resources to manage an FDW-reply cannot be allocated for implementation-defined reasons, then an implementation-defined exception condition is raised.
43. If the resources to manage an FDW-execution cannot be allocated for implementation-defined reasons, then an implementation-defined exception condition is raised.
44. If the resources to manage an FDW-data cannot be allocated for implementation-defined reasons, then an implementation-defined exception condition is raised.
45. If TYPE is 'HEADER,' then header information from the descriptor area *D* is retrieved; if *FI* indicates an implementation-defined descriptor header field, then the value retrieved is the value of the implementation-defined descriptor header field identified by *FI*.

46. If TYPE is 'ITEM,' then item information from the descriptor area *D* is retrieved; if *FI* indicates an implementation-defined descriptor item field, then the value retrieved is the value of the implementation-defined descriptor item field of *IDA* identified by *FI.*
47. If *FI* indicates TYPE and *V* indicates NUMERIC or DECIMAL, then the SCALE field of *IDA* is set to 0 (zero) and the PRECISION field of *IDA* is set to the implementation-defined default value for the precision of NUMERIC or DECIMAL data types, respectively.
48. If *FI* indicates TYPE and *V* indicates FLOAT, then the PRECISION field of *IDA* is set to the implementation-defined default value for the precision of the FLOAT data type.
49. If *FI* indicates TYPE and *V* indicates SMALLINT or INTEGER, then the SCALE field of *IDA* is set to 0 (zero) and the PRECISION field of *IDA* is set to the implementation-defined value for the precision of the SMALLINT or INTEGER data types, respectively.
50. If *FI* indicates TYPE and *V* indicates REAL or DOUBLE PRECISION, then the PRECISION field of *IDA* is set to the implementation-defined value for the precision of the REAL or DOUBLE PRECISION data types, respectively.
51. If *FI* indicates TYPE and *V* indicates an implementation-defined data type, then an implementation-defined set of fields of *IDA* are set to implementation-defined default values.
52. If *TYPE* is 'HEADER' and *DI* indicates an implementation-defined diagnostics header field, then the value retrieved is the value of the implementation-defined diagnostics header field.
53. If *TYPE* is 'STATUS' and *DI* indicates an implementation-defined diagnostics header field, then the value retrieved is the value of the implementation-defined diagnostics header field.
54. If *TYPE* is 'STATUS' and *DI* indicates NATIVE_CODE, then the value retrieved is the implementation-defined native error code corresponding to the status condition.
55. If *TYPE* is 'STATUS' and *DI* indicates MESSAGE_TEXT, then the value retrieved is an implementation-defined character string.
56. If *TYPE* is 'STATUS' and *DI* indicates CLASS_ORIGIN, then the value retrieved shall be an implementation-defined character string other than 'ISO 9075' for any implementation-defined class value.

57. If *TYPE* is 'STATUS' and *DI* indicates SUBCLASS_ORIGIN, then the value retrieved shall be an implementation-defined character string other than 'ISO 9075' for any implementation-defined subclass value.
58. The maximum lengths of foreign-data wrapper diagnostics area fields whose data types are CHARACTER VARYING are implementation-defined.
59. SQL/MED supports implementation-defined header fields in foreign-data wrapper diagnostics areas.
60. The maximum lengths of foreign-data wrapper item descriptor fields whose data type is CHARACTER VARYING are implementation-defined.
61. SQL/MED supports implementation-defined header fields and implementation-defined item fields in row and parameter descriptor areas.
62. SQL/MED supports implementation-defined diagnostics header fields and implementation-defined diagnostics status fields.
63. SQL/MED supports implementation-defined descriptor header fields and implementation-defined descriptor item fields.
64. 'ID' means that it is implementation-defined whether or not the descriptor field is retrievable.
65. SQL/MED supports implementation-defined descriptor header fields and implementation-defined descriptor item fields.
66. 'ID' means that it is implementation-defined whether or not the descriptor field is settable.
67. SQL/MED supports implementation-defined descriptor header fields and implementation-defined descriptor item fields.
68. 'ID' means that the descriptor field's default value is implementation-defined.
69. SQL/MED supports implementation-defined descriptor header fields and implementation-defined descriptor item fields.

Online Analytical Processing

1. If PERCENT_RANK is specified, then the declared type of the result is approximate numeric with implementation-defined precision.
2. If CUME_DIST is specified, then the declared type of the result is approximate numeric with implementation-defined precision.
3. The declared type of the result of `<natural logarithm>` is approximate numeric with implementation-defined precision.

4. The declared type of the result of <exponential function> is approximate numeric with implementation-defined precision.
5. The declared type of the result of <power function> is approximate numeric with implementation-defined precision.
6. The declared type of the result of <floor function> is exact numeric with implementation-defined precision and scale 0 (zero).
7. The declared type of the result of <ceiling function> is exact numeric with implementation-defined precision and scale 0 (zero).
8. If <hypothetical set function> is specified, then if RANK or DENSE_RANK is specified, then the declared type of the result is exact numeric with implementation-defined precision and with scale 0 (zero); otherwise, the declared type of the result is approximate numeric with implemenation-defined precision.
9. If the declared type of the <value expression> simply contained in the <sort specification> of an <inverse distribution function> that specifies PERCENTILE_CONT is numeric, then the result type is approximate numeric with implementation-defined precision.
10. If COUNT is specified, then the declared type of the result is exact numeric with implementation-defined precision and scale of 0 (zero).
11. If SUM or AVG is specified, then: If SUM is specified and the declared type of the argument is exact numeric with scale *S*, then the declared type of the result is exact numeric with implementation-defined precision and scale *S*; if AVG is specified and the declared type of the argument is exact numeric, then the declared type of the result is exact numeric with implementation-defined precision not less than the precision of *DT* and implementation-defined scale not less than the scale of *DT*; if the declared type of the argument is approximate numeric, then the declared type of the result is approximate numeric with implementation-defined precision not less than the precision of *DT*; if the declared type of the argument is interval, then the declared type of the result is interval with the same precision as *DT*.
12. If VAR_POP or VAR_SAMP is specified, then the declared type of the result is approximate numeric with implementation-defined precision not less than the precision of *DT*.
13. If <binary set function type> is specified, then: If REGR_COUNT is specified, then the declared type of the result is exact numeric with implementation-defined precision and scale of 0 (zero); if REGR_AVGX is specified, then (1) if the declared type *DTIVE* of the second parameter is exact

numeric, then the declared type of the result is exact numeric with implementation-defined precision not less than the precision of *DTIVE* and implementation-defined scale not less than the scale of *DTIVE*. (2) Otherwise, the declared type of the result is approximate numeric with precision not less than the precision of *DTIVE*; if REGR_AVGY is specified, then (1) if the declared type *DTDVE* of the first parameter is exact numeric, then the declared type of the result is exact numeric with implementation-defined precision not less than the precision of *DTDVE* and implementation-defined scale not less than the scale of *DTDVE*. (2) Otherwise, the declared type of the result is approximate numeric with precision not less than the precision of *DTDVE*; otherwise, the declared type of the result is approximate numeric with implementation-defined precision.

14. If `<null ordering>` is not specified, then an implementation-defined `<null ordering>` is implicit.
15. The implementation-defined default for `<null ordering>` shall not depend on the context outside of `<sort specification list>`.

Java-Related Specifications

1. The preparation needed, prior to execution of an SQLJ application, that is not addressed by either SQLJ translation or customization is implementation-defined.
2. Whether a portion of the name space is reserved by an implementation for the names of procedures, subroutines, program variables, branch labels, `<SQL-client module definition>`s, or `<externally-invoked procedure>`s for `<embedded SQL host program>`s other than `<embedded SQL Java program>`s is implementation-defined; if a portion of the name space is so reserved, the portion reserved is implementation-defined.
3. When moving character data between an SQL/OLB implementation and an SQL server, support for implicit conversions other than the implicit conversion between Java string data and UTF8, UTF16, and/or UCS2 is implementation-defined.
4. The specification of the default connection context is implementation-defined. If the name jdbc/defaultDataSource is not defined to JNDI, then the database connection used by the default connection context is implementation-defined.
5. The mechanism used to provide an SQLJ translator with a mapping of connection context classes to exemplar schemas is implementation-defined.

6. Runtime support of the sqlj. runtime. ExecutionContext class methods setMaxRows, setMaxFieldSize, and setQueryTimeout if invoked to set an ExecutionContext object's corresponding underlying values to anything other than their default values is implementation-defined.
7. Given a JDBC ResultSet object **rs**, once an iterator object is created due to **rs** having been referenced in an `<iterator conversion clause>` the result of invoking methods against **rs** is implementation-defined.
8. Support for the sqlj. runtime. ResultSetIterator interface method getResultSet is runtime implementation-defined.
9. If an SQLJ runtime supports the sqlj. runtime. ResultSetIterator interface method getResultSet then any synchronization between an iterator object and the JDBC ResultSet object produced by invoking getResultSet against that iterator object is runtime implementation-defined.
10. If invocation of a ResultSetIterator object's isClosed method would return the value true, then the effect of invoking any methods other than isClosed and close against that object is implementation-defined.
11. The semantics of calling close on a JDBC ResultSet object that has already been closed is implementation-defined.
12. The Role OTHER is reserved for SQLJ `<executable clause>` extensions that are implementation-defined.
13. The established default mapping between Java types and JDBC-defined SQL type constants might be disregarded or remapped by implementation-defined profile customizations.
14. The support for each `<predefined iterator with keyword>` is implementation-defined.
15. If the connection context object isn't created using `<data source constructors>` or `<url constructors>` that have a user parameter and a user name isn't provided as part of the info parameter, and if the connection context object isn't created using the constructor that takes an existing connection context object, and if the connection context object isn't created using the constructor that takes an existing JDBC Connection object then the connection context user identifier is implementation-defined.
16. The opaque profile key object returned by invocation of a generated connection class's getProfileKey method, and subsequently used in the generated connection class's getProfile and getConnectedProfile methods, is implementation-defined.

17. The class name of the default connection context is implementation-defined.
18. When processing a `<sort specification list>`, at least one of whose `<sort key>`s contain a column reference that is not a column of the result of evaluating the `<query expression>`, and is not equivalent to a `<value expression>` immediately contained in any `<derived column>` in the `<select list>` of the `<query expression>`, then the `<column name>` for any `<derived column>` that does not have a `<column name>` is implementation-defined, except that it cannot be equal to any other `<column name>` of any other `<derived column>` in the `<select list>` of the `<query expression>`.
19. Whether a sort key value that is null is considered greater or less than a non-null value is implementation-defined, but all sort key values that are null shall either be considered greater than all non-null values or be considered less than all non-null values.
20. Given a JDBC ResultSet object **rs**, once an iterator object is created due to **rs** having been referenced in a `<result set expression>` the result of invoking methods against **rs** is implementation-defined.
21. If an `<embedded Java expression>` containing an `<Lval expression>` has either an implicit or explicit `<parameter mode>` of OUT or INOUT in a given `<SQL procedure statement>` then let *LV* denote the location of the `<Lval expression>`. If another `<embedded Java expression>` containing an `<Lval expression>` has either an implicit or explicit `<parameter mode>` of IN or INOUT in a subsequent `<SQL procedure statement>` and the location of the `<Lval expression>` is *LV*, then the value of the `<Lval expression>` is implementation-defined.
22. Runtime support of the sqlj. runtime. ExecutionContext class methods setMaxRows, setMaxFieldSize, and setQueryTimeout if invoked to set an ExecutionContext object's corresponding underlying values to anything other than their default values is implementation-defined.
23. The effect of an update operation being performed against a Scrollable iterator object is implementation-defined.
24. During customization, the user identifier for inclusion in a customized profile, to be used for runtime privilege checking, may be specified in an implementation-defined manner.
25. The Map object provided in the typemap parameter is passed to the returned RTStatement object in an implementation-defined manner.
26. The Map object provided in the typemap parameter is passed to the returned RTStatement object in an implementation-defined manner.

27. The manner in which a java.util.Map object is provided to an RTResultSet object at the time of that RTResultSet object's creation is implementation-defined.
28. Support for an RTResultSet object's getJDBCResultSet method is implementation-defined. If an implementation does provide support for an RTResultSet object's getJDBCResultSet method, then any synchronization between the RTResultSet object and the returned JDBC ResultSet object is implementation-defined.
29. The manner in which a `java.util.Map` object is provided to an RTStatement object at the time of that RTStatement object's creation is implementation-defined.
30. The manner in which an RTStatement object's `java.util.Map` object is provided to an RTResultSet object created as the result of execution of that RTStatement object is implementation-defined.
31. The manner in which an RTStatement object's `java.util.Map` object is provided to an RTResultSet object is implementation-defined.
32. The effect of setting an RTStatement object's MaxFieldSize to other than its default value is implementation-defined.
33. Support for setting an RTStatement object's MaxRows to other than its default value is implementation-defined.
34. Support for setting an RTStatement object's QueryTimeout to other than its default value is implementation-defined.
35. A conforming implementation is permitted to provide support for additional implementation-defined `<user defined with keyword>`s.
36. An SQLJ translator can perform syntactic and semantic checking based on an exemplar schema provided as a connection context class in an implementation-defined manner.
37. If the `<user-defined type definition>` does not specify an `<interface specification>`, then it is implementation-defined whether the Java interface `java.io.Serializable` or the Java interface `java.sql.SQLData` will be used for object state conversion.
38. The privileges required to invoke the `SQLJ.INSTALL_JAR`, `SQLJ.REPLACE_JAR`, and `SQLJ.REMOVE_JAR` procedures are implementation-defined.
39. Invocations of Java methods referenced by SQL names are governed by the normal EXECUTE privilege on SQL routine names. It is implementation-defined whether a Java method called by an SQL name executes with "definer's rights" or "invoker's rights"—that is, whether it executes

with the user-name of the user who performed the <SQL-invoked routine> or the user-name of the current user.

40. An implementation-defined implementor block can be provided in a deployment descriptor file to allow specification of custom install and remove actions.
41. The character set supported, and the maximum lengths of the <package identifier>, <class identifier>, <Java field name>, and <Java method name> are implementation-defined.
42. If Feature J571, "NEW operator," is not supported, then the mechanism used to invoke a constructor of an external Java data type is implementation-defined.
43. If validation of the <Java parameter declaration list> has been implementation-defined to be performed by <routine invocation>, then the Syntax Rules of Subclause 8.5, "Java routine signature determination," are applied with <routine invocation>, a method specification index of 0 (zero), and subject routine *SR*.
44. For an external Java routine, let CPV_i be an implementation-defined non-null value of declared type T_i.
45. The method of execution of a subject Java class's implementation of `writeObject( )` to convert a Java value to an SQL value is implementation-defined.
46. The method of execution of a subject Java class's implementation of `writeSQL( )` to convert a Java value to an SQL value is implementation-defined.
47. The method of execution of a subject Java class's implementation of `readObject( )` to convert an SQL value to a Java object is implementation-defined.
48. The method of execution of a subject Java class's implementation of `readSQL( )` to convert an SQL value to a Java object is implementation-defined.
49. If *R* is an external Java routine, then if the JDBC connection object that created any element of *RS* is closed, then the effect is implementation-defined.
50. If *R* is an external Java routine, and if any element of *RS* is not an object returned by a connection to the current SQL system and SQL session, then the effect is implementation-defined.

51. If *R* is an external Java routine, then whether the call of *P* returns update counts as defined in JDBC is implementation-defined.
52. If an `<interface using clause>` is not explicitly specified, then an implementation-defined `<interface specification>` is implicit.
53. If *UDT* is an external Java data type, then it is implementation-defined whether validation of the explicit or implicit `<Java parameter declaration list>` is performed by `<user-defined type definition>` or when the corresponding SQL-invoked method is invoked.
54. The method of execution of a subject Java class's implementation of `writeObject( )` to convert a Java value to an SQL value is implementation-defined.
55. The method of execution of a subject Java class's implementation of `writeSQL( )` to convert a Java value to an SQL value is implementation-defined.
56. The method of execution of a subject Java class's implementation of `readObject( )` to convert an SQL value to a Java object is implementation-defined.
57. The maximum value of `<maximum dynamic result sets>` is implementation-defined.
58. If *R* is an external Java routine, then it is implementation-defined whether validation of the explicit or implicit `<Java parameter declaration list>` is performed by `<SQL-invoked routine>` or when its SQL-invoked routine is invoked.
59. The maximum length for the CHARACTER VARYING parameters is an implementation-defined integer value.
60. The privileges required to invoke the `SQLJ.INSTALL_JAR` procedure are implementation-defined.
61. The `SQLJ.INSTALL_JAR` procedure is subject to implementation-defined rules for executing SQL schema statements within SQL transactions.
62. If an invocation of `SQLJ.INSTALL_JAR` raises an exception condition, then the effect on the install actions is implementation-defined.
63. The values of the `url` parameter that are valid are implementation-defined and may include URLs whose format is implementation-defined. If the value of the `url` parameter does not conform to implementation-defined restrictions and does not identify a valid JAR, then an exception condition is raised: *Java DDL—invalid URL*.

64. The privileges required to invoke the `SQLJ.REPLACE_JAR` procedure are implementation-defined.

65. The `SQLJ.REPLACE_JAR` procedure is subject to implementation-defined rules for executing SQL schema statements within SQL transactions.

66. The values of the `url` parameter that are valid are implementation-defined and may include URLs whose format is implementation-defined. If the value of the `url` parameter does not conform to implementation-defined restrictions and does not identify a valid JAR, then an exception condition is raised: *Java DDL—invalid URL.*

67. The privileges required to invoke the `SQLJ.REMOVE_JAR` procedure are implementation-defined.

68. The `SQLJ.REMOVE_JAR` procedure is subject to implementation-defined rules for executing SQL schema statements within SQL transactions.

69. If an invocation of `SQLJ.REMOVE_JAR` raises an exception condition, then the effect on the remove actions is implementation-defined.

70. The privileges required to invoke the `SQLJ.ALTER_JAVA_PATH` procedure are implementation-defined.

71. The `SQLJ.ALTER_JAVA_PATH` procedure is subject to implementation-defined rules for executing SQL schema statements within SQL transactions.

72. If an invocation of the `SQLJ.ALTER_JAVA_PATH` procedure raises an exception condition, the effect on the path associated with the JAR is implementation-defined.

73. SQL systems that implement this part of ISO/IEC 9075 support the package `java.sql`, which is the JDBC driver, and all classes required by that package. The other Java packages supplied by SQL systems that implement this part of ISO/IEC 9075 are implementation-defined.

74. In an SQL system that implements this part of ISO/IEC 9075, the package `java.sql` supports the default connection. Other data source URLs that are supported by `java.sql` are implementation-defined.

75. An `<implementor name>` is an implementation-defined SQL identifier.

76. Whether an `<implementor block>` with a given `<implementor name>` contained in an `<install actions>` (`<remove actions>`) is interpreted as an install action (remove action) is implementation-defined. That is, an implementation may or may not perform install or remove actions specified by some other implementation.

XML-Related Specifications

1. The mapping of an SQL character set to Unicode is implementation-defined.
2. The mapping of Unicode to a character set in the SQL-environment is implementation-defined.
3. If *S* is a character in an SQL `<identifier>` *SQLI* and *S* has no mapping to Unicode, then the mapping of *S* to create an XML Name corresponding to *SQLI* is implementation-defined.
4. The treatment of an escape sequence of the form _***xNNNN***_ or _***xNNNNNN***_ whose corresponding Unicode code point U+*NNNN* or U+ *NNNNNN* is not a valid Unicode character is implementation-defined.

B.2.2 Implementation-Dependent

The following lists contain some of the implementation-dependent features of SQL:1999 that are related to the material in this volume.

User-Defined Types, Typed Tables, and Routines

1. If the element type of a collection is a large object type or a user-defined type whose `<ordering clause>` does not specify ORDER FULL, then the element order is implementation-dependent.
2. Each SQL argument A_i in *SAL* is evaluated, in an implementation-dependent order, to obtain a value V_i.
3. The `<user-defined type name>` of a user-defined type specified in a `<table definition>` without specifying "OF NEW TYPE *UDTN*" is implementation-dependent.
4. The relative ordering of two non-null values of a user-defined type *UDT* whose comparison as determined by the user-defined ordering of *UDT* is *unknown* is implementation-dependent.

Management of External Data

1. The manner in which an external DTD is made available to the SQL server is implementation-dependent.
2. The manner in which the SQL server interacts with a foreign-data wrapper to import information about a foreign schema is implementation-dependent.

3. The mechanism by which the SQL server controls access and maintains integrity of files is implementation-dependent. This mechanism is called the *datalinker.*
4. The generation of the access token and the method of combining it with File Reference are implementation-dependent.
5. After the execution of a foreign-data wrapper interface routine, the values of all output arguments not explicitly defined by this part of ISO/IEC 9075 are implementation-dependent.
6. If multiple status records are generated, then the order in which status records are placed in a diagnostics area is implementation-dependent, with two exceptions.
7. The generation of the access token and the method of combining it with File Reference or the `<hpath>` or `<fpath>` of a File Reference are implementation-dependent.
8. The representation of the result of invoking a `<datalink value constructor>` is implementation-dependent.
9. If `<using arguments>` is specified, then all fields, except DATA and DATA_POINTER, in the *i*-th item descriptor area of *SPD,* that can be set according to Table 35, "Ability to set foreign-data wrapper descriptor fields," are set to implementation-dependent values.
10. If *D* is not zero, then those fields and fields that are not applicable for a particular value of TYPE are set to implementation-dependent values.
11. If *D* is not zero and the column name is implementation-dependent, then NAME is set to the implementation-dependent name of the column and UNNAMED is set to 1 (one).
12. If the name of the field is implementation-dependent, then NAME is set to the implementation-dependent name of the field and UNNAMED is set to 1 (one).
13. If *TDT* is a locator type and *SV* is not the null value, then a locator *L* that uniquely identifies *SV* is generated and the value *TV* of the *i*-th bound target is set to an implementation-dependent four-octet value that represents *L*.
14. If TYPE indicates ROW and *TV* is the null value, then the value of *IP* for *IDA* and that in all subordinate descriptor areas of *IDA* that are not subordinate to an item descriptor area whose TYPE indicates ARRAY or ARRAY_LOCATOR is set to the appropriate 'Code' for SQL NULL DATA in Table 26, "Miscellaneous codes used in SQL/CLI," in ISO/IEC 9075-3, and

the value of the host variable addressed by *DP* and the values of *D* and of *LP* are implementation-dependent.

15. If TYPE does not indicate ROW and *TV* is the null value, then the value of *IP* is set to the appropriate 'Code' for SQL NULL DATA in Table 26, "Miscellaneous codes used in SQL/CLI," in ISO/IEC 9075-3, and the value of the host variable addressed by *DP* and the values of *D* and of *LP* are implementation-dependent.
16. If *TT* indicates BINARY LARGE OBJECT and *L* is not greater than *TL,* then the first *L* octets of *T* are set to *V* and the values of the remaining octets of *T* are implementation-dependent.
17. It is implementation-dependent what `AllocWrapperEnv( )`makes of the values of Wrapper-Name *WN* and WrapperLibraryName *WL.*
18. It is implementation-dependent what use the foreign-data wrapper makes of the values of AuthorizationID *UN,* ServerName *SN,* ServerType *ST,* and ServerVersion *SV.*
19. If *P* is a `<dynamic select statement>` or a `<dynamic single row select statement>`, then a unique implementation-dependent name becomes the cursor name associated with FDWexecution.
20. If an exception condition is raised during the derivation of any target value, then the values of all the bound targets are implementation-dependent and *CR* remains positioned on the current row.
21. If *FI* indicates TYPE, then all fields of *IDA* other than those prescribed are set to implementation-dependent values.
22. If *FI* indicates DATETIME_INTERVAL_CODE and the TYPE field of *IDA* indicates a `<datetime type>`, then all the fields of *IDA* other than DATETIME_INTERVAL_CODE and TYPE are set to implementation-dependent values.
23. If an exception condition is raised, then the field of *IDA* indicated by *FI* is set to an implementation-dependent value.

Online Analytical Processing

1. The window name of a window defined implicitly by an `<in-line window specification>` is implementation-dependent.
2. If the window ordering clause of a window structure descriptor is absent, then the window ordering is entirely implementation-dependent.
3. The window ordering of peer rows within a window partition is implementation-dependent, but the window ordering shall be the same for all

window structure descriptors that are order-equivalent. It shall also be the same for windows *W1* and *W2* if *W1* is the ordering window for *W2*.

4. The `<column name>` of a `<derived column>` that is not a `<column reference>` and that has no `<as clause>` is implementation-dependent, but shall not be equivalent to the `<column name>` of any column, other than itself, of a table referenced by any `<table reference>` contained in the SQL-statement.
5. If the declared type of the argument of MAX or MIN is a user-defined type and the comparison of two values results in *unknown,* then the maximum or minimum is implementation-dependent.
6. If PV_i and QV_i are not null and the result of "PV_i <comp op> QV_i" is *unknown,* then the relative ordering of Pv_i and QV_i is implementation-dependent.
7. The relative ordering of two rows that are not distinct with respect to the `<sort specification>` is implementation-dependent.

Java-Related Specifications

1. If invocation of a ConnectionContext object's isClosed method would return the value true, then the effect of invoking any methods other than isClosed and close against that object is implementation-dependent.
2. Customization objects are implementation-dependent.
3. The deployment tool, or customizer, used to load the profile, inspect and precompile the SQL operations it contains, register an appropriate customization object, and store the profile back to disk, is implementation-dependent.
4. Creating the database connection with which a profile will be customized is implementation-dependent.
5. The effect of violating SQLJ's reserved variable name space is implementation-dependent.
6. The effect of violating SQLJ's reserved internal class name space is implementation-dependent.
7. If a generated connection class's getProfileKey method is called with a profile loader **PL** and a profile name **PN**, and a profile key object does not already exist for the profile named **PN** loaded with profile loader **PL**, then the profile key object that is returned is implementation-dependent.
8. If a runtime exception condition is raised during the execution of an `<executable clause>`, then the values of any OUT or INOUT `<embedded Java expression>`s are implementation-dependent.

9. If `<select statement: single row>` is not contained in an `<embedded SQL java program>`, then the order of assignment of values to targets in the `<select target list>` is implementation-dependent.
10. If `<fetch statement>` is not contained in an `<embedded SQL java program>`, then the order of assignment of values to targets in the `<fetch target list>` is implementation-dependent.
11. If the execution of a `<fetch statement>` results in a row not found, then the values of the `<embedded Java expression>`s contained in the `<fetch target list>` are implementation-dependent.
12. If `<query clause>` does not contain an `<order by clause>`, or contains an `<order by clause>` that does not specify the order of the rows completely, then the rows of the table have an order that is defined only to the extent that the `<order by clause>` specifies an order and is otherwise implementation-dependent.
13. The order of the TypeInfo objects in the Result Set Info of the Result Set Column Java fields of Profile EntryInfo for a `<query clause>` whose associated iterator object is a `<named iterator>` is implementation-dependent.
14. After invocation of a NamedIterator object's next( ) method has returned false, the behavior of any subsequent invocations of that object's named accessor methods is implementation-dependent.
15. After invocation of a ResultSetIterator object's isClosed( ) method has returned true, the behavior of any subsequent invocations of that ResultSetIterator object's methods is implementation-dependent.
16. If a ResultSetIterator object has not had its fetch size set by invocation of its setFetchSize method, or has a fetch size of 0 (zero), then the value resulting from invocation of getFetchSize is implementation-dependent
17. If SQLJ runtime does not support this ResultSet iterator object's declared sensitivity `<with value>` of SENSITIVE or INSENSITIVE, then the result of invoking getSensitivity against that ResultSet iterator object is implementation-dependent.
18. If the int value specified in invocation of setFetchSize against this ResultSet iterator object is 0 (zero), then the fetch size used is implementation-dependent.
19. At runtime a registered Customization object can make a user identifier, stored in a customized profile, the user identifier for privilege checking of that profile object's statements in an implementation-dependent manner.

20. The processing of escape clauses during customization is implementation-dependent.
21. Once an RTStatement object's executeComplete method has been called, the effect of further calls to any of its other methods are implementation-dependent.
22. The effects of a call to any getXXX method of an RTStatement object whose associated EntryInfo object's getStatementType( ) method returns PREPARED_STATEMENT is implementation-dependent.
23. The manner in which built-in procedures are defined is implementation-dependent.
24. The scope and persistence of any modifications to static attributes made during the execution of a Java method is implementation-dependent.
25. If *R* is an external Java routine, then the scope and persistence of any modifications of class variables made before the completion of any execution of *P* is implementation-dependent.
26. If the language specifies ADA (respectively C, COBOL, FORTRAN, JAVA, MUMPS, PASCAL, PLI) and *P* is not a standard-conforming Ada program (respectively C, COBOL, Fortran, Java, MUMPS, Pascal, PL/I program), then the results of any execution of *P* are implementation-dependent.
27. The effect of `SQLJ.REPLACE_JAR` on currently executing SQL statements that use an SQL routine or structured type whose implementation has been replaced is implementation-dependent.
28. The effect of `SQLJ.REMOVE_JAR` on currently executing SQL statements that use an SQL routine or structured type whose implementation has been removed is implementation-dependent.
29. The effect of `SQLJ.ALTER_JAVA_PATH` on SQL statements that have already been prepared or are currently executing is implementation-dependent.

XML-Related Specifications

1. All annotations are implementation-dependent.
2. It is implementation-dependent whether to encode a binary string in hex or base64.
3. It is implementation-dependent whether to encode a bit string in hex or base64.

B.3 SQL:1999 Conformance Claims

In the first volume of this book, conformance to Core SQL was described, and the additional features and packages of SQL:1999 beyond Core SQL were listed. The additional SQL:1999 facilities discussed in this volume do not impact Core SQL at all, but they do add new features to the non-Core components of the standard. In Table B.1, you may find the Feature ID and a short description of each feature of SQL:1999 that was not included in the corresponding table in Volume 1 of this book.

Table B.1 *Additional Features Not in Core SQL:1999*

Feature ID	*Feature Description*	*Part Defining Feature*
J001	Embedded Java	SQL/OLB
J511	Commands	SQL/JRT
J521	JDBC data types	SQL/JRT
J531	Deployment	SQL/JRT
J541	SERIALIZABLE	SQL/JRT
J551	SQLDATA	SQL/JRT
J561	JAR privileges	SQL/JRT
J571	NEW operator	SQL/JRT
J581	Output parameters	SQL/JRT
J591	Overloading	SQL/JRT
J601	SQL-Java paths	SQL/JRT
J611	References	SQL/JRT
J621	External Java routines	SQL/JRT
J622	External Java types	SQL/JRT
J631	Java signatures	SQL/JRT
J641	Static fields	SQL/JRT
J651	SQL/JRT Information Schema	SQL/JRT
J652	SQL/JRT Usage tables	SQL/JRT
M001	Datalinks	SQL/MED
M004	Foreign data support	SQL/MED
M002	Datalinks via SQL/CLI	SQL/MED
M003	Datalinks via Embedded SQL	SQL/MED

B.4 Appendix Summary

With the information in this appendix and the corresponding appendix in Volume 1 of this book, you should now have an understanding of what is and is not contained in Core SQL:1999 and how the various implementation-defined and implementation-dependent aspects of the language are defined. The topics discussed in this appendix are useful in several ways. First, you can evaluate commercial DBMS products that claim SQL:1999 compliance and support, based on the degree to which SQL:1999 is supported. Additionally, you can check product features that are implementation-specific against the lists provided here. Since these variables are likely to be among the major differentiators for DBMS products, you can concentrate on these aspects in your product-to-product comparisons. Finally, you can also use the list of deprecated features to avoid future applications-related problems with respect to potentially unsupported SQL facilities.

Appendix C

Relevant Standards Bodies

C.1 Introduction

If you would like to acquire a copy of the SQL:1999 standard, you may do so by contacting the accredited standards body for your country. You can request a copy of the ISO SQL:1999 standard by specifying the documents listed in the "ISO Number" column of Table C.1. If you live in the United States, you can get the ANSI standard (which is identical to the ISO standard except for such trivial matters as the name of the standard and the list of referenced standards) by specifying the documents listed in the "ANSI Number" column of Table C.1. SQL-92 and earlier versions of the SQL standard were available only in hardcopy form, that is, printed on paper, from ISO and from ANSI. While hardcopy is still available from certain National Bodies (I believe that BSI has published at least the first five parts in hardcopy form, for example), you may prefer to acquire it in electronic, or machine-readable, form, specifically as an Adobe Acrobat Portable Document Format (PDF) file. All parts of SQL:1999 are available in PDF form, either for download or on CD-ROM (depending on the source).

Table C.1 *ISO and ANSI Standards Numbers for SQL:1999*

Part Name	*ISO Number*	*ANSI Number*
SQL/Framework	ISO/IEC 9075-1:1999	ANSI/ISO/IEC 9075-1:1999
SQL/Foundation	ISO/IEC 9075-2:1999	ANSI/ISO/IEC 9075-2:1999
SQL/CLI	ISO/IEC 9075-3:1999	ANSI/ISO/IEC 9075-3:1999
SQL/PSM	ISO/IEC 9075-4:1999	ANSI/ISO/IEC 9075-4:1999
SQL/Bindings	ISO/IEC 9075-5:1999	ANSI/ISO/IEC 9075-5:1999
SQL/MED	ISO/IEC 9075-9:1999	ANSI/ISO/IEC 9075-9:1999
SQL/OLB	ISO/IEC 9075-10:1999	ANSI/ISO/IEC 9075-10:1999
SQL/JRT	ISO/IEC 9075-13:2002	ANSI/ISO/IEC 9075-13:2002

Similarly, copies of all parts of the SQL/MM standard are available electronically in PDF form, either for download or on CD-ROM (again, depending on the source). The SQL/MM standards are not available with an ANSI number, only with any ISO number. Table C.2 contains the designations for SQL/MM's parts.

Table C.2 *ISO Standards Numbers for SQL/MM*

Part Name	*ISO Number*
SQL/MM Framework	ISO/IEC 13249-1:2000
SQL/MM Full-Text	ISO/IEC 13249-2:2000
SQL/MM Spatial	ISO/IEC 13249-3:1999
SQL/MM Still Image	ISO/IEC 13249-4:2001
SQL/MM Data Mining	ISO/IEC 13249-5:2002

The prices of purchasing the standards documents from ISO directly and from most national bodies is quite high, on the order of several hundred U.S. dollars for all eight parts. If you need a paper copy, this might be a viable alternative.

However, it is possible to purchase each part of the SQL standard (but not, I'm sorry to say, the SQL/MM standard) from the U.S. body responsible for its development (INCITS, the International Committee for Information Technology Standards) by means of a Web transaction using a credit card and a file download. At the URL *http://www.cssinfo.com/ncitsgate.html,* you can purchase each part for U.S. $18.00 (a total of U.S. $126 for all seven parts).

Both SQL and each part of SQL/MM are subject to error correction through the publication of Technical Corrigenda. The Technical Corrigenda documents are available from the same sources as the various parts of each standard.

In this appendix, I provide the names, addresses, telephone numbers, and (where available) fax numbers and Web addresses for the national standards bodies for several countries. If I have omitted your country, I apologize, but it is not feasible to list every country, so I have focused on those countries I believe most likely to have interested readers.

Some countries have adopted the ISO standard and put their own standard number on it. However, this practice is not widespread and often follows publication of the ISO standard by as much as two or three years, so I won't attempt to provide that information.

The information provided here was current at the time of publication but is always subject to change.

C.2 Contacting ISO

You can contact ISO at these addresses:

International Organization for Standardization (ISO)
1, rue de Varembé
Case postale 56
CH-1211 Geneva 20
Switzerland
Telephone: +41.22.749.0111
Telefax: +41.22.733.3430
E-mail: central@iso.org
WWW: *http://www.iso.org*

C.3 Selected National Standards Bodies

Australia
Standards Australia (SAI)
GPO Box 5420
Sydney—N.S.W. 2001
Telephone: +.61.2.8206.6000
Fax: +61.2.8200.6001
E-mail: sales@standards.com.au
WWW: *http://www.standards.com.au*

Canada
Standards Council of Canada (SCC)
270 Albert Street, Suite 200
Ottawa, Ontario K1P 6N7
Telephone: +1.613.238.3222
Fax: +1.613.569.7808
E-mail: info@scc.ca
WWW: *http://www.scc.ca*

China, People's Republic of
State Administration of China for Standardization (SAC)
4, Zhichuan Road
Haidan District
Beijing 100088
Telephone: +86.10.6200.0675
Fax: +86.10.6203.3737
E-mail: sacs@mail.csbts.cn.net
WWW: *http://www.csbts.cn.net*

Denmark
Dansk Standard
Kollegievej 6
DK-2920 Charlottenlund
Telephone: +45.39.96.61.01
Fax: +45.39.96.61.02
E-mail: dansk.standard@ds.dk
WWW: *http://www.ds.dk*

France
Association Française de Normalisation (AFNOR)
11, avenue Francis de Pressensé
93571 Saint-Denis La Plaine Cedex
Telephone: +33.1.41.62.80.00
Fax: +33.1.49.17.90.80
WWW: *http://www.afnor.fr*

Germany
Deutsches Institut für Normung (DIN)
Burggrafenstrasse 6
D-10787 Berlin
Telephone: +49.30.2601-0
Fax: +49.30.2601-1231
E-mail: postmaster@din.de
WWW: *http://www.din.de*

Hungary
Magyar Szabványügyi Testület (MSZT)
Hungarian Standards Insitution
H-1091 Budapest
Üllöi út 25
Telephone: +36.1.456.6800
Fax: +36.1.456.6884
E-mail: isoline@mszt.hu
WWW: *http://www.mszt.hu*

India
Bureau of Indian Standards (BIS)
Manak Bhavan
9 Bahadur Shah Zafar Marg
New Delhi 110002
Telephone: +91.11.323.0131
Fax: +.91.11.323.4062
E-mail: bisind@vsnl.com
WWW: *http://www.bis.org.in*

Ireland
National Standards Authority of Ireland (NSAI)
Glasnevin
Dublin 9
Telephone: +353.1.807.3800
Fax: +353.1.807.3838
E-mail: nsai@nsai.ie
WWW: *http://www.nsai.ie*

Israel
Standards Institution of Israel (SII)
42 Chaim Levanon Street
Tel Aviv 69977
Telephone: +972.3.646.5154
Fax: +972.3.641.9683
E-mail: iso/iec@sii.org.il
WWW: *http://www.sii.org.il*

Italy
Ente Nazionale Italiano di Unificaziono (UNI)
via Battistotti Sassi 11/B
I-20133 Milano MI
Telephone: +39.02.70024.1
Fax: +39.2.70105992
E-mail: uni@uni.com
WWW: *http://www.uni.com*

Japan
Japanese Industrial Standards Committee (JISC)
c/o Standards Department
Ministry of Economy, Trade, and Industry
1-3-1, Kasumigaseki, Chiyoda-ku
Tokyo 100-8901
Telephone: +81.3.3501.9471
Fax: +81.3.3580.8637
E-mail: jisc@meti.go.jp
WWW: *http://www.jisc.org*

Korea, Republic of
Korean Agency for Technology and Standards (KATS)
2, Joongang-dong
Gwacheon
Kyonggi-do 427-716
Telephone: +82.2.509.7399
Telefax:+82.2.503.7977
E-mail: standard@ats.go.kr
WWW: *http://www.ats.go.kr*

The Netherlands
Nederlands Normalisatie-instituut (NEN)
Postbus 5059
NL-2600 GB Delft
Telephone: +31.15.2.690.390
Fax: +31.15.2.690.190
E-mail: info@nen.nl
WWW: *http://www.nen.nl*

Norway
Norges Standardiseringsforbund (NSF)
Drammensveien 145 A
Postboks 432 Skøyen
NO-0213 Oslo
Telephone: +47.22.04.92.00
Fax: +47.22.04.92.11
E-mail: firmapost@standard.no
WWW: *http://www.standard.no*

Russian Federation
Committee of the Russian Federation for Standardization, Metrology, and Certification (GOST R)
Leninsky Prospekt 9
Moskva B-49, ГСП, 119991
Telephone: +7.95.236.0300
Fax: +7.95.236.6231
E-mail: info@gost.ru
WWW: *http://www.gost.ru*

Spain
Asociación Española de Normalización y Certificación (AENOR)
Génova, 6
28004 Madrid
Telephone: +34.914.32.6000
Fax: +34.913.10.4032
E-mail: aenor@aenor.es
WWW: *http://www.aenor.es*

Sweden
SIS, Swedish Standard Institute (SIS)
SE-118 80 Stockholm
Sankt Paulsgatan 6
Telephone: +46.8.555.520.00
Fax: +46.8.555.520.01
E-mail: info@sis.se
WWW: *http://www.sis.se*

Switzerland
Swiss Association for Standardization (SNV)
Bürglistrasse 29
8400 Winterthur
Telephone: +41.52.224.5454
Fax: +41.52.224.5474
E-mail: info@snv.ch
WWW: *http://www.snv.ch*

United Kingdom
British Standards Institute (BSI)
389 Chiswick High Road
GB-London W4 4AL
Telephone: +44.181.996.9000
Fax: +44.181.996.7400
E-mail: info@bsi.org.uk
WWW: *http://www.bsi.org.uk*

United States of America
American National Standards Institute (ANSI)
25 West 43rd Street, 4th Floor
New York, NY 10036
Telephone: +1.212.642.4900
Fax: +1.212.398.0023
E-mail: info@ansi.org
WWW: *http://www.ansi.org*

Appendix D

Status Codes

D.1 Values of SQLSTATE

In this appendix, you will find the various values of SQLSTATE. This status code was discussed in the first volume of this book (Chapter 20, "Diagnostics and Error Management"). The corresponding appendix of that first volume, Appendix E, "Status Codes," listed the SQLSTATE values as of the publication of that volume. This appendix repeats and updates that information based on the new parts of SQL and the various parts of SQL/MM discussed in this volume. Of course, the SQLSTATE values for parts of SQL and of SQL/MM that have not yet been published (such as SQL/XML and SQL/MM Data Mining) are only speculative; they won't be finalized until the standard has been published.

In Table D.1, the column named *Category* contains a code to indicate the specific type of SQLSTATE to which the Condition and Class correspond. *Category X* means that the Condition and Class identify an exception condition; *N* means the no data completion condition, *W* means a warning completion condition, and *S* means a successful completion condition. As you'd expect, rows for subconditions take on the SQLSTATE type of their associated Condition and Class.

Table D.1 *SQLSTATE Values for SQL*

Category	*Condition*	*Class*	*Subcondition*	*Subclass*
S	successful completion	00	*(no subclass)*	000
N	no data	02	*(no subclass)*	000
			no additional dynamic result sets returned	001
W	warning	01	*(no subclass)*	000
			additional result sets returned	00D
			array data, right truncation	02F
			attempt to return too many result sets	00E
			cursor operation conflict	001
			default value too long for information schema	00B
			disconnect error	002
			dynamic result sets returned	00C
			external routine warning (the value of *nn* to be chosen by the author of the external routine)	H*nn*
			implicit zero-bit padding	008
			insufficient item descriptor areas	005
			null value eliminated in set function	003
			privilege not granted	007
			privilege not revoked	006
			query expression too long for information schema	00A
			search condition too long for information schema	009
			statement too long for information schema	005
			string data, right truncation	004
X	ambiguous cursor name	3C	*(no subclass)*	000
X	cardinality violation	21	*(no subclass)*	000
X	connection exception	08	*(no subclass)*	000
			connection does not exist	003
			connection failure	006

Table D.1 *(Continued)*

Category	*Condition*	*Class*	*Subcondition*	*Subclass*
			connection name in use	002
			SQL-client unable to establish SQL-connection	001
			SQL-server rejected establishment of SQL-connection	004
			transaction resolution unknown	007
X	cursor sensitivity exception	36	*(no subclass)*	000
			request failed	002
			request rejected	001
X	data exception	22	*(no subclass)*	000
			array data, right truncation	02F
			array element error	02E
			character not in repertoire	021
			datalink value exceeds maximum length	01D
			datetime field overflow	008
			division by zero	012
			error in assignment	005
			escape character conflict	00B
			indicator overflow	022
			interval field overflow	015
			invalid character value for cast	018
			invalid data specified for datalink	017
			invalid datetime format	007
			invalid escape character	019
			invalid escape octet	00D
			invalid escape sequence	025
			invalid indicator parameter value	010
			invalid limit value	020
			invalid parameter value	023

(continued)

Table D.1 *(Continued)*

Category	*Condition*	*Class*	*Subcondition*	*Subclass*
			invalid regular expression	01B
			invalid time zone displacement value	009
			invalid update value	014
			invalid use of escape character	00C
			most specific type mismatch	00G
			null argument passed to datalink constructor	01A
			null image value *(same value as "null instance used in mutator function," for use by SQL/MM)*	02D
			null instance used in mutator function	02D
			null row not permitted in table	01C
			null value in array target	00E
			null value in reference target	00A
			null value in field reference	006
			null value, no indicator parameter	002
			null value not allowed	004
			numeric value out of range	003
			row already exists	028
			string data, length mismatch	026
			string data, right truncation	001
			substring error	011
			trim error	027
			unterminated C string	024
			zero-length character string	00F
X	dependent privilege descriptors still exist	2B	*(no subclass)*	000
X	external routine exception	38	*(no subclass)*	000
			containing SQL not permitted	001
			modifying SQL-data not permitted	002

Table D.1 *(Continued)*

Category	*Condition*	*Class*	*Subcondition*	*Subclass*
			prohibited SQL-statement attempted	003
			reading SQL-data not permitted	004
X	external routine invocation exception	39	*(no subclass)*	000
			invalid SQLSTATE returned	001
			null value not allowed	004
X	feature not supported	0A	*(no subclass)*	000
			multiple server transactions	001
X	integrity constraint violation	23	*(no subclass)*	000
			restrict violation	001
X	invalid authorization specification	28	*(no subclass)*	000
X	invalid catalog name	3D	*(no subclass)*	000
X	invalid condition number	35	*(no subclass)*	000
X	invalid connection name	2E	*(no subclass)*	000
X	invalid cursor name	34	*(no subclass)*	000
X	invalid cursor state	24	*(no subclass)*	000
X	invalid grantor	0L	*(no subclass)*	000
X	invalid role specification	0P	*(no subclass)*	000
X	invalid schema name	3F	*(no subclass)*	000
X	invalid SQL descriptor name	33	*(no subclass)*	000
X	invalid SQL statement name	26	*(no subclass)*	000
X	invalid SQL statement	30	*(no subclass)*	000
X	invalid target specification value	31	*(no subclass)*	000
X	invalid target type specification	0D	*(no subclass)*	000
X	invalid transaction initiation	0B	*(no subclass)*	000

(continued)

Table D.1 *(Continued)*

Category	*Condition*	*Class*	*Subcondition*	*Subclass*
X	invalid transaction state	25	*(no subclass)*	000
			active SQL-transaction	001
			branch transaction already active	002
			held cursor requires same isolation level	008
			inappropriate access mode for branch transaction	003
			inappropriate isolation level for branch transaction	004
			no active SQL-transaction for branch transaction	005
			read-only SQL-transaction	006
			schema and data statement mixing not supported	007
X	invalid transaction termination	2D	*(no subclass)*	000
X	locator exception	0F	*(no subclass)*	000
			invalid specification	001
X	prohibited statement encountered during trigger execution	0W	*(no subclass)*	000
X	Remote Database Access	HZ	*Defined by ISO/IEC 9579 (Remote Database Access)*	
X	savepoint exception	3B	*(no subclass)*	000
			invalid specification	001
			too many	002
X	SQL routine exception	2F	*(no subclass)*	000
			function executed no return statement	005
			modifying SQL-data not permitted	002
			prohibited SQL-statement attempted	003
			reading SQL-data not permitted	004
X	SQL statement not yet complete	03	*(no subclass)*	000

Table D.1 *(Continued)*

Category	*Condition*	*Class*	*Subcondition*	*Subclass*
X	syntax error or access rule violation	42	*(no subclass)*	000
X	transaction rollback	40	*(no subclass)*	000
			integrity constraint violation	002
			serialization failure	001
			statement completion unknown	003
			triggered action exception	004
X	triggered action exception	09	*(no subclass)*	000
X	triggered data change violation	27	*(no subclass)*	000
X	with check option violation	44	*(no subclass)*	000
X	CLI-specific condition	HY	*(no subclass)*	000
			associated statement is not prepared	007
			attempt to concatenate a null value	020
			attribute cannot be set now	011
			column type out of range	097
			dynamic parameter value needed	*(see note at table's end)*
			function sequence error	010
			inconsistent descriptor information	021
			invalid attribute identifier	092
			invalid attribute value	024
			invalid cursor position	109
			invalid data type	004
			invalid data type in application descriptor	003
			invalid descriptor field identifier	091
			invalid fetch orientation	106
			invalid FunctionId specified	095

(continued)

Table D.1 *(Continued)*

Category	*Condition*	*Class*	*Subcondition*	*Subclass*
			invalid handle	*(see note at table's end)*
			invalid information type	096
			invalid LengthPrecision value	104
			invalid parameter mode	105
			invalid retrieval code	103
			invalid string length or buffer length	090
			invalid transaction operation code	012
			invalid use of automatically-allocated descriptor handle	017
			invalid use of null pointer	009
			limit on number of handles exceeded	014
			memory allocation error	001
			memory management error	013
			non-string data cannot be sent in pieces	019
			non-string data cannot be used with string routine	055
			nullable type out of range	099
			operation canceled	008
			optional feature not implemented	C00
			row value out of range	107
			scope out of range	098
			server declined the cancellation request	018
X	case not found for case statement	20	*(no subclass)*	000
X	resignal when handler not active	0K	*(no subclass)*	000
X	unhandled user-defined exception	45	*(no subclass)*	000
X	attempt to assign to non-updatable column	0U	*(no subclass)*	000

Table D.1 *(Continued)*

Category	*Condition*	*Class*	*Subcondition*	*Subclass*
X	attempt to assign to ordering column	0V	*(no subclass)*	000
X	dynamic SQL error	07	*(no subclass)*	000
			cursor specification cannot be executed	003
			invalid descriptor count	008
			invalid descriptor index	009
			prepared statement not a cursor specification	005
			restricted data type attribute violation	006
			undefined DATA value	00C
			undefined DATA target	00D
			undefined LEVEL value	00E
			undefined DATETIME_INTERVAL_CODE	00F
			using clause does not match dynamic parameter specifications	001
			using clause does not match target specifications	002
			using clause required for dynamic parameters	004
			using clause required for result fields	007
			data type transform function violation	00B
X	invalid SQL-invoked procedure reference	0M	*(no subclass)*	000
X	invalid character set name	2C	*(no subclass)*	000
X	invalid schema name list specification	0E	*(no subclass)*	000
X	invalid transform group name specification	0S	*(no subclass)*	000
X	target table disagrees with cursor specification	0T	*(no subclass)*	000
X	CLI-specific condition	HY	invalid datalink value	093

(continued)

Table D.1 *(Continued)*

Category	*Condition*	*Class*	*Subcondition*	*Subclass*
X	datalink exception	HW	*(no subclass)*	000
			external file not linked	001
			external file already linked	002
			referenced file does not exist	003
X	FDW-specific condition	HV	*(no subclass)*	000
			column name not found	005
			dynamic parameter value needed	002
			function sequence error	010
			inconsistent descriptor information	021
			invalid attribute value	024
			invalid column name	007
			invalid column number	008
			invalid data type	004
			invalid data type descriptors	006
			invalid descriptor field identifier	091
			invalid handle	00B
			invalid option index	00C
			invalid option name	00D
			invalid string length or buffer length	090
			invalid string format	00A
			invalid use of null pointer	009
			limit on number of handles exceeded	014
			memory allocation error	001
			no schemas	00P
			option name not found	00J
			reply handle	00K
			schema not found	00Q
			table not found	00R
			unable to create execution	00L
			unable to create reply	00M
			unable to establish connection	00N

Table D.1 *(Continued)*

Category	*Condition*	*Class*	*Subcondition*	*Subclass*
X	invalid foreign server specification	0X	*(no subclass)*	000
X	pass-through specific condition	0Y	*(no subclass)*	000
			invalid cursor option	001
			invalid cursor allocation	002
X	Java DDL	46	*(no subclass)*	000
			invalid URL	001
			invalid JAR name	002
			invalid class deletion	003
			invalid replacement	005
			attempt to replace uninstalled JAR	00A
			attempt to remove uninstalled JAR	00B
X	Java execution	46	*(no subclass)*	000
			invalid JAR name in path	102
			unresolved class name	103
X	SQL/XML mapping error	0N	*(no subclass)*	000
			unmappable XML Name	001

Note: No subclass value is defined for the subcondition *invalid handle,* since no diagnostic information can be generated in this case, or for the subcondition *dynamic parameter value needed,* since no diagnostic information is generated in this case.

In Table D.2, I've provided the SQLSTATE status code values for the SQL/MM standard.

Table D.2 *SQLSTATE Values for SQL/MM*

Category	*Condition*	*Class*	*Subcondition*	*Subclass*
X	SQL/MM, Part 1		*(none)*	
X	SQL/MM, Part 2	2F	invalid search expression	F01
			invalid language specification	F02
			effectively empty search specfication	F03
X	SQL/MM, Part 3	2F	invalid position	F01
			invalid parameter	F02
			null parameter	F03
			invalid intersection matrix	F04
			duplicate value	F05
			empty array	F06
			null exterior ring	F07
			element is not a valid type	F08
			element is a null value	F09
			mixed spatial reference systems	F10
			non-contiguous curves	F11
			curve value is not a linestring value	F12
X	SQL/MM, Part 5	22	null image value	02D
		2F	incorrect image format	F01
			incorrect average color feature specification	F02
			incorrect color histogram feature specification	F03
			incorrect feature list specification	F04
			incorrect color specification	F05
			bad input image; average color feature cannot be determined	F06
			bad input image; positional color feature cannot be determined	F07
			bad input image; color histogram feature cannot be determined	F08
			bad input image; texture feature cannot be determined	F09

Table D.2 *(Continued)*

Category	*Condition*	*Class*	*Subcondition*	*Subclass*
			illegal image format specification	F10
			unsupported image format conversion specified	F11
			illegal specification for thumbnail generation	F12
			fatal error during image format conversion	F13
X	SQL/MM, Part 6	2F	alias already in use	F01
			data and data specification of model not compatible	F02
			field already defined	F03
			field not categorical	F04
			field not defined in data specification	F05
			field not numeric	F06
			invalid source table name	F07
			invalid field name	F08
			invalid import format	F09
			invalid input data	F10
			mining field position out of range	F11
			model computation failed	F12
			no logical data specification defined	F13
			null error weight	F14
			null parameter	F15
			null settings	F16
			null training data	F17
			parameter out of range	F18
			invalid application input data format	F19

Appendix E

The SQL Standardization Process

E.1 Introduction

In this appendix, I present an overview of the ANSI and ISO standardization processes with an emphasis on SQL. While this material isn't essential to use SQL, it will give interested readers some background about how certain facets of the language have been developed. Those who wonder why SQL doesn't have such-and-such a feature or why SQL does things in a particular way will likely understand a bit more about the standardization process from this discussion.

E.2 The Various Standards Bodies

E.2.1 National Standards

ANSI, the American National Standards Institute, is the primary formal standards-making body in the United States. Other countries (especially the developed countries, but also many developing countries) have their own standards bodies: for example, BSI (the British Standards Institute) in the United Kingdom, AFNOR (Association Française de Normalization) in France, and DIN (Deutsches Institut für Normung) in Germany. I limit this national standards overview to

ANSI, since no other national standards body has developed its own independent SQL standard.

ANSI is really an oversight organization and a standards publishing organization rather than a developer of standards itself. The actual work of developing standards is the responsibility of ASDOs (accredited standards development organizations). Responsibility for standards in the area of information processing has been given to an organization called INCITS (International Committee for Information Technology Standards), formerly known by the code-without-a-meaning X3 and, until recently, NCITS (National Committee for Information Technology Standards). The day-to-day affairs of INCITS are managed by an industry group called ITIC (Information Technology Industry Council), headquartered in Washington, DC.

INCITS's responsibilities are very broad and extensive, so it further delegates the actual technical work to technical committees (TCs) and to special working groups. When INCITS was still known as X3, it created a special group called SPARC (Standards Planning and Requirements Committee), whose job it was to determine the need for standards in certain areas and to oversee the development of those standards. SPARC had its own subgroups, one of which was named DBSSG (Database Systems Study Group), which was concerned with broad issues of database standardization (as opposed to specific standards like SQL). However, with the change in name to NCITS and then to INCITS, the special groups were also dropped, leaving INCITS as a whole responsible for reviewing proposals for new standards, progress on standards development, and so forth.

There are many INCITS technical committees. One of these is named H2, which has the title "Database." H2's responsibilities include SQL and other projects not relevant to this book. (For more information about H2's other responsibilities, please contact ITIC.)

When somebody believes that the time is ripe to develop a standard for some area of information processing, they write a project proposal for submission to INCITS. This document, called an *SD-3* (for *Standing Document number 3*) sets forth the details of the standards development activity proposed for the specific area. This includes information such as the proposed name, the relationship to existing standards or developing standards, the affected industry, the likely participants in the project, and so forth.

If INCITS agrees that an effort should be made to standardize the area in question, it will either assign the project to an existing INCITS technical committee (who may have been the "somebody" who wrote the SD-3 in the first place) or recommend the formation of a new technical committee to do the work.

The TC responsible for the project then produces a working draft of the standard (indeed, many SD-3s are accompanied by a proposed working draft, which considerably accelerates the work). At some point, the technical committee conducts a formal ballot to decide if the working draft is ready for broader review. This decision requires a ballot agreement of at least two-thirds of the committee. If ready, the TC asks INCITS to approve the initiation of a public review of the document. The purpose of a public review is to permit the general public, in the United States and elsewhere, to review the document and comment on it. The TC is required to respond to every comment within a relatively short period following a public review (although they are obviously not required to satisfy every request!).

The document may iterate through several cycles of development and public review. At some point, though, the TC members will decide that the document is complete and will make no further changes as a result of public review comments. The document is then forwarded to BSR (the Board of Standard Review) for its review. BSR's review ensures that the ANSI and INCITS rules have been followed and that no one has been deprived of due process. Assuming that these requirements have been met, the document is then published as an ANSI standard. INCITS's standards are published with an identifying number, INCITS *n*, where INCITS identifies the standard as coming from INCITS, and *n* identifies the *n*-th standard published by INCITS (possibly in its earlier incarnations as X3 and NCITS). Before X3 became NCITS, its standards were numbered "X3.*n*." After the change to NCITS, but before INCITS, its standards were numbered "NCITS.*n*." In addition, the year of publication is attached to the number: X3.135-1986 is the number of the first version of the SQL standard, published in 1986, for example.

In recent years, some standards—SQL among them—that were developed principally in the international community (that is, in ISO) were merely adopted by ANSI and given the ISO number prefixed with "ANSI/."

E.2.2 International Standards

Once upon a time, when the world was a larger and simpler place to do business, national standards were quite sufficient for most people's purposes. In fact, one often found that ANSI developed a standard for some area of information processing technology and other national standards bodies simply adopted the ANSI standard unchanged. This process occasionally worked the other way, too: ANSI sometimes adopted other countries' standards unchanged.

However, as the world became smaller and more complex, businesses and other users of information processing systems realized that they were faced with using products that had to conform to one standard in one country and a different standard in another country. That fact cost many organizations countless millions of dollars and untold difficulties. These organizations, and others who became aware of the problems, realized that only international standards would address their requirements. The International Organization for Standardization (ISO) was formed specifically to address these concerns.[1]

Some such organizations are called *treaty organizations* because they are established by treaty among various nations and their specifications are mandatory for adoption by signatories to those treaties. Others, such as ISO, are *voluntary standards organizations,* because adoption of their standards is not mandated by a treaty (although this can be mandated within a given country, as determined by the laws of that country).

Like ANSI, ISO has far too broad a scope to permit actual work to be done at that level. Instead, ISO also assigns areas of work to technical committees (TCs). In some areas, such as information technology, the scope is still too broad, so subcommittees (SCs) are formed. In a few cases, data management among them, the work is still too extensive, so working groups (WGs) are given the responsibility. (As incredible as it sounds, some working groups' responsibilities are so broad that they form less formal subgroups called *rapporteur groups*, so-called because it is their responsibility to reach *rapport* among participants before making recommendations to their parent WGs.)

In ISO, work on information technology was assigned in the mid-1980s to a technical committee numbered TC97. This committee was later reorganized, in cooperation with IEC, as JTC1 (Joint Technical Committee 1). An area of information technology called Open Systems Interconnect (OSI) was divided into two groups; the responsibility for "Information Processing, Transfer, and Retrieval for OSI" was given to a subcommittee numbered SC21. In turn, responsibility for database issues was given to a working group, WG3 (full title: ISO/IEC JTC1/SC21/WG3).

In the late 1990s, the failure of OSI became apparent to even the most casual observer—a different networking standard, often known as TCP/IP, had won the day while the *de jure* standards organizations were fighting over the details of their intended new protocols. In the wake of OSI's demise, SC21 was dismantled and its projects either cancelled entirely or assigned to other subcommittees. The various data management–related projects, including some that had not been part of SC21, were assigned to a new subcommittee numbered SC32. SC32 has divided itself into several working groups, of which WG3 is responsible for SQL and WG4 for SQL/MM.

1 ISO was not, and is not, the only such organization. The International Electrotechnical Commission (IEC) exists specifically to address international standards in the electrotechnical area (obvious, isn't it?); CCITT (Comité Consultatif International de Téléphone et Télégraph) exists to standardize communications issues (that's why we can place telephone calls between countries!).

E.2.3 Standards Development in ISO

As you might expect, the ISO process is quite different from the ANSI process. In the former, only the standards body from each country is allowed to vote at ISO meetings, to propose projects, or to raise issues.[2] By contrast, in ANSI, individuals who attend meetings represent their employers or may even represent themselves. Of course, individual humans represent their countries at ISO meetings, but the decisions must have been previously coordinated in the national standards body. The United States is represented in ISO by ANSI, the United Kingdom by BSI, France by AFNOR, and so forth.

When some country believes that it's time to standardize some aspect of information technology, it raises an issue as a national position either directly with ISO/IEC JTC1 or with one of the SCs, such as SC32, who (if approved at that level) forwards the request to JTC1. A JTC1 ballot is initiated to determine if JTC1 member countries believe that such a project should be initiated and if there is likely to be sufficient resources (read "active representation") to develop a standard based on the project. If enough countries agree (at least five countries must commit to participation in the development), then the work is assigned to an existing SC or, in some situations, a new SC is formed and the project assigned to it. The SC then decides whether the work can be done by the SC as a whole or whether it should be assigned to an existing or new WG for development.

As in ANSI, a working draft is developed (and may accompany the project proposal) by the assigned group. At some point, the group believes that the document is ready for wider review, so it distributes the document within the SC (meaning that all member national bodies are given the document) and formally registers it as a Working Draft (note the capital letters); the document still has no real formal standing at this point. Once the group believes that the document is sufficiently complete, it may be advanced to the first formal stage of progression: Committee Draft (CD), which implies the initiation of a CD ballot. If the development group is *really* confident of its status, the document can bypass the CD stage and advance directly to Final Committee Draft (FCD). All standards must pass an FCD ballot before they are allowed to progress to the next stage. A successful FCD ballot means that the document (after a ballot resolution meeting, often called an *editing meeting*, at which ballot comments are resolved) progresses to become a Draft International Standard, or DIS. That, in turn, implies the initiation of a DIS ballot. If the CD or FCD ballot is unsuccessful (as a result of too many substantial changes, regardless of the actual vote), then the assigned group does more work and tries again. (Common wisdom says that a document that

2 Actually, ISO recognizes a very few non–national body organizations through a formal liaison relationship; such organizations are sometimes permitted to propose new work and even to vote on certain ballots.

fails three CD or FCD ballots is probably dead in the water.) Once the document reaches DIS status, a DIS ballot (or an FDIS—Final Draft International Standard—ballot) is initiated (sometimes after a bit more editing, but without substantial changes to the document). Again, if that ballot is unsuccessful, there may be more work and additional DIS or FDIS ballots; indeed, the document may be pushed back to CD status or even WD status. However, a successful DIS ballot means that (often after an editing meeting to resolve comments) the document is advanced to FDIS status. Whether or not a document undergoes a DIS ballot, it must be submitted for an FDIS ballot before it become a standard. A successful FDIS ballot means that, without any additional editing, the document progresses to International Standard (IS) status and is forwarded to the ISO Central Secretariat (via the SC and TC or JTC responsible for it) for a review of the process used. If it passes this review, then the document is published with an ISO or ISO/IEC number. SQL, for example, was initially published as ISO 9075-1987. Later, ISO changed the convention so that a colon was used to separate the standard number from the year of publication, so that the next revision was ISO 9075:1989. Still later, when JTC1 was formed, its standards used ISO/IEC, so the title of SQL-92 was ISO/IEC 9075:1992.

Usually, this process works very well. Every generation of SQL, for example, has been published both as an ANSI and an ISO standard. Except for such obvious matters as the standard number and references to other ANSI and ISO standards, the two publications are identical. This represents an ideal model of cooperation between a national standards group and the international process. Other standards have been less fortunate, and national bodies have developed many standards that are incompatibly different from the international version.

E.3 History of the SQL Standard

In 1978, ANSI X3 SPARC recommended the formation of a new technical committee called X3H2; the project assigned to this new committee was the development of a data definition language (DDL) for CODASYL databases (Common Data System Languages); CODASYL developed COBOL and also developed a specification for the network database model. It quickly became apparent to the participants of this TC that developing a DDL alone would not satisfy the requirements of the marketplace, so the scope of work was enlarged to include a data sublanguage for network databases. This language was called Database Language NDL (it was widely understood that NDL stood for Network Database Language).

During development of NDL, it became apparent that the relational data model was increasingly important, so the DBSSG (q.v.) recommended a second project for the development of a relational database standard, and in 1982 that project was also assigned to X3H2. X3H2 decided to base the standard on the SQL database language, since it had been implemented by more than one vendor and appeared to be gaining widespread acceptance. For a couple of years, X3H2 "improved" SQL with many changes based on 20-20 hindsight, and, since a good many of those changes made the draft standard incompatible with SQL, the working name was changed to RDL, for "Relational Database Language." In 1984, the committee reassessed this effort and concluded that the changes it had made to the SQL specification did not in fact improve the language enough to justify the incompatibilities. The committee therefore decided to revert to the original SQL specifications. These specifications were refined somewhat and then published as the initial SQL standard in 1986. Subsequently, almost all of the improvements and generalizations that had been developed for RDL were added to SQL in the SQL-92 revision; as it turned out, most of them could be accomplished in an upward compatible manner.

In roughly 1984, ISO TC97/SC5 (which previously had responsibility for programming languages, graphics, database languages, and various other areas) was reorganized along with TC97/SC16. Some of the projects were assigned to one new subcommittee—TC97/SC22 (programming languages)—while others were assigned to another new SC—TC97/SC21 (related to OSI). The database work went into SC21.

In fact, TC97/SC5 was already reviewing the NDL and RDL work as early as 1982. When SC21 was formed, the actual project assigned was titled "Data Definition Language" and was only later evolved into NDL. As ANSI X3H2 began serious development on RDL and, later, on SQL, TC97/SC21 also picked up that work.

These efforts resulted in the late-1986 publication of ANSI X3.135-1986, "Database Language SQL" in the United States.[3] Because of differences in the process, it was early in 1987 before ISO published ISO 9075-1987, "Database Language SQL" internationally.[4] This standard was very close to the IBM implementation, but with sufficient restrictions, escape hatches, and unspecified areas that it served as a sort of least common denominator for several implementations. Unfortunately, it left users with little ability to write meaningful applications that were portable among products from different vendors (indeed, IBM's several implementations were not fully compatible even among themselves).

This standard was defined to have two levels, called (cleverly enough) Level 1 and Level 2. Level 1 was designed to be an intersection of features that were already widely implemented by most SQL vendors, while Level 2 added a few additional features and relaxed some restrictions.

---

3 The formal title was actually *Information Systems—Database Language—SQL*.

4 Its full title was *Information technology—Database languages—SQL*.

One significant comment in the various public reviews and ISO ballots was that the language was missing a very important feature: referential integrity. A compromise was reached that allowed the first version of SQL (often referred to as SQL-86 or, less often, SQL-87 because of the publication date) to go forward; the compromise required the rapid turnaround of a revised standard that included at least basic referential integrity.

Work had begun on that revision even before SQL-86 was published. However, because the TCs (and WGs) were unfamiliar with publishing revised standards and because both ANSI and ISO had undergone some reorganization, delays mounted until the so-called "rapid turnaround" became three years. It was thus mid-1989 when ISO published ISO 9075:1987, "Database Language SQL with Integrity Enhancement"[5] and late 1989 when ANSI published the corresponding X3.135-1989.

Some U.S. government users were critical of SQL-86 because the specification of how to embed SQL in conventional programming languages was contained in an appendix that was explicitly "informative." These users worried that this fact might mean that portable implementations of embedded SQL wouldn't be supported because they weren't "normative" (required). These concerns caused X3H2 to develop a second standard that made the embedding specifications normative; that standard was published in 1989 as ANSI X3.168-1989, "Database Language Embedded SQL."[6] ISO chose not to publish an analogous standard because of a lack of similar concerns in the international community. Unfortunately, this decision meant that ISO had no definition for embedding SQL into Ada or C until SQL-92 was published, while ANSI did.

SQL-89 retained the two levels of SQL-86. It also made the Integrity Enhancement Feature optional, so that vendors could claim conformance to the standard without having to implement that feature.

E.3.1 SQL2

Because of the delays in publishing SQL-89 (as it became known), work was already in full swing for a second revision of SQL by late 1987. This project, code-named SQL2 by both X3H2 and ISO/IEC JTC1/SC21, was intended to define a major revision to the language, making it a more complete language instead of a least common denominator.

---

5 In spite of the name given in the text, the formal title of this standard was identical to that of the 1987 edition: *Information technology—Database languages—SQL.*

6 Actually, *Information Systems—Database Language—Embedded SQL.*

Work was completed on that project in late 1991 (though fine-tuning persisted into early 1992), and the document was published in late 1992 by ANSI as X3.135-1992, "Information Systems—Database Language—SQL," and by ISO as ISO/IEC 9075:1992, "Information technology—Database languages—SQL."

While the next generation of the SQL standard was being developed, industry demand arose for enhancements to SQL-92. The first enhancement was a standard for a call-level interface to SQL database systems, which resulted in the 1995 publication of a new *part* of the SQL standard (ISO/IEC 9075-3:1995, known as SQL/CLI). Only a year after that, another new part (ISO/IEC 9075-4:1996, called SQL/PSM, or Persistent Stored Modules) was published to define the manner in which applications could define and invoke stored routines from their SQL code. Nineteen ninety-eight saw the publication of a third new part dealing with embedding SQL code in Java programs—ISO/IEC 9075-10, SQL/OLB (Object Language Bindings). That was followed in 1999 and 2000, respectively, by the two parts of a different ANSI standard, called SQLJ; NCITS 331.1 was entitled "SQL Routines Using the Java Programming Language," and NCITS 331.2 was called "SQL Types Using the Java Programming Language."

E.3.2 SQL3

Even before publication of SQL-92, work had begun on the next generation of the SQL standard, which was naturally called SQL3 in its project stage. SQL3 was planned to be a major enhancement of the language, adding object technology along with a host of more traditional relational database features (such as triggers).

The object additions proved to be vastly more difficult—both technically and politically—than anybody had anticipated. As a result, the "tradition" of publishing a revision of the SQL standard at three-year intervals fell apart and it took a full seven years to finish this version of the standard.

Of course, the committees were not idly limiting themselves strictly to the major enhancement of SQL. In 1995, a new "part"—a separate document closely aligned with the rest of the standard—was published in alignment with SQL-92. This new part, called SQL/CLI or CLI-95, defined a call-level interface to SQL database systems. Then, in 1996, another new part was published to align with SQL-92; this part was called SQL/PSM, or PSM-96, and specified the ability to define functions and procedures written in SQL or in a host programming language and invoked from SQL programs—commonly called *stored procedures* because they are actually stored right in the database itself. It also defined a number of procedural SQL statements, thus making SQL computationally complete for the first time.

When SQL3 was finally completed in 1999, it contained five parts: SQL/Framework, SQL/Foundation, SQL/CLI, SQL/PSM, and SQL/Bindings. However, other parts were already in development and have been published since 1999: SQL/MED (Management of External Data), SQL/OLB (Object Language Bindings), and SQL/JRT (Java Routines and Types). SQL/MED is covered in this volume, while SQL/OLB and SQL/JRT are covered only briefly here but are discussed in detail in another of my books[7] (SQL/JRT was then known by different names and standard numbers).

E.4 NIST and the FIPS

In the United States, the federal government is a major user of computer systems, including database systems. Agencies of the U.S. federal government depend on the National Institute of Standards and Technology (NIST, formerly known as the National Bureau of Standards, or NBS) to advise them on information technology procurements. In many cases, this advice took the form of a Federal Information Processing Standard (FIPS).

A FIPS often specified a particular way to conform to an existing ANSI standard, or to an existing ISO standard, or it sometimes defined a completely independent specification itself. In the case of SQL, NIST wrote a FIPS in early 1987 that specified conformance to ANSI X3.135-1986. This FIPS was published as FIPS PUB 127 (PUB standing for "publication"). It ignored Level 1 of SQL-86 and required conformance to Level 2 of that standard.

In 1989, NIST published a revised FIPS called FIPS PUB 127-1, which specified conformance to Level 2 of X3.135-1989 and to X3.168-1989. Like the SQL-89 standard, FIPS PUB 127-1 specifies the Integrity Enhancement Feature as an optional feature. It also specifies the required minimum values for many elements of the language that the standard left as implementation-defined.

NIST published yet another revision in 1992, called FIPS PUB 127-2. That revision specified conformance to ANSI X3.135-1992, with the emphasis on the Entry SQL level. It also specified minimum values for additional implementation-defined elements as well as requiring additional "system tables" to document some aspects of the implementation. NIST also developed a conformance test suite that allows it to test implementations that claim conformance to SQL-89. FIPS PUB 127-2 permitted claims of conformance to the Intermediate SQL and Full SQL levels but did not provide additional requirements or clarification.

---

7 Jim Melton and Andrew Eisenberg, *Understanding SQL and Java Together: A Guide to SQLJ, JDBC, and Related Technologies* (San Francisco: Morgan Kaufmann Publishers, 2000).

However, changes determined by Congress removed NIST's responsibilities for developing and publishing FIPS, as well as their mandate to do conformance testing for many standards, including SQL. At this time, there is no widely recognized authority doing conformance testing on SQL database systems, although the NIST test suite is freely available and is used by at least some organizations for their procurement requirements.

E.5 Other SQL-Related Organizations

So far, I've talked about the *de jure,* or formal, standards organizations that produce SQL standards. However, there are also several additional bodies that are concerned with SQL. These groups do not publish formal standards, but their work is sometimes referred to as a *de facto* standard because it gets widely implemented.

X/Open Company, Ltd., now known as The Open Group, is a consortium of companies (initially Unix system vendors) that publishes Portability Guides for many computer-related areas, including operating system interfaces (Unix), programming languages (C and COBOL), networking, security, and data management. The X/Open Data Management Working Group was responsible for producing the XPG (XPG stands for X/Open Portability Guide) text for SQL. The fourth generation of these guides (XPG4) was published late in 1992 and includes a definition of SQL closely based on the Entry SQL level of SQL-92, but with several extensions. These extensions are based on commonly implemented vendor extensions (such as `CREATE INDEX` and `DROP INDEX`) and several features of Intermediate SQL (such as the diagnostics area, the `GET DIAGNOSTICS` statement, and parts of dynamic SQL).

X/Open worked closely with another consortium, called the SQL Access Group (SAG), in database-related matters. SAG was formed to prototype the (then) emerging ISO standard for Remote Database Access (RDA); that work inevitably led to SQL-related questions and issues, so X/Open and SAG joined forces to update X/Open's SQL definition to better conform to the ANSI and ISO SQL-92 standards and to "fill in the blanks" where the ANSI and ISO standards left elements implementation-defined. SAG's most important contribution, however, was development of the call-level interface that eventually became SQL/CLI.

As mentioned in the preceding paragraph, ISO has produced a standard called *Remote Database Access,* or *RDA* (ISO/IEC 9579-1, *Remote Database Access, Part 1: Generic*, and ISO/IEC 9579-2, *Remote Database Access, Part 2: SQL Specialization*). This standard specifies the formats and protocols for accessing an SQL database system across an OSI (Open Systems Interconnect) network. The 1992 version of RDA supported Entry SQL-92; later work supported Intermediate and Full SQL-92. RDA has not proven to have commercial support.

I should also point out that, although SQL defines language for metadata operations (CREATE, ALTER, and DROP) and a place where the metadata is "reflected" (the Information and Definition Schemas, discussed in the first volume of this book), you shouldn't look at SQL as the answer to all data dictionary or repository questions. ANSI X3.H4 produced a standard called IRDS that addresses repository issues without using SQL at all. ISO/IEC JTC1/SC21/WG3 produced a *different* standard, also called IRDS, that addresses repository issues, but with a close relationship to SQL (in fact, it uses SQL language in many places for the definition). As with RDA, neither IRDS standard had commercial support. Other metadata standards continue to be pursued, none with significant commercial presence.

E.6 Appendix Summary

As mentioned at the outset of this appendix, you don't need to know much about the background and history of SQL, nor about the standards process, to use SQL:1999. You can, however, amaze your friends and co-workers with your in-depth knowledge about the standards process. Who knows, you may even get elected (or drafted) to participate in a standards development process.

Index

B

C

D

E

G

J

K

L

M

N

O

P

S

T

V

W

X

Y

About the Author

Jim Melton is editor of all parts of ISO/IEC 9075 (SQL) and representative for database standards at Oracle Corporation. Since 1986, he has been his company's representative to the ANSI NCITS Technical Committee H2 for Database and a U.S. representative to ISO/IEC JTCI/SC32/WG3. He was the editor of SQL-92 and the recently published SQL:1999 suite of standards and is increasingly involved in standards related to querying XML and integrating SQL and XML. He is also the editor of the next generation of the SQL standards, currently under development, as well as an editor for the Functions and Operators specification currently being developed by the W3C XML Query Working Group. He is the author of several SQL books.